SECURITY VALUATION AND RISK ANALYSIS

ASSESSING VALUE IN INVESTMENT DECISION MAKING

KENNETH S. HACKEL

New York Chicago San Francisco Lisbon London Madrid
Mexico City Milan New Delhi San Juan Seoul
Singapore Sydney Toronto

The McGraw-Hill Companies

1 2 3 4 5 6 7 8 9 0 QFR/QFR 0 9 8 7 6 5 4 3 2 1 0

ISBN: 978-0-07-174435-5
MHID: 0-07-174435-5

This publication is designed to provide accurate and authoritative information in regard to the subject matter covered. It is sold with the understanding that neither the author nor the publisher is engaged in rendering legal, accounting, securities trading, or other professional services. If legal advice or other expert assistance is required, the services of a competent professional person should be sought.

—*From a Declaration of Principles Jointly Adopted by a Committee of the American Bar Association and a Committee of Publishers and Associations*

This book is printed on acid-free paper.

CONTENTS

Chapter 3

Statement of Cash Flows 47

Chapter 4

Free Cash Flow 143

Chapter 5

Return on Invested Capital 249

PREFACE

This book has taken me almost four decades to write. And that makes the task of writing this Preface so difficult. If I might, I would like to offer some simple but hopefully helpful advice and insight into this profession: Learn from anyone and everyone. You'll be surprised what information you can glean about business from about anyone you might meet. Ask about their job, what (if not nonpublic and material) their company could be doing to become more efficient, what it might be doing wrong or well, as well as the firm's customers, clients, and competition.

While all security analysts like to spend time with the chief financial officer (CFO), in a large organization it's really the professionals that report to the CFO who carry the valuable information and expertise. For instance, if possible, I like to speak to the individual who wrote particular footnote sections of the 10K or 10Q, such as the manager of global tax or the pension manager.

The chief motivational factor over the course of my professional career has been my desire to learn and experience all there was when it came to analyzing stocks. A good security analyst always should seek out individuals from whom to learn, books to study, and schools and conferences from which to receive training. An analyst must use his or her resources and ask sound questions based on an understanding of the subject or an obvious quest for such an understanding. As a young analyst, I chaired the Education Committee at the New York Society of Security Analysts, so I had access to high-ranking individuals whom I could invite, visit with, and learn from.

An analyst needs to be as inquisitive as a police detective—and as probing and as suspicious. An analyst never should get complaisant during bull markets or be so doubting during bear markets as to lose sight of the long-term opportunities.

Having heard countless Depression-era stories from my father, I came into the investment business with a congenital concern that a business might not be able to provide its owners with sufficient cash to warrant an investment. And the ever-increasing list of scandals and abuses only tended to raise my level of suspicion.

It was with this background that I began, during the 1970s, the study of cash flow and credit, during which I spent several years as a loan officer.

As the growth in U.S. corporate pension funds became apparent, I worked as the pension fund analyst for a large utility company, where I delved into actuarial methodologies, which was an arcane science at the time. The United States was going through a very difficult recession, yet stocks were, for the most part, being valued on growth of earnings, even though the owners of companies, the shareholders—who were hoping for some capital gains—discovered that there was little excess cash to be distributed. Mergers were being completed for stock under pooling of interest accounting, which allowed the assets and liabilities to be recorded at their carrying values. By artificially boosting earnings through avoidance of goodwill, this made for lower P/Es, but again providing no distributable cash.

As I delved into the minutiae of corporate reporting, it became apparent to me that many firms were wasting cash, either through excessive hiring, wasteful acquisitions of other firms, or unneeded expansion fueled by top-of-cycle decisions. These firms had just an outside chance of earning a decent return on their investment, not to mention the downside risk if the investment didn't turn out as planned. One public company chairman once told me he was in a "transactions mode" and wound up almost bringing down the whole company from the eventual deal. His investment bankers were quite happy as they left his office that day. It was from experiences such as these that I learned that a company must have a cash return at least equal to its cost of capital.

Now that the industrialized world is entering its second decade of slowing economic growth, the analysis of cash flow and credit is coming to the forefront. With that Depression mentality in mind, I explain in this book my concept for how the entity can maximize free cash flow without impairing its growth. For without free cash flow, outside of selling assets, principal on debt cannot be reduced, and investors cannot be compensated.

The reason for this book, however, is my genuine concern that investors have not learned to program risk into their expectations. Even when they believe that they have, normally omitted are a multitude of factors that deserved careful attention but did not receive it. Without a careful assessment and evaluation of fundamental business and operating risks, the potential for negative surprise looms. When building in such risks to expectations of reward in the form of cash flow, a superior investment model is created, including the estimate of fair value.

ACKNOWLEDGMENTS

Any success this text may enjoy is made possible through my personal relationships with professionals whose aim is the advancement of the profession. Here I had the aid of some wonderful individuals and corporations.

I received great encouragement from my parents, David and Bernice Hackel, both of whom believed in the power of knowledge and of the people who continually strive for that "better" world.

I was lucky to have the great support of my wife, Gail, to whom this book is dedicated. Gail spent many weekends and evenings without me as I performed research and typed away.

I am also indebted to Eli Hackel, CFA, for his feedback and analysis regarding several portions of the text.

While the parents instill confidence in their children, the children often do the same for the parents. My Emily, Eli, Betsy, and David have done so for me.

I am extremely grateful to Simon Adams at CT Capital, LLC, who was with me on the project from day one. Simon helped to prepare most of the charts and tables in this book and is a whiz in Excel, Word, and whatever software is necessary for the preparation of financial text. He is also a friend I have come to admire and respect.

To my friends at McGraw-Hill, I am most impressed. Here I speak particularly of Jennifer Ashkenazy, Mary Glenn, and Knox Huston. I relied on you, and you all came through. I have been with your company as an author for almost 20 years. As you know, authors need lots of encouragement, and you were there for me and provided the resources I needed when I needed them.

I must not forget the years of friendship, encouragement, and help from my former editor, Ralph Rieves, now a managing director at Farragut, Jones and Lawrence. It was Ralph who first broached the idea of me writing a book some 20 years ago, and it was he who urged me, after hearing my ideas, to bring this project forward. Ralph, this turned out to be a project of joy and learning—you were right!

I am truly appreciative to the professionals at Standard & Poor's Financial Services for the open access and wealth of information provided. I am eternally grateful to Sol Samson, managing director of ratings, as well as Ben Brubeck, Scott Sweeney, Marissa Kandel, Scott Drucker, and Alison Sullivan.

To the remarkable folks at the Financial Accounting Standard Board, popularly known as FASB, I thank you all for your help and research efforts. Their job is not an easy one, being pulled from one side by investors seeking more information and tugged from the other side by firms who wish to protect themselves or not pay their freight. At the FASB, I would particularly like to thank Marc Siegal, board member, and Nicholas Cappiello, as well as all their assistants and researchers.

At Fitch Ratings, I appreciated the fine help of Cindy Stoller, who provided me with access and information that was included in this book.

To Alan Spen, former senior director at Fitch and now a consultant, your capital insights and text feedback are truly appreciated. Alan has been as exceedingly generous with his time and his revelations, and I consider him a good friend.

At Research Insight I must pay homage to John Kim, whom I was free to call evenings and weekends. John is one of the finest financial programmers I have known. For John, no assignment was too big or too complex.

To the people at the Institute of Chartered Financial Analysts, who are responsible for the issuance of the Chartered Financial Analyst (CFA) designation, I can see why the pursuance of the degree has flourished. I have long maintained that I learned more about security analysis from the CFA program than from graduate school. I highly encourage any serious student of finance and security analysis to pursue the CFA.

Many of the CFOs and CEOs I had spoken with in the book's preparation and who have provided insight have preferred that they not be given attribution. Their feedback will always be appreciated.

And finally, I would like to acknowledge anyone who reads this text. I am confident that you will be a better investor for having done so and for embracing the principles of cash flow and risk in your financial decision making.

CHAPTER 1

Overview

Security Valuation and Risk Analysis is a book written to help investors appraise the expected return from an investment in an equity security. In undertaking this endeavor, half this book is allocated to risk, as measured by cost of capital, and half is allocated to to return, as measured by the investment's expected cash flows.[1]

Many new lessons were taught and many old lessons were learned as a result of the financial system meltdown of 2008–2009, but none more important than possessing the deep skill set to practice the rigorous application of cash flows and credit analysis. The investors having such a deep-seated knowledge were, in many instances, able to earn outsized returns while avoiding the concerns that were forced into bankruptcy or forced to accept government aid. Many other entities were severely weakened, with massive loss of market share. And when the economy stabilized, the firms that had strong cash flows and low cost of capital quickly rebounded to their former levels, and over the course of a business cycle, such enterprises normally outperform the general equity market by a considerable margin.

Investors who understand cash flow and credit have an important competitive advantage. They can place a confident value on the enterprise and spot discrepancies in value. To the extent that economic uncertainty is prevalent, investment opportunities are especially widespread. Those who succeed in this environment are those who are best equipped with the new analytic skills to do so. Successful investors understand cash-flow adequacy is the most important benchmark in both security valuation and credit decisions; they also understand there are risks associated with expected cash flows.

[1] Throughout the text, I refer to cash flows as meaning ***both*** cash flow from operating activities and free (maximum distributable) cash flow. Otherwise, they are referred to separately, as will be defined.

This book will provide you with the tools designed to give you a real edge relative to other security analysts by demonstrating how you can

- Enhance your forecasting skills by showing how to spot and take advantage of early-warning signals provided by cash-flow and credit metrics
- Have a better understanding of how financial statements are prepared
- Take advantage of a better definition of cost of equity capital from which to discount free cash flow
- Capitalize on a better definition of free cash flow by understanding how management could free up cash resources
- Earn superior investment returns through practical use of an advanced definition of cash flow from operating activities that is superior to that reported under generally accepted accounting principles (GAAP)
- Spot and quantify important balance-sheet and off-balance-sheet items that most often are neglected or lightly scrutinized by securities analysts and investors
- Think like a corporate "insider" by showing how corporate executives view the various risks that confront them
- Take advantage of the many failings of earnings before interest, taxes, depreciation, and amortization (EBITDA)
- Take advantage of how rating agencies assign credit grades

To say that much has developed in the world of finance since I cowrote *Cash Flow and Security Analysis* (2nd ed., McGraw-Hill, 1995) with distinguished Professor at the Stern School of Business, Dr. Joshua Livnat, would be a very gross understatement. Who knows how close the United States, and, for that matter, the industrialized world, came to financial collapse during the fall of 2008?

What can be stated with complete and utter confidence is the study of cash flow and credit has become more important than ever. It is with this perspective that I produced this book.

Investments—and their study—are a living, changing experience. What we take for granted one day may not be so certain the next. And thus we must adapt, even when our central rule makers, the Securities and Exchange Commission (SEC) and the Financial Accounting Standards Board (FASB[2]), are slow to do the

[2]Accounting promulgations in the United States are issued by the Financial Accounting Standards Board (FASB), a Norwalk, CT–based private organization that is officially recognized by the U.S. government and the accounting profession as the rule-making body. Any company with publicly traded stock or bonds must comply in full with GAAP, which means complying with the FASB's regulations.

same. The U.S. Congress also operates with a lag, normally reacting to events by swinging too hard and too late.

At other times, as we have seen, accounting rule makers are forced to refine accounting standards that have stood for many years, reacting to events of the moment, in order to satisfy investors in problem sectors. We have witnessed the public weigh in, voicing support for modification of existing accounting standards, supported by a Congress feeling the heat of the voters.

Let me state with authority what this book is *not*. It is *not* a text written for or designed to appeal to academic statisticians who practice money management. This book is for *practitioners* of security analysis. I have seen more than a couple of Nobel Prize–winning scholars run gigantic hedge funds into the ground with their theories. I have been through too many once-in-a-hundred-years events.

The great investors throughout time started, built, or acquired companies whose products enjoyed consistent and growing free cash flow. By relying on financially prudent business practices, their companies enjoyed a low cost of capital. They created a competitive advantage and did not deviate. And if they did deviate, more often than not, they ran into trouble. I never hear successful builders of businesses mention beta or other academic statistical risk tools. They talk about products, customers, risk, and cash. They talk about growth rates in free cash flow, taxes, and stability. This is how the reader will be taught to measure return and risk in this book.

This book is *not* centered on financial companies, although I will provide many detailed examples and explanations of financial instruments, including why it is important to monitor creditors with whom the industrial entity relies on for financial backing.

While I am painfully aware of how problems in the financial sector spilled over to the rest of the economy, banks and insurers have investment accounts equal to many times their shareholders' equity, and it is too often those assets that drive valuations and stock prices. If their investments are overstated, their reserves understated, or their commitments, contingencies, or hedges in trouble, their valuations will see sharp declines. It doesn't seem so long ago that many of the largest U.S. banks, quite a while before television commentators were talking about derivatives, were in danger of failing from loan overexposure to the energy sector. Readers will understand how risk to cash flows can be mitigated through the judicious use of financial instruments, but also how risk can be amplified when those instruments are used improperly.

This book is designed to assist you in analyzing operating concerns. Large changes in market value resulting from balance-sheet assets deserve recognition but are not this book's focal point. For instance, when the price of gold runs up, EZCORP, Inc., a large pawn shop operator, often sees its stock rise owing to the company's high inventory of gold pawned merchandise; as gold falls, so too does the price of its stock.

During the real estate boom preceding the outset of the 2008–2009 recession, many stocks sensitive to the sector traded with little regard to cash flow or risk. Some shrewd managers of such entities recognized the discrepancy and placed their companies for sale to the greater fool, as did the board of directors at Central Parking Corp., which was being valued as an asset play.

Example:

Nashville, TN (Business Wire)—March 14, 2005. Central Parking Corporation (NYSE:CPC) announced today that its board of directors has retained Morgan Stanley as its exclusive financial advisor to assist the company in evaluating various strategic alternatives in order to maximize shareholder value.

"Our Board believes that the intrinsic value of our operating platform, as well as the value of our owned real estate, is substantially higher than is currently reflected in our stock price. With the goal of maximizing shareholder value, the Board has decided to evaluate strategic alternatives at this time," commented Monroe J. Carell, Jr., chairman and chief executive officer. "Since I founded Central Parking in 1968, the senior management team and I have spent considerable time developing the company into the industry leader that it is today, particularly in streamlining operations and reducing debt since my return in 2003. I now believe that it is time for the company to enter into the next phase of its corporate life in order to capitalize on the significant growth opportunities in today's recovering and improving economy."

This book will not neglect a proper discussion, analysis, and treatment of financial instruments because one would be foolish not to recognize the importance of the financial sector to the consumer (final demand) and to industrial companies, especially entities having financial subsidiaries. Indeed, industrial concerns do use hedging strategies, but in their case, such hedges are not supposed to drive the train. For financials, they do.

THE MACRO ENVIRONMENT

Although this book is principally about the analysis of free cash flow and risk to the equity holder, the latter measured by the cost of equity capital, it goes without saying that all companies are at the mercy of the macro environment. As we saw during 2010, the fiscal crises in Greece impacted the euro, and with it the financial markets in Europe and the United States. The macro environment affects cost of capital in a multitude of ways—from top-line (revenue) growth to bottom-line free cash flow. For these reasons, as will become clear from my credit model, I evaluate consistency of revenues and interest-rate spreads, among other such metrics that are inextricably tied to the vagaries of the economic and business cycle.

All companies are affected by macroeconomic events, such as embargoes, wars, taxes, threats, consumer confidence, legislation, and general economic prosperity, and inflation. The latter, unless accompanied by substantial increase in free cash flow, often forces the real return on invested capital below the cost of capital, thereby depressing market values. Companies whose customers are regional in scope are more subject to local and state issues, in addition to the unavoidable macroeconomic factors.

For instance, the primary factors affecting demand for power (revenues) for local utility companies are weather and the economic conditions in the regions they serve. In 2004, Consolidated Edison, the large New York City utility, estimated that cooler than average summer weather reduced their earnings by $5 million. While it is difficult to forecast the weather, long-term normal demand for electricity is easier to predict. Is the utility company located in a growth area? Is the state in which the company is located successful in attracting new business? Are taxes, environmental policy, and other regulatory matters conducive to growth of both consumers and business?

While the operating environment for a company under review may be satisfactory currently, it is imperative that analysts understand the climate for potential change—economic, political, and social.

Example:

Altria Corp, the parent company of Phillip Morris, owns a financial services division that leases aircraft [Phillip Morris Credit Corporation (PMCC)]. When the price of oil rose, many airlines, including United Airlines (UAL), had massive cash-flow drains, impairing their ability to service their lease obligations. This, of course, affected Altria.

> PMCC leases 24 Boeing 757 aircraft to UAL with an aggregate finance asset balance of $569 million on December 31, 2004. PMCC has entered into an agreement with UAL to amend 18 direct finance leases subject to UAL's successful emergence from bankruptcy and assumption of the leases. UAL remains current on lease payments due to PMCC on these 18 amended leases. PMCC continues to monitor the situation at UAL with respect to the six remaining aircraft financed under leveraged leases, in which PMCC has an aggregate finance asset balance of $92 million. PMCC has no amended agreement relative to these leases because its interests are subordinate to those of public debt holders associated with the leveraged leases. Accordingly, since UAL has declared bankruptcy, PMCC has received no lease payments relative to these six aircraft and remains at risk of foreclosure on these aircraft by the senior lenders under the leveraged leases.

Source: Altria Corp, 2004 10K.

Example:

When Intel raised its first-quarter 2005 revenue and profit-margin guidance, stock investors greeted the news by pushing up its shares by 3 percent in after-hours trading. The next day, however, when both oil prices and the U.S. trade gap rose sharply, Intel shares dropped by 5 percent from its after-hours high. The macro effect overcame the firm's positive news.

Over the long term, the real driver of the train is management. It is management that strives to add value by virtue of its investments in assets whose returns are in excess of the firm's cost of capital. It is management that recruits, trains, and motivates. As such, we begin this book's journey, Chapter 2, with a discussion of management, showing how executives can create or destroy value. We show how the marketplace reacts to management changes in tacit recognition of expected shifts in free cash flow and risk. Also presented is an example of management leading a firm to bankruptcy by not calibrating the risks of leverage properly while both buying back shares and undergoing a large capital spending budget.

In addition, Chapter 2 discusses productivity and shows that equity values are indeed enhanced when free-cash-flow increases resulting from productivity enhancements. For non-free-cash-flow producers, enhancements to productivity have little value and generally are ignored.

MAKING EFFECTIVE USE OF FINANCIAL STATEMENTS

The role of financial statements is to provide users with relevant, reliable, comparable, and understandable information on which they can make rational economic decisions about a reporting entity. However, as we will see, the analyst can increase the predictive value of financial statements by incorporating adjustments to the balance sheet, income statement, and footnoted items into their analyses. These adjustments will provide the analyst with more reliable information on which to base his or her investment decisions. Too often, as we shall learn, the FASB, in its desire to present investors with greater transparency, has been forced to reverse or partially reverse earlier pronouncements that at the time they were originally put into effect were enacted with the intent of providing investors with greater insight and hoped-for comparability. Unless new accounting rules provide additional relevant information that the analyst could not gather easily on his or her own, they would rarely affect the cash-flow and credit analyst.

There is no doubting financial statement rule makers, both in the United States and around the world, can have a remarkable effect on stock prices and the cost of capital in the short run.

Chapter 3 begins our discussion on cash flows. I embark by providing a detailed understanding of the *Statement of Financial Accounting Standards No. 95, Statement of Cash Flows* (SFAS 95), including its intent and shortfalls and firms misapplications of the standard. Shown are various means by which cash flow from operations can be artificially bolstered or understated through misclassification, expense timing, lease classification, or change in funding pattern. Managerial ploys are also discussed in relevant later chapters.

Example:

March 18, 2005 (Bloomberg)—Shares of Cattles, Plc., which provides unsecured loans to low-income households in the United Kingdom, had its biggest drop in more than three years after the company said new accounting rules would have cut 29 percent of its 2004 profit.

Shares in the lender fell as much as 6.7 percent to 351.75 pence as of 10:20 a.m. in London, their biggest drop since September 21, 2001. International financial reporting standards that came into effect this year would have trimmed about £41 million ($78.6 million) from pretax profit last year, the Batley, England–based company said today.

About 7,000 public companies in the United Kingdom and other European Union countries are adopting the standards this year to make accounts more comparable across the region. The rules replace the U.K.'s GAAP.

Illustrated in Chapter 3 is how to prepare a direct method statement of cash flow from operations from balance-sheet and income-statement information and the importance of doing so. Taken is a critical view of the many firms currently reporting operating cash flows under the indirect method. Also illustrated are a wide cross section of examples of firms' investing, financing, and operating activities, as well as examples of supplementary cash-flow information. The examples were chosen specifically for the information content in an attempt to provide the reader with a very wide swath of presentations, lessons, and accounting and cash-flow treatments. Although many examples are given, I want the reader to be prepared, in his or her own everyday analysis, for reporting related to anything from tax windfalls to hedge accounting, from voluntary employee benefits associations (VEBAs) to the effect of closing out of a multiemployer pension plan.

Important is the understanding of the role of the treasury manager, including the credit and collection process. Therefore, I discuss the cash conversion cycle, showing how it is calculated, as well as advances in Treasury Department software that aids the cash balance and can have the same impact as growth in sales.

It is here that I introduce the concept of power operating cash flow. This concept begins with cash flow from operating activities, as reported, and adjusts important working-capital items to the same percentage of revenues as its 5-year average. This gives the analyst greater visibility into normalized cash flow from operations, that is, exclusive of changes spurred on by management or induced by temporary business conditions. For example, during 2007, UPS reported a sharp decline in operating cash flows resulting from its withdrawal from a pension fund necessitating a large payment, yet power operating cash flow was largely unaffected, reflecting the underlying strength in the company's operations. For this reason, power operating cash flow is often a superior tool for measuring the recurring cash flow than is operating cash flow.

I will show the relationship between the Standard and Poor's (S&P) 500 Index and power operating cash flow going into and coming out of the 2007 recession. You will see that entering the recession, power operating cash flows were negative, reflective of weakness in business operations, and how this number provided greater clarity than reported cash flow from operating activities, which were holding up owing to balance-sheet management. During the first quarter of 2009, power operating cash flow signaled an end to the recession, although growth was weak. A chart on power operating cash flow underscores the reason that returns on the S&P 500 were negative for the decade ending December 2009, the first since data recording began in 1927.

FREE CASH FLOW

Chapter 4 expounds on one of the two focal points of the book—free cash flow. I focus on free cash flow because it is the purest form of return to shareholders. It is not influenced, over the course of the business cycle, by accounting whims, such as accruals, and various other events, such as the timing of expense items intended to inflate cash flow from operations. It will take into account what a firm should have contributed to its pension fund versus what it expensed, a large worker's compensation or other payout relative to its normal expense. Free cash flow is what equity investors generally can count on if the cost of capital for the firm is low.

While I have observed a greater percentage of companies talk about free cash flow over the past several decades, nowhere is the talk more heated than during economic slowdowns. Regrettably, there is no standard definition of free cash flow, so I will provide one that has served me well over several decades, one that makes business and economic sense. I also show how an analyst should account for discretionary expenditures and why part of such spending should be included as free cash flow.

Entities that cannot generate consistent free cash flow are more prone to financial irregularity. It is rare for a consistently positive generator of free cash flow to manipulate its results. There is no reason for such a company to do so. Once a financial irregularity is discovered for a net borrowing entity, its risk profile becomes extremely high as the door to outside financing slams shut.

Example:

Freddie Mac Says SEC May Seek Injunction after Restatement

August 19 (Bloomberg). Freddie Mac, the second-largest U.S. mortgage finance company, said that it may face civil action by the Securities and Exchange Commission (SEC), which began an investigation after the company restated earnings last year by $5 billion.

The SEC is probing possible violations of a regulation prohibiting fraud and deceptive practices and may impose a fine and a permanent injunction, McLean, Virginia–based Freddie Mac said in a statement.

Example:

New York (Dow Jones Newswire)—March 11, 2005. Interpublic Group of Cos., which has been struggling to turn itself around since a 2002 accounting scandal, warned Friday that it might have to restate past results because of the discovery of bookkeeping errors.

Interpublic said that it will delay filing its annual report while it investigates the problems. The company plans to seek waivers from its lenders and bondholders to avoid a possible default.

The most significant of the accounting errors concerned acquisitions made from 1996 through 2001. The company said that so far it has found about $145 million in revenue and $25 million in net income that might have been improperly recognized during those years. But Interpublic said that the review is in its early stages and could uncover further problems.

The company said that it will miss the March 31 deadline for filing its annual report and will delay releasing fourth-quarter and full-year results.

Chapter 4 also shows how many firms devise a definition of free cash flow to suit their own needs and circumstances, not normally resulting in a useful measure of distributable cash to equity holders. Also explored in Chapter 4 are taxes, a critical area of analysis to the cash-flow and credit analyst. Tax rates often flash early-warning signs of trouble or improvements to cash flow. Sudden changes in the rate, even for interim reporting, often result in unpleasant surprises affecting the value of a security, cost of debt capital, and estimated return on projects or invested capital. Shown is the significance of using cash taxes paid (including a cash tax rate) versus the effective tax rate that is reported to shareholders. Tax-rate stability is shown to have the utmost value in setting cost of capital and in relation to owners of equity. Taxes other than income taxes also are discussed for their often unrecognized importance in addition to its impact on free cash flow.

I conclude Chapter 4 with a detailed example of how to construct a worksheet to estimate free cash flow, including the estimation of excess discretionary expenditures. Sources of liquidity aside from cash and cash flow from operations are presented. I compare the model with the most popular definitions in use today, and the advantages of using the enhanced formula become apparent.

RETURN ON INVESTED CAPITAL

Chapter 5 explores the critical concept of return on invested capital (ROIC). Explained is why one of the best decisions corporate executives can make on behalf of shareholders is to invest in projects having a return on invested capital in excess of the cost of capital. Like free cash flow, though, ROIC is defined differently by many firms, and these variations are explained with examples and comments.

To this end, I enumerate the many failings of EBITDA and show why the free-cash-flow-based definition of ROIC that I propose produces superior results. After all, investors invest cash and expect cash in return—the projects of an enterprise must do the same. The denominator of the metric, invested capital, also can pose problems in analysis, and I show how it should be computed.

I look into the folly of stock buybacks and show why it is really ROIC in excess of cost of capital that provides value to shareholders, even though share repurchases can enhance accounting-based metrics.

Depicted is how the analyst should adjust for "Other comprehensive income" in the calculation of ROIC. Under FASB guidelines, companies are able to shift impairment charges on items from foreign currency, pension losses, and other events that are explained to other comprehensive income on the balance sheet.[3]

Many investors, large and sophisticated to small and naive, with the latter dependent on and trusting of the former, fail to understand the complicated relationship between GAAP-based valuation metrics and ROIC. It is easy to understand why investors desire a simplified approach to investing, such as the price/earnings multiple, but quite another to apply facility in a manner that actually works. Having knowledge of the bearings behind the numbers allows the analyst to understand why so many entities sell for what appears to be an incredibly low GAAP-inspired multiple (such as price/book value or price/earnings ratio) yet continue to underperform the general averages. GAAP is an accounting concept; this book deals with cash inflows and cash outflows.

In essence, entities having a low ROIC or that depend on large capital expenditures resulting in small amounts of distributable cash flows deserve low valuation metrics despite their higher rates of growth in revenues and/or earnings. For entities that have a low capital base, I show that using economic profit provides high information content when free cash flow is used as the base. Shown are how various entities calculate their ROIC and economic profits with critiques and explanations.

FINANCIAL STRUCTURE

Credit analysis has become more time consuming since the 1990s, in addition to requiring a deeper understanding of financial instruments that a couple of decades ago either did not exist or were used sparingly. While most industrial entities with

[3] The section of the shareholders equity account "Other comprehensive income" has become a repository of accounting gains and losses that have not been realized and may never be.

variable-rate debt take proper advantage of such instruments to protect (hedge) against harmful movements in interest rates, currencies, or commodities, a few have run into trouble gambling on the outcome of such movements.

Investment bankers always can be counted on to devise new financial instruments that intend to blur the distinction between cash flows and GAAP net income, all under the guise of risk reduction or aiding bottom-line growth. Along with these new creations, expect such "helpful" financiers to continue to find "innovative" ways to keep liabilities off the balance sheet (until the FASB or SEC catches up) and use financial devices as a means of protection of owning otherwise risky assets. However, what happens when the devices don't work as intended, turning them into yet another set of risky securities dressed in lamb's clothing. I recall a number of conference calls held by Merrill Lynch and Enron executives lecturing investors on the benefits of Enron's "Special Purpose Entities," often chastising security analysts for their tough questions.

Financial engineering's obfuscations are not limited to U.S. recordkeeping. In Europe, accounting rule makers approved a standard known as *embedded value*, a measure of net asset value that includes the present value of future profits of life insurance policies—as if that could be forecasted accurately given the multitude of variables that could not be known until the insured's demise.

Financial chicanery is ageless, and barely a year goes by without another publicized event—from Enron, which brought to light the aggressive exploitation of "Special Purpose Entities," to Refco, which concealed $430 million in bad debts. The accountants at Lehman Brothers classified repurchase agreements as a sale of assets just prior to the close of reporting periods in an attempt to show lower leverage.

In Chapter 6 the book thus begins a necessary shift of focus to the credit side, with a detailed discussion of financial structure, including an analysis and comments on the securities the analyst finds on and off the main body of the financial statement. The optimal financial structure is discussed in relation to current popular thinking. Examples illustrate the points discussed, especially the critical point that low leverage does not necessarily translate into a low cost of capital.

Throughout Chapter 6, a thorough discussion of the appropriate accounting rules is presented, including more recent promulgations related to off-balance-sheet debt held by nonconsolidated subsidiaries and their effects on financial structure, credit, and cash flows.

The reader is given a thorough understanding of the roles debt, equity, and hybrid securities play in the capital structure, including possible calls on capital, such as commitments, contingencies, guarantees, convertible securities, and exposure to lawsuits, and other cash requirements, such as sinking-fund requirements. Also explored are contingent capital, debt covenants, adjusted debt, special-purpose entities, bank facilities, contingent liabilities, and the importance of sensitivity analysis in evaluating financial structure.

A thorough understanding of financial structure would not be complete without a detailed discussion of hedging and derivative securities, replete with accounting and cash-flow treatments. The proper role of hedging is analyzed along with relevant examples, including instances where hedges might be characterized improperly.

Financial leverage and debt coverages then are discussed and evaluated in relation to the firm's cash flows and financial flexibility. The chapter then looks at and discusses the weighty role played by the credit rating agencies—how they may evaluate a firm and why their decisions enter into my cost-of-capital model. Volatility of cash flows is discussed in relation to leverage and the setting of the financial structure. The cash burn rate is defined.

Taxes are reintroduced for their significance in the financial structure, including tax accounting, deferred taxes, loss carryfowards, and the ability to affect cash flow through various scenarios. Next shown and discussed in detail is the accounting for pension and other postretirement benefits, including health care. This section will provide the reader with a complete understanding of these far-reaching issues and how to understand the footnote, including actuarial terms. A template is presented that reflects the important information for analysis. The impact of these issues on cash flows and leverage is made clear through examples.

Yield spreads are discussed in this chapter for their important real-time signals and potential early-indicator capacity. Yield spreads flashed a historic warning signal for many firms coming into the financial crises and later signaled its end.

Next, I look at two financial companies that were affected by the credit crisis, with their accounting under current mark-to-market rules explained and what the analyst should be on the lookout for for both financial and nonfinancial firms. Too many industrial companies hold investment portfolios to not have a proper discussion and analysis of the subject. Also, of course, industrial companies are frequent visitors to the credit markets and are affected by yield spreads, derivatives, swaps, and hedges.

Finally, leases are discussed, with a detailed study contrasting UPS and FedEx because the latter leans more on operating leases for its capital equipment. UPS is more conservative in its financial structure, including having defeased some capital leases. Shown is how the analyst should treat operating and capital leases and current accounting rules and how comprehensive income should be adjusted in calculating ROIC for these companies. The advantages and disadvantages to both types of leases are brought out, including their differing accounting, requiring adjustments, on the income statement, balance sheet, and statement of cash flows.

COST OF EQUITY CAPITAL

Building on Chapters 1 through 6, the second central tenet of this book—cost of equity capital—comes next. Chapters 7 and 8 explain in detail cost of capital, including my credit model worksheet. This worksheet will present the analyst with an important tool to assess risk while providing a superior discount rate in a present-value model. Advancement in the analysis of cost of capital was the primary reason this book was undertaken, and Chapter 7 provides both the background of current theory and the tools for an analytic edge. Conventional thinking is challenged, and a better solution is offered.

Understanding the many elements of risk facing the enterprise is essential for the investor to gauge the value of the asset and reasons for its possible volatility both to its cash flows and to its security price. Chapter 7 discusses one of the largest companies in the world, IBM, showing, in slides presented by the company, the company's own inability to accurately determine its cost of capital. I provide an estimate of IBM's cost of equity capital using the popular models, as well as my credit-based model.

Contained in this chapter is a detailed study of a company with quite volatile cash flows in the refinery industry and how it might have analyzed the risks associated with the financing of the construction of a large new refinery. Weighted-average cost of capital is determined, including a number of methods for how the company might have calculated cost of equity. The reader is also introduced to the real decisions that management and the board of directors would confront in deciding if the project should be given the "go ahead."

The cost of capital is the return required by equity investors and is based on the inherent risk to the entity's projected cash flows. This is the logic of the credit-based cost-of-capital model I introduce in Chapter 8. It is grounded on a detailed cash-flow and credit worksheet that assesses the underlying credit risk of the entity and its placement above the risk-free rate. Entities that have low credit risk, along with consistent and prospectively growing positive free cash flow, deserve a lower cost of capital; those with higher credit risk deserve a higher cost of capital. The cost should not be based on an implied rate grounded on nondistributable earnings. This makes sense, right? But this is not how business enterprises and students of finance discern it today.

The factor underpinning the capital asset pricing model (CAPM), at the individual security level, is the beta coefficient, a function of stock price volatility. Cost of equity as calculated via the misty lens of stock volatility has been followed by consultants who received their MBAs at universities teaching this faulty gospel. These leading management consultants, in turn, have advised boards of directors that these methodologies are the most appropriate approaches and, because such methodologies are taught at leading universities, have not been questioned.

A search on Edgar, the SEC database, found that the only alternative getting recognition is the implied cost of equity model (ICEM), which is based on solving for the denominator of the present-value model given a forecast for the entity's GAAP earnings and current stock price. As with the CAPM, the ICEM suffers from serious shortfalls, and these are outlined.

To investors who have not studied credit, the theory behind the CAPM could well make sense. In reality, there is just a loose connection. Hundreds of companies have low betas and are thus accorded a low cost of equity capital, yet they can't pay their bills! Hundreds of other firms are erroneously accorded a high cost of capital yet are strong and consistent producers of cash flow and do so with just moderate financial leverage. True, many hundreds of companies are in bankruptcy, technical default, or a stiff wind away from that status yet have, according to the CAPM, a lower cost of capital than, say, a Microsoft or other deserved AAA-rated entity.

The reliance on stock volatility in the placement of a discount rate is so ingrained in Wall Street (sell-side) analyst research reports that it renders a high percentage of those reports useless. Security analysts then are forced to find a GAAP-associated yardstick such as price/earnings or price/book to back up their investment ratings. However, GAAP and the CAPM do not often reflect underlying financial risk, cash flows, competitive market position, possible loss of a patent or supplier, financial structure, or resources available to the enterprise. Accounting concepts are not a measure of cash that could be used to repay debt or distribute wealth to shareholders.

Consider the following:

Georgia Gulf has a beta of just 0.3, indicative of a low-risk entity, yet it is rated just B by Standard and Poor's (S&P). A B rating by S&P is defined as, among other things, having greater vulnerability to default than other speculative-grade debt that could lead to inadequate capacity or meet timely interest and principal payments.

Comcast is rated BBB ("adverse economic conditions could lead to default"), yet analysts may consider it to have a lower cost of equity capital than 3M owing to its having less stock volatility, as reflected by its beta coefficient. A BBB rating is regarded by S&P as having predominantly speculative characteristics. 3M is rated AA–, which S&P indicates as having a very strong capacity to repay interest and principal.

Example:

Flexpoint Sensor Systems has a beta coefficient of just 0.48, indicative by users of the CAPM[4] of a company having a small degree of risk and a low cost of equity capital. Does reading what management had to say remind you of a low-risk enterprise?

> Management believes that our current cash burn rate is approximately $85,000 per month and that the remaining proceeds from the private placement, notes, and accounts receivable will fund our operations for at least the next three months. Our auditors have expressed doubt about our ability to continue as [a] going concern and that we may not realize significant revenue or become profitable within the next 12 to 18 months. We will require additional financing to fund our long-term cash needs. We may rely on debt financing, additional loans from related parties, and private placements of common stock for additional funding. However, we cannot assure you that we will be able to obtain financing or that sources of financing, if any, will continue to be available and, if available, that they will be on terms favorable to us.

Source: Flexpoint Sensor Systems, 2009 10K.

A business is worth the present value of its free cash flows discounted by its cost of capital. However, if the cost of capital used to discount those cash flows is incorrect, the resulting valuation also will be incorrect. From the point of view of the enterprise, if the company misjudges its cost of capital, it might be accepting projects that destroy shareholder value.

Prior to the worldwide financial meltdown, because analysts did not have a reliable cost-of-capital measure on which to draw, they all too often relied on price/book. However, as book values came crashing down, analysts, who believed that the stocks they were recommending would not trade below book, were caught off guard. Had they approached the analysis with superior credit tools, they would have better understood the exposure. With the credit crisis, the popular risk models became unmasked.

What does the use of an incorrect cost of capital mean in terms of actual valuation? Since Rite Aid (Table 1-1) has not been able to generate free cash flow, a cash-flow analyst would question whether, aside from selling off assets, it should stay in business because the company must, unless cash-flow neutral, continue to borrow cash to stay afloat. If we estimated Toyota's free cash flow at $3 per share, a 5-year growth rate of 5 percent in its free cash flow, leveling off

[4] The Capital Asset Pricing Model, developed by William Sharpe, was intended to help measure portfolio risk and the return an investor can expect for assuming that risk. The beta reflected the (market) risk that could not be diversified away. According to the CAPM, a portfolio's return is solely a function of its beta.

to 2 percent thereafter, along with its 7.5 percent discount rate, fair value would be $84.60 under the CAPM compared with $60.14 under the credit model. On the other hand, IBM, with $9 per share in free cash flow and a 10 percent cost of equity capital, under the same growth pattern as Toyota, would be fairly valued at $130.16 under the CAPM and $160.77 under the credit model. These are significant differences for such large companies that are followed by many investors and security analysts.

TABLE 1-1

Cost of Equity Capital: Capital Asset Pricing Model versus Comprehensive Credit Model

Company	CAPM	Credit Model
Toyota	7.5 percent	9.7 percent*
Rite Aid	6.8 percent	18.5 percent
IBM	10.0 percent	8.4 percent

*Data in table as of September 30, 2009.

Based on Toyota's beta of 0.73, a return on the S&P 500 Index of 9 percent and a 3.5 percent 10-year bond.

Are the risks of these widely followed companies in the table accurately reflected by their cost of equity, as measured by stock volatility? It appears that they are not. Commensurate with the 2007 credit crisis, many firms were unable to raise funds, and even investment-grade borrowers faced historically high credit spreads over U.S. Treasuries. It was the fundamental credit health of the entity that investors in debt and equity instruments were concerned with, not its stock price movements. The following example illustrates further.

Example:

Cal-Maine Foods, a large egg producer, has seen its cost of equity capital, based on the CAPM, swing between 8 and 19 percent, hardly making for a reliable fair-value forecast of its underlying stock. During the same period, cost of equity capital based on the company's credit metrics, while having shifted somewhat during the period, has remained considerably more stable, providing a truer picture of the company's fundamental condition. During the 5-year period under analysis (Fig. 1-1), Cal-Maine's shareholders' equity was rising, its free cash flows were growing, and its total debt was growing just modestly, not indicting the growth in risk that was being reflected under the CAPM.

FIGURE 1-1

Cal-Maine Foods' Cost of Equity Capital versus Market Capitalization

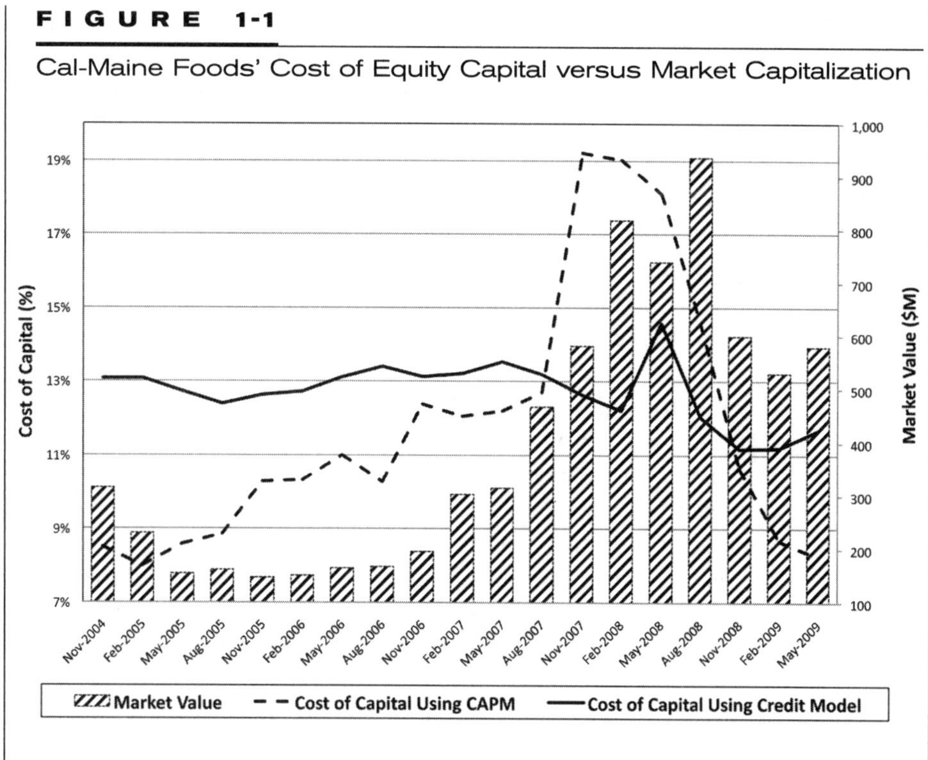

The company's market value rose from a low of $147 million to a high of $936 million as its cost of equity capital based on my credit model remained in the relatively narrow range between 11.2 and 13.5 percent. Meanwhile, Cal-Maine's cost of equity capital based on beta (CAPM) reflects a progressive increase in risk, which would serve to reduce its fair-value estimate. Equity investors were, in this example, obviously following the credit and cash-flow cost of capital and not the cost of equity implied by the CAPM.

It is no wonder the analysis of risk represents the single most important underexplored factor in security analysis and the primary reason for investor disappointment in investment returns. The closer the free cash flows are to meeting expectations, the less is expected volatility. And that risk is best defined through the cost of capital.

COST-OF-CAPITAL MODEL

Chapter 8 presents a cost-of-capital credit model, including a worksheet and related definitions. The purpose of the worksheet is to allow the user to formulate a superior cost-of-equity-capital projection with the goal of improving investment performance. I am confident that this will be the case, and I present the analyst with an important view of how risk might be currently misperceived by the investment marketplace.

In fact, the reader may wish to begin this book with a thorough reading of Chapter 8. It is this chapter that explains many of the terms, adjustments, and analyses used and discussed in prior chapters. Incorporating many departments in finance gathered over the past 35 years, the credit model platform of Chapter 8 has been devised taking a deep and wide array of fundamental items into consideration, including cash flows, sales, taxes, cost of sales and cash flow volatility, cash burn rate, credit, yield spreads, insurance, potential for lawsuits, and about 50 other metrics. Cost of capital is measured as a function of the firm's operating and financial risk, not how its stock price zigzags. If you know the true cost of capital and free cash flow, you then can take advantage of those zigzags. The model is designed to evaluate all credits, with the express purpose of offering a systematic approach for spotting trends that the marketplace in general may not see. Included are metrics that allow users to see "around the corner" through the inclusion and evaluation of areas that normally are not covered by security analysts today.

Betas constantly change, whereas credit risk typically changes slowly. An additional advantage of the credit model is that it eliminates unnecessary high portfolio turnover. If an investor does not have a consistent fundamental credit-risk measure, he or she would be uncertain of an investment's true value, resulting in high trading costs.

The cost-of-capital model in Chapter 8, along with the estimation of free cash flow shown in Chapter 4, should provide the reader of this book with the primary valuation yardsticks needed to achieve superior investment performance.

APPLICATION OF FREE CASH FLOW AND COST OF CAPITAL

I conclude this journey with the results of a live portfolio using the principles outlined. While I was not surprised that a diversified portfolio of companies that produced consistently large and growing amounts of normalized free cash flow, with low cost of capital and high return on invest capital, outperformed the general market, I was pleasantly surprised that it did so in both up and down quarters. The results are presented in Chapter 9.

With that, let us begin!

CHAPTER 2

Management

Corporate executives have direct control over the financing, operations, and resources (assets) of the company—bad decisions destroy value and good ones create it. Certain industries, because their cash flows have higher than normal uncertainty or volatility and are leveraged, are more difficult to manage (including planning) than others, such as airlines and commodity-based firms. As such, mergers in these type of entities are notoriously risky.

Management that is as transparent in its decision making as it is in its good execution makes analysts' jobs a lot easier and at the same time can provide invaluable insights into current industry conditions and trends; management insight is especially needed when operating results are less consistent. Management that is not transparent raises lots of questions, including: Why aren't executives open to questioning? Stocks react to changes in management, often resulting in very large shifts in market value. Analysts get to know and judge management, including level of trust and candidness, in addition to managers' proven ability to drive results in either direction.

The abilities of management can be clearly measured, starting with the revenue line and comparing it with historical trends and those of the industry. If the company operates in more than one segment, assessment of all individual segments is required, allowing for an evaluation of the managers or group heads of the reporting operating units. This would include performance of recent acquisitions and capital outlays that called for the expenditure of cash. A company that reports consistently positive nominal, real, and relative growth in revenues and cash flows, along with a return on invested capital above its cost of capital, is one that is managed effectively; that is, one can attribute the gains to management (and employee) effectiveness.

However, executives must also be judged on their ability to perceive and control risk. And toward that end, we look at those factors which influence the cost of capital. It is these factors—from insurance adequacy (including self-insurance), to litigation hedging and tax rate management, that can expose the entity to risks we will quantify through our cost of capital model. Risk is just as important a barometer of management ability as is return in invested capital.

Superior management will be manifested, relative to its competition, through

1. Greater growth rate in cash flows from operations
2. Greater growth in free cash flow
3. Higher return on invested capital (ROIC)
4. Lower cost of capital

For non-capital-intensive firms, including companies that deal in services and entities that are able to leverage off the capital intensity of other concerns (i.e., those which outsource), economic profit as a percentage of revenues would be added to these evaluation yardsticks. (Chapter 5 discusses economic profit.)

Superior managers have a clear sense of the marketplace and recognize that it is often important to see demand established prior to committing capital. Creating demand for a product or service that does not yet exist takes greater skill and is often risky. For example, Gemstar was unsuccessful at bringing its handheld e-reader, a device that could download books to itself, to market. Now, the e-reader is a successful product, made so by another company, but Gemstar wound up failing with its attempt.

Clearly, Apple and Google created their most successful products many years after a market was established. They, as well as other superiorly managed firms, showed that they had an edge bringing the products to market. McKinsey[1] noted, after surveying more than 300 employees at 28 companies across North America and Europe, that companies with the best product-development track records did three things better than their peers:

- They create a clear sense of project goals early on.
- They nurture a strong project culture in their workplace.
- They maintain close contact with customers throughout a project's duration.

COMPARATIVE ANALYSIS

Table 2-1 highlights comparative data for Motorola, Inc., a large technology company specializing in mobile devices, including the manufacture of cell phones. Motorola is in an extremely competitive industry, pitted against such companies as Apple, Research in Motion, LG, and Nokia. It is where management is of utmost importance, from research to manufacturing.

As discerned from the table, Motorola has a higher cost of capital than its peers, reflective of its revenue volatility, declining trend in cash flows, and deteriorating credit. The company's return on investment is negative, whereas it is

---

[1]McKinsey & Co., "Operations Extranet," Gordon, Gupta & Rebentisch, December 2009.

positive for its peer group. In fact, it is difficult to find a financial measure where Motorola is superior to its peers.

One must conclude, based on its financial performance and risk profile, that Motorola management has been sub-par—a reflection of the company's superiorly managed competition, not industry demand, which has been strong. Management's inability to earn a higher return on company assets than the firm's cost of capital has not been lost on investors, and the company's stock has declined 90 percent from its high. Having been unsuccessful remedying its financial performance, Motorola is in the midst of spinning off its telecom unit.

TABLE 2-1

Mototola Comparative Analysis

	MOTOROLA INC	MOT	6 Co PEER Avg (Incl Target)	
	Sep09 LTM	5 Yr Avg	LTM	5 Yr Avg
LIQUIDITY				
Current Ratio	2.02	1.93	2.52	3.00
Quick Ratio	1.44	1.40	2.36	2.81
Working Capital Per Share	3.34	4.84	2.18	2.17
Cash Flow Per Share	0.09	0.73	0.21	0.69
ACTIVITY				
Inventory Turnover	5.37	7.61	22.66	20.80
Receivables Turnover	5.46	5.89	6.78	6.16
Total Asset Turnover	0.87	1.04	0.39	0.47
Average Collection Period (Days)	63.24	62.18	55.66	65.30
Days to Sell Inventory	65.88	48.94	7.37	9.91
Operating Cycle (Days)	129.12	111.12	65.87	75.22
PERFORMANCE				
Sales/Net PP & E	10.55	15.14	20.51	16.69
Sales/Stockholder Equity	2.39	2.52	0.63	0.76
PROFITABILITY				
Gross Profit Margin (%)	32.96	32.01	86.10	85.47
Operating Margin Before Depr (%)	3.64	8.46	34.70	30.92
Operating Margin After Depr (%)	0.34	6.44	31.78	21.55
Pretax Profit Margin (%)	−8.91	5.80	32.56	23.69
Net Profit Margin (%)	−16.58	2.54	25.05	15.15
Return on Assets (%)	−15.61	2.58	9.78	8.41
Return on Equity (%)	−39.86	3.54	15.26	13.14
Return on Investment (%)	−28.30	3.87	13.73	12.67
Cost of Capital	11.40	10.02	8.11	8.48
Return on Avg Assets (%)	−14.51	3.15	9.36	9.37
Return on Avg Equity (%)	−38.58	6.43	15.27	15.00
Return on Avg Investment (%)	−27.63	5.10	13.53	14.07

(Continued)

TABLE 2-1 *(Continued)*

Mototola Comparative Analysis

	MOTOROLA INC	MOT	6 Co PEER Avg (Incl Target)	
	Sep09 LTM	5 Yr Avg	LTM	5 Yr Avg
LEVERAGE				
Interest Coverage Before Tax	−6.39	7.71	22.61	208.31
Interest Coverage After Tax	−12.82	4.25	14.05	162.06
Adj OCF/Int Cov	3.46	7.05	34.88	177.77
LT Debt/Common Equity (%)	39.77	28.36	23.00	21.89
LT Debt/Shareholder Equity (%)	39.77	28.36	23.00	21.89
Total Debt/Adj OCF	3.49	2.47	2.03	3.44
Total Debt / Market Capitalization	0.20	0.17	0.03	0.04
Total Debt/Total Equity (%)	40.01	32.58	24.89	23.87
Total Debt/Invested Capital (%)	28.40	25.10	11.69	12.76
Total Debt/Total Assets (%)	15.67	13.58	9.13	9.10
Total Assets/Common Equity	2.55	2.38	1.70	1.71
MARKET				
P/E	−4.48	−55.41	41.40	17.68
Price/Earnings from Operations	−8.29	23.57	33.05	7.10
Price to Book	2.07	2.57	5.02	5.43
Price to Sales per Share	0.76	1.07	8.27	8.94
Price to Cash Flow per Share	89.09	16.23	106.13	230.73
Price to Free Cash Flow per Share	−30.77	−17.59	13.63	12.99
Dividend Yield (%)	0.58	1.66	2.23	0.03
Dividend Payout (%)	−2.91	−83.16	51.92	1.01
GROWTH RATES YR OVER YR				
Sales Growth (%)	−28.17	3.50	25.21	17.82
Net Income Growth (%)	−690.55	−1682.44	7.85	57.63
EPS Primary Excl Ex Growth (%)	−719.05	−705.50	9.03	59.87
EPS (Basic from Op) Growth (%)	−2225.00	−67.54	33.68	104.00
Cash Flow per Share Growth (%)	−949.83	−107.26	4.99	461.86
Free CF per Share Growth (%)	−58.63	−32.85	−29.98	77.16
Capital Spending Growth (%)	−41.27	−3.68	33.30	13.48
Reinvested Earnings Growth (%)	−76.07	22.42	95.96	39.38
Equity Capital Growth (%)	−33.08	−3.08	52.74	23.09
Total Assets Growth (%)	−24.37	−1.97	46.16	25.87
Dividend Growth Rate (%)	75.00	4.80	1925.00	#DIV/0!

Source: CT Capital, LLC, Research Insight.

Example:

When Ronald Tutor, chairman of Perini Corporation, sought to combine the company with another entity he controlled, he had no problem convincing his "independent" board members. Investors did not agree with his judgment because, on announcement of the merger, and despite a conference call with investors and analysts touting the benefits of the combination, Perini stock suffered a precipitous decline. Shareholders were diluting their interest in favor of Mr. Tutor and the cash-flow dilution caused by the additional shares relative to the acquired entity's cash flows.

Perini released the following press release:

Merger with Tutor-Saliba Corporation

> On September 8, 2008, we completed the merger with Tutor-Saliba pursuant to an agreement and plan of merger between us, Tutor-Saliba, Ronald N. Tutor and shareholders of Tutor-Saliba. The merger and related transactions were recommended to the Board by the Special Committee which included only independent and disinterested directors. Subsequent to the approval of the merger by our shareholders, we issued 22,987,293 shares of our common stock to the shareholders of Tutor-Saliba in exchange for 100 percent of the outstanding capital stock of Tutor-Saliba. Mr. Tutor served as our Chairman and Chief Executive Officer prior to the merger and continues in that role pursuant to an employment agreement (see "Employment Agreement," page 23). In addition, Mr. Tutor controls two trusts that collectively owned 96 percent of the outstanding stock of Tutor-Saliba prior to the merger. As a result of the merger, Mr. Tutor, through these two trusts, became the beneficial owner of approximately 43 percent of our outstanding common stock. (Mr. Tutor's beneficial ownership has since increased to 46 percent of our outstanding common stock due to the effect of our share repurchase program, which decreased the number of outstanding shares by approximately 2 million shares.) The shares owned by the two trusts are subject to certain restrictions contained in a shareholders agreement between Mr. Tutor, us and other former Tutor-Saliba shareholders as described on page 28.

Changes in upper management often signal upcoming disappointments in operations, especially if the change comes just prior to the actual release of financial results. If, however, investors perceive that the change will result in enhanced cash flows, the stock most often will react quite positively.

When management is highly controlled, as at Perini, by strong insiders and a weak board of directors, the controlling person or group typically has a magnified effect, being able to steer the entity's cash flow and cost of capital. Station Casinos, a hotel/gaming concern based in Nevada, enjoyed strong growth as a result of the rapid population influx into the state during the period 1980–2007. The company benefited because its properties catered to the "locals" market as opposed to out-of-state tourism.

It is important for an investor to feel management, and especially the board of directors, is exercising independent judgment and is professionally skilled and trained in various areas that will maximize the value of their shares. We have all observed situations where corporate officers are undeservedly enriched while shareholders see the value of their shares fall. Management profiting when the company is doing well should be respected, but managers should do so in proportion to shareholders and not more. It is the responsibility of the compensation committee of the board of directors to see such is the case.

As we see below, some firms do align management and shareholders' interests.

Example:

On November 7, 2007, officers and certain employees were granted 48,000 shares of restricted common stock that can be earned only if either one of two defined multiyear performance goals is met within five years of the date of grant ("Performance Shares"). If the performance goals are not earned by the end of this five-year period, the Performance Shares will be forfeited. Vesting of Performance Shares is subject to certain performance measures being met and can be based on an interim earn-out of 25, 50, 75, or 100 percent. The defined performance goals are tied to two different performance measures: (1) growth of free cash flow per share on a trailing twelve-month basis and (2) growth of royalty ounces in reserve on an annual basis.

Source: 2008 10K, Royal Gold, Inc.

Example:

The management of Station Casinos (STN) saw its business grow through two generations of family leadership. As population growth in the State of Nevada took hold, so did the revenues of STN. Rather than balancing the company's massive growth in capital spending with cash flow from operations and additional equity, however, controlling shareholders and senior management spent as much cash as it could in as many places as their creditors would allow, leveraging the balance such that fixed-charge coverage (discussed in Chapters 6 and 8) became unhealthy. When the economy stalled and unemployment grew, STN's financial structure could not withstand the weight of its financial obligations.

As the following financial exhibits clearly illustrate, the company borrowed large amounts of cash not just for new hotels but also to finance dividends and share buybacks. While cash flow from operations was showing solid growth resulting in a large runup in its stock price (Figure 2-1), the controlling shareholders' profligate spending resulted in an increasingly higher leverage profile. Moreover, to build leverage is to increase the cost of capital, and hence risk, because the financial structure allows for less margin for error, an unusual event or a deteriorating business climate. Unfortunately, many investors tend to ignore a shift in the risk profile when the numerator of the valuation equation (earnings or cash flow) is growing.

Gaming was considered an industry whose future growth was forecast by analysts as fairly certain, and as the Station Casino's stockholders' chart Table 2-1 reveals, investors agreed. In 2006, management of Station spent $881 million buying back its stock at the same time that it expended $755 million on capital expenditures. During that year, the company generated $293 million in operating cash flow as the cash burn was financed by $1.5 billion in new borrowings. The company's cash interest expense, as reported in its supplemental cash-flow information in its Statement of Cash Flows (see table), was $137 million, or almost half the operating cash flows. Free cash flow was negative by over $1.2 billion. Meanwhile, management paid $65 million in dividends, all of which contributed to the company having negative shareholders' equity from a modestly positive capital cushion the year before.

TABLE 2-2

Principal Stockholders of Station Casinos (2006)

	Amount and Nature of Beneficial Ownership		
Name and Address of Beneficial Owner	**Currently Owned**	**Acquirable within 60 days**	**Percent of Class**
Frank J. Fertitta III	5,674,443	45,000	8.5
Lorenzo J. Fertitta	5,475,979	30,000	8.2
FMR Corp (4)	5,587,350	—	8.4
Blake L. Sartini (5)	3,911,411	—	5.9
Delise F. Sartini (5)	3,856,763	—	5.8
Scott M Nielson (6)	678,527	10,000	1.0
Glenn C. Christenson (7)	533,857	15,000	*
William W. Warner (8)	472,959	60,000	*
Richard J. Haskins (9)	205,847	10,000	*
James E. Nave, D.V.M.	45,000	—	*
Lowell H. Lebermann, Jr	34,500	—	*
Lee S. Isgur (10)	24,500	—	*
Robert E. Lewis	17,500	—	*
Executive officers and directors as a group (10 persons)	13,163,112	170,000	19.6

Source: Proxy material, Station Casinos, 2006.

During the preceding three years, management and the board of directors also felt compelled to spend over $1 billion buying back stock during the ambitious capital spending period, taking away the capital cushion that could have braced the company during the coming business slowdown.

In 2007, the company was taken private in a $5.4 billion deal, whereas its debt continued to trade publically, which it did until it fell to near zero as the company filed bankruptcy only a couple of years after the buyout.

The company, in its merger documents (see "Successor"), cited a positive net worth only through writing up almost $3 billion in goodwill and writing up its property, plant, and equipment account by almost $600 million. The large unnecessary cash outflows resulted in a high cash burn rate[2] and, with its leverage, resulted in the company's cost of capital, based on my credit model, rising to over 23 percent.

Unfortunately, Station Casinos had no check on the profligate spending by senior management. Not only did insiders control almost 20 percent of the stock, but the company also had very onerous antitakeover provisions, as well as a

[2] The cash burn rate is explained in Chapter 6.

position of paying senior management and board members high compensation packages, including stock. Was there any reason for these very well-paid insiders and board members to disagree with what controlling insiders were doing? With no strong system of checks and balances, the controlling shareholders had free reign, which they took advantage of.

FIGURE 2-1

Comparison of Station Casino's 5-Year Cumulative Total Return

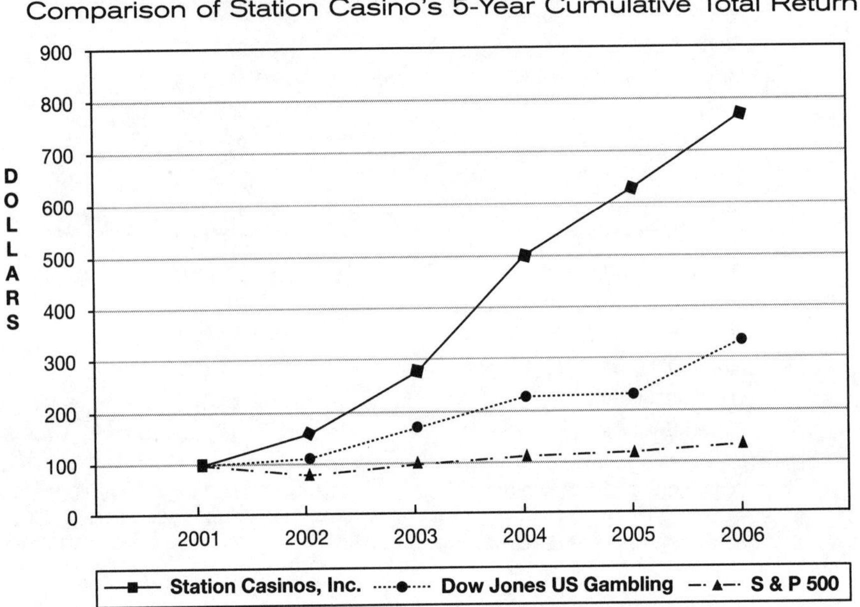

STATION CASINOS, INC.
CONSOLIDATED BALANCE SHEETS
(Amounts in thousands, except share data)

	Successor	Predecessor
	December 31, 2007	December 31, 2006
ASSETS		
Current assets		
Cash and cash equivalents	$96,392	$116,898
Restricted cash	966	—
Receivables, net	48,680	40,762
Inventories	12,496	9,676
Prepaid gaming tax	21,541	21,519
Prepaid expenses	14,472	12,696
Total current assets	194,547	201,551

	Successor	Predecessor
	December 31, 2007	December 31, 2006
Property and equipment, net	3,563,497	2,586,473
Goodwill	2,964,938	154,498
Intangible assets, net	1,002,617	—
Land held for development	516,186	214,374
Investments in joint ventures	391,953	253,577
Native American development costs	200,667	181,153
Other assets, net	154,261	125,070
Total assets	$8,988,666	$3,716,696
LIABILITIES AND STOCKHOLDERS' EQUITY (DEFICIT)		
Current liabilities:		
Current portion of long-term debt	$2,610	$341
Accounts payable	16,954	19,558
Construction contracts payable	23,151	58,318
Accrued expenses and other current liabilities	178,018	173,689
Total current liabilities	220,733	251,906
Long-term debt less current portion	5,241,814	3,468,487
Deferred income tax, net	789,644	109,788
Due to unconsolidated affiliate	100,000	—
Other long-term liabilities, net	65,413	73,373
Total liabilities	6,417,604	3,903,554
Commitments and contingencies		
Stockholders' equity (deficit):		
Successor:		
Common stock, par value $0.01; authorized 10,000 shares; 41.7 shares issued	—	—
Nonvoting common stock, par value $0.01; authorized 1 million shares; 41,674,838 shares issued	417	—
Predecessor:		
Common stock, par value $0.01; authorized 135,000,000 shares; 80,507,427 shares issued	—	593
Treasury stock, 23,245,751 shares, at cost	—	(1,039,804)
Additional paid-in capital	2,948,265	582,739
Accumulated other comprehensive loss	(59,666)	(10,782)
Retained (deficit) earnings	(317,954)	280,396
Total stockholders' equity (deficit)	2,571,062	(186,858)
Total liabilities and stockholders' equity (deficit)	$8,988,666	$3,716,696

STATION CASINOS, INC.
CONSOLIDATED STATEMENTS OF CASH FLOWS
(amounts in thousands)

	Successor		Predecessor	
	Period from November 8, 2007, Through December 31, 2007	Period from January 1, 2007, Through November 7, 2007	Year Ended December 31, 2006	Year Ended December 31, 2005
Cash flows from operating activities:				
Net (loss) income	$(317,954)	$(57,656)	$110,212	$161,886
Adjustments to reconcile net (loss) income to net cash provided by operating activities:				
Depreciation and amortization	32,292	136,498	131,094	101,356
Tax benefit from exercise of stock options	—	—	—	31,803
Excess tax benefit from exercise of stock options	(23,303)	—	(3,145)	—
Share-based compensation	288,130	143,714	24,294	12,669
Earnings from joint ventures	(1,132)	(10,744)	(35,046)	(31,938)
Distributions of earnings from joint ventures	—	82,115	890	11,867
Amortization of debt discount and issuance costs	5,907	4,392	4,731	3,262
Loss on early retirement of debt	20,311	—	—	1,278
Impairment loss	—	16,631	—	—
Changes in assets and liabilities:				
Receivables, net	2,786	(10,704)	(21,158)	1,848
Inventories and prepaid expenses	1,439	(6,057)	(9,836)	(4,419)
Deferred income tax	7,392	(24,023)	38,739	59,481
Accounts payable	(10,422)	7,818	6,947	2,260
Accrued expenses and other current liabilities	18,454	(13,342)	39,589	19,885
Other, net	(5,211)	4,831	6,062	5,653
Total adjustments	336,643	331,129	183,161	215,005
Net cash provided by operating activities	18,689	273,473	293,373	376,891
Cash flows from investing activities:				
Acquisition of Station Casinos, Inc., including direct merger costs	(4,217,469)	—	—	—
Capital expenditures	(55,510)	(530,364)	(754,988)	(830,805)
Proceeds from sale of land, property, and equipment	105	10,019	18,002	22,143
Investments in joint ventures, net	(27,983)	(81,552)	(39,759)	(1,295)

	Successor		Predecessor	
	Period from November 8, 2007, Through December 31, 2007	Period from January 1, 2007, Through November 7, 2007	Year Ended December 31, 2006	Year Ended December 31, 2005
Distributions in excess of earnings from joint ventures	488	106,999	—	—
Construction contracts payable	(19,619)	(15,548)	(24,833)	46,853
Native American development costs	(2,454)	(17,060)	(15,909)	(111,900)
Other, net	(1,523)	(2,912)	(18,774)	(10,323)
Net cash used in investing activities	(4,323,965)	(530,418)	(836,261)	(885,327)
Cash flows from financing activities:				
Cash equity contributions	2,706,145	—	—	—
Proceeds from issuance of CMBS loans	2,475,000	—	—	—
Borrowings under the revolver with maturity dates less than 3 months, net	293,100	—	—	—
Borrowings under the term loan with maturity dates greater than 3 months	250,000	—	—	—
(Payments) Borrowings under revolving facility with maturity dates less than 3 months, net	(1,383,300)	227,500	825,800	278,500
Proceeds from issuance of related party promissory note	—	100,000	—	—
Proceeds from financing transaction	—	70,000	—	—
Proceeds from the issuance of senior and senior subordinated notes, net	—	—	698,500	358,250
Redemption of senior and senior subordinated notes	—	—	—	(34,272)
Purchase of treasury stock	—	(110,164)	(880,676)	(21,414)
Payment of dividends	—	(49,050)	(65,403)	(62,643)
Debt issuance costs	(60,086)	(8)	(8,660)	(11,381)
Exercise of stock options	—	560	1,562	18,957
Excess tax benefit from exercise of stock options	23,303	—	3,145	—
Other, net	(1,229)	(56)	(34)	(426)
Net cash provided by financing activities	4,302,933	238,782	574,234	525,571
Cash and cash equivalents:				
(Decrease) increase in cash and cash equivalents	(2,343)	(18,163)	31,346	17,135
Balance, beginning of period	98,735	116,898	85,552	68,417
Balance, end of period	$96,392	$98,735	$116,898	$85,552

CHANGES IN SENIOR MANAGEMENT

As we saw with Station Casino, insider-controlled management can usurp the corporate checkbook and capital. Changes in key management positions often send shareholders an important signal—the board is unhappy with current results and has decided to move in a new direction. New executives have their own ideas as to how corporate assets are best used, where cash should be spent, which assets need to be disposed of, and any other uses of cash, such as acquisitions that should be considered.

> **Example:**
>
> The stock and business operations of Walt Disney, Inc., suffered a noticeable decline shortly after the 1994 departure of Jeffrey Katzenberg, who ran Disney's movie studio. When he left to form DreamWorks, a rival movie studio, he took many of the best animators at his former employer with him. Katzenberg had been at Disney for 10 years prior to his departure, helping to propel the company's results and stock price to record highs.

> **Example:**
>
> In March 2005, shares in NCR Corp. tumbled over 17 percent the day it was announced that Mike Hurd, its CEO, would leave the company to join Hewlett-Packard. At NCR, Hurd had cut costs while increasing revenues, and as a result, free cash flow grew substantially. As the shares in NCR were falling on the date of announcement, stock in Hewlett-Packard rose over 10 percent.

Were shareholders overreacting to the management changes at NCR and Hewlett-Packard, or were they correct? In the 3 years subsequent to joining Hewlett-Packard, as observed in Figure 2-2, free cash flow grew, whereas back at NCR, free cash flow fell.

The ability of Mr. Hurd to take actions that resulted in increased free cash flow at Hewlett-Packard (HP) has enriched HP investors. As seen in the relative performance of the stocks (Figure 2-3), Hewlett-Packard has substantially outperformed NCR.

> **Example:**
>
> When Feld Entertainment, a privately held entertainment entity whose operating companies include Barnum and Bailey Circus and Disney on Ice, acquired Monster Trucks, Inc., management was easily able to improve free cash flow through selective increases in ticket prices and intensive cost savings, including right-sizing discretionary expenditures such as the combining of advertising departments. Since the prior owner could have initiated many of the same actions, the cash-flow enhancement was clearly a reflection of managerial skill set.

F I G U R E 2-2

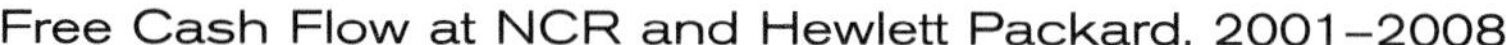

Free Cash Flow at NCR and Hewlett Packard, 2001–2008

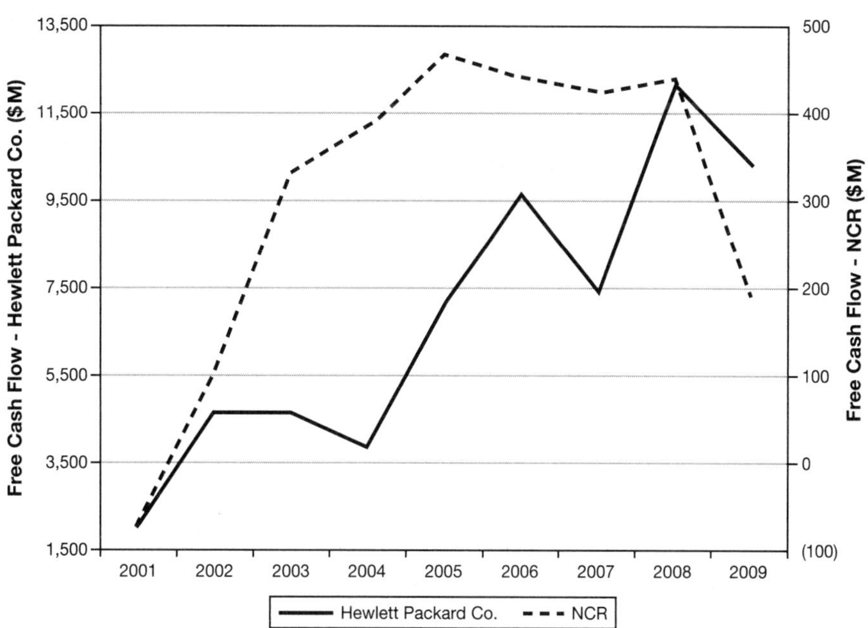

F I G U R E 2-3

Cumulative Returns of NCR and Hewlett-Packard (HPQ)

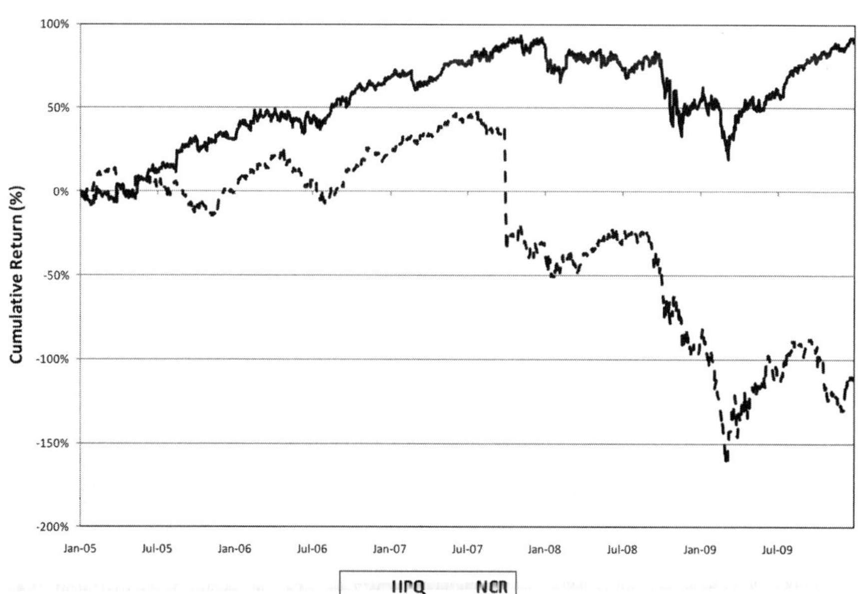

CASH FLOWS, PRODUCTIVITY, AND STOCK PRICES

Productivity growth is probably the single most important indicator of an economy's health.

The Economist, November 4, 2004

Most corporate managers and economists believe that productivity measures lie at the top of determinants of value creation and corporate health. For this reason, it is a recurring theme during meetings with investors and in regulatory filings, as expressed in a September 2009 8K filing for Kraft Foods concurrent with its bid for Cadbury PLC: "A strong pipeline of cost-savings initiatives will result in higher productivity and better margins as part of its three-year plan."

We will see that while productivity is certainly an important factor that could lead to higher cash flows, its positive bearings are confined primarily as a measure of consequence to the current or soon-to-be free-cash-flow producer. If a firm's products are met with insufficient demand and the inputs under which they are produced do not generate satisfactory cash flows, it would be rare for productivity improvements to be able to turn the business around. If the entity is a satisfactory producer of free cash flow, then productivity improvements can indeed lead to even greater free cash flow and a higher security price. For this reason, top-line growth and cash flow from operations are more important valuation and cost-of-capital metrics than productivity.

During periods of slow growth or expectations of slowing growth, managers often pursue a downsizing strategy, including layoffs, efficiencies, and reductions in the number of manufacturing facilities, all in an effort to improve long-term productivity. But what realistically can be expected from such actions?

Economics students learn that productivity, as commonly defined, grew about 2.2 percent per year in the second half of the twentieth century. Economic teachings have us believe that increases above this rate lead to higher than expected corporate profits and hence higher than expected stock prices. If this is the case, we would expect to see companies that are noted for and continuously employ such productivity-enhancing measures, also referred to as *rightsizing*, tending to have investment returns that are higher than those of the general stock market. Certainly, few companies, if any, come to mind ahead of General Electric (GE), which has seen many of its former executives hired to lead other large business enterprises.

Figure 2-4 shows that during the period 2004–2009, a good period to study because it includes both economic expansion and recession, GE underperformed the returns of the Standard and Poor's (S&P) 500 Index. While GE is perceived as a company with excellent managerial skills, if those skills cannot be translated into higher free cash flow, shareholders do not benefit, as they have not since the end of 2002, a full 4 years prior to the outset of the 2007 recession. GE's performance was not, as many would suspect, solely due to its financial exposure; its underperformance began years earlier.

FIGURE 2-4

Stock Price: GE versus S&P 500 Index

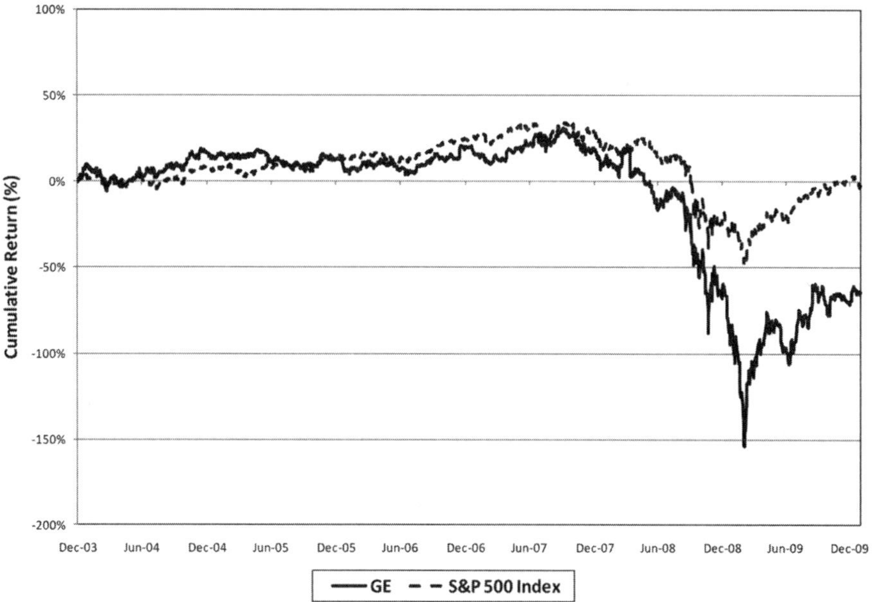

Is GE's stock price performance an anomaly? My analysis concludes that companies such as GE should match their workforce to their operating and free cash flow and not their workforce to output, which GE bases on business strategies such as Six Sigma, a productivity-enhancement tool tied to output, not cash flows. If a firm requires additional labor to match output, which would result in negative free cash flow, one should question making an investment in such an entity until it is evident that free cash flow will be realized.

While it takes a greater workforce to produce a greater level of goods and services, it is not the purpose of a for-profit enterprise to provide employment but rather to produce free cash flow as a residual of that labor. The distinction is subtle but significant.

Figure 2-5 illustrates an interesting dichotomy, leading into the 2007 recession, between the growth rate in sales per employee (year over year) for the aggregate S&P 500 companies relative to cash flow from operations adjusted for normalized balance-sheet changes, power operating cash flow (OCF). Power OCF rose between 2004 and 2007, coincident with the economic expansion. However, beginning 2008, as corporate officers recognized a weakening in their business, they began to step up balance-sheet management to enhance operating cash flows, but, as reflected in the figure, power OCF tumbled. Since power OCF normalizes the working-capital changes, its use provides better predictive value because it is based on the liquidity normalized generation of the operating company.

Also shown in Figure 2-5, the right axis reflects indicate positive growth in productivity, as measured by the growth rate in sales per employee. Sales per employee rose during the recession year of 2008, *and despite the cuts in labor that were taking place at the time, and which translated into rising productivity measures, the improvements were not finding their way into normalized operating cash flows.* Investors who thus made decisions on the basis of changes in productivity-enhancing actions were sorely disappointed. Not so were investors who focused on normalized (power operating) cash flows, which had been in a declining trend since the beginning of the decade.

Corporate executives who are continually reviewing their internal portfolio, enhancing their products and lines of business, and filling in strategic gaps where necessary to improve core competencies while eliminating and streamlining assets that underperform, with an eye on cash flows, typically see higher returns on invested capital than executives who simply look to shed labor as a quick-fix solution. This is an important distinguishing factor in the cost-of-capital-credit model.

FIGURE 2-5

Year-over-Year Rate of Growth in Sales per Employee versus Power OCF: S&P 500

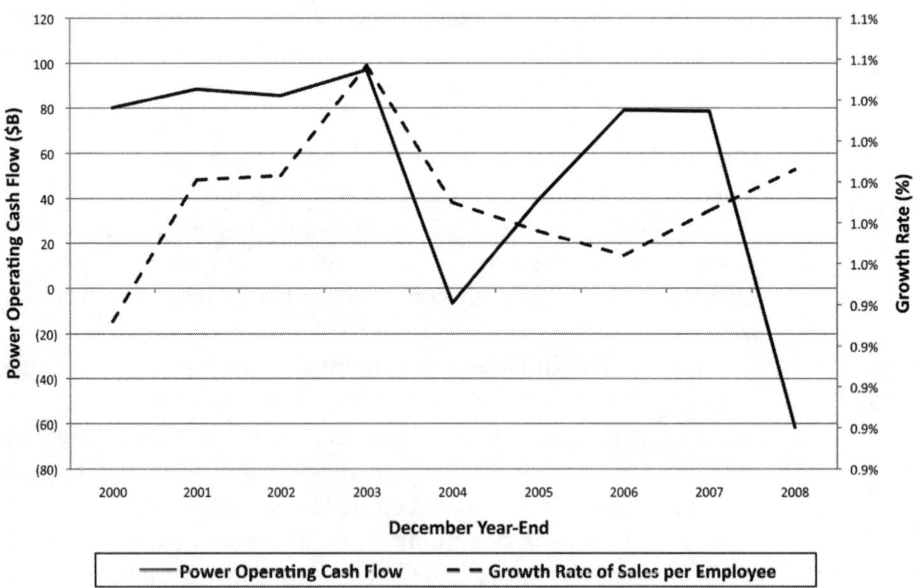

Source: CT Capital, LLC.

While the model considers productivity-boosting measures as value enhancing, it is not awarded the large weighting most investors believe exists, and for companies that are not positive producers of cash flows, its weighting is zero. *The weaker the cash flows, the lower is the importance of enhancing productivity to cost-of-capital improvement.* If an entity has no prospect of ever generating free cash flow, its equity value, as a going concern, is at best zero regardless of how many units it produces.

Management often faces quick decisions concerning its workforce, including the growth outlook for its products and services and the various product lines within the company's markets. As the following examples show, however, if the free cash flows are absent, layoffs hopefully can provide a bridge to a turnaround.

Example:

DuPont, despite substantial layoffs, did not report positive free cash flow for the second quarter of 2009 or the first 6 months of 2009. The company did beat earnings estimates, owing to reduced headcount.

> DuPont Co.'s (DD) second-quarter profit plunged 61 percent on lower volumes as the chemical company continued to struggle with weak demand. Earnings results beat expectations, though revenue fell short of analysts' views.
>
> Chemical companies have been scrambling to cope with falling demand in recent months as major customers in the construction, automotive, and textile industries have slashed inventories. For its part, DuPont has announced 12,000 layoffs since late 2008 and cut its earnings target in April.
>
> Chief Executive Ellen Kullman said the company's actions to boost productivity and cut costs are paying off as it contends with continued weak demand in key segments.
>
> The company reported earnings of $417 million, or 46 cents a share, down from $1.08 billion, or $1.18 a share, a year earlier. The latest period included 15 cents of restructuring charges.
>
> Revenue decreased 22 percent to $6.86 billion.

Source: Wall Street Journal, July 21, 2009.

Example:

Sometimes an entity's desire to avoid a cut in its credit rating forces a particular decision concerning its labor force as management strives to raise assurance that it has the ability to control costs while business is soft. MGIC, the large mortgage insurer, reduced its workforce, hoping it would reflect to the agencies an aggressive act which would help preserve its investment-grade rating, without which it would be virtually assured of not being able to write new business. In fact, the company was able to maintain its grade longer than warranted even though its cash flows and stock price were collapsing from defaults on mortgage payments related to its investments that took place prior to the 2008 housing slump. MGIC's long-term credit rating eventually was reduced to CCC after its stock had lost over 90 percent of its value, too late for shareholders who believed that the cuts in the company's overhead would result in a continuation of its investment-grade credit.

Example:

NEW YORK—Lucent Technologies, Inc., has announced another round of layoffs even as Standard and Poor's cut the wireless vendor's credit rating one notch to "B–," its sixth-highest junk rating. The company said it will cut 10,000 more jobs, or 22 percent of its workforce, and it expects to report a wider-than-expected fourth-quarter loss.

The job cuts will bring down the staff strength to 35,000 instead of the projected 45,000 at the end of the year. Lucent has been slashing its workforce repeatedly since the telecom industry's meltdown began last year. It had anticipated a bounce back to profitability after cutting half of its about 106,000 staff last year, but the company's fortunes have continued to dwindle.

Source: BNET.com.

Corporate executives are initially reluctant to cut staffing levels, especially if they sense that demand will be restored within a reasonable period of time, even if current levels are obviously mismatched with output and cash flows. There is a natural reluctance to cut payroll, even though the facts dictate otherwise, premised on the "invisible handshake" theory of the cost of retraining new employees and allegiance to existing ones.

The workforce and productive capital and plant can be set once current and projected operating and free cash flows are reasonably estimated; it would be imprudent to match workforce and plant with units of production or revenues if the entity is not capable of generating long-term free cash flow.

WHY IT'S CASH FLOW, NOT PRODUCTIVITY, THAT MATTERS

Shown next are leading productivity and cash-flow metrics for two technology companies, Photronics and IBM. Photronics' rate of revenue growth was slightly in excess of IBM's, 3.1 versus 2 percent, for the period 2000–2008. Despite IBM's lower growth rate in revenues, the firm increased total employment at a greater rate than Photronics but did so with less expensive foreign labor. Management at IBM recognized the need for additional employees but did so in a way that matched its estimates of production and sales with its free cash flow. As a result, subsequent free cash flow grew. Photronics increased its labor force despite a weakening of free cash flow, relying on its historical revenue growth in making this decision. The company was concerned about loss of market share to aggressively priced foreign competition and was matching workforce to revenues. Eventually, Photronics was forced to respond to the weakening of its free cash flow and lay off employees, but by then, free cash flow had turned negative, causing the company's stock price to drop rather dramatically.

Photronics

Photronics, a supplier to the semiconductor industry, showed a long history of rising productivity (Figure 2-6), as measured by revenues per employee. Sales/property, plant, and equipment, before depreciation, however, continued to slide (Figure 2-7). Unlike Photronics, IBM (Figure 2-7) saw its revenues per employee generally dropping throughout the decade, except for a brief spurt in 2004, reflecting a substantial drop in productivity. On the other hand, IBM experienced a consistent rise in its sales/property, plant, and equipment (PPE) as the firm became more software-centric given its new lower requirements for capital assets. Shown is PPE *prior* to accumulated depreciation because (1) companies use differing depreciation schedules, (2) depreciation, in many instances, does not reflect the true lifespan of the asset, and (3) we better capture the true cash spent on the asset. A fully depreciated economic asset could make it appear as if management used its resources more efficiently than actually was the case.

Table 2-3 shows Photronic's free cash flow per employee declining after 2001, whereas it rose for IBM. During 2006, Photronic's free cash flow rose owing to "working" the balance-sheet items. Normalizing the changes in balance-sheet items, as we do for power OCF, would have shown that free cash flow declined that year.

The fall (see Figure 2-6) in Photronic's total employment during 2008 allowed the ratio of sales per employee to generally rise compared with the dotted line, which reflects revenues as a percentage of property, plant, and equipment, which is not as easily reduced and, as I pointed out, can be managed through writeoffs and disposals. The more widely used measure of productivity, sales per employee, was not reflecting the financial difficulty experienced by Photronics.

There is a clear positive relationship between rising productivity and subsequent stock price performance when the accompaniment is followed by an increase in free cash flow. However, while cutting the labor force may give the analyst the impression of stronger productivity by increasing sales per employee, this can only result in a temporary salve to a firm's market value if free cash flow for the enterprise is not produced.

TABLE 2-3

IBM and Photronics Productivity Characteristics

	PHOTRONICS INC (October Year-End)			INTL BUSINESS MACHINES CORP (December Year-End)		
	Sales ($M)	Sales/ Employees ($M)	Free Cash Flow/Employees ($M)	Sales ($M)	Sales/ Employees ($M)	Free Cash Flow/Employees ($M)
2000	331	201	3.6	88,396	280	17.9
2001	378	224	38.4	85,866	268	31.6
2002	387	245	6.3	81,186	257	30.1
2003	349	246	25.5	89,131	279	35.4
2004	396	279	32.5	96,293	293	37.7
2005	441	306	14.7	91,134	277	38.0
2006	455	303	14.4	91,424	257	33.0
2007	422	274	26.3	98,786	256	32.9
2008	423	293	(9.1)	103,630	260	38.2
2009	361	278	5.5	95,758	240	44.2

FIGURE 2-6

Photronics Productivity Measures

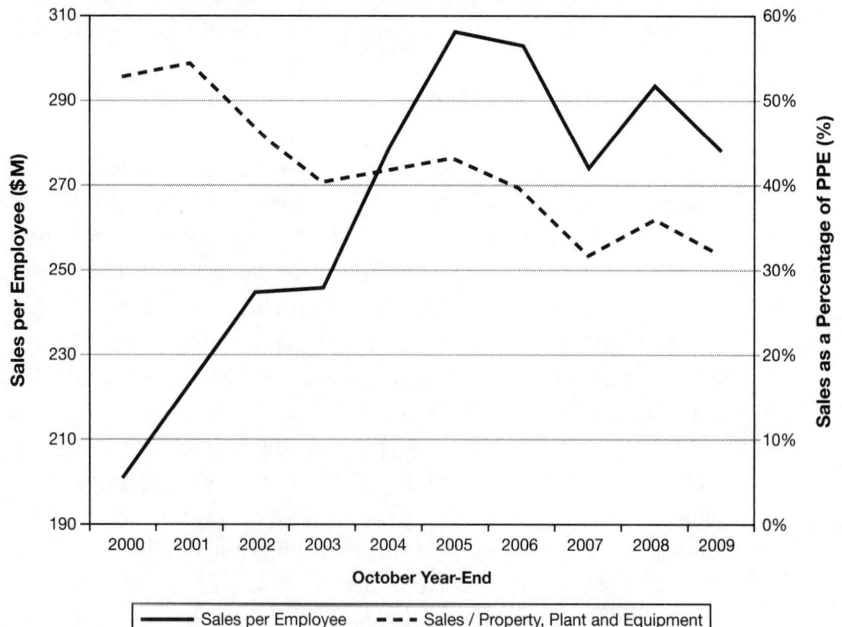

Source: Photronics' 10Ks.

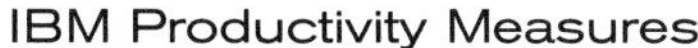

FIGURE 2-7

IBM Productivity Measures

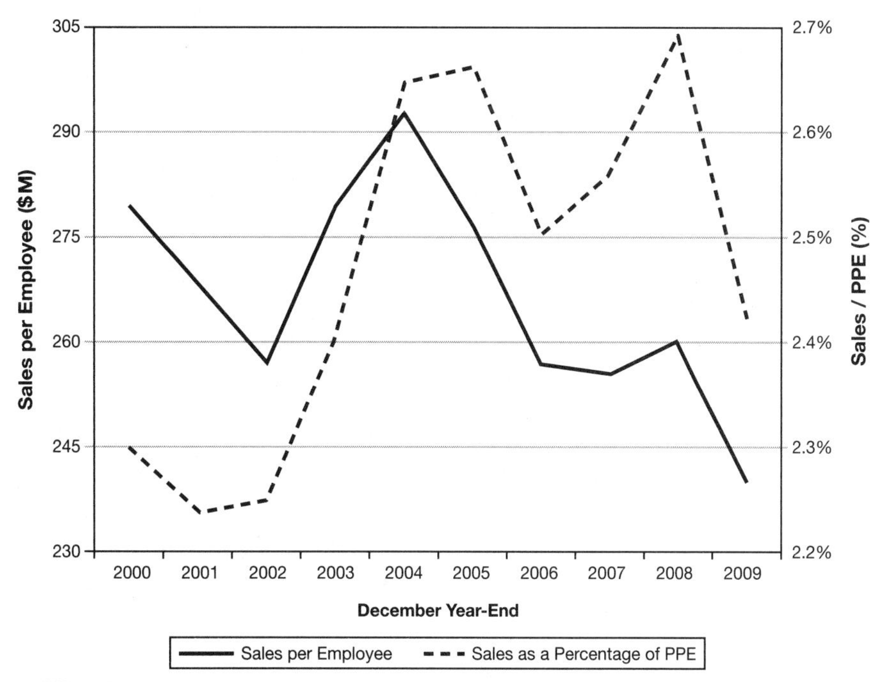

Source: IBM's 10Ks.

Reflected in Figure 2-8 are the headcount and free cash flow for Photronics. Despite downward trending free cash flow since 2004, Photonics' management continued growing its labor force until 2007.

Shares of Photonics (Figure 2-9) were under enormous pressure beginning in the middle of 2007, reflecting the company's drop in free cash flow, because the job cuts and higher sales per employee became irrelevant to equity holders, who rely on free cash flow for compensation. As indicated, free cash flow rose during 2007 only because management "worked" the balance sheet to provide cash. During the following year, it turned negative.

IBM

IBM, unlike Photronics, has shown itself to be quite adept at matching its cost structure with its operating and free cash flow, and as a result, its stock price held up in the face of the severe recession (Figure 2-10). During 2010, shares in IBM

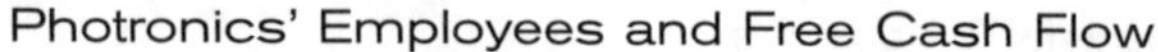

FIGURE 2-8

Photronics' Employees and Free Cash Flow

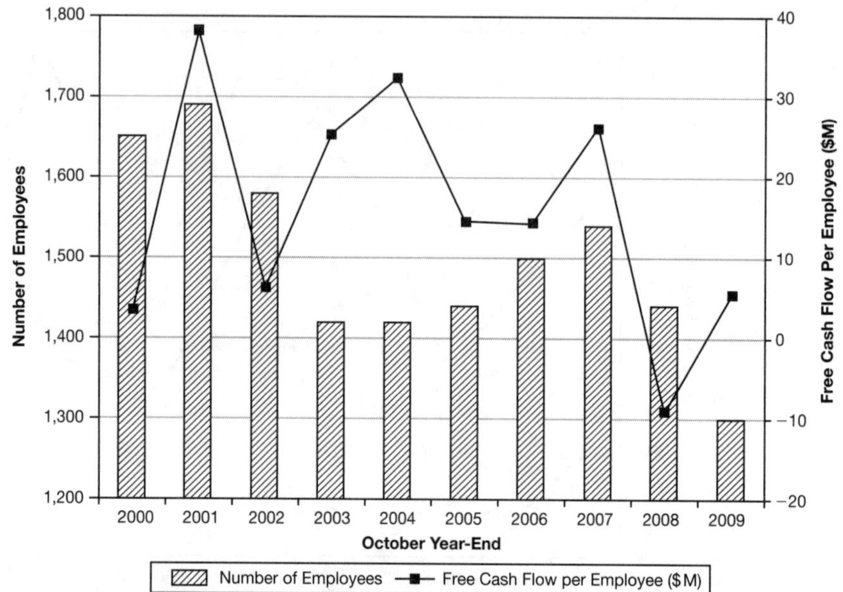

Source: Company 10Ks, CT Capital, LLC.

FIGURE 2-9

Photronics–Cumulative Total Return

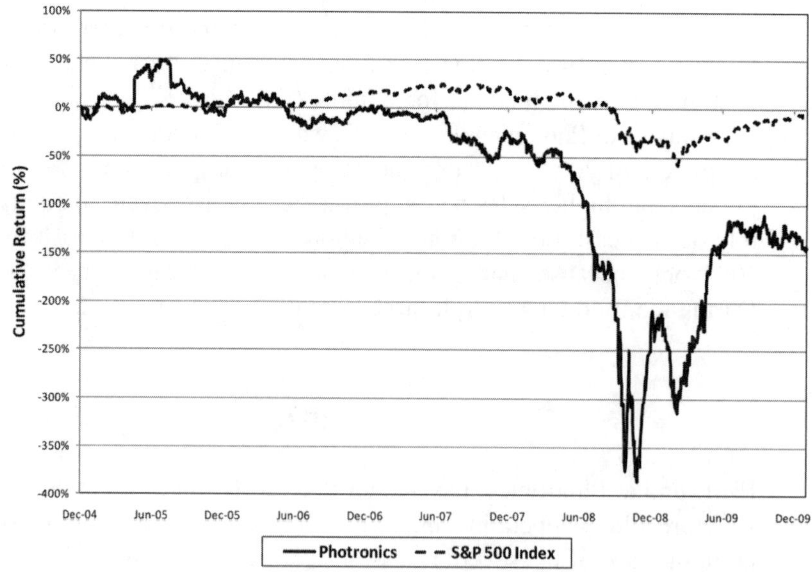

Source: Research Insight, CT Capital, LLC.

FIGURE 2-10

IBM's Stock Price

were back to its prerecession levels, whereas Photronics' shares still were trading at a 10-year low. IBM management's clearly stated vision[3] of substituting cheaper foreign labor for high-cost domestic labor resulted in an upward and consistent increase in its operating cash flows, as depicted in Figure 2-11, and a greater increase in free cash flow, as depicted in Figure 2-12. During the June 30, 2009, quarter, despite a 13 percent fall in revenues, IBM saw its free cash flow increase by over 10 percent. As a result, IBM was the best-performing stock in the Dow Jones Index over the prior year. And for the year 2009, IBM, despite reporting no growth in sales/employees and sales/PPE, by squeezing out cost efficiencies emanating in strong free cash flow, saw its stock rise by over 54 percent, or about twice that of the S&P 500 Index.

Inflation-adjusted revenue growth is often cited as an important gauge of productivity, whereas buying revenue through pricing below cost is usually a recipe for financial failure. If these firms were defending or attempting to increase their market shares through pricing actions, we would most like see it in Figures 2-13 and 2-14. Figure 2-13 highlights the ratio of selling, general, and

[3] As stated during quarterly conference calls and analysts' day conferences.

FIGURE 2-11

IBM Corp.: Employees, Market Value, and Operating Cash Flow

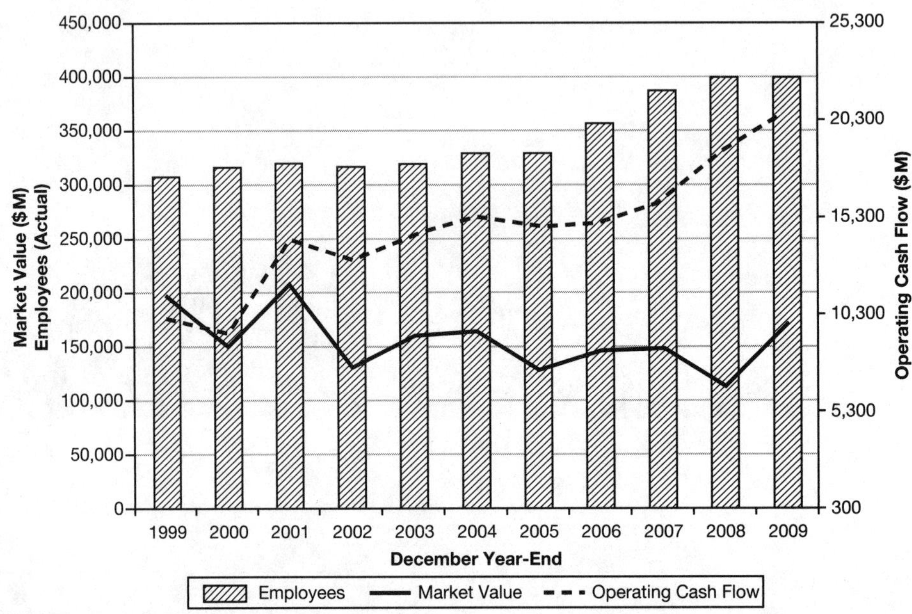

Source: Company 10Ks, Compustat Data Services.

FIGURE 2-12

IBM Corp.: Market Value and Free Cash Flow

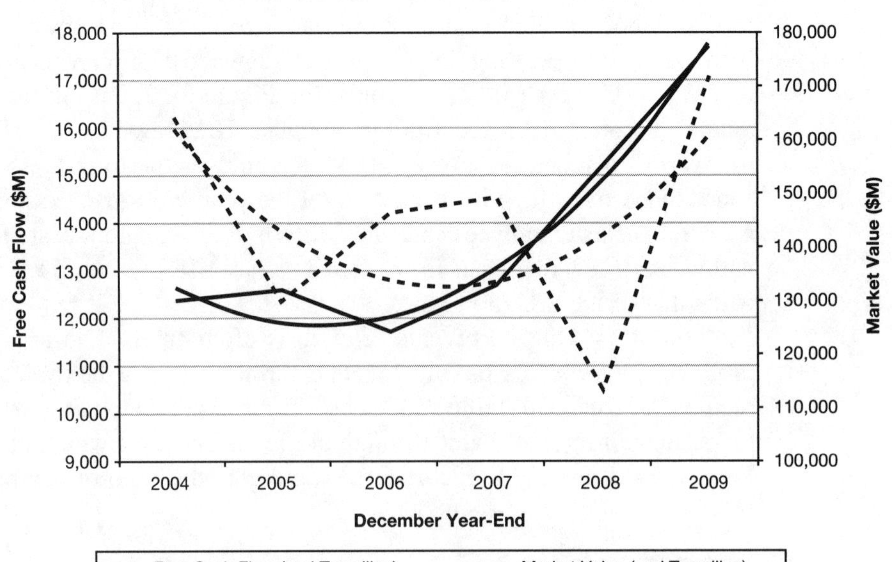

FIGURE 2-13

IBM and Photronics: SG&A/Sales

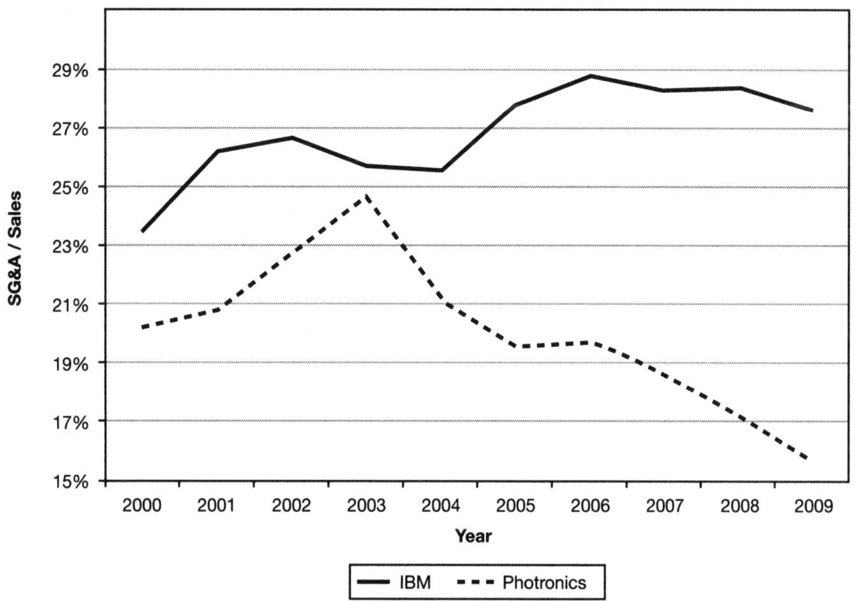

FIGURE 2-14

IBM and Photronics COGS as a percent of Sales, 2004–2008

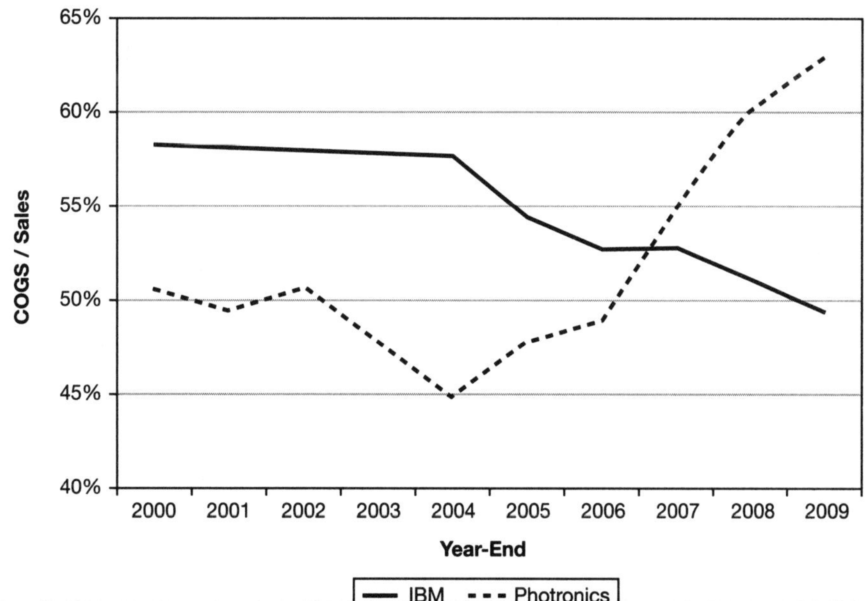

administrative expense SG&A/Sales for IBM and Photronics, and Figure 2-16 highlights cost of goods sold (COGS)/sales. Photronics has had declining selling and general and administrative expenses relative to IBM. Normally, security analysts would view lower and declining levels of SG&A relative to its output (revenues) as a positive sign indicative of rising productivity. If this is true, increased productivity has not helped Photronic's.

For IBM, weak hardware sales were offset by its very lucrative software and service revenues, excellent balance-sheet management, and tight expense control, with the majority of its revenue growth and most of the cost savings stemming from emerging countries. Figure 2-14 depicts IBM's downward-sloping cost of sales, which, for the company, has a significantly greater impact on free cash flow than SG&A owing to its magnitude (about double SG&A) and substantial cost savings, including the labor component. COGS measures normally are looked at as signals of operating margins, not productivity, especially when the depreciation component is removed. The picture, for Photronics, is one of a firm interested in defending its market share despite falling revenue.

This example clearly shows that for Photronics and IBM, it was free cash flow that mattered most to equity owners. A history of good productivity metrics quickly became unimportant to Photronics' investors after its free cash flow peaked. IBM, with consistently poor productivity metrics, enriched investors with its growth in free cash flow. The company had falling revenues per employee but growing free cash flow per employee, whereas Photronics had, over the period studied, the opposite.

Determining the optimal labor force as being a function of sales or unit output does not reflect on an enterprise as a cash-flow-maximizing entity but rather as a unit-producing entity. Determining output based on profits may not leave distributable cash to the owner of equity. The corporate managers and analysts therefore must determine the level of output that places free cash flow at its highest level (Figure 2-15) both today and prospectively. Free cash flow is maximized at the point on the chart where labor is most efficient. If the current level of employment cannot produce satisfactory free cash flow, management must seek a lower-cost labor pool, downsize the labor force, become more productive, raise prices, reduce other expenses, or lastly, sell the asset. If, by virtue of such action(s), the entity turns into a free-cash-flow producer, it has value to its equity owners given the distributable cash.

FIGURE 2-15

Free Cash Flow and Units of Production

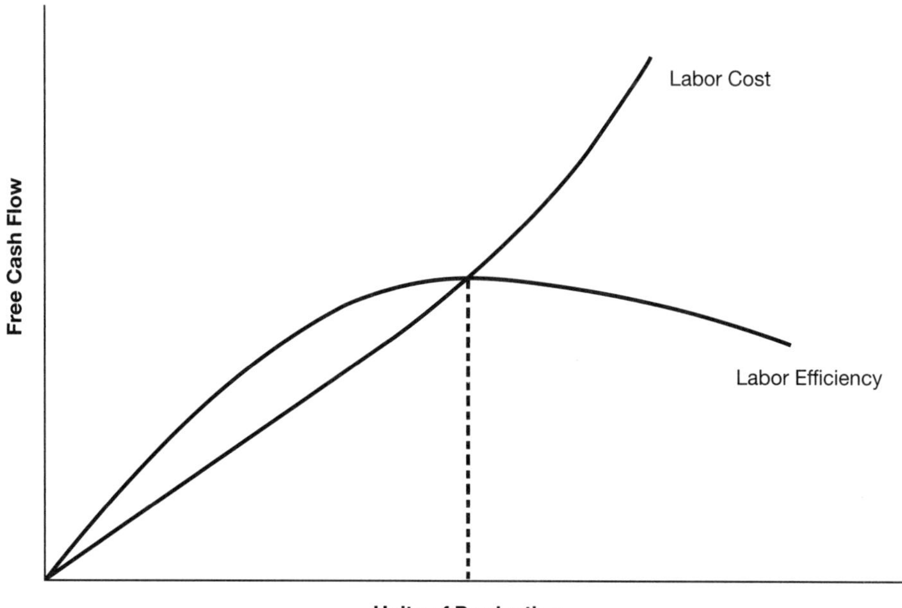

CHAPTER 3

Statement of Cash Flows

Understanding the role of the cash-flow statement is crucial for the general analysis of cash flows and in particular for analysis that is based on free cash flow and cost of capital. This is so because the statement reveals important information about the firm's operations, in addition to reconciling balance-sheet changes and financing and investment activities. In financial reporting, there can be a distortion to the cash-flow statement resulting from events that are classified as investing or financing activities instead of operating activities, with the result of such an action providing a boost to both cash flows from operations and free cash flow.

The purpose of the statement of cash flows is to disclose information about economic events that affect cash during the accounting period. Three general types of economic events or activities are described in the statement: operating cash flows, financing cash flows, and investing cash flows. *Operating cash flows* are ongoing operations of a business entity that affect cash, such as collections from customers and payments to suppliers, employees, and the like. *Financing cash flows* are events that affect the financial structure of the firm, such as borrowing cash, repurchasing common stock, and making dividend payments. *Investing cash flows* are the events that affect the long-term assets of a firm, such as purchases of property, plant, and equipment (PPE), sale of investments in subsidiaries, and so forth.

As the Financial Accounting Standards Board (FASB) states in its introduction of *Statement of Financial Accounting Standards No. 95, Statement of Cash Flows* (SFAS 95): "The primary purpose of the statement of cash flows is to provide relevant information about the cash receipts and cash payments of an enterprise during a period." The statement of cash flows provides information about these events if they affect cash during the accounting period. These events that affect cash during a period are important to investors, creditors, suppliers, and employees. Information about operating cash flows indicates the business's ability to generate cash from its continuing operations. Information about investing cash flows indicates how the business used (received) cash for capital items or liquidated capital to survive downturns. Information about financing cash flows illustrates how the business financed its expansion and partially rewarded stockholders. If a financing event, for example, does not involve cash (such as the conversion of preferred stock to common stock), the information is disclosed in a separate section called "Supplemental information" at the bottom of the cash-flow statement or in the footnotes of the statement of cash flows.

It is important to understand the classifications, especially because it is not uncommon for one entity to place an item as an operating activity, whereas a peer-group entity might place the same item as a finance activity. In general, it is up to the analyst to become familiar with FAS 95 to make any adjustments regarding proper classification. Without doing so, peer comparison and security valuation become difficult.

The sections to follow provide detailed explanations of the components of cash flows, as well as examples from published financial statements. Finally, I discuss how the cash-flow analyst should interpret the cash flows from investing, financing, and operating activities. A follow-up discussion appears in Chapter 8 because various activities here relate to cost-of-capital analysis.

The reader will see why a complete understanding of the items in the cash-flow statement is imperative in risk assessment used to infer a cost of equity and the subsequent determination of fair value. This will allow you to see if a firm is artificially boosting the cash flows it is reporting to shareholders.

CASH FLOWS FROM INVESTING ACTIVITIES

In SFAS 95, the FASB defines cash flows from investing activities as follows:

> Investing activities include making and collecting loans and acquiring and disposing of debt or equity instruments and property, plant, and equipment and other productive assets, that is, assets held for or used in the production of goods or services by the enterprise (other than materials that are part of the enterprise's inventory) [SFAS 95, para. 15].

Thus the definition of investing cash flows includes cash outflows used as investments in financial or fixed assets, as well as cash receipts from disposition of such investments. Furthermore, investing cash flows are for investments in financial instruments as well as investments in real assets (PPE). The FASB further describes cash inflows and outflows from investing activities as

Inflows

a. Receipts from collections or sales of loans made by the enterprise and of other entity's debt instruments (other than cash equivalents) that were purchased by the enterprise.
b. Receipts from sales of equity instruments of other enterprises and from returns of investment in those instruments.
c. Receipts from sales of property, plant, and equipment and other productive assets [SFAS 95, para. 16].

Outflows

a. Disbursements for loans made by the enterprise and payments to acquire debt instruments of other entities (other than cash equivalents).
b. Payments to acquire equity instruments of other enterprises.
c. Payments at the time of purchase or soon before or after purchase to acquire property, plant, and equipment and other productive assets [SFAS 95, para. 17].

It is more natural to discuss the cash outflows for investing activities prior to financing or operating activities. By analyzing the firm's investment activities, we can see how management deploys its cash. The statement requires the classification of investments in PPE and other productive assets as investing activities. It further restricts the inclusion of these investments in the statement of cash flows to amounts that were paid at the time of purchase or soon before or after the time of purchase. Thus an advance payment for PPE or a down payment will be included. However, a loan by the seller of the PPE will not be included as a cash flow from investing activity because the buyer had not paid for it in cash.

The FASB includes in investing cash flows investments in equity instruments of other enterprises (repurchases of the firm's own securities are classified as financing cash flows), investments in debt instruments of other enterprises, or loans made to other enterprises. The FASB notes that investments in debt instruments of other entities should be "other than cash equivalents." This is an important distinction because the statement of cash flows can be prepared using "cash and cash equivalents." *Cash equivalents* are short-term, highly liquid investments that are both

a. Readily convertible to known amounts of cash.
b. So near their maturity that they present insignificant risk of changes in value because of changes in interest rates [SFAS 95, para. 8].

The FASB states that generally only investments with original maturities of 3 months or less qualify under the definition of a cash equivalent. Thus, when a treasurer purchases a Treasury note that has 60 days to maturity using cash, an increase in cash and cash equivalents is recorded for the period.[1] However, if the treasurer purchased a 120-day Treasury note, an investing cash flow is recorded on the statement of cash flows. Clearly, these rules leave management some room for manipulation close to the end of the accounting period. It should be noted that the FASB ruled that if a 7-year note, for example, is purchased less than 90 days before maturity, it does not get reclassified as a cash equivalent when the balance-sheet date falls within 90 days of its maturity.

Example:

Cash and Cash Equivalents

The company considers all highly liquid investments with a maturity of three months or less when purchased to be cash equivalents. The company's cash equivalents consist primarily of money market funds, unrestricted deposits, debt instruments of the U.S. Treasury, and commercial paper. Cash includes amounts restricted for letters of credit for purchases and deposits for equipment maintenance of $528,000 and $72,000 at June 30, 2009 and 2008, respectively.

Source: 2009 Oplink Communications, Inc., 10K.

It seems reasonable that cash and cash equivalents will include only items that could be readily converted to cash because there should be no question both as to the item's value and its liquidity. In some cases, a portion of the available cash is restricted by compensating balance agreements or other agreements. Restricted cash should not be included in "Cash and cash equivalents" for purposes of the statement of cash flows. However, in some cases, firms deviate from this line of reasoning.

Example:

Compensating balance arrangements that do not legally restrict the withdrawal or usage of cash amounts may be reported as Cash and Cash Equivalents, while legally restricted deposits held as compensating balances against borrowing arrangements, contracts entered into with others, or company statements of intention with regard to particular deposits should not be reported as cash and cash equivalents.

Source: Home Depot, June 2009 10Q.

---

[1] The decrease in cash is exactly offset by the increase in cash equivalents, the Treasury note, because the maturity of the note is less than 90 days.

Example:

Berkshire Hathaway defines cash equivalents quite differently. As reported, cash held out as backing for loans and other liabilities is listed as part of "Other assets" on its balance sheet. For Berkshire, this can be substantial because the company lists $9.3 billion of other assets on its 2008 10K. Found in various locations of the company's 10K, we learn that also included in "other assets" are $1.7 billion of premium acquisition costs and $0.3 billion of derivative contract assets minus $0.1 billion in pension assets and $2.1 billion in regulatory assets. The company footnotes cash and cash equivalents as follows:

> Cash equivalents consist of funds invested in U.S. Treasury Bills, money market accounts, and in other investments with a maturity of three months or less when purchased. Cash and cash equivalents exclude amounts where availability is restricted by loan agreements or other contractual provisions. Restricted amounts are included in other assets.

It should be noted that cash flows from investing activities include both cash outflows and cash inflows. The inflows occur when a firm disposes of its investments in financial instruments or fixed assets.[2] The cash proceeds from sales are included among the cash flows from investing activities and represent disinvesting activities by the firm. Can a firm net cash inflows against cash outflows? For example, can a firm net the proceeds from sales of PPE against additions to PPE? Usually, accountants and investors are against offsetting any type of inflows with outflow, assets against liabilities, or revenues against expenses because to do so could deprive the decision maker of important information regarding current and prospective cash flows. However, if the amount of the proceeds is immaterial, the firm may report the net purchases of PPE.

Most firms disclose in this section cash outlays on capital expenditures, acquisitions, investments in financial instruments, investments in unconsolidated subsidiaries, and purchases of additional shares from minority shareholders. Clearly, each of these investing activities has an opposite counterpart of a disinvesting activity, for instance, the sale of investments.

The cash-flow analyst should investigate the capital expenditures of a firm and the retirement of PPE during the accounting period. Capital expenditures should be sufficient at least to sustain the current levels of operations. They can be compared with past capital expenditures, levels of investments by competitors, improvements in technology, current levels of PPE, the firm's unit growth rates, and which divisions or reportable segments are consuming cash. Are the investments in those segments appropriate in relation to their ability to produce free cash flow? Has outsourcing of production had its intended effect, resulting in capital savings, or has it created additional problems?

---

[2] Capital payments on debt instruments in which the firm invested are also considered cash inflows from investing activities; these are, in effect, disinvesting activities. However, interest payments on such debt are classified as operating cash inflows.

A significant increase in the sale of PPE may indicate that the firm is suffering from a cash shortage and decides to generate cash by selling fixed assets. This strategy means that the firm is reducing the scale of operations or that it is gradually liquidating. However, the firm just may be selling underutilized capital or making a strategic shift in its business, such as outsourcing or purchasing more productive capital. Thus the cash-flow analyst will examine these events carefully because of the implications for future cash flows. As we will also see, overspending is also a red flag indicative of mismanagement in the form of wasteful resources.

The firm has three major options in its future expansion: (1) to expand internally through further investments in capital expenditures, (2) to invest in the existing operations of other firms through acquisitions, or (3) to use other firms' capital resources. Most studies to date show that, on average, it is detrimental for a firm to expand through acquisition of other firms; most such acquisitions do not work as originally intended.[3] It has been estimated by management consultants that about half the business combinations either fail or fall short of expectations. Thus the cash-flow analyst may want to assess the probability of success for an acquisition and the related costs of that acquisitions in terms of additional debt that is assumed or issued. The analyst also should assess the potential synergies that can be created through acquisition. These may have favorable effects on future cash flows by eliminating redundant operations.

Finally, the cash-flow analyst should examine additional investments in unconsolidated subsidiaries (which are subsidiaries in which the firm owns less than 50 percent of the stock), investments in joint ventures, and investments in other financial instruments. The analyst should carefully assess potential future cash-flow consequences of such investments. Usually, investments in other entities, where the investing firm does not control the investee, are considered less desirable (unless there are debt consequences) than investments in entities where the firm has full control. Similarly, the analyst should examine the reasons for investments in financial instruments; are these made merely to park cash that will be needed in the near future for investments, because of regulatory requirements or because of covenants, or are they made because the firm has no superior investment opportunities?

Sometimes the distinction between investing and operating cash flows is not clearcut. For example, a cash payment may pertain to an item that could be considered either as inventory or as a productive asset. If so, the appropriate classification should depend on the activity that is likely to be the predominant source of cash flows for the item. For example, the acquisition and sale of equipment to be used by the enterprise or rented to others is generally considered an investing

[3] The list of failed corporate mergers grows daily. Some of the more notable examples include AT&T/NCR, Sterling Drug/Kodak, AOL/Time Warner, Daimler Benz/Chrysler, HP/Compaq, and Alcatel/Lucent.

activity. However, equipment sometimes is acquired or produced to be used by the enterprise or rented to others for a short period of time and then sold. In such circumstances, the acquisition or production and subsequent sale of those assets can be considered an operating activity.

Needless to say, this ambiguity in reporting requirements leads to different interpretations in practice by many firms. Some leasing companies include the collections of principal on their capital leases as cash flows from operating activities on the grounds that the equipment leased is in fact inventory. Other leasing entities include such payments in investing activities on the grounds that the leases represent investments in the traditional sense. Thus the cash-flow analyst needs to carefully assess the classification of such items as a proper investing or operating cash flow. For example, Bally Technologies and IGT Corp. are two slot-machine manufacturers. When building machines for lease to casinos, Bally's purchase of parts is reported as an operating activity, yet IGT reports the event as an investing activity. When making adjustments to cash flow from operations, the analyst should consider both events as operating cash flows.

Similarly, the analyst should examine the implications of disinvesting events as carefully as investing events. Also, the cash-flow analyst should note that the current requirements of SFAS 95 are that *only* the cash portion of these events is disclosed in the statement of cash flows. It is reasonable in most cases to focus not only on the cash portion of the transaction but also on the noncash portion because of its future consequences. For example, the sale of a division for cash, notes receivable, and stocks likely will yield future cash inflows. During 2008, Prudential Insurance agreed to sell its retail brokerage unit to Wells Fargo, with Prudential receiving $4.5 billion in cash, but not until January 2010. These payments, to the extent they are probable, should be incorporated by the cash-flow analyst, as well as the initial payment of cash from the sale of the division, which was reported in the statement of cash flows during 2008. During 2010, the $4.5 billion was received.

Let us now examine several examples of investing activities.

Example:

Merck & Co., Inc., is a global pharmaceutical company. The following schedule is taken from its 2008 10K:

> Merck considers the pledge of assets backing up letters of credit to be restricted assets. These restricted assets evolved with a large legal settlement relating to a drug which was sold by Merck and was withdrawn from the market. As the letter of credit amount declines with payment under the Agreement, so too will the restricted assets (shown as "Other assets" on Merck's balance sheet) and reported in its statement of cash flows as the sale of securities shown under investment activities.

	2008	2007	2006
Cash Flows from Investing Activities			
Capital expenditures	**(1,298.3)**	(1,011.0)	(980.2)
Purchases of securities and other investments	**(11,967.3)**	(10,132.7)	(19,591.3)
Proceeds from sales of securities and other investments	**11,065.8**	10,860.2	16,143.8
Acquisitions of subsidiaries, net of cash acquired	**—**	(1,135.9)	(404.9)
Distribution from AstraZeneca LP	**1,899.3**	—	—
Increase in restricted assets	**(1,629.7)**	(1,401.1)	(48.1)
Other	**95.8**	10.5	(3.0)
Net cash used by investing activities	**(1,834.4)**	(2,810.0)	(4,883.7)

Example:

In June of 2008, Verizon Corp. paid $5.9 billion in cash plus the assumption of $22.2 billion in debt, net of cash acquired, to acquire Alltel Corporation. Immediately prior to the closing, Verizon borrowed $12.4 billion to complete the acquisition and repay a portion of the Alltel debt. In connection with the borrowings, Verizon entered into swap (hedging) contracts to protect against interest-rate and currency movements because some of this new debt was denominated in pound sterling and euros. In December 2008, additional borrowings were needed.

Verizon also repaid debt totaling $4.1 billion during the year and repurchased $1.4 billion of its stock. It is not unusual for boards of directors to "send a signal" to the financial markets on announcement of a large business combination. That signal is designed to show investors that the board is confident that the merger will add to the value of the enterprise and that the board is willing to risk additional capital as a show of faith. This is not a recommended strategy because normally arbitrageurs will offset the stock buyback and investors will wait to see if the combined company does produce the anticipated free cash flows. In Verizon's case, its stock fell on the announcement and had not recovered 2 years later.

Shown below is the financing section of the balance sheet for Verizon Corp. for fiscal years 2006–2008.

	2008	2007	2006
Cash Flows from Financing Activities			
Proceeds from long-term borrowings	**21,598**	3,402	3,983
Repayments of long-term borrowings and capital lease obligations	**(4,146)**	(5,503)	(11,233)
Increase (decrease) in short-term obligations, excluding current maturities	**2,389**	(3,252)	7,944
Dividends paid	**(4,994)**	(4,773)	(4,719)
Proceeds from sale of common stock	**16**	1,274	174
Purchase of common stock for treasury	**(1,368)**	(2,843)	(1,700)
Other, net	**93**	(2)	(201)
Net cash provided by (used in) financing activities—continuing operations	**13,588**	(11,697)	(5,752)
Net cash used in financing activities—discontinued operations	**—**	—	(279)
Net cash provided by (used in) financing activities	**13,588**	(11,697)	(6,031)

Example:

Clayton Williams Energy, Inc., is an independent oil and gas company engaged in the exploration and production of oil and natural gas primarily in Texas, Louisiana, and New Mexico. Shown below is the company's entire consolidated statement of cash flows to illustrate its accounting of derivatives, which the company uses to mitigate the risk of falling energy prices. How the derivatives are set up determines whether they are characterized as cash-flow hedges or non-cash-flow hedges (defined in Chapter 6). This is an example of certain hedges not working out, as well as a pitfall of a business acquisition.

During 2004, Clayton made an acquisition of another energy company that had put in place derivative contracts having a price of $28 a barrel, meaning that a rise in the price of a barrel of crude above $28 would result in a loss as the contracts were settled. As those contracts reached expiration, they indeed saddled Clayton with a huge loss as the price of crude ran up. Fortunately for Clayton, though, it had other hedges in place that were quite profitable.

In its year-end 2009 income statement, the company booked a gain of $74.7 million, with that amount a sum of both realized and unrealized gains for the year. We see $49.7 million of "unrealized gains" reversed under operating cash flows. Therefore, the company had a cash realizable gain for the year approximating $25 million.

The company also shows $43.486 million under financing cash flows, representing cash that was paid to counterparties to settle hedged contracts. Under SFAS 133, *Accounting for Derivative Instruments and Hedging Activities*, because the contracts Clayton acquired pursuant to the merger agreement did not meet the requirement of a cash-flow hedge, those contracts are characterized as non-cash-flow hedges and must be presented under financing activities. If they were cash-flow hedges, under SFAS 133, they would be recognized in "Other comprehensive income" until the hedged item is recognized in earnings. If they are not recognized as cash-flow hedges, they are recognized in earnings, as reported by Clayton Williams.

How did Clayton do on its hedged contracts during 2008?

	Amount
From income statement	$74,743
Add: Unrealized—from operating activities	(49,738)
Equals: Realized gains	25,005
Less: Settled losses—from financing activities	43,486
Normal hedged gains	68,491

Thus Clayton took in $68.491 million on normal hedged activities, from which it had cash payments of $43.486 million, which more than cover the loss-ridden contracts taken on by the acquisition.

Because settlements on derivative contracts deemed to contain a financing element are reported as financing activities in the statement of cash flows and must be reversed under operating activities (the loss is already taken into account in the income statement), it has the effect of increasing (decreasing with a gain) cash flow from operations. This can under certain circumstances, such as not merely reversing an item in the income statement, result in over(under)stated operating cash flows to analysts who use a simple definition of free cash flow defined as either operating cash flow minus depreciation or an EBIDTA-based definition. One therefore must inspect for such reversals if the hedge is deemed a noncash hedge.

Companies that use derivative contracts as partial speculation should be accorded a higher cost of capital. It is not a coincidence, therefore, that Clayton Williams has greater volatility of free cash flow and tax rate, although an inspection of its tax footnote reveals that the latter is due in part to the tax incentives.

CLAYTON WILLIAMS ENERGY, INC.
CONSOLIDATED STATEMENTS OF CASH FLOWS
(In thousands)

	Year Ended December 31,		
	2008	**2007**	**2006**
Cash flows from operating activities			
Net income	$140,534	$5,990	$17,799
Adjustments to reconcile net income to cash provided by operating activities:			
Depreciation, depletion, and amortization	120,542	84,476	66,163
Impairment of property and equipment	12,882	12,137	21,848
Exploration costs	80,112	68,870	65,173
Gain on sales of property and equipment, net	(42,381)	(4,209)	(1,668)
Deferred income taxes	77,327	3,768	215
Noncash employee compensation	5,834	1,865	2,279
Unrealized (gain) loss on derivatives	(49,738)	24,249	(57,568)
Settlements on derivatives with financing elements	43,486	28,468	29,407
Amortization of debt issue costs	1,354	1,281	1,308
Accretion of abandonment obligations	2,355	2,508	1,653
Excess tax benefit on exercise of stock options	—	(963)	(1,807)
Minority interest, net of tax	708	3,812	574
Changes in operating working capital:			
Accounts receivable	13,087	(10,028)	(8,101)
Accounts payable	(4,946)	10,992	3,543
Other	(19,176)	1,650	5,172
Net cash provided by operating activities	381,980	234,866	145,990
Cash flows from investing activities			
Additions to property and equipment	(350,106)	(233,453)	(254,840)
Additions to equipment of Larclay JV	(1,683)	(29,302)	(60,655)
Proceeds from sales of property and equipment	117,226	22,773	4,451
Change in equipment inventory	(8,247)	18,166	(662)
Other	3,935	(14,443)	1,753
Net cash used in investing activities	(238,875)	(236,259)	(309,953)

	Year Ended December 31,		
	2008	2007	2006
Cash flows from financing activities			
Proceeds from long-term debt	—	25,800	129,300
Proceeds from long-term debt of Larclay JV	7,500	8,727	66,254
Repayments of long-term debt	(71,700)	—	—
Repayments of long-term debt of Larclay JV	(22,500)	(13,125)	—
Proceeds from sale of common stock	15,936	6,000	3,914
Settlements on derivatives with financing elements	(43,486)	(28,468)	(29,407)
Excess tax benefit on exercise of stock options	—	963	1,807
Net cash provided by (used in) financing activities	(114,250)	(103)	171,868
Net increase (decrease) in cash and cash equivalents	28,855	(1,496)	7,905
Cash and cash equivalents			
Beginning of period	12,344	13,840	5,935
End of period	$41,199	$12,344	$13,840
Supplemental disclosures			
Cash paid for interest, net of amounts capitalized	$24,027	$35,213	$19,653
Cash paid for income taxes	$16,652	$348	$196

Example:

Black and Decker reported the following investing cash flows in its 2008 10K:

	2008	2007	2006
Investing Activities			
Capital expenditures	**(98.8)**	(116.4)	(104.6)
Proceeds from disposal of assets	**20.4**	13.0	14.7
Purchase of businesses, net of cash acquired	**(25.7)**	—	(158.5)
Reduction in purchase price of previously acquired business	—	—	16.1
Cash inflow from hedging activities	**72.4**	2.0	1.4
Cash outflow from hedging activities	**(29.7)**	(47.4)	(14.8)
Other investing activities, net	—	(1.0)	4.7
Cash flow from investing activities	**(61.4)**	(149.8)	(241.0)

As is typical, the largest item in the subsection of investment activities is capital expenditures, which we discuss in relation to excessive expenditures (corporate "fat") in Chapter 4. The company also disposed of assets as well as made a small acquisition. The company uses derivatives in its hedging activities as protection against changes in commodity prices, in addition to interest-rate hedging on its variable-rate debt. One may question whether commodity price hedging is more suitably related to an operating activity, as are its other related input costs. Over the 3 years shown, the hedges have resulted in a $16.1 million outflow, rather insignificant for a company having over $6 billion in revenues and $1.5 billion in balance-sheet debt.

Example:

Accuray, Inc., develops and manufactures robots used in medical procedures, which the company calls the CyberKnife system. In the sales process, customer's deposits are backed with a letter of credit. As the letters of credit are released, so too are the deposited funds.

During 2009, the company's decrease in restricted cash results from releases of deposited funds as delivery of the CyberKnife unit takes place. Accuray's balance sheet showed that restricted cash declined from $4,830 to $527, or a $4,303 difference, shown under investment activities. Some entities report a change in restricted cash as a financing activity, so the analyst should ensure comparability.

	2009	2008	2007
Cash flows from investing activities			
Purchases of property and equipment	(4,232)	(5,030)	(7,230)
Restricted cash	4,303	(4,830)	1
Purchase of investments	(155,934)	(177,651)	(283)
Sale and maturity of investments	157,732	54,089	—
Net cash provided by (used in) investing activities	1,869	(133,422)	(7,512)

Source: Accuray 2009 10K.

Example:

Phelps Dodge is one of the world's leading producers of copper and molybdenum and is the world's largest producer of molybdenum-based chemicals and continuous copper rod. Its investment activities reveal several entries that bear interest. The first is the reversal of capitalized interest, which appears on the balance sheet as an asset but actually represents a cash expenditure; thus the cash effect is reported in that section. Also reported are $300 million in expenditures during 2006 and $100 million during 2005, representing cash contributions of those amounts into a trust fund earmarked for environmental and mine-closure regulatory compliance. The analyst must inquire how these contributions will be financed, the estimated total obligation, any possible future claims, and the extent of insurance.[4]

Phelps Dodge ramped up its capital expenditure program during 2006. The $1.2 billion in cash expenditures was partially offset by $641 in asset sales, with the balance financed via the large cash flow from company operations.

Also in the investment activities section is $12.1 million of "Other investing, net." This could represent a new investment or an addition to an old investment. The analyst would need further clarification from the company to learn the nature of the outlay(s).

[4] BP PLC was self- insured, having set up insurance subsidiary companies, according to its 20-F. As soon as the oil rig explosion in the Gulf of Mexico occurred, it was incumbent on the analyst to place a worst case outcome scenario. The insurance sub had its parent covered up to $1 billion per incident. In its SEC filings, BP wrote prior to the disaster it considers "external insurance as not being an economic means of financing losses."

Regarding capital expenditures, there is no reason to believe that it must be *consistently* below cash flow from operations. Over the operating cycle, such must be the case because sooner or later the entity will confront a business downturn, and if the gap were continually debt financed, this could place the firm in a severe strain.

However, if the entity is conservatively financed and capable of investing in projects having a higher return on invested capital than its cost, the capital expenditure gap will prove to be value-adding and will reward shareholders over time. It is the divisions that are capital-intensive and do not generate free cash flow and returns on invested capital greater than their cost that should be scrutinized with an eye on disposal. Balance-sheet cash and financial flexibility have a calculable strategic value and so must be put to use properly. When this advantage becomes minimized, the entity's ability to take on additional value-enhancing projects becomes impaired.

Investing Activities	**2006**	**2005**	**2004**
Capital outlays	(1,191.1)	(686.0)	(303.6)
Capitalized interest	(54.4)	(17.6)	(1.0)
Investments in subsidiaries and other, net of cash received	3.3	(12.2)	(13.7)
Proceeds from the sale of Columbian Chemicals	505.2	—	—
Proceeds from the sale of Magnet Wire North American assets	136.5	—	—
Proceeds from the sale of High Performance Conductors	47.9	—	—
Proceeds from sale of cost-basis investments, net of expenses	—	451.6	—
Proceeds from other asset dispositions	25.1	18.2	26.9
Restricted cash	(4.6)	(20.8)	—
Global reclamation and remediation trust contributions	(300.0)	(100.0)	—
Other investing, net	(12.1)	(1.2)	0.4
Net cash used in investing activities	(844.2)	(368.0)	(291.0)

Source: Phelps Dodge 2006 10K.

Example:

Chevron, the large integrated energy company, explains in a footnote the sizable capitalization of items representing cash spent but placed on the balance sheet as an asset. These include expenses related to exploration activities that may be accounted for, under generally accepted accounting principles (GAAP), using two methods: full cost or successful efforts.

Under successful-methods reporting, a firm expenses the costs of unsuccessful drilling and exploration costs, such as geologic and geophysical expenditures, engineering expenses, and the costs of carrying and retaining undeveloped properties.

Under the successful-efforts method, only exploratory drilling costs that result in the discovery and development of a commercial oil and gas field may be capitalized and amortized based on the field's proven reserves on a unit-of-production basis; all expenditures that are unsuccessful (dry holes) are expensed as incurred. Using the full-cost accounting method, all exploration and development expenditures are capitalized and amortized over the reserves of the related pool of properties.

The following is from Chevron's 2009 10K, where dry-hole expense is shown under operating activities.

> *Properties, Plant, and Equipment* The successful efforts method is used for crude oil and natural gas exploration and production activities. All costs for development wells, related plant and equipment, proved mineral interests in crude oil and natural gas properties, and related asset retirement obligation (ARO) assets are capitalized. Costs of exploratory wells are capitalized pending determination of whether the wells found proved reserves. Costs of wells that are assigned proved reserves remain capitalized. Costs also are capitalized for exploratory wells that have found crude oil and natural gas reserves even if the reserves cannot be classified as proved when the drilling is completed, provided the exploratory well has found a sufficient quantity of reserves to justify its completion as a producing well and the company is making sufficient progress assessing the reserves and the economic and operating viability of the project. All other exploratory wells and costs are expensed.

	Year ended December 31,		
	2008	**2007**	**2006**
Operating activities			
Net income	**$23,931**	$18,688	$17,138
Adjustments			
Depreciation, depletion, and amortization	**9,528**	8,708	7,506
Dry-hole expense	**375**	507	520
Distributions less than income from equity affiliates	**(440)**	(1,439)	(979)
Net before-tax gains on asset retirements and sales	**(1,358)**	(2,315)	(229)
Net foreign currency effects	**(355)**	378	259
Deferred income tax provision	**598**	261	614
Net (increase) decrease in operating working capital	**(1,673)**	685	1,044
Minority interest in net income	**100**	107	70
Increase in long-term receivables	**(161)**	(82)	(900)
(Increase) decrease in other deferred charges	**(84)**	(530)	232
Cash contributions to employee pension plans	**(839)**	(317)	(449)
Other	**10**	326	(503)
Net cash provided by operating activities	**29,632**	24,977	24,323
Investing activities			
Capital expenditures	**(19,666)**	(16,678)	(13,813)
Repayment of loans by equity affiliates	**179**	21	463
Proceeds from asset sales	**1,491**	3,338	989
Net sales of marketable securities	**483**	185	142
Net sales (purchases) of other short-term investments	**432**	(799)	—
Net cash used for investing activities	**(17,081)**	(13,933)	(12,219)

Example:

Overseas Shipholding Group is one of the world's leading bulk shipping companies, engaged primarily in the ocean transportation of crude oil and petroleum products. The unusual entry found under investing activities relates to the "Capital construction fund." To encourage private investment in U.S. metric vessels, the Merchant Marine Act of 1970 permits deferral of taxes on earnings from U.S. metric vessels deposited into a capital construction fund and amounts earned thereon, which can be used for the construction or acquisition of or retirement of debt on qualified U.S. metric vessels (primarily those limited to foreign, Great Lakes, and noncontiguous domestic trades).

Overseas Shipholding was using funds in its capital construction fund for business acquisitions (which included ships covered under the act), as well as the original construction of new vessels.

In another such maneuver, during the 1980s, Harold Simmons, a well-known corporate raider, made an unsolicited takeover offer for Sea-Land Corporation, with the motivating factor the cash in Sea-Land's large capital construction fund. Mr. Simmons believed that he would be able to use the cash in the fund for purposes other than that specified in the Merchant Marine Act, presumably to make other corporate acquisitions outside the industry. Eventually, CSX Corp. purchased Sea-Land and in the process paid a healthy premium to its shareholders, including Mr. Simmons.

The following is from the Overseas Shipholding's 2008 10K.

	2008	2007	2006
Cash flows from investing activities			
Purchases of marketable securities	(15,112)	—	—
Proceeds from sale of marketable securities	7,208	—	—
Expenditures for vessels, including $313,045 in 2008, $260,716 in 2007, and $48,100 in 2006 related to vessels under construction	(608,271)	(545,078)	(55,793)
Withdrawals from Capital Construction Fund	105,700	175,950	—
Proceeds from disposal of vessels	461,872	224,019	258,877
Acquisition of Heidmar Lightering, net of cash acquired of $2,600	—	(38,471)	—
Acquisition of Maritrans, Inc., net of cash acquired of $24,536	—	—	(444,550)
Expenditures for other property	(10,809)	(15,864)	(11,591)
Investments in and advances to affiliated companies	(37,871)	(31,083)	(8,613)
Proceeds from disposal of investments in affiliated companies	—	194,706	—
Distributions from affiliated companies	20,148	—	4,772
Other, net	113	926	196
Net cash used in investing activities	(77,022)	(34,895)	(256,702)

Example:

Toll Brothers, Inc., is in the business of designing, building, and marketing homes and rental apartments. Toll has investments in and makes advances to a number of joint ventures with unrelated parties to develop land, either for sale or on which to build. It accounts for these investments under the equity method at $152 million on its balance sheet.

Toll also guarantees the debt of several of its unconsolidated subsidiaries, which as of October, 31, 2009, amounted to $63.3 million. These subsidiaries, according to Toll's 2009 10K, had net borrowings of $850 million that are not consolidated on Toll's balance sheet. Toll also shows $54 million of accrued expenses on its balance sheet to the unconsolidated entities.

These investments and guarantees represent an integral part of the security analysis, given the size of the liabilities and Toll's higher-than-average cost of capital. Although a small percentage of the unconsolidated subsidiaries' total liabilities are guaranteed, there may be some moral commitments involved, especially if Toll has dealings outside the unconsolidated subsidiaries with their creditors.

	2008	2007	2006
Cash flow (used in) provided by investing activities:			
Purchase of property and equipment, net	(2,712)	(8,158)	(14,975)
Proceeds from sale of ancillary businesses			32,299
Purchase of marketable securities	(101,324)	(1,468,440)	(5,769,805)
Sale of marketable securities		1,463,487	5,769,805
Investment in and advances to unconsolidated entities	(31,342)	(54,787)	(34,530)
Return of investments in unconsolidated entities	3,205	3,268	42,790
Net cash (used in) provided by investing activities	(132,173)	(64,630)	25,584

Source: Toll Brother's 2009 10K.

Example:

Central Iowa Energy, LLC, is in the business of developing and constructing biodiesel plants. The company recorded, in its 2009 10K, a sales tax refund as an investment activity because the transaction that gave rise to that cash inflow was an investment activity, the purchase of equipment. The cost of the asset was depreciated at the net amount and is classified properly. A tax refund due to an operating loss would be classified as an operating activity.

	2009	2008
Cash flows from investing activities:		
Capital expenditures	(43,190)	(76,688)
Sales tax refund from equipment purchases	—	461,517
Increase in restricted cash	(460,188)	—
Net cash provided by (used in) investing activities	(503,378)	384,829

Example:

As an insurance firm, the Travelers Corp. makes investments in financial assets, out of which it pays its claims. The financial assets include securities with fixed maturities, mortgage loans, equity securities, and investments in real estate. The items on the portion of the cash-flow statement that relate to investing activities usually describe these financial investments or the collections of principal on these investments. However, one of the items in the list is securities transactions in course of settlement, which represents additional investments in securities where cash was used to purchase certain financial instruments but where the financial instruments were not yet the property of the firm on the balance-sheet date. It also represents financial instruments that were lent to other business entities and were not available for use by the Travelers as of the balance-sheet date. Thus it properly represents a cash flow from an investing activity and not a cash flow resulting from operating activity. The following is from Traveler's 2008 10K:

	2008	**2007**	**2006**
Cash flows from investing activities			
Proceeds from maturities of fixed maturities	**4,869**	5,305	5,810
Proceeds from sales of investments:			
Fixed maturities	**6,932**	7,323	4,401
Equity securities	**53**	106	285
Real estate	**25**	11	—
Other investments	**655**	1,460	1,111
Purchases of investments:			
Fixed maturities	**(11,127)**	(14,719)	(13,845)
Equity securities	**(95)**	(135)	(83)
Real estate	**(38)**	(74)	(75)
Other investments	**(667)**	(740)	(705)
Net (purchases) sales of short-term securities	**(406)**	(562)	(85)
Securities transactions in course of settlement	**(318)**	(123)	447
Other	**(45)**	(378)	(325)

Example:

W. R. Grace & Co. is engaged in the production and sale of specialty chemicals and specialty materials on a global basis through its two operating segments. Grace, along with 61 of its U.S. subsidiaries and affiliates, filed voluntary petitions for reorganization under Chapter 11 of the U.S. Bankruptcy Code and, since 2001, has been subject to the jurisdiction of the U.S. Bankruptcy Court for the District of Delaware.

Grace terminated (surrender value) life insurance policies of its executives to raise cash. One might argue that this is better represented as a financing activity. The proceeds were used to fund the potentially large liabilities and awards related to asbestos claims against the company.

As we will see in a later chapter, lawsuits and the potential for large damage awards have a vitriolic effect on the cost of capital. Shareholders of Grace can understand why this is so. Seen below is the investment activities section taken from the W. R. Grace 2009 10K.

	2009	2008
Investing activities:		
Capital expenditures	**(36.5)**	(58.7)
Proceeds from sales of investment securities	**8.3**	46.7
Purchases of equity investments	**(1.0)**	(3.0)
Proceeds from termination of life insurance policies	**68.8**	8.1
Net investment in life insurance policies	**(0.4)**	0.1
Proceeds from disposals of assets	**5.4**	2.6
Net cash provided by (used for) investing activities	**44.6**	(4.2)

Example:

Martek Biosciences Corporation develops nutritional products using microbes such as algae and fungi. In its 2009 10K, the company capitalized a variety of expenses, including significant legal costs (amortized over 5 years) and patent and interest expenses related to projects under construction.

The cash-flow analyst should view the capitalization of interest expenses no differently than interest expense paid on debt running through the income statement. As such, capitalized interest on plant and legal should have been included as operating activities, and to the extent they are listed as an investing activity, operating cash flows are artificially boosted.

The decision as to whether or not to capitalize certain cash outflows allows wide management discretion, potentially distorting peer comparability.

	2009	2008	2007
Investing activities:			
Sales and maturities of investments	200	8,475	6,850
Purchases of investments	—	(16,925)	(275)
Expenditures for property, plant, and equipment	(8,932)	(9,785)	(8,279)
Repurchase from sale-leaseback transaction and other	—	—	(3,010)
Capitalization of intangible and other assets	(18,535)	(3,895)	(6,010)
Net cash used in investing activities	(27,267)	(22,130)	(10,724)

Example:

Jackson Hewitt Tax Service, Inc., provides computerized preparation of federal, state, and local individual income tax returns in the United States through a nationwide network of franchised and company-owned offices operating under the brand name Jackson Hewitt Tax Service. While the company has had a history of adequate cash-flow generation, a caveat is detected in the investment activity section of its 2009 10K, "Funding provided to franchisees." While Jackson Hewitt reports on its balance sheet less than 5 percent of its shareholders' equity in the form of notes receivable, many companies, such as Krispy Kreme, have failed to do so owing to their financing the operations of franchisees. Many franchisors have had to take back the retail locations of its failed franchises having deficit cash flows, resulting in the firm having greater total operating leases (debt) while absorbing much management time. Such companies include Burger King, Midas, Sharper Image, and Nathan's Famous.

As to be discussed in Chapter 8, Jackson Hewitt relied on a single bank lending program for much of its cash flows. Such reliance on a customer or supplier for an important part of business success will raise risk (cost of equity capital). When that program was ended by its bank, shares in Jackson Hewitt stock fell rather dramatically.

	2009	2008	2007
Investing activities:			
Capital expenditures	(7,603)	(6,441)	(8,949)
Funding provided to franchisees	(6,550)	(9,364)	(6,489)
Proceeds from repayments by franchisees	2,271	2,426	2,133
Cash paid for acquisitions	(14,504)	(17,669)	(3,828)
Net cash used in investing activities	(26,386)	(31,048)	(17,133)

Example:

Cree, Inc., develops and manufactures semiconductor materials and devices based primarily on silicon carbide, gallium nitride, and related compounds. There are several items of interest in the investment activity section of its 2008 10K. As reported, Cree has been an active acquirer both of capital and of intangible assets. The largest items in the section represent the purchase and sale of fixed-income investments, which is common for entities that have either raised funds, sold assets, or are steady free-cash-flow generators. As seen below, fewer of these investments matured during the most recent fiscal year, which, relative to the prior year, was the difference in the investments being able to provide cash for the company's acquisitions. You also can see a $60 million payment related to the acquisition of COTCO 2 years earlier. Cree achieved certain EBITA targets related to the acquisition and was obligated to make the payment to the former shareholder. The cash payment represents an addition to the purchase price and a commensurate addition to goodwill on its balance sheet and is an event the analyst should have been aware of. Analysts will model for any such payments in their projected statement of cash flows, having been aware of deal terms.

	2008	2007	2006
Cash flows from investing activities:			
Purchase of property and equipment	(55,283)	(55,741)	(82,604)
Purchase of Intrinsic Semiconductor Corporation, net of cash acquired	—	—	(43,850)
Purchase of COTCO Luminant Devices, Ltd., net of cash acquired	—	—	(79,289)
Purchase of LED Lighting Fixtures, Inc., net of cash acquired	—	(7,180)	—
Payment of COTCO contingent consideration	(60,000)	—	—
Payment of LLF contingent consideration	(4,386)	—	—
Purchase of investments	(217,059)	(413,735)	(167,608)
Proceeds from maturities of investments	134,561	507,091	254,840
Proceeds from sale of property and equipment	169	1,465	550
Proceeds from sale of available-for-sale investments	35,815	17,000	26,646
Purchase of patent and licensing rights	(8,660)	(7,647)	(6,399)
Net cash (used in) provided by investing activities	(174,843)	41,253	(97,714)

Example:

ConAgra Foods, Inc., is a leading food distributor. ConAgra has a strong business-to-business presence, supplying potato, other vegetable, spice, and grain products to a variety of well-known restaurants, food-service operators, and commercial customers. ConAgra, in its 2009 10K, reports that it purchased businesses totaling $84 million that was financed in part by the sale of businesses for which it accounted using the equity method. For 2008 and 2007, ConAgra also reports both the purchase of and sale of leased warehouses. ConAgra leases warehouses for its manufacturing, storage, and distribution operations. While, from the investing activity section, we see ConAgra has not been successful in buying and selling warehouses, one would need to know the rental (and tax) savings, if any, ConAgra was able to effect by owning those properties. One may question whether the buying and selling of warehouses more appropriately might be suited as an operating activity because there were quite a few transactions relating to the ongoing nature of those transactions. Placing these transactions into operating activities would have reduced operating cash flow and, in any event, requires further insight from the company related to this business strategy.

	2009	2008	2007
Cash flows from investing activities:			
Purchase of marketable securities	—	(1,351.0)	(4,075.5)
Sales of marketable securities	—	1,352.0	4,078.4
Additions to property, plant, and equipment	(441.9)	(449.6)	(386.1)
Purchase of leased warehouses	—	(39.2)	(93.6)
Sale of leased warehouses	—	35.6	91.6
Sale of investment in Swift note receivable	—	—	117.4
Sale of businesses and equity-method investments	29.7	—	73.6
Sale of property, plant, and equipment	27.1	30.0	74.3
Purchase of businesses and intangible assets	(84.2)	(255.2)	—
Other items	1.9	1.5	11.2
Net cash flows from investing activities—continuing operations	(467.4)	(675.9)	(108.7)
Net cash flows from investing activities—discontinued operations	2,258.6	32.1	631.6
Net cash flows from investing activities	1,791.2	(643.8)	522.9

CASH FLOWS FROM FINANCING ACTIVITIES

The FASB defines financing activities broadly as follows:

> Financing activities include obtaining resources from owners and providing them with a return on, and a return of, their investment; borrowing money and repaying amounts borrowed, or otherwise settling the obligation; and obtaining and paying for other resources obtained from creditors on long-term credit [SFAS 95, para. 18].

The FASB further clarifies the nature of cash inflows or cash outflows from financing activities in the following manner:

Cash inflows from financing activities are

- **a.** Proceeds from issuing equity instruments.
- **b.** Proceeds from issuing bonds, mortgages, notes, and other short- or long-term borrowing.

Cash outflows for financing activities are

- **a.** Payments of dividends or other distributions to owners, including
- **b.** Outlays to reacquire the enterprise's equity instruments.
- **c.** Repayments of amounts borrowed.
- **d.** Other principal payments to creditors who have extended long-term credit [SFAS 95, paras. 19–20].

Financing activities are cash transactions that involve liabilities or shareholders' equity. The logic underlying the definition of financing activities seems very clear: All the events that represent increases of internal or external capital are financing cash flows, whereas events that represent decreases of internal or external capital are disfinancing cash flows. Loosely speaking, internal capital is capital invested by shareholders in the firm, whereas external capital represents lending to the firm by creditors.

Cash flows from financing activities first should be segregated into cash inflows and cash outflows from financing activities. The net cash flows from financing activities will be determined by the net cash generated from operating activities minus the net cash used for investing activities minus the increase in the cash balance. Thus, once the cash-flow analyst examines the cash generated from operations and cash investments, net cash financing is of little relevance. However, the composition of net cash from financing activities is of great relevance.

The most significant source of financing for most firms is borrowing. The academic literature is unclear about the implications of debt financing. Debt financing generally is considered favorable because interest on debt is tax deductible; that is, no tax is due on profits paid to creditors. The same argument is extended for return on invested capital; that is, return on invested capital is enhanced through borrowing. However, a firm that is overly leveraged increases the risk of bankruptcy and thus the expected costs of bankruptcy to shareholders, including total loss of their investment. Since debt payments and interest cannot be met from an accounting concept, I rely on the ability of the entity to produce cash. To the extent that cash from operations and disinvesting activities is insufficient to satisfy obligations, financial officers will turn to financial activities.

Many potential business acquisitions are approved or disapproved by the ease with which the free cash flow of the new asset can pay down the incremental debt. To the extent that it takes longer to repay debt from cash flows, the attractiveness of the company to potential acquirers is mitigated.

Most firms have some optimal level of debt; increases beyond this level are undesirable for the firm, whereas increases up to that point could be favorable. Some fortunate firms are such strong cash-flow producers that investment opportunities are easily financed through internal operations. The cash-flow analyst may wish to consider whether the firm's increase in debt financing is favorable or not depending on the analyst's assessment of the optimal level of debt in relation to the firm's pro forma ability to meet scheduled debt payments from a conservative cash-flow forecast. The cost of debt will also be compared to the expected after-tax cash return (its free cash flow) of a particular project.

Another implication of debt financing is that current owners/shareholders of the firm indicate that they wish to retain full ownership in the firm, possibly because they perceive a high probability that the value of the firm will grow or the current market value does not fully recognize the entity's real value. Thus, increases in debt financing or, at least, increases in debt financing that are not accompanied by increases in equity financing may be perceived as favorable signals about the future prospects of a firm. However, increases in debt financing may cause conflicts of interest between stockholders and bondholders, which, in turn, may lead management to invest in suboptimal projects. This arises when equity holders are beholden to creditors, and are in fact fearful a mis-step of an investment would place bondholders in control through bankruptcy. Such conflicts may lead to undesirable consequences or to wasted resources that are dedicated to reducing this conflict. Thus, issuance of debt sometimes may be viewed negatively by the cash-flow analyst.

One important asymmetry in the treatment of internal and external capital under SFAS 95 should be highlighted at this point: Dividends paid to shareholders are classified as financing cash outflows because they represent disfinancing events. However, payments of interest on a loan do not represent cash outflows from financing activities; instead, as we shall see in the next section, they represent an operating cash outflow. This is an asymmetric treatment because both represent a return on capital to providers, and there should not be any distinction between a return to creditors and a return to shareholders. The inclusion of interest payments among operating cash flows will bias the concept of cash flows generated from ongoing operations and the concept of free cash flow as it is generally defined. Therefore, interest, dividends, and tax cash flows that have been reported as financing or investing activities may be moved to operating activities to avoid distortion and improve comparability. On adjustment, misclassifications do not affect the free-cash-flow definition I propose in Chapter 4, with further clarification in Chapter 8 as to the cost-of-capital effect.

Let me provide now examples of financing cash flows from the statement of cash flows.

Example:

The following is taken from US Precious Metal's, 2009 10K. It is an exploration-stage company engaged in the acquisition, exploration, and development of mineral properties. The company raised about $5.3 million in equity capital between 1998 and 2009. Unfortunately, its balance sheet reveals deficit shareholders' equity of $1.8 million as of May 2009 because it has not yet recorded operating revenue. The company has exhausted its cash resources.

	Year Ended		Exploration Stage
	May 2009	**May 2008**	**Jan 1988–May 2009**
Financing activities:			
Proceeds from sales of common stock	400,000	1,417,500	3,492,500
Proceeds from exercises of warrants	184,998	80,000	267,498
Proceeds from convertible notes	730,000	—	730,000
Loan from affiliated company	—	—	70,000
Repayment of loan to the affiliated company	—	—	(68,000)
Cash provided by financing activities	1,314,998	1,497,500	4,491,998

Example:

Harris Corporation, together with its subsidiaries, is an international communications and information technology company serving government and commercial markets in more than 150 countries. From its 2009 10K, we see that Harris assumed borrowings (net of $450 million) that were used to finance $745 million in businesses acquired and $98.7 million for property, plant, and equipment.

Harris also recorded a $5.6 million inflow in connection with the proceeds of employee stock options. One might question whether this entry is more properly allocated as an operating activity because it is related to salaries needed for the production process.

The management of Harris feels confident in its future prospects, having bought back $132.3 million of its stock in the same year as the acquisition, of which over half was financed with debt. Normally, if debt financing is needed to fund an acquisition, share buybacks should not be undertaken. An exception would be if the entity is underlevered, the cash yield is low, and the free cash flow resulting from the investment is relatively certain to improve return on invested capital (ROIC).

You also can see that Harris made a $100 million payment to Harris Stratex Networks as part of the spin-off of this division to its shareholders. A *spin-off* is the distribution of shares of a company owned by the parent to shareholders. Companies may undertake a spin-off if they feel that the value of the division is not being properly reflected in its current market value. Of course, the parent also may attempt to sell the division, and if that is not successful, a spin off may be pursued.

	2009	2008	2007
Investing activities:			
Cash paid for acquired businesses	(745.3)	(19.4)	(404.6)
Cash received in the combination with Stratex Networks, Inc.	—	—	33.1
Additions of property, plant, and equipment	(98.7)	(112.9)	(88.8)
Additions of capitalized software	(23.1)	(33.3)	(40.3)
Cash paid for short-term investments available for sale	(1.2)	(9.3)	(356.0)
Proceeds from the sale of short-term investments available for sale	3.7	26.6	473.7
Proceeds from the sale of securities available for sale	—	13.7	—
Net cash used in investing activities	(864.6)	(134.6)	(382.9)
Financing activities:			
Proceeds from borrowings	531.8	460.5	442.0
Repayment of borrowings	(81.4)	(599.4)	(39.3)
Payment of treasury lock	—	(8.8)	—
Proceeds from exercise of employee stock options	5.6	45.2	35.7
Repurchases of common stock	(132.3)	(234.6)	(251.3)
Cash dividends	(106.6)	(81.5)	(58.2)
Cash decrease related to spin-off of Harris Stratex Networks, Inc.	(100.0)	—	—
Net cash provided by (used in) financing activities	117.1	(418.6)	128.9

Example:

Kaman Corporation is in the aerospace and industrial distribution markets under four reporting segments: aerostructures, precision products, helicopters, and specialty bearings. The windfall profit tax benefits seen in the 2007–2009 financing activity section of its 2009 10K relate to the tax savings resulting from the exercise of nonqualified stock options and disqualifying dispositions of stock acquired by exercise of incentive stock options and employee stock purchase plan stock purchases in excess of the deferred tax asset originally recorded. A windfall tax benefit is created if the deduction for tax purposes exceeds the compensation cost recognized in the income statement. These benefits are reflected under financial activities under FAS 1239(R). Since normally stock compensation is an operating activity, it may be preferable to adjust these benefits to that section because the reporting under financing activity may understate cash flow from operations.

You also will see a book overdraft increase of $5 million. Book overdraft positions occur when total outstanding issued checks exceed available cash balances.

	2009	2008	2007
Cash flows from financing activities:			
Net borrowings (repayments) under revolving credit agreements	31,636	(45,286)	11,735
Proceeds from issuance of long-term debt	50,000	—	—
Debt repayment	—	(1,722)	(1,821)
Net change in book overdraft	5,003	(4,613)	4,872
Proceeds from exercise of employee stock plans	3,616	5,256	3,238
Dividends paid	(14,181)	(12,552)	(12,002)
Debt issuance costs	(645)	(150)	—
Windfall tax benefit	349	1,171	378

Example:

Briggs & Stratton is the world's largest producer of air-cooled gasoline engines for outdoor power equipment. Reproduced below is the financial activity section from its 2009 10K. The section is fairly straightforward, with cash outlays of approximately $137 million for dividends and repayment of principal on debt. You also will see $991,000 in proceeds from stock options and their related tax benefit. Companies receive an expense deduction on their tax returns that is equal to the market price of the shares less the exercise price of the option. I will discuss this at greater length in the following two examples.

	2009	2008	2007	2006	2005
Cash flows from financing activities:					
Net (repayments) borrowings on loans, notes payable, and long-term debt	(92,883)	74,118	8,481	(8,778)	(19,062)
Issuance cost of amended revolver	(1,286)	—	—	—	(1,286)
Cash dividends paid	(43,560)	—	—	—	(43,560)
Capital contributions received	—	383	5,638	(6,021)	—
Stock option exercise proceeds and tax benefits	991	—	—	—	991
Net cash provided (used) by financing activities	(136,738)	74,501	14,119	(14,799)	(62,917)

Example:

The operating and financing activities sections from The Dress Barn's 2009 10K illustrate the reporting of excess tax benefits from stock-based compensation, which, as we have seen, is a commonly used method of cash salary savings and motivation incentive. The basis for recognizing the issuance of stock options as an expense is the value attached to these instruments to both employers and employees. Many employees accept a lower cash salary in return for stock options, perceiving future stock value in excess of forgone cash compensation. The employer also benefits by preserving cash or using that capital in other areas.

Accounting rules require that excess tax benefits be reported as a financing cash flow rather than a reduction of taxes paid. The income tax effect is related to the expense portion of the stock option transaction and, accordingly, is classified as an operating activity.

Note that in The Dress Barn's statement of cash flows, financing activities, excess tax benefit is the same as found under operating activities but in a different direction (the excess tax benefit is negative under operating activities and positive in financing activities). The cash tax benefit from stock-based compensation typically will be split between operating cash flows and financing cash flows. The "excess" is the difference between what the company estimated and the actual tax benefit. For example, if the firm underbooked, the excess will be positive and is reported in cash flow from financing activities. Hence, for The Dress Barn, the company is moving the excess benefit from an operating activity to a financial activity while continuing to show stock-based compensation expense as an operating activity.

The employer generally is eligible for a tax deduction equal to the full amount of the stock when the employee vests in the restricted stock or the intrinsic value of the stock when the option is exercised. Firms that trade at higher valuation multiples will be accorded a greater tax savings. Under SFAS 123(R), for book purposes, a company generally measures the cost of employee services received in exchange for an award of equity instruments based on the grant-date fair value of the award. Fair value normally is determined using a Black-Scholes option-valuation model. That cost is amortized over the vesting period. When a restricted stock vests or a nonqualified option is exercised, the amount of the employer's corporate tax deduction is fixed. At that time, it is evident whether the amount deductible on the tax return is greater or less than the cumulative compensation cost amortized over the vesting period. Excess tax benefits, if any, are credited to additional paid-in capital.

Does stock-based compensation artificially boost cash flow from operations? In almost all cases, the answer is yes because although the stock represents real value, to the extent that a peer pays its employees all cash-based compensation, it distorts comparability. However, to deduct the amount ($6.577 million for The Dress Barn) would result in lower cash flows than actually occurred, with no future cash outlay required, as would be the case of underfunding a pension plan. The cost to existing and future shareholders is that the value of their equity investment is potentially diluted; thus we would not subtract stock-based compensation from the stated cash flow from operations. Creditors, on the other hand, would welcome share-based compensation because it leaves added cash that could be used to enhance repayment prospects.

Reported under financing activities, The Dress Barn received cash from executives exercising stock options of $2.65 million. The company also shows the tax savings owing to the deductibility of value of its stock on its tax return. One might question whether the tax savings also should be placed under operating activities owing to their relationship to salaries. You also will see under financing activities the cash from employees to purchase company stock. Again, one might question whether this is really compensation and should be placed as an operating activity, based on its fair value. In my model, I do not make such an adjustment because, unlike an underfunded pension plan, the entity is under no obligation to change its method of compensation. If its stock price fell so low that employees demanded cash in lieu of future stock benefits, the direct impact on cash flow from operations could be substantial. Also, a potential acquirer would need to make a similar analysis to adjust for realistic operating and free cash flow had cash compensation been required.

Getting back to the question of the two companies, one that pays its employees all cash compensation and the other that pays partly in stock, the latter entity would reflect higher operating cash flows. This is why we need to look at cash-flow multiples because that added cost of share-based compensation presumably will convert into additional shares, diluting the existing shareholder population.

Firms normally will attempt to offset the dilution of stock issuance, and in those instances, the economic cost is clear. The Dress Barn, in fact, has been an active acquirer of its shares.

Amounts in Thousands	Fiscal Year Ended		
	July 25, 2009	July 26, 2008	July 28, 2007
Operating activities:			
Net earnings	$69,688	$74,088	$101,182
Adjustments to reconcile net earnings to net cash provided by operating activities:			
Depreciation and amortization	48,535	48,200	45,791
Impairments and asset disposals	8,291	4,110	2,363
Deferred taxes	2,981	9,999	(1,533)
Deferred rent and other occupancy costs	(4,120)	(4,606)	(4,520)
Share-based compensation	6,577	6,612	6,307
Tax benefit on exercise of unqualified stock options	—	—	5,863
Excess tax benefits from stock-based compensation	(863)	(383)	(5,721)
Amortization of debt issuance cost	353	366	372
Amortization of bond premium cost	624	415	108
Change in cash surrender value of life insurance	907	732	(441)
Realized loss on sales of securities	153	304	215
Gift card breakage	(1,788)	(2,184)	(3,724)
Other	18	1,307	(354)
Changes in assets and liabilities:			
Merchandise inventories	(6,574)	10,160	(26,656)
Prepaid expenses and other current assets	1,782	(7,084)	2,171
Other assets	(313)	378	450
Accounts payable	17,856	(12,718)	12,604
Accrued salaries, wages, and related expenses	4,182	(2,128)	4,358
Other accrued expenses	227	(96)	7,313
Customer credits	965	1,865	2,605
Income taxes payable	13,785	1,642	(8,839)
Deferred rent and lease incentives	9,901	13,157	10,028
Deferred compensation and other long-term liabilities	(476)	1,319	5,290
Total adjustments	103,003	71,367	54,050
Net cash provided by operating activities	172,691	145,455	155,232
Financing activities:			
Payment of long-term debt	(1,298)	(1,211)	(1,148)
Purchase of treasury stock	(4,657)	(40,179)	(8,090)
Proceeds from employee stock purchase plan	238	277	299
Excess tax benefits from stock-based compensation	863	383	5,721
Proceeds from stock options exercised	2,657	1,615	6,511
Net cash (used in) provided by financing activities	(2,197)	(39,115)	3,293

Source: The Dress Barn, 2009 10K.

Example:

The cost of stock-based compensation is clearly measurable for Oracle Corporation. Management wrote in its 2009 10K, "We repurchased 225.6 million shares for $4.0 billion, 97.3 million shares for $2.0 billion, and 233.5 million shares for $4.0 billion in fiscal 2009, 2008, and 2007, respectively."

From the cover page of its 10K, Oracle reports the following number of outstanding common shares at the end of their past 4 fiscal years, as well as shares purchased:

Fiscal Year End	Shares Outstanding	Shares Purchased (million)
May 2009	5,007,230	225.6
May 2008	5,155,842	97.3
May 2007	5,113,035	233.5
May 2006	5,238,329	

While Oracle was active acquiring other entities over the time period shown, the company did so for cash. You can see, then, that Oracle paid $10 billion to acquire 556.6 million shares, even though its total share count was reduced by just 231,000 shares. It is here that the primary (exclusive of tax) cost of stock-based compensation is seen.

Figure 3-1 shows the marked gap of SGA/sales for Oracle and SAP, its chief rival, reflecting the bias from the stock-based compensation costs. It is in the SG&A that most of the savings from stock-based compensation would be captured. SAP reports a small fraction of stock-based compensation compared with Oracle. The cost of the large stock-based compensation program is not captured in Oracle's income statement, distorting many of its GAAP-based metrics and allowing it to report higher GAAP-based measures. The true effect is reflected after considering the cost of the acquired shares. Of course, there is no requirement that Oracle do this, but given its history, it should be considered in cash-flow forecasts.

FIGURE 3-1

Oracle Corp. versus SAP Corp. SG&A/Sales, 2004–2009

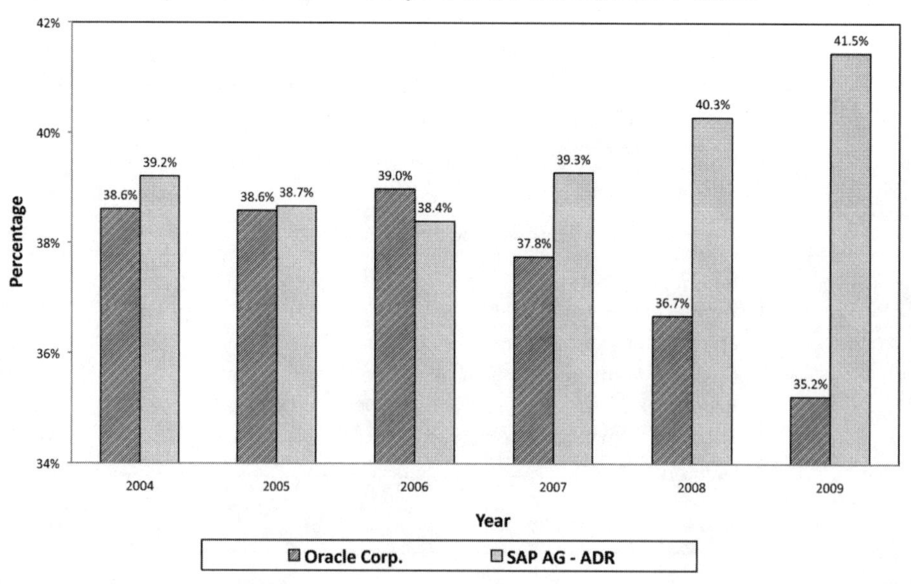

Example:

Trinity Industries, Inc., is a large manufacturer of heavy metal products such as railcars, marine products, and containers; it also has a leasing subsidiary. In its statement of cash flows, Trinity separates its capital spending from its leasing operation from that of its manufacturing operation. It is imperative that an investor or creditor review and analyze the statement of cash flows for Trinity's leasing operation, which it files (with the Securities and Exchange Commission) separately. For the operating company to receive cash flows from the leasing company, certain excess cash flows and fixed-charge coverage ratios must be met. Otherwise, as we read next, the operating company is required to send cash to the subsidiary, which could well result in a cash strain and an increase in leverage.

The investment activities sections for Trinity and its leasing division are closely intertwined. For example, Trinity (the operating company) historically has entered into agreements (the "Fixed charges coverage agreement") with the leasing subsidiary whereby Trinity is obligated, as stated in the agreement, to make such payments to the subsidiary as may be required to maintain "the Registrant's" (the leasing subsidiary) net earnings available for fixed charges (as defined) at an amount equal to but not less than one and one-half times the fixed charges (as defined) of the subsidiary. These fixed-charge coverage agreements terminate in accordance with their terms at such time as all amounts payable by the subsidiary under the equipment trust certificates[5] have been paid in full, and the subsidiary shall have delivered a certificate to its CPAs demonstrating that net earnings available for fixed charges, without considering any payments by Trinity, have not been less than one and one-half times the fixed charges in each of the five most recently completed fiscal years, provided that the subsidiary and Trinity agree in connection with "Future financing agreements" to maintain the fixed-charges coverage agreement in force and in effect during the term of such "Future financing agreements."

Certain ratios and cash deposits must be maintained by the leasing group's subsidiaries in order for excess cash flow, as defined in the agreements, from the leasing group to third parties to be available to Trinity.

TRINITY INDUSTRIES, INC., AND SUBSIDIARIES
CONSOLIDATED STATEMENTS OF CASH FLOWS (IN MILLIONS)

	Year Ended December 31,		
	2008	**2007**	**2006**
Operating activities:			
Net income	**$285.8**	$293.1	$230.1
Adjustments to reconcile net income to net cash provided by continuing operating activities:			
Loss (gain) from discontinued operations, including gain on sale	**1.5**	0.7	(14.6)
Depreciation and amortization	**140.3**	118.9	87.6
Stock-based compensation expense	**18.7**	18.6	14.0
Excess tax benefits from stock-based compensation	**(0.9)**	(4.0)	(7.6)
Provision for deferred income taxes	**251.3**	59.3	75.5

(Continued)

[5] An equipment trust certificate is used as a financing method by transportation companies. It is basically a bond, the proceeds of which are used to purchase the railcars, with the maturity reflecting the useful life of the asset.

	Year Ended December 31,		
	2008	2007	2006
Gain on disposition of property, plant, equipment, and other assets	**(10.5)**	(17.0)	(13.5)
Other	**(26.5)**	(45.7)	(26.6)
Changes in assets and liabilities:			
(Increase) decrease in receivables	**43.4**	(45.7)	(33.8)
(Increase) decrease in inventories	**(25.8)**	(50.9)	(124.0)
(Increase) decrease in other assets	**(138.0)**	(53.2)	(78.7)
Increase (decrease) in accounts payable and accrued liabilities	**(128.3)**	87.2	5.2
Increase (decrease) in other liabilities	**6.9**	(16.7)	(0.2)
Net cash provided by operating activities—continuing operations	**417.9**	344.6	113.4
Net cash (required) provided by operating activities—discontinued operations	**1.3**	(0.1)	17.4
Net cash provided by operating activities	**419.2**	344.5	130.8
Investing activities:			
Proceeds from sales of railcars from our leased fleet	**222.1**	359.3	88.8
Proceeds from disposition of property, plant, equipment, and other assets	**20.8**	51.0	20.0
Capital expenditures—lease subsidiary	**(1,110.8)**	(705.4)	(543.6)
Capital expenditures—manufacturing and other	**(132.3)**	(188.7)	(117.5)
Payment for purchase of acquisitions, net of cash acquired	**—**	(51.0)	(3.5)
Net cash required by investing activities—continuing operations	**(1,000.2)**	(534.8)	(555.8)
Net cash provided by investing activities—discontinued operations	**—**	—	82.9
Net cash required by investing activities	**(1,000.2)**	(534.8)	(472.9)
Financing activities:			
Issuance of common stock, net	**3.1**	12.2	18.1
Excess tax benefits from stock-based compensation	**0.9**	4.0	7.6
Payments to retire debt	**(390.8)**	(129.5)	(410.2)
Proceeds from issuance of debt	**922.5**	304.8	920.1
Stock repurchases	**(58.3)**	(2.9)	—
Dividends paid to common shareholders	**(24.2)**	(20.2)	(16.3)
Dividends paid to preferred shareholders	**—**	—	(1.7)
Net cash provided by financing activities	**453.2**	168.4	517.6
Net (decrease) increase in cash and cash equivalents	**(127.8)**	(21.9)	175.5
Cash and cash equivalents at beginning of period	**289.6**	311.5	136.0
Cash and cash equivalents at end of period	**$161.8**	$289.6	$311.5

Example:

Union Tank Corp. is engaged in the manufacture and leasing of railway tank cars. The company engages in sale-leaseback transactions in which railcars are sold by the company to outside investors and then leased back to customers under operating leases. There are several interesting facets to Union Tank Corp. All the company's stock is owned privately, with Berkshire Hathaway the majority owner. The company files with the Securities and Exchange Commission (SEC) because of debt that is publicly held.

A captive finance operation is meant to facilitate the firm's marketing efforts. It does this by providing the financing by issuing loans or leases to the dealers and customers. From an analytic viewpoint, it is necessary to analyze both entities, the operating and financing companies separately and together, as presented in the consolidated statements. The captive can be structured as a legally separate subsidiary or as a distinct operating division. It can provide the operating, or parent company with a valuable asset that could be monetized or, if liberal in its credit policy along with a weak financial structure, an investment that can bring down the entire organization.

Changes in interest rates also could affect the operating company if they affect product demand or client finances, loans are guaranteed, or variable-rate debt is not hedged. For these reasons, the credit and cash flows of the financial subsidiary must be reviewed separately, including loan covenants and cross-guarantees.

Viewed under financing activities for Union Tank are borrowings from the privately held parent for the construction of railcars. Union Tank is well financed, having $1.3 billion in equity. The majority of the debt owed to the parent is for the manufacture of railcars, which Union then places under lease. The lessees have easily covered these fixed obligations, even under the strain of the 2007–2009 recession; the company's clients have, according to Union Tank's financial statements, a very low default rate because the company's credit standards are high, selling primarily to investment-grade customers having stable cash flows. Equipment-leasing cash flows are also shown in the table. As with all financial filings, a complete reading of the submission, including the management discussion and analysis, is vital.

As seen for Trinity Industries and other entities with leasing divisions, it is necessary to analyze the leasing component separately from the operating company because the leasing entity exhibits separate and distinct operating and free-cash-flow characteristics. Leasing affiliates are dependent on the financial health of the parent for its success, as is Union Tank on its parent company, the financially strong Berkshire Hathaway. It is also important to understand who its clients are for the products out on lease because, if they were to experience cash-flow strains, the ability of the lessor to service its debt would be compromised. Additionally, the more costly the leased product, such as railcars, the more important it is to understand the financial condition of the lessees. It is essential, when analyzing the operating cash flows of an entity such as Union Tank, to understand the current market values of its products. For instance, in the 2007–2009 period, Union Tank suffered $60 million in asset write-downs from cars coming off lease. If, on the other hand, Union Tank was in a period of strong demand for its equipment, the company would have the option of reselling the equipment for large gains or putting the equipment back out on lease for higher lease payments.

	2007	2006	2005
Cash flows from financing activities:			
Increase in advances from parent and affiliates	526,924	465,083	—
Proceeds from issuance of debt	—	—	312,121
Principal payments of debt	(216,058)	(85,143)	(40,583)
Cash dividends	(165,000)	(137,000)	(140,000)
Net cash provided by financing activities	145,866	242,940	131,53

The following table presents the scheduled cash inflows and outflows for the railcar and intermodal tank container leasing businesses over the next 5 years based on leases and equipment-related indebtedness outstanding as of December 31, 2007.

	(Dollars in Millions)				
	2008	2009	2010	2011	2012
Equipment leasing cash inflows					
Minimum future lease rentals	$589.8	$479.1	$367.2	$248.7	$155.5
Equipment leasing cash outflows					
Minimum future lease payments	40.7	37.6	39.9	42.8	56.0
Principal and interest amount of obligations	173.2	259.9	216.1	108.0	103.5
Excess (deficit) of inflows over outflows	$375.9	$181.6	$111.2	$97.9	$(4.0)

Lease Commitments

	Operating Leases		
	Sale-Leaseback	Others	Total
2008	$38,413	$7,485	$45,898
2009	35,412	6,449	41,861
2010	37,758	5,757	43,515
2011	40,753	4,859	45,612
2012	53,956	4,879	58,835
2013 and thereafter	88,231	14,244	102,475
	$294,523	$43,673	$338,196

Source: Union Tank Corp. 2009 10K.

Example:

Beacon Enterprise Solutions Group, Inc. (and subsidiaries) is a provider of global, international, and regional telecommunications and technology systems. Its 2009 10K illustrates a number of transactions, culminating in the company's $4.3 million preferred offering. As shown by the difference between proceeds and repayment amounts, the company's investment bankers and investors in the prefinancings did well. Beacon sold several issues via a private placement with yields of 12 percent plus issuance of warrants. During the year, the company borrowed $400,000 and repaid $450,000 on its line of credit. The cost of capital is onerous for entities with a history of operating losses and deficit net worth, such as Beacon, which paid very large fees to investors to lure investor interest.

	2009	2008
Cash flows from financing activities:		
Proceeds from issuances of convertible notes		500,000
Proceeds from issuances of bridge notes and other short-term notes	422,000	700,000
Proceeds from sale of preferred stock, net of offering costs	4,276,460	—
Proceeds from sale of common stock, net of offering costs	1,035,216	4,346,672
Proceeds from lines of credit	400,000	343,000
Proceeds from note payable	600,000	—
Payment of note offering costs		(75,000)
Repayment of line of credit	(450,000)	(393,000)
Repayment of convertible notes		(202,001)
Payments of notes payable	(985,514)	(534,389)
Payments of capital lease obligations	(13,562)	(11,928)
Net cash provided by financing activities	5,284,600	4,673,354

Example:

Tucson Electric is an electric utility company owned by Unisource, Inc. The following example, from its 2009 10K, illustrates the reporting of capital lease obligations in the statement of cash flows. GAAP requires recording the reduction in the lease obligation as a financing activity, whereas the interest portion must be reported as an operating activity. For operating lease obligations, the payment is recorded in its entirety as an operating activity. Therefore, capital leases for the identical asset and under similar monthly payment (term of lease may differ) will allow the entity to report higher operating cash flows.

When a lessor enters into an operating lease, payments received are recorded as operating activities, and if it enters into a capital lease, it classifies any cash paid to purchase that asset that is subsequently leased out as an investment activity.

	2009	2008	2007
Cash flows from financing activities:			
Proceeds from issuance of long-term debt	—	220,745	—
Proceeds from borrowings under revolving credit facility	**171,000**	170,000	160,000
Repayments of borrowings under revolving credit facility	**(146,000)**	(170,000)	(180,000)
Payments of capital lease obligations	**(24,091)**	(74,228)	(71,464)
Repayments of long-term debt	—	(10,000)	—
Dividends paid to UniSource Energy	**(60,000)**	(2,500)	(53,000)
Equity investment from UniSource Energy	**30,000**	—	18,000
Other cash receipts	**2,447**	1,237	7,795
Payment of debt issue/retirement costs	**(1,329)**	(3,120)	(451)
Other cash payments	**(1,347)**	(3,421)	(968)
Net cash flows—financing activities	**(29,320)**	128,713	(120,088)

CASH FLOWS FROM OPERATING ACTIVITIES

The FASB defined cash flows from operating activities as "all transactions and other events that are not defined as investing or financing activities." It broadly explained that "operating activities generally involve producing and delivering goods and providing services. Cash flows from operating activities are generally the cash effect of transactions and other events that enter into the determination of net income" (SFAS 95, para. 21). The FASB provided a list of specific cash flows from operations:

> **a.** Cash receipts from sales of goods or services, including receipts from collection or sale of accounts and both short- and long-term notes receivable from customers arising from those sales.
> **b.** Cash receipts from returns on loans, other debt instruments of other entities, and equity securities—interest and dividends.
> **c.** All other cash receipts that do not stem from transactions defined as investing or financing activities, such as amounts received to settle lawsuits; proceeds of insurance settlements except for those that are directly related to investing or financing activities such as from destruction of a building; and refunds from suppliers [SFAS 95, para 22].

It further described cash outflows for operating activities as

> **a.** Cash payments to acquire materials for manufacture or goods for resale, including principal payments on accounts and both short- and long-term notes payable to suppliers for those materials or goods.
> **b.** Cash payments to other suppliers and employees for other goods or services.
> **c.** Cash payments to governments for taxes, duties, fines, and other frees or penalties.
> **d.** Cash payments to lenders and other creditors for interest.
> **e.** All other cash payments that do not stem from transactions defined as investing or financing activities, such as payments to settle lawsuits, cash contributions to charities, and cash refunds to customers [SFAS 95, para 23].[6]

[6] There are other cash outflows that should be noted here. For example, there is a 20 percent excise tax when severance pay totals more than three times an executive's average income—including all forms of compensation-over the prior five years. Since outstanding options normally vest upon severance, the tax almost always kicks in. Also, so called "gross-ups," whereby the firm pays the executives income taxes, whether due to severance, a bonus, or a merger, can be very costly.

Clearly, the FASB treated cash flows from operations as the "residual" cash flow; it consists of all events that are not classified as either investing or financing activities. For many firms, the net cash flow from operating activities is likely to contain special items that are not easily assignable to investing or financing cash flows and that may not recur in the future, such as the settlement of a law suit. Thus the analyst ideally should separate the nonrecurring and special items from other operating cash flows. However, this is not easily done in practice because most firms follow the indirect approach to disclosing the cash flows from operating activities.

As noted, repayments under capital leases are treated as a financing activity, and the payment for interest under the same lease is estimated and is included as an operating activity. It would be more appropriate if the entire payment were placed under financing activities.

Assets that are sold at a gain can distort operating cash flows because the tax implications are listed as an operating activity, whereas the gain related to the sale is placed as an investing activity. A more proper placement would be to place both, as separate items, under investing activities.

In reporting cash flows from operating activities, enterprises are encouraged to report major classes of gross cash payments and their arithmetic sum—the net cash flow from operating activities (the direct method). Enterprises that do so should, at minimum, report the following classes of operating cash receipts and payments separately:

1. Cash collected from customers, including lessees, licensees, and the like
2. Interest and dividends received
3. Other operating cash receipts, if any
4. Cash paid to employees and other suppliers of goods or services, including suppliers of insurance, advertising, and the like
5. Interest paid
6. Income taxes paid
7. Other operating cash payments, if any

Additionally, for some items, such as postretirement benefits and asset retirement obligations, we include the (net) cost for the period rather than actual cash outflows in order to separate what we view as financing of these obligations from the operating-cost component. If the company is funding postretirement obligations at a level substantially below its net expense (service cost and net interest cost), this is equivalent to borrowing, which bolsters reported cash flow from operating activities.

Enterprises are encouraged to provide further breakdowns of operating cash receipts and payments that they consider meaningful and feasible. For example, a retailer or manufacturer might decide to further divide cash paid to employees and suppliers (category 4 above) into payments for costs of inventory and payments for selling, general, and administrative expenses (SFAS 95, para. 27).

Net cash flow from operating activities indicates the amount of cash that the firm was able to generate from (or needed to spend on) its ongoing business activities. Ideally, a firm should be able to generate cash from its business activities in every period because operating cash flows are prior to debt repayment and capital spending. However, in reality, many financially healthy firms generate cash from their business activities in most periods but spend more cash on their business activities than they receive from customers in some periods. Also, a firm may be in the development stage of its business. It may invest in developing its products or in setting up production facilities and distribution channels (investment activities), whereas larger cash receipts from customers are expected to occur only in the future. Another example is a seasonal business that invests in setting up inventories during one or two quarters, whereas most sales are made during other quarters (such as during the holiday season). Operating cash flows are likely to be negative during the quarters when inventories are built but positive in quarters when inventories are sold.

For some periods, and for some firms, a negative net cash flow from operations is acceptable, such as a manufacturer that works on long-term contracts (a shipbuilder) and must retool and build inventories during the initial stages of production. However, in the majority of cases, a positive net cash flow from business activities is expected. A business that spends more cash on its ongoing activities than it generates has to finance these activities somehow. It can just use up its cash reserves, it can borrow additional cash, it can raise additional equity, or it can liquidate investments or fixed assets. But none of these options can be sustained for prolonged periods. For example, it is unlikely that creditors will keep lending to a business that continuously does not generate an acceptable level of cash from its operations, resulting in a low ROIC. Similarly, liquidation of necessary assets may reduce the chances of generating cash flows from operations in the future. Thus continuous negative cash flows from operating activities (which are unrelated to a seasonal business or the operating cycle of the business) should be examined carefully by the cash-flow analyst.

In addition to net cash flows from operating activities, one should examine the components of cash flows. Actual cash inflows begin with the collection of cash from accounts receivable. The ease with which the entity collects its accounts receivable is an important determinant of its financial flexibility. Improvements in the collection period begin at the credit approval. For small, unknown, or startup entities, a greater degree of due diligence by the credit analyst is needed to enhance operating cash flows. We shortly discuss the credit process.

Reductions in accounts receivable, next to planned reductions in inventory, are the most sought-after ways to manage operating cash flow. Faster collection periods, made possible by improved credit-analysis software that enables the firm's credit analyst to review prospective and existing accounts, has improved the operating-cash-flow cycle. Additionally, the conservative use of customer credits and discounts has helped to improve the flow of collections.

TABLE 3-1

Largest Producers of Operating Cash Flow, 2008 ($000)

Company Name	Operating Cash Flow ($000)
AT&T, Inc.	33,656
BHP Billiton Group (AUS), ADR	18,159
BHP Billiton Group (GBR), ADR	18,159
BP PLC, ADR	38,095
Canadian Natural Resources	8,283
Chesapeake Energy Corp.	5,236
Chevron Corp.	29,632
China Mobile, Ltd., ADR	28,384
China Petroleum & Chem., ADR	9,925
China Telecom. Corp., Ltd., ADR	11,250
China Unicom (Hong Kong), ADR	8,403
ConocoPhillips	22,658
Daimler AG	4,461
Deutsche Telekom AG, ADR	21,391
Devon Energy Corp.	9,408
E.ON AG, ADR	9,400
Encana Corp.	8,855
ENEL Spa, ADR	14,629
ENI SPA -ADR	30,343
Exxon Mobil Corp.	59,725
Ford Motor Credit Co., LLC	9,128
France Telecom, ADR	20,877
Gazprom O A O, ADR	24,419
General Electric Cap. Corp.	31,262
General Electric Co.	48,601
GMAC, LLC	14,095
Hertz Global Holdings, Inc.	2,096
Honda Motor Co., Ltd., ADR	3,869
Lukoil Oil Co, ADR	14,312
Marathon Oil Corp.	6,782

(Continued)

TABLE 3-1 *(Continued)*

Largest Producers of Operating Cash Flow, 2008 ($000)

Company Name	Operating Cash Flow ($000)
Nippon Telegraph & Telephone, ADR	25,357
Nissan Motor Co., Ltd., ADR	13,443
ORIX Corp., ADR	3,143
Petrobras Brasileiro, ADR	28,220
Petrochina Co., Ltd., ADR	24,992
Repsol YPF SA, ADR	8,341
Rio Tinto Group (AUS), ADR	14,883
Rio Tinto Group (GBR), ADR	14,883
Royal Dutch Shell, PLC, ADR	43,918
Statoilhydro ASA, ADR	14,699
Telefonica SA, ADR	22,780
Total SA, ADR	25,985
Toyota Motor Corp., ADR	15,035
Vale SA, ADR	14,137
Verizon Communications, Inc.	26,620
Vodafone Group, PLC, ADR	17,465
Volkswagen AG, ADR	22,925
Wal-Mart Stores, Inc.	23,147
XTO Energy, Inc.	5,235

DIRECT METHOD

The FASB has provided firms with the option of reporting cash flows from operations using the direct or the indirect method, although the accounting rule maker has clearly advocated a preference for the clarity of the direct method. A joint task force between FASB and the International Accounting Standards Board (IASB) also has advocated a preference for the direct method and has urged companies to switch to the direct method. The cost of preparing under the direct method has resulted in very few companies preparing under the preferred method. Also, perhaps, some entities do not want to reveal the information the direct method provides, although the analyst can estimate such a report, as we will see.

Under the direct method, the main categories of operating cash flows reported in the statement are very similar to how the small local business would evaluate them: cash collections from customers minus payments to suppliers. The basis for the direct method is the simple identity

$$\text{Net income} = \text{revenues} - \text{expenses}$$

We can examine individual revenues and expenses and exclude those which are noncash revenues or expenses, as well as those which are not due to operating events. For example, a firm may record income from unconsolidated subsidiaries that is carried on the balance sheet using the equity method. This income is included in net income but is a noncash event if cash dividends are not paid by the subsidiary. Similarly, suppose that the firm sold some old property, plant, and equipment (PPE) at a gain. This gain is included in net income but reflects an investing cash flow and not an operating cash flow. You also will see how entities book hedging gains into net income, which are reversed in the operating cash flow section because those too are noncash events.

Examples of noncash expenses include depreciation and deferred taxes. Thus we can rewrite the accounting identity as

$$\text{Net income} = \text{CR} + \text{NCR} - (\text{CE} + \text{NCE})$$

where

CR=cash revenues from operating activities

NCR=noncash revenues or nonoperating cash flows

CE=cash expenses from operating activities

NCE=noncash expenses or nonoperating expenses (which are included among expenses)

Simple algebra yields

$$\text{CR} - \text{CE} = \text{net income} + \text{NCE} - \text{NCR}$$

By definition, CR – CE is identical to the cash from operating activities. It can be derived by adjusting net income for revenues and expense events that are either non-cash or nonoperating cash flows. In particular, we *add* noncash (or nonoperating) expenses because they were subtracted from income to derive net income and *subtract* noncash (or nonoperating) revenues because they were added to income in deriving net income.

The FASB's encouragement to use the direct approach in reporting operating cash flows has not met with success. This is unfortunate because a more logical starting point is that of cash collections from customers rather than a reconciliation beginning with net income. Perhaps the reluctance is because the FASB requires firms that use the direct method to add a schedule that reconciles net income with operating cash flow. Thus, when a firm adopts the direct method for reporting operating cash flows from operating activities, it has to supply *all* the information that is required from a firm that uses the indirect method, but in addition, it has to supply information about the major components of operating cash flows. Obviously, reasonable managers will opt to minimize their exposure to costly additional disclosure and mostly will use the indirect method for reporting.

An analyst can create a direct-method worksheet by using the balance-sheet changes and the income statement, if so desired. Creating a worksheet using the direct method may not be precisely comparable with that of a company reporting under the indirect format for several reasons. For example, the change in accounts receivable may not match the statement of cash flows where the indirect method is used if some of the company's receivables are caused by the sale of fixed assets; these receivables should not be considered as a change in operating cash flows because these receivables are related to disinvesting cash flows. Accordingly, a discrepancy in other balance-sheet items may not be due to operating activities but rather to investing or financial activities. It is prudent for the analyst, nonetheless, to review changes in the balance-sheet items to see how those differences compare with the changes as listed in the statement of cash flows under the indirect method.

Next, I show a template for estimating cash flow from operations for a company that reports under the direct method, Nu Horizons Electronics.[7] One might ask why it is necessary to construct a direct-method approach if basic cash-flow information is already given under the indirect method. To begin, it is important to know how to do this because often, when an entity releases preliminary financial results, it does not provide a statement of cash flows (merely an income statement and balance sheet), so even if one is constructed based on a lack of complete data, it will provide very useful information other investors do not have; it will show how the company is collecting cash, where it is coming from, its magnitude, and where it is being spent. The analyst will be able to compute the approximate cash burn or free cash flow that took place during the reporting period. Also, during interim periods, the entity often reports a limited statement of cash flows. We see this for Berkshire Hathaway, which reported cash flow from operating activities as a single-line entry. Additionally, a direct-method approach is a more natural method—cash in and cash out. For instance, isn't a line entry for taxes paid as part of operating activities more reflective of cash flows than deferred taxes? Compare the two formats using Nu Horizons with others in this book.

---

[7] The 2009 10K for Nu Horizons Electronics Corp. may be found on Edgar at www.sec.gov/Archives/edgar/data/718074/000114420409022970/v147330_10-k.htm.

NU HORIZONS ELECTRONICS CORP. AND SUBSIDIARIES
CONSOLIDATED STATEMENTS OF CASH FLOWS

	For the Years Ended		
	February 28, 2009	**February 29, 2008**	**February 28, 2007**
			(As restated)
Increase (decrease) in cash and cash equivalents:			
Cash flows from operating activities:			
Cash received from customers	**$789,991,000**	$716,847,000	$722,922,000
Cash paid to suppliers and employees	**(728,820,000)**	(732,359,000)	(700,393,000)
Interest paid	**(3,035,000)**	(4,500,000)	(4,129,000)
Interest received	**100,000**	241,000	580,000
Income taxes paid	**(2,148,000)**	(11,191,000)	(2,701,000)
Net cash provided by (used in) operating activities	**56,088,000**	(30,962,000)	16,279,000
Cash flows from investing activities:			
Capital expenditures	**(2,186,000)**	(2,808,000)	(1,069,000)
Acquisition payment DT Electronics	**(3,410,000)**	(1,744,000)	(6,098,000)
Acquisition of Dacom-Süd Electronic Vertriebs GmbH	**—**	(2,593,000)	—
Acquisition payment C–88	**(4,042,000)**	—	—
Net cash (used in) investing activities	**(9,638,000)**	(7,145,000)	(7,167,000)
Cash flows from financing activities:			
Borrowings under revolving credit line	**298,720,000**	317,605,000	214,933,000
Repayments under revolving credit line	**(345,223,000)**	(280,029,000)	(236,305,000)
Proceeds from exercise of stock options	**355,000**	210,000	2,726,000
Realized tax benefit of compensation expense	**(5,000)**	—	1,413,000
Proceeds from settlement of subordinated note	**—**	—	2,000,000
Net cash (used in) provided by financing activities	**(46,153,000)**	37,786,000	(15,233,000)
Effect of exchange-rate changes	**610,000**	(540,000)	(5,000)
Net increase (decrease) in cash and cash equivalents	**907,000**	(861,000)	(6,126,000)
Cash and cash equivalents, beginning of year	**3,886,000**	4,747,000	10,873,000
Cash and cash equivalents, end of year	**$4,793,000**	$3,886,000	$4,747,00

NU HORIZONS ELECTRONICS CORP. AND SUBSIDIARIES
CONSOLIDATED STATEMENTS OF OPERATIONS

	For the Years Ended		
	February 28, 2009	**February 29, 2008**	**February 28, 2007**
			(As restated)
Net sales	**$750,954,000**	$747,170,000	$668,591,000
Costs and expenses:			
Cost of sales	**637,261,000**	626,771,000	554,266,000
Selling, general and administrative expenses	**113,010,000**	112,473,000	94,891,000
Goodwill impairment charge	**7,443,000**	—	—
	757,714,000	739,244,000	649,157,000
Operating income (loss)	**(6,760,000)**	7,926,000	19,434,000
Other (income) expense:			
Interest expense	**3,141,000**	4,570,000	3,850,000
Interest income	**(100,000)**	(241,000)	(580,000)
	3,041,000	4,329,000	3,270,000
Income (loss) before provision (benefit) for income taxes and minority interests:	**(9,801,000)**	3,597,000	16,164,000
Provision (benefit) for income taxes	**(837,000)**	766,000	7,991,000
Income (loss) before minority interests	**(8,964,000)**	2,831,000	8,173,000
Minority interest in earnings of subsidiaries	**271,000**	312,000	456,000
Net (loss) income	**$(9,235,000)**	$2,519,000	$7,717,000
Net (loss) income per common share:			
Basic	**$(0.51)**	$0.14	$0.43
Diluted	**$(0.51)**	$0.14	$0.41
Weighted average common shares outstanding:			
Basic	**18,043,834**	17,931,356	17,871,671
Diluted	**18,043,834**	18,582,130	18,641,475

NU HORIZONS ELECTRONICS CORP. AND SUBSIDIARIES

CONSOLIDATED BALANCE SHEETS

	For the Years Ended	
	February 28, 2009	**February 29, 2008**
		(As restated)
Assets		
Current assets:		
Cash	**$4,793,000**	$3,886,000
Accounts receivable—less allowances of $3,438,000 and $4,269,000, respectively	**111,572,000**	150,270,000
Inventories	**107,877,000**	134,691,000
Deferred tax asset	**3,323,000**	3,135,000
Prepaid expenses and other current assets	**4,979,000**	4,306,000
Total current assets	**232,544,000**	296,288,000
Property, plant, and equipment, net	**4,827,000**	4,529,000
Other assets:		
Cost in excess of net assets acquired	**5,020,000**	9,925,000
Intangibles, net	**3,742,000**	2,500,000
Other assets	**5,222,000**	5,101,000
Total assets	**$251,355,000**	$318,343,000
Liabilities and shareholders' equity		
Current liabilities:		
Accounts payable	**$67,133,000**	$79,236,000
Accrued expenses	**8,202,000**	8,615,000
Due to seller	**296,000**	3,245,000
Bank debt	**8,450,000**	603,000
Income taxes payable	**1,322,000**	133,000
Total current liabilities	**85,403,000**	91,832,000
Long-term liabilities:		
Bank debt	**14,950,000**	69,300,000
Due to seller	**190,000**	—
Executive retirement plan	**2,400,000**	1,684,000
Deferred tax liability	**1,903,000**	2,072,000
Total long-term liabilities	**19,443,000**	73,056,000
Minority interest in subsidiaries	**2,532,000**	2,261,000

(Continued)

NU HORIZONS ELECTRONICS CORP. AND SUBSIDIARIES
CONSOLIDATED BALANCE SHEETS *(Continued)*

	For the Years Ended	
	February 28, 2009	**February 29, 2008**
Commitments and contingencies		
Shareholders' equity:		
Preferred stock, $1 par value, 1 million shares authorized; none issued or outstanding	—	—
Common stock, $0.0066 par value, 50 million shares authorized; 18,578,946 and 18,392,457 shares issued and outstanding as of February 28, 2009 and February 29, 2008, respectively	**122,000**	121,000
Additional paid-in capital	**56,386,000**	54,979,000
Retained earnings	**87,386,000**	96,621,000
Other accumulated comprehensive income (loss)	**83,000**	(527,000)
Total shareholders' equity	**143,977,000**	151,194,000
Total liabilities and shareholders' equity	**$251,355,000**	$318,343,000

How to Estimate Cash Flow from Operations

1. To estimate cash collections from customers, we use the following template:

	Item	Source
Cash collections from customers:		
+ Net sales	$750,954,000	Income statement
± Decrease in accounts receivable	$38,698,000	Balance sheet
± Increase in deferred revenue		Balance sheet or footnote
Total	**$789,652,000**	

Entities account for revenue recognition under various FASB and SEC guidelines. In the case of Nu Horizons, the company records revenues at the time its products are shipped. Some firms, as seen in the template, receive cash from customers as prepayments for future products or services, known as *deferred revenue*. This would be the case for prepayment of a magazine or software subscription.

Nu Horizon does not show a line entry for deferred revenue, so the line is left blank in the template. If the change in deferred revenues had increased, we would have added it to cash collections. The $38,698,000 is derived from the changes in the yearly balance sheets. Often, as stated, an entity will include in its receivables cash not due to trade but rather, for instance, due to the sale of an asset. We would exclude this from our estimate of cash flow from operations because such a transaction would be due to disinvesting cash flows. We see on the balance sheet that there was a small change in the bad debt allowance for receivables. If it were large (2 percent or more of sales), we would attempt to determine the amount of the charge-off and the reasons behind it. As seen, the template is very close to the $790 million reported under the direct method.

2. To estimate cash payments to suppliers, we use the following template, which should be used in conjunction with cash collections from customers (shown above). Cash payments to suppliers is equal to the cost of purchases (cost of goods sold plus the increase in inventory) and the payments to suppliers (cost of purchases plus the decrease in accounts payable).

Nu Horizons reports a single-line entry for cash paid to suppliers *and* employees, whereas other firms using the direct method show a separate line entry as cash paid to suppliers. To estimate this single entry for Nu Horizons, we would need to complete steps 2 and 3 of this template. This estimated as $723 million, or slightly below that actually reported. The estimation computation is shown. It represents the net cash outlay of goods used to sell to customers.

	Item	Source
Cash payments to suppliers:		
+ Cost of goods sold		Income statement
± Inventory increase/decrease		Balance sheet
± Accounts payable decrease/increase		Balance sheet
Total		

To accurately reconcile cash paid to suppliers and employees as appeared in the statement of cash flows, I enlisted the aid of Nu Horizons' CFO. However, the estimation method most often—but not always—results in a fairly close approximation that is necessary for the evaluating cash flow from operations. Feel free to copy the worksheets and complete them for Nu Horizons also using the actual reconciliation as a guide.

Cost of sales	(637,261,000)
Operating expenses	(120,453,000)
Adjustments:	
Depreciation and amortization	2,239,000
Bad debt provision	(341,000)
Goodwill write-off	7,443,000
Deferred taxes	(431,000)
Loss on sale of fixed asset	27,000
Income tax benefit from stock options exercised	5,000
Stock-based compensation	1,127,000
Retirement plan	716,000
Changes in assets and liabilities—increase/(decrease):	
Inventory	26,813,000
Prepaid expenses/other current assets	(673,000)
Accounts payable and accrued expenses	(8,675,000)
Income taxes payable	(2,148,000)
Retirement plan	0
Other adjustments (taxes paid, reversals, interest accrual)	2,878,000
(Rounding adjustment)	2,000
Cash paid to suppliers	**(728,820,000)**

3. Cash paid for other operating expenses may be estimated using the following template:

	Item	Source
Cash paid for other operating expenses:		
+ Sales and marketing		Income statement
+ Other general and administrative		Income statement
− Depreciation and amortization		Income statement
± Other working capital		Balance sheet
Total		

4. If available, the analyst should use the actual cash taxes taken directly from the statement of cash flows or footnote. Alternatively, the analyst can use the following template to estimate taxes:

	Item	Source
Cash paid for other operating expenses:		
± Provision for income taxes		Income statement
± Increase in deferred taxes		Balance sheet
± Increase in accrued income taxes		Balance sheet
Total		

Here is one of the big advantages of SFAS 95: the reporting of the actual tax payment, which at $2.148 million is a bit greater than the $1.015 million that would have been estimated prior to the pronouncement, given the $837,000 provision and $188,000 increase in the deferred tax asset. For Nu Horizons, the $2.148 million is deducted because it is included as part of other adjustments ($2,878) as taxes paid, and the company needs to show it as a separate line item.

5. Other cash flows. For Nu Horizons, this would consist of cash interest paid and received.

	Item	Source
Other cash flows:		
+ Other income		Income statement
Total		

The analyst constructing his or her own statement of cash flows might find a large variation between reported and estimated taxes. Normally, differences occur when not all tax-related balance-sheet accounts are disclosed separately. For example, some prepaid or deferred taxes that represent an asset may be included with prepaid and other assets on the balance sheet. Some deferred tax liabilities may be included with other liabilities. In these cases, it is difficult to estimate the cash taxes paid during a period in a reasonable manner. Again, the actual cash paid for taxes is disclosed separately in the statement of cash flows (or in a footnote) for firms that use the indirect method to derive cash-flow operating activities. Also, during interim periods, the effective tax rate is an estimate of the year-end rate.

Finally, regarding the estimation template, very little information might be available to approximate the "other operating cash flows." Often it will be a "plug" figure and is likely to contain an estimation error. If it is of consequence, the analyst would need to speak to a financial officer at the company to determine the source(s) of any discrepancy, and in any event, if the number is significant, one would want to understand how the company is being managed. Normally, the estimation error is small because the taxes paid can be reasonably estimated, and other sources of income and expense are reported.

CREDIT, COLLECTIONS, AND TREASURY DEPARTMENT SOFTWARE

A discussion of cash flow from operations would be incomplete without reviewing credit and collection. Good credit decisions enhance cash flows, permitting the addition of value-adding opportunities. Related are asset sales and a rebalancing of the corporate portfolio that are designed to aid operating cash flows.

With advances in software, credit department analysts today have at their fingertips real-time information needed to make quick, informed decisions. This information includes cash held in banks worldwide, investment schedules, invoices, inventory, payables, customer credit limits, delivery schedules, and an aging schedule of the entity's accounts receivable. Credit managers claim that accounts receivable software, including electronic invoicing, has helped them to reduce their days of sales outstanding by as much as 20 days and has reduced the number of disputed bills and dealings with sales representatives. The software quickly shows if a client is late on payment, with a decision if shipping additional product is warranted. The credit department also may be responsible for monitoring current and forward credit exposure related to financial instruments, as well as providing for letters of credit or other necessary such financings to aid sales and the firms' clients.

While "involuntary" increases in receivables and inventories do occur, advances in computer software monitor all phases of the firms' production to minimize and capture their occurrence so that they are less frequent than they once were. When large bad credits do arise, their effects are felt throughout the enterprise, with possible ramifications on planned outlays. Such software improvements are part of the explanation for the longevity of business expansions after the 1980s. Even the recession that started during 2007 did not find most businesses with severe excess inventory.

The collection process is where the cash inflows begin, and collections is the department within treasury that receives much attention. Although some credit analysts measure the success of such departments by the average collection period,[8] such a metric does not provide them with the more important timely collection and credit information, such as (1) which clients pay their bills on time and might be accorded credit, and (2) which clients have run into such severe payment problems that further delivery of goods is unjustified—and whose accounts probably should be classified as a bad debt.

Computer software has made this function of the credit manager much easier. With the push of a button, most credit managers can check the payment history of their clients over many years, thereby making the credit-approval process quicker, simpler, and more accurate. Software prioritizes daily collection calls and facilitates collaboration between departments. Credit managers still use time-honored techniques to reduce their bad debt expense and aid the accounts receivable process (i.e., minimize the nominal amount of receivables outstanding). Credit service agency reports, such as Dun & Bradstreet (D&B) credit reports, are still used widely, although many credit managers feel that the data in such reports are to a

[8] The average collection period is defined as 360/average accounts receivable turnover. In turn, the accounts receivable turnover is defined as net sales/average accounts receivable.

great extent outdated. D&B reports can be helpful if they show lawsuits against the company, show the company's financial statement, or show the employment and educational backgrounds of key employees.

Trade references, which also help the credit analyst gather information about potential clients, come in a variety of sources. The new-account customer application designates areas for both trade and bank referrals. Sales professionals, who visit the prospective new account's offices and facilities, are likely to spot the products of companies that can be called for references, even though those firms might not be listed on the credit application. The credit application itself usually provides useful information to the credit analyst.

Good credit analysis is vitally important in helping an enterprise's cash flow because errors by credit department analysts can be very costly. Trade shows (friends in the industry) and reference checks of the client's competitors are also very useful. So are telephone leads resulting from the questioning of competitors. Analyzing financial statements for trends in operating free cash flow, free cash flow, and leverage are essential to the credit analyst because cash-flow trend is a leading indicator of financial failure. Newspapers, magazines, and the Internet are also likely to bring a flow of financial information into the credit department, especially for larger customers. Some credit managers take a very careful approach to rumored takeover candidates because direct credit downgrades often result after a takeover.

A pattern of declining receipts from customers may indicate a maturing product, softening of demand, a more stringent credit policy toward customers, or some other problem, such as the loss of a key employee. The cash-flow analyst would be interested in ascertaining the reasons for any such development and may do so by examining and speaking with other firms in the industry along with client discussions of client contact.

A simple ratio that can illustrate the credit-granting policy of the firm or its ability to collect its accounts receivable is the ratio of collections to sales. Collections from customers can be estimated as sales minus the change in accounts receivable, similar to computation of the direct method of cash flow from operations. One then can divide collections during a period by sales in the same period. When operations are relatively stable, this ratio is likely to hover around 1; that is, most sales are collected within the year. However, if the ratio reveals a declining trend, the quality of a firm's receivables should be questioned by the cash-flow analyst. For firms using the direct method, cash collections is already given.

Similarly, if one observes a significant increase in cash payments to employees and suppliers that is beyond the proportionate increase in cash receipts from customers, the cash-flow analyst should examine whether the firm is experiencing an alteration in demand for its products or perhaps a prior "push" on collections that is currently being reversed or normalized. For example, the firm may have problems marketing its products and therefore is caught with unwanted buildup of

FIGURE 3-2

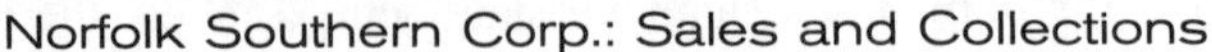

Norfolk Southern Corp.: Sales and Collections

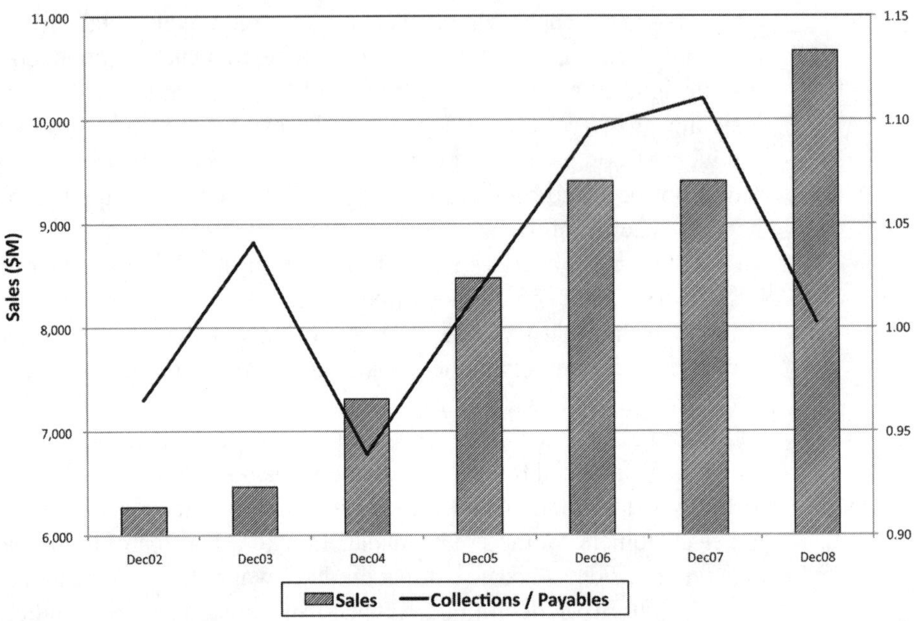

inventories, inability to compete, or a downswing in the economy. It may spend more cash on selling, general, and administrative expenses than is warranted by the level of customer demand. Sometimes a firm may incur greater administrative costs in one period because it may make substantial changes in its operations (such as computerizing its operations). However, one should not observe continuous increases in cash payments to suppliers and employees beyond those called for by increases in demand for the company's products and services.

In Figure 3-2, notice that sales for Norfolk Southern, a large transportation firm, showed a consistent increase during the 6 years ending December 2008. The ratio of collections to payables is very stable at around 1.This is to be expected given the relatively stable business of railroads, as well as the consistent payment record of its clients.

ASSET SALES

For entities needing to raise cash, asset sales are always considered in addition to external financing. The least costly capital raise always will be considered first, especially if the financial turbulence is expected to be short term and the cost of debt and equity is high.

The continual sale of inventory for below-market prices or accounts receivable factoring normally provides an unmistakable warning that should raise a flag for students of cash flow and risk because the realization price reflects a cost that would not normally be acceptable to a well-financed organization. Asset sales are often a de facto partial liquidation. Continuing asset sales that take place for lower-than-balance-sheet values are indeed telltale signs.

To improve operating cash flows, companies often sell operating divisions as they rebalance their portfolio of companies in search of the highest return opportunities. Small asset sales and balance-sheet management typically constitute good business practice and add to free cash flow and reduced cost of capital. Managers committed to weeding out poorly performing business units can enhance their company's market valuation significantly.

Significance, in accounting parlance, relates to size and whether the failure to report an event as a separate line item would mask a change in earnings or trend. The analyst should determine if the company under analysis has indeed sold assets during any particular reporting period owing to weakness in its borrowing capacity or an attempt to bolster disappointing operation cash flow. Both Enron and Delphi Corp., prior to their bankruptcies, were selling inventory with the understanding that it would be repurchased at a later period, a clever way to raise cash but a telling sign of liquidity shortfall.

The securitization of assets for sale into a special-purpose entity, as was invoked by Enron, may not, by itself, represent a reason to sell a security or dismiss the purchase of one, especially in light of otherwise undervaluation by the marketplace. In fact, many companies have raised cash via the securitization of accounts receivable, redeploying those funds back into a business that resulted in high rates of growth in cash flows. When viewed under the light of other metrics, asset sales could form part of a mosaic indicative of a financial risk urging avoidance of the particular security or to place a higher discount rate on its free cash flow, accounting for the new, higher level of uncertainty.

Entities that have substantial accounts receivables, such as retailers, often discount these future cash receipts for immediate cash, as Macy's did during 2006. Figure 3-3 reveals the impact on its average collection period resulting from that sale. Of course, average collection period and similar credit metrics, such as cash conversion cycle, will be distorted by the sale of receivables.

Selling receivables boosts current-period operating cash flow and thus must be normalized by the analyst in evaluating historical and prospective cash flows. To do so, one would compute the past 4 years' average accounts receivable to sales and apply that to the current year as if the financing did not occur. At this point, the analyst can evaluate the operating and power cash flows for that year, including the sales of receivables.

More important, since the upcoming year's cash collections will be lower, an updated cash-flow projection must reflect the new expected collections, with emphasis on the ability of the entity to retire or recast upcoming debt and other obligations coming due. Macy's has, according to its "Financing" footnote, $2.6 billion in principal payments due over the coming 3 years. Since prospective cash flows will be diminished by the present value of the change in future collections, fair value could shift, depending on how the cash from the sale is deployed. In its statement of cash flows, the drop in cash flows from operations is apparent, with management reacting by cutting budgets company-wide.

MACY'S, INC.
CONSOLIDATED STATEMENTS OF CASH FLOWS
(In Millions)

	2008	2007	2006
Cash flows from continuing operating activities:			
Net income (loss)	$(4,803)	$893	$995
Adjustments to reconcile net income (loss) to net cash provided by continuing operating activities:			
(Income) loss from discontinued operations	—	16	(7)
Gains on the sale of accounts receivable	—	—	(191)
Stock-based compensation expense	43	60	91
Division consolidation costs and store closing–related costs	187	—	—
Asset impairment charges	211	—	—
Goodwill impairment charges	5,382	—	—
May integration costs	—	219	628
Depreciation and amortization	1,278	1,304	1,265
Amortization of financing costs and premium on acquired debt	(27)	(31)	(49)
Gain on early debt extinguishment	—	—	(54)
Changes in assets and liabilities:			
Proceeds from sale of proprietary accounts receivable	—	—	1,860
Decrease in receivables	12	28	207
(Increase) decrease in merchandise inventories	291	256	(51)
(Increase) decrease in supplies and prepaid expenses	(7)	33	(41)
Decrease in other assets not separately identified	1	3	25
Decrease in merchandise accounts payable	(90)	(132)	(462)
Decrease in accounts payable and accrued liabilities not separately identified	(227)	(396)	(410)
Increase (decrease) in current income taxes	(146)	14	(139)
Decrease in deferred income taxes	(291)	(2)	(18)
Increase (decrease) in other liabilities not separately identified	65	(34)	43
Net cash provided by continuing operating activities	1,879	2,231	3,692

	2008	2007	2006
Cash flows from continuing investing activities:			
Purchase of property and equipment	(761)	(994)	(1,317)
Capitalized software	(136)	(111)	(75)
Proceeds from hurricane insurance claims	68	23	17
Disposition of property and equipment	38	227	679
Proceeds from the disposition of After Hours Formalwear	—	66	—
Proceeds from the disposition of Lord & Taylor	—	—	1,047
Proceeds from the disposition of David's Bridal and Priscilla of Boston	—	—	740
Repurchase of accounts receivable	—	—	(1,141)
Proceeds from the sale of repurchased accounts receivable	—	—	1,323
Net cash provided (used) by continuing investing activities	(791)	(789)	1,273

In many cases it is less expensive to borrow funds with the creditor taking a security interest in accounts receivables and inventory. This would be a loan, not a factoring agreement where the accounts receivable are sold. In a factoring arrangement, the cost to the firm is typically higher.

When receivables are financed through borrowings, it is shown as a finance activity, even though the actions are basically identical to their sale. Also, by factoring, the firm keeps the loan off its balance sheet. Another issue to consider is whether the receivables being sold were done so on a nonrecourse basis so that if they are ultimately uncollectable, Macy's has no further legal obligation. A moral obligation may exist, however, and must be considered.

Figure 3-3 shows Macy's average collection and payables period for the 2003–2009 fiscal years. When Macy's sold about $ 4.1 billion of its in-house receivables during 2005–2006, it dropped its collection period, but of course, the company paid a price for the immediate cash. It did reduce total debt by about $1.5 billion, but unfortunately, the company also succumbed to shareholder pressure and expended $2.5 billion on the repurchase of shares, hopeful the buyback would boost the stock price, which it did not because the company's cash flows were weak.

To Macy's, which had substantially increased its leverage resulting from its $5.2 billion purchase of May Department Stores the year earlier, the cash resulting from the sale of receivables ultimately might have staved off bankruptcy 2 years later when its business fell owing to the recession and loss of market share to competitors, the latter not an atypical by-product of a large business combination. For sure, management wished the $2.5 billion stock buyback never took place. The $2.5 billion outflow robbed Macy's of needed financial flexibility by eliminating a large cushion when its business turned down.

FIGURE 3-3

Macy's Disclosures: Cash Flow from Operating Activities

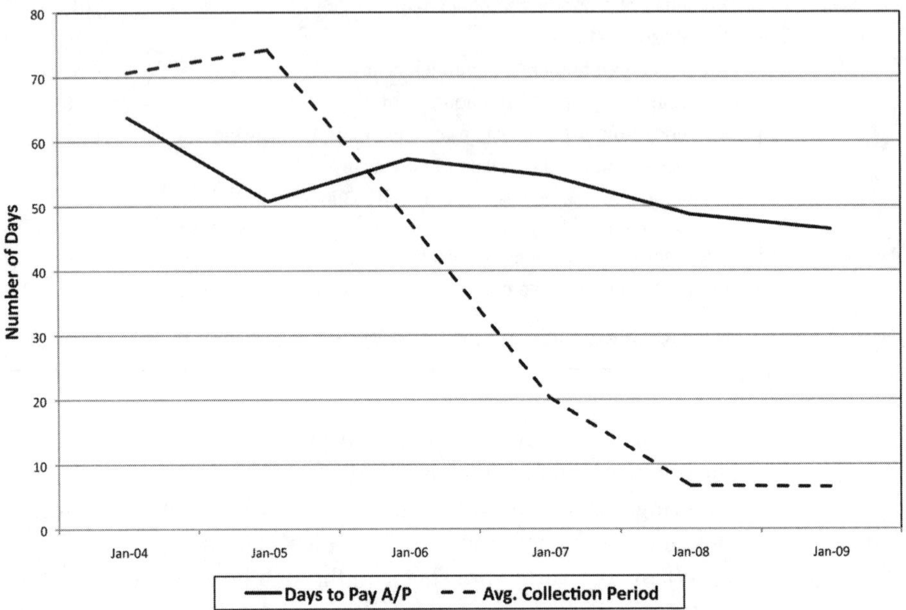

While the sale of receivables does indeed provide immediate cash, it is important to consider why the action was taken, especially for companies that operate on tight margins. For such entities, the sale may eliminate the profits those sales initially produced. For them, if the cash is not used to pay down trade payables or other business-related obligations, the analyst must question where such cash eventually will come from. Because Macy's wasted funds from the sale on share buybacks, it cut its purchases of PPE in half over the next 2 years. It is difficult to imagine that a large sale of accounts receivable to buy back shares is ever a good idea.

Example:

CPI Corp. is a leader in professional portrait photography of young children and families, operating 3,108 studios throughout the United States, Canada, Mexico, and Puerto Rico, principally under license agreements with Sears and Wal-Mart. CPI's operating activities show the cash effect and accounting of their pension contribution. CPI expensed approximately $505,000 million on its income statement during 2008 and $2 million during 2007 related to the plan, which is reversed under operating cash flows. The company did, however, make an actual cash contribution of $3,157,000 for fiscal 2009 and approximately $5 million during 2008, which is reflected under operating activities. Revealed is a supplemental cash payment into the pension plan of $1,283,000, which was financed through the sale of investments in a rabbi trust, which was recorded as an investment activity. The rabbi trust was established for company executives.[9] Also reported under operating activities is the reversal of the noncash income statement expense for stock-based compensation.

For tax-reporting purposes, the exercise or the point of vesting (not granting) of certain stock-based awards often generates a tax-deductible expense regardless of whether the company has been expensing stock-option grants for financial reporting purposes. As specified earlier, tax credits are shown as an operating item on the cash-flow statement under U.S. GAAP only to the extent that they relate to the accounting expense; if the tax deduction exceeds the amount attributable to the accounting expense, such excess is a financing item.

CPI CORP.
CONSOLIDATED STATEMENTS OF CASH FLOWS
Fifty-Three Weeks Ended February 7, 2009, and Fifty-Two Weeks Ended February 2, 2008, and February 3, 2007
(In Thousands)

	2008	2007	2006
Reconciliation of net (loss) income to cash flows provided by (used in) operating activities:			
Net (loss) income	$(7,685)	$3,576	$16,327
Adjustments for items not requiring (providing) cash:			
Depreciation and amortization	29,432	27,291	16,861
Loss from discontinued operations	961	441	103
Stock-based compensation expense	1,037	2,724	776
Issuance of common stock to Sears	865	—	—
Loss on impairment of property and equipment	739	—	—
Loss on disposition of property and equipment	1,387	319	220
Deferred income tax provision	(2,550)	1,455	9,357
Pension, supplemental retirement plan, and profit-sharing expense	505	2,009	2,337
Lease guarantee reserve reduction	—	—	(887)
Other	678	683	401

(Continued)

[9] The *rabbi trust* had its origin in a determination by the Internal Revenue Service (IRS) that an irrevocable trust established for a rabbi by the rabbi's congregation was not subject to current income taxation of the assets because the assets remained subject to the claims of the congregation's general creditors. This ruling was important because, in effect, it permitted a trust to accumulate assets that ultimately would be distributed to a designated person—the participant, in this case the rabbi—without the necessity of the trust or the participant currently paying income taxes on the funds contributed. Further, the assets of the trust are protected from any claims other than those of the employer's general creditors and are otherwise outside the reach of the employer where the trust is irrevocable. The concept was popular as an approach to executive compensation issues, and the IRS was inundated with requests for rulings approving a variety of these so-called rabbi trusts. The IRS responded with the issuance, in 1992, of a Revenue Procedure15 laying down the requirements of a model rabbi trust, thereby providing detailed guidance for employers who wished to make use of an unfunded deferred compensation arrangement (the rabbi trust technique).

	2008	2007	2006
Increase (decrease) in cash flow from operating assets and liabilities:			
Accounts receivable	4,523	(1,987)	436
Inventories	5,448	2,000	81
Prepaid expenses and other current assets	(1,255)	550	(636)
Accounts payable	(5,153)	6,020	(555)
Contribution to pension plan	(3,157)	(5,050)	—
Supplemental retirement plan payments	(1,283)	(249)	(283)
Accrued expenses and other liabilities	(4,365)	(5,833)	(2,003)
Income taxes payable	(708)	(1,001)	(373)
Deferred revenues and related costs	(7,720)	2,655	(3,118)
Other	964	4,269	(1,051)
Cash flows provided by continuing operations	12,663	39,872	37,993
Cash flows used in discontinued operations	(816)	(406)	(43)
Cash flows provided by operating activities	11,847	39,466	37,950

Next shown are CPI's cash flow provided by investment activities for the years 2006–2008. These transaction into and out of the rabbi trust are reported as investment activities because the assets in the trust are investable assets, as defined under SFAS 95. The $1.295 million in investments was sold to finance the $1.283 million supplemental payment listed under operating activities. The reason the amounts do not match is that there were some expenses related to sale of the assets, such as administrative and other fees.

We also see another sale of assets from the rabbi trust of $1.311 million recorded under investment activities. These funds were not used to pay supplemental or other benefits, but (since we see no other entry related to it) we can assume that those funds were used by the company perhaps as working capital or to fund the underfunded pension plan. Underfunded pension plans, as we will see, can be a significant drain on cash because additional contributions need to take place. Companies making catchup contributions into plans to reduce unfunded obligations that are placed as an operating activity more appropriately should book those payments under financing cash flows because the payment is similar to debt retirement. Originally, the payments should have been considered an operating activity, but once the payments became in arrears, in essence, they became debt financed.

	2008	2007	2006
Cash flows (used in) provided by investing activities:			
Acquisition of certain net assets of Portrait Corporation of America, Inc., net of cash and cash equivalents acquired	(52)	(83,010)	—
Additions to property and equipment	(36,074)	(14,884)	(2,760)
Proceeds from rabbi trust used for supplemental retirement plan payments	1,295	262	295
Distribution of rabbi trust funds in excess of related obligations	1,311	—	—
Other	32	(21)	107

Example:

Palm, Inc., is a manufacturer and marketer of mobile products, primarily cell phones. The following is from the Company's 2009 10K.

PALM, INC.
CONSOLIDATED STATEMENTS OF CASH FLOWS
(In Thousands)

	Years Ended May 31,		
	2009	**2008**	**2007**
Cash flows from operating activities:			
Net income (loss)	$(732,188)	$(105,419)	$56,383
Adjustments to reconcile net income (loss) to net cash flows from operating activities:			
Depreciation	19,677	19,699	13,316
Stock-based compensation	23,853	32,181	24,255
Amortization of intangible assets	12,134	16,510	8,315
Amortization of debt issuance costs	3,139	1,834	—
In-process research and development	—	—	3,700
Deferred income taxes	401,670	(58,227)	11,313
Realized (gain) loss on short-term investments	3,594	(68)	(110)
Excess tax benefit related to stock-based compensation	(142)	(40)	(5,241)
Realized loss (gain) on disposition of property and equipment and sale of land	619	(4,446)	—
Impairment of noncurrent auction-rate securities	35,885	32,175	—
Loss on Series C derivative	2,515	—	—
Changes in assets and liabilities:			
Accounts receivable	48,425	89,312	2
Inventories	47,571	(28,147)	18,842
Prepaids and other	4,542	736	1,790
Accounts payable	(54,883)	(35,840)	11,654
Income taxes payable	(346)	3,033	16,421
Accrued restructuring	(361)	6,303	(1,803)
Deferred revenues/costs, net	12,530	—	—
Other accrued liabilities	(16,746)	12,866	9,354
Net cash provided by (used in) operating activities	(188,512)	(17,538)	168,191

In 2009, after 2 years of losses, Palm, Inc., management decided to take the full deferred income tax valuation allowance against its deferred tax asset. While this had no effect on current operating cash flow, it reduced shareholders' equity on the balance sheet. The $401,670 deferred income taxes under operating cash flows is a reversal of the income-statement entry. Also, while Palm has a large tax loss carryover for federal purposes, its income tax footnote reveals that it is paying both state and foreign income taxes.

Palm also recognized a loss on its investment in auction-rate securities owing to the issuer's failure to pay interest in a timely manner. The cash effect was reversed under operating activities because there is no cash impact. There is a valuation and equity impact because those assets have become of questionable value.

Example:

QAD, Inc., is a global software company. In its July 2006 10Q, QAD reported slightly lower cash flow from operations owing to a decline in deferred revenues and other liabilities ($1.2 million from the prior year) that, according to the company's 10K, represented a change in severance pay accruals. The company stepped up its collection efforts, as manifested by the cash provided by accounts receivables. Also reported is an increase in stock compensation expense, which preserved cash.

	Six Months Ended July 31 ($000)	
	2006	**2005**
Cash flows from operating activities:		
Net income	$2,529	$6,350
Adjustments to reconcile net income to net cash provided by operating activities:		
Depreciation and amortization	3,598	3,802
Provision for doubtful accounts and sales adjustments	189	(168)
(Gain) loss on disposal of property and equipment	9	(20)
Tax benefit from reversal of tax allowances and reserves	—	(373)
Exit costs	355	940
Stock compensation expense	2,596	55
Other, net	(39)	(107)
Changes in assets and liabilities, net of effects from acquisitions:		
Accounts receivable	20,024	17,680
Other assets	517	1,973
Accounts payable	(2,657)	(2,633)
Deferred revenue	(12,788)	(11,934)
Other liabilities	(4,098)	(2,884)
Net cash provided by operating activities	10,235	12,681

Source: QAD 10Q, July 31, 2006.

Example:

Phelps Dodge made a large contribution to its Voluntary Employee Benefit Association (VEBA)[10] and pension plans in 2005. Also seen is the effect of its copper protection programs, or copper "collars," under which the company uses both put and calls options to lock in price guarantees for its output. During 2006, a large run-up in the price of copper resulted in a large loss on these hedges, which was made up, and more, from higher price realization for the metal. Phelps Dodge also points out, in their 2006 10K, that it hedged 486 million pounds, its expected output for the following year.

Given the loss on the collar, was Phelps Dodge happy that it had hedged? Probably. Look at it this way: If you were happy to sell your house for $500,000 and someone was willing to pay you $50,000 for the right to buy it for $750,000 over the next year, you might do it. And if the option were taken advantage of, you would both be happy. Of course, if the price of the house dropped to $300,000, you might not be so happy, even though you got to keep the $50,000.

Also of note is the large increase in minority interests. Phelps Dodge owns minority interests in companies located around the world, accounted for on an equity basis. In some geographic areas, the governments do not permit ownership above a fixed percentage. During 2006, minority interest benefited from higher commodity prices, and the value of those assets reflected the rise. The amounts included under operating activities merely reverse those entries on the income statement because it is noncash, and the amount was already debited on the income statement.

Phelps Dodge also recorded $54 million in "early debt extinguishment costs" the prior year as a gain on its income statement, so it was reversed under operating activities. The entry resulted from the company completing a tender offer for debt having a book value of approximately $280 million. That purchase ($280 million plus the $54 million) would be seen as a financing activity (section not shown). Phelps Dodge, in its 10K, estimated that the prepayment of this debt would reduce its pretax annual interest expense by about $24 million.

Operating activities:			
Net income	$3,017.8	1,556.4	1,046.3
Adjustments to reconcile net income to net cash provided by operating activities:			
Losses on copper collars and copper put options (realized but unpaid and unrealized)	1,008.9	410.5	—
Depreciation, depletion, and amortization	449.0	490.9	507.1
Deferred income tax provision (benefit)	(147.0)	16.4	(17.8)
Equity in net earnings (losses) of affiliated companies, net of dividends received	(1.9)	(0.1)	2.2
Gain on sale of cost-basis investment, net of expenses	—	(438.4)	—
Change in interest gains, net of expenses	—	(168.3)	—
Special items and provisions, net	93.6	612.1	59.9
Early debt extinguishment costs	—	54.0	43.2

(Continued)

[10] A VEBA is a specialized tax-free health care trust fund that will pay for the future benefit costs of a company's current or retired workers. VEBAs were created in the 1920s after many large employers defaulted on promised benefits. In a VEBA, the employer makes a tax-free contribution to a trust fund, which also grows tax-free. Since these funds are outside the control of the company, they release the firm from such liabilities.

Minority interests in consolidated subsidiaries	792.7	190.6	201.8
Loss on disposition of discontinued operations	30.3	5.8	—
Cumulative effect of accounting changes	—	13.5	—
Changes in current assets and liabilities:			
Accounts receivable	(236.1)	(399.0)	(276.2)
Repayment of securitized accounts receivable	—	(85.0)	—
Mill and leach stockpiles	(50.1)	(10.5)	1.0
Inventories	(0.7)	(46.5)	(0.4)
Supplies	(48.8)	(33.8)	(23.6)
Prepaid expenses and other current assets	(36.4)	(35.2)	(6.7)
Interest payable	1.1	(3.8)	(8.2)
Other accounts payable	21.7	159.6	212.1
Accrued income taxes	401.9	(0.9)	17.5
Realized losses on 2005 copper collars	(187.2)	—	—
Other accrued expenses	(9.9)	(97.9)	(42.8)
Master trust pension plan contributions	—	(250.0)	(85.4)
VEBA trust contributions	—	(200.0)	—
Other operating, net	(19.7)	29.3	70.1
Net cash provided by operating activities	5,079.2	1,769.7	1,700.1

Source: Phelps Dodge 2006 10K.

Example:

When a firm acquires or disposes of a significant business asset, the analyst should be careful interpreting the relevant items on the statement of cash flows because the amounts shown might represent only a portion of the transaction that involved cash payments or receipts. The entire transaction may have involved a much larger amount because many business combinations include stock, deferred payments, or other expenses as part of the transaction. For example, the merger agreement may indemnify the acquirer against certain risks by providing for backstop payments.

In 2008, Finisar Corp., a leading provider of optical subsystems, completed a business combination with Optimum, a designer of high-performance optical subsystems for the cable industry, in an all-stock transaction in exchange for 160,808,659 shares of its stock, which (valued at closing) was worth approximately $242.8 million. The transaction consisted of $150 million of goodwill. Because Finisar management decided to eliminate all goodwill from its balance sheet, the $88 million, along with the goodwill of a previous business acquisition, totaling ($238.5 million), was reversed under operating activities from the income-statement expense. Because it was a stock deal, no cash outlay is reflected in the statement of cash flows.

In a business combination, vested stock options or awards issued by an acquirer in exchange for outstanding awards held by the target's employees are considered to be part of the purchase price and accounted for under SFAS 141R. Accordingly, the fair value of the new replacement awards is included in the purchase price. Unvested stock options or awards granted by an acquirer in exchange for stock options or awards held by the target's employees are also considered part of the purchase price, with the fair value of the new replacement awards included in the purchase price. Unearned compensation is recorded as an asset on the balance sheet and is amortized over the remaining future service (vesting) period.

Under operating activities, Finisar points out in its 10K, deferred income taxes decreased mainly because of a reversal of previously recorded deferred tax liabilities as a result of the impairment of goodwill. Stock-based compensation is added to operating activities because it represents stock compensation (grants not yet exercised) to employees expensed at fair value but is noncash. Cash will not change hands until the options are exercised. It should be expected that pressure from shareholders and Congress and the associated liquidity savings of noncash compensation will align the owners of capital and firms' employees such that stock-based compensation will continue to grow over the coming years.[11]

FINISAR CORPORATION
CONSOLIDATED STATEMENTS OF CASH FLOWS

	Fiscal Years Ended April 30 (In Thousands)		
	2009	**2008**	**2007**
Operating activities:			
Net loss	$(254,808)	$(74,558)	$(48,908)
Adjustments to reconcile net loss to net cash provided by operating activities:			
Depreciation and amortization	30,490	25,377	25,047
Stock-based compensation expense	14,978	11,564	11,822
Acquired in-process research and development	10,500	—	5,770
Amortization of beneficial conversion feature of convertible notes	1,817	4,943	4,791
Amortization of purchased technology and finite-lived intangibles	2,687	1,749	1,814
Impairment of goodwill and intangible assets	238,507	40,106	—
Impairment of acquired developed technology	1,248	—	—
Amortization of acquired developed technology	6,038	6,501	6,002
Amortization of discount on restricted securities	—	(11)	(92)
Loss (gain) on sales of equipment	996	(516)	1,214
Other than temporary decline in fair market value of equity security	1,920	—	—
Gain on sale of minority investment	—	—	(1,198)
Loss on convertible debt exchange	—	238	31,606
Gain on repurchase of convertible debt	(3,838)	—	—
Loss on sale of product line	919	—	—
Loss (gain) on remeasurement of derivative liability	(1,135)	1,135	—
Share of losses of equity investee	—	—	237
Loss on sale of equity investment	12	15	—

(Continued)

[11]Succumbing to such pressure, Goldman Sachs, a recipient of TARP funds, announced that its top executives would receive stock in lieu of cash bonus compensation for 2009.

	Fiscal Years Ended April 30 (In Thousands)		
	2009	2008	2007
Changes in operating assets and liabilities:			
Accounts receivable	(33,399)	8,891	2,449
Inventories	459	(1,159)	(17,364)
Other assets	922	(5,496)	(333)
Deferred income taxes	(7,277)	1,756	2,176
Accounts payable	4,396	1,432	3,227
Accrued compensation	(4,611)	3,847	(737)
Other accrued liabilities	(9,759)	9,021	113
Deferred revenue	(680)	(214)	1,375
Net cash provided by operating activities	382	34,621	29,011
Investing activities:			
Purchases of property, equipment, and improvements	(23,918)	(27,198)	(22,340)
Purchases of short- and long-term investments	(4,125)	(84,236)	(164,796)
Sale/maturity of short- and long-term investments	42,567	115,051	153,141
Maturity of restricted securities	—	625	4,951
Acquisition of subsidiaries, net of cash acquired	30,137	521	(10,708)
Proceeds from sale of property and equipment	229	643	512
Proceeds from sale of minority investment	—	—	1,198
Proceeds from sale of equity investment	90	1,569	—
Purchases of minority investments	—	(2,000)	—
Net cash provided by (used in) investing activities	44,980	4,975	(38,042)
Financing activities:			
Repurchase of convertible notes	(95,956)	(8,224)	—
Repayment of convertible notes related to acquisition	(11,918)	(5,959)	—
Proceeds from term loan and revolving line of credit	20,000	—	—
Repayments of liability related to sale-leaseback of building	(101)	(359)	(296)
Repayments of borrowings under notes	(4,225)	(1,897)	(2,036)
Proceeds from exercise of stock options, warrants, and stock purchase plan, net of repurchase of unvested shares	4,525	179	4,108
Net cash provided by (used in) financing activities	(87,675)	(16,260)	1,776
Net increase (decrease) in cash and cash equivalents	(42,313)	23,336	(7,255)
Cash and cash equivalents at beginning of year	79,442	56,106	63,361
Cash and cash equivalents at end of year	$37,129	$79,442	$56,106
Supplemental disclosure of cash-flow information:			
Cash paid for interest	$6,776	$9,190	$9,514
Cash paid for taxes	$1,100	$182	$659

	Fiscal Years Ended April 30 (In Thousands)		
	2009	2008	2007
Supplemental schedule of noncash investing and financing activities:			
Issuance of convertible promissory note on acquisition of subsidiary	$—	$—	$16,950
Issuance of common stock in connection with acquisitions	$242,821	$—	$—

Example:

Unifi, Inc., is a diversified producer and processor of multifilament polyester and nylon yarns. The operating activity section is taken from their 2009 10K. As seen, Unifi reports under the direct method of reporting cash flow from operations along with the indirect method as is required.

Several observations are worth noting. Receipts from customers fell considerably (owing to lower sales). Concurrently, we see lower payments to suppliers. The ratio of payments to suppliers and other operating costs as a percentage of cash receipts fell to 75.5 percent from 77.5 percent in 2008, indicating that management was "working" the balance sheet and controlling expenditures as busness softened. We indeed see that this is the case, as shown by the indirect approach because the company collected accounts receivable at a quicker pace, which, together with a significant reduction in inventories of $27.7 million, added about $46.5 million to operating activities. This was offset in part by a slight increase in other assets and a $27.3 million reduction in accounts payable. We also see in the indirect approach an $18.6 million noncash effect of goodwill impairment that would not appear under the direct model. Noncash items are not included in the direct approach.

UNIFI, INC.
STATEMENT OF CASH FLOWS USING THE DIRECT APPROACH

	Fiscal Years Ended (In Millions)		
	June 28, 2009	June 29, 2008	June 24, 2007
Cash provided by continuing operations:			
Cash receipts:			
Receipts from customers	$572.6	$708.7	$691.8
Dividends from unconsolidated affiliates	3.7	4.5	2.7
Other receipts	2.7	6.5	4.3
Cash payments:			
Payments to suppliers and other operating cost	432.3	549.4	530.5
Payments for salaries, wages, and benefits	99.9	117.2	130.3
Payments for restructuring and severance	4.0	11.2	1.6
Payments for interest	22.6	25.3	23.1
Payments for taxes	3.2	2.9	2.7
Cash provided by continuing operations	$17.0	$13.7	$10.6

(Continued)

UNIFI, INC.
STATEMENT OF CASH FLOWS USING THE INDIRECT APPROACH

	Fiscal Years Ended (In Thousands)		
	June 28, 2009	June 29, 2008	June 24, 2007
Cash and cash equivalents at beginning of year	$20,248	$40,031	$35,317
Operating activities:			
Net loss	(48,996)	(16,151)	(115,792)
Adjustments to reconcile net loss to net cash provided by continuing operating activities:			
Income from discontinued operations	(65)	(3,226)	(1,465)
Net (earnings) loss of unconsolidated affiliates, net of distributions	437	3,060	7,029
Depreciation	28,043	36,931	41,594
Amortization	4,430	4,643	3,264
Stock-based compensation expense	1,425	1,015	1,691
Deferred compensation expense, net	165	—	1,619
Net gain on asset sales	(5,856)	(4,003)	(1,225)
Noncash portion of (gain) loss on extinguishment of debt	(251)	—	25
Noncash portion of restructuring charges (recoveries), net	91	4,027	(157)
Noncash write-down of long-lived assets	350	2,780	16,731
Noncash effect of goodwill impairment	18,580	—	—
Noncash write-down of investment in unconsolidated affiliates	1,483	10,998	84,742
Deferred income tax	360	(15,066)	(23,776)
Provision for bad debts	2,414	214	7,174
Other	400	(8)	(866)
Changes in assets and liabilities, excluding effects of acquisitions and foreign currency adjustments:			
Receivables	18,781	(5,163)	(2,522)
Inventories	27,681	14,144	5,619
Other current assets	(5,329)	1,641	187
Accounts payable and accrued expenses	(27,283)	(22,525)	(12,158)
Income taxes payable	100	362	(1,094)
Net cash provided by continuing operating activities	16,960	13,673	10,620

Source: Unifi Corp. 2009 10K.

Example:

Standex International is a manufacturer of a variety of products and services for diverse industrial market segments. The company has 12 operating segments, aggregated and organized for reporting purposes into 5 segments: Food Service Equipment Group, Air Distribution Products Group (ADP), Engraving Group, Engineering Technologies Group, and Electronics and Hydraulics Group. The company reports its cash flow from operating activities as follows:

STANDEX INTERNATIONAL CORPORATION AND SUBSIDIARIES
STATEMENT OF CONSOLIDATED CASH FLOWS

	For the Years Ended June 30 (In Thousands)		
	2009	**2008**	**2007**
Cash flows from operating activities:			
Net income (loss)	($5,405)	$18,510	$21,242
Income (loss) from discontinued operations	(3,515)	(774)	5,317
Income (loss) from continuing operations	(1,890)	19,284	15,925
Adjustments to reconcile net income (loss) to net cash provided by operating activities:			
Depreciation and amortization	15,541	17,113	15,198
Stock-based compensation	2,398	2,437	385
Deferred income taxes	(3,563)	(467)	(1,133)
Impairment charges	21,339	—	—
Noncash portion of restructuring charge	3,730	94	—
(Gain) loss on sale of investments, real estate and equipment, and debt extinguishment	375	(344)	(1,023)
Increase (decrease) in cash from changes in assets and liabilities, net of effects from discontinued operations and business acquisitions:			
Accounts receivables, net	18,360	4,738	(1,591)
Inventories	11,605	4,299	(4,261)
Contributions to defined benefit plans	—	(620)	(3,862)
Prepaid expenses and other	1,001	471	1,277
Accounts payable	(6,034)	(912)	8,378
Accrued payroll, employee benefits, and other liabilities	(18,039)	836	1,151
Income taxes payable	(1,550)	(1,746)	2,053
Net cash provided by operating activities—continuing operations	43,273	45,183	32,497
Net cash (used in)/provided by operating activities—discontinued operations	(3,829)	(477)	(7,002)
Net cash provided by operating activities	39,444	44,706	25,495

Standex reports a large impairment charge under the section. The test for impairment is a two-step process. The first step compares the carrying amount of the reporting unit with its estimated fair value. To the extent that the carrying value of the reporting unit exceeds its estimated fair value, a second step is performed, wherein the reporting unit's carrying value is compared with the implied fair value. To the extent that the carrying value exceeds the implied fair value, impairment exists and must be recognized. If the book value of assets falls below the discounted present value of cash flows, a charge may be necessary.

Since the $21.3 million is already expensed in the income statement, the entry needs to be reversed because it represents a write-off of cash that previously flowed through the statement of cash flows when the asset was acquired—there is no current direct cash-flow impact. While this represents a noncash restructuring charge, to the extent that investors believed the asset would return free cash flow, the charge-off represents a diminishment in expectations as well as a change in the stability of prospective business results.

Example:

99¢ Only Stores is a low-price retailer of consumable general merchandise with an emphasis on name-brand products selling primarily at 99 cents or less. 99¢ Only Stores has (1) been profitable in each of the past 10 years, (2) has no meaningful debt outside normal trade and operating leases, and (3) has had higher operating cash flows than net income in each year. The purpose of the example is a representation of the substantial number of entities that report the ratio of operating activities to net income, representing the quotient as a quasi-cash conversion cycle metric. As a matter of fact, it is not unusual to find such a table in 10Ks and company investor presentations with an implicit representation that the ability to show greater operating cash flows than net income indicates that net income is not capturing the real value of the enterprise or even perhaps that it is a superior free-cash-flow-producing entity.

As seen in this example, despite 99¢ Only Stores' large plowback of earnings into capital spending, resulting in high depreciation expense, the company has not, for the decade under inspection, been able to turn this into growth in free cash flow, and hence its market value has fallen. We see in Table 3-2 its 3-year average free cash flow, which includes overspending on discretionary areas (explained in Chapter 4), lower for 2007–2009 than the 3-year average of 1998–2000.

Regarding the tax credits related to share based compensation, as mentioned earlier, they are shown as an operating item only to the extent that they relate to the accounting expense; such excess is a financing item. When a company grants share-based awards, generally no cash is paid or received. Cash-flow consequences, if any, only arise when the options are exercised (e.g., as a result of payment of the exercise price and from associated tax benefits). For some other grants such as stock appreciation rights (SARs) payable in shares and restricted share grants, no cash changes hands at all.

99¢ ONLY STORES

CONSOLIDATED STATEMENTS OF CASH FLOWS (In Thousands)

	Years Ended		
	March 28, 2009	**March 29, 2008**	**March 31, 2007**
Cash flows from operating activities:			
Net income	$8,481	$2,893	$9,762

	Years Ended		
	March 28, 2009	March 29, 2008	March 31, 2007
Adjustments to reconcile net income to net cash provided by operating activities:			
Depreciation and amortization	34,266	33,321	32,675
Loss on disposal of fixed assets	791	124	171
Gain on sale of partnerships	(706)	—	—
Fixed assets impairment	10,355	531	—
Fixed investments impairment	1,677	—	—
Minority interest in partnership	1,357	—	—
Excess tax deficiency (benefit) from share-based payment arrangements	10	(130)	(645)
Deferred income taxes	(11,419)	(11,024)	(5,934)
Stock-based compensation expense	3,136	4,184	5,224
Tax benefit from exercise of nonqualified employee stock options	—	263	1,032
Changes in assets and liabilities associated with operating activities:			
Accounts receivable	(346)	543	506
Inventories	(11,617)	13,750	(11,887)
Deposits and other assets	(435)	3,031	(3,533)
Accounts payable	10,619	(5,676)	(9,398)
Accrued expenses	11,678	1,644	4,672
Accrued workers' compensation	1,550	(673)	(738)
Income taxes	1,551	72	6,013
Deferred rent	(345)	2,343	586
Other long-term assets	2,339	—	—
Net cash provided by operating activities	62,942	45,196	28,506
Cash flows from investing activities:			
Purchases of property and equipment	(34,222)	(54,388)	(47,007)

TABLE 3-2

99¢ Only Stores Comparison of Fundamental Data

December Year End	Net Income (Loss)	Operating Cash Flow	Free Cash Flow	Capital Expenditures	Depreciation	Market Value
1998	27	27	21	13	5	—
1999	22	26	10	18	6	958
2000	38	50	31	27	9	937
2001	48	67	38	47	12	1,983
2002	59	72	38	42	18	1,883
2003	57	80	11	99	24	1,942
2004	28	94	54	57	28	1,123

(Continued)

TABLE 3-2 *(Continued)*

99¢ Only Stores Comparison of Fundamental Data

December Year End	Net Income (Loss)	Operating Cash Flow	Free Cash Flow	Capital Expenditures	Depreciation	Market Value
2005	11	83	57	48	31	943
2006	10	29	(1)	47	33	1,030
2007	3	45	5	54	33	693
2008	8	63	32	34	34	646
Total	**311**	**636**	**295**	**485**	**233**	—

Example:

Berkshire Hathaway, in its 10Qs, shows its net cash flows from operating activities as a single-line entry.[12] It therefore would behoove the analyst to prepare a more detailed presentation, working through the changes in the balance sheet and other operating items affecting operating activities. The largest item, as reported on the company's balance sheet, is the $2.3 billion gain on derivative contracts, which is merely an adjustment to the liability section and a reflection of the large rise in the equity market on which the underlying contracts are based (over the prior period). This would not be shown in the direct-method presentation but would if an indirect worksheet were constructed. Loss and loss adjustment expenses, depreciation, and changes in other assets and liabilities typically would be the largest items on the worksheet, aside from investment gains and losses and changes in derivative contract assets and liabilities.

Berkshire sold a large number of long-term put contracts, collected the cash premium, and now must report the quarterly net changes in the income and cash-flow statements and reflected in the balance sheet as part of other assets and liabilities. These entries represent an adjustment to the value of the derivative contracts—if no cash changes hands, that amount would be reversed under operating activities. To the extent that Berkshire either sold additional put contracts or changed the maturity date or strike price of the options, it would, and actually did, collect cash during the quarter that would be reflected under operating activities.

It is necessary to thoroughly review the footnote related to derivative positions to grasp the potential risks to cash flow and leverage ratios, especially a worst-case scenario whereby the contract prices went against the holder. In this analysis, one should determine what various scenarios (sensitivity analysis) would mean to shareholders' equity and related loan covenants.

In Berkshire's case, we see that this increased the company's exposure throughout 2008 and 2009. Berkshire's derivatives do not meet the criteria of hedging contracts, so changes flow through the income statement.

---

[12]Regulation S-X, Rule 10–01: Interim Financial Statements:

(a) *Condensed statements.* Interim financial statements shall follow the general form and content of presentation prescribed by the other sections of this Regulation with the following exceptions:

(4) *The statement of cash flows may be abbreviated starting with a single figure of net cash flows from operating activities* and showing cash changes from investing and financing activities individually only when they exceed 10 percent of the average of net cash flows from operating activities for the most recent three years. Notwithstanding this test, Rule 4–02 applies, and de minimis amounts therefore need not be shown separately.

Unlike the June 2009 10Q filing, Berkshire, in its 2008 10K, delineates cash flows from operating activities, and as reported, the largest contributor affecting operating cash flows is derivative contract assets and liabilities. The amount in the statement of cash flows almost fully offsets the gain in the "P&L," but not fully, indicating that Berkshire realized cash of approximately $1 billion, reflecting premiums received for selling these additional derivative contracts and changes in the (maturity) terms on existing contracts. However, this cash didn't come without additional risk, as the company indicated in its derivatives footnote, which shows a large increase in liabilities and notational value (see 2008 balance sheet and footnote). This unrealized loss caused a drop in shareholders' (book value) equity; no cash impact would be felt until the contracts were settled.

BERKSHIRE HATHAWAY, INC., AND SUBSIDIARIES

CONDENSED CONSOLIDATED STATEMENTS OF CASH FLOWS

(In Millions)

	First 6 Months (Unaudited)	
	2009	**2008**
Net cash flows from operating activities:	$7,497	$4,991
Cash flows from investing activities:		
Purchases of fixed maturity securities	(7,450)	(26,754)
Purchases of equity securities	(974)	(5,513)
Purchases of other investments	(6,068)	—
Sales of fixed-maturity securities	2,282	11,950
Redemptions and maturities of fixed-maturity securities	2,716	6,807
Sales of equity securities	1,343	1,764
Purchases of loans and finance receivables	(148)	(1,045)
Principal collections on loans and finance receivables	356	370
Acquisitions of businesses	(221)	(5,424)
Purchases of property, plant, and equipment	(2,633)	(2,538)
Other	1,156	959
Net cash flows from investing activities	(9,641)	(19,424)
Cash flows from financing activities:		
Proceeds from borrowings of finance businesses	1,504	4,118
Proceeds from borrowings of utilities and energy businesses	992	1,047
Proceeds from other borrowings	58	84
Repayments of borrowings of finance businesses	(216)	(2,602)
Repayments of borrowings of utilities and energy businesses	(230)	(1,120)
Repayments of other borrowings	(306)	(133)
Change in short-term borrowings	(339)	(107)
Acquisitions of noncontrolling interests and other	(387)	(31)
Net cash flows from financing activities	1,076	1,256
Effects of foreign currency exchange-rate changes	40	7
Decrease in cash and cash equivalents	(1,028)	(13,170)
Cash and cash equivalents at beginning of year	25,539	44,329
Cash and cash equivalents at end of first 6 months	$24,511	$31,159

(Continued)

BERKSHIRE HATHAWAY, INC., AND SUBSIDIARIES
CONDENSED CONSOLIDATED BALANCE SHEETS
(In Millions, Unaudited)

	June 30, 2009	December 31, 2008
Assets:		
Insurance and other:		
Cash and cash equivalents	$21,439	$24,302
Investments:		
Fixed maturity securities	32,018	27,115
Equity securities	45,794	49,073
Other	30,365	21,535
Receivables	15,778	14,925
Inventories	6,387	7,500
Property, plant, and equipment	17,016	16,703
Goodwill	27,535	27,477
Other	13,306	13,257
	209,638	201,887
Utilities and energy:		
Cash and cash equivalents	875	280
Property, plant, and equipment	29,987	28,454
Goodwill	5,363	5,280
Other	5,597	7,556
	41,822	41,570
Finance and financial products:		
Cash and cash equivalents	2,197	957
Investments in fixed-maturity securities	4,150	4,517
Loans and finance receivables	13,631	13,942
Goodwill	1,024	1,024
Other	3,184	3,502
	24,186	23,942
	$275,646	$267,399
Liabilities and shareholders' equity:		
Insurance and other:		
Losses and loss adjustment expenses	$58,867	$56,620
Unearned premiums	8,831	7,861
Life and health insurance benefits	3,898	3,619
Accounts payable, accruals, and other liabilities	14,676	14,987
Notes payable and other borrowings	4,379	4,349
	90,651	87,436

	June 30, 2009	December 31, 2008
Utilities and energy:		
Accounts payable, accruals, and other liabilities	5,800	6,175
Notes payable and other borrowings	19,708	19,145
	25,508	25,320
Finance and financial products:		
Accounts payable, accruals, and other liabilities	2,580	2,656
Derivative contract liabilities	12,299	14,612
Notes payable and other borrowings	14,697	13,388
	29,576	30,656
Income taxes, principally deferred	11,074	10,280
Total liabilities	156,809	153,692
Shareholders' equity:		
Common stock and capital in excess of par value	27,089	27,141
Accumulated other comprehensive income	7,505	3,954
Retained earnings	79,933	78,172
Berkshire Hathaway shareholders' equity	114,527	109,267
Noncontrolling interests	4,310	4,440
Total shareholders' equity	118,837	113,707
	$275,646	$267,399

BERKSHIRE HATHAWAY, INC., AND SUBSIDIARIES
CONSOLIDATED BALANCE SHEETS
(In Millions Except Per-Share Amounts)

	December 31,	
	2008	2007
Assets:		
Insurance and other:		
Cash and cash equivalents	$24,302	$37,703
Investments:		
Fixed-maturity securities	27,115	28,515
Equity securities	49,073	74,999
Other	21,535	—

(Continued)

	December 31,	
	2008	2007
Loans and receivables	14,925	13,157
Inventories	7,500	5,793
Property, plant, equipment, and assets held for lease	16,703	9,969
Goodwill	27,477	26,306
Deferred charges, reinsurance assumed	3,923	3,987
Other	9,334	7,797
	201,887	208,226
Utilities and energy:		
Cash and cash equivalents	280	1,178
Property, plant, and equipment	28,454	26,221
Goodwill	5,280	5,543
Other	7,556	6,246
	41,570	39,188
Finance and financial products:		
Cash and cash equivalents	957	5,448
Investments in fixed-maturity securities	4,517	3,056
Loans and finance receivables	13,942	12,359
Goodwill	1,024	1,013
Other	3,502	3,870
	23,942	25,746
	$267,399	$273,160
Liabilities and shareholders' equity:		
Insurance and other:		
Losses and loss adjustment expenses	$56,620	$56,002
Unearned premiums	7,861	6,680
Life and health insurance benefits	3,619	3,804
Other policyholder liabilities	3,243	4,089
Accounts payable, accruals, and other liabilities	11,744	10,672
Notes payable and other borrowings	4,349	2,680
	87,436	83,927
Utilities and energy:		
Accounts payable, accruals, and other liabilities	6,303	6,043
Notes payable and other borrowings	19,145	19,002
	25,448	25,045

	December 31,	
	2008	2007
Finance and financial products:		
Accounts payable, accruals, and other liabilities	2,656	2,931
Derivative contract liabilities	14,612	6,887
Notes payable and other borrowings	13,388	12,144
	30,656	21,962
Income taxes, principally deferred	10,280	18,825
Total liabilities	153,820	149,759
Minority shareholders' interests	4,312	2,668
Shareholders' equity:		
Common stock: Class A, $5 par value; Class B, $0.1667 par value	8	8
Capital in excess of par value	27,133	26,952
Accumulated other comprehensive income	3,954	21,620
Retained earnings	78,172	72,153
Total shareholders' equity	109,267	120,733
	$267,399	$273,160

BERKSHIRE HATHAWAY, INC., AND SUBSIDIARIES
CONSOLIDATED STATEMENTS OF EARNINGS
(In Millions Except Per-Share Amounts)

	Year Ended December 31,		
	2008	2007	2006
Revenues:			
Insurance and other:			
Insurance premiums earned	$25,525	$31,783	$23,964
Sales and service revenues	65,854	58,243	51,803
Interest, dividend, and other investment income	4,966	4,979	4,382
Investment gains/losses	(647)	5,405	1,697
	95,698	100,410	81,846

(Continued)

	Year Ended December 31,		
	2008	2007	2006
Utilities and energy:			
Operating revenues	12,668	12,376	10,301
Other	1,303	252	343
	13,971	12,628	10,644
Finance and financial products:			
Interest income	1,790	1,717	1,610
Investment gains/losses	7	193	114
Derivative gains/losses	(6,821)	(89)	824
Other	3,141	3,386	3,501
	(1,883)	5,207	6,049
	107,786	118,245	98,539
Costs and expenses:			
Insurance and other:			
Insurance losses and loss adjustment expenses	16,259	21,010	13,068
Life and health insurance benefits	1,840	1,786	1,618
Insurance underwriting expenses	4,634	5,613	5,440
Cost of sales and services	54,103	47,477	42,416
Selling, general, and administrative expenses	8,052	7,098	5,932
Interest expense	156	164	195
	85,044	83,148	68,669
Utilities and energy:			
Cost of sales and operating expenses	9,840	9,696	8,189
Interest expense	1,168	1,158	979
	11,008	10,854	9,168
Finance and financial products:			
Interest expense	639	588	550
Other	3,521	3,494	3,374
	4,160	4,082	3,924
	100,212	98,084	81,761
Earnings before income taxes and minority interests:	7,574	20,161	16,778
Income taxes	1,978	6,594	5,505
Minority shareholders' interests	602	354	258
Net earnings:	$4,994	$13,213	$11,015
Average common shares outstanding	1,548,960	1,545,751	1,541,807
Net earnings per common share:	$3,224	$8,548	$7,144

BERKSHIRE HATHAWAY, INC.,AND SUBSIDIARIES
CONSOLIDATED STATEMENTS OF CASH FLOWS
(In Millions)

	Year Ended December 31,		
	2008	**2007**	**2006**
Cash flows from operating activities:			
Net earnings	$4,994	$13,213	$11,015
Adjustments to reconcile net earnings to operating cash flows:			
Investment (gains) losses	640	(5,598)	(1,811)
Depreciation	2,810	2,407	2,066
Minority interests	602	354	258
Other	(1,248)	(268)	(627)
Changes in operating assets and liabilities before business acquisitions:			
Losses and loss adjustment expenses	1,466	(1,164)	(2,704)
Deferred charges reinsurance assumed	64	196	424
Unearned premiums	1,311	(713)	637
Receivables and originated loans	(2,222)	(977)	(59)
Derivative contract assets and liabilities	7,827	2,938	(563)
Income taxes	(2,057)	553	303
Other assets and liabilities	(2,935)	1,609	1,256
Net cash flows from operating activities	11,252	12,550	10,195
Cash flows from investing activities:			
Purchases of fixed-maturity securities	(35,615)	(13,394)	(7,747)
Purchases of equity securities	(10,140)	(19,111)	(9,173)
Purchases of other investments	(14,452)	—	—
Sales of fixed-maturity securities	14,796	7,821	1,818
Redemptions and maturities of fixed-maturity securities	18,550	9,158	10,313
Sales of equity securities	6,840	8,054	3,778
Purchases of loans and finance receivables	(1,446)	(1,008)	(365)
Principal collections on loans and finance receivables	740	1,229	985
Acquisitions of businesses, net of cash acquired	(6,050)	(1,602)	(10,132)
Purchases of property, plant, and equipment and assets held for lease	(6,138)	(5,373)	(4,571)
Other	849	798	1,017
Net cash flows from investing activities	(32,066)	(13,428)	(14,077)

(Continued)

	Year Ended December 31,		
	2008	2007	2006
Cash flows from financing activities:			
Proceeds from borrowings of finance businesses	5,195	1,153	1,280
Proceeds from borrowings of utilities and energy businesses	2,147	3,538	2,417
Proceeds from other borrowings	134	121	215
Repayments of borrowings of finance businesses	(3,861)	(1,093)	(244)
Repayments of borrowings of utilities and energy businesses	(2,147)	(1,149)	(516)
Repayments of other borrowings	(233)	(995)	(991)
Changes in short-term borrowings	1,183	(596)	245
Other	(132)	387	84
Net cash flows from financing activities	2,286	1,366	2,490
Effects of foreign currency exchange-rate changes	(262)	98	117
Increase (decrease) in cash and cash equivalents	(18,790)	586	(1,275)
Cash and cash equivalents at beginning of year	44,329	43,743	45,018
Cash and cash equivalents at end of year*	$25,539	$44,329	$43,743
**Cash and cash equivalents at end of year are comprised of the following:*			
Insurance and other	$24,302	$37,703	$37,977
Utilities and energy	280	1,178	343
Finance and financial products	957	5,448	5,423
	$25,539	$44,329	$43,743

Derivatives

Derivative contracts of Berkshire's finance and financial products businesses, with limited exceptions, are not designated as hedges for financial reporting purposes. Changes in the fair value of such contracts that do not qualify as hedges are reported in the consolidated statements of earnings as derivative gains/losses. A summary of these contracts as of December 31, 2008 and 2007 follows (in millions).

	2008			2007		
	Assets	Liabilities	Notional Value	Assets	Liabilities	Notional Value
Equity index put options	$—	$10,022	$37,134[2]	$—	$4,610	$35,043
Credit default obligations:						
High-yield indexes	—	3,031	7,892	—	1,838	4,660
Individual corporate	—	105	3,900	—	—	—

	2008			2007		
	Assets	Liabilities	Notional Value	Assets	Liabilities	Notional Value
States/municipalities	—	958	18,364	—	—	—
Other	503	528		749	489	
Counterparty netting and funds held as collateral	(295)	(32)		(50)	(50)	
	$208	$14,612		$699	$6,887	

Sources: Berkshire Hathaway financial statements from its June 30, 2009, 10Q and 2008 10K.

Example:

SWS Group is a diversified financial services company. The firm's operating activities section is shown to highlight dividends received as an operating activity because SWS is a member bank of the Federal Home Loan Banking system and is required to own its stock.

Joint-venture dividends would be shown under investing activities. Entities that own investments in other firms may receive dividends, which are presented under operations. If dividends are from a foreign entity, the risk to payment should be assessed. There have been instances where foreign nations have put pressure on companies to pay out dividends, so such cash receipts may not be certain because they may reflect cash flows that impair the entity's future prospects. Exchange controls also may alter a U.S. firm's ability to collect dividends.

	2009	2008	2007
Cash flows from operating activities:			
Net income	$23,631	$31,932	$37,609
Income from discontinued operations	—	(17)	(102)
Extraordinary gain	—	(1,061)	—
Adjustments to reconcile net income to net cash (used in) provided by operating activities:			
Depreciation and amortization	6,036	4,955	4,790
Amortization of premiums on loans purchased	(487)	(725)	(1,278)
Amortization of premiums municipal bonds	(6)	—	—
Provision for doubtful accounts and write-downs on REO properties	15,419	4,659	1,538
Deferred income tax (benefit) expense	(6,115)	1,471	632
Deferred compensation	330	1,812	3,139
Gain on sale of loans	(628)	(951)	(999)
Loss on sale of fixed assets	2	196	146

(Continued)

	2009	2008	2007
Loss (gain) on sale of real estate	1,346	(396)	(668)
Gain on sale of factored receivables	(260)	(666)	—
Loss on investment in marketable equity securities available for sale	4,971	—	—
Equity in losses (earnings) of unconsolidated ventures	1,375	(235)	861
Dividend received on investment in Federal Home Loan Bank stock	(79)	(179)	(163)
Windfall tax benefits	(67)	(218)	(225)
Net change in minority interest in consolidated subsidiaries	—	(50)	(234)
Cash flow from operating activities of discontinued operations	—	4	298
Change in operating assets and liabilities:			
Decrease (increase) in assets segregated for regulatory purposes	9,422	(3,310)	25,763
Net change in broker, dealer, and clearing organization accounts	16,410	8,923	(19,862)
Net change in client accounts	(1,776)	41,480	(8,245)
Net change in loans held for sale	97,165	(211,932)	(23,139)
Decrease (increase) in securities owned	23,543	(66,432)	39,383
(Increase) decrease in securities purchased under agreements to resell	(11,760)	32,624	21,150
Decrease (increase) in other assets	5,695	5,274	(7,383)
Increase (decrease) in drafts payable	7,800	(6,061)	(3,426)
Increase (decrease) in securities sold, not yet purchased	26,725	(36,959)	(33,439)
Increase (decrease) in other liabilities	7,997	(1,828)	780
Net cash provided by (used in) operating activities	226,689	(197,690)	36,9

Example:

A. Schulman, Inc., supplies plastic compounds and resins to consumer products, industrial, automotive, and packaging markets. The downturn in the markets forced the company to restructure its business, including employee layoffs, and to withdraw from its multiemployer pension plan. The costs of these actions were reflected in a restructuring charge in the income statement, with the noncash portion reversed under operating activities. We see in the operating activity section how management aggressively stepped up collection of accounts receivable and drew down inventories to provide cash. This would be adjusted when using power operating cash flow.

A. SCHULMAN, INC.
CONSOLIDATED STATEMENTS OF CASH FLOWS
(In Thousands)

	Year Ended August 31,		
	2009	**2008**	**2007**
Provided from (used in) operating activities:			
Net income (loss)	$(2,776)	$18,049	$22,069
Adjustments to reconcile net income (loss) to net cash provided from (used in) operating activities:			
Depreciation and amortization	23,632	27,721	25,802
Deferred tax provision	(2,974)	(2,597)	(1,865)
Pension and other deferred compensation	3,955	3,259	11,347
Postretirement benefit obligation	773	2,839	(2,837)
Net losses on asset sales	740	318	68
Minority interest in net income of subsidiaries	349	872	1,027
Restructuring charges, including accelerated depreciation of $1,326, $0, and $1,071 in 2009, 2008, and 2007, respectively	10,011	6,817	2,669
Goodwill impairment	—	964	—
Asset impairment	12,925	11,699	—
Curtailment gains	(2,805)	(4,009)	—
Proceeds of insurance settlements	—	—	750
Changes in assets and liabilities:			
Accounts receivable	91,218	16,614	(29,088)
Inventories	78,756	54,682	37,942
Accounts payable	(17,856)	25,838	(3,018)
Restructuring payments	(6,684)	(6,384)	(974)
Income taxes	3,720	(5,247)	(2,006)
Accrued payrolls and other accrued liabilities	(1,582)	1,704	789
Changes in other assets and other long-term liabilities	(9,905)	2,646	2,222
Net cash provided from operating activities	181,497	155,785	64,897

CASH CONVERSION CYCLE

The cash conversion cycle is an important operating cash-flow credit metric because it measures the duration, in days, between a company purchasing goods for sale and the ultimate collection of cash for the product. It is an important indicator because entities that can reduce the cash conversion cycle resulting from more optimal and efficient supply management, production, accounting, and collection procedures are also able to increase their free cash flow.

The *cash conversion cycle* is more appropriately defined as days of inventory and trade receivables outstanding less days of trade payables outstanding. Increases in the cash conversion cycle indicate that additional cash is consumed in the sales and manufacturing process that requires additional working capital.

Industries that, by their nature, have long cash collection cycles, as in the manufacturing of products that take a long time to produce, will need to more carefully manage their cash requirements over the cycle because there can be a negative gap between receipt of payments and cash disbursements. Such companies normally require progress payments, but even with such interim cash inflows, it would not be unusual for profits and a positive investment return to be deferred until delivery. These retainage payments could be held up if the quality of the product is in dispute, leading to further cash-flow funding gaps that would need to be financed.

Startup projects and newer companies are often required to finance development of products that might take years to come to market, requiring large outlays for labor and materials. For these entities, the cash conversion cycle, as typically defined, is not appropriate. For such entities, the analyst would evaluate the required funding, including cash on hand, cash flow from operations, and outside financing.

For industrial companies that manufacture new-generation products with long lead times, such as Lockheed, the initial number of deliveries often results in poor cash flows. However, as they move up the production learning curve, their efficiency and cash flows are greatly improved.

Example:

Textron, Inc., during a February 2010 conference call, credited its being able to achieve an 80 percent cash conversion ratio in helping bring down its targeted debt ratio, improve its liquidity ratio, and push up a projected return to profit growth.

Example:

Waste Management, during its third-quarter 2009 quarterly conference call, attributed its step up in free cash flow to "a good conversion ratio and being tight on working capital and capex." The company had been converting 120 percent of net income into cash over the prior 3 years, according to its chief financial officer.

Example:

The Kellogg Company and its subsidiaries are engaged in the manufacture and marketing of ready-to-eat cereal and convenience foods. The cash conversion cycle, even for a strong cash-flow generator such as Kellogg, is an important credit and cash-flow metric, and its components are essential to analyze for their impact on the final result. For instance, a lengthening of the collection period could mean that one (or more) of the company's customers is experiencing business difficulties or a problem with supply or delivery. Shortening of the cycle would allow the company to invest additional funds short term, thus earning cash.

Companies with a short conversion cycle (that more quickly turns sales into cash), such as Kellogg, see a closer matching between net income and operating cash flows, although specific results for any particular year may be significantly affected by the level of benefit plan contributions, working capital movements (operating assets and liabilities), and other factors.

KELLOGG COMPANY AND SUBSIDIARIES
CONSOLIDATED STATEMENT OF CASH FLOWS
(Millions)

	2007	2006	2005
Operating activities:			
Net earnings	**$1,103**	$1,004	$980
Adjustments to reconcile net earnings to operating cash flows:			
Depreciation and amortization	**372**	353	392
Deferred income taxes	**(69)**	(44)	(59)
Other (a)	**183**	235	199
Pension and other postretirement benefit contributions	**(96)**	(99)	(397)
Changes in operating assets and liabilities	**10**	(39)	28
Net cash provided by operating activities	**$1,503**	$1,410	$1,143

Calculating the Cash Conversion Cycle

Most companies do not calculate the cash conversion cycle for investors despite its importance. I have found that most companies that do discuss this metric tend to have greater focus on and run their business with all decisions based on its cash-flow impact.

One of the more interesting companies that does report the benchmark is Dell Computer, which, historically, has been so adept in its manufacturing process, along with excellent credit collection while extending payables, that it has a negative conversion cycle, indicating that it uses its suppliers' cash (not its own) to manufacture the products it sells. As explained in its 2009 10K:

> We ended the fourth quarter of Fiscal 2009 with a negative cash conversion cycle of 25 days, which is a contraction of 11 days from the fourth quarter of Fiscal 2008. The contraction is due to a decrease in our accounts payable balance, which is primarily driven by a reduction in purchases related to declining unit volumes. A negative cash conversion

cycle combined with a slowdown in revenue growth could result in cash use in excess of cash generated. Generally, as our growth stabilizes, our cash generation from operating activities will improve.

In a footnote in its 10K addressing its cash conversion measurement, Dell explains:

> *Key Performance Metrics*—Although our cash conversion cycle deteriorated from February 1, 2008, and February 2, 2007, our direct business model allows us to maintain an efficient cash conversion cycle, which compares favorably with that of others in our industry. As our growth stabilizes, more typical cash generation and a resulting cash conversion cycle are expected to resume.
>
> The following table presents the components of our cash conversion cycle for the fourth quarter of each of the past three fiscal years:

	January 30, 2009	February 1, 2008	February 2, 2007
Days of sales outstanding[a]	35	36	31
Days of supply in inventory[b]	7	8	5
Days in accounts payable[c]	(67)	(80)	(78)
Cash conversion cycle	(25)	(36)	(42)

[a]Days of sales outstanding ("DSO") calculates the average collection period of our receivables. DSO is based on the ending net trade receivables and the most recent quarterly revenue for each period. DSO also includes the effect of product costs related to customer shipments not yet recognized as revenue that are classified in other current assets. DSO is calculated by adding accounts receivable, net of allowance for doubtful accounts, and customer shipments in transit and dividing that sum by average net revenue per day for the current quarter (90 days). At January 30, 2009, February 1, 2008, and February 2, 2007, DSO and days of customer shipments not yet recognized were 31 and 4 days, 33 and 3 days, and 28 and 3 days, respectively.

[b]Days of supply in inventory ("DSI") measures the average number of days from procurement to sale of our product. DSI is based on ending inventory and most recent quarterly cost of sales for each period. DSI is calculated by dividing inventory by average cost of goods sold per day for the current quarter (90 days).

[c]Days in accounts payable ("DPO") calculates the average number of days our payables remain outstanding before payment. DPO is based on ending accounts payable and most recent quarterly cost of sales for each period. DPO is calculated by dividing accounts payable by average cost of goods sold per day for the current quarter (90 days).

> Our cash conversion cycle contracted by eleven days at January 30, 2009, from February 1, 2008, driven by a thirteen day decrease in DPO offset by a one day decrease in DSO and a one day decrease in DSI. The decrease in DPO from February 1, 2008, is attributable to procurement throughput declines as a result of declining demand, reduction in inventory levels, and a decrease in non-production supplier payables as we continue to control our operating expense spending and the timing of purchases

from and payments to suppliers during the fourth quarter of Fiscal 2009 as compared to the fourth quarter of Fiscal 2008. The decrease in DSO from February 1, 2008, is attributable to the timing of revenue due to seasonal impact, partially offset by a shift to customers with longer payment terms.

Our cash conversion cycle contracted by six days at February 1, 2008 compared to February 2, 2007. This deterioration was driven by a five day increase in DSO largely attributed to timing of payments from customers, a continued shift in sales mix from domestic to international, and an increased presence in the retail channel. In addition, DSI increased by three days, which was primarily due to strategic materials purchases. The DSO and DSI declines were offset by a two-day increase in DPO largely attributed to an increase in the amount of strategic material purchases in inventory at the end of Fiscal 2008 and the number of suppliers with extended payment terms as compared to Fiscal 2007.

We defer the cost of revenue associated with customer shipments not yet recognized as revenue until they are delivered. These deferred costs are included in our reported DSO because we believe it presents a more accurate presentation of our DSO and cash conversion cycle. These deferred costs are recorded in other current assets in our Consolidated Statements of Financial Position and totaled \$556 million, \$519 million, and \$424 million at January 30, 2009, February 1, 2008, and February 2, 2007, respectively.

Source: Dell Computer 2009 10K.

Example:

A simple technique for a close approximation of the cash conversion cycle is based on the formula:

Days of supply in inventory + days of sales outstanding − days in accounts payable

Looking back at Kellogg we see[13] that

$$\text{Days of supply in inventory} = \frac{\text{days in year}}{\text{cost of goods sold / average inventory}}$$

$$= \frac{365}{7{,}455 \text{ / average inventory}}$$

[13] All data are in thousands except where noted. Also, for seasonal concerns, the firm may wish to weight the daily average toward those seasonal periods when most of its collections are received.

To calculate average inventory, we used the average of the year-end inventory for the past 2 fiscal years. A closer approximation would be the average of the four quarters, whereas the reporting entity would have the precise daily average inventory. That is why this formula results in an approximation. For year-end 2009 and 2008, reported inventory was \$897 million and \$924 million, or \$910.5 million average. So days in inventory for Kellogg are approximately

$$\frac{365}{(7{,}455\,/\,910.5)} = \frac{365}{8.187} = 44.57 \text{ days}$$

$$\text{Days of sales outstanding} = \frac{\text{days in year}}{\text{sales / average accounts receivable}}$$

$$= \frac{365}{12{,}822 \text{ / average accounts receivable}}$$

Again, a more precise reading would result from an average of the entity's four fiscal quarters and even more so with the daily data in possession of the entity itself because its cash management software would have such information. We see from Kellogg's last two fiscal years that its accounts receivable at the end of the fiscal year was \$1,143 and \$1,001, or a \$1,072 average, so that

$$\text{DSO} = \frac{365}{(12{,}822\,/\,1{,}072)} = \frac{365}{11.96} = 30.51 \text{ days}$$

$$\text{Days in accounts payable} = \frac{\text{days in year}}{\text{cost of goods sold / accounts payable}}$$

$$= \frac{365}{(7{,}455\,/\,1{,}145)} = \frac{365}{6.57} = 55.57 \text{ days}$$

Kellogg had its cash tied up an average of 44.57 days in inventory and waited 30.51 days to be paid. During the period, the company took, on average, 55.57 days to pay its trade payables.

Summary of Kellogg's Cash Conversion Cycle

$$\begin{aligned}\text{Cash conversion cycle} &= \text{days of supply in inventory} + \text{days receivable} - \text{days to pay}\\ &= 45.57 + 30.51 - 55.57\\ &= 20.51 \text{ days}\end{aligned}$$

In its 2008 10K, Kellogg reported that its cash conversion cycle was actually 22 days. The reason the estimation was fairly close was that Kellogg's working-capital items and cost of sales remained in a relatively tight range. If quarterly data were used, the difference would have been less than 1 day compared with my estimation. In any event, Kellogg reports in its 10K that it was able to reduce its cash conversion cycle during the year owing to a decrease in days of inventory outstanding. This is additional cash the entity has on its balance sheet that can be invested and represents an improvement to operating cash flows and metrics based on operating cash flow.

SUPPLEMENTAL INFORMATION

SFAS No. 95 required firms to disclose additional information about their important economic events during the period beyond the direct cash-flow implications of these events. For example, when a firm engages in a transaction that is, in effect, a financing or an investing event, but where the entire consideration is not in cash, the firm should report the transaction in a separate schedule, usually at the bottom of the statement of cash flows. Supplemental disclosure is necessary because financing and investing events are significant economic events, they affect the long-run viability of the firm, and they should be disclosed to investors and creditors regardless of whether they involve cash alone or combine cash and other considerations. For this reason, it is important to scrutinize the supplemental information. Contained here can be very significant information, such as the consideration for acquisitions for which a majority of the payment was not in cash. Some would argue that such events really should be contained under financing activities. The important considerations are the cash effects, peer comparability, and any changes to the capital structure.

The FASB also required firms that report net operating cash flows using the indirect approach to report the tax payments and interest payments during the period. Prior to SFAS 95, an analyst could only guess at the cash taxes paid—and more often than not, it remained a guess.

The biggest shortcoming under SFAS 95 is the failure under the statement to reveal the actual cash tax rate as implied in the firm's federal tax return. Cash taxes paid, as given under supplemental information, represented a big step forward, but in order to see how the effective tax rate really compared with the statutory rate, the analyst would need to calculate an implied rate. As I show in the section "Income Taxes" below, companies are required to state how the effective tax rate differs from the statutory rate. In my cost-of-capital model I estimate the cash tax rate by dividing cash taxes paid by pretax income, plus, where applicable, certain permanent timing differences, such as amortization, where that represents a permanent difference.

Let us examine several disclosures of these supplementary items. Because an entity is required to reveal significant items as a supplemental activity, reporting practices vary.

Example:

Baldor Electric Company is a leading marketer, designer, and manufacturer of industrial electric motors, mechanical power transmission products, drives, and generators. In 2007, Baldor purchased Reliance Electric for cash and stock. At the time of closing, Baldor estimated the stock value at $50.9 million, which, because it was a partial noncash event, was listed as supplemental information. We do see the cash part of the transaction (which excludes the cash held by Reliance at closing) under investing activities, with the borrowing to finance the cash-payment portion of the deal under financing activities.

We also see, presumably to save cash needed as working capital, that Baldor contributed stock from treasury into its employee profit-sharing plan. Doing this artificially boosts cash flow from operations versus firms that contribute cash. Firms investing their own stock into profit-sharing or pension plans add additional risk to their employees because the employees are already dependent on the firm; their pension security should be diversified away from this.

Supplemental cash-flow disclosure revealed important information regarding this business acquisition, including its financing.

	2009	2008	2007
Investing activities:			
Purchases of property, plant, and equipment	(42,877)	(39,490)	(26,649)
Proceeds from sale of property, plant, and equipment	69	3,493	45
Marketable securities purchased	—	—	(470)
Proceeds from sale of marketable securities	—	23,034	10,286
Acquisitions net of cash acquired	(41,285)	(1,779,837)	—
Divestitures	—	49,886	—
Proceeds from sale of equity investment	1,373	—	—
Net proceeds from real estate transaction	23,310	—	—
Net cash used in investing activities	(59,410)	(1,742,914)	(16,788)
Financing activities:			
Proceeds from long-term obligations	137,535	1,550,000	30,000
Principal payments of long-term obligations	(177,960)	(283,000	(28,000
Proceeds from note payable	—	12,321	—
Debt issuance costs	—	(30,519	—
Principal payments on note payable	(11,586)	—	—
Proceeds from common stock issued	—	379,857	—
Dividends paid	(31,392)	(31,184)	(21,891)
Common stock repurchased	—	—	(38,464)
Stock option exercises	11,133	11,397	13,995
Excess tax benefits on share-based payments	399	668	2,149
Net increase (decrease) in bank overdrafts	7,500	(4,624)	4,624
Net cash (used in) provided by financing activities	(64,371)	1,604,916	(37,587)
Net (decrease) increase in cash and cash equivalents	(24,659)	25,020	1,263
Beginning cash and cash equivalents	37,757	12,737	11,474
Ending cash and cash equivalents	$13,098	$37,757	$12,73

Supplemental Cash Flow Information

Noncash Items

- Additional paid-in capital resulting from shares traded for option exercises amounted to $1,411 in 2008, $3,040 in 2007, and $2,763 in 2006.
- Common stock valued at $50,932 was issued January 31, 2007, in conjunction with the acquisition of Reliance Electric (see Note B).
- Treasury shares issued in March 2008 in the amount of $3,284 to fund 2007 accrued profit-sharing contribution.

Note B—Acquisitions

On January 31, 2007, Baldor completed the acquisition of all the equity of Reliance Electric ("Reliance") from Rockwell Automation, Inc., and certain of its affiliates ("Rockwell"). Reliance was a leading manufacturer of industrial electric motors and other mechanical power transmission products. The acquisition extended Baldor's product offerings, provided a manufacturing base in China for the Asian markets, increased the company's manufacturing capabilities and flexibility, strengthened the management team, and provided strong opportunities for synergies and cost savings. The purchase price was $1.83 billion, consisting of $1.78 billion in cash and 1.58 million shares of Baldor common stock valued at $50.93 million, based on the average closing price per share of Baldor's common stock on the New York Stock Exchange for the 3 days preceding and the 3 days subsequent to November 6, 2006, the date of the definitive purchase agreement. The cash portion of the purchase price was funded with proceeds from the issuance of 10,294,118 shares of Baldor common stock at a price of $34.00 per common share, proceeds from the issuance of $550.0 million of 8.625 percent senior notes due 2017, and borrowings of $1.00 billion under a new $1.20 billion senior secured credit facility. In conjunction with an overallotment option in the common stock offering, 1,430,882 additional common shares were issued at a price of $34 per share. Proceeds from the overallotment offering of approximately $46.5 million were utilized to reduce borrowings under the senior secured credit facility. Reliance's results of operations are included in the consolidated financial statements beginning February 1, 2007.

Example:

Arch Chemicals, a biochemical concern, reports in its September 2009 10Q as supplemental cash flow information the final working capital adjustments of a business acquisition. Of the $8.7 million in intangible assets, $4.2 million represented trademarks, which are not subject to amortization, thus representing a permanent tax timing difference.

	($ in Millions)
Working capital (including cash):	$11.7
Property, plant, and equipment, net	4.1
Intangible assets	8.7
Goodwill	4.6
Noncurrent assets and liabilities (including debt)	(8.0)
Investment a advances—affiliated companies at equity	(5.6)
Cash paid	$15.5

Example:

American Home Food Products is engaged in the manufacturing and marketing of private-label and specialty food products. The company lacked liquidity to pay its cash dividends to common and preferred stockholders and so made the payments in kind by issuing additional shares. We also see that the company satisfied trade payables with equity as well. Since these stock contributions represent a noncash payment, they are included as supplemental cash-flow information. Also seen are the liabilities assumed that are related to an acquisition. I would reduce cash flow from operations by the $137,036 and the $530,000 to arrive at adjusted operating cash flow because these are expenses normally paid with cash.

Payments in kind (issuing shares in exchange for assets) are one example of a supplemental activity. Another example would be converting debt to equity and exchanges, for instance, exchanging noncash assets or liabilities for other noncash assets or liabilities.

SUPPLEMENTAL CASH FLOW INFORMATION

	2009	2008
Cash paid during the period for:		
Interest	$—	$—
Income taxes	—	—
Noncash financing activities:		
Preferred and common shares issued for services	$—	137,036
Common shares issued for registration penalty	104,300	—
Preferred shares issued for dividend	680,246	449,850
Seller financing for the purchase of Artisanal	—	1,200,000
Payables paid with issuance of equity	—	530,000
Artisanal liabilities assumed	$—	$688,72

Source: American Home Food Products 2009 10K.

Example:

Tandy Leather Factory is a retailer and wholesale distributor of a broad line of leather and related products, including working tools, buckles, and adornments for belts, leather dyes and finishes, saddle and tack hardware, and do-it-yourself kits. The top of its supplemental schedule is quite typical. The company next shows equipment that was acquired under capital lease and property acquired with debt. The reason land and buildings acquired with long-term debt is shown as a noncash activity is that the property was acquired without using cash. I would adjust this transaction to show the asset purchase and the borrowing as investment and financing activities The property was acquired under a line of credit that was to be converted to a term loan at a later period. Since these are noncash-based investing activities, Tandy reports the transactions in its 2008 10K as supplemental cash-flow disclosures. While entering a capital lease is regarded as a supplemental activity, repayment of principal on capital leases would be reported as a financing activity.

SUPPLEMENTAL DISCLOSURES OF CASH FLOW INFORMATION

Interest paid during the period	$332,107	$122,209	$—
Income tax paid during the period, net of (refunds)	878,110	1,830,688	2,282,113
Noncash investing activities:			
Equipment acquired under capital lease financing arrangements	$803,713	—	—
Land and building acquired with long-term debt	—	$4,050,000	

Example:

Illustrated next is the supplemental disclosure section for Schlumberger, Ltd., a large oil services company. Above its supplemental information from its 2008 10K, the company provides a separate line entry for cash flow from discontinued operations, allowing the analyst better comparability and forecasting of future cash flows.

The supplemental disclosure section reflects the currency translation effect of balance-sheet cash. Currency translation, a noncash activity, being a change in foreign currencies relative to the host currency (U.S. dollars), is also shown as part of other comprehensive income (loss) on the balance sheet and statement of shareholders' equity. These gains or losses also could include the effects of derivative contracts related to changes in currency movements. Foreign currency is sensitive to both exchange-rate and interest-rate risk. To the extent that a foreign currency relative to the U.S. dollar (host currency) changes, it would have an impact on the value on translation back to the host. As SFAS 95 states: "A statement of cash flows of an enterprise with foreign currency transactions or foreign operations shall report the reporting currency equivalent of foreign currency cash flows using the exchange rates in effect at the time of the cash flows." An appropriately weighted average exchange rate for the period may be used for translation if the result is substantially the same as if the rates at the dates of the cash flows were used.

Translation of foreign currency can affect working-capital analysis. To the extent that it reflects volatility in the exchange rate and not cash generated, such swings should be ignored, especially if the parent has not shown a desire to or for any reason cannot remit cash back to the United States. Other effects, such as a change in the value of a foreign entity that could be monetized, would enter the cost of capital model.

SUPPLEMENTARY INFORMATION

	Year Ended December 31 (In Millions)		
	2009	**2008**	**2007**
Cash flows from operating activities:			
Cash flow from discontinued operations—operating activities	**(45)**	63	—
Net increase (decrease) in cash before translation effect	**54**	(6)	28
Translation effect on cash	—	(2)	3
Cash, beginning of year	**189**	197	166
Cash, end of year	**243**	$189	$197

Example:

Thor Industries manufactures and sells a wide range of recreation vehicles and small and mid-sized buses in the United States and Canada. Capital expenditures that have not used cash (an accrued item shown in accounts payable) are reflected as a supplemental item. If a cash outlay was associated with the event, the transaction would be listed as an investing activity. You also can see the cancellation of restricted stock that had been issued previously. At the time of issuance, it also was recorded as a noncash event.

Noncash transactions:			
Capital expenditures in accounts payable	$53	$543	$203
Cancellation of restricted stock	$—	$—	$35
Deferred taxes, net	$—	$562	$—

Example:

Abercrombie and Fitch, the large clothing retailer, capitalizes construction work in progress, which appears in the property, plant, and equipment account on its balance sheet. This is a common practice for the utility and extractive industries, where the outflow of cash is also capitalized in the drilling process. For Abercrombie, when the accrual declined (a noncash item), it was reported as a supplemental activity.

Significant noncash investing activities:			
Change in accrual for construction in progress	$(27,913)	$8,791	$28,455

Source: Abercrombie and Fitch 2009 10K.

Example:

Palatin Technologies, a biopharmaceutical company, recognized the value of tenant allowances (rent otherwise due) for leasehold improvements as supplemental cash flow because no cash was exchanged in return for occupancy. Palatin also paid for license fees (to other firms holding the patents) with stock. The firm sold $37 million in stock and warrants the subsequent year, paying cash for the licensing fees.

Supplemental cash flow information:			
Cash paid for interest	$30,522	$14,171	$22,649
Assets acquired by capital lease	326,214	—	—
Tenant allowances recognized in deferred rent	—	210,924	—
Common stock issued for license fees	—	317,900	—

Source: Palatin Technologies 2006 10K.

Example:

Monsanto, a large provider of agricultural products, reports supplemental cash flow information as a footnote, and the company then redirected analysts to other footnotes. The most significant entry relates to Monsanto's restructuring involving various divisions, shown as its Note 5. Presumably, the restructuring will lead to greater increases in prospective cash flows, and the analyst should determine why the restructuring was undertaken. Monsanto booked a $361 million restructuring expense on its P&L during 2009, which, since it was noncash, was reversed under operating activities. The company also realized a tax benefit from the book loss owing to the restructuring, for which the company showed a lower effective tax rate; however, as reported, actual tax payments rose, primarily resulting from foreign tax payments, as reported in the tax footnote.

Cash payments for interest and taxes during fiscal years 2009, 2008, and 2007 were as follows:

	Year Ended August 31, (In Millions)		
	2009	**2008**	**2007**
Interest	**$136**	$105	$111
Taxes	**657**	596	482

During fiscal years 2009, 2008, and 2007, the company recorded the following noncash investing and financing transactions:

- During fiscal year 2009, the company recognized noncash transactions related to restructuring. See Note 5—Restructuring.
- In 2009, the company recognized noncash transactions related to a new capital lease. Long-term debt, short-term debt, and assets of $18 million, $2 million, and $20 million, respectively, were recorded as a result of payment provisions under the lease agreement.
- During fiscal years 2009, 2008, and 2007, the company recognized noncash transactions related to restricted stock units and acquisitions. See Note 20—Stock-Based Compensation Plans—for further discussion of restricted stock units and Note 4—Business Combinations—for details of adjustments to goodwill.
- In fourth quarter 2009, 2008, and 2007, the board of directors declared a dividend payable in first quarter 2010, 2009, and 2008, respectively. As of August 31, 2009, 2008, and 2007, a dividend payable of $145 million, $132 million, and $96 million, respectively, was recorded.
- In 2008, intangible assets in the amount of $20 million and a liability in the amount of $10 million were recorded as a result of payment provisions under a joint venture agreement. See Note 11—Investments and Equity Affiliates—for further discussion of the agreement.
- In 2009 and 2008, intangible assets of $4 million and $16 million, long-term investments of $2 million and $7 million, and liabilities of $6 million and $23 million, respectively, were recorded as a result of payment provisions under collaboration and license agreements. See Note 11—Investments and Equity Affiliates—for further discussion of the investments.
- In 2007, intangible assets and a liability in the amount of $15 million were recorded as a result of minimum payment provisions under a license agreement. See Note 10—Goodwill and Other Intangible Assets—for further discussion of the agreement.

Note 5: Restructuring

Restructuring charges were recorded in the Statement of Consolidated Operations as follows:

	Year Ended Aug. 31, 2009 (In Millions)
Cost of goods sold[1]	**$(45)**
Restructuring charges[1]	**(361)**
Loss from continuing operations before income taxes	**(406)**
Income tax benefit	**116**
Net loss	**$(290)**

[1]The $45 million of restructuring charges recorded in cost of goods sold were split by segment as follows: $1 million in Agricultural Productivity and $44 million in Seeds and Genomics. The $361 million of restructuring charges were split by segment as follows: $113 million in Agricultural Productivity and $248 million in Seeds and Genomics.

POWER OPERATING CASH FLOW

Cash flow from operations adjusted for balance-sheet items is referred to as *power operating cash flow* (power OCF) because it includes a normalized adjustment for inventory, accounts receivable, accounts payables, and other important working-capital items, thereby creating a less managed version of the FASB definition of GAAP-defined operating cash flows. For example, during business slowdowns, reported cash flow from operations typically exhibits strength, while reported earnings and power operating cash flows more accurately reflect the underlying weakness. During other periods, GAAP measured cash flow from operating activities may show the entity as not being a good cash generator, when in fact, that is not the case, as normalization or unusual activities are accounted for.

Power operating cash flow is a "normalized" cash flow if the company would have maintained these working-capital accounts at average levels (in proportion to sales) that the company experienced in the previous 5 years. Because working-capital items are normally subject to period volatility and are easily managed, power operating cash flow is often more useful and can result in a better assessment of comparability among companies—it is often a more powerful marker owing to the elimination of distortions that would relate to any management bias. It is thus a better indication of normalized period liquidly generation, including if used as a beginning value from which to estimate free cash flow instead of cash flow from operations. The actual free cash flow would require beginning with reported cash flow from operations because it would represent the actual distributable cash during the period. For this reason, I begin my estimation of free cash flow with cash flow from operations, not power OCF, although in my cost-of-capital model, power OCF is an important metric.

Aside from the working-capital items included in my definition of power OCF, it is also important to consider other significant company-specific current assets or liabilities that are subject to rapid management discretion and need to be normalized such that power OCF could provide a more accurate indication of and clearer visibility into the current financial picture, including where the near-term direction of the business lies. When an entity shows relative stability and similar growth of both cash flow from operations and power OCF, management typically is conducting business under a normal state of affairs, balance-sheet levels are in equilibrium relative to revenues, and cash collections are at acceptable levels. However, when there is a large deviation in a working-capital item or items, there is commonly some event that is associated with it or an expectation of a change in business conditions. The definition of what constitutes a large deviation would be decided by the analyst and could vary in time and magnitude. It is conceivable that a single quarter could be significant if the information relayed from the working-capital change is sufficiently large.

Sometimes the event causing a break between power OCF and OCF simply may be a desire for better asset utilization, with the intended effect of improving free cash flow. For this reason, I look at the 5-year average when normalizing balance-sheet ratios, assuming that there have been no major changes to the business composition; a deviation may be the result of a significant divestiture, acquisition, or change in the manufacturing process or expected level of business. Whatever the event, there is always a reason working-capital items have made a telling swing relative to reported operating cash flow, and they can provide an important clue as to current or impending changes in the risk profile. If there has been a significant change to the business, I would shorten the 5-year period or include that information from the combined entity.

As seen in Figure 3-4, there is a fairly consistent and smooth relationship between the Standard and Poor's (S&P) 500 Index and the average power OCF, with power OCFs topping out in 2003, several years ahead of the large bear market. The power OCFs in the figure are weighted using S&P divisors,[14] identical to the index. Between 1999 and 2004, power OCF declined, with a large fall in 2000, preceding the 2001 recession, which began in March and lasted a brief 8 months. While power OCF fell in 2004 and stocks rallied, the increase in the S&P was 9 percent.

During 2007, power OCF declined, in contradiction to the S&P 500, which rose. For 2008, power OCF turned decidedly negative, consistent with the steep recession and in contradiction with reported operating cash flows (not shown) for the S&P 500 group of companies, which were positive by $137 million, its

[14] The companies in the figure are weighted using official S&P divisors, which is not the weighted average. For example, to calculate the power OCFs, I calculated the sum for all companies in the index and then divided by the S&P divisor for the index, which is not released publicly.

FIGURE 3-4

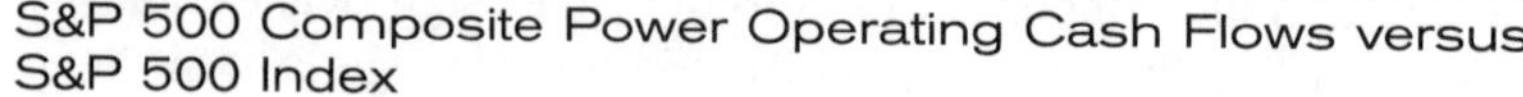

S&P 500 Composite Power Operating Cash Flows versus S&P 500 Index

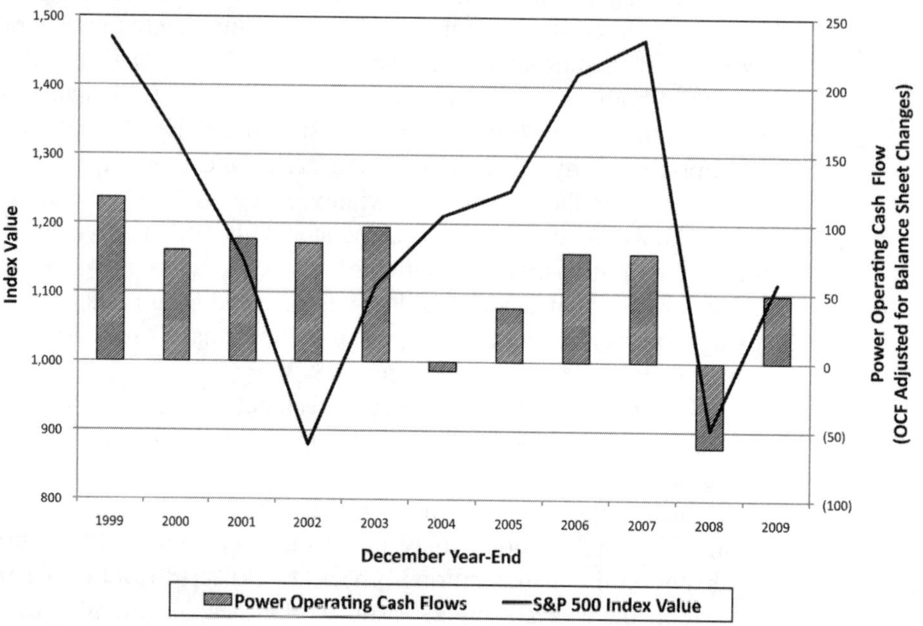

highest of the decade, because managers were extremely aggressive in their management of working capital. During 2009, power OCF rose, coming out of the recession, followed by a large rise in equity prices.

Example:

Starwood, one of world's largest hotel companies, significantly enhanced its operating cash flows through large tax benefits related to asset sales. When backing these benefits out, the result is a normalized view of the health of the operating companies that make up Starwood. Starwood's management, by taking advantage of tax benefits related to these sales, was able to provide a very large boost in operating cash flows, illustrating the importance of normalizing the balance sheet to gain a longer-term perspective. Figure 3-5 shows the smooth relationship between OCF(exclusive of the tax benefit) and market value for Starwood.

Security analysts who follow the hotel and lodging industry have, as a primary focus, RevPar, defined as revenues per available room. They believe that greater revenues per room will result in greater earnings and cash flows, bringing a higher stock price. However, this is not always the case. During business slowdowns, as was observed during the recession that began in 2007, many hotel executives lowered their room pricing, resulting in total revenues showing only minor declines, yet their stock prices had very meaningful falls owing to the drop in free cash flow.

Figure 3-5 shows for Starwood Hotels the stronger relationship between power OCF and market capitalization than with revenues, the primary driver of RevPar, which, for instance, fell by just 1.2 percent for Starwood for their fiscal year ending 2008, according to the company's 10K. On the other hand, power OCFs tumbled.

Except for 2008, the relationship is extremely strong, when power OCFs rose despite the fall in GAAP-reported cash flow from operating activities. During the first 6 months of 2009, however, Starwood stock rose by 24 percent, again following power OCF.

On a related note, Starwood has been reporting a very inconsistent tax rate, normally a negative indicator. We will discuss this in Chapter 6.

FIGURE 3-5

Starwood Power OCF after Adjustment for Tax Benefits of 2006–2008

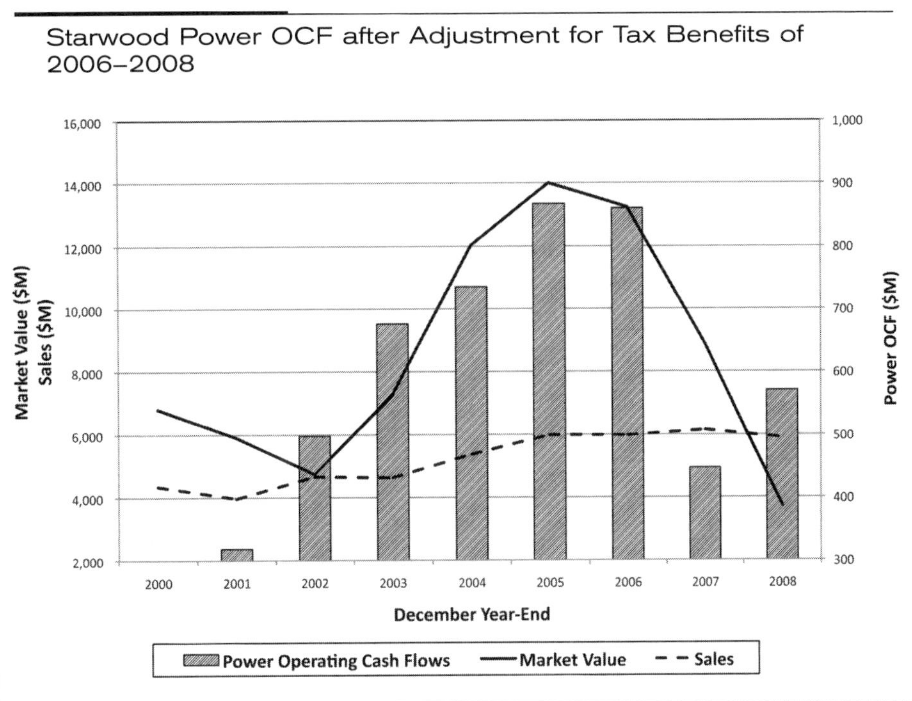

CHAPTER 4

Free Cash Flow

It should come as no surprise there is no better predictor of stock prices than free cash flow. It is, after all, the reason for-profit entities are started in the first place. As the saying goes, "Cash pays the rent." The free cash flow of the corporation is the shareholder's income.

Yet somewhere along the line came accrual accounting and the matching principle, and investors became further and further alienated from free cash flow and pushed toward financial reporting under generally accepted accounting rules, more formerly known as *generally accepted accounting principles* (GAAP).

Free cash flow is a very intuitive concept; it focuses on the amount of cash that owners of a business can consume without reducing the value of the business. It recognizes that a business needs to invest in current and long-term assets in order to continue and grow its operations. Thus free cash flow focuses on the ability of a business to generate cash flows beyond those needed to invest in such assets as inventories, plant and equipment, advertising, labor, other cost of sales, research and development, and the like. When a firm is able to generate more cash flows from its ongoing operations than are needed to remain in business, the firm has free cash flow. Such a firm can distribute the free cash flow to its owners through dividends immediately or retain the free cash flow within the firm for future growth and hope to generate more free cash flow in the future. Thus a firm with growing free cash flow may be a good candidate for investment because rising free cash flow eventually will lead to higher security prices. Absent those investors who became wealthy on the greater fool theory, all great investors attained their status because their companies were strong and growing producers of free cash flow.

Despite free cash flow being a primary objective of management and analytical measurements, net income must too be studied as it can emit signals which cash flow overlooks—but its usefulness is more of short-term significance. For example, if a firm is in distress, management will take measures to maximize cash, the result of which would provide high levels of cash flow from operating activities, and hence free cash flow, while GAAP reported net income portrays a weakened condition. This sort of stepped-up cash management could only take place for several reporting periods, and, to the extent it did occur, would be picked up through the balance sheet changes reflected in power operating cash flows. Additionally, as stock-based compensation grows in importance, and to the extent net income influences short-term stock price movements, the GAAP net income measure has cash flow relevance, particularly in terms of the cost of any stock buybacks put in place to offset dilution of issued shares. For the longer-term, however, it is free cash flow and metrics based off of free cash flow that determines the security price and its associated valuation.

Firms that generate free cash flow and have financial flexibility are able to use their credit strength (low cost of capital) to finance customer's purchases.

Example:

Boeing Co. reports in its 2008 10K customer financing slightly above $5.8 billion out of total assets of $53.8 billion. In order to compete with Airbus, Boeing must make attractive financing available to its customers, with the majority of such financing given to commercial airlines having a low credit rating.

Firms that do not produce free cash flow and do not have other assets available to satisfy their fixed charges will default on their obligations, with bankruptcy the likely outcome. My credit model in Chapter 8 evaluates such a financial possibility.

The ability of the firm to grow free cash flow is better understood through the use of various sensitivity models. These models show how important economic and market events, resulting from changes to either input costs or pricing, affect revenues, net income, or cash flows or the financial structure. In the following example, JM Smucker reports the impact of a 10 percent change in market prices for its raw materials. Since most firms do not report sensitivity analysis on their important inputs, it is the analyst's responsibility to do so, as I will show throughout this text, including a sensitivity analysis in this chapter for Clorox that shows the effects of various scenarios on the company's free cash flow, leverage, and cost of capital. Normally, analysts formulate their sensitivity models using best estimates from many sources, including the company, trade associations, and traded exchange pricing. It is, however, just as important to consider a wide range of sensitivity scenarios, not just the ones related to the biggest numbers on the financial statements.

The following sensitivity analysis presents the company's potential loss of fair value of its hedged commodity portfolio resulting from a hypothetical 10 percent change in market prices (in thousands of dollars).

	October 31, 2009	April 30, 2009
Raw material commodities:		
High	$20,620	$16,374
Low	1,459	3,949
Average	10,699	9,785

Source: JM Smucker, November 20, 2009, 10Q.

Fair value was determined using quoted market prices and was based on the company's net derivative position by commodity for the previous four quarters. The calculations are not intended to represent actual losses in fair value that the company expects to incur. In practice, as markets move, the company actively manages its risk and adjusts hedging, derivative, and purchasing strategies as appropriate. The commodities hedged have a high inverse correlation with price changes of the derivative commodity instrument; thus the company would expect that any gain or loss in the fair value of its derivatives generally would be offset by an increase or decrease in the fair value of the underlying exposures.

When BP, which previously was assigned a cost of equity of 6 percent, suffered a tragic explosion in the Gulf of Mexico, we created a sensitivity analysis which both reduced free cash flow and raised cost of capital. By doing so, even using rough estimates for free cash flows, we concluded it was better to avoid commitment to its shares until a better understanding of the ramifications was apparent.

An integral part of my methodology in the estimatation of free cash flow is the overspending on behalf of the firm. When such unnecessary spending is curtailed, additional cash is released, often leading to higher stock prices. For example, during a third-quarter 2009 conference call, Waste Management, Inc., executives attributed its $30 million reduction in selling, general, and administrative (SG&A) expenses to lower labor costs associated with an earlier restructuring. "Been running $10 million a month—looking for ways to drive out additional costs," their CFO stated during the conference call, and investors reacted positively to the news, bidding up the stock despite the company having reported lower profits.

Accounting for overspending can result in very significant free-cash-flow recapture (as is evident in Table 4-2). This is not surprising because the traditional measure of free cash flow—net cash flow from operating activities minus capital expenditure and cash dividends—does not capture the wasteful spending on everything from overstaffing to acquisitions to capital expenditures as well as it should because we are striving to gain a clear understanding of the maximum distributable cash. The more appropriate method, as we will see, is to determine the amount of the discretionary pie that can be considered wasteful. This is reflected as the "Free Cash Flow Adjusted for Corporate 'Fat'" in Table 4-2, and as is apparent, the gap is often quite substantial.

BP Sensitivity Analysis Resulting from Rig Explosion

			Scenario 1		Scenario 2		Scenario 3	Scenario 4
Year	Free Cash Flow Per Share	Discount Factor @ 11%	Present Value Using 11% COE	Discount Factor @ 10%	Present Value Using 10% COE	Free Cash Flow Per Share	Present Value Using 10% COE	Present Value Using 11% COE
2010	$4.00	0.90	$3.60	0.91	$3.64	$4.00	$3.64	$3.60
2011	$1.00	0.81	$0.81	0.83	$0.83	$2.00	$1.65	$1.62
2012	$0.00	0.73	$0.00	0.75	$0.00	$3.00	$2.25	$2.19
2013	$1.00	0.66	$0.66	0.68	$0.68	$3.00	$2.05	$1.98
2014	$2.00	0.59	$1.19	0.62	$1.24	$3.00	$1.86	$1.78
2015	$2.00	0.53	$1.07	0.56	$1.13	$3.00	$1.69	$1.60
2016	$4.00	0.48	$1.93	0.51	$2.05	$4.00	$2.05	$1.93
2017	$4.00	0.43	$1.74	0.47	$1.87	$4.00	$1.87	$1.74
2018	$4.00	0.39	$1.56	0.42	$1.70	$5.00	$2.12	$1.95
2019	$4.00	0.35	$1.41	0.39	$1.54	$5.00	$1.93	$1.76
2020	$4.00	0.32	$1.27	0.35	$1.40	$5.00	$1.75	$1.59
2021	$4.00	0.29	$1.14	0.32	$1.27	$6.00	$1.91	$1.72
2022	$4.00	0.26	$1.03	0.29	$1.16	$6.00	$1.74	$1.55
2023	$4.00	0.23	$0.93	0.26	$1.05	$6.00	$1.58	$1.39
2024	$4.00	0.21	$0.84	0.24	$0.96	$6.00	$1.44	$1.25
2025	$5.00	0.19	$0.94	0.22	$1.09	$6.00	$1.31	$1.13
2026	$6.00	0.17	$1.02	0.20	$1.19	$6.00	$1.19	$1.02
2027	$6.00	0.15	$0.92	0.18	$1.08	$6.00	$1.08	$0.92
2028	$6.00	0.14	$0.83	0.16	$0.98	$6.00	$0.98	$0.83
2029	$6.00	0.12	$0.74	0.15	$0.89	$6.00	$0.89	$0.74
2030	$7.00	0.11	$0.78	0.14	$0.95	$7.00	$0.95	$0.78
2031	$7.00	0.10	$0.70	0.12	$0.86	$7.00	$0.86	$0.70
2032	$7.00	0.09	$0.63	0.11	$0.78	$7.00	$0.78	$0.63
2033	$7.00	0.08	$0.57	0.10	$0.71	$7.00	$0.71	$0.57
2034*	$30.00	0.07	$2.21	0.09	$2.77	$30.00	$2.77	$2.21
FV			**$28.52**		**$31.81**		**$41.05**	**$37.19**
Probability			**15%**		**15%**		**30%**	**40%**
							Weighted Average	**$36.24**

*terminal value

Source: Research Insight, CT Capital LLC.

Some of the companies in the table are known to be greater producers of excess cash than is determined using a GAAP approach. For instance, Altria, according to the commonly used definition, produced a paltry $86 million in free cash flow for its fiscal year ending 2008. That magnitude of free cash certainly would not support the company's $36 billion market value. Thus there must be another factor at work. Altria, according to its statement of cash flows, paid $4.4 billion in dividends, which, along with stock repurchases of $1.2 billion and subtracting the net debt increase of $2.7 billion, all else equal, would have resulted in generation of $2.9 billion in free cash flow. During the year, Altria also paid a large $3 billion dividend to Phillip Morris International, which is why the company's net debt increased.

Below I summarize Altria's free cash flow of $5.098 billion (the amount in Table 4-1), which represents the actual cash Altria normally could have distributed to its shareholders without impairing its future growth opportunities. Net operating cash flows may not match published financial statements owing to adjustments (discussed in Chapter 8).

TABLE 4-1

Altria Corp.

Cash Flow Items-Discretionary

Year	Dec-04	Dec-05	Dec-06	Dec-07	Dec-08	Most Recent Quarter Jun-09	Previous Quarter Jun-08
Net Operating Cash Flow	10890.0	11060.0	13586.0	10304.0	4755.0	(1908.0)	(2381.0)
Capital Expenditures	1913.0	2206.0	2454.0	1458.0	241.0	69.0	40.0
Sale of PPE	NA	NA	NA	NA	525.0	0.0	NA
Free Cash Flow – Including Discretionary Items	8977.0	8854.0	11132.0	8846.0	5039.0	(1977.0)	(2421.0)
Free Cash Flow – Excluding Discretionary Items	9463.3	9188.1	11298.2	9056.1	5098.4	—	—
Discretionary Capital Expenditures	0.0	0.0	62.3	185.9	0.0	—	—
Discretionary R&D	49.2	33.0	25.3	24.2	2.4	—	—
Discretionary Cost of Goods Sold	437.1	301.0	25.1	0.0	57.1	—	—
Discretionary SG&A	0.0	57.1	0.0	53.5	0.0	—	—
Discretionary Advertising	0.0	0.0	0.0	0.0	0.0	—	—
Large Buildup (Reduction) in Accounts Receivable	0.0	778.1	(277.8)	337.9	101.7	(1321.8)	(1711.1)
Large Buildup (Reduction) in Inventory	(1805.2)	945.7	635.2	1822.9	4575.9	(1863.3)	(2486.3)
Large Buildup (Reduction) in Accounts Payable	(3117.7)	2353.3	650.9	1883.5	4576.1	2176.8	(659.6)

Source: CT Capital, LLC.

ALTRIA CORP.
STATEMENT OF CASH FLOWS
Consolidated Statements of Cash Flows, 2008
(Millions of Dollars)

	Year Ended December 31,		
	2008	**2007**	**2006**
Cash provided by (used in) operating activities:			
Earnings from continuing operations—consumer products	**$3,065**	$2,910	$3,059
Earnings from continuing operations—financial services	**25**	221	123
Earnings from discontinued operations, net of income taxes and minority interest	**1,840**	6,655	8,840
Net earnings	**4,930**	9,786	12,022
Impact of earnings from discontinued operations, net of income taxes and minority interest	**(1,840)**	(6,655)	(8,840)
Adjustments to reconcile net earnings to operating cash flows:			
Consumer products:			
Depreciation and amortization	**215**	232	255
Deferred income tax provision (benefit)	**121**	101	(332)
Equity earnings in SABMiller	**(467)**	(510)	(460)
Dividends from SABMiller	**249**	224	193
Escrow bond for the *Engle* tobacco case		1,300	
Escrow bond for the *Price* tobacco case			1,850
Asset impairment and exit costs, net of cash paid	**197**	333	7
Gain on sale of corporate headquarters building	**(404)**		
Loss on early extinguishment of debt	**393**		
Income tax reserve reversal			(1,006)
Cash effects of changes, net of the effects from acquired and divested companies:			
Receivables, net	**(84)**	162	150
Inventories	**185**	375	216
Accounts payable	**(162)**	(82)	(105)
Income taxes	**(201)**	(900)	(398)
Accrued liabilities and other current assets	**(27)**	(247)	(45)
Accrued settlement charges	**5**	434	50
Pension plan contributions	**(45)**	(37)	(288)
Pension provisions and postretirement, net	**192**	165	318
Other	**139**	302	299
Financial services:			
Deferred income tax benefit	**(259)**	(320)	(238)
Allowance for losses	**100**		103
Other	**(22)**	(83)	(102)
Net cash provided by operating activities—continuing operations	**3,215**	4,580	3,649
Net cash provided by operating activities—discontinued operations	**1,666**	5,736	9,937
Net cash provided by operating activities	**4,881**	10,316	13,586

See notes to consolidated financial statements.

	Year Ended December 31,		
	2008	**2007**	**2006**
Cash provided by (used in) investing activities:			
Consumer products			
Capital expenditures	**$(241)**	$(386)	$(399)
Proceeds from sale of corporate headquarters building	**525**		
Purchase of businesses, net of acquired cash		(2,898)	
Other	**110**	108	(6)
Financial services			
Investments in finance assets	**(1)**	(5)	(15)
Proceeds from finance assets	**403**	486	357
Net cash provided by (used in) investing activities—continuing operations	**796**	(2,695)	(63)
Net cash used in investing activities—discontinued operations	**(317)**	(2,560)	(555)
Net cash provided by (used in) investing activities	**479**	(5,255)	(618)
Cash provided by (used in) financing activities:			
Consumer products			
Net issuance of short-term borrowings		2	1
Long-term debt proceeds	**6,738**		
Long-term debt repaid	**(4,057)**	(500)	(2,052)
Financial services			
Long-term debt repaid		(617)	(1,015)
Repurchase of Altria Group, Inc., common stock	**(1,166)**		
Dividends paid on Altria Group, Inc., common stock	**(4,428)**	(6,652)	(6,815)
Issuance of Altria Group, Inc., common stock	**89**	423	486
Kraft Foods, Inc., dividends paid to Altria Group, Inc.		728	1,369
Philip Morris International, Inc., dividends paid to Altria Group, Inc.	**3,019**	6,560	2,780
Debt issuance costs	**(46)**		
Tender and consent fees related to the early extinguishment of debt	**(371)**		
Changes in amounts due to/from discontinued operations	**(664)**	(370)	(166)
Other	**(51)**	278	164
Net cash used in financing activities—continuing operations	**(937)**	(148)	(5,248)
Net cash used in financing activities—discontinued operations	**(1,648)**	(3,531)	(9,118)
Net cash used in financing activities	**(2,585)**	(3,679)	(14,366)
Effect of exchange-rate changes on cash and cash equivalents			
Continuing operations			34
Discontinued operations	**(126)**	347	126
	(126)	347	160
Cash and cash equivalents—continuing operations:			
Increase (decrease)	**3,074**	1,737	(1,628)
Balance at beginning of year	**4,842**	3,105	4,733
Balance at end of year	**$7,916**	$4,842	$3,105
Cash paid—continuing operations:			
Interest—Consumer products	**$208**	$348	$377
— Financial services	**$38**	$62	$108
Income taxes	**$1,837**	$2,241	$3,074

Source: Altria Corp 2008 10K.

In the following section I discuss an improvement to commonly used free-cash-flow definitions, one that enhances the widespread definition by including the discretionary departments we see with Altria (Table 4-1). As affirmed during the 2007–2009 severe economic downturn, the vast number of entities reducing overhead and discretionary expenses created significant additional free cash flow, leading, for the year 2009, to a big run in equity valuations. For instance, during 2009, it was common for companies to report declines or disappointments in revenues with surprisingly strong free cash flow; on this list were IBM, Coca-Cola, Quest, Hill-Rom, and Waste Management. The potential improvements were picked up by the model.

My adjusted measure effectively captures such excess and adds it back as free cash flow. By doing so, I am able to more correctly value the entity as a cash-flow-maximizing enterprise, just as firms actually were being managed during the recession and ensuing slow period of revenue growth.

Table 4-2 compares large free-cash-flow generators using the most prevalent formula in security analyst models compared with my adjusted definition, which includes corporate "fat."

TABLE 4-2

Large Free-Cash-Flow Generators: Traditional versus Adjusted Definition (Fiscal Year 2008)

Company Name	Ticker	Free Cash Flow Adjusted for Corporate "Fat"	Traditional Free Cash Flow
Abbott Laboratories	ABT	6,393	3,882
Allianz SE-ADR	AZ	36,257	30,018
Altria Group, Inc.	MO	5,098	86
Amgen, Inc.	AMGN	5,568	5,316
Anglo American PLC-ADR	AAUK	4,561	1,369
Apple, Inc.	AAPL	8,810	8,505
Arcelormittal-ADR	MT	10,506	6,545
Astrazeneca PLC-ADR	AZN	7,996	4,908
AXA-ADR	AXA	29,635	25,156
Berkshire Hathaway	BRK.A	9,069	5,114
BHP Billiton Group (GBR)-ADR	BBL	10,103	6,116
BP PLC-ADR	BP	19,933	5,095
British Amern TOB PLC-ADR	BTI	4,610	2,482
Chevron Corp.	CVX	13,777	4,804
China Life Insurance Co.-ADR	LFC	12,532	10,272
China Telecom Corp., Ltd.-ADR	CHA	5,183	3,509
CISCO Systems, Inc.	CSCO	11,272	10,821
Coca-Cola Co.	KO	6,077	2,082

Company Name	Ticker	Free Cash Flow Adjusted for Corporate "Fat"	Traditional Free Cash Flow
COMCAST Corp.	CMCSA	4,667	3,934
Discover Financial Services, Inc.	DFS	4,557	4,294
Exxon Mobil Corp.	XOM	41,630	32,349
Gazprom OAO-ADR	OGZPY	6,357	(581)
Glaxosmithkline PLC-ADR	GSK	8,786	4,168
Google, Inc.	GOOG	5,817	5,494
Hewlett-Packard Co.	HPQ	12,155	10,805
Imperial Tobacco Group-ADR	ITYBY	5,670	1,779
ING Group NV-ADR	ING	18,365	10,449
Intel Corp.	INTC	5,920	2,629
International Business Machines Corp.	IBM	15,237	12,056
Johnson & Johnson	JNJ	12,202	6,882
Lilly (Eli) & Co.	LLY	7,634	4,292
Lukoil Oil Co.-ADR	LUKOY	6,118	2,350
Merck & Co.	MRK	5,453	1,995
Microsoft Corp.	MSFT	16,959	11,450
Nestle SA-ADR	3NSRGY	6,101	1,251
Nippon Telegrph & Telephone-ADR	NTT	12,146	9,751
Novartis AG-ADR	NVS	8,121	4,081
NTT Docomo, Inc.-ADR	DCM	6,636	4,559
Occidental Petroleum Corp.	OXY	6,474	5,048
Oracle Corp.	ORCL	7,773	7,476
Pepsico, Inc.	PEP	4,848	2,012
Phelps Dodge Corp.	PD	4,791	2,913
Philip Morris International	PM	6,889	1,757
Prudential Financial, Inc.	PRU	12,229	10,521
Rio Tinto Group (AUS)-ADR	RTOLY	6,969	4,376
Roche Holding, Ltd.-ADR	RHHBY	8,911	4,673
Royal Dutch Shell PLC-ADR	RDS.A	17,043	(663)
Sanofi-Aventis-ADR	SNY	10,762	5,867
Siemens AG-ADR	SI	7,464	4,845
Statoilhydro ASA-ADR	STO	6,976	1,448
Taiwan Semiconductor-ADR	TSM	5,069	2,610
Telecom Italia SPA-ADR	TI	8,284	5,399
Time Warner, Inc.	TWX	6,746	5,054
Tokio Marine Holdings–ADR	TKOMY	8,215	7,747
Total SA-ADR	TOT	10,999	2,593
United Parcel Service, Inc.	UPS	6,233	3,571
United Technologies Corp.	UTX	4,965	3,735
Verizon Communications, Inc.	VZ	10,190	4,388
Vodafone Group PLC-ADR	VOD	11,259	4,284
Volkswagen AG-ADR	VLKAY	12,549	11,392
Wal-Mart Stores, Inc.	WMT	13,085	7,902

Source: CT Capital LLC

Example:

In its 2009 10K filing, JCPenney used the expression *free cash flow* 15 times, writing that it is central to maintaining a strong competitive position. They stated

> To enhance our liquidity position and ensure we maintain a strong financial position, we addressed these difficult operating conditions by focusing on those areas within our control, specifically by reducing inventory and tightly controlling operating expenses. As a result of our efforts, we finished the year with approximately $2.4 billion of cash and cash equivalents on our balance sheet. Our strong liquidity and solid financial position allow us to focus our efforts on appropriately managing inventory levels, operating expenses, and capital expenditures under our Bridge Plan without the need for substantial changes to our business model. A significant accomplishment and indication of our solid financial position is shown by our free cash flow (a non-GAAP financial measure defined and discussed on page 28), which provided a positive $21 million despite the harsh economic conditions.

And Penney defines free cash flow as follows:

Free Cash Flow (Non-GAAP Financial Measure)

We define free cash flow as net cash provided by operating activities of continuing operations less capital expenditures and dividends paid, plus proceeds from sale of assets. Free cash flow is considered a non-GAAP financial measure under the rules of the Securities and Exchange Commission. We believe that free cash flow is a relevant indicator of our ability to repay maturing debt, revise our dividend policy, or fund other uses of capital that we believe will enhance stockholder value. Free cash flow is limited and does not represent remaining cash flows available for discretionary expenditures due to the fact that the measure does not deduct the payments required for debt maturities and other obligations or payments made for business acquisitions. Therefore, we believe it is important to view free cash flow in addition to, rather than as a substitute for, our entire statement of cash flows and those measures prepared in accordance with GAAP.

The following table reconciles net cash provided by operating activities of continuing operations, the most directly comparable GAAP measure, to free cash flow, a non-GAAP financial measure.

	($ in millions)		
	2008	**2007**	**2006**
Net cash provided by operating activities of continuing operations (GAAP measure)	$1,155	$1,249[a]	$1,258[a]
Less:			
Capital expenditures	(969)	(1,243)	(772)
Dividends paid, common	(178)	(174)	(153)
Plus:			
Proceeds from sale of assets	13	26	20
Free cash flow (a non-GAAP financial measure)	$21	$(142)	$353

[a] Includes a $300 million discretionary cash contribution to our qualified pension plan in 2006. The approximately $110 million tax benefit related to the 2006 contribution was realized in 2007. No such contributions were made in 2008 or 2007.

Notwithstanding the difficult operating conditions in 2008, we generated $21 million of positive free cash flow, an improvement of $163 million over 2007.

Source: JCPenney 2009 10K.

For Penney, beginning with Operating Cash Flow, adding asset sales and subtracting capital expenditures would have endorsed the most commonly used industry and analyst definition. Its subtraction of common stock dividends is acceptable because free cash flow is meant to include distributable cash. A review of financial filings reveals that a large number of company's tailor-make their own formula.

For example, U.S. Concrete includes properties acquired, including the purchase of competitor's assets, in its interpretation.

Example:

We define free cash flow as net cash provided by operating activities less purchases of property, plant, and equipment (net of disposals). Free cash flow is a liquidity measure not prepared in accordance with GAAP. Our management uses free cash flow in managing our business because we consider it to be an important indicator of our ability to service our debt and generate cash for acquisitions and other strategic investments. We believe free cash flow may provide users of our financial information additional meaningful comparisons between current results and results in prior operating periods. As a non-GAAP financial measure, free cash flow should be viewed in addition to, and not as an alternative for, our reported operating results or cash flow from operations or any other measure of performance prepared in accordance with GAAP.

Our historical net cash provided by operating activities and free cash flow is as follows (in thousands):

	Year Ended December 31		
	2008	**2007**	**2006**
Net cash provided by operating activities	$29,678	$44,338	$39,537
Less: Purchases of properties and equipment, net of disposals of $4,403, $2,574, and $3,699	(23,380)	(27,145)	(38,232)
Free cash flow	$6,298	$17,193	$1,305

Source: U.S. Concrete 2008 10K.

Example:

Dun & Bradstreet

We define free cash flow as net cash provided by operating activities minus capital expenditures and additions to computer software and other intangibles.

Example:

Monsanto

We define free cash flow as the total of net cash provided or required by operating activities and net cash provided or required by investing activities.

Monsanto's definition leaves much to its own interpretation regarding cash required in its investing activities. Is it purely capital expenditures? The answer is no, because the timing of Monsanto's short-term debt maturity schedule can influence its defined free cash flow. During 2008, capital expenditures from its statement of cash flows were $918 million and for 2007 they were $507 million. Obviously, Monsanto's definition can lead to easy manipulation. The timing and classification of the investment items must be reviewed with a determination of whether they are normal for Monsanto.

Cash Flow

	Year Ended Aug. 31,		
(Dollars in Millions)	**2008**	**2007**	**2006**
Net cash provided by operating activities	**$2,799**	$1,854	$1,674
Net cash required by investing activities	**(2,027)**	(1,911)	(625)
Free cash flow[a]	772	(57)	1,049
Net cash required by financing activities	**(102)**	(583)	(117)
Effect of exchange-rate changes on cash and cash equivalents	**77**	46	3
Net increase (decrease) in cash and cash equivalents	**747**	(594)	935
Cash and cash equivalents at beginning of period	**866**	1,460	525
Cash and cash equivalents at end of period	**$1,613**	$866	$1,460

[a]Free cash flow represents the total of net cash provided or required by operating activities and provided or required by investing activities (see the "Overview—Non-GAAP Financial Measures" section of MD&A for a further discussion).

From Monsanto's statement of cash flows:

Cash flows provided (required) by investing activities:			
Purchases of short-term investments	**(132)**	(59)	(171)
Maturities of short-term investments	**59**	22	300
Capital expenditures	**(918)**	(509)	(370)
Acquisitions of businesses, net of cash acquired	**(1,007)**	(1,679)	(258)
Purchases of long-term equity securities	**(78)**	—	—
Technology and other investments	**(41)**	(54)	(147)
Proceeds from sale of Stoneville and NexGen businesses (see Note 27)	—	317	—
Other investments and property disposal proceeds	**90**	51	21
Net Cash Required by Investing Activities	**(2,027)**	(1,911)	(625)

Source: Monsanto 2008 10K.

A customed-tailored definition reported by Century Aluminum.

Example:

Century Aluminum excludes capital expenditures related to a certain plant expansion and increase in that project's short-term cash. As the company reports in its 2007 10K:

> We define free cash flow as net cash (used in) provided by operating activities less capital expenditures (other than capital expenditures related to the expansion of Grundartangi) and including the net increase in short-term investments due to their liquidity. Our calculation of free cash flow may not be comparable to similarly titled measures reported by other companies due to differences in the components used in its calculation.

Example:

Comfort Systems adds back taxes paid from the sale of businesses because it was subtracted from net operating cash flows. Unlike JCPenney, Comfort Systems reports free cash flows exclusive of its dividend payments. It deducts "customary" capital spending.

	Year ended December 31 (in Thousands)		
	2005	**2006**	**2007**
Cash provided by (used in):			
Operating activities	$37,446	$17,734	$83,642
Investing activities	$(6,769)	$17,721	$(18,132)
Financing activities	$(7,660)	$(762)	$(16,165)
Free cash flow:			
Cash provided by operating activities	$37,446	$17,734	$83,642
Taxes paid related to the sale of businesses	—	7,020	—
Purchases of property and equipment	(6,188)	(8,113)	(11,088)
Proceeds from sales of property and equipment	696	477	265
Free cash flow	$31,954	$17,118	$72,819

> *Cash Flow*—We define free cash flow as cash provided by operating activities excluding items related to sales of businesses, less customary capital expenditures, plus the proceeds from asset sales. Positive free cash flow represents funds available to invest in significant operating initiatives, to acquire other companies, or to reduce a company's outstanding debt or equity. If free cash flow is negative, additional debt or equity is generally required to fund the outflow of cash. Free cash flow may be defined differently by other companies.

Our business does not require significant amounts of investment in long-term fixed assets. The substantial majority of the capital used in our business is working capital that funds our costs of labor and installed equipment deployed in project work until our customers pay us. Customary terms in our industry allow customers to withhold a small portion of the contract price until after we have completed the work, typically for six months. Amounts withheld under this practice are known as retention or retainage. Our average project duration together with typical retention terms generally allow us to complete the realization of revenue and earnings in cash within one year. Accordingly, we believe free cash flow, by encompassing both profit margins and the use of working capital over our approximately one year working capital cycle, is an effective measure of operating effectiveness and efficiency. We have included free cash flow information here for this reason, and because we are often asked about it by third parties evaluating us. However, free cash flow is not considered under generally accepted accounting principles to be a primary measure of an entity's financial results, and accordingly free cash flow should not be considered an alternative to operating income, net income, or amounts shown in our consolidated statements of cash flows as determined under generally accepted accounting principles.

Free cash flow plays such a leading role in decision making and planning that a few creditors have begun taking it into consideration when formulating debt repayment schedules. This should help borrowers in their long-range planning and allow for a healthier enterprise. One might wonder, though, if, by basing interest payments on free cash flow, it might cause a borrower to manipulate its balance sheet to lower upcoming obligations or perhaps assume greater risks, which could negate free cash flow. As a term of some loans by private equity groups, free cash flow is being used as a condition of an earn-out—if free cash flow exceeds a predetermined level, the acquirer or lender receives additional equity.

Example:

Debt

	December 31, 2005	December 31, 2004
Debt consists of the following:		
1. Revolving credit at lender prime rate (7.00 percent) at December 31, 2005, plus 0.75 percent, interest payable monthly. Secured by receivables and inventory.	$6,193,000	$10,195,000
2. $900,000 mortgage note secured by Hope, AK, property. Monthly principal payments of $13,687. Monthly interest due at bank prime (7.00 percent) plus 2 percent on unpaid principal balance. Term of note 7 years.	762,000	866,000
3. Promissory notes payable, non-interest-bearing. Payable in 28 payments quarterly through 1st qtr. 2005.	-0-	6,000
4. Earn-out notes payable, non-interest-bearing. Contingent on the availability of defined free cash flow, payable up to $500,000 annually in years 2005–2009.	1,793,000	1,793,000

	December 31, 2005	December 31, 2004
5. Asset purchase promissory note payable. Payable monthly. Contingent on attaining certain sales levels.	130,000	130,000
Total debt	**$8,878,000**	**$12,990,000**
Less portion due within one year	**109,000**	**110,000**
Total long-term debt	**$8,769,000**	**$12,880,00**

Source: Champion Parts 2007 10K.

Figure 4-1 illustrates, by industry, major Standard and Poor's (S&P) industry groups based on their 3-year average free cash flow.[1] Although the consumer

FIGURE 4-1

Free-Cash-Flow Multiples by S&P 500 Industries

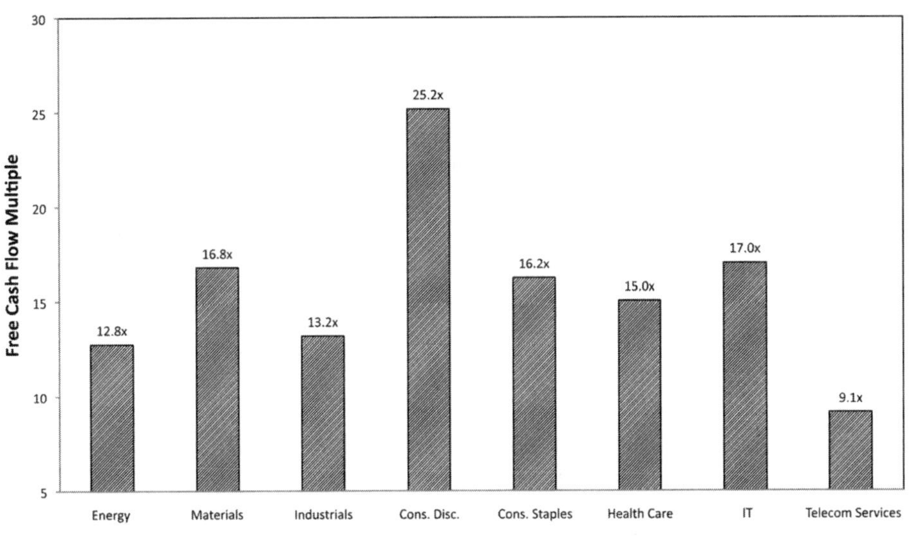

[1] The determination of the period on which to average cash flows is based on the company, industry, and desire to include an economic cycle while incorporating the current and forward capital structure. In this book I use both 3- and 4-year average free cash flow because both metrics currently include economic expansion and contraction. Since the economic expansion began in 2009, in 2011, the analyst would prefer the 4-year measure. In my cost-of-capital worksheet, I include periods as far back as 10 years, although the older periods carry less weight.

discretionary stocks shows the highest valuation multiple, it is a result of falling cash flows; the consumer staple stocks actually turned in the best relative performance, not surprising given the period of economic weakness. Financial stocks are excluded because many of the companies had negative free cash flow.

When accounting rules distort the relation between cash and reported income, cash-flow analysis becomes increasingly important. Because entities typically define free cash flow using a mix of GAAP and non-GAAP components, though, they fall short of the measure's purpose—that of providing the maximum return to the business owners without impairing future growth in free cash flow.

TAXES

Taxes are an important focal point of securities analysis owing to their scope, size, and direct and measurable impact on cash flows. Taxes impair current and prospective operating cash flows because taxes are imposed on residual profits—the only question is the degree. Investment projects are always considered on an after-tax basis from both the income tax effect and the financing effect. Special tax incentives also may affect the hurdle rate and project return in invested capital (ROIC). *Because taxes are not imposed on the income an enterprise pays as interest to creditors, the income tax system creates a bias in favor of debt financing.* This bias often results in the overuse of leverage by some firms and a greater probability of bankruptcy.

A change in the marginal tax rate will influence the amount of capital firms invest by changing the cost of debt capital. This is so because the tax shield will become either larger or smaller, resulting in greater or diminished project free cash flow.

Some industries are, by their nature (i.e., mature, stable, no non-U.S. income), subject to heavier taxation, whereas others, owing to their jurisdiction, are subject to tax benefits. Changes in tax rates can impair cash flows or allow for relief. Tax holidays can provide a temporary salve and must be monitored for the holiday's end. For example, Stanley Works, Inc., stated in its 2008 10K: "Tax holidays resulted in a reduction of tax expense amounting to $2.7 million in 2008, $4.3 million in 2007, and $3.1 million in 2006. The tax holiday in Thailand is in place until 2010, while the tax holiday in China expires between 2009 and 2015."

Tax disputes leave shareholders in doubt as to the firm's real cash flows, whereas completion of a tax audit can provide relief in the form of certainty of prospective free cash flow. The loss of a tax dispute can trigger a loan-covenant violation if the payment reduces cash flows, or earnings, below that called for in the loan agreement.

The tax status may affect the choice of financing alternatives. For instance, a firm with loss carry-forwards, tax credits, or expected losses for tax purposes may wish to choose equity as a financing vehicle because it might not benefit from the deductibility of interest expense.

Taxes provide an impetus for shifting income between countries, including where to borrow. Entities that transact business in both high- and low-taxation jurisdictions may shift income by borrowing in high-tax countries. They also may shift income out of high-tax jurisdictions by financing a project in a high-tax country from loans from affiliates in a low-tax country. Some countries limit such a practice, including the United States.

Taxes represent one of the highest costs of doing business. In 2007, total corporate taxes amounted to $370 billion, according to the Congressional Budget Office (CBO). Entire organizations are uprooted in search of low-tax territories, often resulting in large cash savings. Certain industries, such as insurance and pharmaceuticals, have found success in such jurisdictions, engaging in a form of income tax "arbitrage," where they hold cash and earn income in low-tax countries and incur other expenses in high-tax countries. ALICO, a large insurer, does this between Japan and Eastern Europe. While this focus on tax minimization often has its intended benefits, it is not always the case. Attracting new employees is not always easy and can result in poor productivity as new hires ramp up the learning curve. The Tonka Toy Company's production shift from Minnesota to Mexico was a failure owing, in part, to poor productivity at the new facility.

The statutory federal rates are up to 35 percent in the United States, 30 percent in Japan, 33 percent in Europe, and 25 percent in China. When the federal statutory corporate income tax rate of 35 percent is added to the weighted average of state corporate income taxes, the resulting rate is 39.3 percent, as shown in Table 4-4. Companies holding cash offshore also may be subject to a repatriation tax that

TABLE 4-3

U.S. Corporate Income Tax Rates

Taxable Income Over	Not Over	Tax Rate
$0	$50,000	15 percent
50,000	75,000	25 percent
75,000	100,000	34 percent
100,000	335,000	39 percent
335,000	10,000,000	34 percent
10,000,000	15,000,000	35 percent
15,000,000	18,333,333	38 percent
18,333,333		35 percent

Source: Internal Revenue Code, Title 26, Subtitle A.

TABLE 4-4

Comparing U.S. State Corporate Taxes to the OECD

OECD Overall Rank	Country/State	Federal Rate Adjusted	Top State Corporate Tax Rate	Combined Federal and State Rate (Adjusted)[a]
	Iowa	35	12	41.6
	Pennsylvania	35	9.99	41.5
	Minnesota	35	9.8	41.4
	Massachusetts	35	9.5	41.2
	Alaska	35	9.4	41.1
	New Jersey	35	9.36	41.1
	Rhode Island	35	9	40.9
	West Virginia	35	9	40.9
	Maine	35	8.93	40.8
	Vermont	35	8.9	40.8
	California	35	8.84	40.7
	Delaware	35	8.7	40.7
	Indiana	35	8.5	40.5
	New Hampshire	35	8.5	40.5
	Wisconsin	35	7.9	40.1
	Nebraska	35	7.81	40.1
	Idaho	35	7.6	39.9
	New Mexico	35	7.6	39.9
	Connecticut	35	7.5	39.9
	New York	35	7.5	39.9
	Kansas	35	7.35	39.8
	Illinois	35	7.3	39.7
	Maryland	35	7	39.6
	North Dakota	35	7	39.6
1	**Japan**	**30**	**11.56**	**39.54**
	Arizona	35	6.968	39.5
	North Carolina	35	6.9	39.5
	Montana	35	6.75	39.4
	Oregon	35	6.6	39.3
2	**United States**	**35**	**6.57**	**39.27**
	Arkansas	35	6.5	39.2
	Tennessee	35	6.5	39.2
	Washington*	35	6.4	39.2
	Hawaii	35	6.4	39.2
3	**Germany**	**26.38**	**17.0**	**38.9**
	Michigan*	35	6	38.9
	Georgia	35	6	38.9
	Kentucky	35	6	38.9
	Oklahoma	35	6	38.9
	Virginia	35	6	38.9

OECD Overall Rank	Country/State	Federal Rate Adjusted	Top State Corporate Tax Rate	Combined Federal and State Rate (Adjusted)[a]
	Florida	35	5.5	38.6
	Louisiana	35	8	38.5
	Missouri	35	6.25	38.4
	Ohio	35	5.1	38.3
	Mississippi	35	5	38.3
	South Carolina	35	5	38.3
	Utah	35	5	38.3
	Colorado	35	4.63	38.0
	Alabama	35	6.5	37.8
4	**Canada**	**22.1**	**14**	**36.1**
	Texas*	35	1.6	36.0
	Nevada	35	0	35.0
	South Dakota	35	0	35.0
	Wyoming	35	0	35.0
5	**France**	**34.43**	**0**	**34.4**
6	**Belgium**	**33.99**	**0**	**33.99**
7	**Italy**	**33**	**0**	**33**
8	**New Zealand**	**33**	**0**	**33**
9	**Spain**	**32.5**	**0**	**32.5**
10	**Luxembourg**	**22.88**	**7.5**	**30.38**
11	**Australia**	**30**	**0**	**30**
12	**United Kingdom**	**30**	**0**	**30**
13	**Mexico**	**28**	**0**	**28**
14	**Norway**	**28**	**0**	**28**
15	**Sweden**	**28**	**0**	**28**
16	**Korea**	**25**	**2.5**	**27.5**
17	**Portugal**	**25**	**1.5**	**26.5**
18	**Finland**	**26**	**0**	**26**
19	**Netherlands**	**25.5**	**0**	**25.5**
20	**Austria**	**25**	**0**	**25**
21	**Denmark**	**25**	**0**	**25**
22	**Greece**	**25**	**0**	**25**
23	**Czech Republic**	**24**	**0**	**24**
24	**Switzerland**	**8.50**	**14.64**	**21.32**
25	**Hungary**	**20**	**0**	**20**
26	**Turkey**	**20**	**0**	**20**
27	**Poland**	**19**	**0**	**19**
28	**Slovak Republic**	**19**	**0**	**19**
29	**Iceland**	**18**	**0**	**18**
30	**Ireland**	**12.5**	**0**	**12.5**

*Michigan, Texas, and Washington have gross receipts taxes rather than traditional corporate income taxes. For comparison purposes, we converted the gross receipts taxes into an effective CIT rate.

[a]Combined rate adjusted for federal deduction of state taxes paid.

Source: OECD, www.oecd.org/dataoecd/26/56/33717459.xls.

would need to be discounted by that rate. For example, Textron, during 2009, reported lower earnings in part owing to the year-earlier temporary tax benefit associated with repatriation of cash. Also seen in the table are the combined tax rates of U.S. states and various leading countries where many U.S. entities conduct business.

No wonder Ireland, with its 12.5 percent tax rate, has been so successful in attracting businesses from around the world. In general, small countries have lower tax rates. Differences in corporate tax rates affect where businesses decide to invest.

Because the U.S. tax code offers preferential treatment to equity holders in the form of capital gains, there is an incentive for corporations to invest in value-enhancing projects rather than pay out dividends.

Many states tax the portion of income attributable to income within their state. There are three states in the United States having a zero corporate tax rate, whereas Texas has a 1.6 percent rate. As states become hard pressed to balance their budgets, tax rates often increase, affecting corporate cash flows. Other times, large employers may enter treaties with states, fixing their rate at a reduced level for a specified period of time.

A low tax rate, defined as being below the statutory rate, raises a flag for an apparently healthy company and, as such, might provide a boost to free cash flow that might be unsustainable. For example, a company that enjoys the advantage of a tax-haven jurisdiction, such as Bermuda-based companies, would receive a severe jolt to their cash flows if that benefit were stripped away. If the tax benefit were removed, its effect on their market values could be dramatic.

Last in, first out (LIFO) accounting can lower the cash tax rate as input prices rise, but bear in mind, the entities adopting LIFO are required to use it for financial reporting purposes. If input prices fall, their taxes would rise. Shareholders' equity also will rise by the LIFO reserve.

Stock-based compensation often yields a tax deduction to the issuer regardless of whether the issuer has been expensing the awards for financial reporting purposes. It will be reported under operating activities only to the extent it relates to the accounting expense. If the credit is larger, it is considered a financing activity. The tax deduction takes place on the exercise, the granting of the options. For shareholder reporting, the issuer expenses the fair value of the options, determined on the grant date. The tax benefit, for shareholder reporting, is shown as an increase to shareholders equity because GAAP does not allow an entity to record a tax deduction for excess tax benefits, as is illustrated in the following example, of Globecomm, Inc., in its 2009 10K.

> During the year ended June 30, 2008, based on positive evidence from our earnings trends, we recognized a portion of our deferred tax assets through a reduction in our deferred tax asset valuation allowance of approximately $12.5 million. As of June 30, 2007, we maintained a full

> valuation allowance against our deferred tax assets due to our prior history of pre-tax losses and uncertainty about the timing of and ability to generate taxable income in the future and our assessment that the realization of the deferred tax assets did not meet the "more likely than not" criterion under FAS 109. At June 30, 2009 and 2008, we had a deferred tax valuation allowance of approximately $6.6 million primarily relating to $6.2 million from net operating losses related to excess stock based compensation expense deductions. If the remaining valuation allowance for the excess stock based compensation were to be reversed, the amount would be recorded to additional paid-in capital as it is attributable to the tax effects of excess compensation deductions from exercises of employee stock options.

Federal income taxpayers that receive income (cash flows) from tax-exempt securities would be placed into a higher tax bracket if that benefit somehow were curbed or if those assets were replaced with productive assets. Also, compensation for corporate officers greater than $1 million cannot be deducted from income unless such compensation is paid pursuant to shareholders approval on attainment of specified performance objectives. If this Internal Revenue Service (IRS) provision were to change, so too might the tax rate.

If there is settlement of a lawsuit, the amount of the payment should be adjusted to taxes because the payments normally are tax deductable. In general, deductibility depends on whether the expenditures stem from actions taken in the ordinary conduct of business or, instead, have their origin in a capital transaction, such as an acquisition. Expenditures of the latter are not deductible. For a settlement, taxes would be due.

In a business combination where there is a recapitalization, in which the assets are restructured and there is no step up with respect to purchase price and the net assets acquired, there is no transactional goodwill. Generally, all goodwill is nondeductible for tax purposes unless it arises from an asset sale or a deemed asset sale under the tax code, where it is amortized over 15 years using the straight-line method. Therefore, nondeductible goodwill has a tax basis of zero.

To the extent that an entity is able to enjoy a consistently low cash tax rate, the advantage will accrue to both creditors and shareholders. When I studied the investment returns for companies having cash tax rates of 35 percent and above and those having a tax rate of 0 to 20 percent, I found that the low-rate companies (having a $250 million minimum market value) outperformed for the five-year period ending October 2009, having a 9.1 percent median total return versus a median 6.6 percent total return for the high taxpayers. It was only when I introduced the tax-stability measures, as described in Chapter 8, that I found that stable payers outperformed the unstable payers by 9.5 to 3.1 percent during the identical period.

Consistent tax rate companies at any level normally also have cash flows that are more predictable. This makes sense because the tax provision is mostly a residual of the firm's operating success. The stable rate allows executives to plan better and accept projects more readily owing to a stable return on investment (ROI). It was not a surprise that when searching for clues of the impending bankruptcy of Enron, an inconsistent tax rate was one that stood out, along with its use of "mark-to-market" accounting to prop up values.

Oracle Corporation's income in low-tax jurisdictions enables the company to lower its cash tax rate significantly, the company claiming that those overseas funds that generated the income were permanently invested in those countries.

	Year Ended May 31 (in Millions)		
	2009	2008	2007
Tax provision at statutory rate	$2,742	$2,742	$2,095
Foreign earnings at other than U.S. rates	(673)	(569)	(580)
State tax expense, net of federal benefit	201	135	98
Settlement of audits and expiration of statutes, net	(28)	(20)	(29)
Other	(1)	25	128
Total provision for income taxes	$2,241	$2,313	$1,712

Source: Oracle Corp. 2009 10K.

By permanently investing capital in low-tax-rate geographies, an enterprise is able to enjoy lower foreign tax rates without being subject to the full U.S. rate. Should entities that, for years, have low tax rates owing to non-U.S. operating profits be penalized with a higher cost of capital? Yes, because it does present a potential risk, although the "hit" to cost of equity capital could be only slight, depending on the individual country risk in which such companies operate, as well as the percentage of total free cash flow received from those countries. In certain foreign jurisdictions, exchange controls make it difficult to repatriate cash back to the United States.

For the analyst, taxes represent more than a use or source (refund) of cash. They can provide an important clue as to the stability of the cash flows and, at times, provide a short-term forecast of year-end results.

As illustrated in an upcoming example, Airgas Corp. received a tax refund in a year they reported $54.8 million in net income to shareholders. The *Statement of Financial Accounting Standards No. 95, Statement of Cash Flows* (SFAS 95), classifies income tax payments as cash flow from operating activities, even though some income tax payments relate to gains and losses on investing and financing activities, such as gains and losses on plant asset disposals and early debt extinguishments. Table 4-5 provides a list of companies where there is a disparity between the effective tax rate and cash income taxes paid given their reported net income. The four columns at the right are the most revealing.

TABLE 4-5

Taxes Disparity Between Taxes Paid and Effective Rate

Company Name	Ticker Symbol	Effective Rate[-1Y]	Effective Rate[0Y]	Income Taxes Paid[-1Y]	Income Taxes Paid[0Y]	Net Income (Loss)	Income (Loss)[0Y]
CAMERON INTERNATIONAL CORP	CAM	31.917	26.027	159.680	231.171	593.726	475.519
CARDINAL HEALTH INC	CAH	32.511	31.446	116.000	429.300	1,300.600	1,151.600
CHICAGO BRIDGE & IRON CO	CBI	166.334	39.000	62.405	113.403	(21.146)	174.289
EASTMAN KODAK CO	EK	16.819	(98.291)	145.000	225.000	(442.000)	(210.000)
EVEREST RE GROUP LTD	RE	77.564	14.088	10.955	111.831	(18.758)	806.989
FAIRFAX FINANCIAL HOLDINGS	FRFHF	30.913	17.825	483.800	823.300	1,473.800	856.800
IDT CORP	IDT	(4.705)	4.126	13.090	113.552	(224.330)	(155.449)
LUBRIZOL CORP	LZ	446.471	29.154	88.100	180.300	(66.100)	500.800
NIPPON TELEGRPH & TELE -ADR	NTT	38.482	33.545	2,376.675	4,073.122	6,361.102	5,432.970
PROGRESSIVE CORP-OHIO	PGR	68.511	32.077	258.000	461.700	(70.000)	1,057.500
PROLOGIS	PLD	(55.043)	(2.307)	67.300	234.600	(406.773)	22.773
SIMS METAL MANAGEMENT -ADR	SMS	33.547	(23.030)	138.149	191.729	414.190	(121.063)
SUNCOR ENERGY INC	SU	31.769	11.094	521.242	833.572	1,745.915	1,095.498
SUPERVALU INC	SVU	39.304	(2.735)	107.000	274.000	593.000	(2,855.000)
SYMANTEC CORP	SYMC	34.900	(3.406)	181.089	321.039	463.850	(6,728.870)
TOSHIBA CORP -ADR	TOSYY	44.366	(19.453)	1,074.310	1,437.990	1,274.130	(3,505.704)
WEATHERFORD INTL LTD	WFT	17.090	6.528	271.418	389.652	1,353.903	253.766
	Median	33.547	11.094	145.000	274.000	463.850	253.766

DEFERRED TAX ASSETS AND LIABILITIES

Deferred tax assets are recorded any time a firm has a greater expense for financial reporting purposes than for tax purposes. The asset reflects a likely reduction in future taxes and can result from a number of circumstances outside a reported loss from operations, including asset retirements, tax credits, and stock-based compensation. Companies must record a valuation allowance against the deferred asset to the extent that they might not be able to use the asset. They will recognize deferred tax assets and liabilities on their balance sheet based on the differences between the financial statement carrying values and the tax basis of the assets and liabilities.

During periods of rising prices, there is a boost to cash flows for those entities using the LIFO method through tax savings, thereby reducing the deferred tax asset (or creating or increasing a deferred liability).

When health care legislation was passed by the House of Representatives, many firms announced that an end to the Medicare subsidy would raise their taxes substantially. This was due to a 28 percent tax-free subsidy the federal government was providing to companies for reimbursement to their retired employees related to Part D (prescription drug) payments. Since under the new health care legislation the government subsidy will be taxed, Caterpillar and Deere announced that they would take over $250 million in charges related to a reduction in their deferred tax asset, which had been established based on the expectation that they would continue getting the tax-free subsidy, as was provided for under the tax law. The charges announced by Caterpillar and Deere were a current noncash impact but would affect cash if the firms continued their retiree reimbursement plan. Since the federal subsidy still would be received but no longer would be a deductable expense, future cash taxes would be affected, and hence the need to eliminate that portion of the deferred tax asset.

A deferred tax liability is incurred whenever a firm uses accelerated depreciation for tax purposes. Over the life of an asset, if the present value of the tax deductions for depreciation exceeds the present value of those deductions for shareholder purposes, the effective marginal corporate tax rate will be less than the statutory rate. Only if they are equal will the effective marginal rate equal the statutory rate.

Owing to losses occurring during 2008, many entities were forced to establish or increase their valuation reserves based on their historical taxable income and projected future taxable income, including the expected timing of the reversals of existing temporary differences. If the entities operated at a loss for an extended period of time, were unable to generate sufficient future taxable income, or if there was a material change in the effective tax rates or time period within which the underlying temporary differences become taxable or deductible, these entities could be required to record a valuation allowance against all or a significant portion of their deferred tax assets, which could increase their effective tax rate for such a period substantially. This could affect cash flows for those firms that used a simple definition of cash flow as net profit plus depreciation.

Any significant changes in statutory tax rates or the amount of a valuation allowance could have a material effect on the value of deferred tax assets and liabilities and the entity's reported financial results. For entities that record a foreign tax credit as part of the deferred tax asset, any change in applicable U.S. standards or governing tax rates overseas also would affect the tax asset or liability. If an entity records a deferred tax asset that currently carries a valuation allowance, it may record a reduction to income tax expense in the period of such realization.

Example:

Supplemental Cash-Flow Information

Airgas, Inc.

Cash Paid for Interest and Taxes

	Three Months Ended June 30 (in Thousands)	
	2009	**2008**
Interest paid	$24,773	$16,184
Discount on securitization	1,615	2,984
Income taxes (net of refunds)[a]	(6,635)	1,965

During the three months ended June 30, 2009, the company applied for and received a $10 million federal income tax refund. The refund related to an overpayment of fiscal year 2009 estimated federal income taxes as a result of a difference between actual and forecasted profitability, primarily in the fourth quarter.

[a]AIRGAS, INC., AND SUBSIDIARIES
CONSOLIDATED STATEMENTS OF CASH FLOWS
(Unaudited)

	Three Months Ended June 30, 2009	Three Months Ended June 30, 2008
Cash flows from operating activities:		
Net earnings	$54,816$	$68,883
Adjustments to reconcile net earnings to net cash provided by operating activities:		
Depreciation	51,583	48,098
Amortization	4,816	5,406
Deferred income taxes	15,641	23,455
(Gain) loss on sales of plant and equipment	252	(12)
Stock-based compensation expense	9,914	7,973
Changes in assets and liabilities, excluding effects of business acquisitions:		
Securitization of trade receivables	(15,900)	—
Trade receivables, net	16,986	(6,526)
Inventories, net	23,375	(9,874)

(Continued)

	Three Months Ended June 30, 2009	Three Months Ended June 30, 2008
Prepaid expenses and other current assets	5,603	2,563
Accounts payable, trade	(8,660)	(7,451)
Accrued expenses and other current liabilities	6,039	(3,613)
Other noncurrent assets	1,190	(542)
Other noncurrent liabilities	(3,396)	259
Net cash provided by operating activities	162,259	128,619
Cash flows from investing activities:		
Capital expenditures	(67,312)	(85,564)
Proceeds from sales of plant and equipment	2,510	3,329
Business acquisitions and holdback settlements	(2,863)	(21,680)
Other, net	(1,433)	(1,518)
Net cash used in investing activities	(69,098)	(105,433)
Cash flows from financing activities:		
Proceeds from borrowings	88,553	594,109
Repayment of debt	(163,977)	(596,080)
Purchase of treasury stock	—	(4,613)
Financing costs	—	(5,000)
Proceeds from the exercise of stock options	2,123	9,927
Stock issued for the employee stock purchase plan	3,888	3,934
Tax benefit realized from the exercise of stock options	1,334	7,280
Dividends paid to stockholders	(14,701)	(10,040)
Change in cash overdraft and other	2,163	(805)
Net cash used in financing activities	(80,617)	(1,288)
Change in cash	$12,544	$21,898
Cash—Beginning of period	47,188	43,048
Cash—End of period	$59,732	$64,946

Example:

Provision for Income Taxes

	Year Ended June 30 (in Thousands)			
	2008	2009	$ Change	Percent Change
Income before provision for income taxes	$48,788	$65,810	$17,022	34.9%
Provision for income taxes	17,688	11,486	(6,202)	−35.1%
Percent of income before provision for income taxes	36.3%	17.5%		
Percent of net revenue	4.9%	2.4%		

The provision for income taxes for the year ended June 30, 2009, was approximately $11.5 million compared with $17.7 million for the year ended June 30, 2008, reflecting higher pre-tax profits in lower tax rate jurisdictions, partially offset by an increase of valuation allowance related to impairment charges on certain investments. The income tax provision represented estimated federal, foreign, and state taxes for the years ended June 30, 2008, and 2009. The effective tax rate for the year ended June 30, 2008, was approximately 36.3 percent and diverged from the combined federal and state statutory rate primarily as a result of the incremental research credits associated with stock option activity and tax-exempt interest income, partially offset by the impact of impairment losses, foreign withholding taxes, and the accounting for share-based compensation. The effective tax rate for the year ended June 30, 2009, was approximately 17.5 percent and diverged from the combined federal and state statutory rate primarily as a result of an increase in profits in lower tax rate jurisdictions, the incremental research credits associated with stock option activity, and the extension of the federal research credit, and tax-exempt interest income, partially offset by the impact of accounting for share-based compensation and foreign withholding taxes.

In accordance with SFAS 123R, we recognize tax benefit upon expensing nonqualified stock options and deferred stock units issued under our share-based compensation plans. However, under current accounting standards, we cannot recognize tax benefit concurrent with expensing incentive stock options and employee stock purchase plan shares (qualified stock options) issued under our share-based compensation plans. For qualified stock options that vested after our adoption of SFAS 123R, we recognize tax benefit only in the period when disqualifying dispositions of the underlying stock occur, which historically has been up to several years after vesting and in periods when our stock price substantially increases. For qualified stock options that vested prior to our adoption of SFAS 123R, we record the tax benefit directly to additional paid-in capital. Tax benefit associated with total share-based compensation was approximately $6.1 million and $8.0 million for the years ended June 30, 2008 and 2009, respectively. Excluding the impact of share-based compensation and the related tax benefit, the effective tax rate for the years ended June 30, 2008 and 2009 would have been 35.9 percent and 21.6 percent, respectively. Because we cannot recognize the tax benefit for share-based compensation expense associated with qualified stock options until the occurrence of future disqualifying dispositions of the underlying stock and such disqualified dispositions may happen in periods when our stock price substantially increases, and because a portion of that tax benefit may be recorded directly to additional paid-in capital, our future quarterly and annual effective tax rates will be subject to greater volatility and, consequently, our ability to reasonably estimate our future quarterly and annual effective tax rates is greatly diminished.

Synaptics also lowered its investment in municipals:

	June 30, 2008			
	Amortized Cost	**Gross Unrealized Gains**	**Gross Unrealized Losses**	**Estimated Fair Value**
Money market	$70,756	$—	$—	$70,756
Commercial paper	28,319	—	—	28,319
U.S. Treasury bills	2,998	—	1	2,997
Municipal securities	41,201	133	—	41,334
Auction rate securities	40,412	—	2,466	37,946
Total available-for-sale securities	$183,686	$133	$2,467	$181,352

	June 30, 2009			
	Amortized Cost	Gross Unrealized Gains	Gross Unrealized Losses	Estimated Fair Value
Money market	$166,334	$—	$—	$166,334
Commercial paper	2,598	—	—	2,598
U.S. Treasury bills	7,992	3	—	7,995
Municipal securities	12,898	43	—	12,941
Auction rate securities	28,715	52	—	28,767
Total available-for-sale securities	$218,537	$98	$—	$218,635

Example:

Resulting from its large loss (carry-foward) for federal tax purposes reported under supplemental cash flow information, YRC Worldwide, Inc., received cash refunds its past two years despite positive effective tax rates. The instability in its effective tax rate would serve to increase the cost of equity capital because such instability, as explained in Chapter 8, is associated with higher-risk enterprises. Much of the tax-rate instability for YRC is caused by the impairment of tax-deductible goodwill, which allowed for the speedup of the deduction, thereby lowering the effective and real rate. SFAS 142 requires annual and periodic tests relating to the impairment of goodwill.

The following charts are taken from YRC's 2008 10K:

Supplemental cash-flow information:			
Income taxes paid (refund), net	$(46,463)	$(48,132)	$109,500
Interest paid	70,945	84,076	90,072
Employer 401(k) contributions settled in common stock	8,108	9,548	7,38

A reconciliation between income taxes at the federal statutory rate and the consolidated effective tax rate follows:

	2008	2007	2006
Federal statutory rate	35.0%	35.0%	35.0%
State income taxes, net	0.5	0.2	2.7
Goodwill impairment	(21.0)	(34.3)	—
Nondeductible business expenses	(0.4)	(0.7)	1.1
Foreign tax credit and rate differential	(1.4)	(0.1)	0.2
Alternative fuel tax credit	0.6	1.4	—
Other, net	1.5	0.5	0.3
Effective tax rate	14.8%	2.0%	39.3%

Example:

Union Drilling, Inc., provides contract land drilling services primarily to natural gas producers in the United States. In its footnoted table on income taxes, taken from its 2008 10K, the company reported a higher than effective statutory 35 percent tax rate, even though, through "bonus" depreciation legislation passed as part of the 2008 U.S. economic stimulus package, Union Drilling used accelerated depreciation for taxes (temporary difference) and was entitled to a small cash refund.

The higher than effective tax rate primarily results, in part, from meal allowances, for which only 50 percent is permitted for tax purposes, but is totally expensed for shareholder reporting and the write-off of goodwill for shareholder reporting, which was not deductible for tax reporting. These are two examples of permanent timing differences.

Total income tax expense differed from the amounts computed by applying the U.S. statutory federal income tax rate to income before income taxes as a result of the following (in thousands):

	2008	2007	2006
U.S. statutory federal income tax rate	35%	35%	35%
Income tax expense at the statutory federal tax rate	$7,126	$18,498	$18,994
State, local, and provincial income taxes, net of federal tax benefit	755	2,322	2,382
Meal allowances	1,962	1,924	1,559
Noncash compensation	130	96	235
Goodwill and intangibles impairment charge	3,062	—	350
Domestic production deduction	—	(549)	(343)
Decrease in unrecognized tax benefits	(276)	—	—
Deferred tax adjustment	—	(169)	(693)
Other	(148)	(102)	(66)
Income tax expense	$12,611	$22,020	$22,418

Example:

In order to incentivize energy exploration, the U.S. Congress passed legislation potentially boosting the cash flows of the industry through tax incentives. Hopeful companies would take advantage by increasing exploration, resulting in the nation having less reliance on imported oil. The use of accelerated depreciation for tax purposes relative to shareholder reporting also helps minimize current cash taxes paid, resulting in a temporary timing difference.

In its 2008 fiscal year, Exxon Mobil reported a $16.062 billion net deferred tax liability on its balance sheet. As long as Exxon continues to grow its exploration budget and Congress does not change the tax law, an analyst can presume that this liability will continue to grow indefinitely. The other item causing the large deferred tax liability relates to intangible development costs.

Exploration companies can expense for tax purposes a large percentage of intangible items related to the exploration process, which are expenditures having no salvageable value. For instance, clearing land, repairs, fuel, and even mud placed on the rig fit into the category, whereas piping would not. The items are capitalized for shareholder reporting purposes. We also see that Exxon Mobil capitalized interest expense related to its exploration programs.

Tax Effects of Temporary Differences for	**2008 (Millions of Dollars)**	**2007 (Millions of Dollars)**
Depreciation	$17,279	$18,810
Intangible development costs	5,578	4,890
Capitalized interest	2,751	2,575
Other liabilities	3,589	3,955
Total deferred tax liabilities	$29,197	$30,230
Pension and other postretirement benefits	$(6,275)	$(3,837)
Tax loss carry-forwards	(2,850)	(2,162)
Other assets	(5,274)	(5,848)
Total deferred tax assets	$(14,399)	$(11,847)
Asset valuation allowances	1,264	637
Net deferred tax liabilities	$16,062	$19,020

Deferred income tax (assets) and liabilities are included in the balance sheet, as shown below. Deferred income tax (assets) and liabilities are classified as current or long term consistent with the classification of the related temporary difference—separately by tax jurisdiction.

Balance Sheet Classification	**2008 (Millions of Dollars)**	**2007 (Millions of Dollars)**
Other current assets	$(2,097)	$(2,497)
Other assets, including intangibles, net	(1,725)	(1,451)
Accounts payable and accrued liabilities	158	69
Deferred income tax liabilities	19,726	22,899
Net deferred tax liabilities	$16,062	$19,020

In its 2008 income statement and income tax footnote, Exxon Mobil reports a 47 percent effective tax rate amounting to $36,530 million. We discover from the footnote, "Cash Flow Information," that the company actually made cash tax payments for the year of $33,942 million, or $2.6 billion less.

Table 4-6 depicts Exxon Mobil's actual tax payments versus the amount it accrued in the income statement for the 10 years ending December 2008. Exxon

Mobil paid $161.8 billion in total taxes versus the $177 billion shown in the income statements under the effective rate.

TABLE 4-6

Exxon Mobil Actual Taxes Paid versus Accrued

	Cash Paid	Accrued
1998	2,718	2,616
1999	3,805	3,240
2000	8,671	11,091
2001	9,855	9,014
2002	6,106	6,499
2003	8,149	11,006
2004	13,510	15,911
2005	22,535	23,302
2006	26,165	27,902
2007	26,342	29,864
2008	33,941	36,530
Total	161,797	176,975

As is taken from CT Capital's credit model (discussed in Chapter 8), from which we determine cost of equity capital, Exxon Mobil is not penalized for income tax stability, meaning that it has a stable rate, whether using accrued or actual tax payments. The stability rate of 0 represents the markup to the cost of capital resulting from the tax payment rate changing by more than 10 percent from the prior year or exceeding other stability measures, as explained in Chapter 8.

Tax stability:	
Tax expense/pretax income	42%
Tax payment/pretax income	39%
Stability of tax rate	0
Tax expense/pretax income (most recent quarter)	46%

Source: CT Capital, LLC, September 18, 2009.

Example:

Archer Daniels Midland Company (ADM) is one of the world's largest processors of oilseeds, corn, wheat, cocoa, and other feedstuffs and is a leading manufacturer of vegetable oil and protein meal, corn sweeteners, flour, biodiesel, ethanol, and other value-added food and feed ingredients. Its 2009 10K shows the reporting effect when deferred taxes are reversed. In this instance, Archer Daniels had invested in an overseas entity (WIHL), where it claimed the funds were permanently invested. During 2009, ADM began liquidation of WIHL, and thus Archer Daniels could no longer make this claim and had to reverse the tax benefit. Fortunately, its consolidated tax rate, owing to other jurisdictional benefits, overcame this, bringing the company below the statutory rate. As we see from its segments and geographic information, owing to the U.S. recession, over half the company's sales came from "other foreign" during 2009, including South America, where the tax rate is low.

	2009	2008	2007
Net sales and other operating income			
United States	**$35,485**	$37,466	$24,244
Germany	**7,431**	8,335	6,569
Other foreign	**26,291**	24,015	13,205
	$69,207	$69,816	$44,018

Archer Daniels Midland Income Taxes

	2009 (Millions of Dollars)	2008 (Millions of Dollars)
Deferred tax liabilities		
Property, plant, and equipment	**$599**	$592
Equity in earnings of affiliates	**142**	272
Inventory reserves	**64**	28
Other	**80**	36
	$885	$928
Deferred tax assets		
Pension and postretirement benefits	**$301**	$156
Purchased call options	**78**	98
Stock compensation	**59**	53
Tax credit carryforwards, net	**36**	43
Reserves and other accruals	**19**	9
Other	**153**	96
	$646	$455
Net deferred tax liabilities	**$239**	$473
Current deferred tax liabilities included in accrued expenses	**(9)**	—
Noncurrent deferred tax liabilities	**$230**	$473

Reconciliation of the statutory federal income tax rate with the company's effective tax rate on earnings is as follows:

	2009	2008	2007
Statutory rate	**35.0%**	35.0%	35.0%
State income taxes, net of federal tax benefit	**1.0**	1.3	1.4
Foreign earnings taxed at rates other than the U.S. statutory rate	**(9.2)**	(4.6)	(2.9)
WIHL liquidation	**6.6**	—	—
Adjustment of income taxes to filed tax returns	**(0.1)**	0.2	(0.4)
Other	**(0.7)**	(0.6)	(1.6)
Effective rate	**32.6%**	31.3%	31.5%

QUARTERLY EFFECTIVE TAX RATES

It is not unusual for entities to overaccrue a reported tax rate during early quarters of the year, leaving themselves a cushion for later in the year. Table 4-7 shows the quarterly effective tax rates reported to shareholders of General Electric (GE) and, in the second column, the eventual effective rate for that year. For the five years shown, GE management overaccrued in each of their first quarters, based on the final rate. Whether GE was attempting to manage earnings for later in the year cannot be stated with certainty, although the consistency is obvious because GE's fourth quarter had its lowest effective rate in all periods shown. The investor should be aware of the effective quarterly rate and what signals it may mean for management's expectation for full-year results. As depicted in the case of Kellogg, which, unlike GE, has a high effective rate, the fourth quarter rate often has been the highest reported rate of its fiscal year, with quarterly swings not as pronounced as with GE, especially the first quarter estimated rate compared with the full-year rate. Unquestionably, quarterly effective rates give management a tool to manipulate earnings and operating cash flows over the very short term and present another reason one should look toward free cash flow and actual tax payments.

OTHER TAX CREDITS

Tax credits allow a firm to potentially lower cash taxes due. They can be in the form of a credit applied against the actual tax rate or a direct dollar-for-dollar credit against taxes otherwise due. This is true for both U.S. and foreign taxes.

TABLE 4-7

Quarterly and Yearly Effective Tax Rate–General Electric and Kellogg

	Kellogg Co.		General Electric	
	Tax Rate (Qtly)	Tax Rate (Year)	Tax Rate (Qtly)	Tax Rate (Year)
Mar 04	35.5		23.6	
Jun 04	33.6		15.1	
Sep 04	34.5		18.6	
Dec 04	35.9	34.8	14.9	17.3
Mar 05	32.0		18.8	
Jun 05	33.1		16.6	
Sep 05	30.0		19.7	
Dec 05	29.1	31.2	14.4	17.2
Mar 06	32.0		18.4	
Jun 06	31.3		17.8	
Sep 06	32.0		15.1	
Dec 06	31.4	31.7	14.7	15.5
Mar 07	24.1		19.3	
Jun 07	31.9		20.1	
Sep 07	26.7		10.8	
Dec 07	33.8	28.7	10.4	15.0
Mar 08	30.3		15.7	
Jun 08	29.9		15.9	
Sep 08	28.1		10.4	
Dec 08	31.4	29.7	−52.7	5.3

For example, under the Tax Reform Act of 1986, the U.S. government incentivized the formation of affordable housing aimed at low-income Americans. The credit, because it provides a direct reduction in taxes otherwise due, has economic value for profitable enterprises. As the U.S. economy was expanding, low-income-housing tax credits (LIHTC) traded at premiums, but as the United States entered recession, companies such as FNMA, which had large unusable credits, were forced to write down their value.

Tax credits are shown as an operating item on the cash-flow statement under U.S. GAAP only to the extent that they relate to the accounting expense; if the tax deduction exceeds the amount attributable to the accounting expense, such excess is a financing item.

Example:

This decreased demand has reduced the value of these investments. We determine the fair value of our LIHTC investments using internal models that estimate the present value of the expected future tax benefits (tax credits and tax deductions for net operating losses) expected to be generated from the properties underlying these investments. Our estimates are based on assumptions that other market participants would use in valuing these investments. The key assumptions used in our models, which require significant management judgment, include discount rates and projections related to the amount and timing of tax benefits. We compare the model results to the limited number of observed market transactions and make adjustments to reflect differences between the risk profile of the observed market transactions and our LITHC investments.

Source: FNMA March 2009 10Q.

In a related story, in November 2009, the financial press reported that Goldman Sachs was interested in buying million of dollars of such credits from FNMA, which would have the effect of lowering Goldman Sachs' tax bill while providing cash to FNMA.

Tax credits are incentives and can come from state, federal, or foreign authorities.[2] The goals of incentives vary—but always involve motivation—from labor force hiring, research or capital equipment expenditures, remittance of overseas earnings, purchase of certain securities, or prevention of unemployment, such as aid following natural disasters. They are aimed at improving the economic activity of the provider, with the ultimate goal of increased taxes in the longer run. The analyst should determine the continuing likelihood of such credits and the durational impact on cash flows. For example, in its 2009 10K, Graham Packaging Company, Inc., reported a higher than 35 percent statutory rate owing to the absence of tax benefits being recorded on losses in jurisdictions with valuation allowances and the inability to offset foreign tax credits against domestic tax expense because of net operating losses.

[2] The corporate foreign tax credit is a set of provisions designed by Congress to eliminate potential double taxation on the foreign-source income of U.S. corporations. Double taxation occurs when an item of income is taxed by both the United States, as the corporation's country of residence, and the country where the income was generated. The current provisions allow U.S. businesses to credit their foreign taxes paid, accrued, or deemed paid against their U.S. income tax liability, subject to limitations that prevent taxpayers from using taxes paid in a country with a higher tax rate than the United States to offset their tax liability on U.S. income. Corporations are required to calculate this credit separately for different income categories to prevent taxpayers from combining income that traditionally is taxed at low rates, such as dividend or interest income, with income that typically is taxed at higher rates, such as active business income. For additional information, go to IRS.gov.

Example:

Provision for Income Taxes

Our provision for income taxes increased $3.1 million, or 39.2 percent, from $8.0 million for the year ended December 31, 2007, to $11.1 million for the year ended December 31, 2008. We had an effective income tax rate of approximately 33.3 percent and 36.1 percent for the years ended December 31, 2007 and 2008, respectively. The 2007 effective income tax rate is lower primarily due to the 2007 federal tax credit related to Hurricane Katrina and higher tax exempt interest income for 2007.

Source: Odyssey HealthCare, Inc., 2008 10K.

STABILITY OF TAX RATE

Entities with stable businesses and cash flows have more predictable and steady tax rates. Entities with unstable businesses, either in sales, cost of sales, or operating cash flows, have more unpredictable tax rates, both the effective rate and the cash rate of the tax return. Unstable tax rates are not a surefire warning sign of trouble, but there is always a precipitating event or events that force the inconsistency—when tax rate levels are routinely low or volatile, the analyst should uncover the reason, especially if owing to business conditions, foreign income or credits, tax holidays, or clever bookkeeping. Investors cannot count on growing distributable cash with such volatility. For this reason, more stable rate payers enjoy lower cost of capital, on average. Uncertainty, even in tax planning, is the enemy of security valuation and credit analysis and, for this reason, is directly associated with the cost of capital.

As with Enron, we see a very volatile cash tax rate for General Motors (GM) prior to its declaring bankruptcy. There was no single period in the 10 years preceding GM's bankruptcy when their actual cash tax rate was stable (Fig. 4-2).

Under SFAS 95, the analyst is able to model the historic and expected stability of the company's financial performance more accurately because of the cash tax and cash interest information. As noted, an estimate (that was not always accurate) was necessary prior to SFAS 95. Since the analyst does not have access to actual tax-based profits or corporate tax returns, one needed to approximate the cash taxes from the income tax footnote.

GM was characterized by a very volatile effective tax rate as well. When reviewing the company's effective tax rate, we see somewhat greater stability until 2003, a time when the stock still was trading above $40 per share. By 2007, the company already reported 5 years of 10 percent swings in its effective tax rate (Fig. 4-3).

In the upcoming examples, for Kraft, Jo-Ann Stores, and Tesoro, depicted are the actual taxes paid/pretax income, the latter from the income statement. As long

FIGURE 4-2

General Motors' Cash Tax Rate

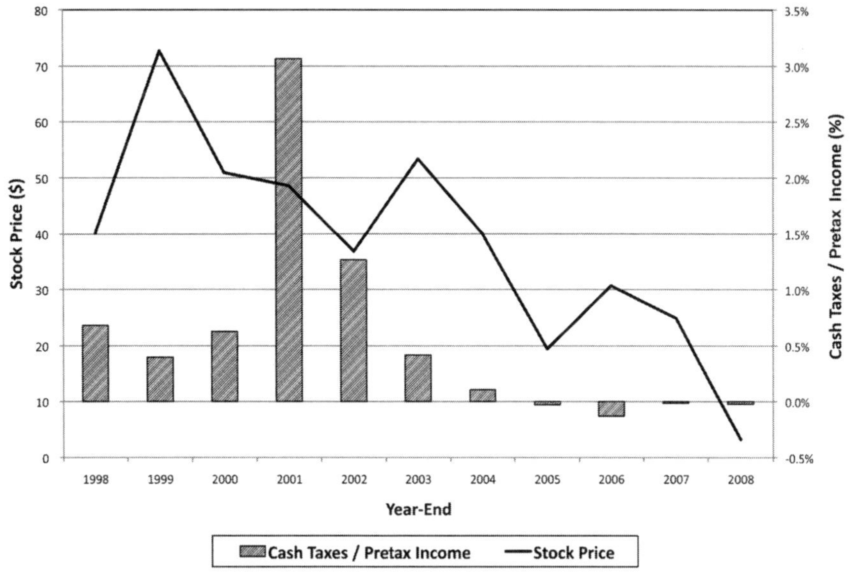

Source: Company filings.

FIGURE 4-3

General Motors' Effective Tax Rate

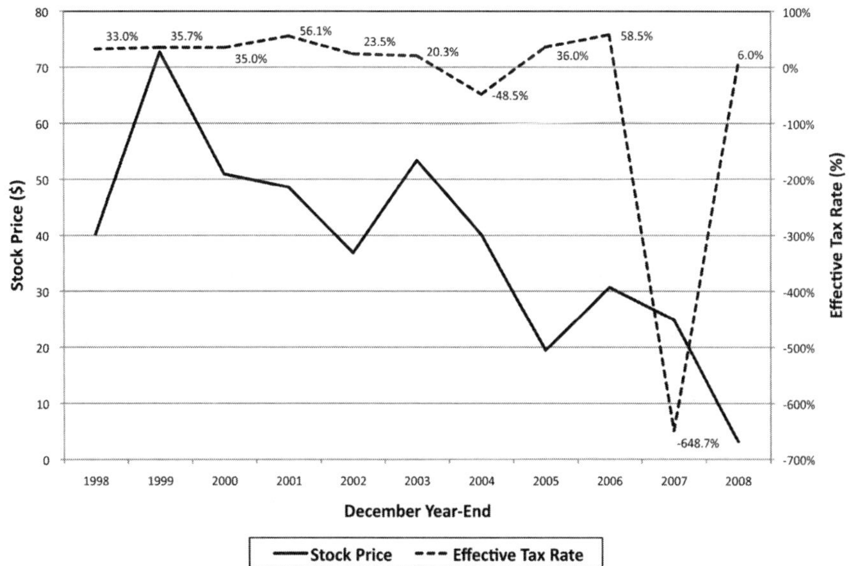

Source: Company filings.

as the cash tax rate, defined as taxes paid/pretax income, is applied consistently (including adding permanent differences), the result is meaningful in assessing stability. There are analysts who prefer to use earnings before interest, taxes, depreciation and amortization (EBITDA) as the denominator as a form of unlevered tax rate. To exclude interest and depreciation would not accurately reflect pretax income, even though those amounts would differ from the tax return.

As we see in the three charts in Figs. 4-4 through 4-6, Kraft, a stable-cash-flow company, shows a fairly steady tax rate (Fig. 4-4), in contrast to both Jo-Ann Stores and Tesoro. Each of these companies had small amounts of permanent timing differences, so there was no need to add that amount to pretax income in arriving at the cash tax rate.

Jo-Ann Stores, a specialty crafts retailer, historically has had an unstable tax rate, reflective of its underlying business, which likewise has shown inconsistent results. Notice the relationship for the years 1999–2005, when the company had a consistently high rate along with its increasing market value, and its subsequent tax volatility, along with the concurrent fluctuation in its market value (Fig. 4-5).

Tesoro, a large refiner and gasoline marketer, saw a large negative cash tax rate jump to a large positive rate, then down again, and then up again (Fig. 4-6).

FIGURE 4-4

Kraft: Approximate Cash Tax Rate versus Market Value

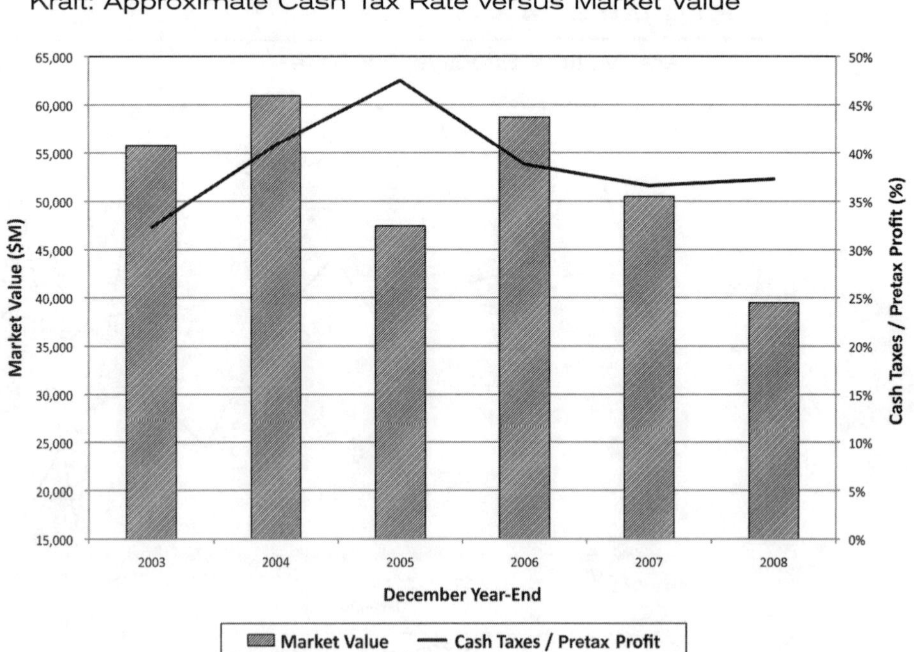

Source: CT Capital, LLC.

FIGURE 4-5

Jo-Ann Stores: Approximate Cash Tax Rate versus Market Value

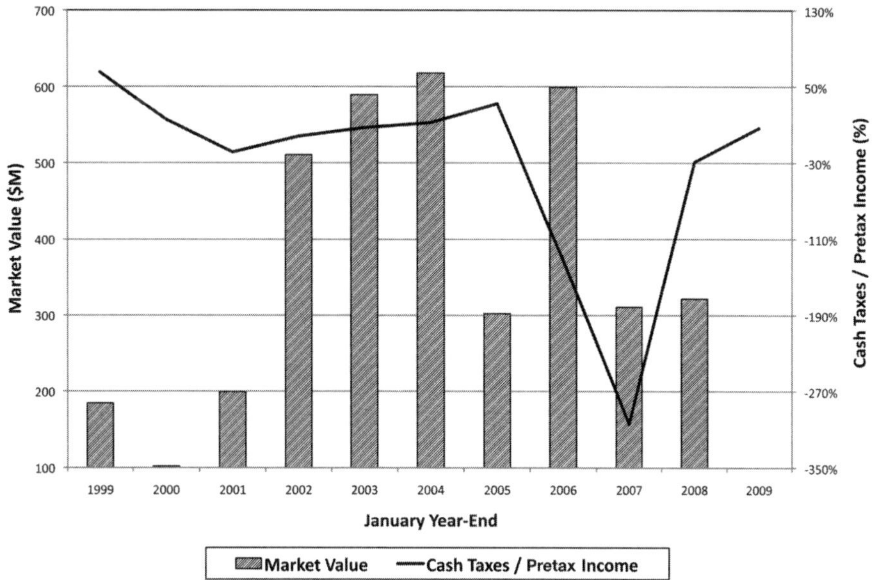

Source: CT Capital, LLC.

FIGURE 4-6

Tesoro Corp.: Approximate Cash Tax Rate versus Market Value

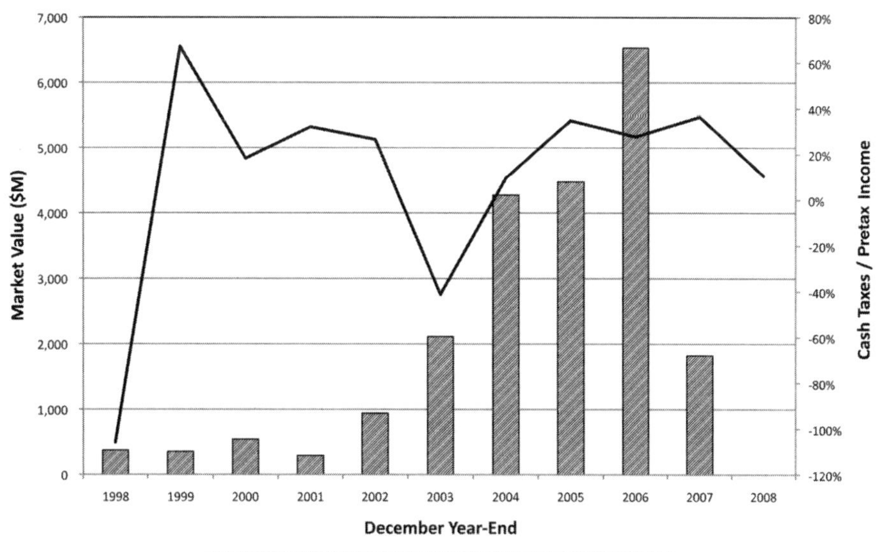

Its market value rose from $374 million to $541 million, back down to $292 million, then up to $6.5 billion, and then down to $1.8 billion. Tesoro, of course, has had a very unstable tax rate, reflective of its underlying business. Also of interest is Tesoro's beta, which at just 1.3, is considerably lower than GE's beta of 1.7, suggesting that Tesoro should be assigned a lower cost of equity capital by users of the popular capital asset pricing model (CAPM). Tesoro has a BB+ credit rating, and GE is rated AA+.

Example:

During 2006, Starwood Hotels sold 38 luxury hotels to Host Marriott, another publicly held company, for cash and stock (based on Host's share price at closing) valued at $4.1 billion The deal also included the assumption by Host of $600 million of debt associated with the hotels being purchased. In the second part of the deal, Starwood purchased from its shareholders, its class B preferred shares, ending the firm's listing as a real estate investment trust (REIT). The book value associated with the class B shares, because it involved a transaction with its shareholders, was treated as a nonreciprocal transaction[3] with owners and was removed through retained earnings up to the amount of retained earnings that existed at the sale date, with the remaining balance reducing additional paid-in capital. This class B portion was treated as a noncash transaction and therefore was excluded from the consolidated statement of cash flows.

The deal with Host resulted in a large year-end capital loss of $2.4 billion for federal tax purposes. Thus Starwood gained a large tax shield should it be in a taxable position going forward. Starwood also sold the stock consideration in Host that year for an approximate $1 billion gain, seen under investment activities as part of the $1.5 billion proceeds from asset sales, net.

On the other hand, Starwood, under the provisions of SFAS 144, *Accounting for the Impairment or Disposal of Long-Lived Assets*, was able to record and use a large income tax benefit for shareholder reporting, as well as tax purposes. We see $620 million of the benefit as noncash for 2006 reversed under cash flow from operations.

During the subsequent year, Starwood reduced its estimate of that capital loss and corresponding valuation allowance, perhaps owing to an IRS examination, to $1.4 billion of particular interest in 2006 is that the sale of the hotels involved a long-term management contract with Host under which Starwood would continue to manage the sold properties. The gain on the sale is allowed to be deferred and amortized over the life of the management contract, which is 20 years, in accordance with SFAS 144. On the statement of cash flows, the book income is reversed as noncash portion of deferred gains. In booking the gain each year, EBITDA is artificially boosted by about $48 million a year, based on the $955 million gain. Since Starwood typically sells properties under this arrangement, its deferred gains each year are significant.

From Starwood's 2006 10K:

> The portion of the transaction between the company and Host was recorded as a disposition under the provisions of SFAS No. 144. As Starwood sold these hotels subject to long-term management contracts, the calculated gain on the sale of approximately $955 million has been deferred and is being amortized over the initial management contract term of 20 years. This transaction also generated a capital loss, net of carry back and current year utilization, of $2.4 billion for federal tax purposes.

---

[3]A *nonreciprocal transaction* is a transferred asset without an attached condition, such as there is only a performance obligation.

Starwood used the cash received from Host Marriot to buy back stock of $1.3 billion and $1.5 billion in debt. The company also paid about 45 percent less in taxes than the year earlier, benefiting from the favorable tax treatment resulting in a low effective and real rate.

In its income tax footnote, Starwood reported that it had a year-end deferred tax asset on its balance sheet of $487 million. We see this in the $518 million asset and the $31 million deferred tax liability reflected on its balance sheet. This book asset, as stated in the footnote, predominantly emanates from the Host transaction; the year prior, the deferred asset was just $173 million. Of the $2.6 billion in capital losses generated by the Host transaction, $200 million was used during 2006 to offset prior-year gains, in the form of tax carry-backs (refunds), resulting in the year-end $2.4 billion remainder.

We also see in the income tax footnote that Starwood is claiming, among other items, a tax benefit of $832 million on the $2.4 billion capital loss generated for tax purposes. The $832 million is derived using a 34.7 percent tax rate ($\$2{,}400 \times 0.347 = \$832$).

Income Taxes

A reconciliation of the tax provision of the company at the U.S. statutory rate to the provision for income tax as reported is as follows (in million):

	Year Ended December 31		
	2006	**2005**	**2004**
Tax provision at U.S. statutory rate	$239	$225	$144
U.S. state and local income taxes	(10)	(14)	(37)
Exempt Trust income	(32)	(64)	(62)
Tax on repatriation of foreign earnings	(16)	11	13
Tax on repatriation of foreign earnings under the American Jobs Creation Act of 2004	—	47	—
Foreign tax rate differential	(15)	(28)	(6)
Change in tax law and regulations	—	—	(15)
Deferred gain on ITT World Directories disposition	—	52	—
Tax settlements	(59)	(8)	(15)
Tax benefit on the deferred gain from the Host transaction	(356)	—	—
Tax benefits recognized on Host transaction	(1,017)	—	—
Basis difference on asset sales	(41)	—	—
Change in of valuation allowance	884	7	24
Other	(11)	(9)	(3)
Provision for income tax (benefit)	$(434)	$219	$43

Source: Starwood 2006 10K.

As discussed in note 5, the company completed the Host transaction during the second quarter of 2006, which included the sale of 33 hotel properties. Since the company sold these hotels subject to long-term management contracts, the gain of approximately $955 million has been deferred over the life of those contracts. As a result of the recognition of this deferred gain, the company has established a deferred tax asset and recognized the related tax benefit of approximately $356 million for the book-tax difference on the deferred gain liability. Additional tax benefits of $1,017 million resulted from the Host transaction, consisting primarily of the tax benefit of $832 million on the $2.4 billion capital loss generated for federal tax purposes. The remaining benefit consisted of an adjustment to deferred income taxes for the increased tax basis of certain retained assets, partially offset by current tax liabilities generated in the transaction.

During 2005, the company was notified by ITT Industries that a refund of tax and interest had been approved by the IRS for payment to ITT Industries related to its 1993–1995 tax returns. In connection with its acquisition of Sheraton Holding, the company is party to a tax-sharing agreement among ITT Industries, Hartford Insurance, and Sheraton Holding as a result of their 1995 split of ITT Industries into these companies and is entitled to one-third of this refund. As a result of this notification, the company recorded an $8 million tax benefit during 2005.

During 2004, the IRS completed its audits of the company's 1999 and 2000 tax returns and issued its final audit adjustments to the company. As a result of the completion of these audits and receipt of the final audit adjustments, the company recorded a $5 million tax benefit. In addition, the company recognized a $10 million tax benefit related to the reversal of previously accrued income taxes after an evaluation of the applicable exposures and expiration of the related statutes of limitation.

STARWOOD HOTELS & RESORTS WORLDWIDE, INC.

CONSOLIDATED BALANCE SHEETS

(In Millions, Except Share Data)

	December 31	
	2006	**2005**
Assets		
Current assets:		
Cash and cash equivalents	$183	$897
Restricted cash	329	295
Accounts receivable, net of allowance for doubtful accounts of $49 and $50	593	642
Inventories	566	280
Prepaid expenses and other	139	169
Total current assets	1,810	2,283
Investments	436	403
Plant, property, and equipment, net	3,831	4,169
Assets held for sale	2	2,882
Goodwill and intangible assets, net	2,302	2,315
Deferred tax assets	518	40
Other assets	381	402
	$9,280	$12,494

	December 31	
	2006	2005
Liabilities and Stockholders' Equity		
Current liabilities:		
Short-term borrowings and current maturities of long-term debt	$805	$1,219
Accounts payable	179	156
Accrued expenses	955	1,049
Accrued salaries, wages, and benefits	383	297
Accrued taxes and other	139	158
Total current liabilities	2,461	2,879
Long-term debt	1,827	2,849
Long-term debt held for sale	—	77
Deferred income taxes	31	602
Other liabilities	1,928	851
	6,247	7,258
Minority interest	25	25
Commitments and contingencies		
Stockholders' equity:		
Class A exchangeable preferred shares of the trust, $0.01 par value, authorized 30,000,000 shares, outstanding 0 and 562,222 shares at December 31, 2006 and 2005, respectively	—	—
Class B exchangeable preferred shares of the trust, $0.01 par value, authorized 15,000,000 shares, outstanding 0 and 24,627 shares at December 31, 2006 and 2005, respectively	—	—
Corporation common stock, $0.01 par value, authorized 1,050,000,000 shares, outstanding 213,484,439 and 217,218,781 shares at December 31, 2006 and 2005, respectively	2	2
Trust class B shares of beneficial interest, $0.01 par value, authorized 1,000,000,000 shares, outstanding 0 and 217,218,781 shares at December 31, 2006 and 2005, respectively	—	2
Additional paid-in capital	2,286	5,412
Deferred compensation	—	(53)
Accumulated other comprehensive loss	(228)	(322)
Retained earnings	948	170
Total stockholders' equity	3,008	5,211
	$9,280	$12,494

The accompanying notes to financial statements are an integral part of the above statements.

STARWOOD HOTELS & RESORTS WORLDWIDE, INC.
CONSOLIDATED STATEMENTS OF CASH FLOWS
(In Millions)

	Year Ended December 31		
	2006	**2005**	**2004**
Operating Activities			
Net income	$1,043	$422	$395
Adjustments to net income:			
Discontinued operations:			
Loss (gain) on dispositions, net	2	—	(26)
Other adjustments relating to discontinued operations	—	11	1
Cumulative effect of accounting change	70	—	—
Stock-based compensation expense	103	31	16
Excess stock-based compensation tax benefit	(87)	—	—
Depreciation and amortization	306	407	431
Amortization of deferred loan costs	5	12	12
Noncash portion of restructuring and other special charges (credits), net	(7)	(3)	(37)
Noncash foreign currency losses (gains), net	(8)	2	(9)
Provision for doubtful accounts	25	6	25
Equity earnings, net of distributions	(30)	(7)	31
Gain on sale of VOI notes receivable	(17)	(25)	(14)
Loss on asset dispositions and impairments, net	3	30	33
Noncash portion of income tax (benefit) expense	(620)	(110)	31
Changes in working capital:			
Restricted cash	(35)	50	(257)
Accounts receivable	49	(152)	(67)
Inventories	(82)	105	(22)
Prepaid expenses and other	(11)	(8)	(52)
Accounts payable and accrued expenses	12	157	118
Accrued income taxes	(64)	(135)	(24)
VOI notes receivable activity, net	(138)	(40)	(114)
Other, net	(19)	11	107
Cash from operating activities	500	764	578
Investing Activities			
Purchases of plant, property, and equipment	(371)	(464)	(333)
Proceeds from asset sales, net	1,515	510	74
Collection (issuance) of notes receivable, net	95	11	(2)
Acquisitions, net of acquired cash	(25)	(242)	(65)
Proceeds from (purchases of) investments	191	47	(73)
Proceeds from (acquisition of) senior debt	—	221	(4)
Other, net	(3)	2	(12)
Cash from (used for) investing activities	1,402	85	(415)

	Year Ended December 31		
	2006	2005	2004
Financing Activities			
Revolving credit facility and short-term borrowings (repayments), net	73	333	(20)
Long-term debt issued	2	9	300
Long-term debt repaid	(1,534)	(583)	(451)
Distributions paid	(276)	(176)	(172)
Proceeds from employee stock option exercises	380	405	379
Excess stock-based compensation tax benefit	87	—	—
Share repurchases	(1,287)	(228)	(310)
Other, net	(80)	(13)	1
Cash used for financing activities	(2,635)	(253)	(273)
Exchange-rate effect on cash and cash equivalents	19	(25)	9
Increase (decrease) in cash and cash equivalents	(714)	571	(101)
Cash and cash equivalents—beginning of period	897	326	427
Cash and cash equivalents—end of period	$183	$897	$326
Supplemental Disclosures of Cash-Flow Information			
Cash paid during the period for:			
Interest	$247	$274	$293
Income taxes, net of refunds	$249	$447	$21

The accompanying notes to financial statements are an integral part of the preceding statements.

	December 31	
	2006	2005
Plant, property, and equipment	$236	$(448)
Intangibles	6	(158)
Allowances for doubtful accounts and other reserves	151	139
Employee benefits	80	51
Net operating loss, capital loss and tax credit carry-forwards	1,052	173
Deferred income	(103)	(154)
Other	74	(40)
	1,496	(437)
Less valuation allowance	(1,009)	(125)
Deferred income taxes	$487	$(562)

OTHER TAXES AND INCENTIVES

While income taxes are a vital consideration to all profitable enterprises, other taxes can impair cash flows as well, including property, sales, and excise taxes, among others. While a firm may be able, to an extent, to manage income taxes, the same cannot be said for so-called use taxes. In addition, states that are in financial difficulty often find the profitable corporation as an easy political mark to close budget deficits. Increases in state taxes, whether income or "use" taxes, often result in unexpected and sometimes significant cash expense.

On the other hand, it is not unusual for large employers to benefit from special tax incentives from states hoping to create employment and boost state revenues through the property, sales, and other taxes paid by a rising employment base. Or the company itself, through, such incentives can amount to substantial cash savings, especially if moving to a low-tax jurisdiction from a high-tax jurisdiction. For tax incentives about to expire, the reverse would be in order.

Example:

Boyd Gaming is a casino gaming company. Some of its properties operate from riverboats.

> In April 2007 the Indiana General Assembly amended the manner in which riverboats are to be taxed for property tax purposes. Retroactive to March 1, 2006, riverboats are to be taxed based on the lowest valuation as determined by an application of each of the following methodologies: (i) cost approach; (ii) sales comparison approach; and (iii) income capitalization approach. Alternatively, the Riverboat Licensee and the respective Township Assessor may reach an agreement regarding the value of the riverboat. All Indiana state excise taxes, use taxes, and gross retail taxes apply to sales made on a riverboat. In 2004 the Indiana Supreme Court ruled that vessels purchased out of the State of Indiana and brought into the State of Indiana would be subject to Indiana sales tax. Additionally, the Supreme Court declined to hear an Indiana Tax Court case that determined wagering tax payments made by a riverboat could not be deducted from the riverboat's adjusted gross income.

Example:

Biostar Pharmaceuticals develops, manufactures, and markets pharmaceutical and medical nutrient products for a variety of diseases and condition. It is based in Maryland and owned by a Chinese (PRC) company.

> Our effective tax rate decreased by 4 percent from the year ended December 31, 2007, to the year ended December 31, 2008, primarily as a result of reduction in the PRC statutory tax rate effective on January 1, 2008. Based on our current operating structure and the preferential tax treatments available to us in the PRC, our PRC operation, Aoxing

> Pharmaceutical, qualifies as a high-tech enterprise entitled to a 50 percent income tax reduction from January 1, 2007, to December 31, 2009. Therefore, the effective tax rate for Aoxing Pharmaceutical was 13 percent for the year ended December 31, 2008, and 17 percent for the year ended December 31, 2007. If the tax benefits currently available to us in the PRC become unavailable, the effective income tax rate for Aoxing Pharmaceutical could increase to 25 percent. We expect our effective tax rate to increase in the future, as we experience further expiration of tax incentives.

Example:

Hanesbrands is a consumer goods company with manufacturing operations in Puerto Rico. Its taxes jumped when an important incentive ended.

> Our effective income tax rate increased from 24.3 percent for the six months ended December 31, 2005, to 33.8 percent for the six months ended December 30, 2006. The increase in our effective tax rate as an independent company is attributable primarily to the expiration of tax incentives for manufacturing in Puerto Rico of $9 million, which were repealed effective for the periods after July 1, 2006, higher taxes on remittances of foreign earnings for the period of $9 million and $5 million tax effect of lower unremitted earnings from foreign subsidiaries in the six months ended December 30, 2006, taxed at rates less than the U.S. statutory rate.

Example:

Pacific Ethanol, Inc., is a producer and marketer of ethanol-based products, especially for use in gasoline. A change in tax incentives related to ethanol production would have very severe ramifications for its business, including its ability to raise capital, as outlined in its 2009 10K:

> The amount of ethanol production capacity in the U.S. exceeds the mandated usage of renewable biofuels. Ethanol consumption above mandated amounts is primarily based upon the economic benefit derived by blenders, including benefits received from federal excise tax incentives. Therefore, the production of ethanol is made significantly more competitive by federal tax incentives. The federal excise tax incentive program, which is scheduled to expire on December 31, 2010, allows gasoline distributors who blend ethanol with gasoline to receive a federal excise tax rate reduction for each blended gallon they sell regardless of the blend rate. The current federal excise tax on gasoline is $0.184 per gallon, and is paid at the terminal by refiners and marketers. If the fuel is blended with ethanol, the blender may claim a $0.45 per gallon tax credit for each gallon of ethanol used in the mixture. The 2008 Farm Bill enacted into law reduced federal excise tax incentives from $0.51 per gallon in 2008 to $0.45 per gallon in 2009. The federal excise tax incentive program may not be renewed prior to its expiration in 2010, or if renewed, it may be renewed on terms significantly less favorable than current tax incentives. The elimination or significant reduction in the federal excise tax incentive program could reduce discretionary blending and have a material adverse effect on our results of operations and our financial condition.

While many states use incentives to lure companies, some jurisdictions impose new taxes that are harmful to cash flows. For example, *tax increment financing* (TIF) has been used in Chicago and elsewhere. If it is deemed that a municipal or other such improvement takes place that enhances the value of existing properties, those properties are accessed additional taxes. These TIFs are aimed at companies doing business in the area. During difficult economic times for municipal and state governments, taxes, especially property and use taxes, come to the forefront.

On the other hand, firms can be expected to take advantage of new tax laws even if they need to be resourceful in the application of legislation which may not have been intended originally for their industry. For instance, a 2005 law intended to encourage alternate use of fuels for motor vehicles is currently helping pulp and paper companies realize substantial cash benefits.

Example:

Verso Paper Company, a large manufacturer and supplier of coated paper, as well as other companies in its industry, such as International Paper, have seized the opportunity to realize cash through such credits.

Subsequent Event

The company burns alternative fuel mixtures at its Androscoggin and Quinnesec mills in order to produce renewable energy and help manage the company's exposure to high energy costs. The federal government has implemented a program that provides incentive payments under certain circumstances for the use of alternative fuels and alternative fuel mixtures in lieu of fossil-based fuels. In the fourth quarter of 2008, the company filed applications with the Internal Revenue Service for certification of its eligibility to receive incentive payments for its use of black liquor in alternative fuel mixtures in the recovery boilers at the Androscoggin and Quinnesec mills. In January and February 2009, the IRS certified that the company's operations at the two mills qualified for the incentive payments. In February 2009, the company received an incentive payment of $29.7 million for operations at the Androscoggin mill in the fourth quarter of 2008. The company's claim for a similar incentive payment for operations at the Quinnesec mill in the fourth quarter of 2008 is expected during March 2009. The federal regulations relating to the alternative fuels mixture incentive program are complex, and further clarification is needed by the company prior to the recognition of any payment received for financial reporting purposes.

Source: Verso Paper Corp. 2008 10K.

While not considered a tax, additional governmental regulation is a quasi-tax in the form of increased fixed costs as the license for conducting business. The proposal or fear of added industry regulation should serve to suppress valuation multiples to the extent cash flows could be impaired or cost of capital raised. In 2005, sales of GM's cars in China, a large, profitable market for the company, dropped in part owing to new restrictions there on corporate and governmental purchase of fleets.

U.S.-imposed duties on foreign goods could lead to retaliation by foreign governments. In September 2009, China threatened tariffs on certain U.S. industries in retaliation for the United States placing duties on Chinese tires. Stocks in those effected industries fell, even though China called for talks. The introduction and overhang of the new risk served to increase the cost of equity.

Duties, taxes, levies, sanctions, or tighter controls and reviews affect cash flows and should be brought into the analytic review process by the security analyst for their effects on cash flows and cost of capital. They can critically affect valuation.

SEGMENTS OF OPERATION

Analysts must understand which of the entity's operating units are producing cash and which require cash—which are capital intensive and which are not. They need to know the magnitude of each, the history of each, and their prospects for growth. They would need to know how the various segments compare with their competitors. Yet accounting rule makers do not require a full set of financial statements for operating segments.

In order to understand the cash flow and cost of capital for the enterprise as a whole, it is important to decompose the organization into individual units based on their relative importance. However, because firms are required to provide information only on reportable segments, which can comprise many operating units, it may be difficult for the analyst to determine with precision how an entity can most maximize its cash flows. For years, Zurn, Inc., reported mediocre cash flows owing to its cash-using golf division. Meanwhile, its plumbing division had record profits and cash flow for at least 15 years in a row. Zurn was later acquired with the golf division disposed of.

The Financial Accounting Standards Board (FASB) requires segment reporting as set forth in SFAS 131. In 2006, the International Accounting Standards Board (IASB) also required segment reporting consistent with the FASB. SFAS 131 states

> This Statement requires that a public business enterprise report financial and descriptive information about its reportable operating segments. Operating segments are components of an enterprise about which separate financial information is available that is evaluated regularly by the chief operating decision maker in deciding how to allocate resources and in assessing performance. Generally, financial information is required to be reported on the basis that it is used internally for evaluating segment performance and deciding how to allocate resources to segments.

Source: Financial Accounting Standards Board.

Unfortunately, the standard has not led to the consistency desired owing to interpretation of the wording because what constitutes a *reporting segment* varies widely; some entities supply investors with a wealth of information, including a full management discussion and analysis of the reportable segments, as in the case of Proctor & Gamble, whereas other entities offer little more than segment profit and revenues, as in the case of Microsoft. If there is a division responsible for greater than 10 percent of operating profits or revenues but it is part of a reportable segment, its results would not need to be reported separately. It would be helpful to the analyst if such results were given, especially if the division were responsible for large positive or negative free cash flow. Thus, while SFAS 131 was intended to provide insight and comparability, it does not go far enough. In such cases, it is up to the analyst to acquire the relevant information from the CFO or appropriate executive.

SFAS 131 required companies to present segment results when a reportable segment meets one or more of the following tests: (1) revenue is 10 percent or more of combined revenue, (2) operating profit is 10 percent or more of combined operating profit (operating profit excludes unallocable general corporate revenue and expenses, interest expense, and income taxes), or (3) identifiable assets are 10 percent or more of the combined identifiable assets (also called *line of business reporting*). Condensed segment reporting is also required for interim statements.

SFAS 131 also requires disclosure if revenues from transactions with a single external customer amount to 10 percent or more of an enterprise's revenues; the enterprise shall disclose that fact, the total amount of revenues from each such customer, and the identity of the segment or segments reporting the revenues. Cash flows would be affected if there was either a change in the business outlook of such customer or the customer was lost.

Example:

Jabil Circuit is one of the leading providers of worldwide electronics manufacturing services and solutions. The company provides comprehensive electronics design, production, product management, and aftermarket services to companies in the aerospace, automotive, computing, consumer, defense, industrial, instrumentation, medical, networking, peripherals, solar, storage, and telecommunications industries. As stated in its 2009 10K:

> Sales of the company's products are concentrated among specific customers. For the fiscal year ended August 31, 2009, the company's five largest customers accounted for approximately 43 percent of our net revenue and 50 customers accounted for approximately 90 percent of our net revenue. Sales to the following customers who accounted for 10 percent or more of the company's net revenues, expressed as a percentage of consolidated net revenue, and the percentage of accounts receivable for each customer, were as follows:

	Percentage of Net Revenue			Percentage of Accounts Receivable	
	Fiscal Year Ended August 31			Fiscal Year Ended August 31,	
	2009	2008	2007	2009	2008
Cisco Systems, Inc.	13%	16%	15%	*	*
Research in Motion, Limited	12%	*	*	10%	*
Nokia Corporation	*	*	13%	*	*
Hewlett-Packard Company	*	11%	*	10%	*

*Amount was less than 10 percent of total.

It is not uncommon to find, within reporting entities, a particular segment that is stable to declining, whereas another segment is growing faster than its peers. Such has been the case for telecom companies that have wireless (high growth) and wireline (negative growth) segments. The analyst must examine the cash needs of such segments and whether the low-growth segment is providing important levels of cash that could be used by the high-growth segment. All segmental market values should be established, even if the value is not directly a cash producer. If cash drains are expected to continue for a particular reporting segment, the analyst should determine the value of the enterprise without that segment and if management's outlook for the cash-using segment is realistic or if the unit could be sold, spun off (if possible),[4] or shut down.

Example:

Microsoft reports its revenues and operating profits for its five segments, not providing sufficient information to determine each segment's free cash flow. As reported in the company's 2009 10K:

> SFAS No. 131, *Disclosures about Segments of an Enterprise and Related Information*, establishes standards for reporting information about operating segments. This standard requires segmentation based on our internal organization and reporting of revenue and operating income (loss) based upon internal accounting methods. Our financial reporting systems present various data for management to operate the business, including internal profit and loss statements prepared on a basis not consistent with U.S. GAAP. The segments are

[4] As of this writing, Motorola has decided to spin off its telecom unit after years of poor performance and attempts at sale.

designed to allocate resources internally and provide a framework to determine management responsibility. Amounts for prior periods have been recast to conform to the current management view. Operating segments are defined as components of an enterprise about which separate financial information is available that is evaluated regularly by the chief operating decision maker, or decision making group, in deciding how to allocate resources and in assessing performance. Our chief operating decision maker is our Chief Executive Officer. Our five segments are Client; Server and Tools; Online Services Business; Microsoft Business Division; and Entertainment and Devices Division.

	Year Ended June 30 (In Millions)		
	2009	**2008**	**2007**
Revenue:			
Client	**$14,414**	$16,472	$14,779
Server and Tools	**14,135**	13,121	11,117
Online Services Business	**3,088**	3,190	2,434
Microsoft Business Division	**18,902**	18,935	16,478
Entertainment and Devices Division	**7,753**	8,213	6,136
Unallocated and other	**145**	489	178
Consolidated	**$58,437**	$60,420	$51,122

	Year Ended June 30 (In Millions)		
	2009	**2008**	**2007**
Operating income (loss):			
Client	**$10,435**	$12,566	$11,295
Server and Tools	**5,047**	4,170	3,520
Online Services Business	**(2,391)**	(1,304)	(617)
Microsoft Business Division	**11,940**	12,169	10,757
Entertainment and Devices Division	**5**	325	(1,945)
Reconciling amounts	**(4,673)**	(5,655)	(4,572)
Consolidated	**$20,363**	$22,271	$18,438

Example:

PepsiCo reports six segments of operations: Frito-Lay North America (FLNA), Quaker Foods North America (QFNA), Latin America Foods (LAF), PepsiCo Americas Beverages (PAB), United Kingdom & Europe (UKEU), and Middle East, Africa and Asia (MEAA). Although Pepsi does not provide a statement of cash flows for each segment, an investor can estimate, based on the information provided, (1) the revenue growth rate of each segment, (2) the capital intensity of each segment, and (3) operating profits. From this information, one could construct a naive statement of cash flows.

Below I estimate the free cash flow for the Frito-Lay North American segment; I allocated 37 percent of corporate overhead, based on that segment's sales (relative to total sales), for 2008 and 35.9 percent for 2007. I used the same percentages for capital spending of the parent and allocated that down as well, which I added to total capex. By allocating corporate overhead, I am implicitly taking into consideration expenses like interest and dividend payments on preferred stock that may not appear on the financial statements of the subsidiary. As you can see, Frito-Lay North America is a very strong generator of free cash flow and has a very high return on its invested capital. A precise determination of its invested capital is not possible without its financial statement, even though assets are given. In Chapter 5 I discuss in detail return on invested capital (ROIC).

Since segment operating profit is before depreciation and amortization, the analyst has no need to add those items back to what is reported by the company. If it were a true statement of cash flows, they would be subtracted from operating profits and added back under operating activities unless reporting under the direct method. I am not adding back excess discretionary spending, as you will see I will do for Clorox in an upcoming example.

For 2008, Pepsi reported an effective tax rate of 26.8 percent and, according to its statement of cash flows, supplemental information, actually paid $1.477 billion in income taxes on pretax income of $5.142 billion, or an approximate tax return rate of 28.7 percent, which I use below.

FLNA	**2008**	**2007**
Operating profit	2,959	2,845
Capex	(654)	(705)
Corp. overhead	(375)	(270)
Pretax	1,930	1,870
Taxes (28.7 percent)	(554)	(537)
Free cash flow	1,382	1,333

	2008	**2007**	**2006**	**2008**	**2007**	**2006**
	Net Revenue			**Operating Profit**[a]		
FLNA	**$12,507**	$11,586	$10,844	**$2,959**	$2,845	$2,615
QFNA	**1,902**	1,860	1,769	**582**	568	554
LAF	**5,895**	4,872	3,972	**897**	714	655
PAB	**10,937**	11,090	10,362	**2,026**	2,487	2,315
UKEU	**6,435**	5,492	4,750	**811**	774	700
MEAA	**5,575**	4,574	3,440	**667**	535	401
Total division	**43,251**	39,474	35,137	**7,942**	7,923	7,240
Corporate—net impact of mark-to-market on commodity hedges	**—**	—	—	**(346)**	19	(18)
Corporate—other	**—**	—	—	**(661)**	(772)	(720)
	$43,251	$39,474	$35,137	**$6,935**	$7,170	$6,502

[a]For information on the impact of restructuring and impairment charges on our divisions, see note 3.

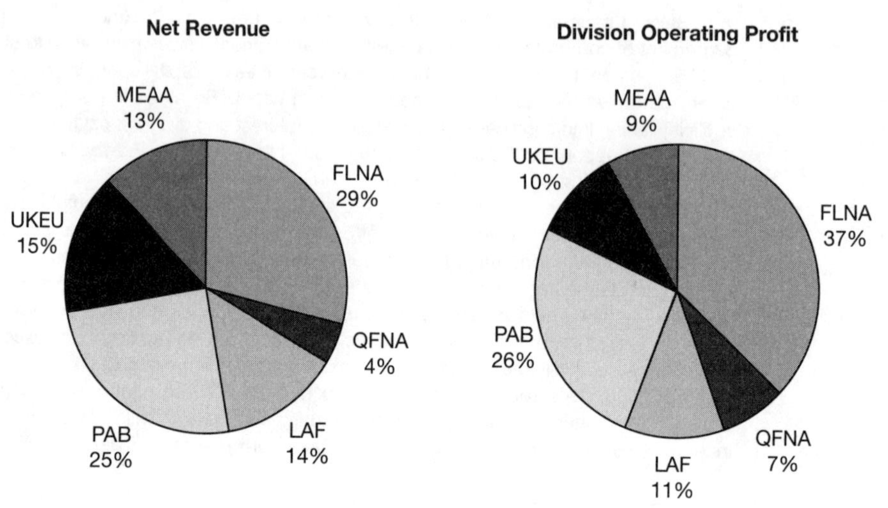

Corporate

Corporate includes costs of our corporate headquarters, centrally managed initiatives, such as our ongoing business transformation initiative and research and development projects, unallocated insurance and benefit programs, foreign exchange transaction gains and losses, certain commodity derivative gains and losses, and certain other items.

Other Division Information

	2008	2007	2006	2008	2007	2006
	Total Assets			Capital Spending		
FLNA	**$6,284**	$6,270	$5,969	**$553**	$624	$499
QFNA	**1,035**	1,002	1,003	**43**	41	31
LAF	**3,023**	3,084	2,169	**351**	326	235
PAB	**7,673**	7,780	7,129	**344**	450	516
UKEU	**8,635**	7,102	5,865	**377**	349	277
MEAA	**3,961**	3,911	2,975	**503**	413	299
Total division	**30,611**	29,149	25,110	**2,171**	2,203	1,857
Corporate[a]	**2,729**	2,124	1,739	**275**	227	211
Investments in bottling affiliates	**2,654**	3,355	3,081	**—**	—	—
	$35,994	$34,628	$29,930	**$2,446**	$2,430	$2,068

[a]Corporate assets consist principally of cash and cash equivalents, short-term investments, derivative instruments, and property, plant, and equipment.

Total Assets

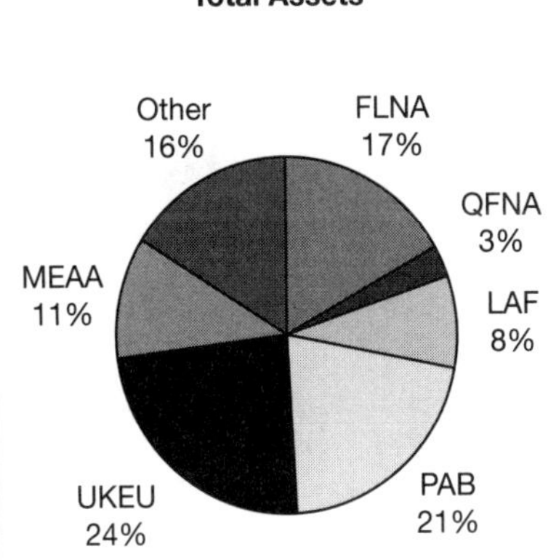

Capital Spending

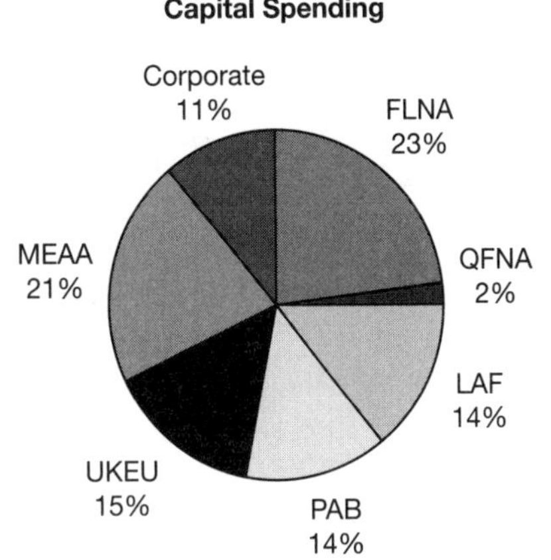

	2008	2007	2006	2008	2007	2006
	Amortization of Intangible Assets			Depreciation and Other Amortization		
FLNA	**$9**	$9	$9	**$441**	$437	$432
QFNA	**—**	—	—	**34**	34	33
LAF	**6**	4	1	**194**	166	140
PAB	**16**	16	83	**334**	321	298
UKEU	**22**	18	17	**199**	181	167
MEAA	**11**	11	52	**224**	198	155
Total division	**64**	58	162	**1,426**	1,337	1,225
Corporate	**—**	—	—	**53**	31	19
	$64	$58	$162	**$1,479**	$1,368	$1,244

	2008	2007	2006	2008	2007	2006
	Net Revenue[a]			Long-Lived Assets[b]		
U.S.	**$22,525**	$21,978	$20,788	**$12,095**	$12,498	$11,515
Mexico	**3,714**	3,498	3,228	**904**	1,067	996
Canada	**2,107**	1,961	1,702	**556**	699	589
United Kingdom	**2,099**	1,987	1,839	**1,509**	2,090	1,995
All other countries	**12,806**	10,050	7,580	**7,466**	6,441	4,725
	$43,251	$39,474	$35,137	**$22,530**	$22,795	$19,820

[a]Represents net revenue from businesses operating in these countries.

[b]Long-lived assets represent property, plant, and equipment; nonamortizable intangible assets; amortizable intangible assets; and investments in noncontrolled affiliates. These assets are reported in the country where they are used primarily.

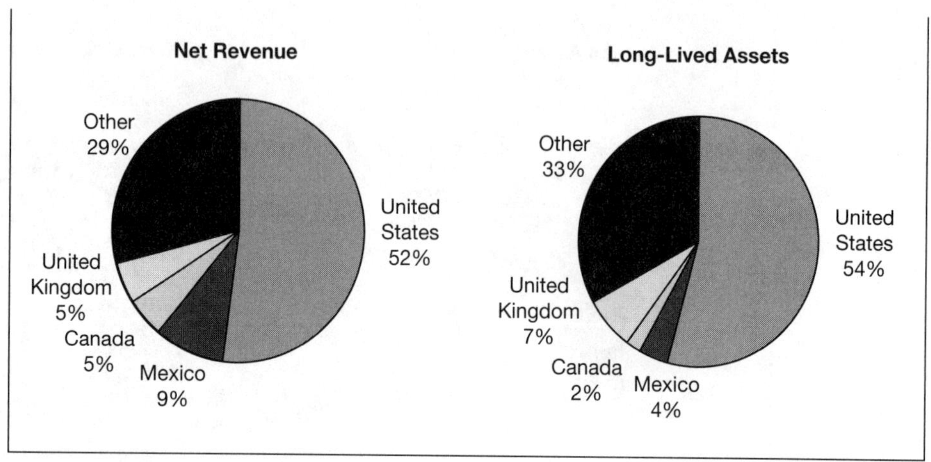

ESTIMATING FREE CASH FLOW

Corporate executives must, over the long term, manage their companies with the goal of maximizing free cash flow. To accomplish that objective, they must balance output, pricing, and expenditures with the intent that current spending will lead not only to satisfactory short-term cash-flow generation but also to sustainable long-term performance. It is when expenditures, unit output, and cash flows become unbalanced that actions should be taken to rebalance the fulcrum. Risks, whether they are business risk, financial risk, or country risk, must be weighed carefully.

Equity investors must gauge the firm's free cash flow, for this is how they are compensated. Everyone else is paid before the shareholders. The greater the free cash flow, the greater is the flexibility to pursue additional growth strategies and return cash to the owners of the equity capital. The weaker the free cash flow, the more difficult it will be to remain in business, and little or nothing will be left for shareholders. To have as a management goal long-term free-cash-flow maximization without current free cash flows introduces risk. Such enterprises have a higher cost of capital because that long-term free cash flow may be illusory.

Estimating free cash flow is not simple for those inside the company and thus even more difficult for analysts. Free cash flow, especially over shortened time periods, is fairly unpredictable and subject to discretionary expenditures. It can be subject to the entity's stock price, which determines the ability of the enterprise to substitute stock for cash compensation. Some capital spending programs are quite large and lumpy, subject to delays and cost overruns, and so affect free cash flow for years. Free cash flow is also subject to the vagaries of the stock market as it impacts pension funding, which is determined by the return on plan assets. Free cash flow is subject to interest rates because it affects consumer demand, interest expense, and the timing and cost of a sinking-fund payment or debt repurchase. Free cash flow is subject to congressional and accounting rule makers to the extent that tax incentives are granted or withdrawn; accounting promulgations affect credit ratings and shareholders equity, which, in turn, alter the potential growth rate of the entity. And of course, free cash flow is most affected by business conditions—demand for the company's product and/or services and the input costs required to produce revenues.

Free cash flow is not the same as EBITDA, because it is derived only from income statement inputs, comes with a big theoretical caveat: It fails to capture capital intensity, the proportion of cash flows that must be reinvested to maintain the business, including working capital. This varies structurally between industries and companies, which is why I look to growth rates when evaluating capital spending requirements. Calculating EBITDA is certainly a lot simpler than calculating free cash flow. Later in the chapter I enumerate other failings of EBITDA.

So why do we do it? Because this is what an operating company is truly worth—the potential *cash* it can return to shareholders in return for the *cash* they invested in the business. Would you quit your job to buy a business you knew would return zero cash back? Our lives are based on cash. We cannot accrue that bill at a restaurant—pay it, or the owner will call the cops!

To estimate free cash flow, one can follow two approaches—the direct and the indirect approach—just like the derivation of net cash from operations. Under the direct approach, the cash-flow analyst estimates the components of cash flows of operating activities and then estimates the portion of those components that are discretionary in nature. The cash-flow analyst also estimates the discretionary components of the firm's major investments in fixed assets. As we saw in Chapter 3, very few companies use the direct method for reporting changes in operating activities, although the FASB and the IASB clearly have been advocating its adoption.

Under the indirect approach, the cash-flow analyst begins with the change in cash during a period and makes adjustments to that amount for various events that affect free cash flow. Generally, all cash outlays that are not necessary for the firm's continuing operations will be added back to the change in cash because the firm could have avoided making those payments and still continued its operations. Consequently, free cash flow would have increased had the firm not made those expenditures. Similarly, increases in cash that result from liquidation of fixed assets or from external financing are subtracted from the change in cash because they do not represent cash flows that were generated from continuing operations of the business or because they represent the gradual liquidation of the firm.

Although free cash flow can be estimated beginning with the changes in the balance-sheet cash, an easier yet still precise method is to begin with cash flows from operating activities, as stated in the statement of cash flows, and from that to make the necessary adjustments.

This approach is based on the following rationale:

Consider the cash sources–uses identity:

$$\text{OCF} + \text{net debt} + \text{net equity} = \text{dividends} + \text{investments} + \text{change in cash}$$

where

OCF = net cash flow from operating activities
Net debt = net cash provided by debt issuance
Net equity = net cash provided by equity issuance
Dividends = cash dividends paid by the firm
Investments = cash investments in capital expenditures and such investments
Change in cash=change in cash balance from beginning to end of period

Simple algebraic manipulation yields

$$\text{OCF} - \text{investments} = \text{change in cash} + \text{dividends} - \text{net debt} - \text{net equity}$$

On the left-hand side of the equation, which I will call FCF1, is equal to net operating cash flows minus net investments during the period, mostly in capital expenditures. By now, we know that some of the investments in capital expenditures can be considered discretionary. Let us denote discretionary investments by *DiscInv* and nondiscretionary investments by *NonDiscInv*. Similarly, some of the cash outlays, such as payments to employees and suppliers, research and development (R&D), and so forth, may be discretionary. Let us denote these discretionary cash outflows by *DiscOCF* and the nondiscretionary cash from operations by *NonOCF*.

Thus the equation can be written as

$$\begin{aligned}(\text{NonOCF} - \text{DiscOCF}) - (\text{NonDiscInv} + \text{DiscInv}) \\ = \text{change in cash} + \text{dividends} - \text{net debt} - \text{net equity}\end{aligned}$$

Simple manipulation yields

$$\begin{aligned}\text{NonOCF} - \text{NonDiscInv} = \text{change in cash} + \text{dividends} - \text{net debt} - \text{net equity} \\ + \text{DiscInv} + \text{DiscOCF}\end{aligned}$$

Note that the left-hand side of this equation now contains the free cash flow as we have defined it—the cash generated by ongoing operations of the business during the period in excess of necessary investments in capital expenditures and other necessary payments. Note that this represents free cash flow because net operating cash flow now includes cash receipts from operations in excess of necessary cash outflows for generating these cash receipts during the period and in excess of investments that are intended to maintain the ability of the firm to generate those cash receipts in the future. Obviously, the excess cash receipts can be distributed to shareholders without affecting the growth of the business.

The right-hand side of the equation shows the indirect method alternative way of estimating free cash flow from operations. Instead of estimating the cash receipts minus necessary cash flows, one begins with the change in cash during the period and makes adjustments to it as it is portrayed on the right-hand side of the equation. For example, decreases in cash owing to financing events, such as payment of dividends or retirement of debt, are added back to the change in cash. Similarly, decreases in cash owing to discretionary capital expenditures or investing activities beyond those needed to sustain the growth of the firm are added back to the change in cash. Decreases in cash owing to operating expenses beyond those needed to sustain the growth of the firm are also added back to the change in cash because they represent discretionary expenditures. Using similar logic, increases in cash owing to disinvesting events, such as the sale of plant, property, and equipment (PPE), or increases in cash owing to financing events, such as the issuance of common stock, are subtracted from the change in cash. This procedure yields another estimate of free cash flow, but it uses an indirect method to estimate the free cash flow.

While we normally would opt for the indirect approach because information is gleaned by viewing the various items that supply and use cash, preparers of financial statements do not always present sufficient data (or lump other data together) for the analyst to prepare an accurate model. For this reason, our credit models use the direct approach, starting with cash flow from operating activities and then making the necessary adjustments.

For the positive free-cash-flow producer, principal sources of liquidity are cash on hand and cash generated from operations. For the non-free-cash-flow generator, it is external financing, cash on hand, asset sales, and tax refunds. Management also focuses on managing the critical components of working capital, which include receivables, inventory, payables, and short-term debt, to make certain that all short-term obligations are able to be satisfied. If long-term credit is needed as a result of a cash shortfall, a decision must be made on the optimal means to secure it. The most optimal way may not always be the cheapest but may be the right decision for the current period. This is so because the entity might be in need of quick access to cash, such as to fund an acquisition or pay debt, and timing may have an added cost.

As we have seen from company reporting, there is no simple or single definition of free cash flow in use today, nor can an analyst simply rearrange a few numbers from the statement of cash flows to arrive at free cash flow. Some models value an entity as the present value of dividends but do not consider if the dividend to pay the cash was generated from free cash flow. Using my definition, bank borrowing to pay a dividend would result in a neutral cash generation, as it should, because the payment does not represent free cash flow. Free cash flow, as defined in my model, can be used to reduce leverage, if desired or required, without depriving the firm of needed cash for expansion.

I now show a detailed procedure to estimate free cash flow using Clorox as an example. I also show Clorox's ability to satisfy its obligations from free cash flow and credit capacity.

Example: CLOROX

The Clorox Company (the company or Clorox) is a leading manufacturer and marketer of consumer products with fiscal year 2008 net sales of $5.3 billion. The company sells its products primarily through mass merchandisers, grocery stores, and other retail outlets. It markets some of consumers' most trusted and recognized brand names, including its namesake bleach and cleaning products, Green Works natural cleaners, Poett and Mistolín cleaning products, Armor All and STP auto-care products, Fresh Step and Scoop Away cat litter, Kingsford charcoal, Hidden Valley and K C Masterpiece dressings and sauces, Brita water-filtration systems, Glad bags, wraps and containers, and Burt's Bees natural personal care products. With approximately 8,300 employees worldwide, the company manufactures products in more than 15 countries and markets them in more than 100 countries. The company was founded in Oakland, Calif., in 1913, and is incorporated in Delaware.

Source: Clorox 2009 10K.

We begin our model with Clorox's cash flow from operating activities as stated in its financial reports (column "d" in Table 4-8). Cash flow from operations reveals the important cash collections and disbursements from its primary business activities, including payments for supplies, taxes, and labor; it ignores the basic outflows of the financing and investment decisions. It thus cannot be considered a measure of free cash flow. It does not make comparability adjustments.

Table 4-8 shows three approaches to calculating free cash flow. The first uses operating cash flows minus capital expenditures. This method ignores excess spending in discretionary areas, which can be captured through cost cutting. I will refer to this approach as *FCF1*.

The second approach, *FCF2*, uses a naive but still widely used version of free cash flow, one where operating cash flows are estimated from after-tax profits plus depreciation, and from which we subtract capital expenditures. In FCF2, free cash flows vary widely from FCF1, which uses actual operating cash flows. Despite this, many finance textbooks still define cash flow as profits plus depreciation. FCF2 would not be an accurate measure of distributable cash flow.

TABLE 4-8

Clorox: Free Cash Flow, as Commonly Defined

	EBITDA	Net Income	Deprec. & Amort.	Opt. Act. Net Cash Flow	CapEx	Est. OCF	FCF1	FCF2	FCF3
Year	**(a)**	**(b)**	**(c)**	**(d)**	**(e)**	**(b) + (c)**	**(d) – (e)**	**(b) + (c) – (e)**	**(a) – (e)**
1998	628	298	123	313	99	421	214	322	529
1999	853	246	176	588	176	422	412	246	677
2000	907	394	176	658	158	570	500	412	749
2001	843	323	194	747	192	517	555	325	651
2002	899	322	159	876	177	481	699	304	722
2003	1,004	493	160	803	205	653	598	448	799
2004	1,041	549	176	899	172	725	727	553	869
2005	991	1,096	174	765	151	1,270	614	1,119	840
2006	954	444	175	522	180	619	342	439	774
2007	1,056	501	180	709	147	681	562	534	909
2008	1,124	461	201	730	170	662	560	492	954
2009	1,219	537	189	738	197	726	541	529	1,022
Avg.							527	477	791

Notice the large after-tax profit Clorox reported for 2005. The company booked a $550 million profit owing to the exchange of certain of its businesses with a low book value and cash in return for 29 percent of its common stock. This amount is reversed in the statement of cash flows. It did, however, result in a large gain for shareholder reporting purposes, and thus the difference between FCF1 and FCF2 is substantial.

The boom of the 1990s through 2007 in merger and acquisition (M&A) activity brought on a concurrent rise in the use of EBITDA. The theory behind EBITDA was the desire to capture unlevered cash flows, believing that it (*FCF3*) represented the amount that could be used to cover debt service, with any balance available for shareholders. EBITDA, of course, ignores capital spending, balance-sheet changes, other operating activities, and discretionary arcas that could be trimmed to provide additional cash flows, or other obligations that might require cash. While at times EBITDA is considered a proxy for cash earnings, changes in accounting promulgations make this increasingly an accrual-based earnings measure. EBITDA minus capital expenditures is one the most commonly used definition of free cash flow despite the fact that it does not represent cash that could be distributed to equity holders. It is not surprising that FCF3 results in the highest of the common free-cash-flow measures. In FCF3, dividends on preferred stock would also be subtracted from operating cash flows.

ADDING DISCRETIONARY EXCESS

Corporate executives are under constant intense pressure to cut costs, improve liquidity, and bolster financial performance. Whether owing to competition, shareholder, or creditor pressure or the effects of the business cycle, discretionary expenses come under steady scrutiny as a means to maximize and lever free cash flow with output, credit position and cost of capital.[5] Investors are quick to react if they perceive that managers are not acting to reduce costs. For example, during their third quarter 2009 conference call, Sprint executives expressed disappointment because the cost savings of earlier quarters could not be duplicated, and stock in Sprint fell on this announcement.

Over the long term, discretionary spending should be related directly to the unit growth rate of the entity and the maximization of its free cash flow. Many discretionary areas—from manufacturing to support—should be identified to help in leveraging free cash flow, given that expected output level. Using published financial information, the analyst can identify obvious targets for management to attack. While the analyst does not have inside access or perhaps the skill to see waste at the lowest level, such as identifying cost reductions and duplications on the factory floor, a diligent analyst can deduce how spending in key areas compares with output and current free cash flow and how these yardsticks measure against the competition. Companies that lose efficiency or competitive positioning will have rising cost-of-sales and SG&A ratios in relation to their cash flows—it is then management's prerogative how to implement techniques to restore those metrics to more appropriate levels that would reinstate or minimize a loss of free cash flow. It is only the production or sales manager who would have the informed knowledge of which specific actions to undertake while not impairing revenues. The CEO must work with middle-management to identify these items, including plans for prospective savings, but would normally be unaware of the specifics, other than having a broad sense of what needs to be done. The goal is a permanent and continuing attack on cost of sales, SG&A and other discretionary areas, with clearly defined and measurable targets.

Helping to boost free cash flow has been the significant trend toward outsourcing (which began in earnest with the 2001 recession), lean management, and

[5]A study by McKinsey & Co. of purchasing performance at more than 400 companies across the globe found that companies with the most effective purchasing functions delivered annual purchasing savings more than twice those of poorly performing firms. These same companies managed to reduce their cost of goods sold significantly at times when poor performers were struggling with rising costs. Most compellingly, profit margins at leading firms were twice as high as those of poor performers. For more information, see "Operations Extranet," Guido and Spiller, McKinsey & Co., October 2009.

other operational techniques, movements that have enhanced the value to both industrial and service entities. Large cost savings can be achieved rather quickly while, for many companies, providing cash, because some outsourcing companies have purchased the manufacturing plants as a seller's condition of entering a long-term supply contract. Because outsourcing companies often have been more efficient in the manufacturing process, they have been able to step up time to market, an important competitive advantage, especially if customer demand is strong or the entity is concerned over losing market share to a competitor who is a lower-cost producer. As aggregate demand slowed following the 2007–2009 recession, cost cutting continued to be recognized as a leading method to increase market share because price increases became unthinkable.

However, while outsourcing has resulted, for many, in increases in free cash flow, the use of outsourced manufacturers can remove control and expertise. Boeing admits that it lost control of the manufacturing process by outsourcing more design and production work on its new Dreamliner series and by not keeping close tabs on suppliers. Senior management discovered that it needed to retake control, but not before the company lost as many as 60 orders owing to delays.

It is important to consider the special case of high-unit-growth industries such as technology or companies with "hot consumer products." When the growth rate of these entities slows owing to the inevitable competitive pressures or market saturation, the firms must waste little time addressing and pressing their cost side. This is so because output and expenses are now unbalanced, leading to deteriorating free cash flow. If the same entity is successful reestablishing growth in operating cash flows, it then, in the most efficient way possible, rebuilds flexible manufacturing coverage. When growth does slow, companies quickly should reduce both fixed costs and discretionary expenditures to match their new lower long-term unit growth rate.

Example:

Kraft Foods, Inc., highlighted on Wednesday its latest efforts to improve productivity and save on costs over the next two years, in a continued effort to make the case that it is in a strong position to engineer its bold takeover bid for Cadbury PLC.

Kraft highlighted the steps it is taking to boost its margins, like cutting the number of suppliers it works with. The company also pointed to the turnaround efforts of the last three years, noting that it cut 19,000 positions between 2004 and 2008 as part of its restructuring plan. Kraft said it is focusing on faster growing brands in Europe and said the efforts will fuel margin expansion.

Source: Wall Street Journal, September 9, 2009.

Although the term *corporate fat* has a negative connotation, every company, like every living being, has and needs some. The question all companies face is, How much corporate fat is justified under the current circumstances, and for what reason? If manufacturing capacity is at 100 percent, or the firm needs to step up its applied research budget, perhaps greater than normalized spending may be justified. Footlocker, Inc., explained during an investor conference call reviewing its 2009 fourth quarter that cutbacks were warranted in "store scheduling," meaning that locations were operating with too many employees. Basically, corporate fat represents overspending, which is found most often in SG&A expenses; cost of goods sold (COGS), in which both material expense and labor expenses may be included; advertising expenses; and R&D expenditures. Thus I will focus on these items in estimating discretionary cash outflows on the continuing operations of a firm. Of course, overspending can be found with every cash outlay and must be checked to free cash. Corporate fat also represents insurance against employees leaving and not having a trained replacement.

The savings from cuts to discretionary areas can be quite substantial. For instance, speeding up collection of accounts payable can add days of sales to cash, in effect creating the same result as adding revenue. For instance, it has been estimated that improving collections by 4 days for a company with $20 billion in revenue adds the equivalent of $200 million in cash. Cutting unneeded capital spending or inventory for a company this size can add additional hundreds of millions of dollars.[6]

Management consultants are well known for studying an entity's productive and administrative processes to determine how cutbacks could be accomplished while maintaining the same or improved level of production. Six Sigma and continuous process improvement (CPI) techniques and efficiency (including outsourcing) in R&D budgets have added to better quality control and superior (less defective) products, which, in turn, serve to reduce corporate waste. Management consulting firms continue to help their clients strive for operational excellence by helping them to reduce overhead and improve supply-chain management through "lean" production techniques and knowledge sharing.

While running lean can help to improve cash flows, the running down of inventory and staff can lead to lost sales. Proctor & Gamble, during conference calls with analysts and investors, has repeatedly stated that its biggest challenge is to make sure that inventory is on retailers' shelves or in back of the store. To that end, the company works closely with retailers so that they are never out of product, even during busy periods. Likewise, eliminating service staff can adversely

[6] See McKinsey & Co, Operations—Extranet, "Freeing Up Cash from Operations," by Alexander Niemeyer, December 2008.

affect relationships with important customers. Many companies are now servicing smaller customers through less expensive service centers.

Example:

Macy's attacked corporate fat by, among other things, combining its 12 payroll support locations into one. The company reduced the number of banks its uses. The result of these actions, according to the company, was a savings of 25 percent.

Although the proper amount of corporate fat must be determined case by case, I have found that when public firms restructure their operations, they are able to trim about 20 percent from what I defined as overspending without affecting future growth[7]. This is the same assumption as that of capital expenditures; not all excess payments to suppliers and employees can be considered discretionary, and to be conservative, only 20 percent of these amounts are classified as overexpenditure.

The cost-cutting trend that begun in earnest during the merger boom of the late 1980s continued during the economic expansion of the 1990s, with the largest companies leading the way. As the world entered the economic recession of 2007, corporate overhead and discretionary areas were slashed further, this time from a real fear of financial failure. Companies merged departments and shifted research and manufacturing to low-cost countries as quickly as they could, while requiring their remaining employees to put in longer hours, all in the hope that when demand returned, the increase in revenues would result in historically wide margins. No industry was immune, whether it be manufacturing, banking, insurance, or service. And when the economy began recovery during 2009, these companies benefited and were able to show increases in free cash flow that would not have been possible a few years earlier.

Improvements in supply-chain management saved hundreds of millions of dollars for some companies. For example, transportation accounts for about 50 percent of supply-chain costs, and through better asset utilization, routes, and modal mix, significant cash savings have been achieved.

While security analysts may not have knowledge of small departments capable of such potential improvements, published financial statements are sufficient to spot trends in expenditures where savings can be delivered without revenue diminishment.

---

[7] Because the amount a particular entity can free up while still maintaining maximum growth must be determined on an ad hoc basis, financial software can serve only as a general guide.

Currently, security analysts are taught to compare various expenses as a percentage of sales over a period of years to get an idea of whether such expenses are out of line. Such analysis is often misleading because it is the company's current and projected unit growth rate that determines the appropriate level of many expenses and expense ratios. Then, as discussed in the productivity section of Chapter 2, the firm must be managed to produce free cash flow based on that output and expense level. If the firm is incapable of doing so, expenses must be controlled further, or other means to enhance revenues (e.g., price increases or additional sales) must be put into place.

Because of inflation's effect on sales, unit growth ideally should be compared with discretionary expenditures. For example, if revenues double with no change in unit growth (in, say, an inflationary spiral), a doubling in selling and administrative expenses would destroy value because the inflation-adjusted cash flow and ROIC could decline. To calculate unit growth, the analyst would deflate revenues by the inflation adjustment for the company or industry depending on available data. This information for various industries is assembled by the Bureau of Economic Analysis.

The entity's unit growth also should be compared with growth of that unit in the industry, on a quarterly reporting basis, using industry or Bureau of Labor Statistics (BLS) data. Market share is important, but only if it results in growing free cash flow. Table 4-9 shows the price data for wireless carriers, revealing price

TABLE 4-9

Chain-Type Price Changes—Cellular Carriers

Series ID: PCU517212517212
Industry: Cellular and other wireless carriers
Product: Cellular and other wireless carriers
Base Date: 199906

Year	Jan	Feb	Mar	Apr	May	Jun	Jul	Aug	Sep	Oct	Nov	Dec	Annual
1999						100.0	100.9	99.4	99.2	98.8	98.0	97.0	
2000	96.3	95.4	95.4	94.5	95.7	94.5	94.9	93.6	94.3	92.5	90.9	91.1	94.1
2001	87.6	91.0	90.2	90.2	90.8	90.6	90.1	89.9	89.8	90.4	90.3	90.0	90.1
2002	89.7	89.5	89.3	89.6	90.2	92.2	92.9	92.5	92.7	93.7	93.3	93.5	91.6
2003	92.9	91.4	91.5	92.1	92.1	92.4	92.6	92.5	92.9	92.3	92.3	92.4	92.3
2004	92.2	91.7	91.6	92.3	91.7	91.7	91.9	91.4	90.3	89.6	88.9	88.1	90.9
2005	86.4	83.7	82.1	81.9	80.8	79.2	79.2	78.3	77.2	76.0	75.3	74.8	79.6
2006	74.5	74.5	74.0	75.3	74.1	74.4	74.6	74.8	74.5	73.8	74.8	74.3	74.5
2007	73.9	73.2	72.5	73.7	74.6	74.4	76.5	73.8	75.1	74.2	73.4	71.6	73.9
2008	71.4	70.7	69.4	70.7	70.4	69.8	68.8	70.2	70.0	69.0	69.0	69.6	69.9
2009	68.8	68.9	68.2	67.7	70.1(P)	67.0(P)	67.0(P)	67.9(P)					

P = preliminary. All indexes are subject to revision 4 months after original publication.

deflation, which is common for new, fast-growing industries attracting many new entrants. In order to calculate unit growth, the analyst would need to deflate a firm's yearly revenues by the amount shown in the table. In this case, there have not been price increases but price declines. For example, $100 in revenue in June 1999 would require about $110 in revenue in July 2001 for the same volume. This would not be accurate if the firm is buying sales through acceptance of lower margins, so discretion is advised when using such tables. Unit growth has been greater for this industry than is implied by the price declines against sales revenue in the table and is why I prefer also evaluating cost-of-sales growth rates when prices are stable or declining with firms fighting over market share.

CAPITAL EXPENDITURES

Of all the discretionary expenditures in a business, capital spending is probably the most scrutinized because of its visibility and its nature. The mere size of capital spending (it is usually the largest use of cash on the statement of cash flows), combined with the fact that cash returns on capital spending occur many periods away, forces investors to investigate whether an entity's capital expenditures are economically justified.

Because capital spending typically represents such a large use of cash and can be cut easily, it is often the main target when business conditions soften, thereby giving the entity time to either work its way through its difficulties or wait until the economy improves.

Example:

NEW YORK (MarketWatch) – Pressured by the declining economic environment, Limited Brands—which operates the Victoria's Secret and Bath & Body Works chains—said Wednesday it plans to reduce capital spending next year by as much as 60 percent from a spending peak just two years earlier. Spending in 2009 will decline to between $300 million and $400 million from a projected $500 million this year, Chief Financial Officer Stuart Burgdoerfer said at the company's annual analyst meeting in Columbus, Ohio, compared with the company's peak spending level of $749 million in 2007. The spending cuts for this year and next will come from curtailing various real estate projects, including scaling back the number of store openings and remodels the company plans, said Chief Administrative Officer Martyn Redgrave at the company's analyst meeting.

Source: MarketWatch, October 22, 2008.

Forecasting capital spending is difficult because it depends on the economy, available investment opportunities, and the specific conditions of the firm, particularly on its expected rate of growth and its ability to produce free cash flow, alongside its cost of capital, leverage, and financial flexibility. Thus, forecasting capital spending is best left up to management estimates, and corporate executives should clearly state their capital expenditure budgets for as many years into the future as practical, including their requirements and the financial standards of projects they have or would accept. Analysts then must determine if management is true to those standards.

For cyclic entities, capital expenditures can be as volatile as cash flows. For such entities, especially when liquidity deteriorates, capital spending often would reflect the minimum that is needed to sustain the business entity. Still, we must devise a way to estimate the component of capital expenditures that is discretionary and that is not necessary to sustain the growth of the business.

When credit-rating agencies evaluate capital spending, they often add to the reported amount what they call *imputed capital spending* from the operating lease payment, on the theory of comparability. I do not agree with this methodology because to do so would distort the actual free cash flow that could be distributed to shareholders if it were to be subtracted. The financing method does indeed, in and of itself, provide or reduce free cash flow; hopefully, it also will result, by virtue of the asset financed, in even greater free cash flow in the future.

If the entity is capable of servicing its operating leases from operating cash flows, management is left with cash to deploy as it sees fit and not keep in reserve, as the credit agencies would imply. The present value of such leases is added to total debt, and its impact would be felt there (including my ROIC measure), as well as the credit metrics based on total debt. To the extent that an analyst believed a portion of operating leases should be considered a capital-spending surrogate, capital ratios would be affected.

Some security analysts prefer to look at what they consider to be "maintenance" capital spending, that is, capital expenditures that are adequate to keep up the current level of production. This is faulty for the growing concern because it does not take into account the appropriate future needs any capital budget should consider. During periods of financial stress, it would not be inappropriate to consider maintenance capital spending because maximum liquidity may be needed to satisfy debt or other legal obligations—maintenance capital spending in fact may be too high, and the entity may shut or partially close certain of its facilities. If the entity is forced to cut back capital spending plans to a minimum for an extended period, it most likely does not have growing free cash flow or, perhaps, any free cash flow. These entities would not have the required cash to stay competitive if their peers are investing in productive assets. Also, the time to reduce capital spending to a maintenance level could be longer than anticipated if agreements to purchase capital already have been entered into.

When evaluating long-term capital projects, the preferable method is to fund projects that have an expected ROIC in excess of its cost of capital while allowing for a margin of error to the return. Theorists claim that the entity should accept any project for which ROIC is greater than its cost of capital.

Example:

Crown Castle defines recurring cash flow to be Adjusted EBITDA, less interest expense and less sustaining capital expenditures. Each of the amounts included in the calculation of recurring cash flow are computed in accordance with GAAP, with the exception of sustaining capital expenditures, which is not defined under GAAP. We define sustaining capital expenditures as capital expenditures (determined in accordance with GAAP) which do not increase the capacity or life of our revenue generating assets and include capitalized costs related to (i) maintenance activities on our towers, (ii) vehicles, (iii) information technology equipment, and (iv) office equipment.

Source: Crown Castle, Q2, 2009, conference call to shareholders.

Clorox's normalized capital expenditure (Fig. 4-7) pattern is typical for a mature consumer goods firm when viewed in relation to its $1.1 billion net property account, characterized by a low growth rate, and as capital expenditure patterns go, is somewhat, but not excessively, "lumpy." Clorox made large capital investments in PPE commencing in 1997 (not shown) and then saw a generally declining account as that build neared its end. The company began a new program during 2003. We see a fairly smooth relationship between capital spending and cost of goods sold when trend lines are introduced. However, to assess the benefits of a capital expenditures program, one has to look at the long-term benefits of free cash flow and commensurate ability to repay the added debt assumed as part of the build. Once those debt levels have been brought down, additional free cash flow should accrue to equity holders.

In some cases, one finds that a firm writes down or writes off some of the capital expenditures made earlier. Not so in Clorox's case because management has made prudent decisions and has not overinvested; free cash flow continued to rise for the period under analysis, although leverage ratios increased, resulting from the large repurchase of stock from the former controlling shareholder. The increase in free cash flow indicates that capital expenditures were justified. It is not unusual for companies to see the SG&A expense rise in the early years of a significant capital program because new hires are not yet covered by the additions to operating cash flows. Again, this was not the case with Clorox because perhaps management was concerned with a restrictive covenant (soon explained) and reigned in all unnecessary expenditures.

TABLE 4-10

Largest Capital Spending Companies, Fiscal Year 2008

Company Name	Capital Expenditures
AT&T INC	19,676
BHP Billiton Group (AUS)–ADR	8,908
BHP Billiton Group (GBR)–ADR	8,908
BP PLC–ADR	22,658
Canadian Natural Resources	9,098
Chesapeake Energy Corp.	17,649
Chevron Corp.	19,666
China Mobile, Ltd.–ADR	18,001
China Petroleum & Chem.–ADR	15,832
ConocoPhillips	19,099
Daimler AG	12,456
Deutsche Telekom AG–ADR	9,615
Devon Energy Corp.	9,375
E.On AG–ADR	12,522
Encana Corp.	8,254
Enel Spa–ADR	9,825
Eni Spa–ADR	17,137
Exxon Mobil Corp.	19,318
Ford Motor Credit Co., LLC	11,230
France Telecom–ADR	10,044
Gazprom O A O–ADR	22,171
General Electric Cap. Corp.	13,184
General Electric Co.	16,010
General Motors Corp.–PRE FASB	7,530
GMAC, LLC	10,544
Hertz Global Holdings, Inc.	10,203
Honda Motor Co., Ltd.–ADR	13,145
Korea Electric Power Co.–ADR	7,072
Lukoil Oil Co.–ADR	10,525
Marathon Oil Corp.	7,146
Motors Liquidation Co.	7,530
Nippon Telegrph. & Tele.–ADR	14,241
Nissan Motor Co., Ltd.–ADR	13,333
ORIX Corp.–ADR	8,875
Petrobras Brasileiro–ADR	29,874

Company Name	Capital Expenditures
Petrochina Co., Ltd.–ADR	31,574
Rio Tinto Group (AUS)–ADR	8,574
Rio Tinto Group (GBR)–ADR	8,574
Royal Dutch Shell, PLC–ADR	35,065
Statoilhydro ASA–ADR	9,368
Telefonica SA–ADR	10,981
Total SA–ADR	16,509
Toyota Motor Corp.–ADR	23,668
Toyota Motor Credit Corp.	7,626
Vale SA–ADR	8,074
Verizon Communications, Inc.	17,238
Vodafone Group, PLC–ADR	7,442
Volkswagen AG–ADR	10,808
Wal-Mart Stores, Inc.	11,499
XTO Energy, Inc.	13,030

FIGURE 4-7

Clorox: Three-Year Growth Rates in Yearly Capital Spending and Cost of Goods Sold

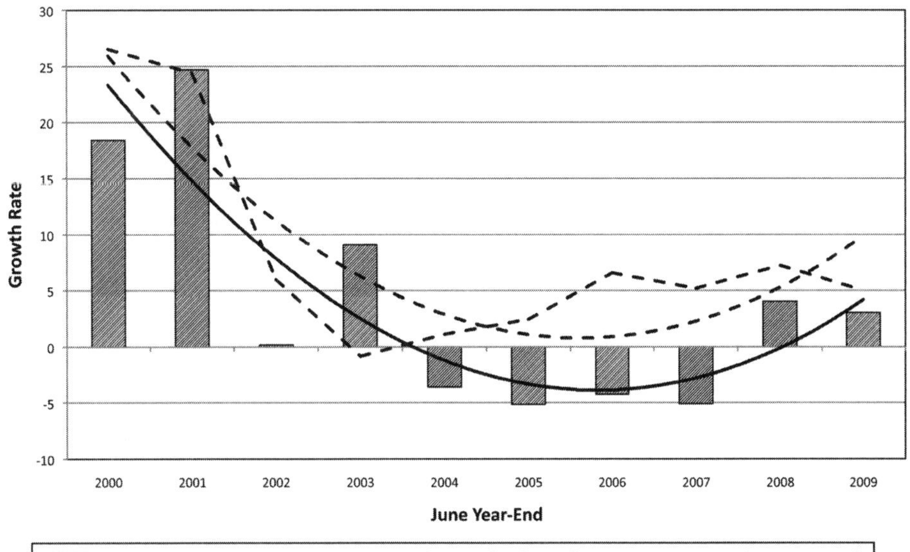

Source: Clorox 10Ks and CT Capital, LLC.

One way of estimating the requisite level of capital expenditures[8] is to compare its growth rate with COGS (Fig. 4-11). Presumably, in order to sustain a specific growth rate of COGS, capital expenditures should grow by approximately the same rate, especially during periods of modest inflation, as was the case during the years shown. If the data are given, depreciation included in COGS should be removed to both improve comparability and to adjust to a figure closer to the actual growth rate of the important inputs. Depreciation related to COGS may be found either in the property, plant, and equipment footnote or in the management discussion and analysis.

Typically, product price inflation in a competitive industry will grow similarly, if not below, the overall inflation rate for fear of losing market share. If we observe a substantially higher growth rate of capital expenditures than cost of sales during a reasonable period, then it can be assumed that the firm had overinvested in PPE during the period, and this overinvestment represents discretionary capital expenditures that can be considered a free cash flow. An entity continually needing to grow its capital spending at a greater rate than its nominal cost of sales almost always would have negative free cash flow.

To show the estimation for Clorox, I follow these steps:

1. I first estimate the annual average growth rate in capital expenditures and cost of sales over the most recent three years (Table 4-11). For example, in 2009, I divide $197 by $180 to obtain 1.094. I take the log of that, divide by the number of years growth rate (three), and then take the antilog of that for an average growth rate of 3.1 percent per year.
2. I follow similar calculations to estimate the growth rate in COGS. If the information is given, depreciation in COGS should be subtracted, and then the growth rates applied. Clorox does not report its depreciation in COGS, SG&A, R&D, or other line items, although a call to the company revealed that 80 percent the total firm depreciation was in COGS. Since depreciation would not have significantly changed the growth rate and it was not reported separately, the example shows reported COGS. For other entities, it will be significant and must be excluded from reported COGS. For 2009, the growth rate of COGS was 5 percent.

[8] Wasteful capital spending also can result from cost and time overruns, especially with projects of a long duration. Delays in such projects can be substantial and harm the estimated return, causing it to fall below its cost of capital. Additionally, if market conditions change during construction, the project could be "mothballed" or placed on hold until demand improves. The model illustrated in this chapter does not take such scenarios into account.

3. I subtract the growth rate of COGS from that of capital expenditures and substitute zero if the result is negative. For example, in 2009, the difference is −1.9 percent (5.0 – 3.1). In 2003, it is 9.9 percent because the growth rate of COGS was −0.8 percent, and the growth rate of capital expenditures was 9.1 percent.
4. I multiply the excess growth rate of capital expenditures by the COGS that year to obtain an estimate of discretionary capital expenditures for the year. For example, in 2003, I multiply the COGS of $2.076 billion by the excess growth rate of 9.9 percent to obtain $205 million, which I then multiply by 20 percent to obtain the excess, or $41.1 million. Since cost of sales was negative, indicating no growth, there was no reason to spend more than $160 million in capital expenditure (capex), which was slightly lower than the prior year. As seen, Clorox did in fact reduce its capex below that figure in subsequent years.

In 2009, the excess is zero, and no discretionary capital expenditures are designated.[9]

TABLE 4-11

Estimating Growth Rates of Capital Expenditure and Cost of Sales

	Fiscal Year Ended June								
Discretionary Capital Expenditure	**2009**	**2008**	**2007**	**2006**	**2005**	**2004**	**2003**	**2002**	**2001**
Capital expenditure	197	170	147	180	151	172	205	177	192
Three-year growth rate of cap. ex.	3.1	4.0	(5.1)	(4.2)	(5.2)	(3.6)	9.1	0.2	24.7
COGS	2,905	2,862	2,581	2,510	2,323	2,218	2,076	2,161	2,146
Three-year growth rate of COGS	5.0	7.2	5.2	6.5	2.4	1.1	(0.8)	5.9	24.4
Excess growth rate of COGS	0.0	0.0	0.0	0.0	0.0	0.0	9.9	0.0	0.3
Discretionary cap. ex.	0.0	0.0	0.0	0.0	0.0	0.0	41.1	0.0	1.3

[9] The astute reader may ask why should we consider some capital expenditures as discretionary (when the growth rate of capital expenditures exceeds that of cost of sales), but when capital expenditures lag behind sales, I do not subtract from operating cash flows an additional amount that is equal to the "required" capital expenditures that were not undertaken. The reason for this seeming inconsistency is that firms can increase productivity owing to technological advances and other measures (outsourcing) without requiring comparable investments in capital expenditures. Thus, in my calculations, I do not penalize firms that become more efficient.

Based on these estimates of the discretionary expenditures on PPE, I obtain the estimated free cash flow by subtracting total capital expenditures from net operating cash flows and adding back discretionary capital expenditures, or FCFIV (Table 4-12). If Clorox had preferred stock in its capital structure, one would need to deduct those dividend payments to arrive at cash available to shareholders.

The procedure I used to estimate discretionary capital expenditures may seem arbitrary at a first glance. I first estimate the growth rate over three years (which requires four years of data) in capital expenditures and cost of sales. The decision to use four years stems from a balancing of two errors; a longer period may yield unfair comparisons because firms change substantially over time. They branch out to other lines of business or decide to dispose of existing lines of business. However, a period shorter than four years is unlikely to include an entire business cycle. Thus I focus on four years in my analysis. In this example I have both an expansion and a recession in the data.

I compare the rate of growth in capital expenditures with that of COGS. Ideally, as stated, I could have used a physical measure of output to examine the required growth rate of inputs needed to support the growth level of output. However, firms do not provide physical output or input measures, and one has to resort to estimates if BLS or trade data pricing is unavailable or not comparable with the entity's product mix. I feel that cost of sales is a good measure of growth in output because it comprises all components of product costs. Given fairly similar price increases between inputs and outputs, the growth rates of cost of sales and capital expenditures should be good proxies for growth rates in physical outputs and inputs.

TABLE 4-12

Estimating Free Cash Flow–FCFIV

	Fiscal Year Ended June								
Calculating Free Cash Flow	**2009**	**2008**	**2007**	**2006**	**2005**	**2004**	**2003**	**2002**	**2001**
Operating cash flow minus cap. ex.	541	560	562	342	614	727	598	699	555
Discretionary cap. ex.	0.0	0.0	0.0	0.0	0.0	0.0	41.1	0.0	1.3
FCFIV	541.0	560.0	562.0	342.0	614.0	727.0	639.1	699.0	556.3

COGS needs to be inspected because it is a product of many items in addition to the cost of merchandise sold, some of which could be temporary aberrations and could account for a biased result. Where a bias exists, the result should be adjusted. Items included in COGS could include taxes (other than income), supplies, maintenance and repairs, insurance, licenses, and light and power. I exclude the depreciation piece of SG&A because doing so may better reflect the discretionary component.

Over 30 years of using this method supports the estimation procedure. When checking the distribution of what was termed *discretionary payments* to suppliers and employees in the entire population of Compustat firms (existing firms and those in the research database of merged and failed firms), about 20 to 25 percent of all firms had discretionary payments to suppliers and employees in any given year. When comparing the magnitude of those discretionary cash flows with total sales of the firm, it was found that fewer than 6 percent of the firms in any given year had any discretionary cash flows that exceeded 10 percent of total sales. Thus errors in estimates probably would not affect the ranking of firms significantly in terms of their free cash flow. Even if one used other percentages or other approaches to estimate the discretionary components of these expenditures, one probably would have obtained similar results to those obtained in the estimation procedure.

One might ask, Why not add the full amount of excess spending? It has been shown that companies can cut too much, leading to a less efficiently run enterprise for the long term.[10] When labor is thin and the remaining workforce is overtaxed, inefficiencies begin to appear. When executives speak of "across the board" cuts, analysts should be concerned that the cuts are taking place in the right areas, in the right amounts, and for the right reasons. Additionally, our research at CT Capital has found 20 percent of the excess to be correct, even if cost of sales growth is negative, as it was for Clorox during 2003. To stipulate that Clorox should have had zero capital spending if there was no growth in cost of sales would be incorrect, especially for an entity with strong free cash flow. Had the company's cost of sales continued to fall, its capital spending should have continued to fall. The model correctly picked up Clorox's peak capital

[10] Low levels of capital spending can lead to staying with a less than optimal mix of more costly labor, whereas cutting back on advertising has shown to lead to loss of market share for many companies. As Ted Turner, the founder of CNN, was known to say, "Early to bed and early to rise, but don't forget to advertise." And of course, R&D budgets are crucial for innovative companies, such as 3M. McKinsey Quarterly, in July 2008, wrote, "Cutting research costs across the board in a recession isn't smart."

spending and adjusted it to a normal level. This was verified because Clorox did reduce capital spending in subsequent years.

Can one identify expenses other than capital expenditures that are discretionary in nature? An immediate candidate is expenditures made in the daily operations of the firm, where management may expend cash flows in its operations beyond those needed to sustain growth. For example, payments for goods that were acquired or produced, payments for SG&A expenses, payments for advertising, and payments for R&D efforts may be in excess of the level that is needed to sustain the current growth rate in sales. Thus it is important to obtain estimates of discretionary cash outflows for the firm's ongoing operations.

Unfortunately, few have attempted to quantify the corporate fat portion of overhead. In fact, little has been written about corporate overhead in textbooks on security analysis, investments, and accounting. The current literature has not tied the financial process to the management process, although management consulting firms have long established that corporate overhead is excessive for most firms. For example, whereas corporate overhead represented about 10 percent of total product cost at the beginning of the twentieth century, corporate overhead now contributes more than 40 percent to total product costs (e.g., see articles that discuss activity-based costing in the *Journal of Cost Management*).

Corporate restructuring, which became so prevalent beginning in the 1980s, still has a long way to go, according to the measures explained in this chapter. Management consultants agree because one sees a greater percentage of companies adopting a variety of management tools and techniques all aimed to cut corporate fat some thirty years later. There is little doubt that labor and production efficiencies are here to stay, whereas bloated overhead practices and featherbedding are a thing of the past.

The severity of the 2007–2008 recession, as well as the lingering effects of the previous expansion's debt buildup, has only stepped up the frontal attack on corporate cost structure both in the United States and abroad. Employers, from small to large, both private to public, including leading-edge management firms such as IBM, Sony, United Technologies, Colgate-Palmolive, and Hitachi, are just some who have taken a hard look at their corporate fat and decided it was too high in relation to their current and projected rate of growth. In fact, it is difficult to find a company of any size that has not been forced to review its cost structure. The investment marketplace has rewarded companies that already had strong cash flows as they announced incremental reductions to their cost structure because such steps are bound to further increase their free cash flow. Also rewarded were companies cutting costs or divisions in slow-growth segments and deploying those additional resources into their proven high-free-cash-flow growth segment.

Example:

AT&T made the following announcement in December 2008:

> AT&T said Thursday that it will cut about 12,000 jobs, or 4 percent of its workforce, due largely to "economic pressures."
>
> AT&T said it wants to streamline its operations as its business morphs to one that's largely dependent on wireless service. AT&T added that it will add jobs in growth areas such as wireless, video, and broadband. *For many quarters*, AT&T's wireless and U-verse broadband service have shown growth as its once-core wireline business erodes.
>
> AT&T also said that it will cut its 2009 capital spending budget from 2008 levels, but didn't give specific guidance.

For other entities announcing cost cuts but which had negative free cash flow, such as GM, the market punished their stocks as further proof that the cuts were too late, and their operating cash flows too weak, to be saved by shaving expenses. These announcements were merely a tacit recognition that their business prospects were extremely weak.

CONSOLIDATED BALANCE SHEETS

The Clorox Company

	As of June 30 (Dollars in Millions, Except Share Amounts)	
	2009	**2008**
Assets		
Current assets		
Cash and cash equivalents	$206	$214
Receivables, net	486	505
Inventories, net	366	384
Other current assets	122	150
Total current assets	1,180	1,253
Property, plant, and equipment, net	955	960
Goodwill	1,630	1,658
Trademarks, net	557	560
Other intangible assets, net	105	123
Other assets	149	158
Total assets	$4,576	$4,712

(Continued)

	As of June 30 (Dollars in Millions, Except Share Amounts)	
	2009	2008
Liabilities and Stockholders' Deficit		
Current liabilities		
Notes and loans payable	$421	$755
Current maturities of long-term debt	577	—
Accounts payable	381	418
Accrued liabilities	472	440
Income taxes payable	86	52
Total current liabilities	1,937	1,665
Long-term debt	2,151	2,720
Other liabilities	640	632
Deferred income taxes	23	65
Total liabilities	4,751	5,082
Commitments and contingencies		
Stockholders' deficit		
Common stock: $1.00 par value, 750,000,000 shares authorized, 158,741,461 shares issued on June 30, 2009 and 2008, and 139,157,976 and 138,038,052 shares outstanding on June 30, 2009 and 2008, respectively	159	159
Additional paid-in capital	579	534
Retained earnings	640	386
Treasury shares, at cost: 19,583,485 and 20,703,409 shares on June 30, 2009 and 2008, respectively	(1,206)	(1,270)
Accumulated other comprehensive net losses	(347)	(179)
Stockholders' deficit	(175)	(370)
Total liabilities and stockholders' deficit	$4,576	$4,712

CONSOLIDATED STATEMENTS OF EARNINGS

The Clorox Company

	Years ended June 30 (Dollars in Millions, Except Per-Share Amounts)		
	2009	2008	2007
Net sales	$5,450	$5,273	$4,847
Cost of products sold	3,104	3,098	2,756

	Years ended June 30 (Dollars in Millions, Except Per-Share Amounts)		
	2009	2008	2007
Gross profit	2,346	2,175	2,091
Selling and administrative expenses	715	690	642
Advertising costs	499	486	474
Research and development costs	114	111	108
Restructuring and asset impairment costs	20	36	13
Interest expense	161	168	113
Other expense (income), net	26	(9)	(2)
Earnings from continuing operations before income taxes	811	693	743
Income taxes on continuing operations	274	232	247
Earnings from continuing operations	537	461	496
Earnings from discontinued operations	—	—	5
Net earnings	$537	$461	$501
Earnings per share			
Basic			
Continuing operations	$3.86	$3.30	$3.28
Discontinued operations	—	—	0.03
Basic net earnings per share	$3.86	$3.30	$3.31
Diluted			
Continuing operations	$3.81	$3.24	$3.23
Discontinued operations	—	—	0.03
Diluted net earnings per share	$3.81	$3.24	$3.26
Weighted average shares outstanding (in thousands)			
Basic	139,015	139,633	151,445
Diluted	141,063	142,004	153,935

See notes to consolidated financial statements.

CONSOLIDATED STATEMENTS OF CASH FLOWS

The Clorox Company

	Years Ended June 30 (In Millions)		
	2009	2008	2007
Operating activities:			
Net earnings	$537	$461	$501
Deduct: Earnings from discontinued operations	—	—	5
Earnings from continuing operations	537	461	496

(Continued)

	Years Ended June 30 (In Millions)		
	2009	2008	2007
Adjustments to reconcile earnings from continuing operations to net cash provided by continuing operations:			
Depreciation and amortization	190	205	192
Share-based compensation	58	47	49
Deferred income taxes	(1)	(51)	(19)
Asset impairment costs	3	29	4
Other	33	23	26
Changes in:			
Receivables, net	(2)	(8)	(15)
Inventories, net	—	(26)	(8)
Other current assets	(4)	11	13
Accounts payable and accrued liabilities	(40)	63	(30)
Income taxes payable	(6)	(24)	11
Pension contributions to qualified plans	(30)	—	(10)
Net cash provided by operations	738	730	709
Investing activities:			
Capital expenditures	(197)	(170)	(147)
Businesses acquired	—	(913)	(123)
Other	—	1	2
Net cash used for investing activities	(197)	(1,082)	(268)
Financing activities:			
Notes and loans payable, net	(334)	681	(87)
Long-term debt borrowings	11	1,256	—
Long-term debt repayments	—	(500)	(150)
Treasury stock purchased	—	(868)	(155)
Cash dividends paid	(258)	(228)	(183)
Issuance of common stock for employee stock plans and other	41	39	119
Net cash (used for) provided by financing activities	(540)	380	(456)
Effect of exchange rate changes on cash and cash equivalents	(9)	4	5
Net (decrease) increase in cash and cash equivalents	(8)	32	(10)
Cash and cash equivalents:			
Beginning of year	214	182	192
End of year	$206	$214	$182
Supplemental cash flow information:			
Cash paid for:			
Interest	$161	$153	$117
Income taxes, net of refunds	275	299	272
Noncash financing activities:			
Dividends declared and accrued but not paid	70	64	61

Clorox has invested heavily in its own stock, using debt and free cash flow to finance the purchases. Over the nine-year period ending June 2008, Clorox spent $2.7 billion buying back its shares (of which $2.1 billion was from its former majority shareholder and was financed with debt) while paying out $1.95 billion in dividends, which was somewhat offset by its issuance of $673 million in equity to employee stock plans. As Fig. 4-8 shows, Clorox's ability to produce strong and consistent free cash flow has benefited shareholders because the stock outperformed the Standard and Poor's (S&P) 500 Index by a wide margin. This has not come without a cost because the cash used to purchase those shares has wiped out shareholders' equity.

Fortunately, the consistency of Clorox's operating and free cash flow has given the firm the financial flexibility to conduct its operations with sufficient borrowing capacity, if needed. Clorox states in its 10K that it has $1.1 billion committed in unused credit lines (expires in 2013) and an additional $600 million it could borrow without being in violation of restrcitive covenants on that line. Given that Clorox has negative net worth, its most restrictive covenant is a maximum ratio of total debt/four-quarter trailing EBITDA of 3.25.

Table 4-13 shows EBITDA and total debt for one quarter, and to calulate the covenant ratio, one needs to compute the past four quarters. Clorox had four quarters of EBITDA totaling $1,161 million, which, when divided by its total debt,

FIGURE 4-8

Clorox: Cumulative Return versus S&P 500

TABLE 4-13

Quarter Ending June 2009: EBITDA and Total Debt Used in Covenant Calculation

	($ Millions)
Net income	128
Add: Interest expense	42
Income taxes	58
Depreciation and amortization	47
Interest income	(1)
EBITDA	274
Total debt	3,149

TABLE 4-14

Clorox Contractural Obligaions, 2010–2014

	2010	2011	2012	2013	2014	Thereafter	Total
Long-term debt maturities and interest payments	$706	$414	$116	$925	$52	$1,069	$3,282
Notes and loans payable	421	—	—	—	—	—	421
Purchase obligations (see note 18)	336	153	71	17	3	4	584
Operating leases (see note 18)	61	58	58	54	50	21	302
ITS agreement (service agreement only) (See note 18)	38	34	33	31	7	—	143
Contributions to nonqualified supplemental postretirement plans	14	15	15	15	16	119	194
Terminal obligation pursuant to venture agreement (see note 13)	—	—	—	—	—	269	269
Total contractual obligations	$1,576	$674	$293	$1,042	$128	$1,482	$5,195

equates to 2.71. Based on the 3.25 ceiling, Clorox could have taken on an additional $624 million in debt (3.25 × 1,161 – 3,149) and still been under the credit revolver covenant.

Clorox's cash flows and unused credit capacity should be able to satisfy its contractural oblications, as reported in Table 4-14.[11]

[11] The appropriate liquidity cushion an entity has available depends on its stage of the economic cycle, trade, debt, and other obligations coming due, and its ability to generate operating cash flow. During its third quarter 2009 conference call with investors and security analysts, Prudential Financial stated that it felt comfortable having an 18- to 24-month cash cushion, which some investors believed was excessive and would retard results.

OTHER DISCRETIONARY ITEMS

1. I now break the discretionary payments to suppliers and employees into several components. The first is the component of R&D expenditures that is discretionary (Table 4-15). To estimate them, I use the same procedure as for capital expenditures, except here I multiply the excess by current R&D expenditures, not by cost of sales, and then by 20 percent, which is considered excess. If there is depreciation expense included with R&D, it should be excluded, meaning that it should be deducted from the reported R&D figure. About 7 percent of reported depreciation is related to R&D, as learned from a call to the company. R&D is a naturally smoother time series than is capital spending and is an area where expenses typically are less subject to economic cycles. For this reason, excess capital spending, a lumpier item, is smoothed to cost of sales, whereas the other excess discretionary areas are smoothed in relation to themselves. I use the three-year growth rate, which required four yearly data points.

2. I next proceed to estimate discretionary cash flows in the firm's expenditures on COGS (Table 4-16). Depreciation expense included in COGS should be excluded wherever possible from stated COGS. Clorox does not report this. The estimation process here is to compare the ratio of COGS to sales with the long-run ratio (average of the most recent four years). If the ratio exceeds the long-run average ratio, some of these expenditures are considered discretionary, and 20 percent of the excess is multiplied by current sales to determine the amount of excess COGS that is considered discretionary cash flows. We can see the jump in Clorox's COGS in 2001, explained by the company in its 10K as "mostly due to the provision for inventory obsolescence of $54 million which included $39 million for inventories associated primarily with discontinued product lines, packaging, and unsuccessful product launches. Higher energy, raw-material and packaging costs, and an unfavorable assortment mix due to a shift to larger sizes also contributed to the increase."

TABLE 4-15

Discretionary R&D

	Fiscal Year Ended June								
Discretionary R&D	**2009**	**2008**	**2007**	**2006**	**2005**	**2004**	**2003**	**2002**	**2001**
Research and development	114	111	108	99	88	84	76	67	67
Three-year growth rate of R&D	4.8	8.0	8.7	9.2	9.5	7.8	6.5	2.6	6.2
Three-year growth rate of COGS	5.0	7.2	5.2	6.5	2.4	1.1	–0.8	0.0	0.1
Discretionary R&D	0.0	0.2	0.8	0.5	1.2	1.1	1.1	0.4	0.8

TABLE 4-16

Discretionary COGS

	Fiscal Year Ended June								
Discretionary COGS	**2009**	**2008**	**2007**	**2006**	**2005**	**2004**	**2003**	**2002**	**2001**
COGS	2,905	2,862	2,581	2,510	2,323	2,218	2,076	2,161	2,146
Sales	5,450	5,273	4,847	4,644	4,388	4,324	4,144	4,061	3,903
Four-year average as percent of sales	53.7%	53.6%	52.9%	52.1%	51.9%	52.4%	52.6%	51.4%	48.2%
Current-year COGS as percent of sales	53.3%	54.3%	53.2%	54.0%	52.9%	51.3%	50.1%	53.2%	55.0%
Discretionary COGS	0.0	6.8	3.6	18.1	9.2	0.0	0.0	14.8	52.9

Of all the discretionary areas, cost of sales is, after capital spending, normally the largest item. For Clorox, unusual bumps in COGS always have been followed by retreat to normal levels.

I use a very similar process for the SG&A expenses, after excluding advertising expenses and R&D expenses, which are usually included in SG&A expenses. I also multiply the excess by 25 percent, not 20 percent as for COGS, because this item is more subject to managerial discretion. We see a clear trend in the reduction in Clorox's SG&A expenses as a percent of sales owing to substantial labor force reduction and synergies from acquisitions (Fig. 4-9 and Table 4-17). This reduction in SG&A expenses, more than any other area, has led to the increase seen in free cash flow for Clorox over the years. In the company's 2001 10K, Clorox stated that the large reduction on SG&A was due to the ongoing benefit of combining the former First Brands businesses with the company and savings from lower commission expense primarily owing to the consolidation of the company's broker network. The analyst should remove all atypical inputs the firm shoves into SG&A, such as early extinguishment of debt, because it should reflect only the actual expenses related to sales.

Clorox has shown that it is continually searching for ways to stay lean because the efficiencies that it put in place today may not be optimal tomorrow. This way of thinking has not been confined to Clorox, as clearly substantiated by the secular international production shift to lower-cost geographies for most manufacturers. For example, in 1997, labor costs were roughly equal between China and Vietnam; a decade later, a Chinese manufacturing worker costs nearly three times as much as his or her Vietnamese counterpart. In 2009, Nike manufactured more shoes in Vietnam than in China for the first time in its history.

FIGURE 4-9

Clorox: SG&A as a Percentage of Sales

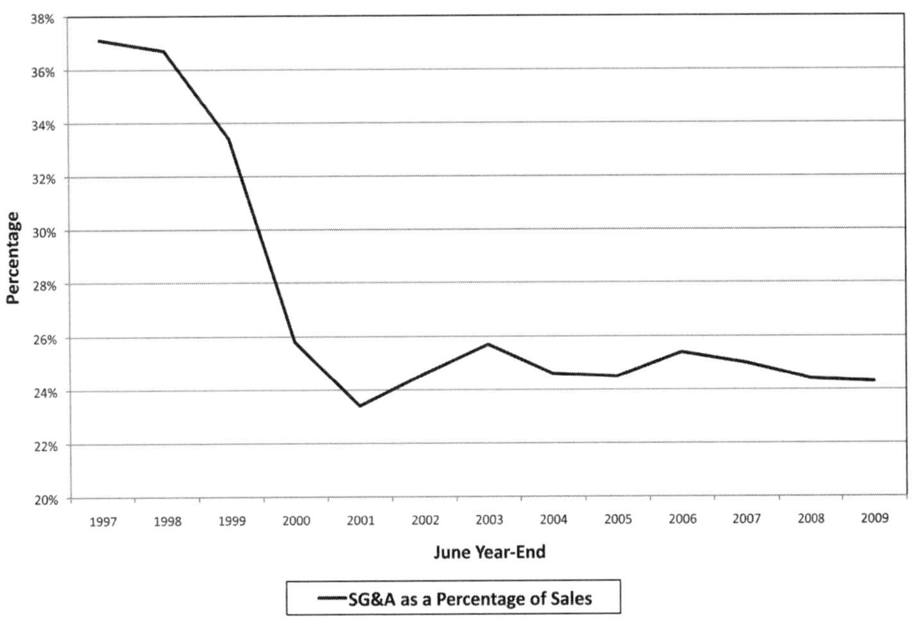

TABLE 4-17

Clorox: SG&A as a Percentage of Sales

	Fiscal Year Ended June								
Discretionary SG&A	**2009**	**2008**	**2007**	**2006**	**2005**	**2004**	**2003**	**2002**	**2001**
SG&A	1,326	1,287	1,210	1,180	1,074	1,065	1,064	1,001	914
Sales	5,450	5,273	4,847	4,644	4,388	4,324	4,144	4,061	3,903
Four-year average as percent of sales	24.8%	24.8%	24.9%	25.0%	24.9%	24.6%	24.9%	26.8%	29.8%
Current year SG&A as percent of sales	24.3%	24.4%	25.0%	25.4%	24.5%	24.6%	25.7%	24.6%	23.4%
Discretionary SG&A	0.0	0.0	1.2	4.6	0.0	0.0	8.3	0.0	0.0

As clearly evidenced, Clorox is a well-managed company having very limited excess SG&A expenditures. This was not always the case. In the mid–1980s through the mid–1990s, Clorox had shown a larger amount of corporate fat that it has combatted each year and continues to do so. The large share buyback, by driving shareholders equity negative, has been the motivating factor.

3. I now estimate the discretionary component in advertising expenses. The estimation process is very similar to that of the prior two components, except that I consider 50 percent of the excess of advertising expenses to be discretionary. Being a consumer product company, Clorox has a large advertising budget that can be altered quickly if business conditions warrant. The company has been very efficient with its advertising expenditures, constantly reducing the budget as a percentage of revenues, and so my model picks up no corporate fat in this area over the past six years. The shift from television and print media to the Internet also has positively affected the expense budget. This is far different from the 1980s and early 1990s, when Clorox had been overspending on advertising almost every year, as shown through this methodology. Bear in mind that total advertising dollars grew in nominal terms over the years shown (Table 4-18), but revenues were showing at an even greater percentage growth, forcing the result.

4. Finally, I estimate the extent to which funding (prepayment) of pension obligations can be considered discretionary. I compute the change in pension prepayment during the year and assume that 25 percent of it is discretionary, if it is positive (Table 4-19). If the change is negative, I disregard it in the estimation of free cash flow.

Let me now summarize all the discretionary items and the resulting net free cash flow. To arrive at net free cash flow, I subtract capital expenditures from cash flow from operating activities (FCF1) and add back overspending on discretionary items, including that related to capital spending. Recall that I also could have come up with the same result beginning with the change in cash between two periods and then adding and subtracting those events which were not necessary for the firm's continuing operations. Increases in cash that result from liquidation of fixed

TABLE 4-18

Discretionary Advertising Expenses

	Fiscal Year Ended June								
Discretionary Advertising	**2009**	**2008**	**2007**	**2006**	**2005**	**2004**	**2003**	**2002**	**2001**
Advertising expense	499	486	474	450	435	429	456	397	352
Sales	5,450	5,273	4,847	4,644	4,388	4,324	4,144	4,061	3,903
Four-year average as percent of sales	9.5%	9.6%	9.8%	10.1%	10.2%	9.9%	10.3%	10.5%	11.3%
Current-year advertising as percent of sales	9.2%	9.2%	9.8%	9.7%	9.9%	9.9%	11.0%	9.8%	9.0%
Discretionary advertising	0.0	0.0	0.0	0.0	0.0	0.0	14.5	0.0	0.0

TABLE 4-19

Discretionary Pension Prepayment

Year:	**6/98**	**6/99**	**6/00**	**6/01**	**6/02**	**6/03**
Pension prepayment:	23	7	16	23	0	17
25% of difference:	5.8	1.8	4	5.8	0	4.3
Year:	**6/04**	**6/05**	**6/06**	**6/07**	**6/08**	**6/09**
Pension prepayment	44	26	17	−74	−125	−193
25% of difference	11	6.5	4.3	0	0	0

assets or from external financing would be subtracted from the change in cash because they do not represent cash flows that were generated from continuing operations of the business. I also would adjust cash flow from operations if any artificial boosts or charges existed, such as the under(over)funding of a pension contribution, payment in kind, or classification as a financing or investment activity (reverse) that should have been listed as an operating activity. These are explained in Chapter 8. I made no such adjustments with Clorox.

At this point I can assess total corporate fat as the excess of discretionary capital expenditures plus discretionary R&D expenditures and discretionary COGS, advertising, pension prepayment, and discretionary SG&A (Table 4-20). These items represent corporate fat or additions to free cash flow because they are not required to sustain the current growth of the firm. On this account, Clorox can be described as a strong, consistent generator of free cash flow.

Aside from being an efficiently managed firm (lack of egregious overspending), the data on Clorox illustrate that well-managed firms are more likely to be good free-cash-flow generators because they fully use their resources; such entities typically show better than average investment performance. In Clorox's case, its free cash flow was used, in good part, to repurchase stock, which might have contributed, with the company's back against the wall, to its tight expense control in discretionary spending. Management has been very diligent in controlling the company's labor expense, advertising, and capital expenditures while they have shrunk the capital base, but not to the detriment of creating shareholder value.

Compare the lack of Clorox's corporate fat with that of a competitor, Proctor & Gamble (P&G), which has $67 billion in shareholder's equity. While Clorox has been forced, by virtue of its deficit equity, to operate lean, not quite the same can be said for P&G, which, using the same methodology shown for Clorox, exhibits excess spending in three areas. P&G, like Clorox, is also an excellent generator of

TABLE 4-20

Summary of Discretionary Items

Year:	6/98	6/99	6/00	6/01	6/02	6/03
Discretionary items:						
Capital expenditures value:	0.0	5.2	0.0	1.3	0.0	41.1
R&D expense value:	7.7	7.0	4.7	0.8	0.4	1.1
COGS (20%):	0.0	24.1	59.7	52.9	14.8	0
SG&A (25%):	.7	0.0	0.0	0.0	0.0	8.3
Pension prepayment (25%):	5.8	1.8	4.0	5.8	0.0	4.3
Advertising value:	0.0	0.0	0.0	0.0	0.0	14.5
Net free cash flow:	227.3	454.1	566.2	615.8	714.2	667.3
Year:	**6/04**	**6/05**	**6/06**	**6/07**	**6/08**	**6/09**
Discretionary items:						
Capital expenditures value:	0.0	0.0	0.0	0.0	0.0	0.0
R&D expense value:	1.1	1.2	0.5	0.8	0.2	0.0
COGS (20%):	0.0	9.2	18.1	3.6	6.8	0.0
SG&A (25%):	0.0	0.0	4.6	1.2	0.0	0.0
Pension prepayment (25%):	11.0	6.5	4.3	0.0	0.0	0.0
Advertising value:	0.0	0.0	0.0	0.0	0.0	0.0
Net free cash flow:	739.1	630.9	369.5	567.6	557.0	541.0

free cash flow and has had superior stock performance by virtue of those free cash flows and low cost of capital. Quite noticeably, its overspending was reduced considerably during 2009 in reaction to its decline in operating cash flows resulting from the severe recession. During fiscal year 2009, P&G executed a number of significant reorganization changes and, as seen in Table 4-21, eliminated its excess SG&A and almost all its excess advertising.

An area I have not included in this section is the analysis of working capital items. Such savings can result in significant cash flows, but in my estimation procedure, I am concerned with built-in structural spending. The analyst is free to add excess working capital to free cash flow, if desired, but only to the extent that it has not been captured by other items. In another section of this book I address the cash-conversion cycle, which, when reduced, has an important positive effect on cash flows. An entity that operates with excessive working capital will have lower free cash flow than need be. Working capital also can be enhanced by changes in interest rates because many companies finance their seasonal or longer-term working capital needs using floating-rate borrowings.

TABLE 4-21

Proctor and Gamble Co.: Cash Flows and Excess Expenditures

	Fiscal Year Ended June				
	2005	2006	2007	2008	2009
Net operating cash flow	8,722	11,375	13,435	15,814	14,919
Capital expenditures	2,181	2,667	2,945	3,046	3,238
Sale of PPE					
Free cash flow—incl. discretionary items	6,541	8,708	10,490	12,768	11,681
Free cash flow—excl. discretionary items	6,770	8,886	10,565	12,600	11,588
Discretionary capital expenditures	0.0	138.5	17.9	0.0	20.4
Discretionary R&D	0.0	0.0	0.0	0.0	0.0
Discretionary COGS	0.0	0.0	0.0	0.0	55.8
Discretionary SG&A	124.2	55.8	187.5	183.2	0.0
Discretionary advertising	0.0	240.7	0.0	35.2	7.9

Source: CT Capital, LLC.

Supply-chain improvements have been significant over the past few decades, although it is still not uncommon to see excess inventory/sales ratios for many companies that wish to satisfy their most demanding customers. While there is a normal managerial inclination to have inventory on hand for clients and customers, this represents a decision that must be weighed carefully against the cash savings. Reducing the cash-conversion cycle, for many companies, has the same impact as offsetting a decline in sales.

As Table 4-22 and Figure 4-10 depict, free cash flow, stock price, and net income indicate a rising trend, and as an earlier illustration showed, Clorox stock has easily outperformed the S&P 500 Index because investors value the free cash-flow consistency. Market value, owing to the reduced share count, actually declined during the period. A negative aspect of large stock repurchases is that they make it easier for a hostile acquirer to buy the company. This is possible here because Clorox has not been able to increase the valuation multiple of its shares. We see that its free-cash-flow multiple has fallen from 26.5 in 2000, based on the three-year average free cash flow, to just 14.6 at fiscal end 2009.

It is almost always critical to prepare a sensitivity analysis to evaluate the change in fair value given changes in free cash flow, cost of capital, or other variables having an important impact on valuation. I prepared such a table for Clorox using a standard net-present-value model. As seen in Table 4-23, a change in Clorox's cost of capital of 0.1 will change the company's fair value by about 2 percent; an increase of 10 percent in the company's total debt will decrease fair value by 15 percent. The cost

TABLE 4-22

Clorox: Summary of Net Income, Free Cash Flow, Market Value, and Stock Price

	Fiscal Year Ended June			
Year	Net Income	Free Cash Flow	Market Value	Stock Price
1998	298	227	9,933	48
1999	246	454	12,604	53
2000	394	566	10,518	45
2001	323	616	8,005	45
2002	322	714	9,524	41
2003	493	667	9,243	43
2004	549	739	11,408	54
2005	1,096	630	8,589	56
2006	444	370	9,198	61
2007	501	568	9,428	62
2008	461	557	7,195	52
2009	537	541	7,763	55

FIGURE 4-10

Clorox: Free Cash Flow, Stock Price, Net Income, and Market Value

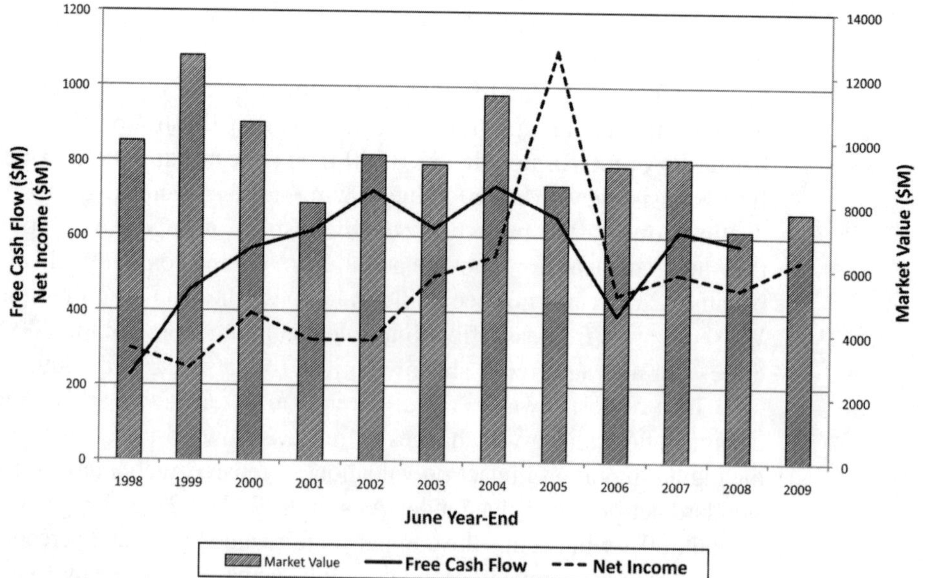

TABLE 4-23

Sensitivity Analysis Clorox Corp.

	Change	Intrinsic Value	Change in Intrinsic Value	Weighted-Average Cost of Capital
Change in cost of equity	0.1	57.8	(2.0)	8.2
Change in total debt	10.0	51.0	(14.9)	7.9
	(10.0)	66.8	11.3	7.6
Change in first-year free cash flow	0.1	68.6	14.3	7.7
Change in cash tax rate	1.0	56.3	N/A	8.0
Change in rate of perpetuity growth	0.01	64.9	0.08	7.7
	(0.01)	61.4	(0.06)	7.7

of equity for Clorox is affected by changes in debt owing to its deficit net worth, which is somewhat offset by its consistent free-cash-flow generation.

Example:

Table 4-24 presents the results of an analysis of corporate fat for IBM, a company that is continually shedding low-return businesses, moving assets and labor to low-cost areas, and trading up its business asset portfolio for more profitable and stable software businesses in its never-ending quest for maximizing free cash flow.

Also shown in Table 4-24 is IBM's free cash flow (using the methodology outlined for Clorox), including and excluding discretionary spending, and as seen, the difference has been substantial. Since IBM has moved a substantial portion of its production and research staff to low-cost geographies, including a large base in India, while at the same time shedding its PC division, we clearly see the savings, with R&D overspending dropping from over $103 million to zero in two years. As a result of IBM's additional cutbacks in overspending, the company was able to increase its free cash flow during the first half of 2009 (not shown in table) despite falling sales, resulting in its stock having the highest return of all companies in the Dow Jones Index. I still see quite a bit of overspending on SG&A, indicating that IBM still has a way to go before it can consider itself a lean organization. We learn later that IBM also has substantial pension liabilities.

TABLE 4-24

IBM Cash Flows Including Discretionary Overspending

Part I – Cash Flow Items:					
Year	**Dec-04**	**Dec-05**	**Dec-06**	**Dec-07**	**Dec-08**
Net Operating Cash Flow	15323.0	14874.0	15007.0	16090.0	18812.0
Capital Expenditures	4368.0	3842.0	4362.0	4630.0	4171.0
Sale Of PPE	1311.0	1107.0	430.0	537.0	350.0
Free Cash Flow–Including Discretionary Items	12266.0	12139.0	11075.0	11997.0	14991.0
Free Cash Flow–Excluding Discretionary Items	12395.7	12522.1	11732.9	12682.8	15237.0
Discretionary Capital Expenditures	0.0	0.0	72.5	242.1	16.2
Discretionary R&D	0.0	0.0	103.4	87.6	0.0
Discretionary Cost of Goods Sold	0.0	0.0	0.0	0.0	0.0
Discretionary SG&A	129.7	0.0	383.1	482.0	356.1
Discretionary Advertising	0.0	0.0	0.0	0.0	0.0
Large Buildup (Reduction) in Accounts Receivable	0.0	(3432.5)	(5025.0)	(1243.2)	(1150.9)
Large Buildup (Reduction) in Inventory	(1648.9)	(1140.8)	(991.2)	(618.7)	(657.8)
Large Buildup (Reduction) in Accounts Payable	(843.7)	2430.4	(825.4)	2152.3	780.0

Figure 4-11 displays the gap between IBM's free cash flow both inclusive and exclusive of its corporate fat. The success of IBM in reducing its cost structure has been a prime reason for its superior investment return.

Few, if any, business owners would deny the very strong and sound relationship between the entity's free cash flow and market value. To establish a current *fair* value for the common stock, the analyst must discount the free cash flow at a deserved cost of equity.

Additionally, in the free-cash-flow valuation discount model, the analyst should net excess cash (adjusted for required working capital and other current obligations requiring cash) on hand and total debt from the net present value of the free cash flow to calculate the unlevered value. For instance, if the entity has a net present value of its free cash flow of $20 per share and $10 per share in net debt, fair unlevered value is $10. An exception, to some investors, would be if the entity could maintain that debt and shareholders still receive their $20 in present value, but this is not the same as unlevered free cash flow, which might be a preferable metric in comparisons of relative value. If the same entity has $10 per share in cash, its fair value is $30, net of the tax effect, because shareholders theoretically could receive a $10 per share dividend (excluding taxes) in addition to the annual free cash flow. The unlevered value is primarily a theoretical exercise because typically a company's debt and cash are assumed by the new owner when the entity

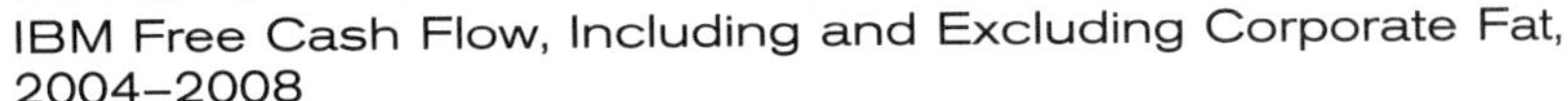

FIGURE 4-11

IBM Free Cash Flow, Including and Excluding Corporate Fat, 2004–2008

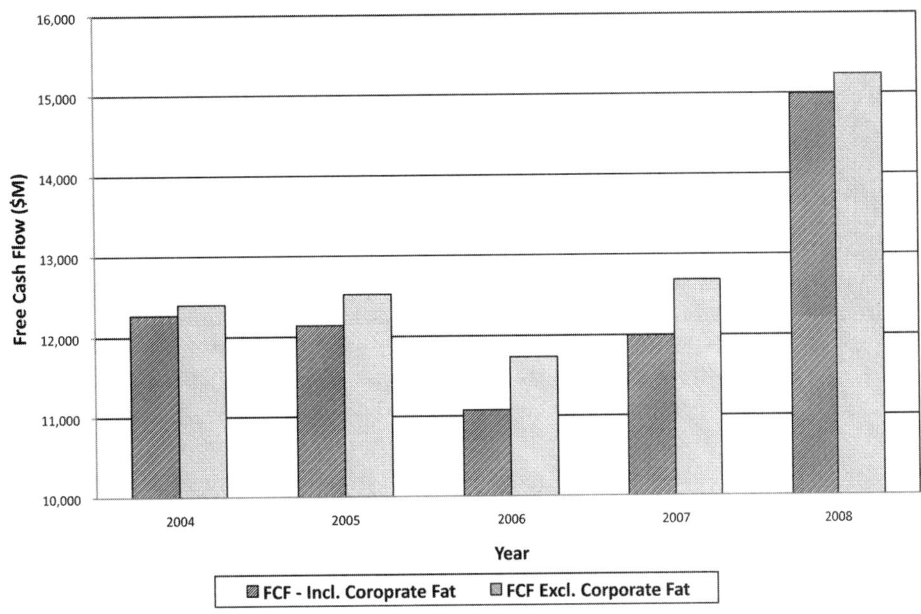

Source: CT Capital, LLC.

is acquired. Where the new owner is capable of replacing high-cost debt with either equity or low-cost debt, the new fair value should be determined.

FREE CASH FLOW, RETURN ON INVESTED CAPITAL, AND SHARE BUYBACKS

An area receiving much scrutiny when free cash flow exists and/or stock performance is sub-par is the potential repurchase of outstanding corporate shares. Share buybacks traditionally have been viewed as an outlet for free cash flow and excess balance-sheet liquidity with the intent of bolstering a firm's valuation. By shrinking the equity base and number of shares outstanding, it is believed, the firm would enhance its earnings and cash flow per share, economic profit, and hence market valuation. As has been seen by the number of companies that bought back significant amounts of their stock for treasury and later returned to investors to sell back shares at a considerably lower price, share buybacks are often a poor choice. The loss of financial flexibility and equity cushion was a central reason for the demise of many firms that had acquired large amounts of their own stock during 2007–2008. For most firms, share buybacks are used to offset the dilution resulting from stock-based compensation.

Financial theory states that companies that shrink equity by buying back shares or paying dividends with balance-sheet cash and new debt tend to see their cost of capital decline. This occurs for two reasons. The first has to do with the mystery of what management might wind up doing with the cash. Too often bad acquisitions burn cash or lower ROIC, waste management time, and increase leverage. This occurs most often when companies acquire outside of their own industry (e.g., Mobil and Montgomery Ward) but also when firms seek to diversify outside of their core competency from within their industry (e.g., AT&T and NCR).

As stated in the 2009 10K of Perrigo, Inc.:

> As part of the company's strategy, it evaluates potential acquisitions in the ordinary course of business, some of which could be and have been material. Acquisitions involve a number of risks and present financial, managerial and operational challenges. Integration activities may place substantial demands on the company's management, operational resources, and financial and internal control systems. Customer dissatisfaction or performance problems with an acquired business, technology, service, or product could also have a material adverse effect on the company's reputation and business.

The other benefit concerns the tax shield of interest payments. Using excess balance-sheet cash to pay common stock dividends does not change the cost of capital, according to popular finance, because payment is made after taxes, and the entity receives no tax benefit, as does a credit against taxes for interest expense. It is the tax shield of interest expense that reduces a firm's cost of (debt) capital because profits paid to creditors in the form of interest are not taxed. Unlike financial theory, if a firm paid a dividend through borrowing, it could raise the cost of capital in my credit model because of the increase in leverage and debt metrics.

The Chapter 8 credit model would not lower the cost of capital owing to a stock repurchase program. It does not provide cash flow and reduces financial flexibility. It has been observed, in widespread practice over the course of several business cycles, that such programs actually wind up raising the cost of capital more often than lowering it.

Entities buying back stock in the midst of a large capital spending program significantly raising leverage ratios would be especially prone to increases in their cost of debt and equity capital. Business runs in cycles, and even investment-grade companies such as The Home Depot have seen higher cost of capital resulting in part to large stock repurchases.

Seen too often are share buybacks forced on management by aggressive and vocal shareholders hoping a share repurchase program will either support the stock or allow them the flexibility to sell their holdings. But what if the entity has surplus cash on its balance sheet, low leverage, no promising investment opportunities, and is a consistent producer of free cash flow? Rather than continually shrinking its equity, which has not shown to improve stock valuation, shareholders are best rewarded by changing to management that can find worthwhile opportunities either within or outside the firm. Providing cash to selling shareholders has not proven to improve the wealth of the remaining shareholders if ROIC falls below the cost of capital.

The road to superior stock performance always has been for management to raise the ROIC, not stock buybacks.[12] Berkshire Hathaway was a slow-growth, stable free-cash-flow producer until new management arrived, deploying excess cash at every opportunity to buy high-ROIC companies, finding hundreds of opportunities, from very small to very large, including furniture manufacturers, newspapers, brokerages, food, and now a railroad. Despite Berkshire outperforming the S&P 500 by a huge margin, Berkshire has never repurchased its own shares. And even today, being a company with a $195 billion market value, it is finding no shortage of investment opportunities of the kind that are generally available to all investors.

Example:

Aside from the probable loss in financial flexibility, do share buybacks otherwise improve valuation? Take the case of a hypothetical company, Worldwide Electric Co. Think of Worldwide as having two parts: (1) the operating company, which produces $100 million in annual free cash flow, and (2) Worldwide's cash and cash equivalents (14.3 percent of equity), which can be used to buy back its shares. The firm has $100 million in payables and no other liabilities.

Assume that the company generates $100 million in free cash flow (putting aside taxes), with a market value of $1.3 billion and 100 million shares outstanding, so it generates $1.00 per share (including interest), and the stock sells at $13 per share.

If the company were to use its $100 million in cash to buy back 7.7 million shares (at its current market price), the multiple on its shares would fall to that of the operating company, or 12.5, and the company now would have approximately 92.3 million shares outstanding.

---

[12] For example, a *Wall Street Journal* article, "America's New Cash Conundrum," on January 20, 2010, pointed out that over the prior 10 years, over half the companies surveyed had a zero or negative return on their stock repurchases.

Worldwide's return on invested capital would remain exactly the same because we exclude interest income from the metric; we are only interested in the cash on cash return. While their GAAP ratios would fall, including the P/E, as a result of the reduced number of shares outstanding, the more vital cash flow return ratio is identical. And by this measure, the company still produces $96 million in free cash flow on the same capital base, or a 13.4 percent return on invested capital. The only differences are the shares outstanding and the reduced cash. If Worldwide had a greater amount of cash on its balance sheet to repurchase stock, the fall in P/E and free-cash-flow multiples would be more dramatic, and yet the ROIC still would remain the same 13.4 percent. The free-cash-flow multiple falls to that of the operating company, so from the shareholders point of view their value is not enhanced. And certainly lost is the company's financial flexibility. If it had balance-sheet debt or operating leases, the debt ratios would have increased in addition to the elimination of cash that might have been used for expansion as a low cost of capital.

Under typical circumstances, as you can see in the example to follow on Clorox, a large stock buyback can completely eliminate shareholders equity.

WORLDWIDE ELECTRIC CO.

	Before Buyback	After Buyback
Balance sheet:		
Cash	100	0
Property, plant, and equipment	700	700
Liabilities	100	100
Equity	700	600
Market value of operating company	1,200	1,200
Value of cash	100	0
Market value	1,300	1,200
Income statement:		
Free cash flow—operations	96	96
Interest income—tax-free	4	0
Free cash flow	100	96
Shares outstanding	100	92.3
Share price	$13.00	$13.00
Free cash flow per share	$1.00	$1.04
Free-cash-flow multiple	13.0	12.5
Return on invested capital	13.4%	13.4%

SHARES OUTSTANDING

Equity is normally the most expensive cost class of capital, but at times it represents the only outlet available because leverage is already at an uncomfortable level, the price of additional debt, if available, is excessive, and there are few, if any, buyers for the firm's noncore assets. Warrants and convertible securities or other forms of calls on an entity's equity can provide a necessary part of financing, and those costs also must be considered because they can equate to selling off a stake in the company, similar to selling stock.

To the equity analyst, if potential claims are far from the striking price, the current market value is to be calculated based on the total shares currently outstanding, as listed on the cover of the entity's latest regulatory filing. Dilutive securities would be added to this base amount.

When an entity reports primary or fully diluted earnings per share, it is based on the weighted-average number of shares outstanding during the quarter. It is more accurate to begin with the actual number listed on the SEC filing, as shown below for Talbots. Talbots, a clothing retailer, had an actual number of 55,303,147 shares outstanding, whereas the company reported, in its 10Q, a weighted-average number of shares for the quarter ending of 53,621,000.

Example:

UNITED STATES SECURITIES AND EXCHANGE COMMISSION

Washington, D.C. 20549

Form 10-Q

☐ **QUARTERLY REPORT PURSUANT TO SECTION 13 OR 15(d) OF THE SECURITIES EXCHANGE ACT OF 1934**

For the quarterly period ended May 2, 2009 or

☐ **TRANSITION REPORT PURSUANT TO SECTION 13 OR 15(d) OF THE SECURITIES EXCHANGE ACT OF 1934**

For the transition period from to

Commission File Number: 1–12552

THE TALBOTS, INC.

(Exact name of registrant as specified in its charter)

Delaware	41–1111318
(State or other jurisdiction of incorporation or organization)	(IRS Employer Identification No.)

One Talbots Drive, Hingham, MA 02043

(Address of principal executive offices)

Registrant's telephone number, including area code 781–749–7600

Indicate by checkmark whether the registrant (1) has filed all reports required to be filed by Section 13 or 15(d) of the Securities Exchange Act of 1934 during the preceding 12 months (or for such shorter period that the registrant was required to file such reports) and (2) has been subject to such filing requirements for the past 90 days. ☐ Yes ☐ No

Indicate by checkmark whether the registrant has submitted electronically and posted on its corporate Web site, if any, every Interactive Data File required to be submitted and posted pursuant to Rule 405 of Regulation S-T during the preceding 12 months (or for such shorter period that the registrant was required to submit and post such files). ☐ Yes ☐ No

Indicate by checkmark whether the registrant is a large accelerated filer, an accelerated filer, a nonaccelerated filer, or a smaller reporting company. See the definitions of "large accelerated filer," "accelerated filer," and "smaller reporting company" in Rule 12b–2 of the Exchange Act. (Check one):

Large accelerated filer ☐ Accelerated filer ☐ Nonaccelerated filer ☐ Smaller reporting company ☐

(Do not check if a smaller reporting company)

Indicate by checkmark whether the registrant is a shell company (as defined in Rule 12b–2 of the Exchange Act). ☐ Yes ☐ No

Indicate the number of shares outstanding of each of the issuer's classes of common stock, as of the latest practicable date.

Class	Outstanding as of June 8, 2009
Common Stock, $0.01 par value	55,303,147

And from the income statement, we see

	Basic	Diluted
Weighted-average number of shares of common stock outstanding:	53,621	53,621

Source: Talbots June 30, 2009 10Q.

The reason, in Talbots case, diluted and basic shares outstanding are identical is the fall in the price of the company's stock price such that there was no dilution from common stock equivalents in the calculation of the weighted average. In the calculation of both free cash flow per share and fair value per share, the analyst needs to divide available free cash flow by the 55.3 million actual share count, as is listed on the cover of the 10Q. If there were options or warrants outstanding, under the treasury method, it is presumed that the company uses the proceeds from the option or warrant exercise to buy back stock at the average price throughout the period. Talbot's reports a greater number of shares than the weighted amount owing to stock-based compensation and awards, demonstrating its real cost to remaining shareholders, as was shown in a previuos example for Oracle.

When an enterprise purchases its stock for treasury, we assume that the stock has been retired, although it may be accounted for under the par-value method, where it is considered a temporary reduction in shares outstanding.

Example:

Paychex is a large payroll processing company also involved in ancillary services such as benefits outsourcing, tax administration, and regulatory compliance services. The company has very strong credit and is a consistent producer of free cash flow (Table 4-25). The company has no debt, other than trade, a very stable cash tax rate, no pension or other postretirement liabilities, and holds excess cash. My credit model has picked up some deterioration in net working capital over the year, but even with that, I assign a cost of equity capital to Paychex of 7 percent, which is the discount rate I use to calculate fair value (Table 4-26), based on its free cash flow.

TABLE 4-25

Paychex Cost of Equity Capital

Part I – Cash Flow Items:

Year	May-05	May-06	May-07	May-08	May-09	Most Recent Quarter May-09	Previous Quarter May-08
Net Operating Cash Flow	467.9	569.2	631.2	724.7	688.8	125.4	134.3
Capital Expenditures	70.7	81.1	79.0	82.3	64.7	11.4	17.7
Sale of PPE	3.5	0.0	0.1	0.7	0.6	0.6	0.0
Free Cash Flow – Including Discretionary Items	400.7	488.1	552.3	643.1	624.7	114.6	116.6
Free Cash Flow – Excluding Discretionary Items	401.4	522.3	579.0	660.1	634.5	—	—
Discretionary Capital Expenditures	0.0	0.0	0.0	0.0	0.0	—	—
Discretionary R&D	0.0	0.0	0.0	0.0	0.0	—	—
Discretionary Cost of Goods Sold	0.0	34.1	26.7	17.0	9.8	—	—
Discretionary SG&A	0.8	9.8	0.0	0.0	0.0	—	—
Discretionary Advertising	0.0	0.0	0.0	0.0	0.0	—	—
Large Buildup (Reduction) in Accounts Receivable	0.0	(7.0)	2.2	(10.0)	(48.5)	(54.7)	(34.4)
Large Buildup (Reduction) in Inventory	(39.0)	0.0	0.0	0.0	0.0	0.0	0.0
Large Buildup (Reduction) in Accounts Payable	0.0	(414.9)	133.5	123.7	(521.3)	(726.1)	(5.2)

TABLE 4-26

Paychex Fair Value Estimate

Current free cash flow	$634.50						
Growth rate in cash flows	−10%	−5%	0%	3%	5%	10%	15%
Cost of capital	7%	7%	7%	7%	7%	7%	7%
Growth after 5 years	−5%	−3%	0%	2%	3%	5%	5%
Value per share	$11.94	$17.16	$26.63	$36.96	$48.15	$138.20	$171.62

With Paychex reporting $472 million in cash on its balance sheet as of May, 31, 2009, and no bank debt, one could reasonably assume, given its consistent historical ability to produce free cash of over $100 million per quarter, even during the 2007–2009 recession, that the company would need no more than $100 million in short-term liquidity, and most likely just a fraction of that, to run its day-to-day operations. Let's say that the CFO felt very comfortable holding $100 million, which would protect the company against an unusual occurrence, such as a client default on an advance from Paychex for funds for payroll taxes.[13] The analyst would evaluate quarterly cash balances and draws on credit lines to have a better understanding of Paychex's maximum daily cash needs, including a discussion, if possible, with it CFO. To the extent that the excess cash is invested in instruments earning a *de minimis* return, equity investors are being penalized if those funds could be put to more productive uses, such as expansion of the firm's existing business, which has a high ROIC.

Paychex	
Current cash balance	$472 million
Maximum cash needed	$100 million
Excess cash	$372 million
Total borrowings	0
Shares outstanding	361.1 million
Net cash per share	$1.03

[13] Today, there are excellent cash-flow requirement software packages available to the cash manager. Such programs take into account collection periods, payables, inventory, capital requirements, labor and other operating expenses, tax payments, and any unusual circumstances. In addition, each CFO needs to build in a factor for any unforeseen expenses, especially if the entity has more uncertain or lumpy cash inflows (collections).

The cover of Paychex's 10K reveals that it had 361.1 million shares outstanding as of the most recent filing period of June 30, 2009. This is less than a 1 million share variation from fully diluted shares outstanding. Thus, if one estimates Paychex's growth in free cash flow to be 3 percent, based on a conservative outlook for the company, its fair value of discounted free cash flow is $36.96, to which you add the net cash per share, resulting in a fair value of $37.99. This compares very favorably with a current price of the shares of $28.1 the day this was written.

For entities having net debt, that amount should be subtracted from fair value. In addition, if the analyst believes that the entity has need of additional cash borrowings to cover a liability not indicated by the financial statement information, such as a derivative contract that must be settled and whose value on the balance sheet understates the true liability, that added amount also should be subtracted from fair value. Of course, if the entity increasingly relied on debt or its credit metrics were either deteriorating or becoming potentially weaker, risk would be adjusted through a higher cost of equity such that even with free cash flow that met expectations, fair value would decline. For instance, increasing credit spreads, which are often based on such expectations, can serve to change the cost of capital.

CASH-FLOW PROJECTIONS

There are many excellent financial programs available for which the analyst can construct a cash-flow projection. The advised format is to use the direct method, as outlined in Chapter 3, using the firm's typical line entries. To those line entitries, the analyst should show any adjustments that are necessary, such as a reclassification of a cash-flow activity.

Reproduced as Table 4-27 is a direct-method template from Microsoft Excel that is similar to but not as detailed as that shown in the Chapter 3 example on Nu-Horizons Corp. Additional lines should be inserted as appropriate to reflect the cash transactions.

While it may be easier to formulate a cash-flow projection under the indirect format because this is the overwhelmingly common method in practice today, you will find that the information under the direct method makes more sense and will provide a better feel for the true cash flows given that noncash activities are absent and format begins where the cash process does.

In my free-cash-flow summary, as shown in Table 4-26, I estimate the five-year free cash flow and a longer-term forecast based on various growth rates. I have found this kind of general forecast, which is based on the past four-year average as

TABLE 4-27

Statement of Cash Flows Template

Statement of Cash Flows	**[Name]**	**[Time Period]**
Cash flows from operating activities		
Cash received from customers		
Cash paid for merchandise		
Cash paid for wages and other operating expenses		
Cash paid for interest		
Cash paid for taxes		
Other		
Net cash provided (used) by operating activities		
Cash flows from investing activities		
Cash received from sale of capital assets (plant and equipment, etc.)		
Cash received from disposition of business segments		
Cash received from collection of notes receivable		
Cash paid for purchase of capital assets		
Cash paid to acquire businesses		
Other		
Net cash provided (used) by investing activities		
Cash flows from financing activities		
Cash received from issuing stock		
Cash received from long-term borrowings		
Cash paid to repurchase stock		
Cash paid to retire long-term debt		
Cash paid for dividends		
Other		
Net cash provided (used) in financing activities		
Increase (decrease) in cash during the period		
Cash balance at the beginning of the period		
Cash balance at the end of the period		

a foundation for normalized growth, to be a more reliable indicator of fair value than attempting to estimate the last dime of next year's free cash flow, which, in itself, is an impossible feat. Once I am confident that my historic free cash flows are computed correctly and my cost of capital is accurate, a reasonable estimate of free-cash-flow growth ranges will confidently let the analyst know if the equity security is fairly valued.

THE SIGNIFICANCE OF ADDING CORPORATE FAT

Figure 4-12 shows the relationship between free cash flow both with and without discretionary items taken into account. Since free cash flow typically is much greater than corporate fat, one would expect the lines to be closely parallel. But the added difference is significant and can add substantially to market value because those unencumbered funds are put to use.

It is not surprising that the line indicating the presence of corporate fat remains consistently above the traditional measure, indicating that even for large, highly regarded companies, there remains substantial extra expense that could be cut.

The chart indicates that many S&P companies could increase their free cash flow by up to 30 percent if they were to benefit by 20 percent of that difference in overspending, using the procedure illustrated in the Clorox example. The analysis of discretionary savings gains momentum with each economic slowdown, and for firms that continually practice lean methods, the additional cash is often placed into high-ROIC projects.

Since the benefits are apparent, one might wonder why it takes a recession for operating officers to take action. Whether it be unions, inertia, miscalculation of

FIGURE 4-12

Average Free Cash Flow: S&P 500 Before and After Corporate Fat ($Million)

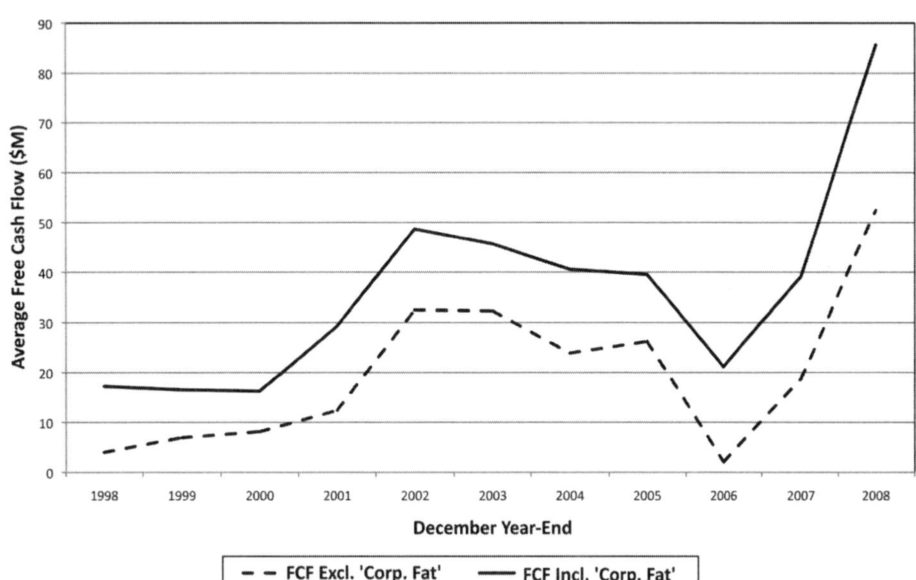

product demand, or some other factor, ultimately, corporate officers responsible to their shareholders accept and recognize the benefits of removing overstaffing and overspending, including that on facilities (supply chain), and welcome the new contribution to cash flows. As we have seen, the savings, without affecting the potential ability to deliver goods and services, are significant and can change the valuation of the entity by a considerable margin because the added free cash flow is recognized by investors. The cost cutting also provides a cushion during a business downturn and can, in effect, save further job cuts because the entity can reduce the price of its products or service by virtue of the lower cost structure and increased operating cash flow. Recall that Clorox used the savings to repurchase shares, boosting its stock value during an otherwise negative equity market. We unmistakably saw this again with IBM.

REVENUE GROWTH AND FREE CASH FLOW

Growth and stability of revenues are included in my cost-of-capital credit model. Revenues that are flat or declining often require reductions in costs for the entity to preserve its operating and free cash flow. Entities that are able to improve their products and services typically are able to generate growing cash flows along with reduced demand for external capital. To the extent that external capital is required, such entities normally have low cost of capital, allowing them to accept projects offering value creation to shareholders. Companies in cyclical industries often find it difficult to improve their products through differentiation, and so revenue growth normally is associated with gains in market share via acquisition or expansion of plant capacity. For them, free cash flows tend to be very strong during periods of economic strength and poor during recessions and slowdowns.

For companies that are riding the crest of a new technology or consumer product, revenue growth can be impressive, as could operating cash flows, but they may not lead to free cash flow if large additions to plant capacity are required. For such companies, sustainability of that growth in revenues is the important consideration because investors may be discounting free cash flow that does not currently exist.

Some companies may have aggressive policies regarding revenue recognition. If this is the case, the gap between growth in revenues and operating cash flows will be material. For some companies, the exchange rate may affect reported revenue growth.

For large technology companies, service revenue growth normally is associated with more stable and stronger free cash flow than revenues achieved from the sale of hardware.

Example:

During recessions, service segment revenues typically hold up compared with hardware sales. As reported in its July 31, 2009 10Q, Hewlett-Packard's hardware sales declined by over 20 percent, whereas services rose by almost 70 percent, driven by the company's acquisition of EDS as well as the need for the company's support by clients, even when business conditions were weak. Clients continue to prefer to have their products serviced by the original equipment manufacturer, even though it might be slightly more expensive. Also, hardware revenue typically reflects sales for a given year, whereas service revenue reflects sales over many years.

HEWLETT-PACKARD COMPANY AND SUBSIDIARIES

Consolidated Condensed Statements of Earnings

(Unaudited)

	Three Months Ended July 31		Nine Months Ended July 31	
	2009	**2008**	**2009**	**2008**
	(In Millions, Except Per-Share Amounts)			
Net revenue:				
Products	$17,606	$22,180	$53,627	$67,866
Services	9,749	5,757	29,700	16,619
Financing income	96	95	275	276
Total net revenue	$27,451	$28,032	$83,602	$84,761

Example:

Producers of coal and iron ore are often able to forecast their short-duration revenues as they work off contract prices set up to a year in advance. Thus, despite current market conditions, revenues for the year can be reasonably estimated. Their stock prices, however, often react to changes in current commodity prices, reflecting a belief the follow-up contract will result in a shift in revenues and free cash flow. This also would affect cost of capital because lenders are more willing to finance projects to a cyclic entity with a revenue stream less in doubt, even if it be for a single year.

> BHP Billiton announced Wednesday it had agreed to prices on 53 percent of its iron-ore sales for the 2009 contract year. Historically, prices were set in opaque negotiations between large miners and big steelmakers, striking a benchmark price for the year.
>
> But this time, just 23 percent of BHP's volumes have been set on an annual contract price so far. A bigger proportion, 30 percent, is being priced using a mix of quarterly, spot market, and index-based prices.

Anglo-Australian BHP, which accounts for about 15 percent of global iron-ore exports, has been pressing for more market-based pricing. Spot prices have outpaced contract prices for much of the past five years. But when spot prices collapsed last year, some steelmakers reneged on contracts. For producers, this left contracts looking like a great way to cap any upside while offering uncertain guarantees on the downside.

Market-based pricing also ought to favor large, low-cost miners like BHP. Shorter contracts and more-competitive pricing could make financing rival mines more difficult.

Source: Wall Street Journal, July 29, 2009.

CHAPTER 5

Return on Invested Capital

For most industrial entities, return on invested capital (ROIC) represents the most important measure of management ability. Projects whose ROIC exceeds their cost of capital create value, and as value-enhancing projects continue to grow, the results are reflected in the acquirer's share price. If the executives in charge of the firm's assets are consistently able to invest in such projects, this represents the most management-proven technique to reward shareholders looking to build long-term value. Improvements in ROIC are seen in companies that are able to achieve higher margins, stronger cash flow, and low cost of capital.

For entities that operate on minimal capital, we shall learn a technique that is based on ROIC but works better because as ROIC approaches zero, it results in extremely large, impractical returns, both positive and negative.

As Oracle Corporation, a very successful acquirer, wrote in its 2009 10K report: "We estimate the financial impact of any potential acquisition with regard to earnings, operating margin, cash flow, and return on invested capital targets before deciding to move forward with an acquisition."

When interest rates are low, corporate planners evaluate taking on projects they might not consider when interest rates are higher. The savings on the cost of marginal debt might make such projects worthwhile for equity holders. However, if the cost of debt is variable (i.e., tied to LIBOR) and interest rates rise, the project might become unprofitable. For this reason, such a possibility is almost always hedged, allowing the enterprise to eliminate the risk.

ROIC is becoming one of the more widely used analyst metrics. It is of particular relevance, however, when under competition with the entity's cost of capital. By itself, only a vital but often partial picture emerges. And for entities or divisions of entities that cannot earn a greater return (on projects) on their invested capital than their cost of capital, its value will decline.

The ROIC is not a measure of security valuation. An entity can continue to accept projects that exceed its cost of capital, but if its valuation multiple is excessive, its stock could very well decline in the short run.

Entities that are underleveraged may be denying shareholders a higher valuation if they decline projects having an ROIC that is greater than the after-tax yield on the excess cash and cost of debt.

Corporate managers evaluate the firm's and the business units' ROIC versus those units' cost of capital. Underperforming assets typically have a specific period to improve performance before strategic alternatives are considered. The inability to divest or improve the returns on such assets successfully in a timely manner, meaning that the unit cannot achieve its cost of capital, could have a negative effect on the entire operation of the enterprise, including its stock price. Management attention is diverted to underperforming units in the hope of turning them around or getting them ready for sale. In addition, the process of divestitures could cause strains on the remaining business segments in need of cash to expand or retool their operations.

The theory behind ROIC is to present investors and creditors with an accurate measurement of the cash-on-cash return management has been able to earn. Management needs to spend cash to purchase assets in the hope of a cash return greater than the cost to acquire those assets.

It is for this reason that the analyst should not begin with a generally accepted accounting principles (GAAP) measurement such as net income or earnings before interest, taxes, depreciation, and amortization (EBITDA) but rather with free cash flow in the computation of ROIC. Creditors, as with stockholders, expect a cash return, which may not be possible with accounting profits.

EBITDA IS INAPPROPRIATE AS A VALUATION TOOL AND IN MERGER ANALYSIS

ROIC, since it is one of the central determinants of valuation, has clear advantages over the use of EBITDA. For example, EBITDA

- Excludes important tax payments that represent a reduction in cash available
- Does not consider capital expenditure requirements for the assets being depreciated and amortized that may have to be replaced in the future
- Does not reflect changes in or cash requirements in working capital needs
- Does not reflect the significant interest expense or the cash requirements necessary to service interest or principal payments on debt

Even in a merger analysis, for which EBITDA was intended originally, its use is limited. In addition to the preceding drawbacks, it may not be useful because it

- Does not include share-based employee compensation expense, goodwill impairment charges, and other charges that can affect prospective free cash flows

- Does not include restructuring, severance, and relocation costs incurred to realize future cost savings and enhance the operations of the entity
- Does not include the impact of business-acquisition purchase accounting adjustments
- Does not reflect company sale transaction expenses and merger-related expenses
- May include other adjustments required in calculating debt covenant compliance such as pro forma adjusted EBITDA for companies acquired during the year

To begin analysis of the ROIC metric, I first look at how ROIC is commonly defined by security analysts and enterprises, as a search on EDGAR, the Securities and Exchange Commission (SEC) database, reveals. Here, too, as with free cash flow, definitions reported in financial statements differ for filers, making comparability often difficult to impossible. As with free cash flow, many firm's tailor-make an ROIC definition, attempting to both place themselves in a favorable light and adjust for peculiarities of their business.

A search through the EDGAR database reveals a commonly used definition of ROIC to be

$$\text{ROIC} = \frac{\text{EBITDA} + \text{interest income} * (1 - \text{tax rate}) + \text{goodwill amortization}}{\text{total assets} - (\text{current liabilities} + \text{short-term debt} + \text{accumulated depreciation})}$$

National Semiconductor, has an even simpler definition, as spelled out in its 2009 10K: "We determine return on invested capital based on net operating income after tax divided by invested capital, which generally consists of total assets reduced by goodwill and non-interest-bearing liabilities."

Not only does beginning with EBITDA suffer from the shortfalls just listed, it is not a measure of distributable cash and thus is not a measure of real return to holders of equity securities. Excluding goodwill, like National Semiconductor, ignores a real cash outflow for which management is expected to earn free cash flows.

A SUPERIOR ROIC METHODOLOGY USING FREE CASH FLOW

Using free cash flow as a base allows for comparability and uniformity and offers what ROIC is really supposed to capture—the cash return on cash spent for capital. A more logical definition for ROIC, and one being proposed for analyst adoption, is

$$\text{ROIC} = \frac{\text{free cash flow} - \text{net interest income}}{\text{invested capital (equity} + \text{total interest bearing debt} + \text{present value of leases} - \text{cash marketable securities)}}$$

This more precise definition includes

1. Intangible assets because those funds were used to acquire cash-producing assets.
2. All interest-bearing debt because this too was sold to purchase productive assets.
3. Present value of operating leases because this represents contractual debt in exchange for required assets needed to produce revenue, hence cash flows. To exclude operating leases would be to unfairly boost the ROIC and to distort the comparison between companies that buy assets or enter into capital leases and those which enter into operating leases.
4. Since free cash flow is used, it includes the payment of cash taxes and the elimination of other accruals.

We do not add back, as true with EBITDA-based measures, interest income to free cash flow because we are attempting to measure the cash return on productive, not financial assets.

Investors, large and sophisticated to small and naive, with the latter often dependent on and trusting of the former, often fail to understand the complicated relationship between valuation metrics and ROIC.

It is easy to want a simplified approach to investing, such as price/earnings (P/E) multiple or price/book (P/B) ratio, but quite another to be able to understand the bearings behind the numbers and why so many entities sell for what appears to be an incredibly low valuation multiple or ratio.

In essence, entities having a low ROIC or dependent on large capital expenditures resulting in small amounts of distributable cash flows deserve low valuation metrics despite their higher rates of growth in GAAP-related yardsticks. This is why many investors are fooled, having invested in low-P/E-multiple companies. It is for this reason that I advocate adoption of the ROIC metric using free cash flow as a base and, in my model portfolio, invest only in entities that have shown the ability to consistently produce an average[1] free-cash-flow yield in excess of the 10-year Treasury yield.

Under the cash-flow-based definition, goodwill, intangible assets, and all other productive assets that require cash expenditures are counted in the capital base. Operating leases also should be included in the capital base because they represent a financing decision for capital expected to return cash to the firm. I would not, however, impute an interest charge on the operating leases to deduct from free cash flow

---

[1]We use a three- or four-year average free cash flow in an attempt to capture part of an economic down cycle or period of softness or unusual spending for an individual entity.

because the entire lease payment is deducted in computation of free cash flow, as reported under operating activities.

HOW OTHER COMPREHENSIVE INCOME FACTORS INTO ROIC ANALYSIS

I do not generally penalize the capital base resulting from pension and health care liabilities, even though they could represent true liabilities that may affect the capital structure. With ROIC, I am evaluating return on capital employed, and this liability is not due to invested capital.[2] I thus would add back to shareholders equity the comprehensive loss. If the loss represented a liability for which payment were reasonably assured, and especially if so within two years, it would affect the leverage ratio, affecting the ability of the enterprise to repay said obligation. This conceivably could cause a large markup to its cost of capital. If the entity had the financial flexibility to finance the liability, including its conversion to long-term debt, the markup to cost of capital would be less severe.

Pension and health care liabilities that run through shareholders' equity are volatile, subject to the vagaries of the financial markets, and if included, would cause unnecessarily large swings in the ROIC, reflective of the financial markets, not the company's ability to generate a return on its assets and capital. For instance, Lockheed Martin's (see example below) accrued pension liability rose from $1.2 billion to $12.2 billion during 2008 owing to a large, unrecognized actuarial loss resulting in part from a large fall in the equity markets and a drop in the discount rate used to project benefit obligations. Recognition of the funding status as of the end of the reporting period was in part due to adoption of *Statement of Financial Accounting Standards No. 158* (SFAS 158): *Employers Accounting for Defined Benefit Pension and Other Post-Retirement Plans*.

For this reason, under the cash-flow-based ROIC, the analyst must review the other comprehensive income/loss section of shareholders' equity for items not reflective of the normalized and true invested capital. Adjustments should be made as appropriate. These would include

1. Foreign-currency translation adjustments
2. Changes in fair value of a financial instrument in a cash-flow hedge
3. Actuarial gains and losses
4. Changes in the fair value of available-for-sale financial assets
5. Revaluations of property, plant, and equipment

[2] One could argue the liability is a result of human capital, but this is not the intent of ROIC.

Comprehensive income/loss consists of changes in the actuarial gains and losses associated with pension and other postretirement benefits plans and unrealized losses on derivatives. The yearly change, in most instances, skews the shareholders' equity account such that if it were included as stated, it would render a poor and inaccurate estimate of the ROIC.

EXAMPLE:

In its 2009 10K, Microsoft reported $171 million in accumulated comprehensive income, which the company added to shareholders' equity for that year. As seen from its statement of shareholder equity, the company separated other comprehensive income into three pieces. The prior year, the comprehensive income required an adjustment to shareholders' equity, which, if taken into account in the calculation of ROIC, would have had a somewhat greater impact. That accumulated comprehensive income can bounce $1 billion from year to year, as was the case between 2007 and 2008, and leaves one questioning its relevance, especially if there is no discernible trend.

Microsoft used derivatives as a cash-flow hedge:

Note 19: Other Comprehensive Income

The activity in other comprehensive income and related income tax effects were as follows:

	Year Ended June 30 (In Millions)		
	2009	**2008**	**2007**
Net unrealized gains on derivatives:			
Unrealized gains, net of tax effects of **$472**, $46, and $66	**$876**	$86	$123
Reclassification adjustment for gains included in net income, net of tax effects of **$(309)**, $(36), and $(59)	**(574)**	(68)	(109)
Net unrealized gains on derivatives	**302**	18	14
Net unrealized gains (losses) on investments:			
Unrealized gains (losses), net of tax effects of **$(142)**, $(234), and $393	**(263)**	(435)	730
Reclassification adjustment for losses (gains) included in net income, net of tax effects of **$16**, $(117), and $(217)	**30**	(218)	(404)
Net unrealized gains (losses) on investments	**(233)**	(653)	326
Translation adjustments and other	**(240)**	121	85
Other comprehensive income (loss)	**$(171)**	$(514)	$425

The components of accumulated other comprehensive income were as follows:

	Year Ended June 30 (In Millions)		
	2009	**2008**	**2007**
Net unrealized gains on derivatives	**$437**	$135	$117
Net unrealized gains on investments	**502**	735	1,388
Translation adjustments and other	**30**	270	149
Accumulated other comprehensive income	**$969**	$1,140	$1,654

STOCKHOLDERS' EQUITY STATEMENTS

	Year Ended June 30 (In Millions)		
	2009	**2008**	**2007**
Common stock and paid-in capital			
Balance, beginning of period	**$62,849**	$60,557	$59,005
Common stock issued	**567**	3,504	6,783
Common stock repurchased	**(2,611)**	(3,022)	(6,162)
Stock-based compensation expense	**1,708**	1,479	1,550
Stock-based compensation income tax benefits (deficiencies)	**(128)**	253	(661)
Other, net	**(3)**	78	42
Balance, end of period	**62,382**	62,849	60,557
Retained deficit			
Balance, beginning of period	**(26,563)**	(29,460)	(18,901)
Cumulative effect of a change in accounting principle—adoption of FIN 48	—	(395)	—
Cumulative effect of a change in accounting principle—adoption of EITF 06–2	—	(17)	—
Net income	**14,569**	17,681	14,065
Other comprehensive income:			
Net unrealized gains on derivatives	**302**	18	14
Net unrealized gains (losses) on investments	**(233)**	(653)	326
Translation adjustments and other	**(240)**	121	85
Comprehensive income	**14,398**	17,167	14,490
Common stock cash dividends	**(4,620)**	(4,084)	(3,837)
Common stock repurchased	**(6,039)**	(9,774)	(21,212)
Balance, end of period	**(22,824)**	(26,563)	(29,460)
Total stockholders' equity	**$39,558**	$36,286	$31,097

Source: Microsoft Corp. 2009 10K.

FIGURE 5-1

Investment Performance of High-ROIC Portfolio versus S&P 500

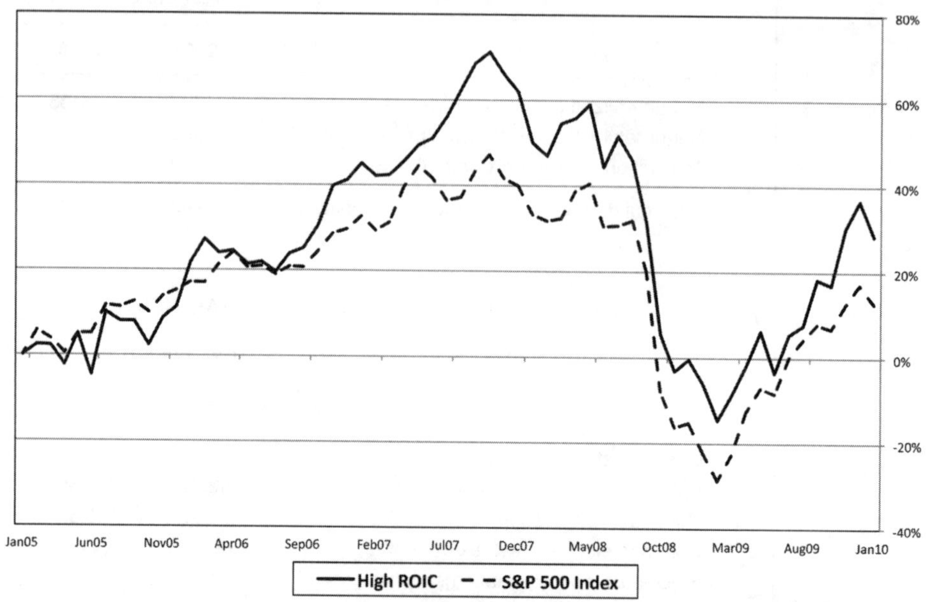

Entities that have exhibited a high ROIC compared with cost of capital have shown to outperform the general market. Figure 5-1 shows the investment returns of the CT Capital portfolio discussed in Chapter 9 (see Table 9–1). The companies that make up the portfolio were selected primarily because they each had an ROIC far in excess of their cost of capital. For the five-year period ending January 2010, this portfolio, equally reweighted monthly, had a total return of 28 percent versus 13 percent for the Standard and Poor's (S&P) 500 Index, a most worthy achievement. A study by McKinsey & Co. found that investors prefer investing in companies with high ROICs, even if the entity had limited prospects for growth.[3] On the other hand, as McKinsey points out, entities that have low returns on invested capital often run into financial difficulty, especially when confronted with an economic, industry, or nonsystematic downturn.

A HODGEPODGE OF METHODS CURRENTLY IN USE

A review of EDGAR filings, as well as reading through a large number of company investor presentations and security analyst reports, finds a wide range of

[3]*McKinsey Quarterly*, Balancing ROIC and Growth to Build Value, March 2006.

ROIC definitions. Goodrich is one of many companies that look to ROIC when determining bonus and incentive awards for its employees. The company's computation begins with net income and adjusts for one-time events. The inclusion of such special items allows for much management discretion, and often such special events occur all too frequently. The analyst might well question some or all of the company's special items, including the cumulative effect of an accounting change. Certainly, using free cash flow in its place would eliminate much of this discretion.

EXAMPLE:

The two equally-weighted performance measures for the Units will be Relative Total Shareholder Return, which measures Goodrich stock performance against a peer group of aerospace companies, and Return on Invested Capital, defined as net income excluding special items, divided by the average invested capital ("Adjusted ROIC"). The term "special items" includes merger-related and consolidation costs, certain gains and losses on the sale of businesses, results of discontinued operations, cumulative effect of change in accounting, asset impairment charges, and other restructuring costs. The Committee is expected to approve the specific target, threshold and maximum performance levels for each performance measure in the first quarter of 2005.

Source: Goodrich 2004 10K.

EXAMPLE:

While most entities use their effective tax rate to calculate ROIC, many entities rely on the statutory 35 percent rate, even though it differs from both the effective rate and the implied cash tax rate. To the extent that the actual cash rate is below 35 percent, a profitable firm would be understating the ROIC. For example, Cardtronics, Inc., a manufacturer of ATMs, uses a 35 percent rate in its ROIC determination, even though it has never shown an effective rate at that, or higher, level. Likewise, for the many entities having greater than a 35 percent rate, they would be overstating the ROIC. By using free cash flow, as I have shown, taxes paid at the cash rate are being considered. The following example illustrates the significant effect of the tax rate on ROIC for a company having a $100 million operating profit.

	2010	2009	2008
Operating profit ($M)	$100	$100	$100
Tax rate	35%	22%	40%
Taxes paid	35	22	40
Net profit	65	78	60
ROIC ($350M inv. cap.)	18.6%	22.2%	17.1%

EXAMPLE:

In its calculation of ROIC, Burlington Northern estimates the interest expense portion of its operating leases, which it approximates as one-third the lease expense. The company then adds that to accrued interest expense from the income statement, to which it adds to operating income. By denying interest expense as a real cost of doing business, because operating income is calculated prior to deduction of interest, Burlington Northern management is avoiding a real cost-of-capital acquisition. Burlington also included the noncash charge related to an increase in estimated asbestos liabilities, resulting in a mixture of accounting and cash approaches. The company also uses the effective tax rate, where my model, by virtue of its use of free cash flow, uses the actual taxes paid.

In the denominator, leases are capitalized because the assets underlying the obligation are necessary for cash generation. Burlington Northern also incorporates sales of accounts receivable in its capital base, even though it represents cash, which is excluded from invested capital.

TABLE 5-1

Burlington Northern: Calculation of Return on Invested Capital

	Year ended December 31		
	2006	**2005**	**2004**
Average capitalization[a]	**$21,200**	$19,831	$19,069
Operating income	**$3,517**	$2,922	$1,686
Other expense	**(40)**	(37)	(4)
Financing charges[b]	**370**	305	274
2004 charge for change in estimate of unasserted asbestos and environmental liabilities	—	—	465
Taxes[c]	**(1,438)**	(1,196)	(917)
After-tax income excluding financing charges and 2004 charge	**$2,409**	$1,994	$1,504
Return on invested capital[d]	**11.4%**	10.1%	7.9%

[a]Average capitalization is calculated as the average of the sum of stockholders' equity, net debt (long-term debt and commercial paper plus long-term debt due within one year less cash and cash equivalents), the net present value of future long-term operating lease commitments, and the receivables sold under the accounts receivable sales program for the most recent preceding 13-month ends.

[b]Financing charges represent the estimated interest expense included in operating lease payments and A/R sales fees.

[c]Taxes are calculated as the sum of monthly operating income, other expense and financing charges, multiplied by an effective tax rate respective to each month.

[d]Return on invested capital is calculated as the total after-tax income excluding financing charges and 2004 charge divided by average capitalization.

Source: Burlington Northern, Inc., 2006 10K.

PepsiAmericas adds interest expense to net income when measuring ROIC because it uses operating profits in its computation. Adding back interest expense, a legitimate ongoing cost without which the entity would not have been able to raise the funds to purchase the related assets, represents an unbalanced approach—that of including the capital but not its cost. If the company were able to change its capital structure so that it had greater equity and lower interest payments, its return on capital undoubtedly would shift, as would its cost of capital.

We are, after all, seeking to determine how effective management has been at using the entity's capital base, not the financing base. If, however, the business under scrutiny has a substantial financing unit that is integral to the business or is a financing company—as opposed to an industrial concern—one should not deduct net interest income from free cash flow.

EXAMPLE:

PepsiAmericas defines ROIC as follows:

- Numerator (rolling 12 periods):
  + Net income
  + Amortization expense
  + Interest expense (net of tax)
  + Special charges (net of tax)
  − Other income (expense)
  − Loss from discontinued operations
  = *Adjusted net operating profit after taxes*
- Denominator (average 4 quarters):
  + Total assets
  + Accumulated amortization
  − Cash
  − Current liabilities, excluding short-term debt
  − Other liabilities, excluding long-term debt
  = *Adjusted average invested capital*

Source: PepsiAmericas 2004 Annual Report.

EXAMPLE:

Lockheed Martin calculated its return on invested capital for the fiscal years 2004–2008 as shown in Table 5-2.

TABLE 5-2

Lockheed Martin: Return on Invested Capital

	Year Ended January 31 (In Millions)				
	2008	**2007**	**2006**	**2005**	**2004**
Net earnings	**$3,217**	$3,033	$2,529	$1,825	$1,266
Interest expense (multiplied by 65%)[1]	**222**	229	235	241	276
Return	**$3,439**	$3,262	$2,764	$2,066	$1,542
Average debt[2,5]	**$4,346**	$4,416	$4,727	$5,077	$5,932
Average equity[3,5]	**8,236**	7,661	7,686	7,590	7,015
Average benefit plan adjustments[4,5]	**3,256**	3,171	2,006	1,545	1,296
Average invested capital	**$15,838**	$15,248	$14,419	$14,212	$14,243
Return on invested capital	**21.7%**	21.4%	19.2%	14.5%	10.8%

[1]Represents after-tax interest expense using the federal statutory rate of 35%.

[2]Debt consists of long-term debt, including current maturities of long-term debt, and short-term borrowings (if any).

[3]Equity includes noncash adjustments, primarily related to average benefit plan adjustments discussed in note 4 below.

[4]Average benefit plan adjustments reflect the cumulative value of entries identified in our Statement of Stockholders' Equity under the captions "Postretirement benefit plans," "Adjustment for adoption of SFAS 158" and "Minimum pension liability." The total of annual benefit plan adjustments to equity were: 2008 = $(7,253) million; 2007 = $1,706 million; 2006 = $(1,883) million; 2005 = $(105) million; and 2004 = $(285) million. As these entries are recorded in the fourth quarter, the value added back to our average equity in a given year is the cumulative impact of all prior year entries plus 20 percent of the current year entry value. The cumulative impact of benefit plan adjustments through December 31, 2003 was $(1,239) million.

[5]Yearly averages are calculated using balances at the start of the year and at the end of each quarter.

By using the average of debt and equity held throughout the year, the company could be overstating its prospective ROIC if total debt significantly increased toward the back half of the year. As the table shows, Lockheed Martin showed a significant rise in its ROIC metric owing to vastly improved net income in relation to its capital base, which it adjusts for the pension liability included in other comprehensive income/loss. Since the company's pension obligation exceeded its plans assets, the difference was shown as a liability. Prior to SFAS 158, the company's unrecognized net losses and unrecognized prior service costs enabled it to report a pension asset. Lockheed Martin is, correctly adding back the charge to net comprehensive income. Under SFAS 158, actuarial gains and losses that arise during a period, as well as amortization of such gains and losses, are recognized as components of other comprehensive income. In my ROIC computation, I am striving to measure the ability of the enterprise to provide a cash return on the invested capital, which may differ from the balance-sheet equity owing to the charge in the other comprehensive income component.

Lockheed Martin produced $4.4 billion in cash flow from operations during 2008, with a boost coming from the noncash stock-based compensation, deferred income taxes, and balance-sheet items. With $926 million in capital spending and $42 million in corporate fat, its free cash flow, using the procedure outlined in Chapter 4, amounted to about $ 3.5 billion, slightly higher than the return derived by the company.

Lockheed Martin uses a 35 percent statutory tax rate in its calculation of ROIC. However, since actual cash taxes that year were $1.234 billion, not the $1.485 expense listed on the income statement, the interest expense, based on the 35 percent tax shield added back to calculate ROIC, was overstated. This is another reason why I prefer a free-cash-flow-based definition; there is no need to estimate the tax rate because free cash flow uses the actual tax payment. The company's effective tax rate was 31.6 percent.

EXAMPLE:

Nordstrom, the large clothing retailer, reports the computation shown in Table 5-3 in its 2009 10K for its return on invested capital:

TABLE 5-3

Nordstrom: Return on Invested Capital

	Twelve Fiscal Months Ended	
	January 31, 2009	**February 2, 2008**
Net earnings	**$401**	$715
Add: Income tax expense	**247**	458
Add: Interest expense, net	**131**	74
Earnings before interest and income taxes	**779**	1,247
Add: Rent expense	**37**	48
Less: Estimated depreciation on capitalized operating leases	**(19)**	(26)
Net operating profit	**797**	1,269
Estimated income tax expense	**(303)**	(497)
Net operating profit after taxes	**$494**	$772
Average total assets	**$5,768**	$5,455
Less: Average non-interest-bearing current liabilities	**(1,447)**	(1,506)
Less: Average deferred property incentives	**(400)**	(359)
Add: Average estimated asset base of capitalized operating leases	**322**	395
Average invested capital	**$4,243**	$3,985
Return on assets	**7.0%**	13.%
ROIC	**11.6%**	19.4%

Nordstrom begins by adding the entire interest expense ($131 million) listed on the income statement, as opposed to the after-tax cost, which would be more appropriate. Since interest costs are a real cost of doing business and are part of any capital expenditure analysis, I disagree with this practice. The actual interest expense, as seen under supplementary information in its footnotes, was $145 million.

Nordstrom also adds back $247 million in income taxes from the income statement and subtracts an estimated payment of $303 million that is derived from applying a projected 38 percent tax rate multiplied by the $779 million in operating profits seen in the table.

Taxes are a real cost of doing business and, like interest, are part of capital spending decision making. The actual tax expense, as gleaned from its supplementary cash flow information, for 2009 was $340 million, or $37 million greater than the amount Nordstrom used to calculate ROIC.

While Nordstrom uses $797 million in its calculation of operating profit, it showed little free cash flow for 2009, as seen in its statement of cash flows. The company generated $848 million in operating cash flows and had $563 million in capital spending, in addition to an additional $232 million increase in accounts receivable from VISA, shown as a financing activity. When including overspending on discretionary items, as we see from Table 5-4, a large part of the capex spent is picked up, as well as some overspending in cost of goods sold (COGS). Prior to 2009, Nordstrom points out in its 10K, it treated accounts receivable from third parties as an operating activity.

Using the free-cash-flow-based definition, I arrive at the following:

ROIC = free cash flow − interest income
= $509 million − $3 million
= $506 million
= shareholder's equity + short term debt + long term debt + operating leases
= $1,210 million + $24 million + $2,214 million + $696 million
= $4,144 million

Return on invested capital (ROIC) is calculated as follows:

$$\text{ROIC} = \frac{\$506 \text{ million}}{\$4{,}144 \text{ million}} = 12.2\%$$

While the difference between the company-defined ROIC of 11.6 percent and the free-cash-flow-based ROIC of 12.2 percent may not appear significant, from a valuation viewpoint, it can be. For example, given Nordstrom's four-year average free cash flow of $408 million and a current 19 × free-cash-flow multiple, a 1 percent increase in its ROIC from its $4,144 of invested capital would translate into a $790 million in market value, or about a 10 percent increase in its stock price. Put another way, a 1 percent increase in Nordstrom's ROIC should translate into a 10 percent rise in its stock price.

The primary reason for the difference in the company's ROIC and my cash-flow-based definition is the invested capital, as depicted in its financial filing versus my calculation, as shown below. The prior year, 2007, there was a substantial difference between Nordstrom's operating profit and free cash flow, even after adding back corporate fat. Nordstrom reported it's ROIC of 19.4 percent while using a free-cash-flow-based definition; the ROIC was negative. It is not surprising, therefore, that the stock price for Nordstrom declined by over 25 percent during 2007 because investors followed the free-cash-flow-based ROIC metric, not the company's. The following year and into 2009, when Nordstrom's free-cash-flow-based ROIC rose, so too did its stock price, even though the company's "tailor made" metric fell by 40 percent.

NORDSTROM, INC.

CONSOLIDATED STATEMENTS OF CASH FLOWS (In Millions)

	2008	2007	2006
Operating activities:			
Net earnings	**$401**	$715	$678
Adjustments to reconcile net earnings to net cash provided by operating activities:			
Depreciation and amortization of buildings and equipment	**302**	269	285
Gain on sale of Façonnable	**—**	(34)	—

	2008	2007	2006
Amortization of deferred property incentives and other, net	**(21)**	(36)	(36)
Stock-based compensation expense	**28**	26	37
Deferred income taxes, net	**(36)**	(42)	(58)
Tax benefit from stock-based payments	**3**	28	44
Excess tax benefit from stock-based payments	**(4)**	(26)	(38)
Provision for bad debt expense	**173**	107	17
Change in operating assets and liabilities:			
Accounts receivable	**(93)**	(1,083)	(61)
Investment in asset-backed securities	**—**	420	128
Merchandise inventories	**53**	—	(39)
Prepaid expenses	**9**	(9)	(5)
Other assets	**29**	(27)	(8)
Accounts payable	**16**	(19)	84
Accrued salaries, wages, and related benefits	**(54)**	(64)	49
Other current liabilities	**28**	36	23
Income taxes	**(76)**	(6)	(6)
Deferred property incentives	**119**	58	31
Other liabilities	**(29)**	(1)	17
Net cash provided by operating activities	**848**	312	1,142
Investing activities:			
Capital expenditures	**(563)**	(501)	(264)
Change in accounts receivable originated at third parties	**(232)**	(151)	—
Proceeds from sale of Façonnable	**—**	216	—
Proceeds from sale of assets	**2**	12	—
Purchases of short-term investments	**—**	—	(110)
Sales of short-term investments	**—**	—	164
Other, net	**1**	3	(8)
Net cash used in investing activities	**(792)**	(421)	(218)
Financing activities:			
Proceeds from commercial paper	**275**	—	—
Proceeds from long-term borrowings, net	**150**	2,510	—
Principal payments on long-term borrowings	**(410)**	(680)	(307)
Increase (decrease) in cash book overdrafts	**20**	5	(51)
Proceeds from exercise of stock options	**13**	34	51
Proceeds from employee stock purchase plan	**17**	17	16
Excess tax benefit from stock-based payments	**4**	26	38
Cash dividends paid	**(138)**	(134)	(110)
Repurchase of common stock	**(264)**	(1,702)	(621)
Other, net	**(9)**	(12)	—
Net cash (used in) provided by financing activities	**(342)**	64	(984)
Net decrease in cash and cash equivalents	**(286)**	(45)	(60)
Cash and cash equivalents at beginning of year	**358**	403	463
Cash and cash equivalents at end of year	**$72**	$358	$4

TABLE 5-4

Free Cash Flow: Nordstrom

Part I - Cash Flow Items:

Year	Jan-05	Jan-06	Jan-07	Jan-08	Jan-09	Most Recent Quarter Jul-09	Previous Quarter Jul-08	Last 12 Months Jul-09	Last 12 Months Jul-08
Net Operating Cash Flow	606.3	776.2	1142.4	161.0	848.0	492.0	218.0	1174.0	884.9
Capital Expenditures	246.9	271.7	264.4	501.0	563.0	94.0	153.0	464.0	574.0
Sale of PPE	NA	NA	NA	NA	NA	0.0	0.0	NA	NA
Free Cash Flow – Including Discretionary Items	359.5	504.6	877.9	(340.0)	285.0	398.0	65.0	710.0	310.9
Free Cash Flow – Excluding Discretionary Items	359.5	504.6	877.9	(259.5)	509.1	—	—		
Discretionary Capital Expenditures	0.0	0.0	0.0	80.5	163.9	—	—		
Discretionary R&D	0.0	0.0	0.0	0.0	0.0	—	—		
Discretionary Cost of Goods Sold	0.0	0.0	0.0	0.0	27.2	—	—		
Discretionary SG&A	0.0	27.2	0.0	0.0	0.0	—	—		
Discretionary Advertising	0.0	0.0	0.0	0.0	0.0	—	—		
Large Buildup (Reduction) in Accounts Receivable	0.0	143.5	153.4	(92.7)	528.1	634.4	683.9		
Large Buildup (Reduction) in Inventory	726.2	(201.7)	(214.5)	(220.9)	(233.4)	(130.6)	(82.8)		
Large Buildup (Reduction) in Accounts Payable	(133.5)	24.6	21.9	(5.5)	(95.2)	(29.7)	162.0		

EXAMPLE:

Flextronics, Inc., calculates ROIC both including and excluding goodwill, referring to the latter as return on invested tangible capital. In its definition of return on capital, the company excludes certain charges, such as bad debts, that can upwardly bias the calculation. It is up to the analyst to determine whether these exclusions are unusual, although it would appear, in the case of Flextronics, that bad debt and other charges for which a cash return was expected should be included. Bad debts unfortunately have been an ongoing cost of the firm's doing business. Using the free-cash-flow-based measure, non-cash write-offs such as goodwill are relevant to the extent that they required a cash outlay for capital.

EXAMPLE:

Because MBIA is a financial company, its preferred measure is return on equity, not return on capital.

> **Operating Return on Equity (ROE):** The Company believes operating return on equity is a useful measurement of performance because it measures return on equity based upon income from operations and shareholders' equity, unaffected by investment portfolio realized gains and losses, gains and losses on financial instruments at fair value and foreign exchange, unrealized gains and losses, and non-recurring items. Operating return on equity is also provided to assist research analysts and investors who use this information in their analysis of the company.

Source: MBIA 2007 Third Quarter Report to Shareholders.

By overlooking its investment portfolio, management is ignoring very large, real effects amounting to almost $6 billion compared with $2.5 billion in shareholders' equity. These investments are necessary if called on to pay claims. As early as 2007, some credit analysts estimated that MBIA, owing to its large position in structured investments in mortgages, was facing loses exceeding its stated equity. Indeed, its stock price and shareholders' equity collapsed when the default rate on those investments rose, and they were being ignored under MBIA's preferred measure of return on equity. Thus, to ignore its investment portfolio would be to disregard the part of its business that brought the company to near bankruptcy.

DIVISIONAL RETURN ON CAPITAL

When evaluating the financial results of a division, a tax rate must be assigned, even though income taxes typically are paid at the parent-company level through a consolidated tax return. We saw how many firms use the statutory rate in many calculations. Table 5-5 shows an analysis by LaFarge Corp., a French-based cement manufacturer, in which they utilize a 26 percent tax rate, the parent's rate, to compute divisional ROIC. Under the analysis, LaFarge calculates each division's return on capital, with little supporting data available to the analyst. As is seen, despite the cement division's appetite for capital, this division, during 2005, had an after tax-return on capital of 9.7 percent. The roofing division had a poor ROIC, probably not covering its ROIC.

TABLE 5-5

LaFarge Corp.: Divisional Return on Capital

2005	Current Operating Income	Current Operating Income after Tax	Income from Associates	Current Operating Income after Tax with Income from Associates	Capital Employed on December 31, 2005	Capital Employed on December 31, 2004	Average Capital Employed	Return on Capital Employed after Tax
	(a)	(b) = (a) × (1 – 28.6%)	(c)	(d) = (b) + (c)	(e)	(f)	(g) = [(e) + (f)]/2	(h) = (d)/(g)
Cement	1,770	1,264	8	1,272	13,982	12,167	13,075	9.7
Aggregates and concrete	398	284	8	292	3,932	3,337	3,634	8.1
Roofing	98	70	7	77	2,181	2,118	2,149	3.6
Gypsum	151	108	15	123	1,267	1,147	1,207	10.2
Other	(60)	(43)	—	(43)	290	139	215	n/a
TOTAL	2,357	1,683	38	1,721	21,652	18,908	20,280	8.5

Source: LaFarge Corp. 2005 20F.

EXAMPLE:

Corn Products, Inc., uses ROIC, having devised a scoring system to calculate divisional bonuses. The size of the bonus rests on the spread between the ROIC and the division's cost of capital. Corn Products estimates a tax rate for the division based on the individual unit's operating results.

> *Return on Invested Capital for each of the company's business segments relative to their weighted-average cost of capital.* The score starts at 1.0 for achieving Return on Invested Capital equal to Weighted Average Cost of Capital and moves up on a sliding scale of 0.5 for every additional 1 percent in Return on Invested Capital, with no maximum. If Weighted Average Cost of Capital is not achieved then the score is zero. In 2008 this measure accounted for 57 percent of the Corporate performance measure.

CORN PRODUCTS, INC.
RETURN ON INVESTED CAPITAL (In Millions)

	2008	2007
Total stockholders' equity	$1,605	$1,330
Add:		
Cumulative translation adjustment	132	214
Minority interest in subsidiaries	21	19
Redeemable common stock	19	44
Share-based payments subject to redemption	9	4
Total debt	649	554

	2008	2007
Less:		
Cash and cash equivalents	(175)	(131)
Capital employed (a)	$2,260	$2,034
Operating income	$434	$347
Adjusted for:		
Income taxes (at effective tax rates of 32.0% in 2008 and 33.5% in 2007)	(139)	(116)
Adjusted operating income, net of tax (b)	$295	$231
Return on capital employed [(b) ÷ (a)]	13.1%	11.4%

RECOVERY RATE

A forerunner of ROIC and a measure in some use today is the *recovery rate*. The recovery rate measures the relationship between funds provided by operations and fund invested in the business (as total assets). The recovery rate can be considered an index of management's ability to deploy effectively (and earn an acceptable return on) corporate assets. Some companies use the recovery rate as a determining factor of a business acquisition. Acceptable recovery rates will differ from entity to entity depending on their cost of funds, investment alternatives, and ROIC.

This measure may be used, in conjunction with the cost of capital, at the individual unit level by the parent or divisional head when determining how corporate cash should best be deployed. This decision will be a function of the units' prospects for growth in free cash flow, amount of cash needed, the effect on the consolidated balance sheet, and time for the operating cash flows to pay down the external capital put into the division and balance. By *balance*, it is meant the remaining divisions' capital requirements and not wanting to "starve" a division that is fitting into the consolidated entity's long-range plan.

The companies in Table 5-6 have recovery rates ranging from negative to strong and are drawn from the beginning list of Standard and Poor's (S&P) 500 companies. The median S&P 500 company had a recovery rate of 9.34 years, meaning that it hypothetically would take that period of time to recover the cash spent for those assets, and is seen in the table as the reciprocal of the data in column 2.

Companies having large amounts of cash can, under an income-statement-based definition of ROIC, increase their metric by reducing (shrinking) shareholders' equity, with perhaps a stock buyback or a cash dividend. ROIC also could increase, all things equal, from the write-down of assets and recognition of a newly introduced accounting regulation. As we saw, Lockheed Martin's

TABLE 5-6

S&P 500 Recovery Rate Companies

Company Name	OCF/ASSETS LFY	OCF/ASSETS LTM	FCF/MK VAL	OCF/TTL DEBT	Market Value	Price Close % Change-3 Yr
3M CO	0.177	0.171	0.061	0.669	53,606.187	(0.833)
ABERCROMBIE & FITCH -CL A	0.172	0.177	0.076	4.908	3,289.517	(52.677)
ADOBE SYSTEMS INC	0.220	0.202	0.063	3.659	18,724.420	(11.799)
ADVANCED MICRO DEVICES	(0.090)	(0.115)	(0.167)	(0.136)	4,132.549	(77.223)
AES CORP	0.062	0.060	0.010	0.119	9,985.095	(27.317)
AETNA INC	0.062	0.056	0.179	0.573	11,226.780	(29.633)
AFFILIATED COMPUTER SERVICES	0.127	0.127	0.118	0.375	4,796.198	4.454
AFLAC INC	0.063	0.071	0.238	2.885	21,314.465	(6.600)
AGILENT TECHNOLOGIES INC	0.102	0.069	0.066	0.356	9,531.994	(14.867)
AIR PRODUCTS & CHEMICALS INC	0.134	0.115	0.034	0.423	17,636.383	16.890
AIRGAS INC	0.132	0.140	0.062	0.331	4,132.980	33.730
ALCOA INC	0.033	0.022	(0.108)	0.117	13,992.054	(53.210)
ALLERGAN INC	0.100	0.128	0.032	0.416	17,900.012	0.808
ALTERA CORP	0.239	0.142	0.066	0.890	6,372.047	11.589
AMAZON.COM INC	0.204	0.245	0.034	2.556	41,457.792	190.660
AMERICAN TOWER CORP	0.094	0.097	0.038	0.178	15,801.106	(0.274)
AMERIPRISE FINANCIAL INC	0.021	0.002	0.226	0.988	9,502.604	(22.537)
AMERISOURCEBERGEN CORP	0.060	0.074	0.102	0.620	6,940.951	(0.973)
AMGEN INC	0.164	0.137	0.089	0.588	62,786.944	(15.798)
AMPHENOL CORP	0.161	0.187	0.054	0.612	7,029.893	21.686
ANADARKO PETROLEUM CORP	0.132	0.116	0.060	0.522	32,296.230	43.121

shareholders' equity dropped from $9.8 billion to $2.9 billion despite strong operating profits as it recognized the impact of SFAS 158. With its shrunken capital base, ROIC, under many definitions, including that used by Corn Products, Inc., would not accurately reflect Lockheed Martin's ability to return cash on its invested capital. A write-down of assets would positively affect Nordstrom, improving its ROIC (if profits were unaffected).

When borrowings are used to fund a capital expenditure program, the increase in long-term debt would need to be met with an increase in free cash flow if the ROIC is to rise. If the borrowings stay in cash, there is no immediate effect on ROIC because cash merely offsets the borrowing in the denominator. For analysts who prefer to look at book value, buying back stock below book will enhance remaining book, a tactic used by some managements to increase that metric. By the same reasoning, selling shares above book will boost book value.

Evaluating companies on the basis of book value is a tricky proposition because it rests on the quality and ease with which that book value can generate free cash flow and, in the case of financial entities, the ease with which that book can be readily converted into cash and its adequacy in supporting the entity's credit rating. While valuation on book value has merit when it can affect cash flows (such as banks), asset impairments will undermine its relation to market value. Such was seen prior to the 2007 mortgage meltdown as security analysts for the largest brokerage firms valued the financial industry based on book value. Almost every "buy side" security analyst had "buy" ratings on financial industry companies when those stocks initially fell to below book, pointing out in their research reports the companies had almost always rebounded from that level. This logic made sense when the companies were generating positive cash flows; however, as the financial firms wrote down their investment accounts, book value fell to a fraction of where it stood prior to the crisis. Meanwhile, the industry, which had collectively repurchased tens of billions of dollars of its own stock near book value, thinking it was getting a bargain because many were rated investment grade, it soon wished it had that capital back. For the financial entities themselves, their ability to grow their business is very much a function of their capital positioning.

It should be noted, however, that many companies earn superior returns on capital in a given year or during a particular phase of the economic cycle only to see quite low or negative returns on capital employed during other phases of the cycle. These entities must be fiscally prudent during periods of strength or be subject to a larger than necessary rise in the cost of equity capital when business turns down. Cyclicality in businesses need not translate into high added cost of capital if managed prudently.

EVALUATION OF ROIC WHEN INVESTED CAPITAL IS LOW

As industrial efficiencies evolve, improvements in technology take place, and management consultants develop techniques to enhance supply and production methods, productivity improves, and the growth rate of productive capital falls. This need for less capital intensity positively affects ROIC, cash required, and financial ratios. McKinsey & Co. found that the median level of invested capital for U.S. industrial entities dropped from around 50 percent of revenues in the early 1970s to just above 30 percent in 2004.[4]

[4]McKinsey & Co. study based on an analysis of more than 600 companies with sales of more than $100 million. "Comparing Performance when Invested Capital is Low," *McKinsey Quarterly*, 2005.

What McKinsey found in 2005 has only picked up momentum since. Worldwide competition for sales and market share, especially as economic growth has slowed, has led to additional expense skimming and creative means to reduce or minimize the capital base given a projected revenue stream.

For certain industries, which have a naturally low capital base, such as service-oriented entities, ROIC will be naturally high. And for manufacturing entities that use outsourcing effectively or other entities' capital for a substantial part of assembly or service, they, too, would have an unnaturally low capital base resulting in a high ROIC. This does not make ROIC any less important. However, I introduce another measure that is intended to evaluate the cash return on the company's deployment of resources—its *economic profit*. The economic profit then should be compared with sales. Doing so can remove many of the distortions of ROIC and improve intercompany comparability. Even when ROIC makes sense, economic profit should be employed as another measure to evaluate firms.

Economic profit also could be related to other firm factors, such as total employees or units sold. Doing so would provide the analyst with comparability measures specific to a particular industry or situation. When used in this way, economic profit can indicate management's ability to create value relative to its peer group or the direction and efficiency of its spending. For example, a pharmaceutical company analyst may wish to look at the economic profit per researcher.

Economic profit is defined as a company's free cash flow exclusive of interest income minus a capital charge, with the charge calculated as the company's weighted-average cost of capital multiplied by the operating invested capital. The traditional definition of economic profit uses after-tax operating profits in lieu of free cash flow.

EXAMPLE:

Calculate the 2008 economic profit for MMM using the following financials:

	($ Million)
2008 revenues	$25,269
Shareholders' equity	$9,879
Free cash flow (incl. interest income)	$3,290
Interest income	$105
Operating leases	$395
Cash and equivalents	$2,222
Invested capital	$14,728
Weighted-average cost of capital	6.4%

From the free cash flow, interest income is subtracted because we are computing the economic return on the invested capital, not the total free cash flows, which include the returns on the financial assets as well.

$$\begin{aligned}\text{Economic profit} &= (\$3{,}290 \text{ million} - \$105 \text{ million}) - 0.064 * (\$14{,}728 \text{ million})\\ &= \$3{,}185 \text{ million} - \$942 \text{ million}\\ &= \$2{,}242 \text{ million}\end{aligned}$$

MMM's economic profit was $2.2 billion during 2008.

When we compare MMM's economic profit to its 2008 revenues of $25,269 million, we arrive at 8.9 percent, which then could be compared with its historic results or with other companies in its industry. The economic profit also could be related to employee headcount or other useful factors important to the company.

EXAMPLE:

This is how Clorox computed its economic profit for fiscal years 2007–2009. As seen below, it used a partial-cash-flow format by excluding some noncash charges.

THE CLOROX COMPANY
ECONOMIC PROFIT

	(Dollars in Millions)		
	FY09	**FY08**	**FY07**
Earnings from continuing operations before income taxes	$811	$693	$743
Noncash restructuring-related and asset-impairment costs[1]	10	48	4
Interest expense[2]	161	168	113
Earnings from continuing operations before income taxes, noncash restructuring-related and asset-impairment costs, and interest expense	$982	$909	$860
Adjusted after-tax profit[3]	$650	$604	$574
Average capital employed[1,4]	3,045	2,680	2,165
Capital charge[5]	274	241	195
Economic profit (adjusted after-tax profit less capital charge)	376	363	379

[1]Noncash restructuring-related and asset-impairment costs are added back to earnings and adjusted capital employed to more closely reflect cash earnings and the total capital investment used to generate those earnings.

[2]Interest expense is added back to earnings because it is included as a component of the capital charge.

[3]Adjusted after-tax profit represents earnings from continuing operations before income taxes, noncash restructuring-related and asset-impairment costs, and interest expense after tax. The tax rate applied is the effective tax rate on continuing operations, which was 33.8, 33.6, and 33.2 percent in fiscal years 2009, 2008, and 2007, respectively.

[4]Total capital employed represents total assets less non-interest-bearing liabilities. Adjusted capital employed represents total capital employed adjusted to add back current-year noncash restructuring-related and asset-impairment costs. Average capital employed represents a two-point average of adjusted capital employed for the current year and total capital employed for the prior year based on year-end balances. See below for details of the average capital employed calculation:

	FY09	FY08	FY07	FY06
Total assets	$4,576	$4,708	$3,581	$3,521
Less:				
Accounts payable	381	418	329	329
Accrued liabilities	472	440	507	474
Income taxes payable	86	48	17	19
Other liabilities	640	600	516	547
Deferred income taxes	23	97	5	34
Non-interest-bearing liabilities	1,602	1,603	1,374	1,403
Total capital employed	2,974	3,105	2,207	$2,118
Noncash restructuring and asset-impairment costs	10	48	4	
Adjusted capital employed	$2,984	$3,153	$2,211	
Average capital employed	$3,045	$2,680	$2,165	

[5] Capital charge represents average capital employed multiplied by the weighted-average cost of capital. The weighted-average cost of capital used to calculate the capital charge was 9 percent for fiscal years 2009, 2008, and 2007.

Source: Clorox Corp 2009 10K.

Clorox could have taken its definition a step further, as we did with MMM, by substituting free cash flow for operating profit because operating profits are subject to generally accepted accounting principles (GAAP), and we are gauging cash return to compare the result with revenues or other useful measures, including invested capital. I believe that my definition of free cash flow and capital employed to be more reflective of invested capital than is Clorox's definition. Clorox uses a weighted average cost of capital (WACC) of 9 percent but doesn't reveal how that was determined. It is most likely that the company is using the capital assets pricing model (CAPM) to compute the equity cost of capital.

Table 5-7 lists companies in the advertising industry, which traditionally has required a small capital base. The companies were selected from their Standard Industrial Code (SIC)[5] for 2008. Even the size of the capital base could not save many companies from a negative economic profit during the recession, as shown in the table. In the first column we see how most investors would define return on

[5]Standard Industrial Classification (SIC) codes are four-digit numerical codes assigned by the U.S. government to business establishments to identify the primary business of the establishment. The first two digits of the code identify the major industry group, the third digit identifies the industry group, and the fourth digit identifies the industry.

investment (see table footnote), whereas we are defining economic profit using free cash flow.

The table, listing companies having a minimum $200 million market capitalization for which data were available, showed for the average firm a positive ROIC yet a vastly different (negative) economic profit as a percentage of total sales. Monster Worldwide, for example, had an acceptable 10.9 percent ROIC yet a near-zero economic profit relative to revenue, indicative of its large capital base, high cost of capital, and free cash flow during the year. Monster Worldwide is predominantly an online employment agency, yet it has the same SIC as companies in pure advertising, illustrating a weakness of comparability based solely on U.S. government classification.

TABLE 5-7

Year 2008: Return on Investment as Traditionally Defined versus Economic Profit as a Percent of Sales

Company Name	Return on Investment[6]	Economic Profit/Sales
Arbitron, Inc.	52.8%	3.2%
Clear Channel Outdoor Hldgs.	−46.9%	−36.3%
Focus Media Holding, Ltd.–ADR	−34.6%	−53.2%
Harte Hanks, Inc.	10.5%	5.6%
Interpublic Group of Cos.	6.3%	3.9%
Lamar Advertising Co.–CL A	0.3%	−19.8%
Monster Worldwide, Inc.	10.9%	0.0
National Cinemedia, Inc.	5.8%	22.2%
Omnicom Group	14.7%	5.1%
Publicis Groupe SA–ADR	12.2%	7.5%
WPP PLC–ADR	4.4%	−0.2%
Median	**6.3%**	**−3.5%**
Median (ex. focus media)	**8.4%**	**3.5%**

[6]Return on Investment is defined in the table as income before extraordinary items available for common divided by total invested capital which is the sum of the following items: Total long term debt; Preferred Stock; minority Interest; and Total Common Equity. We believe return should be measured as free cash flow, the amount of cash that could be distributed to shareholders without effecting future growth.

EXAMPLE:

TABLE 5-8

Cash Flows: Monster Worldwide

Part I - Cash Flow Items:							
Year	**Dec-04**	**Dec-05**	**Dec-06**	**Dec-07**	**Dec-08**	**Most Recent Quarter Jun-09**	**Previous Quarter Jun-08**
Net Operating Cash Flow	92.5	221.6	268.8	269.2	225.8	(13.6)	70.7
Capital Expenditures	24.3	39.8	55.6	64.1	93.6	11.5	29.7
Sale Of PPE	NA	NA	NA	0.0	0.0	0.0	0.0
Free Cash Flow – Including Discretionary Items	68.2	181.8	213.2	205.1	132.2	(25.1)	41.0
Free Cash Flow – Excluding Discretionary Items	77.9	182.5	227.6	220.6	150.5	—	—
Discretionary Capital Expenditures	0.0	0.7	14.5	15.5	18.1	—	—
Discretionary R&D	0.0	0.0	0.0	0.0	0.0	—	—
Discretionary Cost of Goods Sold	9.7	0.0	0.0	0.0	0.2	—	—
Discretionary SG&A	0.0	0.2	0.0	0.0	0.0	—	—
Discretionary Advertising	0.0	0.0	0.0	0.0	0.0	—	—
Large Buildup (Reduction) in Accounts Receivable	0.0	59.5	(48.7)	(47.9)	(109.2)	(215.1)	(94.4)
Large Buildup (Reduction) in Inventory	(193.0)	4.0	(26.6)	(24.3)	(24.3)	(16.9)	(6.2)
Large Buildup (Reduction) in Accounts Payable	(19.5)	84.5	(97.8)	(94.9)	(182.2)	(301.2)	(84.6)

Monster Worldwide generated free cash flow of $150 million during its fiscal year 2008, when adjusted for overspending in discretionary areas (Table 5-8). When we subtract its interest income and its weighted-average cost of capital of 13.2 percent multiplied by its capital base of $1.047 billion, we see that it had an economic profit of negative $5 million, surely a disappointing return given the size of its capital base. This is calculated as follows:

$$\begin{aligned}\text{Economic profit} &= (\$150 \text{ million} - \$17 \text{ million}) - (0.132 * \$1{,}047 \text{ million})\\ &= \$133 \text{ million} - \$138 \text{ million}\\ &= -\$5 \text{ million}\end{aligned}$$

And with Monster Worldwide's 2008 revenues of $1,343 million, we get

$$\text{Economic profit as a percentage of sales} = \frac{-\$5 \text{ million}}{\$1{,}343 \text{ million}}$$
$$= -0.004$$
$$= -0.04 \text{ percent}$$

Thus, when we look at Monster Worldwide's economic profit as a percentage of revenue, we see that its return was, for 2008, very unimpressive. Importantly, the difference between the traditional definition of ROIC relative to economic profit as a percentage of sales is quite dramatic, indicating that Monster's financial performance is more reflective of reality when substituting economic profits for return on investment. However, as we see from Monster's free cash flow, its four-year average was considerably higher than the 2008 recession-induced year, so if we were to normalize economic profit, the results would have been considerably stronger. Given that its most recent fiscal year showed a sharp drop in free cash flow and its most recent quarter was negative, Monster's cost of capital undoubtedly has risen, reflecting the increase in instability.

Figure 5-2 shows that companies in the capital-intensive paper products industry have a wide disparity in their ability to produce sales given their invested capital. The average for the group is 0.963, meaning that they need almost $1 dollar of capital to produce $1 dollar in revenue per year.

FIGURE 5-2

Invested Capital as a Percentage of Sales: Paper Products Industry

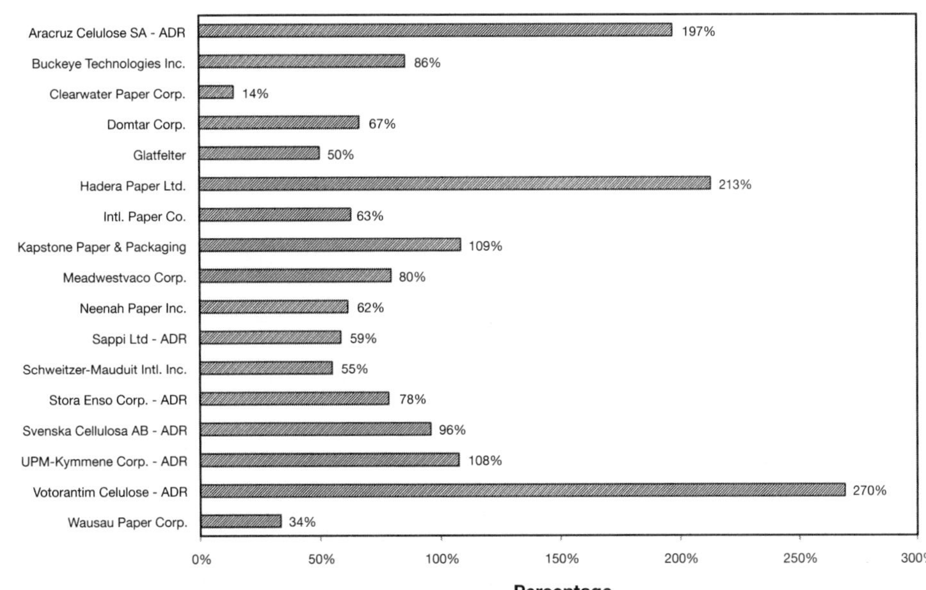

FIGURE 5-3

Invested Capital as a Percentage of Sales: Internet Retail

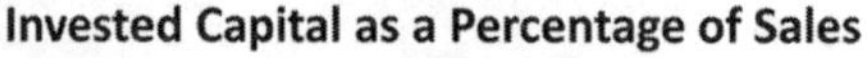

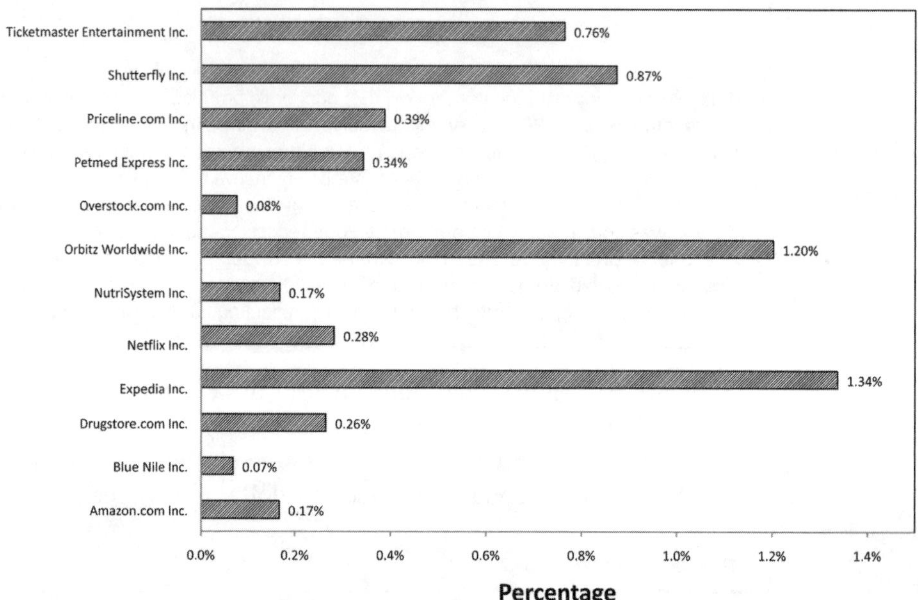

Shown in Fig. 5-3 is the percentage of invested capital required for each dollar of sales for Internet retailers, which, while having a definite need for infrastructure, especially for warehousing and computers, require only, on average, 49 cents in capital to produce $1 in annual revenues. And for other service industries, such as advertising, accounting services, money management, and consulting, it may be as low as 10 cents—or lower—in capital to produce a dollar in sales.

Entities requiring a small invested capital base are capable of reducing their capital infrastructure, requiring less need for financing, thus are a management goal for all companies. Improving the return on the capital base while increasing revenues often results in a boon in free cash flow for shareholders. The improvement could take the form of moving production equipment to a lower-cost (labor or tax) jurisdiction, outsourcing labor, margin improvement, revenue enhancement, improvements in the credit department, and effective balance-sheet management.

The sale of manufacturing facilities to an outside contract manufacturer and at the same time receiving a cash payment in return for the assets with exclusive right for the contractor to manufacture the company's products also can improve ROIC.

EXAMPLE:

Xerox, Flextronics Reach $1bn Outsourcing Deal

Xerox has reached an outsourcing agreement with contract manufacturer Flextronics International of Singapore encompassing more than $1bn in annual manufacturing costs.

The deal includes the sale of some of Xerox's manufacturing assets to Flextronics for $220m, and encompasses about half of Xerox's overall manufacturing operations. The agreement includes a five-year contract for Flextronics to manufacture certain Xerox office equipment and components, at a modest premium over book value.

Source: Electronics Weekly.

Companies can be expected to continue to reduce their property, plant, and equipment (PPE) relative to revenues, especially as the trend toward low-cost manufacturing countries evolves, with a resulting increase in balance-sheet cash, short-term investments, and expansion opportunities. Certainly, Apple Computer has been a leading company in this regard and in the process has been generating very high amounts of excess cash. Investors are, in Apple's case, ignoring the very low returns on its cash in their valuation of the company, focusing instead on its high economic profit.

As we see from its June 30, 2009, balance sheet (Table 5-9), Apple, reports $24 billion in balance-sheet cash, another $6.9 billion in marketable securities, and just $26 billion in shareholders' equity. It generates about $34 billion in revenue on just $2.6 billion in PPE. Apple's cash and equivalents are so large in relation to its equity that when subtracting cash from its capital base, its invested capital is small. Of course, this also would be the case for a company with operating losses, but in Apple's case, its management has been extraordinarily effective at taking advantage of others' capital.

This trend toward using other entities' capital is not confined to the manufacturing sector because service entities are also redeploying labor outside their cost structure.

TABLE 5-9

Apple, Inc., Consolidated Financial Statements

APPLE, INC.
CONDENSED CONSOLIDATED BALANCE SHEETS
(Unaudited)
(In Millions, Except Share Amounts)

	June 27, 2009	September 27, 2008
Assets		
Current assets:		
Cash and cash equivalents	$5,605	$11,875
Short-term marketable securities	18,617	10,236
Accounts receivable, less allowances of $58 and $47, respectively	2,686	2,422
Inventories	380	509
Deferred tax assets	1,731	1,447
Other current assets	6,151	5,822
Total current assets	35,170	32,311
Long-term marketable securities	6,899	2,379
Property, plant, and equipment, net	2,653	2,455
Goodwill	207	207
Acquired intangible assets, net	259	285
Other assets	2,952	1,935
Total assets	$48,140	$39,572
Liabilities and Shareholders' Equity		
Current liabilities:		
Accounts payable	$4,854	$5,520
Accrued expenses	3,338	3,719
Deferred revenue	8,469	4,853
Total current liabilities	16,661	14,092
Deferred revenue—noncurrent	3,667	3,029
Other noncurrent liabilities	1,924	1,421
Total liabilities	22,252	18,542
Commitments and contingencies		
Shareholders' equity:		
Common stock, no par value, 1,800,000,000 shares authorized, 895,735,210 and 888,325,973 shares issued and outstanding, respectively	7,957	7,177
Retained earnings	17,878	13,845
Accumulated other comprehensive income	53	8
Total shareholders' equity	25,888	21,030
Total liabilities and shareholders' equity	$48,140	$39,57

CHAPTER 6

Financial Structure

A firm's financial structure is its integrity. It is the backbone that provides the strength to withstand both the forces of economic nature and those self-imposed. It is where creditors look to first when evaluating and rating an enterprise. "Does the capitalization support the rating" is a common theme heard from rating agencies. The more leverage an entity has, the greater is the risk. And leverage is balanced by cash flows, the stability of those cash flows, and liquid assets. If the financial structure is not sitting on solid ground, a marginal turn of events can put the health of the enterprise at risk. Its ability to satisfy claims, including fixed obligations, is put into question.

An entity whose financial structure is overly capitalized normally is prepared for a sudden and swift negative turn of events; it is in a position to both buy time and take advantage of its competitors' weakened market condition. It also can, if it so chooses, gain market share or severely weaken its competitors, such as through pricing decisions that its weakened competitors cannot afford to match profitably. As we have seen, though, being overcapitalized has its costs, in the form of foregone free cash flow based on the returns of lower-yielding cash assets versus what could have been achieved had the cash been invested in value-enhancing investments. Not infrequently, the cost of the insurance for holding cash is worth the price, as it was during 2008 and 2009.

This is admittedly a long chapter, but it is necessary to the cost-of-capital matrix. In it I cover balance-sheet assets, liabilities of all forms, financial securities, off-balance-sheet obligations, and applicable accounting rules. For concerns that doubt the need for capital strength, financial history and a storied legacy will not be sufficient to bail them out.

Example:

Lehman Brothers survived for 157 years, through wars, the Great Depression, famines, assassinations of presidents, deep recessions, and oil embargoes, but it got into trouble by buying and financing commercial and residential real estate, including subprime mortgages. By placing the riskiest of all financial instruments on its balance sheet, it in essence put itself out of business when the real estate market collapsed. The company did not suitably gauge the extreme risk involved, nor did investors focus on their derivative activities. Its financial structure, despite such a long period of profitable growth, could not handle the immense strain of risky assets to which its management had taken it.

Many financial executives do not wish their firms to be significantly overcapitalized because their management consultants advise a larger than necessary equity cushion harms their financial ratios. Also, the yield on cash is unpredictable, aside from not being the purpose for which the organization was founded. Income from cash is not included in the return on invested capital (ROIC) metric.

Corporate executives must explicitly understand and determine the entity's desired and current financial and operating risk when setting the desired capital base. Excess leverage may not allow the firm's cash flows to service its obligated requirements. Certainly, this type of stress analysis took on new meaning with the 2008 credit crises and the subsequent effects on financial as well as industrial entities. And since shocks come "unannounced," the capital cushion is a necessary part of risk analysis and should be included in every research report by those undergoing such reviews. Every firm and analyst must ask themselves: Is the company prepared for a severe financial or industry crisis? Are the necessary financial backstops in place from reliable providers? What if it wasn't business as usual for a year or two or three? Could the firm survive?

In hindsight, it is easy to see that in too many historical instances, assumptions had been incorrect or perhaps not even considered. Firms ran into financial difficulties, and debt payments could not be met from operating cash flows. For banks and mortgage insurers, the projected default rates underpinning the cash flows of securitized debt turned out to be a multiple higher than originally perceived. Pension plans went from large overfunded positions to large underfunded positions, resulting in negative shareholders' equity for many firms. The expected ROIC for many projects no longer made economic sense, but cash had been spent and the projects were half complete. Borrowing froze for even the most creditworthy risks.

The optimal financial structure is established based on a firm's ability to predict its cash flows accurately. If it does not have this foresight—and few, if any, firms do—it must be set by its ability to withstand a probable worst-case scenario. So-called one in a hundred-year events seem to come around all too frequently. A probable worst-case scenario might be one in which the credit market freezes for two years with revenues at half the projected levels. If a firm has sufficient cash and calls on capital from a group of reliable providers, it can see its way through such a scenario.

If, however, ROIC is greater than the cost of capital for a project, the firm's *cost of capital could very well decline by increasing leverage.* We see this with most successful high-credit-rated entities, such as Walmart, Cisco, and Pepsi. Financial executives are always weighing business risk, leverage, and the cost of capital when making capital decisions—it is then up to investors, who also must weigh the rewards and risks, setting a required return for the cash they are considering investing. When Pepsi made a $7.8 billion bid to acquire its bottling unit, it did so, in part, because the expected return on the acquisition exceeded its cost of capital.

The firm's financial structure, as portrayed by its balance sheet, is out of date a moment after it is prepared because the value of its assets and liabilities shifts with the respective markets and the company's clients' business and financial condition. For instance, FNMA, in the years prior to its U.S. government bailout, showed large deferred tax assets on its balance sheet, without which it would have had large negative shareholders' equity. Given its poor cash flows, its financial leverage was considerably weaker than the company portrayed because the value of those deferred assets was questionable. A retailer's or manufacturer's inventory would be overstated if demand for its product slowed.

Errors in forecasts or shifting industry conditions affect the optimal financial structure. Many companies that experienced financial difficulty had a conservative financial structure, including adequate interest-charge coverage (operating cash flows/interest and operating lease expense[1]). However, when their business did not meet expectations, a reasonable financial structure became onerous and, and as bondholders increased their debt positions by virtue of the higher credit risk, they, in effect, controlled the company, putting equity holders at risk. It is therefore important that the analyst be able to "see down the road" in the event additional capital is needed and where, how, and at what cost that capital could be raised.

Electric utilities (Fig. 6-1), owing to their fairly assured return on capital, typically operate with higher leverage than the cyclic footwear, gold, and steel industries.

---

[1] In my model I add back interest and operating lease payments to cash flow from operations to arrive at the coverage.

FIGURE 6-1

Total Debt/Shareholders' Equity for Various Industries, Fiscal Year Ending (FYE) 2008

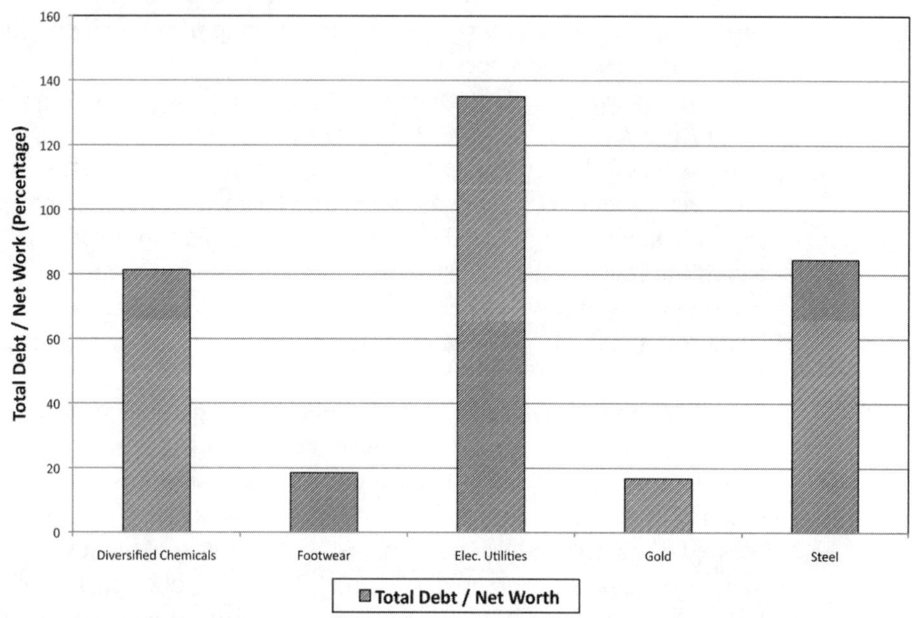

INTERNAL AND EXTERNAL CAPITAL

Most publicly held companies are financed by a mixture of internal and external capital. *Internal capital* consists of all financial instruments that, in effect, provide holders with an equity position in the firm. Examples include common stocks, convertible instruments such as preferred stocks and bonds that, for all practical purposes, can be considered as already converted into common stock, stock warrants, stock rights, and so on. *External capital* can be defined as all financial obligations to outsiders who are not likely to become equity holders in the firm. Examples are short-term debt owed to banks and bonds that are not likely to be converted to common stock. Other examples of external capital are obligations of the firm under leases, guarantees made by the firm, and other off-balance-sheet liabilities such as debt related to a joint venture and various derivative securities.[2]

[2] In some cases, a supplier will provide a customer with free equipment and even inventory in exchange for the customer using the firm as a supplier.

Traditional financial theory states that a firm has an optimal financial structure when there is is an optimal balance between internal and external capital.[3] In practice, corporate executives attempt to minimize the weighted-average cost of capital using all forms of internal and external capital consistent with the risk level of the firm.

The term *optimal financial structure* is an illusory term. It shifts with changes in cost of capital, which encompasses market perception (i.e., valuation multiples and yield spreads), cash flows, taxes, debt levels, litigation risk, risk-free rate, and other variables discussed in Chapter 8.

One well-known study suggests that owing to the tax benefits of debt and the fact that debt holders pay bankruptcy costs, leverage ratios should be high to attain the optimal capital structure.[4] Leland claims that leverage for most companies is optimal at about 75 to 95 percent and that firms with high risk and high bankruptcy costs should have leverage on the order of 50 to 60 percent when their effective tax rate is 35 percent. Leland does not broach volatility of tax rates, an important determinant of my credit model. He does not discuss cash flow or cash tax rate in his paper despite the fact it is cash-flow adequacy that keeps entities from avoiding bankruptcy. Litigation risk is not mentioned, but debt covenants are.

Benefits and costs are associated with external capital. For example, as Leland explains, interest payments on debt are tax deductable, whereas dividend payments to preferred and common stockholders are not deductable to the firm and are taxable to shareholders. Thus the firm has a clear incentive to raise external capital. However, external capital may dilute the implicit control of equity holders because the firm is subject to greater scrutiny by rating agencies and creditors. Also, if at any period the firm's cash flows are insufficient to service its debt, the firm may be forced into operating decisions it would prefer not to make or even confront bankruptcy, exposing equity holders to additional unexpected costs (including the issuance of additional equity). Firms steering down such as path may be forced to sell assets that have been reliable producers of free cash flow because these properties meet with the greatest demand by potential acquirers.

---

[3] Miller and Modigliani showed in 1961 (*Journal of Business*) that it does not matter how a firm finances itself. Ross (*Bell Journal of Economics*, 1977) and Leland and Pyle (*Journal of Finance*, 1977) show that an optimal financial structure exists because of signaling costs. Lewellen (*Journal of Finance*, 1975) and Galai and Masulis (*Journal of Financial Economics*, 1984) show that an optimal financial structure exists because of bankruptcy costs and taxation.

[4] See "Corporate Debt Value, Bond Covenants and Optimal Debt Structure," by Hayne Leland (*Journal of Finance*, September 1994).

Other financial theories suggest that entrepreneurs have incentives to issue shares in their firms to the public, in effect, raising more internal capital when they consider current stock prices too high. Thus they issue additional shares of the firm to the public and enjoy the benefits of cash infusion into the firm that is not justified by the firm's cash flows. Conversely, when firms purchase stock in themselves, they likely consider the price too low compared with their cash flows. Thus they repurchase the firm's stock, reducing internal capital. In reality, while many soundly financed firms with good cash flows have repurchased their own stock, too many others have done so succumbing to the pressure of vocal shareholders who believed that buyback programs will lend support to the stock price, implying that the stock price was not correctly discounting prospective free cash flow. Also, for a firm to constantly buy and sell its own stock would send a signal to the financial markets that could harm the stock valuation. Besides, no company has a crystal ball.

Information asymmetry almost always exists between insiders and outside investors, and it also may exist between shareholders and bondholders. For example, stock repurchases reduce total shareholders' equity, and shareholders may wish to accept certain capital projects or acquisitions that are too risky for bondholders.

One common characteristic of all financial theorists is that the financial structure of a firm does not usually lie in either extreme case; that is, firms are neither all equity nor all debt. Rather, they are a mixture of internal and external capital. Another common characteristic of the theories is that firms are not at their optimal structure at all times. Instead, they continuously make adjustments to their financial structure in an attempt to react to changing economic and market conditions so that they can reach their new optimal financial structure. Thus we should observe that firms adjust their capital structure in almost every period, as can, indeed, be verified from any casual examination of the financing cash flows of firms. These adjustments are more earmarked toward leverage, not equity issuance.

Can one predict how adjustments to the financial structure of a firm should be related to operating and free cash flow? To answer this question, recall that one of the major disadvantages of external capital is the possibility of bankruptcy and reorganization costs to shareholders. These expected costs relate to the likelihood of financial difficulties for the firm; the higher the likelihood of financial difficulties, the greater are the expected bankruptcy costs, and the more costly external financing becomes. An immediate variable to consider for the likelihood of financial difficulties is the stability of operating and free cash flow. The more stable[5] operating

---

[5] I define *stability* in Chapter 8.

and free cash flows are, the lower is the probability of financial difficulties, and the lower is the probability of bankruptcy. Thus firms with stable but growing operating and free cash flows are expected to be characterized by higher financial leverage than their counterparts, where financial leverage can be measured by the relative proportion of debt to equity, including all forms of external financing. Such firms are also more likely to be increasing external capital at the expense of internal capital. Assumed in all this is the soundness of the nation's banking system and, for individual entities, the soundness, reliability, and diversity of any backup financing agreements in place.

For entities that have entered bankruptcy but have shown a history of adequate but cyclicality in their cash flows, creditors have a reasonable opportunity at recouping some to all of their capital. Pilgrim's Pride, a large poultry company, saw its senior unsecured debt trade as low as 14 cents on the dollar with the firm being in Chapter 11 bankruptcy; when the firm was offered $2.6 billion in a buyout, those bonds went back up to par. Unfortunately, stockholders received very little from the deal.

Firms that exhibit volatile operating cash flows and firms that are characterized by negative free cash flow are expected to have lower financial leverage and, on average, are expected to show decreases in debt and increases in equity financing when conditions permit.

While the optimal financial structure is one of constant debate, in reality, it can be only determined with perfect foresight. This is so because the optimal mix of debt and equity is a function of future cash flows and the assets required to produce those cash flows. If the firm knew for certain its operating cash flows, it would adjust its capital structure accordingly, including lining up any necessary financing that needed to take place from secure sources. *The optimal structure would, in essence, be that level where the entity is capable of producing the highest free cash flow consistent with its ability to retire its contractual obligations and allowing a measure of financial flexibility.* There is a continual dynamic tradeoff between that financial structure and the time it takes for normalized operating cash flows to retire all outstanding obligations. Investors and corporate executives must evaluate the risk of nonpayment of debt if the operating cash flows are less than expected and whether the increase in leverage ratios is worth the added cash flows. As we saw in the case of Clorox, part of the analysis is available liquidity aside from what is listed on the balance sheet. Committed unused credit lines, including contingent equity, must be considered when evaluating the optimal structure for a particular company. Two companies having the same expected operating and free cash flows should have different leverage ratios if they have dissimilar credit lines available. Likewise, if they have dissimilar costs of capital, the company having the less risk (lower cost of capital) would be expected to withstand higher leverage.

Cash-flow analysis can provide worthwhile clues to impending financial risk and return. Unfortunately, many entities reporting a healthy operating gain after years of negative free cash flow often find themselves unprepared to operate during an ensuing business downturn. Because traditionally they have been heavy users of cash (with commensurate increases in debt), they cannot build the sufficient liquidity cushion necessary as conditions improve. Some entities, however, have been successful using a financing "window" to enhance their capital structure.

Example:

Temple Inland, Inc., manufactures corrugated packaging and building products and had $3.8 billion in revenues during fiscal year 2008. As reported on its balance sheet, Temple Inland has $41 million in cash and minimal short-term debt coming due.

TEMPLE INLAND, INC., AND SUBSIDIARIES
CONSOLIDATED BALANCE SHEETS

	At Year-End (in Millions)	
	2008	**2007**
ASSETS		
Current assets:		
Cash and cash equivalents	$41	$227
Trade receivables, net of allowance for doubtful accounts of $14 in 2008 and 2007	407	433
Inventories:		
Work in process and finished goods	104	116
Raw materials	217	224
Supplies and other	137	121
Total inventories	458	461
Deferred tax asset	66	99
Income taxes receivable	57	—
Prepaid expenses and other	44	57
Total current assets	1,073	1,277
Property and equipment:		
Land and buildings	671	641
Machinery and equipment	3,577	3,423
Construction in progress	36	120
Less allowances for depreciation	(2,620)	(2,552)
Total property and equipment	1,664	1,632

	At Year-End (in Millions)	
	2008	**2007**
Financial assets of special-purpose entities:	2,474	2,383
Goodwill	394	365
Other assets	264	285
Total assets	$5,869	$5,942
Liabilities		
Current liabilities:		
Accounts payable	$162	$244
Accrued employee compensation and benefits	84	108
Accrued interest	30	31
Accrued property taxes	12	11
Accrued income taxes	—	258
Other accrued expenses	140	173
Current portion of long-term debt	1	3
Current portion of pension and postretirement benefits	17	62
Total current liabilities	446	890
Long-term debt:	1,191	852
Nonrecourse financial liabilities of special-purpose entities	2,140	2,140
Deferred tax liability	750	762
Liability for pension benefits	172	71
Liability for postretirement benefits	101	123
Other long-term liabilities	292	324
Total liabilities	5,092	5,162
Noncontrolling Interest of Special-Purpose Entities	91	—
Shareholders' equity:		
Preferred stock—par value $1 per share, authorized 25,000,000 shares, none issued	—	—
Common stock—par value $1 per share, authorized 200,000,000 shares, issued 123,605,344 shares in 2008 and 2007, including shares held in the treasury	124	124
Additional paid-in capital	461	475
Accumulated other comprehensive loss	(189)	(139)
Retained earnings	936	987
Cost of shares held in the treasury: 17,098,808 shares in 2008 and 17,464,189 shares in 2007	(646)	(667)
Total shareholders' equity	686	780
Total liabilities and shareholders' equity	$5,869	$5,942

We see, however, that the company has significant debt maturing over its coming three years. Also on the balance sheet is an entry associated with its special-purpose entity, which relates to the sale of timberland through nonrecourse notes and would need to be investigated for any potential financial liabilities.

Temple Inland reports:

> Maturities of our debt during the next five years are (in millions): 2009—$33; 2010—$191; 2011—$163; 2012—$293; 2013—$0; and thereafter—$512. We have classified $32 million of 2009 stated maturities as long-term based on our intent and ability to refinance them on a long-term basis.

Given the cyclicality of its business, the company has been dependent on economic conditions to generate free cash flow. When reviewing this company, the analyst would be apprehensive that the company may be forced to pay a high cost of debt to refinance the coming obligations. Temple Inland states in a footnote that its $835 million in committed credit agreements expires by 2011. If the company decided to completely take down the $835 million to repay the debt coming due, it would have less than a year to repay that entire obligation—the date the credit line expired. Obviously, an analyst would prefer to see these debts coming due extended as soon as possible.

Example:

SkyTerra Communications, Inc., through its subsidiaries, provides mobile satellite communications services in the United States and Canada. For the 11 years shown in Table 6-1, SkyTerra Communications has shown just one year of limited free-cash-flow generation as its market value fell from almost $1.4 billion down to $18 million and then rose to $740 million. The sole reason SkyTerra recorded positive free cash flow during 2004 was that it was working its balance sheet; otherwise, its free cash flow would have been negative for all years shown in the table.

TABLE 6-1

SkyTerra Communications, Inc.

December Year End	Net Income (Loss)	Free Cash Flow	Total Debt	Total Market Value
1998	−0.6	−9.6	—	—
1999	−49.5	−84.6	2.6	1,375.0
2000	−124.7	−113.1	0.1	121.2
2001	−210.3	−52.3	0.0	47.1
2002	−4.0	−20.8	0.0	18.0
2003	−0.7	−15.4	0.0	22.6
2004	17.2	5.5	0.0	403.1
2005	59.3	−15.3	0.0	677.3
2006	−57.1	−33.4	483.9	740.3
2007	−123.6	−71.1	604.8	696.5
2008	−204.9	−89.4	838.2	193.4

Source: CT Capital, LLC.

Executives at the company took advantage of two positive years in earnings, especially 2005, when earnings showed a substantial jump, allowing management to raise almost $500 million in the debt market. Free cash flow again was negative that year, but both equity and fixed-income investors looked the other way, perhaps fixating on reported income. Investors who looked at the common free-cash-flow definition of net income plus depreciation also were fooled because that measure during 2004–2006 showed relative stability. In 2007 and 2008, as cash flows remained negative, the company was continually allowed to reenter the debt markets, forcing up leverage on lower capital.

This company was successful at raising almost $275 million in the year 2000, which allowed it to stay in business during 2001, when it reported a large loss along with continued negative free cash flow. With the loss, the credit markets were closed to the company, and as we see from Table 6-2, capital spending was, in essence, eliminated as revenues remained at basically zero.

SkyTerra was able to raise large amounts of equity and debt despite having a minimal revenue base. Normally, when firms such as SkyTerra have consistent negative free cash flow, it is an irrefutably negative signal because the original projections were not met. When such firms continually enter the debt markets, it bears closer watching, and it is indeed a risky proposition for creditors if they are not accorded a security interest in assets worth at least the principal amount of the loan. When revenues rose to $35 million in 2006, management jumped at the chance to raise capital again. Unfortunately, free cash flow continued to be negative, and SkyTerra's market value subsequently declined by over 75 percent.

SkyTerra Communications, Inc.

Ticker: 3SKYT

December Year End	Sales ($M)	Free Cash Flow ($M)
2002	0.0	(20.8)
2003	0.7	(15.4)
2004	2.1	5.5
2005	0.6	(15.3)
2006	34.9	(33.4)
2007	34.1	(71.1)
2008	34.5	(89.4)

It is not surprising that financial structure and cost of capital are closely related because credit and possible impairment to cash flows play a central role in risk analysis. Cost of capital, as with financial structure, is established by an entity's ability to produce cash flows—magnitude, growth rate, consistency, and capital intensity, as well as the other fundamental credit metrics enumerated in Chapter 8.

Entities having uncertain cash flows should carry less total debt, whereas entities having more predictable streams could have greater leverage.[6] For new

[6] For purposes of discussion, I refer to operating companies as opposed to companies in full or partial liquidation. Also excluded are companies that have raised sufficient equity capital with a low cash burn rate so that the cash could satisfy all outstanding claims. The cash burn rate is explained later in this chapter.

TABLE 6-2

Selected Investing and Financing Data: SkyTerra

SKYTERRA COMMUNICATIONS INC
TICKER: 3SKYT
SIC: 4,899.000
GICS: 50102010

	Stockholders' Equity	Capital Expenditures	Sale of Com/ Pref Stock	Issuance of LT Debt	Reduction in LT Debt	Financing Activ-Other
Dec98	29.822	0.912	0.118	0.000	0.108	0.000
Dec99	141.215	8.792	94.789	6.000	1.245	0.000
Dec00	280.407	24.491	247.038	@CF	0.915	0.000
Dec01	128.862	0.095	0.022	0.000	0.000	10.000
Dec02	81.297	0.000	16.971	0.000	0.000	0.177
Dec03	79.566	0.007	0.006	0.000	0.000	(1.195)
Dec04	134.084	0.839	35.328	0.000	0.000	(2.913)
Dec05	191.485	0.003	0.140	0.000	0.000	0.076
Dec06	(119.943)	99.063	0.713	423.052	0.225	0.000
Dec07	616.218	240.494	1.123	1.058	0.247	0.000
Dec08	471.353	177.101	0.064	150.000	0.910	0.000

organizations, the financial structure should be geared toward equity and the raising of equity capital if additional financing is needed. Unless the new enterprise is virtually assured of being in a position to repay borrowings, including principal, leverage is discouraged. For a fortunate entity whose debt retirement is very likely and prospective free cash flow is large, maximum leverage is judicious.

More cyclical firms or those with unstable cash flows will have a higher cost of debt owing to their questionable ability to repay principal and interest. If the cyclical concern is at the top of the operating cycle, where operating margins, free cash flow, and stock price are strongest, it should seriously consider selling shares, even if the cash is not currently needed. It should do this for three reasons: (1) so that it is not forced to sell high-cost equity during an ensuing downturn, (2) so that it can later take advantage of investment opportunities, including in-house research, which its weakened competitors cannot, with its low cost capital, and (3) so that its financial strength can grow market share through pricing. Being overcapitalized has its virtues, but as mentioned, if the entity continually taps the market at perceived peaks, it will send the wrong signal to investors (of prospective diminishment of cash flows), causing a stock decline and making such future sales unlikely.

If the entity under analysis is being studied for its ability to retire principal payments in a timely manner, it is total debt that must be used in the calculation of leverage ratios. Debt is debt—whether it is short-term bank debt, long-term subordinated debt, sinking-fund requirements, operating leases, pension obligations, or purchase commitments. They all represent legal liabilities that must be satisfied prior to shareholders' interest. For this reason, the maturing debt must match the enterprise's ability to service it. Again, this is addressed in Chapter 8.

Many popular financial ratios consider only long-term debt, thereby subjecting the leverage ratio to classification decision and conceivably manipulation. To consider only long-term debt might result in a large and inappropriate shift in leverage ratios depending on such classification. Under *Statement of Financial Accounting Standards No. 78* (SFAS 78): *Classification of Long Term Debt Callable by the Creditor*, if there is a violation of the debt agreement (covenant), such long-term debt might need to be reclassified as a current liability, altering both working capital and other ratios, which could impair the firm. Likewise, if the debt has a call feature and is callable within a year, it must be reclassified as a current liability, affecting working capital and similar ratios, which also could impair the firm or affect debt covenants.

Low leverage does not ensure an entity a low cost of capital if the firm does not generate free cash flow or have other positive metrics, as discussed in Chapter 8. As of October 1, 2009, there were 323 industrial companies having 40 percent or lower total debt/shareholders equity, a market value in excess of $100 million, greater than 10 percent cost of equity capital, and three-year negative average of free cash flow. Their five-year total stock return, thereby encompassing not just the three-year period of negative free cash flow but two years prior, showed a negative 4.9 percent total rate of return compared with a positive 2.4 percent for the Standard and Poor's (S&P) 500 Index.

For entities undergoing large capital expansion programs in the belief that the project will contribute to free cash flow, such as Wynn Resorts, total leverage will increase until the operating cash flows from the project are able to return the debt ratios back to acceptable levels. Such temporary strains to shareholders' equity should be balanced with additional equity raises in the event that market conditions work against projected revenues and cash flows. If the equity raise comes after market conditions turn down, the incremental cost of capital would be much higher than if part of the initial raise occurred when optimism for the project was at its peak. We see this with every recession, when capital becomes scarce and costs extreme.

TABLE 6-3

Companies with Low Leverage and High Cost of Equity Capital

Company	Cost of Capital (%)	Three-Year Average Free Cash Flow	Total Debt/ Net Worth	Five-Year Total Return
ATS Medical	17.5	(6.3)	32.3	(5.8)
Ballard Power	18.3	(35.3)	0	(23.2)
Enzo Biochem	15.3	(7.1)	0	(17.3)
Golden Star Res.	12.9	(95.9)	29.1	(10.7)
Lexicon Pharma.	11.5	(62.8)	11.5	(24.2)
Microvision	18.2	(23.5)	18.2	(11.2)
Tejon Ranch	13.2	(0.4)	13.2	(7.2)

In the midst of the credit crunch in 2009, Wynn was forced to raise $175 million by selling 9.6 million shares at $19 per share, when a year earlier its stock sold at as high as $119; a mere four months after the equity sale, its stock was back to $57. If it had a more balanced approach to the initial capital raise during 2007, taking into account the possibility of an economic downturn, dilution would have been very minor, and given its low cost of capital resulting from its then-stronger balance sheet, Wynn stock would not have sold off as greatly during the capital crunch. Six months after the $175 million raise, Wynn raised an additional $1.6 billion by selling 25 percent of its high-growth Macau properties through an initial public offering (IPO).

Debt taken on to fund the purchase of assets should be able to be tied directly to operating cash flows used in the retirement of that debt. The financing decision must match the investment decision. Banks that borrow short and loan long learn this lesson with each downturn.

As stated, startups, including companies that are expected to incur negative cash flows, should have as little debt as possible (preferably none), along with a substantial capital cushion. These companies often go through longer than expected periods of cash burn, with their only cash inflow resulting from interest income.

This was the case with a 2005 IPO, Nucryst Corporation, a medical products company based on a proprietary metal technology. While the capital raise brought it time and cash to expand, its business never took hold and was unable to produce free cash flow. We see in the firm's 2008 10K balance sheet an accumulated deficit of $41 million. When an entity is continually burning cash, it remains to be seen how long it will continue as a viable independent concern.

NUCRYST PHARMACEUTICALS CORP.

CONSOLIDATED BALANCE SHEETS

	December 31, 2008	December 31, 2007
	(Thousands of U.S. Dollars, Except Share Data)	
Assets		
Current		
Cash and cash equivalents	$23,388	$17,841
Accounts receivable—net (note 4)	5,062	14,924
Inventories (note 5)	2,887	4,426
Prepaid expenses	414	427
	31,751	37,618
Restricted cash (note 2g)	145	140
Capital assets—net (note 6)	9,379	12,734
Intangible assets—net (note 7)	525	807
	$41,800	$51,299
Liabilities and Shareholders' Equity		
Current		
Accounts payable and accrued liabilities (note 8)	$2,859	$3,650
Accounts payable and accrued liabilities to related party (note 12)	—	67
Deferred lease inducement (note 2m)	90	111
	2,949	3,828
Long-term deferred lease inducement (note 2m)	495	726
	3,444	4,554
Guarantees (note 13)		
Commitments (note 14)		
Shareholders' Equity		
Common shares no par value, unlimited shares authorized, issued and outstanding—18,320,531 and 18,367,563 shares on December 31, 2008 and 2007, respectively (note 10)	82,776	82,776
Additional paid-in capital	2,178	1,511
Accumulated other comprehensive (loss) income (note 2d)	(5,528)	557
Accumulated deficit	(41,070)	(38,099)
Total shareholders' equity	38,356	46,745
	$41,800	$51,299

Source: Nucryst Pharmaceuticals 2009 10K.

DEFERRED ASSETS

The deferred-asset account appearing on a balance sheet must be monitored for its potential impact on cash flows and financial structure, including the underlying causes resulting from changes to the account. The merit of the asset(s) should be evaluated. There is little doubt that material issues could be uncovered through such analysis, including that related to pension funding and income taxes. The interperiod change also will be reflected under the operating activity section, but the underlying cause may not. Unlike other working-capital items appearing under operating activities, which are self-explanatory, deferred assets, because they consist of many items grouped together, could represent trends, benefits, or potential problems ahead.

Examples of deferred assets that might benefit the firm in future periods include advertising expenses, rents paid in advance, capitalized items such as interest or dry holes, and intangible assets such as goodwill. Changes in deferred assets could be attributed to changes in policy regarding payment of expenditures for such items as insurance, maintenance, and the cost to redesign and improve existing products, which the firm *hopes* will result in future cash flows. However, the addition to deferred assets usually requires an outlay of cash, whose expense recognition for accounting purposes is deferred for later periods. The deferred-asset account can be a refuge for many items, and for certain entities it can be quite large.

Advocates of cash-flow analysis differ with the accounting convention of recording an asset of this kind for cash already spent and will consider it an immediate cash outflow in their analysis. As we will see, deferred tax assets might represent an important asset that might be offset by a valuation allowance. Judgments as to the size of the valuation allowance are subjective and influence accounting ratios that are popular with analysts and credit-rating agencies, especially leverage ratios. If used, it represents a tax shield resulting in higher than otherwise cash flows.

CONTINGENT EQUITY

Contingent equity can be considered part of standby capital for entities that have such commitments. Equity commitments to the enterprise will be found in the footnotes. Under a contingent equity agreement, also referred to as a *contingent capital commitment*, cash would be received under predefined circumstances, similar to the action of the Federal Reserve in providing a backstop for acquiring banks, thereby facilitating their purchase of weaker institutions that otherwise would have failed. However, contingent equity agreements can exist for any sector.

A firm given a contingent equity commitment would receive the capital (cash) on the realization of a predetermined event. A triggering event could be an increase in raw materials prices, a natural hazard, a financial market setback, a labor strike, a change in the state of the economy, and so on. The capital can be in the form of subordinated debt, preferred shares, or pure equity. For this "insurance," the firm pays an option fee to the institution or group providing the commitment, whereas the company receives the comfort of standby capital at a predetermined cost. If the contingent capital takes the form of straight preferred stock, it could have no dilution effect on reported earnings and, being equity, could aid leverage ratios. To the entity receiving the contingent capital, its price normally consists of a commitment fee based on LIBOR that is paid during the period that the commitment remains in effect.

Contingent capital allows the entity to use its assets more fully because the need for a normal reserve it might maintain for contingencies would be lessened. This could increase the firm's ROIC and, commensurably, its stock price.

Normally, the cost to firms receiving contingent equity is high because investors need to be induced to offer a capital contingency arrangement; entities participating thus far generally have not been top-tier credits because the cost is greater than a standard bank commitment. It appears, however, based on Securities and Exchange Commission (SEC) filings that contingent equity arrangements are growing in popularity. It is up to the analyst to pro forma the balance sheet to determine if the contingent capital would provide sufficient financing for the firm to continue normal operations if the triggering event were to take place. The analyst also must review the reason for the need for this type of financing, its cost, and how long it might be needed. Growth of this form of financing has not been greater because large buyers of contingent convertibles are sometimes prohibited from owning equity.

Example:

On June 19, 2009, we entered into a Contingent Equity Agreement with Thermo Funding whereby Thermo Funding agreed to deposit $60 million into a contingent equity account to fulfill a condition precedent for borrowing under the Facility Agreement. Under the terms of the Facility Agreement, we will be required to make drawings from this account if and to the extent we have an actual or projected deficiency in our ability to meet indebtedness obligations due within a forward-looking 90 day period. Thermo Funding pledged the contingent equity account to secure our obligations under the Facility Agreement. If we make any drawings from the contingent equity account, we will issue Thermo Funding shares of our Common Stock calculated using a price per share equal to 80% of the volume-weighted average closing price of the Common Stock for the 15 trading days immediately preceding the draw. Any undrawn amounts in the account will be returned to Thermo Funding after we have made the second scheduled repayment under the Facility Agreement, which we currently expect to be no later than June 15, 2012.

> The Contingent Equity Agreement also provides that we will pay Thermo Funding an availability fee of 10 percent per year for maintaining funds in the contingent equity account. This fee is payable solely in warrants to purchase Common Stock at $0.01 per share with a five-year exercise period from issuance, with respect to a number of shares equal to the available balance in the contingent equity account divided by $1.37, subject to an annual retroactive adjustment at each anniversary of the date of the agreement. We issued Thermo Funding a warrant to purchase 4,379,562 shares for this fee upon the establishment of the Contingent Equity Account. No Common Stock is issuable if it would cause Thermo Funding and its affiliates to own more than 70 percent of our outstanding voting stock. If our Board of Directors and stockholders approve the creation of a class of nonvoting common stock in the future, we may issue nonvoting common stock in lieu of Common Stock to the extent issuing Common Stock would cause Thermo Funding and its affiliates to exceed this 70 percent ownership level.

Source: Globalstar 14A, September 3, 2009.

Example:

Deltic Timber Corporation is a natural resources company engaged primarily in the growing and harvesting of timber and the manufacture and marketing of lumber. Deltic owns approximately 437,700 acres of timberland, primarily in Arkansas and north Louisiana.

> Prior to August 26, 2004, the company had agreed to a contingent equity contribution agreement with Del-Tin Fiber and the group of banks from whom Del-Tin Fiber had obtained its $89,000,000 credit facility. Under this agreement, Deltic and the other 50 percent owner of the joint venture had agreed to fund any deficiency in contributions to either Del-Tin Fiber's required sinking fund or debt service reserve, up to a cumulative total of $17,500,000 for each owner. In addition, each owner had committed to a production support agreement, under which each owner had agreed to make support obligation payments to Del-Tin Fiber to provide, on the occurrence of certain events, additional funds for payment of debt service until the plant was able to successfully complete a minimum production test. Both owners had also agreed, in a series of one-year term commitments, to fund any operating working capital needs until the facility was able to consistently generate sufficient funds to meet its cash requirements.

Source: Deltic Timber Corp. 2005 10K.

BANK CREDIT FACILITIES

Bank credit facilities represent short-term calls on cash. When drawn, they are similar to short-term debt and become part of that balance-sheet entry. The maturity of the debt typically ranges from a few months to three years, although it can be longer. As the entity enters the final year of a credit facility, it normally looks to extend and perhaps increase the amount of the current agreement. If the facility is near expiration, obvious risk develops, including that which may be due to market conditions.

The ability of the entity to have a bank credit facility in place represents an important source of cash and has proven to be invaluable if a pending liability needs to be funded quickly or a fear of credit market tightening or change in perception takes hold. It also may be needed to satisfy maturing liabilities.

Bank credit facilities become increasingly important as the credit of the entity drops. During the financial crisis, many firms drew down their bank credits, fearing they would be removed and long-term credits would be unavailable. Entities that feared a large derivatives trading loss quickly established increases to their existing facilities.

When reviewing bank facilities, it is preferable for the entity to have contractual commitments with several high-grade institutions with which the entity has had a long relationship. The use of a single bank poses risk, as might agreements with just two institutions. The larger the facility, the larger is the consortium needed. This is done to minimize both client and bank risk. The greater the number of institutions taking part in the lending facility, the lower is the exposure for any particular bank, and the more willing banks would be to provide the financing commitment. The soundness of the lending institutions must be part of the analysis because the loss of any one could result in collapse of the entire agreement.

The analyst should evaluate the size of the credit facility in relation to the needs of the entity, its purpose, and the length of the agreement. The analysis should include the circumstances under which the banks can block any further credit or demand immediate repayment of amounts borrowed. If the entity needs to take down part or all of the facility, it must be reviewed for repayment prospects and to determine whether the added debt will violate any existing covenants.

DEBT, FINANCIAL FLEXIBILITY, AND COVENANTS

Financial flexibility refers to the ability of an enterprise to take advantage of investment opportunities. Companies that lose financial flexibility become increasingly reliant on sources outside the company for help, including additional financing and asset purchases. They do not control their own destiny. If they lack such flexibility, whether owing to market conditions or their own state of affairs, available projects that can enhance their ROIC or acquisitions become limited, affecting prospective cash flows, shareholder returns, and credit rating. Entities that are managed conservatively, with a long history of stable growth of revenues and free cash flow, or entities that are in industry sectors perceived to have above-average growth prospects have access to a strong investor supply of capital that may be used for expansion, acquisition, or to lower prices to gain market share. Such enterprises can operate with greater financial leverage.

Entities with consistent cash flows have an invaluable advantage—a lower hurdle rate than their competition. This was seen vividly in the credit crisis of 2007–2008, in which many companies under generally accepted accounting principles (GAAP) earnings growth became cash strapped owing to an unbalanced financial structure and, because of large capital expenditures, did not generate normalized (four-year average) free cash flow. They were reliant on others. Financially flexible firms during that same period were able to invest in assets at substantially below-market prices resulting from the crisis, as they are during every economic downturn.

When an entity enters the marketplace to raise capital, it must take into consideration its remaining financial flexibility—is it increasing or decreasing as a result of the offering? To what extent? Did the yield spread change? Will the entity be able to tap the market further, if necessary? Is the current project worth cashing in some or all of that flexibility? No matter how high the credit rating of the entity, investors often will demand higher rates of return for continued trips to raise capital. For this reason, in my credit model, I penalize (raise the cost of equity capital for) such entities because there always comes a time when credit conditions work against them.

Understanding the financial flexibility of a firm requires an analysis of all debt covenants that restrict the firm's ability to operate its business in a manner allowing it to maximize free cash flow while maintaining a sufficiently low cost of capital. Covenants can affect the financial flexibility in addition to bankruptcy risk. Covenants also can protect a firm from taking unwarranted risk under the fear of bankruptcy resulting from a violation. Restrictive covenants are included in every lending agreement, especially restrictions related to conversion of assets that are used to collateralize the obligation. The covenants affecting working capital and leverage could impair an entity's ability to do business, and the analyst must understand the effects those limitations have on the firm's operations. As would be expected, the weaker the credit, the more restrictive are the covenants; such restrictions and requirements might include agreements requiring the company to meet monthly liquidity hurdles, even if the borrower is public and required to report results to shareholders on a quarterly basis.

Bond indentures contain the terms of the obligations set forth between the issuer and the trustee, with the latter selected to represent the rights of the bondholders. Indenture terms include the interest rate, maturity, collateral, procedures to modify the indenture, use of proceeds, and the responsibilities of the borrower. Other common clauses relate to required insurance, events of default, payment of dividends, incurring additional debt, and restrictions of business combinations.

The covenants of the indenture can be either positive or negative. A negative covenant, such as a maximum leverage ratio, can restrict the borrower and hence its ability to operate without creditor approval. A positive covenant requires the firm to take certain actions, such as minimum net worth and working capital.

If the bond issue calls for an annual sinking fund, the terms, including the amount of principal or number of bonds to be retired each year, will be listed in the indenture. If the issuer's bonds are selling below par, the company can repurchase the bonds at a discount and book the gain into its income statement. For the cash-flow analyst, these retirements could have positive ramifications owing to the effects on leverage ratios, such as debt/operating cash flows and fixed-charge coverage. Additionally, if the issuer is able to retire additional debt resulting from excess free cash flow, the deleveraging will add financial flexibility should additional capital be needed in the future. On the other hand, if the entity is required to make a sinking-fund payment and its balance sheet cash is needed for working capital, payment would cause additional loss to financial flexibility, resulting in greater prospective risk to both equity and debt holders. In this circumstance, where the entity might be forced to raise equity to satisfy debt payments, it is not unusual for large dilution to take place, resulting from the new higher risk (cost of equity).

When analyzing debt covenants, it is imperative to understand the definitions set forth by the creditors. For example, restricted cash on the balance sheet may not count as equity in the calculation of leverage ratios by certain lenders. Other times, events that have yet to take place may allow for debt not to count against leverage ratios, such as debt related to a division to be sold. Other times, balance-sheet cash is allowed to be netted against debt in the calculation of leverage. When firms negotiate credit agreements, those agreements must be suited to their particular situation, especially the timing of expected cash flows.

The failure of the entity to comply with a loan covenant might not necessarily mean that the loan will be declared in default. If the lender believes that the company will eventually be in compliance, it may waive the (soon to be) violated covenant for a period of time until the covenant will again be in full force. The lender also may choose to amend the covenant to less restrictive terms under which the borrower will not continue to be in violation. After all, if the lender is a bank, it is in its best interest not only to see the loan repaid but also to continue to help the customer to grow. The bank's business will benefit as well, especially since its reputation will be enhanced. Cost of equity will benefit if, as a result of a covenant waiver, the price of the stock rises, allowing for equity financing and payment of those same fixed obligations.

Often, when loan covenants are extended, they are done so at a high cost to the entity. Either borrowing capacity is restrained, as in lines of credit, or other terms, such as the rate of interest or collateral, are reworked. Such actions would have a negative impact on the value of the firm if the present values of future free cash flow are affected.

If the lender is so inclined, for example, out of fear that the collateral is being impaired or because there is greater doubt that the entity can repay, it may demand the violation be cured within a period of time, which is normally spelled out in the loan agreement. Such periods normally run from 10 to 90 days. If the violation has not been cured, the lender again may choose to defer the cure for another specified period, rewrite the covenant, or declare the loan to be in default. Regardless of the lender's decision, a violation of a loan covenant or indenture is a negative event often resulting in bankruptcy.

Example:

Nordstrom lists the following covenants in its 2009 10K:

Debt Covenants

Our borrowing facilities include restrictive covenants, including the following significant restrictions:

Facility	Description of Covenant
2007-A $300 variable funding note	Standard and Poor's BB+ and Moody's Ba1ratings or better
$100 variable funding note	Standard and Poor's BB+ and Moody's Ba1 ratings or better
$650 commercial paper/ unsecured line of credit	Leverage ratio ("Adjusted Debt to EBITDAR" not greater than approximately four times)

Example:

The debt indenture includes covenants that limit our ability to grant liens on our facilities and to enter into sale and leaseback transactions, subject to significant allowances under which certain sale and leaseback transactions are not restricted. We are in compliance with all of our covenants as at June 30, 2009.

Source: KLA Tencor 2009 10K.

Example:

Restrictive covenants that lenders refuse to waive might make it more difficult to operate and grow a company. Many capital projects do not produce significant cash flows for several years, and therefore, creditors would be reluctant to waive covenants until it is clear that payback is reasonably assured or they have little choice. Lenders often will defer covenants and provide additional cash if a project is near completion or is about to be sold. Restrictive covenants could hamper management's desire to diversify out of existing businesses or add onto current lines. Management also conceivably could lose the flexibility of making an undervalued acquisition that could contribute significantly to cash flows.

> *Restrictive Covenants.* The agreements governing our credit facility, the term loans and the operating lease agreements contain restrictive covenants that, among others, (a) prohibit distributions under defined events of default, (b) restrict investments and sales of assets, and (c) require us to adhere to certain financial covenants, including defined ratios of asset coverage of at least 1.25 to 1.00, fixed charge coverage of at least 1.85 to 1.00 and of total funded debt to EBITDA (as defined in the agreements) of no greater than 4.00 to 1.00 through June 30, 2009 and of no greater than 3.75 to 1.00 thereafter. We continuously monitor our debt covenants and when considering future transaction, our decision making process evaluates the impact such transactions will have on our debt covenants. As of June 30, 2009 and 2008, we were in compliance with all of our debt covenants.

Source: K-Sea Transportation Partners 2009 10K.

Example:

For IMG Resort, if a company having a weak or uncertain credit were to buy a significant equity interest in it, it might hamper the company's ability to raise equity owing to a loan restriction. If IMG needed working capital and the covenant was in existence, it would be up to creditors to decide if they were willing to void or amend the provision, calling for payment on the entire note, called an *acceleration clause*.

> On November 3, 2003, IMG Resort and Casino issued $200.0 million of its 12% Senior Notes (the "*Notes*"). The Notes bear interest at 12% per year, payable on May 15 and November 15 of each year, beginning on May 15, 2004. The Notes will mature on November 15, 2010. The Notes may be redeemed at any time on or after November 15, 2007 at fixed redemption prices plus accrued and unpaid interest, if any. If a change in control occurs, holders of the Notes will have the right to require the repurchase of their Notes at a price equal to 101% of the principal amount thereof, plus accrued and unpaid interest, if any. The Notes are guaranteed by all of IMG Resort and Casino's subsidiaries.

Source: IMG Resorts 2009 10K.

Example:

When Vail Resorts required additional capital, the indenture needed to be modified as follows:

> The Additional Guarantor, as provided by Section 4.18 of the Indenture, jointly and severally, hereby unconditionally expressly assumes all of the obligations of a Guarantor under the Notes and the Indenture to the fullest as set forth in Article 12 of the Indenture; and the Additional Guarantor may expressly exercise every right and power of a Guarantor under the Indenture with the same effect as if it had been named a Guarantor therein.

Example:

Loan covenants, if not reviewed carefully and understood, can result in a massive wipeout of an entire equity investment. For example, Las Vegas Sands saw its market capitalization fall from over $80 billion to under $1 billion because it was about to violate certain covenants related to leverage and interest-charge coverage before its founder and chairman personally injected capital into the company. The firm has covenants related to many large debt tranches for its various operating properties, each of which calls for default if any other loan is in default, referred to as a *cross-default provision.* When assessing Las Vegas Sands credit quality, one must consider the consolidated entity and each of its operating companies separately owing to cross-defaults, with maximum leverage covenants varying from division to division. Restrictions also include the company's ability to transfer cash from one division to another.

Even with its current $10.5 billion market capitalization, these covenants bear close watching because they become more restrictive over time, and despite the company's existing ability to cover the next two years of debt maturities from available cash, a violation of a covenant would force all debt to become due. At the end of September 2009, the Las Vegas division had 5.73 times leverage (as defined in the covenant agreement) versus a 6.5 requirement, which steps down to 6 times in March 2009 and 5 times in March 2011. Given the company's substantial capital spending program, Las Vegas Sands most likely would need to sell assets, improve its earnings before interest, taxes, depreciation, and amortization (EBITDA) or renegotiate its credit terms.[7] The fact that Las Vegas Sands sold a portion of its Macau subsidiary subsequent to the Form 10K being filed does not play into the rating assessment other than the cash flow that boosted the liquidity of the parent. While technically a portion of the cash flows is now owned by investors of the Macau subsidiary, so too is a proportion of the debt obligation. Therefore, credit measures the rating agencies rely on, such as EBITDA coverage, are not affected.

The following is from Las Vegas Sands' China subsidiary and its Form 10K:

> The U.S. credit facility and FF&E facility require the company's Las Vegas operations to comply with certain financial covenants at the end of each quarter, including maintaining a maximum leverage ratio of net debt, as defined, to trailing twelve-month adjusted earnings before interest, income taxes, depreciation and amortization, as defined ("Adjusted EBITDA"). The maximum leverage ratio is 6.5× for the quarterly periods ending September 30 and December 31, 2009, and decreases by 0.5× every subsequent two quarterly periods until it decreases to, and remains at 5.0× for all quarterly periods thereafter through maturity (commencing with the quarterly period ending March 31, 2011). The Macau credit facility, as amended in August 2009, requires the company's Macau operations to comply with similar financial covenants, including maintaining a maximum leverage ratio of debt to Adjusted EBITDA. The maximum leverage ratio is 4.5× for the quarterly periods ending September 30 and December 31, 2009, and decreases by 0.5× every subsequent two quarterly periods until it decreases to, and remains at 3.0× for all quarterly periods thereafter through maturity (commencing with the quarterly period ending March 31, 2011).

[7] For purposes of its debt covenant, Las Vegas Sands is allowed to offset cash against debt.

Financial Ratios	Ratio Requirement as of June 30, 2009	As of June 30, 2009	Ratio requirement as of September 30, 2009	As of September 30, 2009
Consolidated interest coverage ratio	Not less than 3.50	5.73	Not less than 4.00	6.47
Consolidated leverage ratio	Not more than 4.00	3.83	Not more than 4.50	3.48

DEBT AND FREE CASH FLOW DURING THE 2007–2009 CREDIT CRISIS

An interesting period to study leverage is June 2007 through June 2009, that of going into and coming out of a severe recession. As Figure 6-2 makes clear, leverage began to build going into the recession as equity fell and debt grew. Even with record equity financing, leverage ratios at the end of June 2009 were higher than two years earlier. This is not atypical because excesses typically take several years to unwind.

FIGURE 6-2

Debt as a Percent of Equity for S&P 500, Quarters June 2007–June 2009

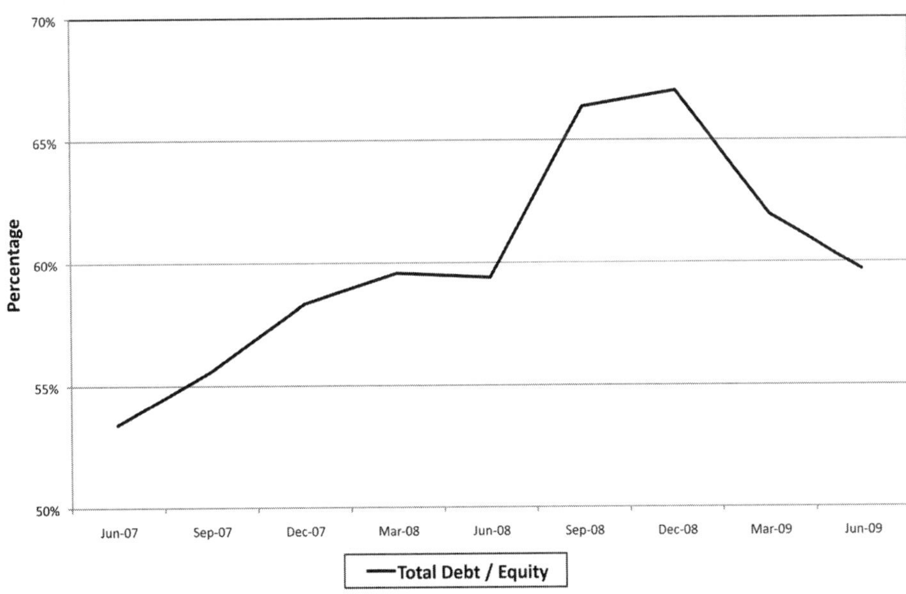

As Figure 6-3 illustrates, free cash flow increased 40 percent year over year for the one-year period ending June 2009, led by aggressive balance-sheet and discretionary expenditure management, without which free cash flow would have remained flat. The figure also shows the initial drop in free cash flow resulting from the recession and subsequent improvement starting in the March 2009 quarter, coinciding with the equity market rally.

Several S&P 500 companies saw their free cash flow decline, accompanied by an increase in leverage, yet saw a sharp rise in their stock price over the period, such as Archer Daniels, Interpublic, Jabil, and Massey Energy. For these companies, their (normalized) three- and four-year average free cash flows divided by their market capitalization were far in excess of the 10-year Treasury yield, and their fixed-charge coverage indicated that they would be able to continue to service their fixed-income obligations. As it became apparent that the United States would not suffer a depression, more leveraged firms saw outsized returns, especially those having a history of adequate normalized cash generation.

FIGURE 6-3

Free Cash Flow for S&P 500 Index by Quarter, June 2007–June 2009

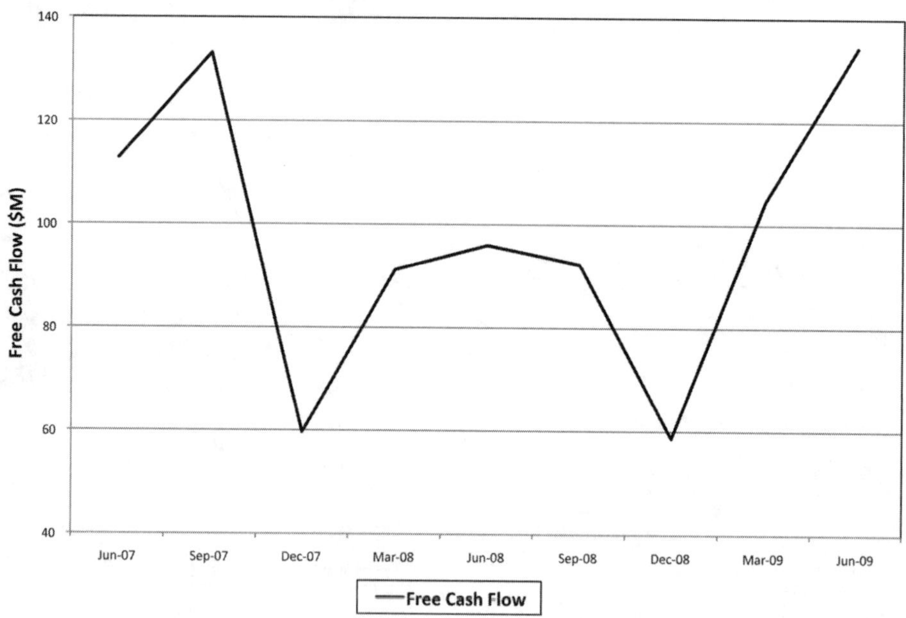

ADJUSTED DEBT

As with most non-GAAP yardsticks, the term *adjusted debt* takes many forms. This is true for reporting companies and credit-rating agencies. In their credit analyses, rating agencies normally define adjusted debt to include debt outstanding plus an adjustment to capitalize the operating leases.

It is fairly common for companies to design leverage yardsticks applicable to their own circumstance or that of their industry. For instance, Ralph Lauren and Nordstrom calculate adjusted debt as balance-sheet debt plus eight times their rent expense, believing that the latter is a fair approximation of their total capitalized operating leases. Brookdale Senior Living, Inc., takes this definition and subtracts available cash and cash equivalents.

FedEx considers adjusted debt to be long-term debt, including the current portion of such debt, plus six times rentals and landing fees. McDonalds states in its 10K that rating agencies exclude certain leases outside the United States that are cancellable with minimal penalty, capitalizing nonrestaurant leases at three times rent expense and reducing total rent expense by a percentage of the annual minimum rent payments due the company from franchisees. Schlumberger, Inc., calculates its adjusted net debt, which it defines as gross debt minus cash and investments that could be used to retire that debt. It also shows a modified cash-flow statement showing the change in net debt.

Regardless of the method used to capitalize the operating leases (Table 6-4) and adjust other debt, the result typically is a more accurate presentation of debt (than the balance sheet itself) to be compared with shareholders' equity and cash flows when making credit decisions.

Net debt also should be used to adjust the present value of free cash flow, as also shown for Schlumberger in Table 6-4, to arrive at fair value. For instance, the fair-equity-value estimate of Schlumberger requires, after arriving at the present value of its free cash flow using an appropriate cost of equity capital, subtracting its net debt (or net debt per share) of $1.1 billion and three months' working capital. Since Schlumberger generates positive and consistent free cash flows, probably no more than three months of working capital on hand is needed, especially given that the firm has sufficiently strong lines of credit available.

BUYING BACK DEBT

Buying back outstanding debt issued when interest rates were high and selling new low-interest debt in its place does not make economic sense if the market values and maturity dates are identical. Although it would appear that the entity would be

TABLE 6-4

Schlumberger Calculation of Adjusted Net Debt from Its 2008 10K (In Millions)

	2008	2007	2006
Net debt, beginning of year	**$(1,857)**	$(2,834)	$(532)
Net income	**5,435**	5,177	3,710
Excess of equity income over dividends received	**(235)**	(189)	(181)
Depreciation and amortization (includes multiclient seismic data costs)	**2,269**	1,954	1,561
Increase in working capital	**(591)**	(541)	(341)
Pension plan contributions	**(290)**	(250)	(251)
Capital expenditures	**(3,723)**	(2,931)	(2,457)
Multiclient seismic data capitalized	**(345)**	(260)	(180)
Proceeds from employee stock plans	**351**	622	442
Stock repurchase program	**(1,819)**	(1,355)	(1,068)
Dividends paid	**(964)**	(771)	(568)
Eastern Echo acquisition	**—**	(699)	—
Acquisition of minority interest in WesternGeco	**—**	—	(2,406)
Other business acquisitions	**(345)**	(286)	(577)
Conversion of debentures	**448**	656	—
Distribution to joint venture partner	**—**	—	(60)
Translation effect on net debt	**166**	(128)	(66)
Other	**371**	(22)	140
Net Debt, end of year	**$(1,129)**	$(1,857)	$(2,834)

Components of Net Debt	**Dec. 31, 2008**	**Dec. 31, 2007**	**Dec. 31, 2006**
Cash	**$189**	$197	$166
Short-term investments	**3,503**	2,972	2,833
Fixed income investments, held to maturity	**470**	440	153
Bank loans and current portion of long-term debt	**(1,598)**	(1,318)	(1,322)
Convertible debentures	**(321)**	(769)	(1,425)
Other long-term debt	**(3,372)**	(3,379)	(3,239)
	$(1,129)	$(1,857)	$(2,834)

saving cash from the gap in coupon rates, this is not always correct. If, however, the firm is desirous of "locking" in rates over a longer maturity, it might wish to do so. The cash impact of any swapping would be reported in the financing activities section of the cash-flow statement.

While normally a firm will show a separate line entry for early extinguishment of debt, this is not always the case. For instance, in 2009, Textron reported its loss of an early extinguishment of debt into selling, general, and administrative (SG&A) expense. When calculating the growth rate in SG&A for the estimation of free cash flow, this loss should be removed, as should all such atypical inputs.

GOODWILL

How should balance-sheet goodwill be viewed by the equity analyst? Goodwill is measured as the excess of the purchase price of a purchased business over the fair value of the tangible and intangible assets acquired minus the liabilities assumed. If there is a bargain purchase, where the acquirer pays less for the assets than the stated amount, *negative goodwill* occurs, and the buyer is required to recognize such excess in earnings as a gain. This would be recognized as a noncash event in operating activities.

Goodwill has measurable value to the extent the assets it represents can produce free cash flow in excess of the firm's cost of capital. Since goodwill represents an economic benefit, to the extent that this benefit is impaired, so too must its value, including a possible increase in stability metrics related to the firm's cash flows. But because the value of goodwill is included in the calculation of ROIC, its write-down could distort the analysis of management's ability to spend and earn a rate of return in excess of its cost of capital. In theory, an entity should write down all assets that do not produce a cash return at least equal to its cost of capital, as assets should reflect economic reality. Impairments, by themselves, do not affect free cash flow and that is why we look to growth rates in that measure when selecting an investment portfolio.

For the cash-flow analyst, the governing rule, SFAS 109, *Accounting for Income Taxes*, does not permit the recognition of deferred taxes related to goodwill that is not deductible for tax purposes. If the assets creating the goodwill are expected to be of indefinite value, the goodwill is not amortized, and the related deferred tax liabilities will not reverse until those assets become impaired. The tax treatment of the goodwill depends on the expenditures that created the goodwill. If an acquisition is structured as a stock purchase, no amortization of goodwill is permitted. If the purchase is structured as an asset purchase, goodwill is amortized over 15 years using straight-line depreciation. For shareholder reporting, goodwill normally is not amortized unless the assets are deemed impaired.

When goodwill is not tax deductible, any book/tax difference is considered a permanent difference, and no deferred taxes are recognized. When goodwill is tax deductible and is being amortized on the corporate return, it creates a deferred tax liability once the amortization period is up. When a company makes an acquisition, it may be required to reclassify its acquired intangible assets as goodwill if the intangibles are not tax deductible, and any deferred tax liability associated with those intangibles will be reversed as a reduction to goodwill.

As part of the Omnibus Budget Reconciliation Act of 1993, Congress added Section 197 to the Internal Revenue Code:

(a) General Rule

A taxpayer shall be entitled to an amortization deduction with respect to any amortizable section **197** intangible. The amount of such deduction shall be determined by amortizing the adjusted basis (for purposes of determining gain) of such intangible ratably over the 15-year period beginning with the month in which such intangible was acquired.

For purposes of this section—

(1) **In general**

Except as otherwise provided in this section, the term "section 197 intangible" means—

- **(A)** goodwill,
- **(B)** going concern value,
- **(C)** any of the following intangible items:
  - **(i)** workforce in place including its composition and terms and conditions (contractual or otherwise) of its employment,
  - **(ii)** business books and records, operating systems, or any other information base (including lists or other information with respect to current or prospective customers),
  - **(iii)** any patent, copyright, formula, process, design, pattern, knowhow, format, or other similar item,
  - **(iv)** any customer-based intangible,
  - **(v)** any supplier-based intangible, and
  - **(vi)** any other similar item,
- **(D)** any license, permit, or other right granted by a governmental unit or an agency or instrumentality thereof,
- **(E)** any covenant not to compete (or other arrangement to the extent such arrangement has substantially the same effect as a covenant not to compete) entered into in connection with an acquisition (directly or indirectly) of an interest in a trade or business or substantial portion thereof, and
- **(F)** any franchise, trademark, or trade name.

The following are listed by the IRS as not Section 197 intangibles and therefore are ineligible for amortization on the tax return:

1. Any interest in a corporation, partnership, trust, or estate.
2. Any interest under an existing futures contract, foreign currency contract, notional principal contract, interest-rate swap, or similar financial contract.
3. Any interest in land.
4. Most computer software (see below).
5. Any of the following assets not acquired in connection with the acquisition of a trade or business or a substantial part of a trade or business:
   a. An interest in a film, sound recording, videotape, book, or similar property.
   b. A right to receive tangible property or services under a contract or from a governmental agency.
   c. An interest in a patent or copyright.
   d. Certain rights that have a fixed duration or amount.
6. An interest under either of the following:
   a. An existing lease or sublease of tangible property.
   b. A debt that was in existence when the interest was acquired.
7. A right to service residential mortgages unless the right is acquired in connection with the acquisition of a trade or business or a substantial part of a trade or business.
8. Certain transaction costs incurred by parties to a corporate organization or reorganization in which any part of a gain or loss is not recognized.

Intangible property that is not amortizable under the rules for Section 197 intangibles can be depreciated if it meets certain requirements. You generally must use the straight-line method over its useful life. For certain intangibles, the depreciation period is specified in the law and regulations. For example, the depreciation period for computer software that is not a Section 197 intangible is generally 36 months.

For more information on depreciating intangible property, see "Intangible Property" under "What Method Can You Use to Depreciate Your Property?" in Chapter 1 of Publication 946.

Section 197 intangibles do not include the following types of computer software:

1. Software that meets all the following requirements:
   a. It is or has been readily available for purchase by the general public.
   b. It is subject to a nonexclusive license.
   c. It has not been substantially modified. This requirement is considered met if the cost of all modifications is not more than the greater of 25 percent of the price of the publicly available unmodified software or $2,000.
2. Software that is not acquired in connection with the acquisition of a trade or business or a substantial part of a trade or business.

To see if investors penalize entities that have large amounts of goodwill relative to shareholders' equity, all companies (including companies that became inactive through merger or bankruptcy) that had greater goodwill than equity were studied, with no other financial considerations taken into account; if goodwill had been valued at zero for these entities, shareholders' equity would have turned negative. For the five years ending November 2009, this group had a median stock return of 1.4 percent, virtually in line with the average return of each sector these companies are a member of. The companies had a median market value of $1.5 billion, $918 million in goodwill and $436 million in shareholders' equity. Based on this one study, it appears that investors do not penalize firms having excessive goodwill when making buy/sell decisions.

Because SFAS 109 requires periodic testing for impairment of goodwill, analysts should consider it in their calculation of shareholders' equity. If these assets fail to produce cash flows in excess of the firm's cost of capital, it will quickly show in the reporting periods and affect the free-cash-flow multiple, growth rate in free cash flow, stability of cash flows, and associated metrics, including cash flow/debt and ROIC. Given the preceding study, any write-down is most likely already reflected in the market price.

OFF-BALANCE-SHEET LIABILITIES

Certain significant current and potential legal liabilities may not appear on the balance sheet. For example, joint-venture entities may have debt obligations that do not appear on either equity owners' balance sheets but may represent legal or moral obligations of the joint-venture partners. The analyst should consider the likelihood that the joint-venture entity will be unable to service such obligations.

Special-purpose entity (SPE) debt is now required, under most circumstances, to be included in the consolidated balance sheet, even if nonrecourse. I will discuss this later in this chapter under SFAS 166.

If the likelihood of default is minimal and the debt is nonrecourse such that the joint-venture entity has at least three times fixed-charge coverage and operating cash flow capable of servicing the principal debt, the analyst may exclude the debt from the owner's balance sheet; otherwise, it could be included based either on the proportionate share of ownership or on exposure of repayment, which would be the case if one of the joint-venture partners was incapable of satisfying a claim. This nonrecourse debt would be included if this were a moral obligation on the part of the equity owner to see that the debts were paid. Some entities may give the debt holder other collateral or new debt to replace the bad debt. In the case of Pulte Homes, its joint venture defaulted under its debt agreement.

Example:

At December 31, 2008 and 2007, aggregate outstanding debt of unconsolidated joint ventures was $519.3 million and $602.5 million, respectively, of which our proportionate share of such joint venture debt was $92.0 million and $134.0 million, respectively. Of our proportionate share of joint venture debt, we provided limited recourse guaranties for $84.3 million and $124.5 million of such joint venture debt at December 31, 2008 and 2007, respectively.

Source: Pulte Homes 2008 10K.

While obligations for payment appearing on the balance sheet and with explanation in debt footnote are clear, off-balance-sheet liabilities are often less so. These obligations will be discussed throughout this chapter and may be explicit, in the case of guarantees, or implicit, in the case of implied or moral commitments. For example, even though an entity has sold accounts receivable on a nonrecourse basis, it may feel an obligation to make the buyer whole out of fear that such future sales will be impossible if the expected return to the buyer falls short.

The projected statement of cash flows should reflect any off-balance-sheet payments. Commitment or contingency payments, a common off-balance-sheet liability, normally become compulsory only on a trigger, as would be called for by a loan guaranty or a supply contract. If business conditions deteriorate and a purchase contract calls for delivery of unneeded product at prices above current market value, the projected cash-flow statement must reflect that payment due, with its commensurate impact on leverage. The firm's ability to make payment on these obligations must be assessed in light of expected cash flow, balance-sheet liquidity, and other calls on capital, such as maturing debt, or other commitments. At a minimum, prospective free cash flows would be affected because cash paid to suppliers could well exceed collections on the firm's receivables.

When energy prices spiked upward during the 1990s, pipelines and utility companies were required under so-called take-or-pay contracts to accept large volumes of oil and gas at prices far in excess of the then-current market price, having signed such contracts under fear they would not have either their needed supply or be required, owing to market conditions, to pay even higher prices than the contracts called for. Several companies filed bankruptcy as a result of these onerous provisions.

Example:

Resolute Energy Corp. is an oil and gas company engaged in exploration and development.

> Resolute is required to take on a monthly basis, or pay for if not taken, a percentage of the total of the maximum daily quantities for each month during the term of the Kinder Morgan contract. The percentage is 80% for 2009 and 75% for the remainder of the contract term. There are make-up provisions allowing any take or pay payments it makes to be applied against future purchases for specified periods of time. Resolute has a one time right to reduce committed volumes under the contract by up to approximately 41 Bcf for 25% of the contract price at the time the volumes are released. It does not have the right to resell CO_2 required to be purchased under the Kinder Morgan contract. As of December 31, 2008, Resolute had made payments of $94,290 under this contract for 134,708 Mcf of CO_2 for which it had not yet taken delivery.

Source: Resolute Energy Form S4, August 28, 2009.

So great were the liabilities resulting from take-or-pay contracts that merger agreements in the energy industry now contain a fairly standard clause stipulating that the party being acquired has either a small or no such obligation in existence.[8]

Companies are required to provide comprehensive explanations of any such arrangements and agreements in their annual and quarterly reports, registration statements, and proxy and information statements. In addition, companies must determine whether the contracts underlying these arrangements are material contracts required to be filed as exhibits.

Not all agreements with suppliers incur contingent or reportable liabilities. For example, to induce large restaurant chains to purchase their syrup, Coke and

[8] During 2001, Columbia Gas Systems unexpectedly filed for bankruptcy owing to natural gas take-or-pay obligations.

Pepsi often pay those customers large upfront cash payments for exclusivity in their stores and their agreement to take a certain volume. However, their clients incur no legal obligation to take such volume, although it is in those customers' best interest to work off the deal quickly so that they can receive another large cash payment. Until the supply is exhausted, the restaurant operator is prohibited from using the competitor's product.

Example:

> During the year ended June 30, 2000, the company entered into long-term, exclusive contracts with The Coca-Cola Company and with Dr Pepper/Seven Up, Inc., to supply the company and its franchise restaurants with their products and obligating Burger King restaurants in the United States to purchase a specified number of gallons of soft drink syrup. These volume commitments are not subject to any time limit. As of June 30, 2009, the company estimates that it will take approximately 13 years to complete the Coca-Cola and Dr Pepper/Seven Up, Inc., purchase commitments. In the event of early termination of these arrangements, the company may be required to make termination payments that could be material to the company's results of operations and financial position. Additionally, in connection with these contracts, the company received upfront fees, which are being amortized over the term of the contracts. As of June 30, 2009 and 2008, the deferred amounts totaled $16.1 million and $17.2 million, respectively. These deferred amounts are amortized as a reduction to food, paper, and product costs in the accompanying consolidated statements of income.

Source: Burger King Holdings, Inc., 2009 10K.

Typically, the most common and largest off-balance-sheet liability is the operating lease, which I will soon discuss. However, off-balance-sheet liabilities, especially coming under the umbrella of a special-purpose entity, can be as creative as lawyers and investment bankers can imagine.

SPECIAL-PURPOSE ENTITIES

A *special-purpose entity* (SPE) is a structured finance vehicle typically designed to provide financing to a firm or its customers. The SPE was conceived originally as a sales tool, such as when companies set up such separate entities as leasing divisions to help customers finance a purchase. Thus the SPE began as a legitimate tool that allowed many companies to propel their growth while allowing the parent or holding company to maintain an acceptable level of risk by separating the two structures. With the Enron debacle, a closer look at SPEs brought forth a wave of changes in their formation and accounting regulations, including SFAS 166 and SFAS 167, which took effect January 2010 and required, under many circumstances, consolidation of debt and other information pertaining to SPEs and securitizations. As originally intended, the SPE still represents a viable and important selling aid that enables firms to compete for business that could not obtain bank financing

In the SPE, assets are siphoned off and placed in a separate legal entity. This entity then can borrow and pay expenses and is subject to risks as with any corporation. Since many of the more infamous SPEs were levered, when tough times arose, the cash flows from their assets were not sufficient to repay their debts, and the owners of their equity and debt capital were stuck with massive losses.

The true amount of Enron's debt escaped most investors who believed the story line coming out of the conference calls, including Merrill Lynch, whom the SEC accused of abetting and aiding Enron. We thus learned that the SPE needed to be analyzed with the precision and diligence one would use when evaluating any concern and especially for the implications it held for its owners and creditors. Many SPEs were poorly capitalized and could not stand up to the strains of a poor economic climate.

Today, many SPEs are used to remove (or place new debt) off the consolidated balance sheet, including lease obligations, sometimes referred to as *synthetic leases*. As a result, the Financial Accounting Standards Board (FASB) issued Interpretations 46 and 46R, *Consolidation of Variable Interest Entities*. The objectives of 46R were to explain how to identify variable-interest entities (VIEs) and how to determine when a business enterprise should include the assets, liabilities, noncontrolling interests, and results of activities of a VIE in its consolidated financial statements. I will provide an example involving this standard later in this chapter.

CONTINGENT LIABILITIES

Another potential off-balance-sheet liability is that related to contingent liabilities, which could be included in leverage ratios, depending on the circumstances. If large enough, contingent liabilities can severely impair an entity or even induce bankruptcy. These include obligations that occurred before the end of the fiscal year but whose effect on the financial statements is not clearly determinable on that date.[9]

[9] On April 1, 2009, the FASB issued Staff Position 141R, which reduced the recognition of contingent assets and liabilities acquired during a business combination to those which can be *reasonably* determined from being more likely than not to give rise to an asset or liability.

Example:

Contingent obligations can either be *contractual* or *non-contractual* in nature. For example, if a subsidiary is facing financial difficulties, its parent company may be contractually obligated to cover the subsidiary's debt service payments under the terms of a guarantee. In another example, financial institutions may provide standby liquidity facilities or letters of credit, which contractually require funding under certain conditions and could result in potentially significant liquidity calls and exposure to credit risk.

Non-contractual contingent obligations are those that arise unexpectedly such as lawsuits or those created by the requirements of regulatory or environmental agencies. Unlike contractual contingent obligations and the other two categories of OBS exposures, non-contractual contingent obligations are difficult to measure due to their uncertainty.

Source: Moodys.com.

For many years, contingent liabilities, because they are normally relegated to the footnotes of financial statements, were merely an afterthought for many investors and analysts—until the financial crisis began in 2007. To many analysts, they were considered an ordinary cost of doing business—mere formalities or simple hedges—and because of that, they were believed to be conservative in nature. At least that was what analysts were hearing from many CFOs.

Contingent liabilities can run the gamut of circumstances and are recorded on the balance sheet only if the contingency is both probable and the amount can be estimated. If the contingent liability is only possible, or if the amount cannot be estimated, only a disclosure is required. If the contingent liability is remote, no disclosure is required.

A common contingent liability found in financial statements is product warranties because manufacturers can reasonably estimate, based on history, their amount and probability. Other examples of contingent liabilities include lease agreements, forward purchase or sale commitments, guarantees, standby liquidity agreements, letters of credit, environmental remediation, and unwinding loss-plagued financial instruments.

Contingency payments with regard to lawsuits are also common, and the financial consequences can be significant. For this reason, exposure to lawsuits is included in my cost-of-equity credit model. It is rare for companies to admit, on being handed a lawsuit, that the plaintiffs have a weak case and thus downplay its significance. Because such contingent liabilities often cannot be estimated (they are subject to judgment), they are normally relegated to a footnote. Unfortunately, financial history has seen many formerly very healthy entities forced into bankruptcy or severely weakened as a result of lost verdicts and settlements, most recently those related to asbestos. A. H. Robbins was a strong credit until faced with thousands of lawsuits and many millions of dollars in claims resulting from its manufacture of the Dalkon Shield. It ultimately filed bankruptcy. Dow Corning was the subject of many hundreds of claims resulting from its manufacture of silicone gel breast implants and also filed bankruptcy.

Not only can lawsuits have a devastating effect on current finances, they also can force a shift in operating decisions if the risk associated with the research into or sale of a product are deemed to be too great. It is an unfortunate aspect of our society that litigation risk has prevented important research from going forward.

Since the 1990s, there have been an increasing number of successful lawsuits related to a company's financial engineering. For instance, Lucent paid $517 million and Oxford Health $300 million as a result of such lawsuits. Class-action lawsuits now take place in every country having an active stock exchange.

The analyst therefore cannot glance over contingencies because such payments not only could prove substantial, but they also divert management focus. Lawsuits have been most notable for the tobacco industry, where several awards were massive, and were thought by analysts at the time to potentially bankrupt the companies involved. In addition, even if the risk of loss from a lawsuit is remote, litigation expense is assured, always costly, and must be considered when preparing a cash-flow projection.

While cash outlays for contingencies are, in many instances, difficult to estimate, the same is not true for commitments. A firm normally would agree to a commitment if it is either concerned about the supply of an important input or is concerned about future prices of the input. When an entity agrees to a commitment, it represents a legal obligation; therefore, a review must take place for its capacity to do so and the extent of future cash obligations that could result. For instance, asset-retirement obligations (AROs) incurred by power companies to decommission power plants would be studied for both the change in cash flows resulting from the plant and all costs agreed to resulting from its dismantling.

The risks to the entity signing a commitment agreement to purchase inputs, such as raw materials or energy, are that demand for its product does not materialize or the cost of the goods falls in price. The analyst must ask, What if demand for the entity's products were to fall? What if the price of the committed material were to fall by half? Or more? How would that affect the firm's cash flow and leverage? Could it be used at a later time? Is the possibility already reflected in the price of the company's debt, equity, and cost of capital (risk profile)? As history has shown, this is more than a theoretical exercise.

Example:

Rancher Energy Corp. acquires, explores for, develops, and produces oil and natural gas in North America. The following is from its 2009 10K:

> Our existing contracts with ExxonMobil and Anadarko contain provisions under which we are required to take delivery of certain volumes of CO_2 or pay the seller for the volume difference between the required quantity and the volume actually purchased. If we are unable to secure sufficient financing to construct a pipeline and to develop and prepare our properties for the injection of CO_2 we will be unable to take delivery of CO_2 and our cash position at that time will not be sufficient to pay for the take-or-pay volume.

Example:

Reddy Ice Holdings, Inc., engages in the manufacture and distribution of packaged ice in the United States. The following is taken from its June 30, 2009 10Q:

> **Commitments and Contingencies**
>
> In order to secure a long-term supply of plastic bags at favorable prices, the company entered into a supply agreement with a plastic bag manufacturer (the "Bag Supply Agreement") in which it committed to purchase 250 million bags per twelve-month period beginning March 1, 2008. The Bag Supply Agreement expires on March 1, 2013. On March 9, 2009, the Bag Supply Agreement was amended to start on January 1, 2008 and end on December 31, 2012 and modify certain other provisions. The annual commitment to purchase 250 million bags remains in effect. The company anticipates being in compliance with the terms of the contract at December 31, 2009.
>
> The following is a discussion of the company's significant legal matters. The company is involved in various claims, suits, investigations, and legal proceedings. The company accrues a liability when it believes that it is both probable that a liability has been incurred and that it can reasonably estimate the amount of the loss. At September 30, 2009, and December 31, 2008, no accruals had been made in connection with the matters discussed below.

Example:

A. O. Smith Corporation engages in the manufacture and sale of water-heating equipment and electric motors for residential, commercial, and industrial end markets. The following is from its 2009 10K. The company is insured against large claims and self-insures against small claims to maintain low insurance premium payments. Insurance is a costly expense, so all companies self-insure to some degree.

Commitments and Contingencies

The company is subject to various claims and pending lawsuits for product liability and other matters arising out of the conduct of the company's business. With respect to product liability claims, the company has self-insured a portion of its product liability loss exposure for many years. The company has established reserves which it believes are adequate to cover incurred claims. For the years ended December 31, 2008 and 2007, the company had $125 million of product liability insurance for individual losses in excess of $5 million. The company periodically reevaluates its exposure on claims and lawsuits and makes adjustments to its reserves as appropriate. The company believes, based on current knowledge, consultation with counsel, adequate reserves, and insurance coverage, that the outcome of such claims and lawsuits will not have a material adverse effect on the company's financial position, results of operations, or cash flows.

Example:

Dollar General paid $32 million to settle a lawsuit rather than undergo a lengthy trial during the period it sought to sell equity to be used to pay down debt. The company's management did not want the "overhang" of a potential large liability to weigh on the IPO.

DOLLAR GENERAL CORPORATION AND SUBSIDIARIES
CONSOLIDATED STATEMENTS OF OPERATIONS
(In Thousands Except Per-Share Amounts)

	Successor		Predecessor	
	For the Year Ended January 30, 2009	March 6, 2007 Through February 1, 2008(a)	February 3, 2007 Through July 6, 2007	For the Year Ended February 2, 2007
Net sales	$10,457,668	$5,571,493	$3,923,753	$9,169,822
Cost of goods sold	7,396,571	3,999,599	2,852,178	6,801,617
Gross profit	3,061,097	1,571,894	1,071,575	2,368,205
Selling, general, and administrative expenses	2,448,611	1,324,508	960,930	2,119,929
Litigation settlement and related costs, net	32,000	—	—	—
Transaction and related costs	—	1,242	101,397	—
Operating profit	580,486	246,144	9,248	248,276
Interest income	(3,061)	(3,799)	(5,046)	(7,002)
Interest expense	391,932	252,897	10,299	34,915
Other (income) expense	(2,788)	3,639	—	—
Income (loss) before income taxes	194,403	(6,593)	3,995	220,363
Income tax expense (benefit)	86,221	(1,775)	11,993	82,420

	Successor		Predecessor	
	For the Year Ended January 30, 2009	March 6, 2007 Through February 1, 2008(a)	February 3, 2007 Through July 6, 2007	For the Year Ended February 2, 2007
Net income (loss)	$108,182	$(4,818)	$(7,998)	$137,943
Earnings (loss) per share:				
Basic	$0.19	$(0.01)		
Diluted	$0.19	$(0.01)		
Weighted-average shares:				
Basic	554,792	554,360		
Diluted	555,630	554,360		

Source: Dollar General August 2009 S1.

Although Dollar General's payment might be considered *de minimus* in relation to its equity, such is not always the case, as a review of Form 10Ks will attest.

Analysts must access litigation risk even when there is minor ongoing litigation because from time to time small lawsuits, if they are successful, can spread rapidly into many large class-action fillings. The analyst must determine if this possibility exists. For the small filing, the analyst must understand, to the extent possible, the facts involved, whether the company is potentially at fault, and if so, whether the lawsuit is contagious. A thorough review of the financial filings must be made because company executives normally do not make recent lawsuits a regular part of scheduled conference calls or investor presentations. Credit reports also report lawsuits, as do other services. Because large legal liabilities could have an important effect on an entity's ability to function, they must be considered in the risk profile, affecting the cost of equity capital. If lawsuits, including legal expenses, represent over 5 percent of the entity's cash flow from operations, the analyst must possess a very detailed understanding of the facts involved and consider a worst-case scenario. Cost of capital will be adjusted upward, as it would be in my credit model.

Example:

In a September 4, 2009, "Heard on the Street" *Wall Street Journal* column, the author noted that shares of Moody's and McGraw-Hill declined 7 and 10 percent after a federal judge ruled that the companies will have to defend themselves against fraud claims relating to ratings on a collapsed investment vehicle. The article noted that while the ruling does not conclude that Moody's or S&P (a division of McGraw-Hill) did anything wrong, it does show how the ratings agencies may be legally vulnerable. The article pointed out that Moody's latest quarterly filing implied that liability from litigation and regulatory actions would not be materially adverse.

How do companies account for commitments and contingencies? The FASB postulated in SFAS 5 three degrees of uncertainty: probable, reasonably possible, and remote. The firm must set a liability for an expected obligation if it is *probable* that a liability has been incurred *and* the amount of the liability can be reasonably estimated.[10] For example, when a firm distributes coupons that can be redeemed with purchases of future merchandise, a contingent liability exists and must be accrued. In such a case, it is almost certain that a large proportion of the coupons will be presented in the next accounting period. Furthermore, the firm can reasonably forecast what percentage of the coupons will be presented by the due date. Thus a liability is accrued on the balance sheet with an offsetting charge against income.

When the liability involves a lawsuit, the analyst must, in his or her best judgment, attempt to estimate any follow-on legal claims, as well as any insurance covering the liability. If the total value of the claims is in excess of the insured loss, it could devastate the entity.

Example:

On April 10, 2007, an individual shareholder of Vitesse, Jamison John Dupuy, filed a complaint in the Superior Court of California, County of Ventura, against Vitesse and three of its former officers (Case No. CIV 247776). Mr. Dupuy's complaint included causes of action for fraud, deceit, and concealment and violation of California Corporations Code §§25400 et seq. Vitesse filed an answer, asserting numerous affirmative defenses. On March 3, 2008, Mr. Dupuy filed an amended complaint that named six new defendants, all former employees, and included new causes of action for negligent misrepresentation and violations of California Corporations Code §1507. On April 4, 2008, after mediation before a retired U.S. District Judge for the Central District of California, the parties entered into a confidential settlement agreement, and the plaintiff filed a dismissal of the action. The company has recorded a liability for this settlement, and the related expense is reflected in the accompanying financial statements.

Source: Vitesse Semiconductor 2008 10K.

The cash-flow analyst must examine the footnote on contingencies closely to determine if any events occurred that may affect cash flows in the future, although

[10] In "Materiality and Contingent Tax Liability Reporting," by Gleason and Mills (*The Accounting Review*), the authors found that many companies failed to disclose IRS claims, even though they exceeded 5 percent of income.

they had not been given accounting recognition in the financial statements. The analysis should include past acquisitions that might require additional future payments of cash, stock, or debt on the attainment of certain predefined targets. If an asset sale was involved, the entity might be due additional cash.

Should the cash-flow analyst add purchase commitments to leverage ratios, as one would add operating leases? I include the obligation to total debt only if the supply is not needed and cannot be expected to be used in the current operating cycle. Since the unneeded product or material would not result in free cash flow, it must be considered a liability.

An announced acquisition or business combination ordinarily results in new commitment obligations for the acquirer. The analyst's examination of the company to be acquired should include:

1. Irrevocable standby letters of credit that guarantee payment of a specified obligation
2. Market-value guarantee of assets owned by the guaranteed party
3. Guarantee of the market price of common stock by the acquirer
4. Guarantee of the collection of cash flows from assets held by any special-purpose entity
5. Indirect guarantees of the indebtedness of others, including moral obligations
6. Indemnification agreements that require the guarantor to make payments to the indemnified party

SFAS 141 (revised in 2007) provides the accounting and disclosure requirements for contingent gains and losses recognized as part of a business combination.

Example:

Cracker Barrel Old Country Store, Inc., operates 591 restaurants. Shown, from their 2009 10K, are their contractual obligations and commitments. As expected for this industry, operating lease obligations are substantial and become particularly relevant for locations that cannot generate free cash flow. Often the entity is not let out of the lease or is required to pay a large settlement to be let out. Cracker Barrel also leases billboards used to advertise its stores. The $257.3 million in purchase commitments for food, capital expenditures, and other trade payables may seem large but is reasonable given that Cracker Barrel has annual revenues of almost $2.4 billion

As seen in the footnote, Cracker Barrel does pay its lenders a usage fee to keep the credit facilities available. During the 2008 credit crises, many financial companies took advantage of such standby agreements, fearing a liquidity issue. Other entities like having the credit available if a suitable business opportunity arises.

Contractual Obligations[a]	Total	2010	2011–2012	2013–2014	After 2014
Term loan B[b]	$600,000	$6,847	$13,695	$579,458	—
Delayed-draw term loan facility[b]	45,000	459	918	43,623	—
Note payable[c]	473	110	218	145	—
Operating leases excluding billboards[d]	765,144	36,890	71,269	72,381	$584,604
Operating leases for billboards	26,780	18,339	8,369	72	—
Capital leases	89	22	44	23	—
Purchase obligations[e]	257,276	98,521	99,185	52,699	6,871
Other long-term obligations[f]	29,002	—	2,177	444	26,381
Total contractual cash obligations	$1,723,764	$161,188	$195,875	$748,845	$617,856

	Amount of Commitment Expirations by Year				
	Total	2010	2011–2012	2013–2014	After 2014
Revolving credit facility[g]	$250,000	—	$250,000	—	—
Standby letters of credit	33,892	$6,930	26,962	—	—
Guarantees[h]	2,919	555	1,705	$659	—
Total commitments	$286,811	$7,485	$278,667	$659	—

[a] At July 31, 2009, the entire liability for uncertain tax positions (including penalties and interest) is classified as a long-term liability. At this time, we are unable to make a reasonably reliable estimate of the amounts and timing of payments in individual years due to uncertainties in the timing of the effective settlement of tax positions. As such, the liability for uncertain tax positions of $26,137 is not included in the contractual cash obligations and commitments table above.

[b] The balances on the Term Loan B and Delayed-Draw Term Loan, at July 31, 2009, are, respectively, $600,000 and $45,000. Using the minimum principal payment schedules on the Term Loan B and Delayed-Draw Term Loan facilities and projected interest rates, we will have interest payments of $44,203, $86,056, and $30,415 in 2010, 2011–2012, and 2013–2014, respectively. These interest payments are calculated using a 7.07% and 4.12% interest rate, respectively, for the swapped and unswapped portion of our debt. The 7.07% interest rate is the same rate as our fixed rate under our interest rate swap plus our credit spread at July 31, 2009 of 1.50%. The projected interest rate of 4.12% was estimated by using the average of the three-year and five-year swap rates at July 31, 2009 plus our credit spread of 1.50%.

[c] The note payable consists of a five-year note with a vendor in the original principal amount of $507 and represents the financing of prepaid maintenance for telecommunications equipment. The note payable is payable in monthly installments of principal and interest of $9 through October 16, 2013, and bears interest at 2.88%. Principal and interest payments for the note payable are included in the contractual cash obligations and commitments table above.

[d] Includes base lease terms and certain optional renewal periods, for which at the inception of the lease, it is reasonably assured that we will exercise.

[e] Purchase obligations consist of purchase orders for food and retail merchandise; purchase orders for capital expenditures, supplies and other operating needs and other services; and commitments under contracts for maintenance needs and other services. We have excluded contracts that do not contain minimum purchase obligations. We excluded long-term agreements for services and operating needs that can be cancelled within 60 days without penalty. We included long-term agreements and certain retail purchase orders for services and operating needs that can be cancelled with more than 60 days notice without penalty only through the term of the notice. We included long-term agreements for services and operating needs that only can be cancelled in the event of an uncured material breach or with a penalty through the entire term of the contract. Due to the uncertainties of seasonal demands and promotional calendar changes, our best estimate of usage for food, supplies, and other operating needs and services is ratably over either the notice period or the remaining life of the contract, as applicable, unless we had better information available at the time related to each contract.

[f] Other long-term obligations include our Non-Qualified Savings Plan ($22,583, with a corresponding long-term asset to fund the liability; see Note 13 to the Consolidated Financial Statements), Deferred Compensation Plan ($3,798), FY2007, FY2008, and FY2009 Long-Term Retention Incentive Plans ($2,158), and FY2009 District Manager Long-Term Performance Plan ($463).

[g] We did not have any outstanding borrowings under our Revolving Credit Facility as of July 31, 2009. We paid $493 in non-use fees (also known as commitment fees) on the Revolving Credit Facility during 2009. Based on having no outstanding borrowings at July 31, 2009 and our current unused commitment fee as defined in the Credit Facility, our unused commitment fees in 2010 would be $545; however, the actual amount will differ based on actual usage of the Revolving Credit Facility in 2010.

[h] Consists solely of guarantees associated with properties that have been assigned. We are not aware of any non-performance under these arrangements that would result in us having to perform in accordance with the terms of those guarantees.

Example:

ING Group is a Dutch banking and insurance company. As seen from its 20F, the company separates commitments and guarantees by their segments of operation. Although ING states that most contingencies are short term, they are normally rolled over.

CONTINGENT LIABILITIES AND COMMITMENTS

	2008	2007
Insurance operations		
Commitments	**4,221**	4,477
Guarantees	**2,460**	173
Banking operations		
Contingent liabilities in respect of		
Discounted bills		
Guarantees	**1**	1
Irrevocable letters of credit	**22,391**	19,018
Other	**10,458**	11,551
Irrevocable facilities		
	89,081	100,707
	129,065	136,277

Guarantees relate both to credit and noncredit substitute guarantees. Credit substitute guarantees are guarantees given by ING Group in respect of credit granted to customers by a third party. Many of them are expected to expire without being drawn on and therefore do not necessarily represent future cash outflows. The guarantees generally are of a short-term nature. In addition to the items included in contingent liabilities, ING Group has issued guarantees as a participant in collective arrangements of national industry bodies and as a participant in government required collective guarantee schemes that apply in different countries.

Irrevocable letters of credit mainly secure payments to third parties for a customer's foreign and domestic trade transactions in order to finance a shipment of goods. ING Group's credit risk in these transactions is limited because these transactions are collateralized by the commodity shipped and are of a short duration.

Other contingent liabilities include acceptances of bills and are of a short-term nature. Other contingent liabilities also include contingent liabilities resulting from the normal operations of the real estate business, including obligations under development and construction contracts. None of the items included in other contingent liabilities are individually significant.

Irrevocable facilities mainly constitute unused portions of irrevocable credit facilities granted to corporate clients. Many of these facilities are for a fixed duration and bear interest at a floating rate. ING Group's credit risk and interest-rate risk in these transactions are limited. Most of the unused portion of irrevocable credit facilities is secured by the customer's assets or counterguarantees by the central government and exempted bodies under the regulatory requirements. Irrevocable facilities also include commitments made to purchase securities to be issued by governments and private issuers.

Example:

In a footnoted table in its 10K, UPS, a company we will soon explore in greater detail, reported that it entered into substantial purchase commitments. From time to time, such purchase commitments actually represent value rather than a liability, as, for instance, would be the case if the product the company has committed to purchase has seen its price rise or is in such great demand that another buyer is willing to pay a premium for its spot in line. For instance, when the demand for aircraft was high, a ready market appeared for earlier spots on line for delivery from Boeing and Airbus. These early delivery spots often were sold.

Year	Capital Leases	Operating Leases	Debt Principal	Debt Interest	Purchase Commitments	Pension Fundings	Other Liabilities
2009	$83	$344	$2,007	$331	$708	$778	$74
2010	121	288	18	326	658	593	71
2011	29	217	5	326	667	828	69
2012	30	147	22	325	406	945	67
2013	31	109	1,768	285	—	964	65
After 2013	246	423	5,658	4,526	—	—	139
Total	$540	$1,528	$9,478	$6,119	$2,439	$4,108	$485

Source: UPS 2008 10K.

HEDGING

As we have seen in several examples, the use of hedging and derivatives is commonplace, regardless of industry. While it is not the intent of this text to delve into the minutiae of derivatives, a working knowledge is essential. An understanding of their accounting treatment, effect, and impact on the balance sheet, credit, and cash flow is an integral element of risk and cash-flow analysis, and lest we forget, they can either be ticking time bombs or an important and conservative management tool. If used with prudence, hedging indeed can reduce overall risk and allow the entity to concentrate on its operations with less concern for swings in the credit and commodity markets. In fact, many creditors, as part of their loan agreements with borrowers, require interest-rate swaps as protection on variable-interest-rate loans.

Keep in mind when evaluating hedging strategies, whether from the viewpoint of the analyst, creditor, or entity employing a hedging strategy, that the more volatile the markets, the more costly is the strategy. For an entity employing a hedge, a period of low volatility results in less cost and higher cash flows, everything else being equal.

However, for entities that use derivatives as more than a hedging device, the risks are enormous. Even the esteemed Harvard University lost at least $500 million betting on the wrong side of swaps. Swaps are a type of derivative where two parties agree to exchange payments tied to a financing, typically receiving a variable-rate for a fixed-rate payment. For example, if an entity has a variable-rate loan and would like to insulate against the effects of increases in the base rate (i.e., LIBOR),[11] it can turn that loan into a fixed-rate loan through a swap. Harvard paid $497.6 million to investment banks during the fiscal year ended June 30, 2009, to get out of $1.1 billion of interest-rate swaps intended to hedge variable-rate debt for capital projects, the school's annual report said. The university also agreed to pay $425 million over 30 to 40 years to offset an additional $764 million in swaps.

Example:

Interest-rate exposure—The Company had outstanding bank debt in excess of $22.0 million as of May 31, 2009, all of which is subject to interest rate fluctuations by the company's lenders. Higher rates applied by the Federal Reserve Board could have a negative effect on the company's earnings. It is the intent of the company to continually monitor interest rates and consider converting portions of the company's debt from floating rates to fixed rates should conditions be favorable for such interest rate swaps or hedges.

Source: Video Display Corporation 2009 10K.

Hedging through interest-rate swaps is recorded on the balance sheet at fair value as either an asset or a liability in accordance with the SFAS 133. Changes in the fair value of such interest-rate swaps are recorded as nonoperating income or expense in each period. The fair value approximates the amount the company would receive if these contracts were settled at the respective valuation dates. Fair value is estimated based on current and predictions of future interest-rate levels

[11] The London Interbank Offered Rate (LIBOR) is based on the interest rates at which banks borrow unsecured funds from other banks in the London wholesale money market (or interbank market).

along a yield curve, the remaining duration of the instruments, and other market conditions and therefore is subject to significant estimation and a high degree of fluctuation between periods.

Example:

Wynn Resorts has used hedges in the form of interest-rate swaps to protect against an increase in the LIBOR for its variable-rate debt. As reported by the company, Wynn booked a $6.3 million credit in its income statement for the March 31, 2006 ending quarter compared with $7.7 million during the prior year. The reported income from the swaps, however, is a noncash event and therefore does not add to operating cash flow, although it does affect reported income and earnings per share. It is merely a change in the value of the financial agreement. This is seen in the statement of cash flows, where the line entry in the income statement is reversed under cash flows from operating activities. If Wynn had purchased additional protection or had changed the terms of the existing derivatives, necessitating a cash payment or receipt, we would see that as well in the cash-flow statement to the extent that it provided or required funds. Why would Wynn use interest-rate swaps? As shown in its long-term debt footnote, Wynn has about $636 million face value of variable-rate debt tied to LIBOR as part of its large total debt. Wynn recorded a $15.1 million asset on its balance sheet as of the statement date related to the gain. This amount can be expected to rise or fall quarterly based on the level of interest rates.

Evaluating Wynn's cash flow and risk resulting from the derivative activity, the analyst should view the interest-rate swaps as constructive. The firm is using the tool only to protect against the cost of rising rates on its variable-rate debt obligations. There is no other risk involved outside the cost of the protection, which is minimal compared with the total value of debt and the conceivable increase in cash payments resulting from a rise in interest rates if the hedges were not in place. The effect on cash flows is otherwise nil. Of more concern, in the case of Wynn, is the large amount of debt (from its expansion of new hotels) on its balance sheet resulting in a high cost of capital and whether the cash flows can adequately service that debt.

I would look at other industrial and service companies in a similar manner. Were the hedges necessary? Were they put in place as a conservative measure, as a fair-value or cash-flow hedge? Did the company put in place no more than what was needed to hedge effectively? Does the company need to constantly add or reduce its hedge exposure? What has been the company's experience using hedging instruments? Have the hedges resulted in a lower cost of debt capital? For Wynn, the answers are all positive.

Example: WYNN RESORTS

Interest-Rate Swaps

The company has entered into interest rate swap arrangements to effectively fix the interest on floating-rate debt borrowings. The following table presents the historical asset or (liability) fair values (reflected in deposits and other assets or in other long-term liabilities as appropriate) as of March 31, 2006 and 2005 and as of December 31, 2005 and 2004 (amounts in thousands):

	Wynn Las Vegas Interest-Rate Swaps	Wynn Macau Interest-Rate Swaps	Total Interest-Rate Swap Asset/ (Liability)
Asset/(liability) fair value on March 31, 2006	$13,878	$1,202	$15,080
Asset/(liability) fair value on December 31, 2005	$10,523	$(1,788)	$8,735
Asset/(liability) fair value on March 31, 2005	$8,283	$—	$8,283
Asset/(liability) fair value ont December 31, 2004	$583	$—	$583

The fair value approximates the amount the company would receive if these contracts were settled at the respective valuation dates. Fair value is estimated based upon current, and predictions of future, interest rate levels along a yield curve, the remaining duration of the instruments and other market conditions, and therefore, is subject to significant estimation and a high degree of variability of fluctuation between periods.

The company accounts for these interest rate swaps in accordance with Statement of Financial Accounting Standards No. 133, *Accounting for Derivative Instruments and Hedging Activities* ("SFAS No. 133"), and its related interpretations. Accordingly, during the three months ended March 31, 2006 and 2005, the company recorded approximately $6.3 million and $7.7 million, respectively, as increase to swap fair value, a component of other income (expense), net.

Long-Term Debt

Long-term debt consists of the following (amounts in thousands):

	March 31, 2006	December 31, 2005
6%/8% First mortgage notes, due December 1, 2014	$1,300,000	$1,300,000
6% Convertible subordinated debentures, due July 15, 2015	235,871	250,000
$600.0 million revolving credit facility, due December 14, 2009, interest at LIBOR plus 2.25% (approximately 7.1% and 6.67%)	—	10,000

(Continued)

	March 31, 2006	December 31, 2005
$400.0 million delay draw term loan facility, due December 14, 2011, interest at LIBOR plus 2.125% (approximately 6.975% and 6.525%)	400,000	400,000
Senior term loan facilities, due September 14, 2011, interest at LIBOR or HIBOR plus 3.0%, decreasing to LIBOR or HIBOR plus 2.75% on opening of Wynn Macau (approximately 7.82% and 7.345%)	193,869	78,944
$44.75 million note payable, due March 31, 2010, interest at LIBOR plus 2.375% (approximately 7.225% and 6.902%)	42,305	43,536
Note payable—aircraft, interest at 5.67%	13,812	13,986
12% Second mortgage notes, net of original issue discount of approximately $417,000 and $440,000, respectively, due November 1, 2010, effective interest at approximately 12.9%	9,725	9,702
Other	156	167
	2,195,738	2,106,335
Current portion of long-term debt	(15,592)	(15,489)
	$2,180,146	$2,090,846

WYNN RESORTS, LIMITED AND SUBSIDIARIES
CONDENSED CONSOLIDATED STATEMENTS OF OPERATIONS
(Amounts in Thousands, Except Per-Share Data)
(Unaudited)

	Three Months Ended March 31	
	2006	**2005**
		(As Restated: See Note 14)
Operating revenues:		
Casino	$126,514	$—
Rooms	68,177	—
Food and beverage	74,634	—
Entertainment, retail, and other	48,957	—
Gross revenues	318,282	—

	Three Months Ended March 31	
	2006	2005
		(As Restated: See Note 14)
Less promotional allowances	(41,057)	—
Net revenues	277,225	—
Operating costs and expenses:		
Casino	63,236	—
Rooms	16,985	—
Food and beverage	44,759	—
Entertainment, retail, and other	32,514	4
General and administrative	46,965	5
Provision for doubtful accounts	2,929	—
Preopening costs	8,946	38,104
Depreciation and amortization	41,785	3,494
Contract termination fee	5,000	—
Property charges and other	4,949	53
Total operating costs and expenses	268,068	41,660
Equity in income from unconsolidated affiliates	575	—
Operating income (loss)	9,732	(41,660)
Other income/(expense):		
Interest income	8,432	6,182
Interest expense	(35,943)	(2,149)
Increase in swap fair value	6,345	7,700
Other income (expense), net	(21,166)	11,733
Net loss	$(11,434)	$(29,927)
Basic and diluted earnings per common share:		
Net loss:		
Basic	$(0.12)	$(0.30)
Diluted	$(0.12)	$(0.30)
Weighted average common shares outstanding:		
Basic	98,736	98,229
Diluted	98,736	98,229

WYNN RESORTS, LTD., AND SUBSIDIARIES
CONDENSED CONSOLIDATED STATEMENTS OF CASH FLOWS
(Amounts in Thousands)
(Unaudited)

	Three Months Ended March 31	
	2006	2005
		(As Restated: See Note 14)
Cash flows from operating activities:		
Net loss	$(11,434)	$(29,927)
Adjustments to reconcile net loss to net cash provided by (used in) operating activities:		
Depreciation and amortization	41,785	3,494
Stock-based compensation	3,919	1,256
Amortization and writeoff of deferred financing costs	3,832	2,043
Provision for doubtful accounts	2,929	—
Property charges and other	4,949	(12)
Equity in income of unconsolidated affiliates, net of distributions received	(325)	—
Increase in the fair value of interest rate swaps	(6,345)	(7,700)
Increase (decrease) in cash from changes in:		
Receivables	19,006	(575)
Inventories and prepaid expenses	(8,351)	(5,801)
Accounts payable and accrued expenses	(16,633)	31,330
Net cash provided by (used in) operating activities	33,332	(5,892)
Cash flows from investing activities:		
Capital expenditures	(115,413)	(291,969)
Restricted cash and investments	34,447	(13,847)
Other assets	(11,056)	(21,323)
Proceeds from sale of equipment	—	23
Net cash used in investing activities	(92,022)	(327,116)
Cash flows from financing activities:		
Proceeds from the exercise of stock options	2,365	534
Proceeds from issuance of long-term debt	114,926	373,436
Principal payments of long-term debt	(11,417)	(176)
Payments on long-term land concession obligation	(4,446)	(4,759)
Net cash provided by financing activities	101,428	369,035
Cash and cash equivalents:		
Increase in cash and cash equivalents	42,738	36,027
Balance, beginning of period	434,289	330,261
Balance, end of period	$477,027	$366,288

Source: Wynn Resorts Limited March, 31, 2006 10Q.

The value of derivatives, whether as a cash-flow or a non-cash-flow hedge, can constitute a significant liability or asset on the balance sheet, whereas the cash-flow effect may be slight. While most derivative agreements are rolled over or settled for a small fraction of their notional value, a large change in bond prices could force nonhedged contracts to be settled with cash that the entity does not have or the credit capacity to settle.

When an entity's risk exposure is large in relation to its financial ability to settle an extreme scenario, caution should be exercised, especially regarding the possibility of a catastrophic event. It is up to the analyst to place a very conservative estimate on the magnitude of such liabilities for the company and their effect on survivability. A sensitivity analysis would be an important part of such a review. This would apply only if the firm is not using the instruments as a hedging strategy or if the hedges became partially unbalanced owing to market conditions.

Derivative assets and liabilities can be exchange traded or traded over the counter. Otherwise, their values are based on models that may, at times, not reflect their true value. Valuation models require a variety of inputs, including contractual terms, market prices and rates, yield curves, credit curves, measures of volatility, prepayment rates, and correlations of such inputs.

AIG, once the world's largest insurer, had to be propped up by the federal government with many tens of billions of dollars of taxpayer money after derivative losses left it on the verge of bankruptcy.[12] Although AIG's derivative contracts were contained in a separate legal entity, the parent guaranteed the subsidiary's obligations. How large was the liability for AIG? The company stated in March 2009 that it had about $1.6 trillion in "notional derivatives exposure."

If AIG or a properly regulated insurance company were forced into bankruptcy, policyholders would be protected, although equity holders most likely would lose the entirety of their investment. This is so because the insurance subsidiaries are not responsible for the debts of their parent, and insurance policy claims are backed both by the subsidiary's required reserves and state insurance funds.

The size of AIG's notional amount is the reason legendary investor Warren Buffett referred to such instruments as "financial weapons of mass destruction." The *notional value* refers to the value of the assets the investor is controlling as a result of holding the contract and is used to calculate payments made on that instrument.

---

[12] AIG played the role of counterparty (insurer) to hundreds of billions of dollars of CDS, which were purchased by firms to protect against a default. As the counterparty, AIG put up a small amount to insure a large amount. Although AIG is a regulated U.S. insurance company, its CDS business was largely conducted by lightly regulated offshore entities, which made it possible for AIG to engage in CDS trades without setting aside sufficient capital to cover widespread losses, such as happened in 2007 and 2008.

As seen from Table 6-5, the fair value of AIG's derivative liabilities, even near the height of the credit crisis, was just 8.7 percent its notional value. Even so, the fair-value liabilities of $77.5 billion exceeded its fair-value assets by $8 billion and were extraordinary in size by almost any measure, having $896 billion in notional liabilities and $609 billion in assets. A 1 percent change in its fair-value assets would add almost $7 billion the firm would need to cover with additional collateral it did not have; a 10 percent change would add about $70 billion.

TABLE 6-5

AIG Derivative Instruments

	Derivative Assets		Derivative Liabilities	
	Notional Amount[a]	Fair Value[b]	Notional Amount[a]	Fair Value[b]
	On March 31, 2009 (In Millions)			
Derivatives designated as hedging instruments:				
Interest-rate contracts	$3,450	$551	$2,573	$195
Foreign-exchange contracts	7,562	1,293	1,963	442
Total derivatives designated as hedging instruments	$11,012	$1,844	$4,536	$637
Derivatives not designated as hedging instruments:				
Interest-rate contracts	$501,644	$56,248	$520,422	$54,841
Foreign-exchange contracts	20,487	2,635	51,690	2,862
Equity contracts	9,311	3,087	13,031	2,862
Commodity contracts	18,969	3,949	14,324	2,781
Credit contracts	4,632	924	269,974	11,046
Other contracts	43,827	865	22,189	2,509
Total derivatives not designated as hedging instruments	$598,870	$67,708	$891,630	$76,901
Total derivatives	$609,882	$69,552	$896,166	$77,538

[a]Notional amount represents a standard of measurement of the volume of swaps business of AIG. Notional amount is not a quantification of market risk or credit risk and is not recorded on the consolidated balance sheet. Notional amounts generally represent those amounts used to calculate contractual cash flows to be exchanged and are not paid or received, except for certain contracts such as currency swaps.

[b]Fair value amounts are shown before the effects of counterparty netting adjustments and offsetting cash collateral in accordance with FIN 39.

Example:

Airlines are well known for attempting to hedge their largest expense, fuel. Southwest Airlines was notably successful and able to avoid bankruptcy, unlike many of its competitors, when the price of fuel tripled and revenues weakened.

Airlines Fuel Risk for Investors

Airlines are stuck in the hedging maze.

Last year, when oil nudged $150 a barrel and was touted to hit $200, airlines aggressively hedged fuel costs with swaps, collars, and other financial instruments. But when oil plunged to below $40, those hedges sank in value, carrying airline profits down, too.

Delta Air Lines' $257 million second-quarter loss included a $390 million loss on fuel hedges. JetBlue Airways lost $42 million on fuel hedges. It's a similar story worldwide. LAN Airlines of Chile took a $53 million hedging loss. Cathay Pacific Airways of Hong Kong doesn't release quarterly figures but took a $980 million hit on fuel hedges in 2008.

Oil's now back around $69 a barrel, so it might seem like time to hedge for 2010. Instead, carriers appear hesitant. It's not just nervousness about taking losses again. In addition, industry liquidity isn't great and airlines don't want to exacerbate balance-sheet weakness with poor use of capital.

Source: Wall Street Journal, August 1, 2009.

While derivative activity may result in an inconsequential cash-flow impact, owing to SFAS 133, *Accounting for Derivatives and Hedging Transactions*, its effect on shareholders' equity, and thus credit rating, may be significant. On the other hand are financially strong firms (including Berkshire Hathaway) whose balance-sheet leverage, although having increased owing to a change in the market value of the swap, benefited from investors and creditors choosing to look past the accounting entry.

Let us now look at the summary statement of SFAS 133, as issued by the FASB. To the analyst, the chief sources of concern should be the potential impact on cash flow and credit. The accounting of derivatives focuses more on classification of the instrument than on the instrument's cash-flows impact.

BACKGROUND ON SFAS 133

Summary of Statement Number 133: Accounting for Derivative Instruments and Hedging Activities

This Statement establishes accounting and reporting standards for derivative instruments, including certain derivative instruments embedded in other contracts (collectively referred to as derivatives) and for hedging activities. It requires that an entity recognize all derivatives as either assets or liabilities in the statement of financial position and measure those instruments at fair value. If certain conditions are met, a derivative may be specifically designated as (a) a hedge of the exposure to changes in the fair value of a recognized asset or liability or an unrecognized firm commitment, (b) a hedge of the exposure to variable cash flows of a forecasted transaction, or (c) a hedge of the foreign currency exposure of a net investment in a foreign operation, an unrecognized firm commitment, an available-for-sale security, or a foreign-currency-denominated forecasted transaction.

The accounting for changes in the fair value of a derivative (that is, gains and losses) depends on the intended use of the derivative and the resulting designation.

- For a derivative designated as hedging the exposure to changes in the fair value of a recognized asset or liability or a firm commitment (referred to as a fair value hedge), the gain or loss is recognized in earnings in the period of change together with the offsetting loss or gain on the hedged item attributable to the risk being hedged. The effect of that accounting is to reflect in earnings the extent to which the hedge is not effective in achieving offsetting changes in fair value.
- For a derivative designated as hedging the exposure to variable cash flows of a forecasted transaction (referred to as a cash flow hedge), the effective portion of the derivative's gain or loss is initially reported as a component of other comprehensive income (outside earnings) and subsequently reclassified into earnings when the forecasted transaction affects earnings. The ineffective portion of the gain or loss is reported in earnings immediately.
- For a derivative designated as hedging the foreign currency exposure of a net investment in a foreign operation, the gain or loss is reported in other comprehensive income (outside earnings) as part of the cumulative translation adjustment. The accounting for a fair value hedge described above applies to a derivative designated as a hedge of the foreign currency exposure of an unrecognized firm commitment or an available-for-sale security. Similarly, the accounting for a cash flow hedge described above applies to a derivative designated as a hedge of the foreign currency exposure of a foreign-currency-denominated forecasted transaction.

For a derivative not designated as a hedging instrument, the gain or loss is recognized in earnings in the period of change.

Source: Financial Standards Accounting Board.

The accounting for derivative instruments was codified by SFAS 133, *Accounting for Derivative Instruments and Hedging Activities*, as amended by SFAS 137, SFAS 138, SFAS 149, and SFAS 155. On issuing SFAS 133, the FASB set forth the Derivatives Implementation Group (DIG) to aid users in understanding and compliance with the statement.

Derivative accounting is categorized as either hedge or nonhedge. Hedge accounting deals with accounting for derivatives that are entered into as a hedging strategy, and I will soon provide examples of this. These are typically intended to reduce or eliminate common market risks such as interest-rate and currency fluctuations and commodity price movements. Hedge accounting is presented under SFAS 133 only if certain strict criteria are met at inception and, in some cases, through the life of the derivative instrument. The purpose of hedge accounting is to relate the gains and losses arising from changes in fair value of the derivative with the related gains and losses of the hedged transactions. While the derivatives must be carried at fair value at any given reporting date, the gains and losses from changes in fair value potentially may be offset against the gains and losses arising from the hedged transaction, thereby minimizing the overall impact of the hedge and the hedged transaction on a company's income statement.

Other derivatives, those not qualifying for hedge accounting, are placed into the nonhedge accounting category. Here, gains or losses arising from changes in fair value of the derivative must be fully reported in current income. Since their impact is applied directly to the income statement, changes in fair value could have a significant impact on an entity's shareholder profits or loss. Derivatives falling under nonhedge accounting fall into one of two types, either freestanding derivatives or embedded derivatives. *Freestanding derivatives* are instruments that in their entirety meet the definition of a derivative set forth in paragraph 6 of SFAS 133, which, along with the entire statement, may be found on the FASB Web site.

Embedded derivatives contain features or provisions that meet specific criteria, namely, (1) the feature or provision meets the SFAS 133 definition, (2) the feature or provision would be accounted for as a derivative were it freestanding, and (3) the derivatives contract is not a derivative in its entirety (i.e., a derivative cannot contain embedded derivatives).

Other comprehensive income is established when the entity has a cash-flow hedge or a foreign-currency hedge of a net investment. From an analytic viewpoint, a hedging strategy should be engaged in only to reduce risk and thereby permit the entity to focus on enhancements to revenue. If used as a tool in this manner, it can result in higher free cash flow and lower cost of capital. It is only when the hedges fall outside normal business parameters that the entity runs into trouble.

To summarize, hedging transactions normally are separated into three broad categories:

1. *Cash-flow hedge.* Under the cash-flow hedge, the variability of the hedged item's cash flow (i.e., oil prices) is offset by the cash flows of the financial instrument (derivative contract). The hedged item is a forecasted transaction or balance-sheet item with variable cash flows. The market value of the derivative is shown under other comprehensive income, with normally no effect on cash flows except during the purchase or sale of the hedge.
2. *Fair-value hedge.* Under a fair-value hedge, the hedged item is exposed to changes in its value (i.e., variable interest rates) or an unrecognized commitment (to purchase a commodity). Changes in fair value of the hedged item and the financial instrument are recorded in earnings, and normally, no effect on cash flows is seen, except during the purchase or sale.
3. *Investment in a foreign operation hedge.* Such as hedge may be employed to reduce any of the risks associated with an entity's foreign operations—cash flows, assets, or currency. Changes in the fair value of the instrument are consolidated with the translation (currency) adjustment as part of other comprehensive income. There would be no effect on cash flows, except during the purchase or sale.

Presented next is Warren Buffett's dire but amazingly accurate assessment of the derivatives market in his 2003 letter to shareholders. Unfortunately, he has not been immune from taking large bets himself.

> **Unless derivatives contracts are collateralized or guaranteed, their ultimate value also depends on the creditworthiness of the counterparties to them. But before a contract is settled, the counterparties record profits and losses—often huge in amount—in their current earnings statements without so much as a penny changing hands. Reported earnings on derivatives are often wildly overstated. That's because today's earnings are in a significant way based on estimates whose inaccuracy may not be exposed for many years.**
>
> **The errors usually reflect the human tendency to take an optimistic view of one's commitments. But the parties to derivatives also have enormous incentives to cheat in accounting for them. Those who trade derivatives are usually paid, in whole or part, on "earnings" calculated by mark-to-market accounting. But often there is no real market, and**

"mark-to-model" is utilized. This substitution can bring on large-scale mischief. As a general rule, contracts involving multiple reference items and distant settlement dates increase the opportunities for counterparties to use fanciful assumptions. The two parties to the contract might well use differing models allowing both to show substantial profits for many years. In extreme cases, mark-to-model degenerates into what I would call mark-to-myth.

I can assure you that the marking errors in the derivatives business have not been symmetrical. Almost invariably, they have favored either the trader who was eyeing a multi-million dollar bonus or the CEO who wanted to report impressive "earnings" (or both). The bonuses were paid, and the CEO profited from his options. Only much later did shareholders learn that the reported earnings were a sham.

Initial implementation of SFAS 133 was not uniform, and as a result, restatements often were necessary. Even sophisticated companies ran amok, including General Electric.

Example:

Restatement and Non-reliance

On the date hereof, GE is filing an amendment to its Annual Report on Form 10K for the year ended December 31, 2005, to amend and restate financial statements and other financial information for the years 2005, 2004, and 2003, and financial information for the years 2002 and 2001, and for each of the quarters in the years 2005 and 2004. In addition, we are filing amendments to our Quarterly Reports on Form 10Q for each of the periods ended September 30, June 30, and March 31, 2006, to amend and restate financial statements for the first three quarters of 2006. The restatement adjusts our accounting for interest rate swap transactions related to a portion of the commercial paper issued by General Electric Capital Corporation (GECC) and General Electric Capital Services, Inc. (GECS), each wholly-owned subsidiaries of GE, from January 1, 2001, the date we adopted Statement of Financial Accounting Standards (SFAS) No. 133, *Accounting for Derivative Instruments and Hedging Activities*, as amended. The restatement has no effect on our cash flows or liquidity, and its effects on our financial position at the ends of the respective restated periods are immaterial. We have not found that any of our hedge positions were inconsistent with our risk management policies or economic objectives.

In light of the restatement, readers should not rely on our previously filed financial statements and other financial information for the years and for each of the quarters in the years 2005, 2004, 2003, 2002, and 2001, and for each of the first three quarters of 2006.

Source: GE January 19, 2007 8K.

The analyst may wonder how to treat potentially harmful derivative contracts that appear on the balance sheet and whose potential value can only be subject to estimation. As stated, such is the case with Berkshire Hathaway, whose eminent chairman, despite the accuracy of his 2003 letter, was making large bets on both currency and equities through derivatives.

Sensitivity analysis showing the range of conceivable scenarios is an essential part of the credit analysis, and most entities will share this information with shareholders. The range and probability of outcomes and the effect each would have on the financial structure and credit capacity of the enterprise would enter into the cost-of-capital determination. If the entity has adequate bank facilities in place to satisfy all but the most extreme scenario, the penalty to cost of capital still would need to be recognized and monitored for changes. The potential liability should be placed on the firm's balance sheet as debt. For Berkshire, settlement was of a very long duration, and balance-sheet cash and its other sources of liquidity, including lines of credit, expected cash from operations, and investments, could have settled even an extreme scenario. Shareholders' equity would have been impaired, however.

If derivatives are used, the analyst must thoroughly understand their purpose, including the extent of hedged and nonhedged instruments, their notional values, company history using hedging instruments, and the company's ability to withstand a large impact to equity, as reflected in the sensitivity model. Equity analysts and creditors should mark up the cost of capital of these firms as appropriate. Once the hedges stop acting as insurance and more like bets, the riskier they become. Even though Warren Buffett has to date been successful in his market bets, one must wonder, given his inordinate success investing in high-ROIC companies, why he would chose to gamble on nonhedged derivatives.

Example:

Medtronic, Inc., a medical device manufacturer, reported the following sensitivity results, in its October, 2009 10Q. The analyst should extend the model to incorporate wider swings in the underlying contracts than Medtronic's is revealing.

> We had foreign exchange derivative contracts outstanding in notional amounts of $5.801 billion and $5.296 billion at October 30, 2009 and April 24, 2009, respectively. The fair value of these contracts at October 30, 2009 was $46 million less than the original contract value. A sensitivity analysis of changes in the fair value of all foreign exchange derivative contracts at October 30, 2009 indicates that, if the U.S. dollar uniformly strengthened/weakened by 10 percent against all currencies, the fair value of these contracts would increase/decrease by $542 million, respectively. Any gains and losses on the fair value of derivative contracts would be largely offset by gains and losses on the underlying transactions. These offsetting gains and losses are not reflected in the above analysis. We are also exposed to interest rate changes affecting principally our investments in interest rate sensitive instruments. A sensitivity analysis of the impact on our interest rate sensitive financial instruments of a hypothetical 10 percent change in short-term interest rates compared to interest rates at October 30, 2009 indicates that the fair value of these instruments would correspondingly change by $15 million.

Example:

BERKSHIRE HATHAWAY, INC., AND SUBSIDIARIES
CONDENSED CONSOLIDATED BALANCE SHEETS
(Dollars in Millions)
(Unaudited)

	June 30, 2009	December 31, 2008
ASSETS		
Insurance and other:		
Cash and cash equivalents	$21,439	$24,302
Investments:		
Fixed-maturity securities	32,018	27,115
Equity securities	45,794	49,073
Other	30,365	21,535
Receivables	15,778	14,925
Inventories	6,387	7,500
Property, plant, and equipment	17,016	16,703
Goodwill	27,535	27,477
Other	13,306	13,257
	209,638	201,887
Utilities and energy:		
Cash and cash equivalents	875	280
Property, plant, and equipment	29,987	28,454
Goodwill	5,363	5,280
Other	5,597	7,556
	41,822	41,570
Finance and financial products:		
Cash and cash equivalents	2,197	957
Investments in fixed-maturity securities	4,150	4,517
Loans and finance receivables	13,631	13,942
Goodwill	1,024	1,024
Other	3,184	3,502
	24,186	23,942
	$275,646	$267,399

(Continued)

	June 30, 2009	December 31, 2008
Liabilities and Shareholders' Equity		
Insurance and other:		
Losses and loss-adjustment expenses	$58,867	$56,620
Unearned premiums	8,831	7,861
Life and health insurance benefits	3,898	3,619
Accounts payable, accruals, and other liabilities	14,676	14,987
Notes payable and other borrowings	4,379	4,349
	90,651	87,436
Utilities and energy:		
Accounts payable, accruals, and other liabilities	5,800	6,175
Notes payable and other borrowings	19,708	19,145
	25,508	25,320
Finance and financial products:		
Accounts payable, accruals, and other liabilities	2,580	2,656
Derivative contract liabilities	12,299	14,612
Notes payable and other borrowings	14,697	13,388
	29,576	30,656
Income taxes, principally deferred	11,074	10,280
Total liabilities	156,809	153,692
Shareholders' equity:		
Common stock and capital in excess of par value	27,089	27,141
Accumulated other comprehensive income	7,505	3,954
Retained earnings	79,933	78,172
Berkshire Hathaway shareholders' equity	114,527	109,267
Noncontrolling interests	4,310	4,440
Total shareholders' equity	118,837	113,707
	$275,646	$267,399

Source: Berkshire Hathaway June, 30, 2009 10K.

Whereas, during the March 2009 quarter, Berkshire recorded a noncash gain of $2.3 billion owing to the company's bullish bet on a rise in equity prices, not all such bets have gone in its direction. In fact, if the current bet needed to be settled as of the balance-sheet date (June 30, 2009),

Berkshire would need to either extend the maturities of its contracts or settle the trade in cash, which would have resulted in a mega-billion-dollar loss. Berkshire has already collected the premiums on the derivatives trades at the outset of the contracts, in essence betting that stock prices do not fall below the striking price of its S&P futures contracts. Assuming that June 30, 2009, was the actual expiration date of the put contracts, Berkshire would need to pay $9.3 billion in cash to settle the trades.

As seen in its footnote concerning derivative contracts, part of the booked gain resulted from the company being able to renegotiate and amend six equity index put option contracts, reducing their duration and striking prices and reducing the intrinsic-values losses by $1.1 billion.

While Berkshire, having stated shareholders' equity of $118 billion, would appear able to withstand the risk, the magnitude of having over $37 billion in notional value in put options is large enough to bear very close scrutiny. If the stock market suffered a dramatic fall, the bet undoubtedly would have a pronounced negative effect on Berkshire, its stockholders, creditors, and potentially, its insurance operations.

Note 9: Derivative contracts of finance and financial products businesses

Derivative contracts of Berkshire's finance and financial products businesses, with limited exceptions, are not designated as hedges for financial reporting purposes. These contracts were initially entered into with the expectation that the premiums received would exceed the amounts ultimately paid to counterparties. Changes in the fair values of such contracts are reported in earnings as derivative gains/losses. A summary of derivative contracts outstanding as of June 30, 2009 and December 31, 2008, follows (in millions):

	June 30, 2009			December 31, 2008		
	Assets[3]	Liabilities	Notional Value	Assets[3]	Liabilities	Notional Value
Equity index put options	$—	$8,233	$37,480[1]	$—	$10,022	$37,134[1]
Credit default obligations:						
High-yield indexes	—	2,507	6,383[2]	—	3,031	7,892[2]
States/municipalities	—	1,049	16,042[2]	—	958	18,364[2]
Individual corporate	—	80	3,775[2]	—	105	3,900[2]
Other	439	461		503	528	
Counterparty netting and funds held as collateral	(239)	(31)		(295)	(32)	
	$200	$12,299		$208	$14,612	

[1] Represents the aggregate undiscounted amount payable at the contract expiration dates assuming that the value of each index is zero at the contract expiration date.

[2] Represents the maximum undiscounted future value of losses payable under the contracts, assuming a sufficient number of credit defaults occur. The number of losses required to exhaust contract limits under substantially all of the contracts is dependent on the loss recovery rate related to the specific obligor at the time of the default.

[3] Included in other assets of finance and financial products businesses.

A summary of derivative gains/losses included in the Condensed Consolidated Statements of Earnings follows (in millions):

	Second Quarter		First Six Months	
	2009	**2008**	**2009**	**2008**
Equity index put options	$1,956	$326	$1,790	$(851)
Credit default obligations	391	339	(960)	(136)
Other	10	24	10	35
	$2,357	$689	$840	$(952)

Berkshire has written equity index put option contracts on four major equity indexes including three indexes outside the United States. These contracts are European-style options and will be settled on the contract expiration dates, which occur between June 2018 and January 2028. Future payments, if any, under these contracts will be required if the underlying index value is below the strike price at the contract expiration dates. Premiums on these contracts were received in full at the contract inception dates, and therefore, Berkshire has no counterparty credit risk.

On June 30, 2009, the aggregate intrinsic value (the undiscounted liability, assuming that the contracts are settled on their future expiration dates based on the June 30, 2009, index values) was $9.3 billion. Aggregate intrinsic value was approximately $13.3 billion on March 31, 2009, and $10.8 billion as of December 31, 2008. However, these contracts may not be terminated or fully settled before the expiration dates, and therefore, the ultimate amount of cash basis gains or losses on these contracts will not be known for many years.

In the second quarter of 2009, Berkshire agreed with certain counterparties to amend six equity index put option contracts. The amendments reduced the remaining durations of these contracts between 3.5 and 9.5 years. As a result, the remaining average life of all of Berkshire's contracts declined from 13 years at March 31, 2009 to 12 years at June 30, 2009. In addition, the amendments reduced the strike prices of those contracts between 29% and 39%. The reductions in the strike prices had the effect of reducing the intrinsic value losses on those contracts by approximately $1.1 billion. In addition, the aggregate notional value related to three of the amended contracts increased by approximately $161 million. No consideration was paid by either party with respect to these amendments.

Credit default contracts include various high yield indexes, state/municipal debt issuers and individual corporate issuers. These contracts cover the loss in value of specified debt obligations of the issuers arising from default events, which are usually for non-payment or bankruptcy. Loss amounts are subject to contract limits.

High yield indexes are comprised of specified North American corporate issuers (usually 100 in number) whose obligations are rated below investment grade. The weighted average contract life at June 30, 2009 was approximately 2 years. State and municipality contracts are comprised of over 500 reference obligations issuers, which had a weighted average duration at June 30, 2009 of approximately 11.5 years. Risks related to approximately 50% of the notional amount cannot be settled before the maturity dates of the underlying obligations, which range from 2019 to 2054.

Premiums on the high yield index and state/municipality contracts were received in full at the inception dates of the contracts and, as a result, Berkshire has no counterparty credit risk. Berkshire's payment obligations under certain of these contracts are on a first loss basis. Several other contracts are subject to aggregate loss deductibles that must be satisfied before Berkshire has any payment obligations.

Credit default contracts written on individual corporate issuers primarily relate to investment grade obligations. Installment premiums are due from counterparties over the terms of the contracts. In most instances, premiums are due from counterparties on a quarterly basis. Most individual issuer contracts expire in 2013.

With limited exception, Berkshire's equity index put option and credit default contracts contain no collateral posting requirements with respect to changes in either the fair value or intrinsic value of the contracts and/or a downgrade of Berkshire's credit rating. Under certain conditions, a few contracts require that Berkshire post collateral. As of June 30, 2009, Berkshire's collateral posting requirement under such contracts was approximately $650 million.

Sometimes, a firm may account for a derivative agreement as a fair-value hedge when, for all practical purposes, it is a cash-flow hedge. This could be the case if, owing to a change in the price of the item hedged, the firm becomes slightly over(under)hedged.

In making the determination each quarter, the Empire Electric Company applies any gain or loss on contracts that become unhedged as reclassified to fuel expense. The company states in its 2009 10K, "All of our gas hedging activities are related to stabilizing fuel costs as part of our fuel procurement program and are not speculative activities. If conditions change, such as a planned unit outage, we may need to de-designate and/or unwind some of our previous derivatives designated under SFAS 133. In this instance, these derivatives would be classified into the category above, which is derivatives classified as non-hedges."

The analyst might need to confer with financial management to understand why a transaction was accounted for as a particular hedge if the accounting is unclear. *The significant issues are not always the accounting treatment but the determination as to whether the derivatives were used to reduce risk, the extent to which such risk has been reduced, and the range of cash-flow and credit outcomes resulting from their implementation.* The sensitivity analysis performed by the company should be released and considered an integral part of the financial statements. Even AutoDesk, Inc., a strong credit that hedges its dollar risk, explained in its October 2009 10Q:

> A sensitivity analysis performed on our hedging portfolio as of October 31, 2009, indicated that a hypothetical 10 percent appreciation of the U.S. dollar from its value at October 31, 2009, would increase the fair value of our forward exchange and option contracts by $13.4 million. A hypothetical 10 percent depreciation of the dollar from its value at October 31, 2009, would decrease the fair value of our forward exchange and option contracts

> by $14.2 million. We do not anticipate any material adverse impact to our consolidated financial position, results of operations or cash flows as a result of this foreign currency forward and option contracts.

Given Autodesk's strong financial position and cash flows, the hedges are of a nonmaterial nature in evaluating the company's credit strength and cost of capital. However, even this strong credit finds it appropriate to release its sensitivity results as part of its financial filings.

FINANCIAL STRUCTURE AND DEBT COVERAGE

Financial leverage may be defined as the proportion of total debt to total capitalization of a firm. A firm is considered highly leveraged when the ratio of debt to total capitalization is high, taking into account the operating cash flows. A firm is unleveraged when it has no debt in its capital structure. *Debt* is defined as total debt, including lease obligations and any off-balance-sheet liabilities, such as unfunded pension and other postretirement benefits, and any other off-balance-sheet liabilities, including derivatives, for which the entity might be liable.

Contingent liabilities should not be included unless the probability of the obligations coming due is reasonably assured. They should be evaluated to both probability and the cash-flow and credit impact. If a contingent liability is assumed, its effect may be short-lived or last many years depending on the circumstances. Short-term debt also must be included in total debt becaues many companies have short-term loans that must be settled with cash or recast into long-term debt. In fact, credit analysis begins with the analysis of near-term obligations. Rollover risk is an important part of the cost of capital. Companies having large balloon payments due within a year must have the financial flexibility to satisfy those upcoming claims or face bankruptcy.

Total capitalization, as typically defined, includes long-term debt plus total shareholders' equity, where the latter is measured by the accounting book value of equity, taking into account assets that are likely to be sold above (below) book within the coming 12 months. Short-term debt is excluded because it could be removed from the firm within an operating cycle.

The market value of the equity should be used, when appropriate, such as when book value is unrealistically low owing to an accounting regulation or not otherwise reflective of the firm's capital strength, as we saw with Clorox, whose book value was affected by the large share repurchase. Thus the typical treatment of total capital where short-term debt is excluded is different from my ROIC measure, in which I include all interest-bearing debt. Short-term debt is almost always rolled over or converted to equity. In instances of weak credits where rollover risk exists, my cost-of-capital model would pick this up and mark up the discount rate of the free cash flows. Even moderately leveraged firms can be sensitive to rollover risk.

Traditional finance thinking views greater amounts of financial leverage as increasing a firm's risk; if operating cash flows during any period are lower than short-term debt payments, the firm has to liquidate some assets or increase its capitalization to continue operations. Thus the more leveraged a firm, the riskier it becomes. At the same time, debt has a desirable benefit because interest payments on debt are tax deductible, whereas dividend payments are not. Generally, the greater the volatility of operating cash flows and free cash flow, the lower should be the financial leverage. Conversely, the greater the stability of operating or free cash flow, the more leveraged a firm can become.

In Chapter 3 we saw Macy's factoring its accounts receivable for cash that was used, in part, to pay down debt incurred from the previous year's acquisition of May Department Stores. Typically, continuous factoring arrangements restrict the ability of the entity to function in various ways, such as the sale of assets, dividend payments, minimum net worth, maximum leverage ratios, and minimum EBITDA requirements. If the entity under consideration has entered into such an arrangement, it is important to understand the terms of any accompanying positive or negative restrictions or covenants and the effect they might have on cash flows and competitive position.[13]

Example:

It is not unusual for financially weak brokerage firms to borrow at the parent level and then send the cash to the broker-dealer where it counts as capital. In the industry, this is known as *double leveraging.* The SEC regulates the industry and is in charge of setting capital requirements—how much equity and debt a firm must have invested in the business.

Since loans are counted as part of capital, Drexel Burnham Lambert, even as it was rapidly heading toward bankruptcy, was able to claim that it was exceeding federal capital requirements. In fact, just before Drexel entered bankruptcy, it stated that it had almost $300 million more in capital than was required by the SEC. However, much of the capital was in the form of loans from its parent, Drexel Burnham Lambert Group, Inc., which was financing itself with short-term loans. Soon afterward, Drexel's house of cards collapsed when the SEC and the New York Stock Exchange refused to allow Drexel's brokerage unit to reduce its capital by repaying loans from its parent.

[13] To see an example of a factoring agreement between CIT Financial and Bernard Chaus, please go to http://www.sec.gov/Archives/edgar/data/793983/000095012309045239/y02288exv10w3.htm.

Example

Many Japanese firms that typically had been financially leveraged throughout the 1990s up to the 2006 economic expansion, such as Hitachi, ran into financial difficulties when the 2007 recession took hold. At the end of 2008, Hitachi had a debt/equity ratio of 269 percent versus just 26.8 percent for Panasonic. In the same year, Intel Corp. and Oracle had ratios of 5.1 and 40.8 percent, respectively. Thus these two U.S. firms relied more heavily on internal capital than Hitachi, which relied more heavily on external capital. Thus it was no surprise that Hitachi shares did not hold up as well as those of Oracle, Panasonic, and Intel during the recession.

The most commonly applied measure of a firm's ability to pay the interest on its debt is the *debt coverage ratio*, measured by operating cash flows plus lease and interest expense divided by interest expense and lease expenses. The greater this ratio, the easier it is for a firm to meet interest and lease payments. However, this ratio measures the short-term ability of a firm to service its debt; it totally ignores the firm's ability to reduce its financial leverage. For example, the firm may generate enough operating cash flows to sustain its current level of growth and to cover existing interest and lease payments, but the firm may not have sufficient operating cash flows to retire old debt or meet minimal levels of EBITDA, as required in loan covenants. Consequently, it may be exposed to greater financial risk than a firm that does generate sufficient operating and free cash flow. Therefore, I suggest an additional measure of a firm's financial risk: the relationship between total debt and free cash flow. For this reason, I measure total debt relative to both operating and free cash flow.

To assess the ability of a firm to attain its desired financial structure, I examine the ratio of total debt to the normalized free cash flow as one of the leverage ratios in my credit model. Other factors I examine are stability measures of: free cash flow, sales, taxes, and operating cash flows. I also look at the entity's cash burn rate and persistence in going to the credit market, among other factors, all of which will determine the optimal financial structure.

The greater the leverage ratios, as measured by the cash-flow coverage ratios, the greater is the financial risk of the firm, and the lower this ratio, the lower is the financial risk of the firm. Ideally, one would like to invest in firms that are able to generate free cash flow consistently but also require a lower debt burden relative to their competition. Such firms can make appropriate capital investments if the management of these enterprises continues to find opportunities, both internally and externally, above their cost of capital. These firms either can use their retained earnings built from their free cash flow or can increase their debt. Firms that are leveraged may benefit from the tax advantage when the going is good but pay the consequences during periods of uncertainty or distress.

CREDIT-RATING FINANCIAL RATIOS

Credit-rating agencies have general financial guidelines under which their ratings are assigned. These are shown in Table 6-6, as compiled by Standard and Poor's, for some common financial ratios.

Enterprises attempt to maintain their leverage and fixed-charge ratios at the desired (target) level or to improve or take actions to improve their averages to that level, comparing their ratios with those in the table. Firms also compare their financial ratios with others in their industry relative to their respective credit ratings. Some overcapitalized entities will be comfortable taking on debt, even though it may mean sacrificing a credit rating, to improve ROIC. If investors believe that a project or acquisition will be value-enhancing, bonds that need to be sold normally will be placed at the expected interest rate, and cost of capital remains stable, even if the ratings are negatively affected. If the capitalization of the entity is inconsistent with its current rating, a rating change most likely will take place.

Entities that are reliant on the credit markets, especially medium credits, can reduce their cost of debt substantially if their credit rating is assigned a higher grade. Many pension funds are prohibited from owning debt below a certain grade,

TABLE 6-6

S&P-Adjusted Key Industrial Financial Ratios, Long-Term Debt, U.S. (Medians of Three-Year Averages, 2006–2008)

	AAA	AA	A	BBB	BB	B
Operating income (before D&A)/revenues (%)	27.8	25.2	18.8	17.7	17.2	15.7
Return on capital (%)	30.5	29.9	21.7	15.1	12.6	8.6
EBIT interest coverage (*x*)	34.9	16.6	10.8	5.9	3.6	1.4
EBITDA interest coverage (*x*)	38.8	20.8	13.3	7.8	5.1	2.2
FFO/debt (%)	190.2	76.9	54.0	34.8	26.9	11.6
Free operating cash flow/debt (%)	154.6	42.5	30.9	14.0	7.8	2.1
Discount cash flow/debt (%)	93.9	26.5	20.2	8.4	5.8	1.0
Debt/EBITDA (*x*)	0.4	1.0	1.5	2.3	3.0	5.4
Debt/debt plus equity (%)	13.3	27.6	36.1	45.3	52.9	75.6
Number of companies	6	15	100	202	271	321

Note: In this table, FFO = funds from operations, which is defined as net income from continuing operations adjusted for depreciation and amortization (D&A) and other noncash and nonrecurring items such as deferred taxes, write-offs, gains and losses on asset sales, foreign-exchange gains and losses on financial instruments, and undistributed equity earnings or losses from joint ventures. *Free operating cash flow* is defined as operating cash flow minus capital expenditures.

Source: "CreditStats: 2008 Adjusted Key U.S. and European Industrial and Utility Financial Ratios," by David Lugg and Paulina Grabowiec.

whereas other funds may own no greater than a small allocation to lower grades. Thus the higher the grade, the greater is the potential demand for an entity's fixed-income instruments and a commensurate lower cost of debt.

As shown in the table, the greater the leverage and lower the fixed-charge coverage, the lower is the credit rating, on average. In actuality, a credit rating takes into account many factors, some being nonfinancial, such as the *willingness* of an entity to reduce its leverage.

CASH BURN RATE

The *cash burn rate* represents the number of days it will take until the company will use up all the cash and marketable securities it has on hand for its operations and new investments in capital expenditures. It is calculated as the magnitude of the negative free cash flow by the number of days so that if the entity had negative free cash flow, as defined, of $40 million for the quarter and had $160 million in cash, its cash burn would be one year. If the entity had bank credit facilities in place, depending on its reliability and date the facility runs out, that also could be added to the balance-sheet cash. The cash burn is also sometimes calculated as 365 (days) times cash and marketable securities divided by the difference between capital expenditures and operating cash flow.

For entities that do not generate free cash flow, this metric should indicate the date that additional cash will be needed, either from external financing or via asset sales. The metric also will be used to plan the magnitude of a cash raise and the needed reduction in fixed and variable costs to allow the entity to reach positive free cash flow.

Tables 6-7 delineates a number of companies that have high cash burn rates, are highly levered, and have negative free cash flow as of September 2009. When companies are under this pressure, they normally must restructure.

TABLE 6-7

High-Cash-Burn-Rate Companies

Company Name	Cash Burn Rate in Days	Total Debt/Total Capital	Three Year Average Free Cash Flows
ADVANCED MICRO DEVICES	303.982	105.951	(685.291)
AERCAP HOLDINGS NV	80.538	86.848	(621.956)
AMERICAN AXLE & MFG HOLDINGS	332.026	161.872	(41.686)
ANOORAQ RESOURCES CORP	188.706	111.422	(4.232)
ATP OIL & GAS CORP	211.672	81.713	(114.239)
BABCOCK & BROWN AIR LTD -ADR	157.703	78.523	(483.021)

Company Name	Cash Burn Rate in Days	Total Debt/Total Capital	Three Year Average Free Cash Flows
CARDIMA INC	155.940	961.824	(6.864)
CARDTRONICS INC	49.561	106.269	(24.912)
CHENIERE ENERGY INC	202.018	112.612	(502.699)
CHENIERE ENERGY PARTNERS LP	213.152	119.228	(416.931)
CHINA BAK BATTERY INC	340.305	76.359	(39.295)
CHINA SOUTHN AIRLS LTD -ADR	238.429	143.294	(114.992)
CONSTELLATION ENERGY GRP INC	140.237	100.656	(921.699)
COOPER TIRE & RUBBER CO	305.417	93.147	(14.997)
DEXCOM INC	247.348	277.731	(41.227)
EDP-ENERGIAS DE PORTUGAL-ADR	110.889	75.620	(283.291)
EMERITUS CORP	16.041	82.197	(85.560)
FOREST CITY ENTRPRS -CL A	260.937	96.450	(715.882)
GASTAR EXPLORATION LTD	24.733	149.322	(33.800)
GATX CORP	224.098	83.536	(372.098)
GOLAR LNG LTD BERMUDA	155.323	79.338	(6.343)
HUANENG POWER INTL INC -ADR	92.680	98.050	(1,093.763)
HUMAN GENOME SCIENCES INC	51.290	146.860	(8.563)
IMAX CORP	354.324	284.693	(4.605)
INSULET CORP	223.208	95.212	(66.025)
ISRAMCO INC	17.342	98.324	(9.029)
JAMES RIVER COAL CO	15.907	78.053	(36.566)
JETBLUE AIRWAYS CORP	329.007	76.134	(414.076)
LDK SOLAR CO LTD -ADR	156.074	91.994	(431.400)
MAP PHARMACEUTICALS INC	264.973	75.164	(40.902)
MONEYGRAM INTERNATIONAL INC	319.796	104.208	(1,763.058)
NIVS INTELLIMEDIA TECHNOLOGY	162.282	115.231	(25.078)
OPKO HEALTH INC	82.147	97.857	(16.029)
PARALLEL PETROLEUM CORP	155.770	77.602	(23.309)
PEREGRINE PHARMACEUTICLS INC	360.040	114.126	(11.818)
PILGRIM'S PRIDE CORP	31.537	463.199	(106.472)
SANDRIDGE ENERGY INC	6.771	75.351	(580.422)
SONIC AUTOMOTIVE INC -CL A	154.629	881.168	(28.039)
STRATUS MEDIA GROUP INC	118.300	151.286	(0.169)
STUDENT LOAN CORP	33.811	189.986	(160.331)
SYNUTRA INTERNATIONAL INC	288.741	261.059	(25.109)
TAL INTERNATIONAL GROUP INC	83.196	78.754	(19.844)
UNIGENE LABORATORIES INC	313.876	285.473	(3.612)
US AIRWAYS GROUP INC	237.087	127.709	(174.203)
VITACOST.COM INC	3.847	123.665	(9.722)
WILLIS LEASE FINANCE CORP	155.128	80.229	(32.628)
XOMA LTD	181.072	198.519	(25.507)
ZYMOGENETICS INC	286.672	80.302	(78.780)

Source: CT Capital, LLC, and company reports.

Example:

Companies that make large acquisitions, despite an already levered balance sheet, often run into financial danger. They simply do not have the financial structure to withstand adversity. During 2006, American Tire Distributors, Atlas Pipeline, Brookstone, Circuit City, Hexion, MF Global, and Spectrum Brands all made large acquisitions and saw their business either fail or severely weakened as a result.

Example:

In 2009, credit-rating agencies lowered their rating on UAL, a commercial airline. A review of the company's debt coming due included debt and lease payments of about $655 million through the rest of the year, $1 billion in 2010, and $869 million in 2011. The company's cash and investment total had slipped to $2.5 billion from $3.8 billion in 2008 because it sold off more than $1 billion in aircraft, parts, and frequent-flier miles to raise money. Fitch ratings stated that UAL's remaining $1.7 billion in unencumbered assets may be difficult to sell.

Companies such as UAL have been forced to consider debt from nontraditional lenders, including private equity and hedge funds. The willingness to accept high interest rates is a clear signal of a cash-strapped company. During periods of declining or low interest rates, many lenders, including nontraditional creditors, such as hedge funds, have been willing to take on second liens in the hope of greater returns. These leveraged lenders normally charge at least 400 basis points over the LIBOR rate. However, this higher rate may be insufficient because Standard and Poor's estimated that investors in second liens could recover less than 25 percent of their principal in the event of bankruptcy.[14]

RISK PROFILE

Because cash flows are, by their nature, uncertain, it is imperative to evaluate not only the ratio of total debt to average free cash flow but also the volatility of free cash flow. The volatility of free cash flow is a measure of the *operating risk* of a firm; the more volatile the free cash flow, the greater is the firm's operating (business) risk. The ratio of total debt to average free cash flow is a measure of *financial risk*; the higher this ratio, the greater is the firm's financial risk. Standard measures of risk—such as systematic risk, beta, or the total variability of stock returns—have

[14] "Return Hungry Investors Snap Up Riskier Loans" (*New York Times*, April 6, 2005). Krispy Kreme, a company in need of cash, paid 5.88 percentage points above LIBOR in such an agreement.

not always been useful predictors of financial and operating risks because they do not take into account the cash flows and credit structure.

Figure 6-4 shows the two dimensions of risk, and Table 6-8 illustrates how Standard and Poor's Rating Service would interpret the table with rating classifications. The figure shows a simplistic risk profile of hypothetical firm X. We can compare the risk profiles of other firms with this firm. Naturally, most people will prefer firms with lower risk to firms with higher risk. Thus firms with risk profiles in region C would be superior to firm X because they have both a lower operating risk and a lower financial risk. Firms in region B are inferior to firm X because both dimensions of risk are greater than those of firm X. The selection of a firm in regions A and D depends on the decision maker's tolerance for the two types of risk. Individuals with more tolerance for financial risk than for operating risk may prefer firms in region D over firm X because they have lower operating risk. The converse would be true for region A.

Instead of quadrants, Table 6-8 places risk profiles into ratings classes. As firms' financial ratios deteriorate, credit-rating agencies increase their risk level to lower rated credits such that, in effect, they shift to the right quadrants of Fig. 6-4. As their cash flows, including volatility, and leverage ratios improve, their business risk moderates, and they would be expected to be placed into a higher credit rating with resulting lower cost of capital, or into the upper-left quadrant. They also would move up to the top left of the table.

The security analyst should examine the behavior of the annual, rolling 12-month, and quarterly operating and free cash flows (stability and growth) relative to their prior periods, including a comparison to total debt of the same periods.

FIGURE 6-4

Risk-Volatility of Cash Flows versus Leverage

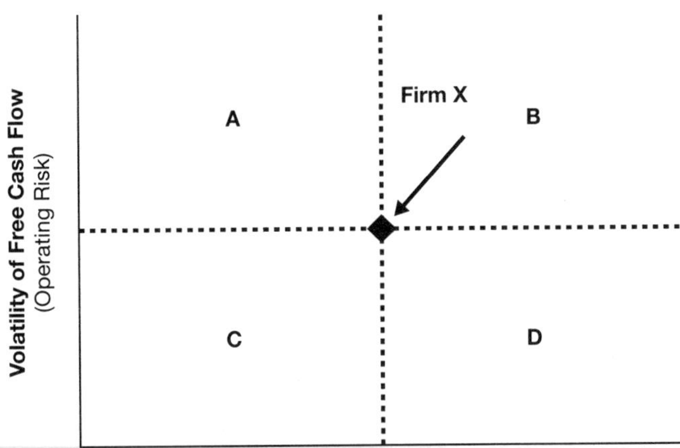

TABLE 6-8

Standard and Poor's Business Risk Profile

	Business Risk Profile			Financial Risk Profile		
	Minimal	Modest	Intermediate	Significant	Aggressive	Leveraged Highly
Excellent	AAA	AA	A	A−	BBB	—
Strong	AA	A	A−	BBB	BB	BB−
Satisfactory	A−	BBB+	BBB	BB+	BB−	B+
Fair	—	BBB−	BB+	BB	BB−	B
Weak	—	—	BB	BB−	B+	B−
Vulnerable	—	—	—	B+	B	CCC+

Note: These rating outcomes are shown for guidance purposes only. Actual rating should be within one notch of indicated rating outcomes.

Source: "Criteria Methodology: Business Risk/Financial Risk Matrix Expanded," by Solomon B. Samson and Emmanuel Dubois-Perelin. Copyright © 2009 by Standard & Poor's Financial Services, LLC. Reproduced with permission of Standard & Poor's Financial Services, LLC.

Also to be examined are the most recent three- or four-year average free cash flow to assess if and how the firm was able to overcome downturns in the industry or economy, including managerial decision making during those periods. Was the firm reliant on the capital markets? To what extent? What happened to its operating cash flows and power operating cash flows? What executive decisions were made? Are the company's revenues of a recurring nature such that the company was protected during the downturn? What happened to the company's market share? Was the company reliant on weak credit clients? Did managers overreact to events or take advantage of them? How were the financial structure, cash flows, and credit rating affected? Have recent events changed the company's risk profile, as would be measured by Tables 6-6 and 6-7 and Fig. 6-4?

PRINCIPAL STRUCTURE OF DEBT

Credit analysis begins with an evaluation of the ability of an entity to satisfy its current obligations. If the entity has adequate financial flexibility and satisfactory prospects for the repayment or rollover of current debt, an analysis of later-maturing liabilities takes place.

The firm's long-term obligations, covered under SFAS 47, requires it to disclose its commitments under unconditional purchase obligations, such as take-or-pay contracts and obligations related to supplier financing. The firm must disclose its long-term obligations, including sinking-fund requirements, maturities, and redemption requirements for each of the next five years.

While interest coverage on debt is a primary consideration in credit analysis, also to be evaluated is the ability of the entity to retire its principal obligations. In the credit model, I evaluate the ease of the entity to retire its obligations from a variety of sources, including credit extension, free cash flow, working capital, cash, and calls on credit.

Figure 6-5 shows Macy's debt structure, as reported, to which I have added the operating lease component. Macy's operating leases are almost entirely composed of rental commitments. Also shown, in Table 6-9, is Macy's upcoming maturity schedule over the next five years, including capital and operating leases, in conformity with the standard. The schedule shows a drop in minimum lease obligations, which is probably an unrealistic assumption. Even for an enterprise such as Macy's, which has seen its growth rate stall, it would be judicious to incorporate no less than the stated lease obligations for the five-year period. The analyst then would discount the operating leases at Macy's weighted-average cost of debt, which should be

FIGURE 6-5

Macy's Debt Structure

Debt Structure (Annual – January 2009)	**$M**	**% of LT Debt**
Convertible Debt Senior	0	0.0
Convertible Debt Subordinated	0	0.0
Total Convertible	0	0.0
Subordinated Debt	0	0.0
Notes	4,776	43.9
Debentures	3,589	33.0
Other – Long-Term	337	3.1
Operating Leases	2,148	19.7
Capital Lease Obligations	31	0.2
Unamortised Debt Disc & Premiums	0	0.0
Total Long-Term Debt	**10,881**	**100.0%**
Debt – Mortgage & Secured	31	
Contingent Liability Guarantees	48	
Total Debt Summary:		
Total Debt	10,960	100.0
Long-Term Debt	10,881	89.1
Debt in Current Liabilities	966	8.9

TABLE 6-9

Macy's Debt and Lease Obligations for the Upcoming Five Years

	2010	2011	2012	2013	2014	After
Debt maturities	238	662	1,663	138	505	5,185
Operating leases	235	226	207	191	170	1,709
Capital leases	8	7	6	5	4	27

added to total liabilities, as I will do for UPS later in this chapter. UPS, a growth company, has seen its operating leases grow by 5.6 percent per year, and as such, the analyst could build such growth into the cash-flow projection and debt-obligation schedule.

SUBSEQUENT EVENTS

Important events taking place subsequent to the reporting period but prior to the SEC filing may affect the financial structure of an enterprise. Such material events subsequent to the date the financial statements were prepared must be reported in a footnote. SFAS 165 (May 2009) sets standards for the disclosure of events that occur after the balance-sheet date but before financial statements are issued or are available to be issued. Aside from this one aspect, it left alone the central tenants of SFAS 5, *Accounting for Contingencies*.

The subsequent-event footnote is not a substitute for an 8K filing, whereby an entity must report, within 4 business days, an unscheduled event that is material (could be expected to affect the value of the company) to shareholders. The following are examples of subsequent events found in 8K financial filings. If it is deemed significant, the event must be reported by the entity through an 8K, but some latitude has been shown to exist where the effect is less clear-cut. Also, what may be a reportable event for one company might be insignificant for another. What is clear is that such events often have cash-flow, financial structure, and/or valuation consequences.

Which of the following eleven actual 8K-reported events affected financial structure, cash flow, or cost of capital (risk)? Which events might have had a significant effect on the firm's stock price?

1. The company effected a one-for-four reverse stock split. The financial statements have been restated, for all periods presented, to reflect the stock split. After the split, the company has 1,371,750 shares outstanding.

2. The IRS completed its examination of the firm's U.S. federal income tax returns for the years 2002 to 2005 and issued a Revenue Agent Report (RAR) that includes various proposed adjustments, including with respect to the going-private merger transactions.
3. The company issued 312,000 common shares at US$0.80 per share pursuant to secured convertible note principal conversions received in the amount of US$250,000.
4. The company will record a $1 billion noncash expense in the first quarter owing to the newly passed health care law.
5. The company entered into a corporate job-creation and lease agreement with the Pearland Economic Development Corporation of Pearland, Texas.
6. The company received a final payment of $820,000, completing the sale of all its domestic oil and gas properties.
7. The executive vice president and chief financial officer of the company resigned.
8. The company completed a $250 million share-repurchase program.
9. The company terminated the pending acquisition of . . . .
10. Mr. XXX (the CFO) died unexpectedly. As a result, the existing board unanimously appointed Ms YYY to replace Mr. XXX.
11. The company entered into a distribution agreement with a large company from South Korea for the exclusive rights to market the firm's products.

DEFERRED TAXES

Deferred taxes are included in this chapter because, if a deferral is reversed, the financial structure is affected, including the possibility of a violation of a debt covenant. I discussed the income tax rate as a credit indicator in Chapter 4, and now I discuss the deferred account as a provider (user) of cash if the rate were to change.

Most large firms include on the balance sheet a provision for future tax payments, or deferred tax liability. Deferred taxes represent an integral part of the capital structure and are also studied both for their potential cash effects and the integrity of the asset or liability causing their existence. If a deferred tax asset is recognized without an offsetting valuation allowance and business conditions turn down, the firm's financial structure would show greater leverage or possibly eliminate shareholders' equity as the tax assets become of questionable value and would need to be offset.

This liability has attracted the attention of investors, creditors, managers, and accountants for a long time. At issue is the difference between the tax expense reported in the financial statements and the actual tax payment to the governmental authorities, including overseas. The two are different because of different tax treatments of items for tax and for financial reporting purposes. Some differences are permanent (i.e., they are not expected to reverse in the future), whereas others are temporary differences that are expected to reverse.

For instance, companies normally would choose to depreciate[15] assets more quickly during the early years of placing the asset in service to enhance cash flows sooner. Any lower tax payments at the beginning of the asset's life are expected to be offset by greater tax payments toward the end of the asset's life; thus the cash flows will be enhanced during the early years. Of course, companies with growing capital expenditures would continue to see such benefits. One sees this when the deferred tax account continues to grow.

The accounting profession requires firms to record a liability for temporary differences based on the assumption that the entry will be reversed in the future, and increased tax payments will be necessitated. Thus the firm creates a liability based on these expected higher future rates. Such a liability is not required for permanent timing differences because they are not expected to be reversed in the future.

A firm is allowed to carry tax losses backward to two years and forward up to 20 years.[16] However, to use tax carry-fowards, the firm must have taxable income. To the extent that it does, the loss carry-fowards represent a very valuable asset because the gains could result in no or little actual federal income tax payments. It was estimated by the Bureau of Economic Research that extending the carry-back period from two to five years would have provided $34 billion in additional liquidity in 2008. For the cash-flow analyst, extending the carry-back period would, for firms able to take advantage of such a provision, help to smooth out (or increase average) free cash flow, thereby also reducing the cost of equity capital.

SFAS 109 allows firms to set up a deferred tax account if it "is more likely than not" that the tax asset would be used in the future. It also requires firms to show the entire amount of deferred tax assets with, if called for, a *valuation allowance*, which is similar to an allowance for uncollectible receivables. This allowance reduces the deferred tax asset to the amount that is likely to be used in the future. Accordingly, firms report separately in a footnote their current and

[15] *Economic depreciation* is the decrease in value of a productive asset as it ages. *Tax depreciation* is the depreciation permitted by the tax code.

[16] The IRS announced on March 16, 2008, that small businesses with deductions exceeding their income in 2008 can use a new net operating loss tax provision to get a refund of taxes paid in prior years. As tax laws change, the analyst must adjust the free cash flow to accommodate such shifts, including changes in state tax rates.

deferred tax expense for the period, as well as their federal, state, and local taxes and, if applicable, their foreign taxes. Firms are also required to reconcile their effective tax rate with the statutory tax rate, in effect providing information about permanent differences between financial reporting and taxable income. Firms are also required to disclose the major components of deferred tax assets and liabilities, in effect providing information about temporary differences.

When evaluating tax losses, the cash-flow analyst should determine if the loss was created through a business still owned by the parent or by an entity that was sold for a loss or closed down. If the remaining enterprise is a consistent and growing producer of free cash flow, the tax loss has real immediate value. Companies typically are conservative in recognizing the likely value of tax assets, with their auditors requiring the offset through the valuation allowance. It is contingent on the analyst to determine the likelihood of cash tax savings that could accrue to the entity and to adjust the expected free cash flow accordingly.

For International Paper Company, losses have been common, occurring in half the years shown in Table 6-10. As seen, the company was able to reduce its tax bill. During 2006, the company sold $3.4 billion in assets yet paid just $249 million in income taxes while showing an effective tax payment of $1.9 billion. The third

TABLE 6-10

International Paper Tax Information

INTL PAPER CO.
TICKER: IP
SIC: 2,600.000
GICS: 15105020

	(1)	(2)	(3)	(4)	(5)	(6)
	Tax Loss Carry Forward	Tax Rate	Income Taxes-Total	Income Taxes Paid	Pretax Income	Free Cash Flow
Dec01	1,873.000	21.344	(270.000)	333.000	(1,265.000)	183.000
Dec02	3,786.000	(14.555)	(54.000)	295.000	371.000	607.000
Dec03	4,702.000	(26.590)	(92.000)	277.000	346.000	176.000
Dec04	4,024.000	27.614	206.000	254.000	746.000	641.000
Dec05	4,644.000	(48.635)	(285.000)	457.000	586.000	(140.000)
Dec06	3,189.000	59.253	1,889.000	249.000	3,188.000	(270.000)
Dec07	610.000	25.091	415.000	328.000	1,654.000	163.000
Dec08	762.000	(14.674)	162.000	131.000	(1,104.000)	1,239.000
Average	2,948.750	3.606	246.375	290.500	565.250	324.875

column discloses income taxes accrued under the effective tax rate, and the fourth column shows income taxes actually paid. Despite International Paper having shown a negative effective tax rate over many years owing to payments to local and foreign tax authorities (foreign constitutes about 21 percent of sales), its cash tax payments actually remained reasonably high, averaging $290 million on $565 million in pretax income, while showing an effective rate to shareholders of just 3.6 percent.

Example:

International Paper has U.S. federal and non-U.S. net operating loss carry forwards of approximately $488 million that expire as follows: 2009 through 2018—$16 million, years 2019 through 2028—$109 million and indefinite carry forwards of $363 million. International Paper has tax benefits from net operating loss carry forwards for state taxing jurisdictions of approximately $274 million that expire as follows: 2009 through 2018—$108 million and 2019 through 2028—$166 million. International Paper also has U.S. federal, non-U.S. and state tax credit carry forwards that expire as follows: 2009 through 2018—$57 million, 2019 through 2028—$90 million, and indefinite carry forwards—$337 million. Further, International Paper has state capital loss carry forwards that expire as follows: 2009 through 2018—$7 million.

Source: International Paper 2008 10K.

Example:

For unprofitable companies, the cash refund represents an important source of cash, given that the conditions that caused it most likely resulted in a need for cash. For example, during 2009, the management of Schnitzer Steel Corp. stated that it expected a $47 million refund owing to available tax loss carry-backs and the current year's reported loss. Since the payment has not yet been received, it is shown on the company's balance sheet as an asset.

SCHNITZER STEEL INDUSTRIES, INC.
CONSOLIDATED BALANCE SHEETS
(in thousands, except per share amounts)

	August 31,	
	2009	**2008**
Assets		
Current assets:		
Cash and cash equivalents	$41,026	$15,039
Accounts receivable, net of allowance of $7,509 in 2009 and $3,049 in 2008	117,666	314,993
Inventories, net	184,455	429,061
Deferred income taxes	10,027	7,808

	August 31,	
	2009	**2008**
Refundable income taxes	46,972	825
Prepaid expenses and other current assets	10,868	11,800
Total current assets	411,014	779,526
Property, plant, and equipment, net	447,228	431,898
Other assets:		
Investment in and advances to joint venture partnerships	10,812	11,896
Goodwill	366,559	306,186
Intangibles, net	20,422	15,389
Other assets	12,198	9,958
Total assets	$1,268,233	$1,554,853
Liabilities and Shareholders' Equity		
Current liabilities:		
Short-term borrowings and capital lease obligations	$1,317	$25,490
Accounts payable	72,289	161,288
Accrued payroll and related liabilities	23,636	64,453
Environmental liabilities	3,148	3,652
Accrued income taxes	776	42,774
Other accrued liabilities	38,963	47,265
Total current liabilities	140,129	344,922
Deferred income taxes	44,523	16,807
Long-term debt and capital lease obligations, net of current maturities	110,414	158,933
Environmental liabilities, net of current portion	38,760	40,052
Other long-term liabilities	11,657	11,588
Minority interests	3,383	4,399
Commitments and contingencies (Note 11)		
Shareholders' equity:		
Preferred stock—20,000 shares authorized, none issued	—	—
Class A common stock—75,000 shares $1.00 par value authorized, 21,402 and 21,592 shares issued and outstanding	21,402	21,592
Class B common stock—25,000 shares $1.00 par value authorized, 6,268 and 6,345 shares issued and outstanding	6,268	6,345
Additional paid-in capital	—	11,425
Retained earnings	894,243	939,181
Accumulated other comprehensive loss	(2,546)	(391)
Total shareholders' equity	919,367	978,152
Total liabilities and shareholders' equity	$1,268,233	$1,554,853

Example:

Centex was able to use its loss carry-back, receiving a significant cash refund, but owing to the enormity of its recent losses and uncertainty as to future profits, it established a full valuation allowance.

> As of March 31, 2009, we had net deferred tax assets of $1.29 billion for which a $1.29 billion valuation allowance has been established. The ultimate realization of the deferred tax assets is dependent upon a variety of factors, including taxable income in prior carryback years, estimates of future taxable income, tax planning strategies, and reversals of existing taxable temporary differences. The FASB provides in SFAS No. 109, "Accounting for Income Taxes," or SFAS 109 that a cumulative loss in recent years is significant negative evidence in considering whether deferred tax assets are realizable. Based on our assessment, the realization of our deferred tax assets is dependent upon future taxable income and, accordingly, we have established a full valuation allowance. The valuation allowance may increase or decrease as conditions change and/or if new tax laws are enacted, such as changes to net operating loss carryback and carryforward rules, which could have a material effect on our financial position and results of operations.
>
> As of March 31, 2009 and 2008, the company had a federal income tax receivable of $198.8 million and $648.5 million, respectively, primarily relating to net operating loss carryback refund claims. During the year ended March 31, 2009, the company received federal tax refunds of $699.3 million. The company's net deferred tax assets before the valuation allowance increased to $1.29 billion as of March 31, 2009 from $1.02 billion as of March 31, 2008. The company had a $266.6 million deferred tax asset resulting from tax credits and net operating loss carryforwards at March 31, 2009. If unused, the various tax credits and net operating loss carryforwards will expire (beginning at various times depending on the tax jurisdiction) in the years 2013 through 2029.

Source: Centex 2009 10K.

Most firms use the liability method for recording deferred income taxes. Under this method, deferred tax assets and liabilities are determined based on differences between financial reporting and tax basis of assets and liabilities and are measured using the enacted tax rates and laws that will be in effect when the differences are expected to reverse. A firm need not establish a full valuation allowance, like Centex, if it is more likely than not that some portion or all of the deferred tax assets will be realized.

For firms that have substantial temporary timing differences, cash flow, of course, would be enhanced in earlier years and impaired in later years. This is not the case with permanent timing differences. For example, interest received on municipal bonds is not taxable and would be excluded in taxable income, but financial reports must incorporate such interest as income.

Opponents of the deferred tax liability argue that, in reality, most firms have a large buildup of deferred taxes that are unlikely to ever be paid to the government. They contend that as long as the firm keeps growing, and as long as additional temporary differences are created, deferred taxes will continue to grow. This is verified empirically by observing the steady growth of the deferred tax liability on most firms' financial statements over the last two decades. Furthermore, opponents of the deferred tax liability argue that this liability is never discounted to the present, unlike other long-term liabilities of the firm. Indeed, this issue has not been resolved satisfactorily by the FASB, which issued SFAS 96 to deal with accounting for income taxed. Also, the FASB deferred the effective date of the standard with the issuance of SFAS 100, deferred it again with SFAS 103, and finally set new accounting rules with SFAS 109.

SFAS 109 changed the accounting for income taxed in several material ways. First, it established the liability approach for deferred tax liabilities. Second, it defined and expanded the disclosure rules for temporary and permanent differences between tax and financial reporting. Finally, it allowed firms to include deferred tax assets on the balance sheet if it is "more likely than not" that the firm can use these deferred tax assets in the future. Let me explain each of these issues and illustrate them with several examples.

In the past (before SFAS 96, which most firms did not adopt, or before SFAS 109), firms used to set a deferred tax liability as the difference between the tax expense on a temporary item and the actual current tax liability on that item. For example, if a financial reporting expense was shown at $5,000, whereas on the tax return the same expense was shown as $6,000, a temporary difference of $1,000 would have been created. Suppose further that the firm was subject to a 46 percent tax rate. The firm would create a deferred tax liability for $460 (46 percent of $1,000), which is equal to the expected tax payment on the item when the expense is smaller on the tax return than on the financial statements. One also can derive $460 by comparing the financial statements tax credit on the item of $2,300 (46 percent of $5,000) and the actual tax credit of $2,760 (46 percent of $6,000). Note that both computations give the same result if one uses the same rate of 46 percent. Prior to SFAS 109 (or its predecessor, SFAS 96), firms used the second method to set up their deferred tax liability.

Suppose now that two years later, but before the item reverses, the government decides to reduce the tax rate to 40 percent. Using the first approach, the expected tax liability in the future is now $400 (40 percent of $1,000) instead of $460, as computed earlier. Thus the liability approach, which is adopted by SFAS 109 (and SFAS 96), would reduce the deferred tax liability on the balance sheet by $60 ($460 – $400) and would incorporate in income a $60 gain owing to lower taxes. Under the approaches prior to SFAS 109 (and SFAS 96), such a decrease in the liability would not have been made because at the time of the initial expense of the item the difference in the tax and financial statement expense that was incorporated into the income statement was exactly $460. Note that if tax rates are expected to increase, the reverse effect would occur—an increase in the deferred tax liability and a loss on the income statement owing to tax increases.

Prior to SFAS 109, firms found it very difficult to record a deferred tax asset. Deferred tax assets occur when a firm has greater expense for financial reporting purposes than for tax purposes. For example, the accrual of postretirement benefits is a financial reporting expense under SFAS 106, but it is not a taxable expense until cash is actually paid to retirees. Firms did not set up deferred tax assets unless they were reasonably certain that the tax benefits from the assets would indeed be obtained in the future. Under the current tax rules, one can carry tax losses backward two years to offset prior taxable income and forward up to 20 years.[17] However, to use tax carryforwards, the firm must have future taxable income. Prior to SFAS 109, firms rarely created deferred tax assets because the uncertainty about utilization of those assets in the future was significant. SFAS 109 allowed firms to set up a deferred tax asset if "it is more likely than not" that the tax asset would be used in the future. It also required firms to show the entire amount of deferred tax assets but then reduce the tax assets by a "valuation allowance," which is similar to an allowance for uncollectible receivables. This allowance reduces the deferred tax asset to the amount that is likely to be used in the future.

SFAS 109 requires firms to continue with prior disclosure about income taxes and mandates some additional disclosure. Accordingly, firms usually report separately in a footnote their current and deferred tax expense for the period, as well as their federal, state, and local taxes and, if applicable, their domestic and foreign taxes. Firms are also required to reconcile the statutory tax rate with their effective tax rate, providing information about permanent differences between financial reporting and taxable income. Firms are also required to disclose the major components of deferred tax assets and liabilities, in effect providing information about temporary differences. Let's examine several such disclosures.

Since the cash-flow and debt effects of deferred taxes are difficult to ascertain, I recommend that the cash-flow analyst should not, under most circumstances, include deferred taxes among long-term liabilities of the firm when considering total debt and any ratio based on total debt. In fact, credit-rating agencies typically add deferred taxes to long-term debt in computing total capital. The one exception would be if an amount of deferred taxes were likely to be realized, the analyst should deduct that from estimated operating and free cash flow and adjust the current debt ratio to include the liability.

---

[17] The loss carryback was extended for five years for eligible small business corporations resulting from the economic stimulus package of 2008.

Example:

Ulta Salon, Cosmetics & Fragrance, Inc., is the largest beauty retailer that provides one-stop shopping for prestige, mass, and salon products and salon services in the United States. In its income tax footnote, management reports a deferred tax asset of $10.5 million for reserves not currently deductible; the reserve is created as vendors advance cash to the company to promote their products. On Ulta's balance sheet, the amount is netted against inventory until the product is sold. The $2.8 million accrued tax asset represents mostly gift cards and would be reduced as redeemed. We also see that the company had a tax-loss carryforward that, given its recent consistent profitability, one would expect to be fully used in the current fiscal year. It will not, however, be utilized in the current period owing to a recent ownership control change that limits such deductibility per year.[18] The company's return to profitability related to the change in ownership illustrates the importance of management and the ability of different skill sets in turning around the cash flows of a company.

Finally, the deferred tax liability regarding deferred rent obligation relates to tenant allowances, whereby Ulta receives cash up front from landlords when building out locations, with the cash used for leasehold improvements. Ulta uses straight line for shareholder reporting and amortizes the upfront payments over the term of the lease. Presumably, as long as Ulta continues to expand locations, this timing difference will grow.

	January 31, 2009	February 2, 2008
Deferred tax assets:		
Reserves not currently deductible	$10,491	$11,655
Employee benefits	2,576	2,315
Net operating loss carryforwards	989	963
Accrued liabilities	2,799	1,038
Property and equipment	—	671
Inventory valuation	—	243
Total deferred tax assets	16,855	16,885
Deferred tax liabilities:		
Property and equipment	15,771	—
Deferred rent obligation	5,815	3,586
Prepaid expenses	4,483	—
Inventory valuation	124	—
Total deferred tax liabilities	26,193	3,586
Net deferred tax (liability) asset	$(9,338)	$13,299

Source: Ulta Salon and Fragrances 2009 10K.

[18] For information on the permissible deduction and change-of-control definitions, see IRS Code Section 382.

PENSION AND OTHER POSTRETIREMENT BENEFITS

Most entities in the United States have plans that promise employees various benefits, most notably pension, life insurance, and health care benefits. It is important to study and understand the entity's benefit expense, including postretirement liabilities, in credit analysis because it relates to capital structure. I shall describe in this section some of those postretirement benefits, their accounting rules, and their effects on cash flow and debt.

The contribution companies make into their retirement plans is almost always material. Its effect on the entity is profound, from a market-value perspective, owing to the impact of the required large cash outlays and leverage through the liability associated with pension obligations. These obligations also affect credit rating and future prospects because investments and additions to the workforce may be curtailed as a result of these prior commitments of cash now being earmarked for plan funding. Worker terminations may result if the cash contributions into the plans are greater than budgeted.

As of September 2009, there were 179 companies having a market value of at least $100 million that contributed 20 percent or more of their pretax profit to such plans. Table 6-11 discloses the magnitude of the cash expense for many large companies having a high ratio of company contributions as a percentage of net income for their latest fiscal year as of September 2009. Unsurprisingly, the average company on the list did not produce positive free cash flow for the year under review.

TABLE 6-11

Pension Expense and Other Related Information for Selected S&P 500 Companies

Company Name	Ticker Symbol	Premium Employer Contrib	Net Income (Low)	Pension Cont.	Free Cash Flow	Debt-Total
AK STEEL HOLDING CORP	AKS	326.800	4.000	56.700	(153.800)	693.300
ALTRA HOLDINGS INC	AIMC	3.947	6.494	0.600	25.825	261.523
AMCOR LTD -ADR	AMCRY	52.041	170.525	0.310	(144.268)	2,281.014
AMETEK INC	AME	79.906	246.952	0.324	177.365	1,111.681
AMPCO-PITTSBURGH CORP	AP	9.434	12.575	0.750	16.838	13.311
ANALOGIC CORP	ALOG	1.156	3.705	0.312	1.314	0.000
ANDERSONS INC	ANDE	10.002	32.900	0.304	154.475	361.751
ARH CHEMICLAS INC	ARJ	26.300	37.000	0.708	(27.800)	393.000
ARKANSAS BEST CORP	ABFS	31.218	29.163	1.070	31.254	16.805
AVISTA CORP	AVA	28.000	73.620	0.300	(140.932)	1,192.068

Company Name	Ticker Symbol	Premium Employer Contrib	Net Income (Low)	Pension Cont.	Free Cash Flow	Debt-Total
CAMBREX CORP	CBM	3.194	7.929	0.403	(24.389)	123.000
CASS INFORMATION SYSTEMS INC	CASS	5.900	19.006	0.310	16.291	3.296
CEMEX SAB DE CV -ADR	CX	60.223	164.691	0.366	217.972	18,659.195
CH ENERGY GROUP INC	CHG	13.027	36.051	0.361	(1.994)	469.394
CONNECTICUT WATER SVC INC	CTWS	3.500	9.424	0.371	(11.601)	104.309
CONSOLIDATED COMM HLDGS INC	CNSL	6.139	12.504	0.491	(1.065)	881.266
CRAWFORD & CO	CRDB	24.577	32.259	0.762	55.761	198.856
CROWN HOLDINGS INC	CCK	71.000	226.000	0.314	248.000	3,337.000
DANA HOLDING CORP	DAN	37.000	18.000	2.056	(1,283.000)	1,251.000
DELTIC TIMBER CORP	DEL	2.372	4.384	0.541	(11.317)	76.944
DEUTSCHE LUFTHANSA AG -ADR	DLAKY	470.462	833.743	0.564	8.359	5,065.124
DOW CHEMICAL	DOW	185.000	579.000	0.320	872.000	11,856.000
ENERGYSOLUTIONS INC	ES	104.632	45.181	2.310	87.849	568.864
FEDEX CORP	FDX	1,148.000	98.000	11.684	157.000	2,583.000
FORTUNE BRANDS INC	FO	114.500	311.100	0.360	380.100	4,725.200
FREIGHTCAR AMERICA INC	RAIL	6.750	4.614	1.463	(68.111)	0.028
GAYLORD ENTERTAINMENT CO	GET	2.674	4.364	0.613	(272.915)	1,262.901
GENCORP INC	GY	1.700	1.500	1.133	5.700	440.600
GERBER SCIENTIFIC INC	GRB	6.419	2.236	2.871	1.587	73.689
GOODRICH CORP	GR	227.200	681.200	0.334	385.200	1,569.400
GRACE (W R) & CO	GRA	67.700	121.500	0.557	(130.000)	11.800
GRAHAM CORP	GHM	7.500	17.487	0.429	1.100	0.059
HANOVER INSURANCE GROUP INC	THG	21.300	20.600	1.034	129.200	591.400
HONDA MOTOR CO LTD -ADR	HMC	481.866	1,381.795	0.349	(10,684.831)	46,565.598
INNOSPEC INC	IOSP	7.500	12.500	0.600	2.900	73.000
KAMAN CORP	KAMN	25.772	35.599	0.724	(43.900)	94.165
KELLOGG CO	K	354.000	1,148.000	0.300	311.000	5,462.000
KRONOS WORLDWIDE INC	KRO	20.000	9.000	2.311	(114.400)	658.500
KYOCERA CORP -ADR	KYO	122.243	298.040	0.410	(37.586)	539.425
LAUDER (ESTEE) CDS INC -CL A	EL	66.900	218.400	0.306	307.800	1,421.400
LAZARD LTD	LAZ	16.208	3.138	5.165	464.325	1,286.720
LIFE SCIENCES RESEARCH INC	LSR	4.926	10.418	0.473	15.061	74.539
LIFE TECHNOLOGIES CORP	LIFE	9.745	31.321	0.311	283.896	3,583.589
MCDERMOTT INTL INC	MDR	160.298	429.302	0.373	(304.858)	15.130
MOLSON COORS BREWING CO	TAP	223.600	388.000	0.519	41.900	1,831.800
MUELLER WATER PRODUCTS INC	MWA	33.900	42.000	0.855	85.800	1,095.500
NAVISTAR INTERNATIONAL CORP	NAV	108.000	134.000	0.806	905.000	6,074.000
NCR CORP	NCR	83.000	228.000	0.364	321.000	308.000
NORTHWESTERN CORP	NWE	32.734	57.601	0.414	23.930	900.047
NSTAR	NST	72.588	239.507	0.303	(21.868)	3,024.583

(Continued)

TABLE 6-11 *(Continued)*

Pension Expense and Other Related Information for Selected S&P 500 Companies

Company Name	Ticker Symbol	Premium Employer Contrib	Net Income (Low)	Pension Cont.	Free Cash Flow	Debt-Total
NV ENERGY INC	NVE	94.143	208.887	0.451	(1,156.303)	5,275.273
OCE NV -ADR	OCENY	54.166	2.498	21.964	(13.535)	775.732
ONEOK INC	OKE	117.597	311.909	0.377	(1,160.244)	6,500.776
PEPSI BOTTLING GROUP INC	PBG	90.000	162.000	0.556	389.000	6,192.000
PMA CAPITAL CORP	PMACA	2.000	5.689	0.352	(61.161)	129.380
POLYMER GROUP INC	3POLGA	5.141	5.353	1.091	24.998	413.665
QUAKER CHEMICAL CORP	KWR	8.355	11.132	0.751	(7.154)	33.167
RAYTHEON CO	RTN	1,174.000	1,872.000	0.702	1,251.000	2,309.000
RHODIA -ADR	RHAYY	57.068	146.150	0.390	101.568	2,510.988
RICOH CO LTD -ADR	3RJCOY	149.020	65.960	2.259	(351.283)	7,870.657
ROGERS CORP	ROG	9.326	26.515	0.352	41.277	0.000
RURAL/METRO CORP	RURL	2.185	5.026	0.435	35.389	277.309
SAPPI LTD -ADR	SPP	76.000	102.000	0.745	(150.000)	2,679.000
SARA LEE CORP	SLE	306.000	364.000	0.841	241.000	2,820.000
SCHWEITZER-MAUDUIT INTL INC	SWM	4.500	0.700	6.571	(11.400)	179.300
SCIENTIFIC GAMES CORP	SGMS	3.200	8.488	0.386	24.858	1,259.848
SEARS HOLDINGS CORP	SHLD	262.000	53.000	4.943	495.000	3,147.000
SENECA FOODS CORP -CL B	SENEA	10.000	18.765	0.533	24.058	230.802
SOUTHWEST GAS CORP	SWX	30.363	60.973	0.596	(39.174)	1,348.307
STANDARD RECHSTER CO	SR	22.316	6.836	9.264	17.784	33.999
STEINWAY MUSICAL INSTRS INC	LVB	7.017	8.186	0.857	1.639	186.750
STURM RUGER & CO INC	ROR	2.936	8.666	0.339	1.594	1.000
TATE & LYLE PLC -ADR	TATYY	44.330	92.950	0.477	228.000	2,362.360
TELEDYNE TECHNOLOGIES INC	TDY	59.700	111.300	0.536	78.500	333.200
TNT NV -ADR	TNTTY	311.786	773.896	0.403	456.543	3,119.248
TOSHIBA CORP -ADR	TOSYY	593.263	1,164.653	0.451	1,307.932	9,817.670
UNISOURCE ENERGY CORP	UNS	10.000	14.021	0.713	(106.321)	1,861.466
UNITED CAPITAL CORP	AFP	1.500	1.616	0.928	(4.530)	32.863
WACDAL HOLDINGS CORP -ADE	WACLY	20.958	52.743	0.397	22.410	53.475
WATSON WYATT WORLDWIDE	WW	68.014	146.458	0.451	175.567	0.000
WHIRLPOOL CORP	WHR	128.000	418.000	0.301	(348.000)	2,597.000
WILLS GROUP HOLDINGS LTD	WSH	154.000	303.000	0.508	(29.000)	2,650.000
XEROX CORP	XRX	299.000	230.000	1.300	579.000	9,092.000
AVERAGE		108.564	182.020	1.941	(68.606)	2,518.959

Firms employ two general types of pension plans—defined-benefit and defined-contribution plans. *Defined-benefit plans* promise employees specific monetary payments to be made to them (or to their remaining spouses) on retirement. The firm has the responsibility to have funds available to pay for those future benefits. *Defined-contribution plans* specify the contribution the employer has to make currently to the plan. Employees are paid from funds available in the plan when they retire based on number of years of service and salary. Under defined-benefit plans, the employer bears the risk of a shortfall in funds if the employee reaches retirement and the plan's assets are insufficient to make the required payments. In such a case, the employer must make supplemental payments so that retirees will receive their promised benefits. Under defined-contribution plans, the employer discharges most responsibilities as soon as the necessary contributions are forwarded to the plan; any risk of shortfall in funds is borne by the employees. Many firms have attempted in the last two decades to terminate their defined-benefit plans and to offer instead defined-contributions plans, which would effectively eliminate their risk, once the required contributions are made.

Typically, firms will set up a separate entity, the pension fund, that is administered jointly by employees and the firm's management (called the *investment* or *employee benefits committee*). A member of a union also may be involved. Employer contributions to the fund (called *funding*) increase the assets of the pension fund. Fund assets are also invested (typically in equities, governmental or corporate bonds, real estate, hedged funds, or company stock), and the return on these investments increases fund assets. Fund assets decrease when payments are made to current retirees, the market value of the investments fall, and to a much smaller extent, because of expenses in managing the fund. Pension plans are subject to the provisions of the Employee Retirement Security Act of 1974 (ERISA).

Defined-contribution plans pose few accounting problems. When employees earn the right to the contribution by the employer, the employer accrues the obligation as a current liability. Funding of the contribution to the designated fund discharges the employer's obligation. The employer is not legally concerned with the value of the assets in the fund or with making additional payments to existing and future retirees. Fund managers are hired to maximize the long-term returns on plan assets. An example of a defined-contribution plan is one in which the employer transfers a specified percentage of the employee's current compensation to a fund chosen by the employee. Typically, these contributions are not taxable to the employee until drawn from the fund.

Defined-benefit plans, on the other hand, pose great difficulties from an accounting point of view. Here, the employer retains the responsibility for the specified future benefits until the employee or the employee's survivors are no longer eligible for those benefits. Thus the employer is liable for these benefits until all future promised payments are made. The major accounting issues are how to estimate the value of this liability and how it should be recorded in the financial statements. The major concern for the cash-flow analyst is the effect of the liability on cash flows and the long-term solvency of the firm, as well as adjusting the current leverage ratio.

Initially, firms reported no liability for pension obligations and included in the income statement an expense that was equal to the actual payment to existing retirees during the accounting period. This practice was stopped by APB Opinion No. 8, which required firms to estimate their liability to employees and disclose in a footnote to the financial statements some information about that liability. The next example will help you to better understand the nature of the liability and the associated accounting.

Example:

This a hypothetical example, although many firms have most features employed in this example. The pension plan is a defined-benefit plan. It promises that employees who reach retirement age (65 years) will get, for each year of service, annual compensation that is equal to 2 percent of their average annual salary during the five-year period prior to retirement. Thus an employee who worked for the firm 30 years is entitled to 60 percent of his or her average annual salary prior to retirement. These benefits will continue until the employees dies, at which point only 50 percent of the benefits will be paid to the surviving spouse. The plan has other restrictions. For example, employees who leave the firm before they have spent at least five years with the firm are not eligible to any pension benefits. Employees who remain in the employment of the firm for more than five years but for less than 10 years will get only 50 percent of their pension benefits when they reach retirement age, even if they are no longer employed by the firm. After 10 years, employees are eligible for 100 percent of the earned pension benefits when they reach retirement age, even if they are no longer employed by the firm.

Several factors affect the estimation of the firm's liability under this plan. First, the firm has to consider the current age of employees so that it will know how many years are left before pension benefits begin. Second, the firm has to estimate the life expectancy of the employees because it is *not* necessary to accrue pension obligations for employees who will not remain with the firm for at least five years and only 50 percent of the benefits for employees who remain with the firm between five and ten years. The firm then should estimate the average annual salary of the employee on which pension benefits will be based.[19] Finally, these future payments should be discounted to estimate the present value

---

[19] In some pension plans, payments received from Social Security reduce payments to employees. In such cases, it is important to estimate the future level of payments from the Social Security system and how they integrate with the company's plan.

of the pension obligation. The estimated liability is called *actuarial present value of pension benefits* because actuarial assumptions are made in estimating future payments under the plan.

Typically, when firms initiate pension plans, or when firms make amendments to existing pension plans (e.g., increasing the rate of compensation from 1.5 to 2 percent for each year of service), the benefits are applied retroactively to employees who were eligible for these benefits when the plan was adopted or amended. Thus, in addition to the continuous accumulation of pension benefits for current services by employees, firms may be liable to pay pension benefits to employees for past and prior services. These lump-sum additions to the pension liability may be spread over future periods by amortizing the liability for prior services over the remaining time until employees retire.

As already explained, the firm makes contributions to the pension fund, and fund assets are invested further to yield greater assets in the future.[20] Thus, at any point in time, the pension plan will have a liability for future pension benefits and assets from which this liability can be paid in the future. One describes the fund as *underfunded* when liabilities exceed assets and as *overfunded* when assets exceed the liabilities.

The funding status of the plan may change every year. The firm may increase contributions to the plan, or investments may yield a rate of return beyond that which was expected initially. Also, there may be actuarial gains and losses that are caused by changes in the actuarial assumptions that underlie the estimated liability. For example, when the turnover rate of employees surpasses expectations, the pension liability decreases because fewer employees will reach the point at which benefits vest, which is the point when benefits will have to be paid even if the employee leaves the firm before retirement.[21] Another example is when employees die earlier than the actuarial projection, known as the *mortality assumption*. This reduces future benefits as well as current liabilities, thus producing an actuarial gain. Such gains and losses are not incorporated into income in the year in which they occur but are amortized over future years if they are material.

APB Opinion No. 8 (1968) required firms to estimate pension liability using an acceptable actuarial method and to include in the pension expense an amortization of

---

[20] Sometimes the contribution to the pension fund will not be in cash but will be in the form of real estate properties or even the firm's own common stock. In an effort to reduce its liability in its underfunded pension plans, General Motors contributed its own common stock to its pension fund.

[21] For the pension liability, one cannot necessarily use the rule of thumb, according to which increases in liabilities are economically bad for the firm, and decreases are necessarily beneficial to the firm. For example, an increase in the turnover rate will decrease pension liability, but it also means that the firm loses skilled, trained employees. Thus the economic loss from the higher turnover ratio actually may exceed the economic benefits from reduced pension payments in the future.

prior service costs. It also required firms to disclose in a footnote to the financial statements the unfunded vested benefit obligation and pension expense for the period. Unfunded vested benefits are equal to the actuarial present value of pension obligations that will be paid whether or not employees remain with the firm minus fund assets that are available for payments to employees. In addition, the SEC required firms to disclose the unfunded prior service cost.

In 1976, the FASB changed the accounting and disclosure requirements as they relate to the pension fund. First, fund assets were required to be disclosed using the fair market value of those assets, not their accounting carrying cost. This usually tended to increase the value of fund assets because equity and real estate investments, typically, were understated when historical cost values were used. Second, the FASB required additional disclosure about pension plans in a footnote to the financial statements. Firms had to supply information about the actuarial present value of their vested and nonvested pension benefits about the fair market value of pension plan assets, about the average discount rate used in the estimation of the liability, and about the projected rate of return on pension plan investments. Still, no liabilities or assets were incorporated into the financial statements by these pronouncements.

In 1985, the FASB issued SFAS 87, which imposed new accounting and disclosure requirements on firms. SFAS 87 required for the first time the recording of a pension liability on the balance sheet under certain conditions (described below). It also broadened the disclosure in the footnotes to the financial statements. The standard became effective in 1987, although some firms chose to adopt it earlier. Let's examine some of these major changes.

Probably the most significant effect of this standard is the requirement to use the "projected benefit obligations" instead of the "accumulated benefit obligations" in some tests employed by the standard and in disclosure of the liability. The difference between *projected* and *accumulated* benefits relates to the forecast of future salary increases. Recall that a pension plan usually sets a formula for pension benefits based on the average salary at some point close to retirement. Naturally, the longer the service is with the firm, the more likely the employee is to have a higher salary owing to promotions and salary increases as a result of inflation. Thus, in estimating the actuarial present value of *projected* benefit obligations, the actuary takes into account expected future salary increases. However, to estimate the actuarial present value of *accumulated* pension benefits, the actuary uses current salary levels. The difference between the two measures is substantial; for the average firm, it increases the actuarial present value of the liability by about 20 to 40 percent.

If the analyst determines that the projected benefit obligation understates the true liability, such as those instances where the workforce is growing, an adjustment should be made to the balance sheet to reflect the additional liability. Shareholders' equity should be adjusted by the difference between the amount accrued on the balance sheet and the net amount of either the over- or underfunded obligation, net of any tax effect.

The second major change in SFAS 87 is the requirement to accrue a liability *on the balance sheet* that is equal to the excess of the actuarial present value of accumulated pension benefits over plan assets. Thus, if a firm's actuarial present value of accumulated pension benefits is larger than the value of plan assets to satisfy this liability, the difference is shown as a liability on the balance sheet. This requirement becomes effective for firms with large shortfalls in their pension plans and is known as the *minimum liability requirement*.

SFAS 87 also required firms to disclose information in a footnote to the financial statements, some of which is just a carryover of prior FASB pronouncements, but most of which is new and broadened information. The required information generally is of three types: (1) information about pension plan assets and liabilities, whether incorporated on the balance sheet or not, (2) information that provides additional details about the pension expense for the period, and (3) information about the pension plan, funding policy, and assumptions used in estimating the liability. Later I will provide a description of these information items.

The standard required firms to disclose information about the actuarial present value of accumulated pension benefits and of projected pension benefits. Since the old disclosure requirements are still in effect, the pension liability is broken down into vested and nonvested benefits. The footnote also discloses the fair market value of pension plan assets so that analysts could determine if the pension plan is overfunded or underfunded. The standard also required firms to reconcile the funding status or the amount of over- or underfunding with the pension plan assets/liabilities that were not yet recognized and incorporated on the balance sheet.

The standard required firms to disclose information about the major components of the pension expense for the accounting period. The first component is the normal service cost for the period. This represents the additional pension benefits that employees earned during the period simply because they spent one additional year of service with the firm. Recall that the pension plan has a formula that provides pension benefits according to the number of service years with the firm. Thus this additional year entitles employees to greater pension benefits, and the actuarial present value of those additional benefits is the normal service cost.

The second component of the pension expense is the interest expense. This component represents the fact that the balance of the pension liability as of the beginning of the year has come one year closer to maturity. As is true of debt, when a loan is one year closer to maturity, its present value increases, and the increase in the present value of the loan from the beginning of the year to its end represents interest expense. Similarly, since the actuarial present value of the pension liability that existed at the beginning of the year is larger at the end of the year, the increase in the present value is considered interest expense and is shown as the second component of the pension expense for the year.

The third component of the pension expense is actually a pension revenue in most cases—the rate of return on pension plan assets. As a mirror image of the interest expense on the pension plan liability at the beginning of the year, the return on plan assets represents the interest revenue on assets that existed at the beginning of the year. Recall that in most cases the pension plan will have assets in the fund at the beginning of the period. These assets were intended to offset the liability that existed at the beginning of the period. Just as we recognize the increase in the present value of the liability over the year as interest expense, we should recognize as revenue the increase in plan assets owing to profitable investments during that same year.

The final component of the pension expense in the footnote to the financial statements is the amortization and deferral of various amounts. Among the amounts that need to be amortized and included in the pension expense are items such as actuarial gains and losses that are incorporated into the balance sheet over a period of time.[22] Other items that will be amortized are prior service costs owing to adoption and amendments of pension plans and the transition amount. Also, if the pension fund had an actual return on assets that exceeded or fell short of the assumed long-term rate of return, the excess (or shortfall) is deferred and is amortized slowly if it exceeds a minimum amount. Finally, firms may from time to time decide to provide current retirees with benefits increases. These also would be added to the pension expense.

The last type of information disclosed in the footnote on pensions is about assumptions made to estimate the pension liability, a description of the pension plans and pension formulas, and the funding policy of the firm. For example, the firm usually will disclose the discount rates, the rate of return on plan assets, and the rate at which salaries are expected to grow in the future. Interestingly enough, most firms assume that the rate of return on plan assets and the rate used to discount the pension liability are higher than the rate at which salaries are expected to grow. Thus employees in these firms are estimated to have an erosion of their real earnings power.

The firm usually describes its pension plans in general terms: who is eligible for participation in the plan, the major elements of the plan formula, and any other plans that are not standard U.S. plans. Thus information is provided separately about foreign pension plans and about multiemployer plans within the United

[22] SFAS 87 allowed firms to amortize actuarial gains and losses only if they exceed a certain minimum amount. This is the *corridor* approach adopted by this standard.

States (multiemployer plans are common to all employees of a particular union regardless of the specific employer; all employers are responsible together for pension liabilities and assets). The firm also will describe its funding policy.

SFAS 158, *Employers' Accounting for Defined Benefit Pension and Other Postretirement Benefits*, effective December 31, 2006, requires an employer to recognize the funded status of each of its defined pension and postretirement benefit plans as a net asset or liability in its statement of financial position with an offsetting amount in accumulated other comprehensive income and to recognize changes in that funded status in the year in which changes occur through comprehensive income. Following the adoption of SFAS 158, additional minimum pension liabilities and related intangible assets are no longer recognized. Adoption of the statement does not affect cash flows.

Although SFAS 158 requires a company to recognize the underfunded status of defined-benefit plans as a liability on its balance sheet and to recognize changes in that funded status in the year that such changes occur, the ultimate liability is still uncertain because it can really be determined only when the last retiree is paid in full. In my determination of operating cash flow, I adjust cash flow from operations if the periodic accrual differs from the actual contribution.

Beginning in 2008, resulting from the Pension Protection Act of 2006, an employer must fund 100% of a liability of its defined pension plan over nor greater than 7 years. The funding shortfall must take place each year. By 2008 the shortfall is recalculated each year and to the extent any additional shortfall has taken place, the total must be contributed to the plan over a new 7 year period. This is in addition to the normal costs that must be funded.

In December 2008, the FASB issued SFAS 132(R)–1, *Employers' Disclosures about Postretirement Benefit Plan Assets*. This requires additional disclosures about plan assets for sponsors of defined-benefit pension and postretirement plans, including expanded information regarding investment strategies, major categories of plan assets, and concentrations of risk within plan assets. We shall see how this plays out in the years ahead, but I believe that the only true way to complete transparency is to make public the complete actuarial valuation. The information that is currently included in and part of financial statements relates to the current closed group of employees. For defined-benefit plans that have a growing business, the difference in the liabilities thus can be substantial.

To summarize terms found in the pension footnote that are important to the cash-flow analyst:

1. *Service cost.* This is the increase in the pension benefit obligation owing to current employees resulting from an added year of service.
2. *Interest cost.* The interest expense related to the pension benefit obligation, which is determined by the settlement rate.

3. *Settlement rate.* The benefits if the plan were closed out today.
4. *Discount rate.* Discount rates are used to calculate the present value of pension obligations and the service and interest cost portions of net periodic pension cost. The discount rate is intended to represent the rate at which pension benefit obligations could be settled by purchase of an annuity contract. A number of measures can be used as bases for determining the discount rate, including a current annuity rate, current Pension Benefit Guaranty Corporation (PBGC) rates, or available rates on high-quality fixed-income investments. This is an important variable because it applies to all employees, and a small change will have a large effect on the liability. The higher the discount rate, the less conservative is the assumption.
5. *Actual and estimated return on plan assets.* The actual return on plan assets is computed as beginning value plus contributions minus benefits paid. Estimated return is calculated as estimated return multiplied by the beginning value. The difference between the two is amortized or can be satisfied through an additional employer contribution. Owing to swings in the financial markets, actuaries smooth investment performance over a period of years, with the difference between the estimated and actual returns placed into unexpected gains and losses. The expected return on assets is a negative component of net periodic pension cost; that is, it lowers the cost.
6. *Unrecognized gains and losses.* This represents deviations of actual amounts from estimated amounts. The entity is required to amortize the unrecognized gains and losses only if they exceed 10 percent of the greater of the pension benefit obligation or market related value (both as of the beginning of the year). Such gains or losses then are amortized over the remaining service life of the active employee workforce. The pension benefit obligation is that amount due to vested and nonvested employees at their retirement salary. This differs from the accumulated benefit obligation, which is the amount owed based on current salary.

The importance of the funding and actuarial methodologies are extremely significant to the cash-flow and credit analyst because liberal assumptions may be hiding large prospective cash requirements the entity is ill-prepared to make. Even if the entity has the financial flexibility to contribute additional amounts of cash into the plan, it represents cash that is unavailable for distribution to shareholders, place into the business to generate additional free cash flow, or leave as surplus equity. Also, since the periodic cost may differ from the actual contribution, the underfunding, if it were to continue and not be offset by an increase in the market value of the plan's assets, would result in a large legal liability.

Defined-benefit obligations for retirees, including pensions and health care coverage, and other forms of deferred compensation are financial obligations that must be paid over time, just as any legal obligation must be serviced, so typically they should be included in debt ratios if they are deemed to result in a probable outflow of capital outside the normal historical funding pattern. Contributions within the normal funding pattern should not be included as part of total debt and represent an expense similar to compensation. A company that wishes to pre-fund its obligation, or part of it, offsets the financial burden and to that extent may understate its normalized operating cash flow.

Campbell Soup contributed $70 million into its retirement plans during 2009 and expected the cash contribution to rise to $80 million in 2010. It states in its 10K filing that the cash payment will increase owing, in part, to a lowering of its discount rate from 6.87 to 6 percent. Even for a company as large as Campbell Soup, with $7.6 billion in revenue, $80 million represents 7.4 percent of pretax income and 10.9 percent of after-tax income. The discount rate change thus has important ramifications for investors and creditors, increasing the total debt of the firm while affecting cash flows with the rising contributions. Credit agencies often place peers on equal actuarial footing.

To the extent that certain of an entity's actual experiences (e.g., mortality rate, changes in Social Security level) are below those assumed, it could be overfunding its pension or postretirement obligations, and operating and free cash flow will be understated. The firm would have the option of adjusting future contributions downward. If actual experience were worse than planned, cash flows would have been overstated.

Example:

Of interest with regard to 3M is the additional substantial cash outlay required to improve the funding status of its pension and postretirement plans resulting from the decline in the financial markets. Since pension and other postretirement actuarial methods allow for various market-value smoothing techniques, the full brunt of a particular year's investment performance may not result in immediate stepped-up contributions. The analyst must review the pension and other postretirement footnote to determine the reasonableness of the size of the company contribution in relation to any liability, and annual outflows from the fund for, as seen for 3M in Table 6-12, a contribution can represent a very significant cash expense, even during years the plans' assets are meeting actuarial expectations.

Additionally, any large change in the investment returns of the financial assets during the course of the fiscal year would affect the following year's contribution level. A gain in the firm's operating performance could be offset by the increased funding to its plans.

During 2008, 3M's plan assets fell despite total contributions in the prior three years exceeding $1.1 billion. Thus it should be presumed that if plan returns for 2009 were to be disappointing relative to their actuarial assumptions, including plan experience (i.e., return on plan assets, new hiring, changes in plan benefits, etc.), another large contribution would be necessary. Fortunately for 3M and plan participants, 2009 was a strong year for the financial markets.

TABLE 6-12

3M Statement of Cash Flows

3M COMPANY AND SUBSIDIARIES
CONSOLIDATED STATEMENT OF CASH FLOWS
Years Ended December 31
(Millions)

	2008	2007	2006
Cash Flows from Operating Activities			
Net income	**$3,460**	$4,096	$3,851
Adjustments to reconcile net income to net cash provided by operating activities			
Depreciation and amortization	**1,153**	1,072	1,079
Company pension and postretirement contributions	**(474)**	(379)	(385)
Company pension and postretirement expense	**105**	255	440
Stock-based compensation expense	**202**	228	200
(Gain)/loss from sale of businesses	**23**	(849)	(1,074)
Deferred income taxes	**118**	11	(316)
Excess tax benefits from stock-based compensation	**(21)**	(74)	(60)
Changes in assets and liabilities			
Accounts receivable	**197**	(35)	(103)
Inventories	**(127)**	(54)	(309)
Accounts payable	**(224)**	(4)	68
Accrued income taxes	**(162)**	(45)	138
Product and other insurance receivables and claims	**153**	158	58
Other, net	**130**	(105)	252
Net cash provided by operating activities	**4,533**	4,275	3,839
Cash Flows from Investing Activities			
Purchases of property, plant, and equipment (PPE)	**(1,471)**	(1,422)	(1,168)
Proceeds from sale of PPE and other assets	**87**	103	49
Acquisitions, net of cash acquired	**(1,394)**	(539)	(888)
Purchases of marketable securities and investments	**(2,211)**	(8,194)	(3,253)
Proceeds from sale of marketable securities and investments	**1,810**	6,902	2,287
Proceeds from maturities of marketable securities	**692**	886	304
Proceeds from sale of businesses	**88**	897	1,209
Net cash used in investing activities	**(2,399)**	(1,367)	(1,460)

	2008	2007	2006
Cash Flows from Financing Activities			
Change in short-term debt, net	**361**	(1,222)	882
Repayment of debt (maturities greater than 90 days)	**(1,080)**	(1,580)	(440)
Proceeds from debt (maturities greater than 90 days)	**1,756**	4,024	693
Purchases of treasury stock	**(1,631)**	(3,239)	(2,351)
Reissuances of treasury stock	**289**	796	523
Dividends paid to stockholders	**(1,398)**	(1,380)	(1,376)
Distributions to minority interests	**(23)**	(20)	(38)
Excess tax benefits from stock-based compensation	**21**	74	60
Other, net	**(61)**	—	(14)
Net cash used in financing activities	**(1,766)**	(2,547)	(2,061)
Effect of exchange rate changes on cash and cash equivalents	**(415)**	88	57
Net increase/(decrease) in cash and cash equivalents	**(47)**	449	375
Cash and cash equivalents at beginning of year	**1,896**	1,447	1,072
Cash and cash equivalents at end of year	**$1,849**	$1,896	$1,447

I now show both 3M's pension and postretirement footnote and a template (Table 6-13) that summarizes relevant information the investor can use when evaluating a plan. It is apparent that 3M's plans are underfunded by $2.2 billion, although the status is subject to very wide swings. At the end of 2006, the plans ended the year $2.3 billion overfunded and were overfunded at the end of 2007.

While 3M shows an accumulated benefits obligation of $15.5 billion, it also reveals in a footnote an ending projected benefit obligation of $14.4 billion.

3M reveals the following footnoted information:

> In September 2006, the FASB issued SFAS No. 158, "Employers' Accounting for Defined Benefit Pension and Other Postretirement Plans, an Amendment of FASB Statements No. 87, 88, 106 and 132(R)." This standard eliminated the requirement for a "minimum pension liability adjustment" that was previously required under SFAS No. 87 and required employers to recognize the underfunded or overfunded status of a defined benefit plan as an asset or liability in its statement of financial position. In 2006, as a result of the implementation of SFAS No. 158, the company recognized an after-tax decrease in accumulated other comprehensive income of $1.187 billion and $513 million for the U.S. and International pension benefit plans, respectively, and $218 million for the postretirement benefit plans.

In its pension footnote, 3M reports that it made discretionary contributions of $421 million to its pension plan in 2008, with its contribution for international growing at a much quicker rate. Aside from actuarial experience, the analyst must possess a complete understanding of plan investments, asset allocation, current financial market levels, and potential claims on plan assets to fully grasp the current funding status and size of a liability. If 3M's contributions for its international employees continues to grow at its current rate, in three years it will be greater than its U.S. contributions and

TABLE 6-13

3M Pension Summary

	Annual Data as of:				
	2008	**2007**	**2006**	**2005**	**2004**
Benefit obligation					
Accumulated benefit obligation	13,525	14,064	13,316	12,716	11,706
Pension plan assets					
Beginning plan assets	15,520	14,030	12,625	11,727	9,825
Actual return	(2,367)	1,564	1,397	1,242	1,846
Employer contributions	421	376	348	654	596
Participant contributions	5	4	4	9	11
Benefits paid (−)	800	740	676	659	731
Other	(514)	286	332	(348)	180
Plan assets	12,265	15,520	14,030	12,625	11,727
Pension-funded status	(2,167)	449	(569)	2,332	2,043
Balance sheet reconciliation					
Long-term asset	36	1,378	395		
Current liability (−)	36	33	31	0	0
Long-term liability (−)	2,167	896	933		
Pension-funded status	(2,167)	449	(569)	2,332	2,043
AOCI-related					
Unrecognized prior service cost	(18)	23	(1)	7	6
Other adjustments	4,957	2,095	2,929	3,636	3,155
Net pension cost (credit)					
Service cost	312	317	320	279	265
Interest cost	849	796	722	679	649
Return on assets	(1,194)	(1,130)	(1,009)	(882)	(829)
Other periodic cost components, net	122	207	314	255	240
Periodic pension cost	89	190	347	331	325
Pension expense					
Pension expense	103	190	347	331	325
Assumptions used for pension plans					
Discount rate					
Discount rate	6.1%	6.0%	5.8%	5.5%	5.8%
Conpensation rate—obligation					
Compensation rate increase	4.3%	4.3%	4.3%	4.3%	4.3%
Asset return rate—periodic cost					
Asset return rate	8.5%	8.8%	8.8%	8.8%	9.0%
Periodic cost discount rate					
Discount rate	6.0%	5.8%	5.5%	5.8%	6.0%

Source: 3M Financial Filings, Research Insight.

represent a considerable percentage of the total firm's cash flows. In fact, international growth in the benefits area deserves special recognition because large multinational employers have not had the success in bringing down those overseas costs as they have in the United States. This step-up for overseas employee funding is to be expected for entities whose international operations are seeing their cash flows grow more quickly than their U.S. operations. Currently, the pension contribution accounts for approximately 10 percent of 3M's operating cash flows.

As investors saw with General Motors, older-line companies can be suffocated by outsized employee benefits. And as reported, 3M had a considerable loss in its plans during 2008, even after raising the discount rate from 6 to 6.14 percent. Despite 3M's investment-grade credit rating, which is confirmed with CT Capital's credit model, the unfunded pension liability represents an item that deserves careful watching because its funding is responsible for consuming a large amount of cash that might cause the company to miss cash-flow estimates (affecting its stock price), even if the liability does not turn out to represent a threat to survivability.

	Qualified and Nonqualified Pension Benefits				**Postretirement**	
	United States		**International**		**Benefits**	
(Millions)	**2008**	**2007**	**2008**	**2007**	**2008**	**2007**
Change in benefit obligation						
Benefit obligation at beginning of year	**$10,215**	$10,149	**$4,856**	$4,450	**$1,809**	$1,841
Acquisitions	**22**	—	**—**	3	—	—
Service cost	**192**	192	**120**	125	**53**	57
Interest cost	**597**	568	**252**	228	**100**	104
Participant contributions	—	—	**5**	4	**56**	47
Foreign exchange rate changes	—	—	**(620)**	337	**(20)**	14
Plan amendments	**9**	18	**(9)**	17	**(148)**	(98)
Actuarial (gain) loss	**(40)**	(154)	**(369)**	(114)	**(93)**	(16)
Medicare Part D reimbursement	—	—	—	—	**12**	10
Benefit payments	**(606)**	(565)	**(194)**	(175)	**(158)**	(159)
Settlements, curtailments, special termination benefits, and other	**6**	7	**(4)**	(19)	**—**	9
Benefit obligation at end of year	**$10,395**	$10,215	**$4,037**	$4,856	**$1,611**	$1,809
Change in plan assets						
Fair value of plan assets at beginning of year	**$11,096**	$10,060	**$4,424**	$3,970	**$1,355**	$1,337
Acquisitions	**13**	—	—	1	—	—
Actual return on plan assets	**(1,495)**	1,376	**(872)**	188	**(377)**	127
Company contributions	**235**	225	**186**	151	**53**	3
Participant contributions	—	—	**5**	4	**56**	47
Foreign exchange rate changes	—	—	**(527)**	300	—	—
Benefit payments	**(606)**	(565)	**(194)**	(175)	**(158)**	(159)
Settlements, curtailments, special termination benefits, and other	—	—	**—**	(15)	—	—
Fair value of plan assets at end of year	**$9,243**	$11,096	**$3,022**	$4,424	**$929**	$1,355
Funded status at end of year	**$(1,152)**	$881	**$(1,015)**	$(432)	**$(682)**	$(454)

Source: 3M 2008 10K.

Example:

Aluminum Co. of America, Alcoa, is the largest manufacturer of aluminum and aluminum products in the United States. In its December 2008 financial statements, it disclosed the following information about its comprehensive income, which includes its prior service cost and change in recognized losses owing to the fall in the company's pension plan assets. Also seen in comprehensive income are the effects of hedging activities and fair-value accounting.

As is seen in Tables 6-14, 6-15, and 6-16, Alcoa's pension fund also suffered from market-value losses during 2008 that could have large funding implications. The beginning of the reporting year saw the plan reporting \$10.6 billion in assets, and resulting from negative investment returns of about 20 percent (\$2,058 loss/\$10,562 beginning market value), benefits paid of \$769 million, and employer contributions of \$523 million, the plan saw the end of the year with \$7.9 billion in assets. This resulted in a net recognized liability of \$2.8 billion versus just \$933 million the prior year. If the plan were to experience another year of negative returns, it would be expected that the 2009 contribution would need to be considerably larger than the \$523 million in 2008, thus having a material negative cash impact. On the other hand, a rebound in the financial markets would save the company from making such an increased payment, benifitting operating cash flows. The pension fund and other postretirement benefit accounts, as we have seen through these examples, can be a cause of major cash-flow uncertainty.

What are the implications of the pension plan's liabilities and assets as they relate to total debt and free cash flow? The firm may have an underfunded pension plan, and the liability that is recorded on the balance sheet (if one is recorded at all) may be smaller than the projected benefit obligation. In such cases, as stated, the cash-flow analyst could (if not brought on by unusual factors or to be settled with company stock) add to total debt the difference between the projected benefit obligations and the pension liability net of any tax effect. This additional liability is considered an off-balance-sheet liability, just like operating leases, and can be added to debt ratios. If the firm has a growing workforce, the liability is forced by market conditions, and the analyst deems the funding policy otherwise sound, the debt should not be added to total liabilities. When reviewing the pension and other postretirement footnotes, plans that are overfunded could see contributions eliminated, with that cash redirected into the underfunded plans, thus having a net neutral effect of cash outlays.[23] Bear in mind, though, that companies are no longer required to report a breakout of over- and underfunded plans.

TABLE 6-14

Alcoa: Actuarial Plan Assumptions

	2008	2007	2006
Discount rate	6.20%	5.95%	5.70%
Expected long-term rate of return on plan assets	9.00	9.00	9.00
Rate of compensation increase	4.00	4.00	4.00

[23] Many actuaries do not agree with this approach, believing that future salary levels are (1) in conflict with Concept Statement 6 and (2) misrepresent the value of the contract. Moreover, (3) including future salary levels in pension liabilities does not provide shareholders with relevant information about the current value of their obligations.

TABLE 6-15

Statement of Shareholders' Equity: Alcoa, December 30, 2008

December 31,	Comprehensive income	Preferred stock	Common stock	Additional capital	Retained earnings	Treasury stock	Accumulated other comprehensive loss	Total shareholders' equity
Balance at end of 2007		55	925	5,774	13,039	(3,440)	(337)	16,016
Comprehensive loss:								
Net loss	$(74)				(74)			(74)
Other comprehensive (loss) income:								
Change in unrecognized losses and prior service cost related to pension and postretirement benefit plans, net of tax benefit and minority interests of $799	(1,382)							
Foreign currency translation adjustments	(1,457)							
Unrealized losses on available-for-sale securities, net of tax benefit of $233	(432)							
Unrecognized gains on derivatives, net of tax expense and minority interests of $180 (X):								
Net change from periodic revaluations	282							
Net amount reclassified to income	157							
Net unrecognized gains on derivatives	439							
Comprehensive loss	$(2,906)						(2,832)	(2,832)
Cash dividends: Preferred @ $3.75 per share					(2)			(2)
Common @ $0.68 per share					(554)			(554)
Stock-based compensation				94				94
Common stock issued: compensation plans				(18)		196		178
Repurchase of common stock						(1,082)		(1,082)
Cumulative effect adjustment due to the adoption of the measurement date provisions of SFAS 158, net of tax and minority interests					(9)			(9)
Balance at end of 2008		$55	$925	$5,850	$12,400	$(4,326)	$(3,169)*	$11,735

*Comprised of unrecognized losses and prior service cost, net, related to pension and postretirement benefit plans of $(2,690); unrealized foreign currency translation adjustments of $74; unrealized losses on available-for-sale securities of $(428); and unrecognized net losses on derivatives of $(125); all net of tax and applicable minority interests.

Alcoa reported in its footnotes that in 2008 it increased the discount rate by 25 basis points. This would have the effect of reducing the accumulated benefits obligation and is not normally recommended when the funding status is deteriorating. If the discount rate were left unchanged, the net charge in comprehensive income, as well as the company's contribution to the plans, would have been greater. In the prior year, Alcoa also increased the discount rate on plan assets by 25 basis points. *The discount rate is a more powerful influence than is the salary assumption because the latter applies only to the active workforce.* The expected return on plan assets was kept at 9 percent, but as Alcoa claims in its footnotes, its 20-year return has exceeded this expectation.

It is also important to track the spread between the discount rate and the expected return on plan assets. As we see in the case of Alcoa, the spread decreased from 3.2 percentage points in 2006 to 2.8 percentage points, a red flag. The spread also would depend on plan history, age of the workforce, Social Security integration level, mortality experience, and so on.

Alcoa reports that the adoption of SFAS 158 resulted in the following impact: a reduction of $119 million in existing prepaid pension costs and intangible assets, the recognition of $1,234 million in accrued pension and postretirement liabilities, and a charge of $1,353 million ($877 million after taxes) to accumulated other comprehensive loss.

TABLE 6-16

Alcoa: Pension Plan and Other Postretirement Benefits

Obligations and Funded Status

	Pension Benefits		**Postretirement Benefits**	
December 31:	**2008**	**2007**	**2008**	**2007**
Change in benefit obligation				
Benefit obligation at beginning of year	$11,601	$11,614	$3,260	$3,511
Service cost	185	200	25	28
Interest cost	693	666	193	195
Amendments	11	67	—	(27)
Actuarial gains	(457)	(311)	(16)	(153)
Divestitures	(71)	(5)	(58)	(5)
Settlements	(27)	(62)	—	—
Curtailments	(2)	—	3	(9)
Benefits paid, net of participants' contributions	(771)	(710)	(308)	(303)
Medicare Part D subsidy receipts	—	—	29	20
Other transfers, net	23	(51)	—	—
Exchange rate	(420)	193	(7)	3
Benefit obligation at end of year	$10,765	$11,601	$3,121	$3,260
Change in plan assets				
Fair value of plan assets at beginning of year	$10,652	$10,097	$203	$189
Actual return on plan assets	(2,058)	836	(41)	14
Employer contributions	523	374	—	—

December 31:	Pension Benefits 2008	Pension Benefits 2007	Postretirement Benefits 2008	Postretirement Benefits 2007
Participants' contributions	33	36	—	—
Benefits paid	(769)	(716)	—	—
Administrative expenses	(22)	(19)	—	—
Divestitures	(46)	(3)	—	—
Settlements	(27)	(64)	—	—
Other transfers, net	18	(51)	—	—
Exchange rate	(396)	162	—	—
Fair value of plan assets at end of year	$7,908	$10,652	$162	$203
Funded status	$(2,857)	$(949)	$(2,959)	$(3,057)
Amounts attributed to joint venture partners	14	16	9	9
Net funded status	$(2,843)	$(933)	$(2,950)	$(3,048)
Amounts recognized in the consolidated balance sheet consist of:				
Noncurrent assets	$122	$216	$—	$—
Current liabilities	(24)	(24)	(220)	(295)
Noncurrent liabilities	(2,941)	(1,098)	(2,730)	(2,753)
Liabilities of operations held for sale	—	(27)	—	—
Net amount recognized	$(2,843)	$(933)	$(2,950)	$(3,048)
Amounts recognized in accumulated other comprehensive loss consist of:				
Net actuarial loss	$3,650	$1,385	$724	$784
Prior service cost (benefit)	89	118	(143)	(150)
Total, before tax effect	3,739	1,503	581	634
Less: Amounts attributed to joint venture partners	13	11	2	2
Net amount recognized, before tax effect	$3,726	$1,492	$579	$632
Other changes in plan assets and benefit obligations recognized in other comprehensive loss (income) consist of:				
Net loss (gain)	$2,364	$(344)	$(16))	$(160)
Amortization of net loss	(99)	(127)	(44)	(55)
Prior service (benefit) cost	(11)	67	(4)	(30)
Amortization of prior service (cost) benefit	(18)	(15)	11	3
Total, before tax effect	2,236	(419)	(53)	(242)
Less: Amounts attributed to joint venture partners	2	—	—	(2)
Net amount recognized, before tax effect	$2,234	$(419)	$(53)	$(240)

Pension Plan Benefit Obligations

	Pension Benefits	
	2008	**2007**
The projected benefit obligation and accumulated benefit obligation for all defined benefit pension plans was as follows:		
Projected benefit obligation	$10,765	$11,601
Accumulated benefit obligation	10,485	11,216
The aggregate projected benefit obligation and fair value of plan assets for pension plans with projected benefit obligations in excess of plan assets was as follows:		
Projected benefit obligation	10,233	9,933
Fair value of plan assets	7,256	8,771
The aggregate accumulated benefit obligation and fair value of plan assets for pension plans with accumulated benefit obligations in excess of plan assets was as follows:		
Accumulated benefit obligation	9,660	9,550
Fair value of plan assets	6,923	8,771

Components of Net Periodic Benefit Costs

	Pension Benefits			Postretirement Benefits		
	2008	**2007**	**2006**	**2008**	**2007**	**2006**
Service cost	$166	$200	$209	$24	$28	$32
Interest cost	678	666	628	193	195	208
Expected return on plan assets	(805)	(787)	(740)	(18)	(17)	(15)
Amortization of prior service cost (benefit)	18	15	14	(11)	(3)	10
Recognized actuarial loss	99	127	118	44	55	63
Settlements	20	—	—	—	—	—
Curtailments	2	—	—	9	(3)	—
Net periodic benefit costs	$178	$221	$229	$241	$255	$298

Amounts Expected to be Recognized in Net Periodic Benefit Costs

	Pension Benefits	Postretirement Benefits
	2009	**2009**
Prior service cost (benefit) recognition	$16	$(11)
Actuarial loss recognition	104	51

Example:

A sensitivity analysis is useful because it reveals how changes in actuarial assumptions would affect future contributions. Siemens, a German electronics company, in its 20F reveals the potential impact on its following year's pension costs recorded in its income statement (NPBC) owing to various scenarios.

Pension Benefits: Sensitivity Analysis

A one-percentage-point change of the established assumptions mentioned above, used for the calculation of the NPBC for fiscal 2010, or a change in the fair value of plan assets of 500, as of September 30, 2009, respectively, would result in the following increase (decrease) of the fiscal 2010 NPBC:

	Effect on NPBC 2010 Due to a	
	One-Percentage-Point/€500 Increase	**One-Percentage-Point/€500 Decrease**
Discount rate	18	(29)
Expected return on plan assets	(195)	195
Rate of compensation increase	26	(23)
Rate of pension progression	139	(109)
Fair value of plan assets	(32)	32

Increases and decreases in the discount rate, rate of compensation increase, and rate of pension progression which are used in determining the DBO do not have a symmetrical effect on NPBC primarily due to the compound interest effect created when determining the net present value of the future pension benefit. If more than one of the assumptions were changed simultaneously, the cumulative impact would not necessarily be the same as if only one assumption was changed in isolation.

Source: Siemens Aktiengesellschaft 20F.

Example:

In some cases, the pension plan is overfunded to such a degree that the plan has more assets than what is forecast by its projected benefit obligation. In such cases, the cash-flow analyst could increase net assets of the firm and net equity by the difference between these two amounts, net of any tax effect. The difference represents additional assets that will save future cash contributions into the plan by the firm aside from benefiting the capital structure.

The analyst must establish *whether the company under analysis has an appropriate asset allocation given its funding status, cash flows, credit strength, financial flexibility, growth in workforce, and time horizon of its liabilities. The analyst also must determine the company's success in managing the plans assets.*

As seen for L. S. Starrett Company, a manufacturer of precision tools and electronic gauges, the 2008 economic recession moved its plan from overfunded to underfunded status. Primarily because the company's domestic defined-benefit plan had been overfunded, retirement benefits in total generated approximately $1.6 million, $2.8 million, and $1.1 million of noncash income in fiscal years 2009, 2008, and 2007, respectively. The company's plans were, in essence, a profit center. The company shifted its asset allocation during 2008 as plan cash rose to 6 percent, debt investments rose by 150 percent, and the equity allocation fell from 70 to 41 percent. It appears as if the management of Starrett feared the impact of further equity market deterioration as a basis for changing its plan asset allocation. Since the equity market rebounded during 2009, one could argue that management overreacted. However, since Starrett's business was quite negatively affected by the recession, the move to reign in risk probably was warranted.

Also provided is Starrett's balance sheet, which shows the transition of overfunded to underfunding status and the commensurate effect on the capital structure.

Domestic and U.K. Plans Combined

The status of these defined-benefit plans, including the ESOP, is as follows (in thousands):

	2009	2008	2007
Change in benefit obligation			
Benefit obligation at beginning of year	$109,837	$120,849	$115,485
Service cost	2,090	2,376	2,727
Interest cost	6,754	6,980	6,807
Participant contributions	244	300	282
Exchange-rate changes	(7,306)	11	2,242
Benefits paid	(6,017)	(5,287)	(5,210)
Actuarial (gain) loss	(9,435)	(15,392)	(1,484)
Benefit obligation at end of year	$96,167	$109,837	$120,849
Weighted-average assumptions—benefit obligations (domestic)			
Discount rate	6.50%	6.75%	6.20%
Rate of compensation increase	2.64%	3.25%	3.25%
Cost of living increase	2.50%	2.50%	2.50%
Change in plan assets			
Fair value of plan assets at beginning of year	$140,829	$157,505	$138,044
Actual return on plan assets	(38,015)	(12,368)	21,700
Employer contributions	511	622	588
Participant contributions	244	300	282
Benefits paid	(6,017)	(5,287)	(5,210)
Exchange-rate changes	(6,691)	57	2,102
Fair value of plan assets at end of year	$90,864	$140,829	$157,505
Funded status at end of year			
Funded status	$(5,303)	$30,992	$36,656
Unrecognized actuarial gain	N/A	N/A	N/A
Unrecognized transition asset	N/A	N/A	N/A

	2009	2008	2007
Unrecognized prior service cost	N/A	N/A	N/A
Net amount recognized	$(5,303)	$30,992	$36,656
Amounts recognized in statement of financial position			
Noncurrent assets	$—	$34,643	$36,656
Current liability	(23)	(23)	—
Noncurrent liability	(5,280)	(3,628)	—
Net amount recognized in statement of financial position	$(5,303)	$30,992	$36,656

THE L. S. STARRETT COMPANY
Consolidated Balance Sheets
(In Thousands Except Share Data)

	June 27, 2009	June 28, 2008
ASSETS		
Current assets:		
Cash (Note 4)	$10,248	$6,515
Investments (Note 4)	1,791	19,806
Accounts receivable (less allowance for doubtful accounts of $678 and $701)	27,233	39,627
Inventories:		
Raw materials and supplies	19,672	15,104
Goods in process and finished parts	20,265	16,653
Finished goods	20,289	29,400
Total inventories	60,226	61,157
Current deferred income tax asset (Note 9)	5,170	5,996
Prepaid expenses and other current assets	8,054	5,535
Total current assets	112,722	138,636
Property, plant, and equipment, at cost, net (Note 7)	56,956	60,945
Property held for sale (Note 7)	2,771	1,912
Intangible assets (less accumulated amortization of $3,724 and $2,477) (Note 5)	2,517	3,764
Goodwill (Note 5)	981	6,032
Pension asset (Note 10)	—	34,643
Other assets	275	1,877
Long-term taxes receivable (Note 9)	2,807	2,476
Long-term deferred income tax asset (Note 9)	15,212	
Total assets	$194,241	$250,285

(Continued)

	June 27, 2009	June 28, 2008
Liabilities and Stockholders' Equity		
Current liabilities:		
Notes payable and current maturities (Note 11)	$10,136	$4,121
Accounts payable and accrued expenses	10,369	18,041
Accrued salaries and wages	5,109	6,907
Total current liabilities	25,614	29,069
Long-term taxes payable (Note 9)	9,140	8,522
Deferred income taxes (Note 9)	—	6,312
Long-term debt (Note 11)	1,264	5,834
Postretirement benefit and pension liability (Note 10)	15,345	13,775
Total liabilities	51,363	63,512
Stockholders' equity (Note 12):		
Class A common stock $1 par (20,000,000 shares authorized, 5,769,894 outstanding at June 27, 2009, 5,708,100 outstanding at June 28, 2008)	5,770	5,708
Class B common stock $1 par (10,000,000 shares authorized, 869,426 outstanding at June 27, 2009, 906,065 outstanding at June 28, 2008)	869	906
Additional paid-in capital	49,984	49,613
Retained earnings reinvested and employed in the business	127,707	134,109
Accumulated other comprehensive loss	(41,452)	(3,563)
Total stockholders' equity	142,878	186,773
Total liabilities and stockholders' equity	$194,241	$2,502
Asset category:		
Cash	6%	1%
Equities	41%	79%
Debt	53%	20%
	100%	100%

Source: L. S. Starrett 2009 10K.

The cash-flow and credit analyst should examine the cash-flow contributions into the pension plan and compare that amount with the accrued pension expense. Any discrepancies should be added to or subtracted from operating cash flow. If the expense is greater than the cash outflow, the difference should be subtracted from operating cash flow or added to operating cash flow if the cash contribution is greater than the amount accrued. For example, during 2008, Boeing expensed almost $1.3 billion on its income statement but contributed just $531 million. Merck, however, contributed $1.1 billion to its plans but expensed just $356 million.

If, in a given year, the firm makes a "catchup" contribution intended to reduce the unfunded obligation, cash flow from operations will be understated. It also may be a sign that management has confidence about future operating prospects because firms that are concerned about near-term events would tend to hold onto cash. The contribution would equate to a debt payment on an outstanding bond issue, although the pension contribution would be classified as an operating activity.

SFAS 158 did not change the computation of the periodic pension cost from SFAS 87.

PENSION PLAN SURPLUS OR DEFICIENCY

The growth in corporate unfunded pension liabilities resulting from the 2007–2009 recession and ensuing period of slow economic growth has made firms, unions and union members, employees, Congress, security analysts, and investment bankers aware of the potential risk in these long-term liabilities. Plan analysis, with a focus on the soundness of liabilities, assets, and funding methodology, are an integral part of business combinations. Prior to the 1970s, a detailed analysis of an entity's pension plan usually was not undertaken until after a merger. With the enormous growth in pension liabilities and its effects on cash flows, this situation changed dramatically. Owing to the large impact of contributions into pension plans on cash flows and debt ratios, the pension liability is examined very closely by potential buyers, investors, analysts, and creditors.

Table 6-17 shows the liability owing to the pension benefit obligation for some large companies, and as seen, the pension benefit obligation can represent a significant percentage of total debt. As of January 2010, there were 786 public companies having a then market value of greater than $100 million whose projected benefit obligations exceeded 20 percent of their total debt. Just like debt, pension obligations must be serviced, and for many companies on the table, leverage ratios are currently understated, especially those with liberal actuarial assumptions.

As seen with Delta Airlines, Federal-Mogul, and countless other entities, the liability of the pension plan can be too great for the firm's cash flows. Many firms have chosen to file for bankruptcy protection to avoid large pension payments. For example, during 2002, Bethlehem Steel shut down its pension plan, leaving the PBGC (Pension Benefit Guaranty Corporation to worry about the $3.7 billion in unfunded obligations to retirees.

For firms whose pension assets exceed pension obligations, there is a temptation to terminate the pension plan, settle existing obligations, and use the assets in the plan to purchase guaranteed insurance contracts and convert new employees to defined-contribution plans. Any excess, of course, may be viewed as hidden free cash flow, which gets recognized with a formal action of the firm. In reality, as we see next, it is quite difficult to take pension plan assets and convert them back to the entity.

TABLE 6-17

Pension Benefit Obligation and Total Debt

Company Name	Ticker Symbol	Market Value	PBO/Total Debt	PBO/ Sharehlders Eq
3M CO	MMM	58,526.887	2.130	1.461
ABB LTD -ADR	ABB	43,599.285	3.284	0.696
ABBOTT LABORATORIES	ABT	83,508.389	0.448	0.317
ACUITY BRANDS INC	AYI	1,519.297	0.643	0.222
AECOM TECHNOLOGY CORP	ACM	3,049.475	3.171	0.314
AES CORP	AES	8,884.198	0.223	1.105
AETNA INC	AET	13,741.950	1.231	0.579
AGCO CORP	AGCO	2,989.898	0.789	0.275
AGILENT TECHNOLOGIES INC	A	10,750.220	0.743	0.861
AIR PRODUCTS & CHEMICALS INC	APD	17,124.735	0.752	0.707
AIR TRANSPORT SERVICES GROUP	ATSG	167.537	1.237	7.884
AK STEEL HOLDING CORP	AKS	2,334.964	5.554	3.634
AKZO NOBEL NV -ADR	AKZOY	15,458.018	3.117	1.537
ALASKA AIR GROUP INC	ALK	1,218.274	0.614	1.709
ALBANY INTL CORP -CLA	AIN	692.689	0.605	0.782
ALBEMARLE CORP	ALB	3,334.511	0.556	0.486
ALCATEL-LUCENT -ADR	ALU	7,502.251	4.379	4.815
ALCOA INC	AA	15,706.957	1.018	0.917
ALEXANDER & BALDWIN INC	ALEX	1,404.867	0.623	0.293
ALLEGHENY ENERGY INC	AYE	3,980.400	0.265	0.395
ALLEGHENY TECHNOLOGIES INC	ATI	4,390.952	4.059	1.055
ALLETE INC	ALE	1,140.532	0.728	0.532
ALLIANT ENERGY CORP	LNT	3,347.785	0.455	0.292
ALLIANT TECHSYSTEMS INC	ATK	2,906.554	1.369	3.238
ALLSTATE CORP	ALL	16,101.440	0.800	0.361
ALTRIA GROUP INC	MO	40,670.004	0.715	1.889
AMCOR LTD -ADR	AMCRY	4,721.984	0.299	0.281
AMEREN CORP	AEE	6,618.560	0.407	0.461
AMERICAN COMMERCIAL LINES	ACLI	233.103	0.399	1.055
AMERICAN ELECTRIC POWER CO	AEP	16,608.709	0.235	0.400
AMERICAN GREETINGS -CL A	AM	859.528	0.359	0.265
AMERICAN STATES WATER CO	AWR	655.510	0.296	0.325
AMERICAN WOODMARK CORP	AMWD	278.452	2.933	0.394
AMERON INTERNATIONAL CORP	AMN	584.784	3.971	0.439
AMETEK INC	AME	4,123.763	0.393	0.339
AMPCO-PITTSBURGH CORP	AP	322.237	12.870	1.182

Company Name	Ticker Symbol	Market Value	PBO/Total Debt	PBO/ Sharehlders Eq
AMPHENOL CORP	APH	7,919.731	0.475	0.277
ANIXTER INTL INC	AXE	1,629.330	0.266	0.300
AON CORP	AON	10,502.202	2.891	1.076
ARBITRON INC	ARB	621.379	0.510	(2.989)
ARCH CHEMICALS INC	ARJ	772.000	1.711	1.574
ARKANSAS BEST CORP	ABFS	737.162	13.155	0.354
ARMSTRONG WORLD INDUSTRIES	AWI	2,232.869	4.195	1.195
ARTHUR J GALLAGHER & CO	AJG	2,291.518	0.378	0.272
ASHLAND INC	ASH	2,971.500	2.228	1.003
ASTRAZENECA PLC -ADR	AZN	68,050.186	0.728	0.542
AT&T INC	T	165,377.004	0.678	0.527
ATLAS COPCO AB -ADR	ATLCY	15,913.829	0.237	0.285
ATMOS ENERGY CORP	ATO	2,721.029	0.215	0.222
AVERY DENNISON CORP	AVY	3,838.420	0.480	0.607
AVISTA CORP	AVA	1,181.858	0.297	0.355
AVON PRODUCTS	AVP	13,452.261	0.550	2.027
BADGER METER INC	BMI	595.269	1.846	0.418
BALL CORP	BLL	4,862.281	0.584	1.297
BARNES GROUP INC	B	924.379	0.742	0.627
BASF SE -ADR	BASFY	57,640.069	0.783	0.647
BAXTER INTERNATIONAL INC	BAX	35,401.575	0.925	0.558
BAYER AG -ADR	BAYRY	66,666.891	0.834	0.865
BCE INC	BCE	21,181.178	1.106	0.786
BECKMAN COULTER INC	BEC	4,534.992	0.975	0.626
BECTON DICKINSON & CO	BDX	18,696.287	0.865	0.318
BELDEN INC	BDC	1,021.625	0.334	0.345

Example:

Alexander and Alexander, Inc., purchased annuity contracts for $37.4 million to settle the accumulated benefit obligations to certain retirees and recorded a pretax gain of $15.7 million. Alexander and Alexander recognized the gain as a reduction of its pension expense.

During the leveraged buyout era of the 1980s, the pension plan, once perceived to be a cost center for a firm, began to be considered a profit center because the investments of the pension plan yielded higher returns than were expected.

Example:

When speculation spread that USX was a candidate for a hostile takeover, many security analysts pointed to the seemingly large surplus of pension assets in the fund. Presumably, the acquirer could have used cash from the pension plan to pay down debt used to buy the company. The same argument was used when Lockheed Corp. was viewed, during the 1990s, as a takeover candidate.

However, the large surplus that seemed to exist when security analysts simply subtracted pension liabilities from the fair market value of pension assets at year end was drastically reduced in reality. What analysts ignored were the following:

1. There were taxes on the gains in the pension assets, including a 15 percent excise tax.
2. The rates on guaranteed insurance contracts (GICs) were lower than the discount rates assumed by the pension plan at that time. Thus, to satisfy the pension obligations, more assets would have had to be invested in low-yielding GICs.
3. For Lockheed, the U.S. government would be entitled to most of the surplus because the Pentagon funded the plan.

It is vital that potential acquirers and investors have a thorough understanding of the magnitude of the pension plan's liabilities, actuarial assumptions, and expected growth in contributions that would be assumed as a result of a business combination. Often, owing to the haste with which many business combinations are put together, the acquiring company is not fully mindful of the magnitude of the prospective liabilities it is assuming. This may be especially so for non-U.S. divisions, where unions and federal restrictions may be involved.

Many suitors are so overly desirous to complete an acquisition that they do not fully appreciate the drag on cash flows resulting from the benefits area. All too often it is not until they "get in there" that are they able to wrap their arms around the pension and related liability issues. Other entities are more than happy to sell divisions because of the size of the associated pension fund liabilities and the future negative impact on cash flows of funding those liabilities. The wording in a purchase agreement concerning the meaning of a particular liability can be so vague that not all parties can later agree on what was meant when the initial agreement was signed.

Example:

Banner Industries charged Pepsi-Cola with dumping a large liability in its lap when Banner purchased Pepsi's trucking subsidiary.

If the acquiring entity continues the plan of the acquired entity, under ERISA Section 4062.6, it assumes a liability for that portion of the plan's vested liability that is not funded (the unfunded vested liability) up to 30 percent of the acquiring entity's net worth.[24] The vested liability is the actuarial present value of benefits that must be paid even if current employees leave the company. In addition, the acquiring company may assume other liabilities. Nonvested benefits or benefits that will become vested only if the employee remains employed by the company may be assumed, and such liabilities may be substantial. If the acquired entity was publicly held, information about vested and nonvested benefits is included, as we saw, in the pension footnote in the financial filings. More typically, the acquiring entity elects to terminate the acquired entity's plan, preferring to meld the new employees into its own plan, with appropriate credits given for length of service.

Liabilities under a multiemployer pension plan must be evaluated by the analyst because of the penalties associated by withdrawal. Severe penalties could be imposed on the acquirer if it decided to terminate its proportionate interest. The extent of outstanding claims and lawsuits related to the plans also must be reviewed. Other postretirement benefits such as life insurance or catastrophic claims also need reviewing. The annual (cash) expenses surrounding all benefit plans of the acquired company, including any additional contributions that may be necessary, must be determined, if it is not well specified.

Example:

As part of a business restructuring during 2009, A. Schulman Company withdrew from its multiemployer plan. When this occurs, it normally places additional burden on the remaining pension sponsors, and so the analyst must study the health of multiemployer plans if the company being studied is included in one or more. The following is from A. Schulman's 2009 10K:

> During fiscal 2009, the company received notification from a U.S. multiemployer pension plan that it was being assessed for partial and complete withdrawal liabilities from the plan. This plan covered the company's employees who previously worked at the company's Orange, Texas warehouse. The company terminated over 70 percent of this location's workforce in fiscal 2004, and then terminated the remaining workforce in fiscal 2007. In accordance with the Employee Retirement Income Security Act ("ERISA") guidelines these workforce reductions qualified as partial and complete withdrawals from the plan. Accordingly, the plan assessed the company for withdrawal liabilities of \$1.8 million for the fiscal 2004 partial withdrawal and \$0.6 million for the fiscal 2007 complete withdrawal for its share of the underfunded multiemployer plan. The company revised the consolidated financial information for the fiscal years 2004 and 2007 to

[24] The liability for termination is true for any single-employer plan. Additional information may be found on the PBGC Web site at www.pbgc.gov/practitioners/law-regulations-informal-guidance/content/page14767.html.

reflect the correction of an immaterial error identified in fiscal 2009 that related to prior periods. The company reflected in its consolidated statements of stockholders' equity a change of $1.8 million to the August 31, 2006 ending retained earnings balance and a change of $0.6 million to fiscal 2007 income from continuing operations, net income and total stockholders' equity. The fiscal 2007 change of $0.6 million was included in the restructuring expense line item in the company's consolidated statements of operations. In addition, the company reflected a change of $2.4 million as a liability in the consolidated balance sheets as of August 31, 2009 and 2008.

The Pension Benefit Guaranty Corporation (PBGC) was established by the Employee Retirement Income Security Act of 1974 (ERISA) to ensure that participants in defined-benefit pension plans receive their pensions if their plans terminate without sufficient assets to pay promised benefits. The PBGC administers separate insurance programs to protect participants in single-employer and multiemployer plans. It has been speculated that the existence of PBGC represents a "put" option to which the entity could use to dump its poorly funded and cash-draining plan into the lap of the federal government. While it is doubtful the PBGC would allow an entity capable of servicing its liabilities to do this, for entities that are not sponsoring well-funded plans, the put option has been taken advantage of.

LIABILITIES FOR POSTRETIREMENT BENEFITS OTHER THAN PENSIONS

While the pension expense has justly received important recognition, health care, and other postretirement obligations also could represent unrecognized debt on the sponsoring employer's balance sheet. Taken together, the potential cost to the system is so great that in 2005, S&P warned that the United States, Germany, France, and the United Kingdom face junk debt status within 30 years unless something is done to control their costs.

In November 1984, the FASB issued SFAS 81, which required firms to disclose information about postretirement health care and life insurance benefits. Under this standard, firms are to disclose the cost of health care and/or life insurance benefits to retirees, their dependents, or survivors. If such costs to retirees cannot be separated from costs to current employees, total costs are required to be disclosed, as well as the number of active employees and the number of retirees covered by the plan. A general description of the plan, covered employees, and benefits also is required.

In December 1990, the FASB issued SFAS 106, which required companies to report and accrue their obligations for postemployment benefits—including retiree health plans—for current and future retirees. The rate of growth in the cost of health care benefits, which must be projected well into the future, can be the most significant assumption in calculating the obligation, a present-value item. Thus the model and assumptions used in these projections are critical. Firms also have to include an expense that is equal to the actuarial present value of additional benefits that *current active employees* earned during the period. In addition, footnote information provides data about the liability associated with these benefits, as well as any assets that were set aside to discharge the liability.

For most firms, "pay as you go" continues to be the preferred funding route for other postretirement obligations as companies endeavor to lay out as little current cash as possible (not prefund) and do not wish to show another (potentially large) liability on the balance sheet. In an effort to control costs, many employers are capping contributions and/or subsidies and are changing plan designs from defined-benefit plans to defined-contribution plans. It also has proven cost-efficient to separate the retiree population from the active group because this results in more effective Medicare integration for the post–65 population given that this population is covered by the federal government.

When SFAS 106 was adopted, most corporate plan sponsors assumed that health care costs would grow by 9 percent in the near term. They also assumed that the rate of growth would ramp down to 5 percent over the coming six years and remain there for the long term. During the ensuing period, the health care cost trend rate used by firms indeed has declined steadily, although the long-term 5 percent assumption remains. Health care costs, however, can be subject to large and unexpected increases given that agreements with health providers are typically set for one year at a time, and unexpected experiences in provider payouts to doctors would lead them to pass on the increase.

SFAS 106 was amended by SFAS 132R (December 2003) and SFAS 158 (September 2006). SFAS 132R required, to the extent that postretirement benefits are funded, the firm to state the percentage of the fair value of plan assets held, as well as provide a narrative of the sponsor's investment strategy and policies. SFAS 158 required full recognition of other postretirement obligations be placed on the balance sheet.

Example:

When General Motors adapted SFAS 106, analysts considered it to be another accounting rule providing little information of value because GM's shareholders' equity was about $28 billion at the time. When the rule was adopted, GM took a $24 billion hit to earnings to set up the reserve for postretirement health benefits.

To understand the provisions of the FASB pronouncements, let us assume initially that it relates only to health care benefits that are paid after retirement. Suppose that the plan promises health care benefits to all employees who attain age 55 while in service and only if they have at least 10 years of service with the firm. Suppose that we wish to determine the obligation for an employee who is 45 years old, who had been with the firm for 13 years already, and who is expected to remain employed by the firm until retirement at age 65. The employee is expected to live until age 75, and health care benefits are assumed to be $1,500 during the first year after retirement and to increase by 8 percent each year. For simplicity, assume that the employee is single and that all benefits are paid at the end of the year. The firm assumes a discount rate of 9 percent for the postretirement benefits.

The first step in estimating the obligation is to determine the expected payments after retirement age (i.e., at ages 66 through 75). We then discount the obligation to the present. The discounting is done by using the assumed rate of, say, 9 percent. At the current age, 45, the present value of those future postretirement costs is $2,357. This is the actuarial present value of *expected* benefit obligations. It is the actuarial present value because we had to make actuarial assumptions about life expectancy, length of service, marital status, and the like. However, note that at present the employee is not yet fully eligible for the postretirement benefits. The employee will become fully eligible only at the age of 55 and then only if he or she is still employed by the firm. Thus the employee has not yet attained the date of *full eligibility.*

The standards attribute postretirement benefits to years of service in an equal manner. Thus, at the age of 45 with 13 years of service, the employee has 10 more years to attain the full eligibility age of 55. Regulations require recognition of the portion of the obligation that accumulated by the employee to date using the number of years of service to date divided by the total expected number of years until the employee become fully eligible. At the age of 45, this yields 13/(13 + 10), and at age 50, the ratio increases to 18/23. Thus the actuarial present value of the accumulated benefit obligations at the age of 45 is 13/23 of the expected benefit obligation, or $1,332. At age 55, the employee becomes fully eligible, and the accumulated and expected benefit obligations are identical, $5,579. From then on, the actuarial present value of the two benefit obligations is identical.

From age 55 to age 56, the actuarial present value of the accumulated benefit obligation increases by $502 (6,081 – 5,579). This increase represents the interest cost component of the expense and is equal to 9 percent of the accumulated benefit at age 55 ($5,579). This seems intuitively reasonable because at age 55 the employee is fully eligible, and an additional year of service does not add any new postretirement benefits. The only change is that the obligation's maturity is one year shorter at age 56 than at age 55, which represents the interest-expense component (this would be the same methodology used to calculate pension benefits). However, before age 55, the increase in the liability comprises both an interest expense and a service cost component because some of the postretirement benefits are attributed to that year's services.

Unlike pension plans, postretirement plans are largely unfunded and typically highly underfunded, as we see in the case of IBM. Whether a firm chooses to recognize the expense immediately or delay its recognition depends on the firm's current and prospective cash flows. If cash flows for the year are high, the firm may choose to increase funding. If cash flows in the future are expected to be low, the firm may delay incorporation of the expense into earnings of future years.

Note that under the standard, as seen in the IBM example, the company shows payments out of the fund. *This has no effect on reported cash flows to shareholders.* The only cash-flow effects are the actual contributions. Since the introduction of the standard, it appears, in general, that credit-rating agencies behave as if they were aware of this liability even prior to its incorporation into a footnote or the balance sheet.

Disclosure requirements are similar to those of pensions. For example, a firm is required to disclose the amount of the net periodic postretirement cost, showing separately the service cost component, the interest cost component, the actual return on plan assets for the period, amortization of the transition amount, and other amortizations and deferrals. A firm is also required to provide information about assets and liabilities: the fair value of plan assets, the actuarial present value of the accumulated benefit obligation (identifying separately the portion attributable to retirees, other fully eligible employees, and other active plan participants), unrecognized prior service cost, unrecognized net gain or loss, unrecognized transition amount, and the amount included on the balance sheet (whether an asset or a liability).

A firm is also required to disclose information about the terms of the plans, the participants, the assumed rates (including health care cost trend rate), the effects of a one-percentage-point increase in the assumed health care cost trend rates, and the types of assets held to discharge postretirement obligations.

What are the implications for the analyst? The direct effects of the accounting standards regarding other postretirement benefits on cash flows are likely to be minimal, although the impact on the balance sheet resulting from the increased liability could prove sizable, as seen in the table for some reporting companies. As with pensions, a high ratio of retirees to active workers will raise the liability. To the extent that the liability interferes with financial flexibility and cash flows, the impact could force cash to be allocated among operating companies in a different manner, especially if particular subsidiaries have younger workforces allowing for lower contributions. Unlike debt obligations, the sponsor could amend plan benefits to reduce the liability but might require employee or union acceptance. If the company is successful in reducing health care costs, operating cash flows will improve.

Regarding the financial structure, if the health care cost trend rate is inappropriately low, the potential liability would be greater than portrayed by the company and future operating cash flows lower than expected. This would include any tax subsidies received by the entity that are used to offset health care costs.

A decrease in the discount rate would result in an increase in the real benefit obligation and a decline in the funded status, whereas an increase in the discount rate would result in a decrease in the benefit status obligation and an improvement in the funded status. But because there is no legal requirement to fund these plans, the company could continue to fund current costs without addressing the liability, unlike pension obligations. To the extent that such benefits are implied, the analyst should consider the effect the postretirement liability might have on leverage ratios and debt covenants.

POSTRETIREMENT BENEFITS OTHER THAN PENSIONS COMPARED WITH TOTAL DEBT AND SHAREHOLDERS' EQUITY

Company Name	Ticker Symbol	Market Value	Postretirement Benefit Liab.	Debt – Total	Bal Sheet Post Ret/Share Eq.
AMERICAN AXLE & MFG HOLDINGS	AXL	445.639	(514.900)	1,139.900	1.182
AMR CORP/DE	AMR	2,543.632	(2,618.000)	10,957.000	0.892
ARVINMERITOR INC	ARM	827.320	(638.000)	1,177.000	0.500
BLOUNT INTL INC	BLT	481.911	(38.071)	325.520	0.875
BOEING CO	BA	37,737.320	(7,780.000)	7,512.000	6.012
CHINA EASTERN AIRLINES -ADR	CEA	1,709.290	(222.145)	8,757.826	0.116
CINCINNATI BELL INC	CBB	705.518	(283.800)	1,960.700	0.400
CLOROX CO/DE	CLX	8,528.288	(70.000)	3,149.000	0.400
COMMERCIAL VEHICLE GROUP INC	CVGI	129.989	(2.311)	164.895	(0.053)
EASTMAN KODAK CO	EK	1,130.960	(1,471.000)	1,303.000	(1.531)
FORD MOTOR CO	F	33,071.011	(16,279.000)	154,196.000	0.940
INTERCONTINENTAL HOTELS -ADR	IHG	4,109.820	(19.000)	1,355.000	3.167
LEAR CORP	LEA	5,243.588	(172.400)	3,526.800	(0.867)
LIBBEY INC	LBY	115.943	(61.881)	550.257	1.069
MONEYGRAM INTERNATIONAL INC	MGI	237.658	(13.416)	978.881	0.339
NAVISTAR INTERNATIONAL CORP	NAV	2,732.555	(1,158.000)	5,406.000	0.643
QWEST COMMUNICATION INTL INC	Q	7,267.150	(2,509.000)	13,659.000	1.732
TENNECO INC	TEN	841.147	(143.000)	1,451.000	0.570
UAL CORP	UAUA	1,911.093	(1,901.000)	8,149.000	0.771
US AIRWAYS GROUP INC	LCC	779.734	(122.000)	3,996.000	0.242
VERISK ANALYTICS INC	VRSK	4,335.702	(28.640)	669.754	0.110

Firms have taken steps to decrease future cash payments to their retirees and to reduce the potential liability. For example, Safeway became a self-insurer and set up programs to encourage healthy behavior. Most companies ask their workforce to pay a percentage of health benefits. Ralston Purina introduced an ESOP instead of a retiree medical plan. Other firms discontinued such benefits to new employees, and still others introduced health maintenance organizations (HMOs) to reduce future medical costs. Despite these cost-savings measures, the direct cash-flow effects have been significant because the cost of providing health care has risen.

Example:

Alcoa states that it assumes a health care cost trend rate of 6.5 percent that is gradually reduced to 5 percent. However, based on current health care surveys from leading actuarial firms, including Aon Consulting, Buck Consultants, and Segal Company, among others, it is the general belief that employers should expect to see increases in their health care expense of at least 10 percent over the coming years. Analysts should be aware of current research by independent sources when evaluating the actuarial assumptions of health plans. To the extent that companies such as Alcoa are understating health care expenditures, the analyst should adjust cash flow from operations as well as ask the firm's financial officer why the firm's assumed rate is vastly different from consultants' expectations. One also should measure the company's historical and recent growth rates in this expenditure, in addition to recent price increases announced by health care firms, as reported in their financial filings or gleaned from conference calls. For instance, poor medical cost experience on the part of health organizations (providers) will assuredly lead to future price increases.

Alcoa points out that during its past three years, its experience has been considerably below the 6.5 percent assumption; three years, however, is a short period of time (including a recession), and while a 1 percent increase might result in a relatively small expense for Alcoa (Table 6-18), for other entities, an increase could be material. Additionally, stock investors normally react harshly to even small bottom-line disappointments, and if Alcoa were to experience a higher than forecasted estimated trend rate, investors surely would take notice and reduce expected cash flows while marking up the cost of equity capital to account for the increased risk.

TABLE 6-18

Alcoa Health Care Trend Rates, 2006–2008

	2008	2007	2006
Health care cost trend rate assumed for next year	6.5%	7.0%	7.0%
Rate to which the cost trend rate gradually declines	5.0%	5.0%	5.0%
Year that the rate reaches the rate at which it is assumed to remain	2013	2012	2011

The health care cost trend rate in the calculation of the 2007 benefit obligation was 7.0 percent from 2007 to 2008 and 6.5 percent from 2008 to 2009. Actual annual company health care cost trend experience over the past three years has ranged from (6.2) to 4.1 percent. Owing to the decline in Alcoa's health care cost trend experience in recent years, a 6.5 percent trend rate will be used for 2009. Recently, the low end of the range of actual annual health care costs turned favorable; however, this change was not considered indicative of expected future actual costs. As a result, the assumed health care cost trend rate for next year was not affected significantly.

Assumed health care cost trend rates have an effect on the amounts reported for the health care plan. A one-percentage-point change in these assumed rates would have the following effects:

	1% Increase	**1% Decrease**
Effect on total of service and interest cost components	$4	$(4)
Effect on postretirement benefit obligations	61	(55)

Example:

Tenant Corp., a manufacturer of cleaning equipment, reports a health care cost trend rate more in line with the predictions of market consultants. While many companies decreased their trend rate during the 2008 recession, resulting in a lower liability, Tennant increased its rate while at the same time very gradually reducing the rate over a longer time period, a conservative action having the effect of forcing a higher liability:

> As of December 31, 2008 and 2007, the U.S. Nonqualified, U.K. Pension, and German Pension Plans had an accumulated benefit obligation in excess of plan assets.
>
> Assumed Health Care Cost Trend Rates on December 31, 2008 and 2007, are as follows:

	2008	**2007**
Health care cost trend rate assumption for the next year	**11.3%**	10.1%
Rate to which the cost trend rate is assumed to decline (the ultimate trend rate)	**5.0%**	5.1%
Year that the rate reaches the ultimate trend rate	**2029**	2028

Example:

Becton Dickinson is a global medical technology company. Its significant pension and postretirement benefits forced management to better control its costs.

> The company has defined benefit pension plans covering substantially all of its employees in the United States and certain foreign locations. The company also provides certain postretirement health care and life insurance benefits to qualifying domestic retirees. Postretirement health care and life insurance benefit plans in foreign countries are not

material. The measurement date used for the company's employee benefit plans is September 30.

During 2007, the company redesigned its U.S. pension plans to provide for a cash benefit formula by offering a one-time, irrevocable election to existing employees to change to this provision and mandating all new employees hired after April 1, 2007 to participate in the new formula. The company also amended its other postretirement benefits plan to provide that new hires, as of April 1, 2007 or later, will no longer be eligible for company subsidized benefits. These amendments did not have a material impact on the net pension and postretirement cost of the company in 2007.

Source: Becton, Dickinson and Company 2009 10K.

Example:

Table 6-19 shows IBM's benefit obligations and plans assets for its pension plans and plans for other postretirement benefits. While the size of the benefit obligation for IBM's nonpension plans is about 10 percent of the size of its pension plans, it is nonetheless substantial because benefits paid from the trust are about 20 percent of its assets, whereas the plan is underfunded by over $5 billion This underfunding of other postretirement benefits amounted to about 37 percent of IBM's shareholders' equity.

As is seen from its footnoted table, IBM contributed $457 million less during 2008 than 2007 into its postretirement plans despite its negative funded status, with the company's contribution covering only a small fraction of benefits paid. One could presume that IBM will need to increase funding to these plans or change the benefits packages offered to employees. If it chooses to increase funding, its effect on cash flows will be significant, as it has in the past when it provided for special contributions. Notice the gap in non-U.S., nonpension plan funding status. For these reasons, IBM stated that it intended to contribute $1 billion into its plans during 2009.

TABLE 6-19

IBM Pension and Nonpension Plan Obligations: 2007 and 2008

	Defined-Benefit Pension Plans				**Nonpension Postretirement Benefit Plans**			
	U.S. Plans		**Non-U.S. Plans**		**U.S. Plan**		**Non-U.S. Plans**	
($ in Millions)	**2008**	**2007**	**2008**	**2007**	**2008**	**2007**	**2008**	**2007**
Change in benefit obligation:								
Benefit obligation at beginning of year	**$47,673**	$47,839	**$42,291**	$40,861	**$5,472**	$5,773	**$769**	$680
Service cost	**—**	773	**660**	688	**55**	69	**10**	12
Interest cost	**2,756**	2,660	**2,042**	1,825	**312**	311	**53**	46
Plan participants' contributions	**—**	—	**63**	67	**216**	199	**—**	—

(Continued)

TABLE 6-19 *(Continued)*

IBM Pension and Nonpension Plan Obligations: 2007 and 2008

	Defined-Benefit Pension Plans				Nonpension Postretirement Benefit Plans			
	U.S. Plans		Non-U.S. Plans		U.S. Plan		Non-U.S. Plans	
($ in Millions)	**2008**	**2007**	**2008**	**2007**	**2008**	**2007**	**2008**	**2007**
Acquisitions/divestitures, net	**—**	5	**(6)**	85	**—**	—	**(1)**	—
Actuarial losses/(gains)	**1,183**	(484)	**(64)**	(2,388)	**(191)**	(203)	**(12)**	(44)
Benefits paid from trust	**(2,999)**	(3,046)	**(1,814)**	(1,638)	**(656)**	(650)	**(31)**	(6)
Direct benefit payments	**(81)**	(75)	**(486)**	(492)	**(24)**	(38)	**(21)**	(16)
Foreign-exchange impact	**—**	—	**(3,357)**	3,279	**—**	—	**(146)**	98
Medicare subsidy	**—**	—	**—**	—	**37**	10	**—**	—
Plan amendments/curtailments/settlements	**224**	—	**(157)**	3	**3**	—	**(13)**	—
Benefit obligation at end of year	**$48,756**	$47,673	**$39,171**	$42,291	**$5,224**	$5,472	**$608**	$769
Change in plan assets:								
Fair value of plan assets at beginning of year	**$57,191**	$52,913	**$41,696**	$38,207	**$504**	$47	**$121**	$99
Actual return on plan assets	**(8,274)**	7,324	**(7,678)**	1,483	**4**	15	**10**	11
Employer contributions	**—**	—	**858**	474	**45**	893	**10**	3
Acquisitions/divestitures, net	**—**	—	**16**	52	**—**	—	**—**	—
Plan participants' contributions	**—**	—	**63**	67	**216**	199	**—**	—
Benefits paid from trust	**(2,999)**	(3,046)	**(1,814)**	(1,638)	**(656)**	(650)	**(31)**	(6)
Foreign-exchange impact	**—**	—	**(3,978)**	3,054	**—**	—	**(30)**	14
Plan amendments/curtailments/settlements	**—**	—	**2**	(3)	**—**	—	**—**	—
Fair value of plan assets at end of year	**$45,918**	$57,191	**$29,164**	$41,696	**$113**	$504	**$79**	$121
Funded status at end of year	**$(2,838)**	$9,519	**$(10,007)**	$(595)	**$(5,111)**	$(4,968)	**$(529)**	$(648)
Accumulated benefit obligation	**$48,756**	$47,673	**$37,759**	$40,598	**N/A**	N/A	**N/A**	N/A

In December 2003, the U.S. Congress enacted the Medicare Prescription Drug, Improvement and Modernization Act of 2003 for employers sponsoring postretirement health care plans that provide prescription drug benefits. The act introduced a prescription drug benefits under Medicare as well as a federal subsidy to sponsors of retiree health care benefit plans. Under the act, the Medicare subsidy amount is received directly by the plan sponsor and not the related plan. Further, the plan sponsor is not required to use the subsidy amount to fund postretirement benefits and may use the subsidy for any valid business purpose. Under the Obama health care legislation, this subsidy is to be taxed, which forced many firms to lower their deferred tax asset.

YIELD SPREADS

Yield spreads are important for the analyst to monitor because they indicate the willingness of banks, funds, and other creditors to lend, at what price, and the associated market liquidity. This is particularly important for current and potential creditors and investors. The spread between the risk-free rate and that of an entity's fixed-income instruments can signal whether there are factors within the firm that investors, in general, may not be aware of. The yield spread has a direct bearing on financial structure and cost of capital; investor perception and pricing of risk will help to determine the ability to issue debt and equity. The greater the spread relative to the risk-free rate, the more costly is the debt capital, if cash needs to be raised. Higher spreads, which imply lower bond prices, result in a lower cost for the enterprise to repurchase its outstanding debt. And in both these instances the capital structure is affected.

A widening of the yield spread is a telltale sign that investors are concerned about the ability of the entity to satisfy its obligations, and for this reason, significant spread widening (defined in Chapter 8) has been incorporated into my credit model. This is especially important for entities that have become increasingly reliant on the capital markets for funding.

During 2007, at the time many entities were reporting positive growth in earnings, the spreads on their bonds were increasing, often very significantly. For financial firms and industrial companies with financing arms (e.g., General Electric), investors were devaluing their investment portfolios, recognizing the real prospect for further deterioration of such assets and feeling increasingly uncertain about financial market stability and liquidity. *Market efficiency often does a good job, in real time, signaling changes in the fundamental outlook*, and investors and analysts must be cognizant of such shifts in perception. Even if the financial marketplace's perception turns out wrong and events correct back, during the time that such shifts exist, their effect on the cost of capital is real. It is commonly accepted that credit-rating agencies erred during the credit crisis by not paying adequate attention to existing market conditions and the ongoing perceptible shift in risk associated with the broad decline in the economic value of financial assets. The growth rate in mortgage delinquencies was picking up at an alarming rate, yet many firms were reluctant to write down the value of those assets. This fundamental shift was picked up through widening yield spreads signaling the increase in default risk.

Credit-rating agencies historically have done a good job accessing risk but typically are lagging indicators. The companies responsible for credit ratings normally react to events, such as earnings announcements or financial filings, rather than act as events are taking place.

One of the more important of the yield-spread indicators is the LIBOR-OIS spread, which has been a closely watched barometer of distress in money markets. The three-month London Interbank Offered Rate (LIBOR) is the interest rate at which banks borrow unsecured funds from other banks in the London wholesale money market. Alternatively, if a bank enters into an overnight indexed swap (OIS), it is entitled to receive a fixed rate of interest on a notional amount called the *OIS rate*. In exchange, the bank agrees to pay a (compound) interest payment on the notional amount to be determined by a reference floating rate (in the United States this is the effective federal funds rate) to the counterparty at maturity. For instance, according to Bloomberg data, the OIS spread contracted from a peak of 384 basis points in June 2008 to 25 basis points during July 2009 as central banks flooded the system with liquidity and the fear of large-scale financial failure abated. The borrowing window was essentially closed to almost all borrowers when the spread was over 200 points.

During that period of widened yield spreads, levered companies saw their cost of capital, both equity and debt, surge, severely compressing valuation metrics. In fact, as the spread widened to historic levels—the world's credit machine became inactive—the very basis of the economy was thrown into doubt, as reflected by the spread.

Although one could track the LIBOR-OIS spread of almost any maturity, the two-year swap spread showed over the credit crisis to be the preferred indicator of economic health, counterparty risk, and market liquidity and a key benchmark for pricing and hedging. In essence, the two-year swap spread is the price to exchange fixed- for floating-rate payments for two years.

As shown in Fig. 6-6, the two-year spread rose to over 150 basis points, and later, as the financial crisis abated, it fell to 25 basis points. Normally, higher Treasury yields induce swap spreads to widen because they are associated with a tighter monetary policy, economic uncertainty, and upcoming liquidity concerns. While the swap spread is used commonly to hedge variable-rate debt, it is also used by hedge funds to speculate. When the spread rises, it is more costly to convert variable-to fixed-rate debt, affecting cost of capital and a firm's financial structure.

FIGURE 6-6

Two-Year Swap Spread

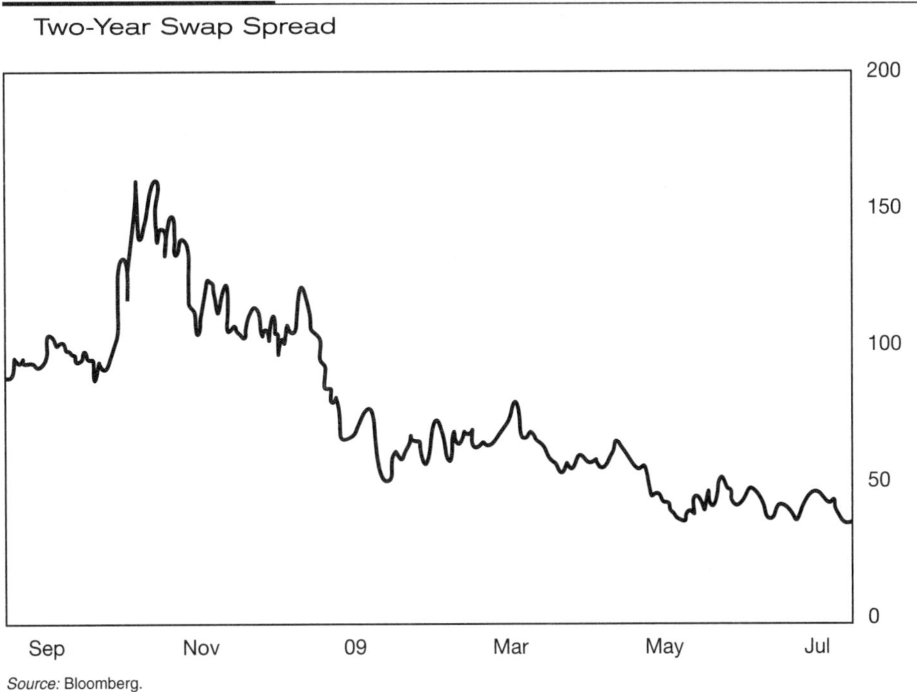

Source: Bloomberg.

IMPROVING FINANCIAL STRUCTURE THROUGH EXCHANGE OF SECURITIES

Companies have been quite innovative in swapping their own securities, enabling them, at times, to reduce their outstanding principal on debt while at the same time boosting equity capital. Such was seen in a swap by Legg Mason during August 2009, when the company exchanged cash on hand and stock (which was issued) for its "Corporate Units." It was only a year earlier that Legg Mason sold the units (raising $1.1 billion), consisting of (1) a purchase contract obligating the holder to purchase Legg Mason stock and (2) 5.6 percent senior notes, which were used by Legg Mason as collateral until the stock was purchased. Through the swap, Legg Mason then was able to reduce its long-term debt by the $1.1 billion and associated interest expense while offering 18.6 million shares. The swap was viewed positively by investors, who were receiving more value than the current units were selling for while giving the company needed debt relief and additional equity.[25]

[25] To view the prospectus and details on Edgar, please see http://www.sec.gov/Archives/edgar/data/704051/000119312509172535/d424b3.htm

At the time of the exchange, the units were selling for $29.50 and the common stock of Legg Mason for $28.25. Holders who exchanged thus received 0.881 times $29.50 (the exchange's offer) plus $6.25, or $32.45, versus the $28.25 current value of the stock. Thus it paid for holders to exchange, and not surprisingly, the offer was fully subscribed. For Legg Mason, the swap saved the company $60 million in interest and dividends (yield on the units was higher than on the common stock), wiped off $1.1 billion in long-term debt from the books (investors were concerned about their leverage), and saved the company the worry about market conditions two years hence when the $1.1 billion would have been due.

CAPITALIZATION

The following table sets forth our capitalization as of June 30, 2009 on an actual basis and on an adjusted basis to give effect to the tender of 21,850,000 Corporate Units to us under the exchange offer. You should read the information set forth in the table below in conjunction with "Selected Consolidated Financial and Operating Data" and our audited financial statements and the accompanying notes incorporated by reference in this prospectus.

	As of June 30, 2009	
	Actual	**As Adjusted**
Legg Mason Inc.	**(Unaudited, in Thousands)**	
Cash and cash equivalents[1]	$1,539,295	$1,397,732
Restricted cash[2]	42,929	42,929
Total	$1,582,224	$1,440,661
Long-term debt		
2.5% Convertible senior notes	$1,025,162	$1,025,162
5.6% Senior notes from equity units	1,150,000	57,500
5-Year term loan	550,000	550,000
Third-party distribution financing	3,288	3,288
Other term loans	18,038	18,038
Subtotal	2,746,488	1,653,988
Less: Current portion	7,964	7,964
Total long-term debt	2,738,524	1,646,024

Legg Mason Inc.	As of June 30, 2009 Actual	As Adjusted
	(Unaudited, in Thousands)	
Stockholders' equity:		
Legg Mason, Inc., stockholders' equity		
Common stock, par value $0.10, authorized 500,000,000 shares, 142,452,080 shares outstanding	14,245	16,186
Preferred stock, par value $10, authorized 4,000,000 shares, 0 shares outstanding	—	—
Shares exchangeable into common stock	2,830	2,830
Additional paid-in capital	3,467,437	4,459,358
Employee stock trust	(33,238)	(33,238)
Deferred compensation employee stock trust	33,238	33,238
Retained earnings	1,177,376	1,163,370
Accumulated other comprehensive income, net	38,527	38,527
Total stockholders' equity	4,700,415	5,680,271
Total capitalization	$7,446,903	$7,334,259

[1]As adjusted amounts include payment of the cash portion of the offer consideration and other transaction related costs.

[2]Includes non-current portion of restricted cash of $8.2 million.

Source: Legg Mason, Prospectus, August 12, 2009.

IMPORTANCE OF CREDIT RATING

After many decades of having unquestioned integrity and analytic ability, the credit-rating companies came under harsh attack with the prominence of the worldwide credit crisis. The credit-rating authorities are relied on by investors worldwide, and hence their effect on individual companies and the financial system is profound. Changes in the credit rating of an entity, one of its large customers or suppliers, or of an asset held by such an entity could have a material impact on the cost of capital.[26]

[26] In 2009, the SEC completed a 10-month study of the three largest rating agencies and found that they struggled significantly with the increase in the number and complexity of subprime residential mortgage-backed securities (RMBS) and collateralized debt obligation (CDO) deals since 2002. The SEC also said that the problems are being fixed, with the agencies agreeing to broad reforms.

Investors rely on the credit-rating services, and many pension funds are prohibited from owning the securities of entities below a given ratings grade. Credit-rating agencies could have access to confidential information shared by the issuer that may not factor into its current risk assessment, giving the agencies additional credence with investors.

Much of the public criticism that took place during 2007–2008 was a result of rating agencies being late in making changes to information that had been negatively affecting the market value of the rated securities for some time. And by the time the rating changes were made, many tens of billions of dollars had been lost. As a result of public outcry, the Credit Rating Reform Act was passed, which provided for censure, suspension, or revocation of SEC registration of any national rating organization or, as they were called, nationally recognized statistical rating organizations (NRSRO). Ten organizations were designated as NRSROs:

1. Moody's Investor Service
2. Standard and Poor's
3. Fitch Ratings
4. A. M. Best Company
5. Dominion Bond Rating Service
6. Japan Credit Rating, Ltd.
7. Egan-Jones Rating Co.
8. LACE Financial
9. R&I, Inc.
10. Realpoint, LLC

Under the law, any credit-rating agency having three years of experience that meets certain standards would be allowed to register with the SEC as a statistical ratings organization. It remains to be seen if a new competitive arena takes hold for the credit-rating industry. In 2010, the Senate approved a provision having the Securities and Exchange Commission establish a credit-rating board that would act as a middleman between issuers and rating agencies. Many legislators and investors believe the rating agencies, due to their system of pay, loses objectivity in favor of revenues. The newly anointed European Securities and Markets Authority is now also responsible for regulating the credit rating agencies, including having the power of investigation, which includes access to their rating methodologies.

Higher credit ratings are strongly associated with a lower cost of capital, both debt and equity. While this has always been the case, nowhere was this seen more acutely than in the financial sector during 2007–2009, when the survivability of the largest financial intermediaries was put into question. As many investors, policyholders, and state regulators looked to the large rating agencies for answers, many other large investors, notably hedge funds, were selling short the shares of companies in question.

Most companies are not rated by any NRSRO, so it is the investor's responsibility to assign his or her own risk proxy. Also, there might be a size bias with ratings firms because they tend to assign higher ratings to firms having high market valuations. If this exists, the credit model in Chapter 8 should be used, and if a credit rating does exist, the model can confirm the accuracy of the credit-rating organizations. If the investor believes that the model's rating deviates from a credit rating assigned by an NRSRO, an investor can take advantage by buying long or selling short the firm's securities. If the analyst deems the credit of a large company to be considerably weaker than commonly perceived, one could leverage one's knowledge through derivatives such as credit default swaps, although that is a proven risky alternative if the markets don't agree.

For companies that are rated, the analyst should examine when the rating was assigned. Have conditions changed? It is also the responsibility of the analyst to determine if the entity under consideration had its securities rated as a one-time evaluation (called a *point-in-time rating*) or is under a *regular review* rating service. Even for entities undergoing regular reviews, ratings may be dated compared with real-time information being reflected in the marketplace.

Rating agencies consider net debt/EBITDA as the leading leverage credit metric. As has been pointed out, this ratio, because of the failings of EBITDA, is deficient. Free cash flow has superior information content because it represents real cash, so it and adjusted operating cash flows are used in my credit model. Operating cash flow includes taxes, depreciation, and working capital changes and may include other adjustments for classification, timing, and comparability.

Example:

Moody's dropped the rating for the New York Times Co.'s (NYSE:NYT) corporate family of debt a notch. The Gray Lady's debt totaled 6.6 times the company's EBITDA at the end of March. Moody's had expected a multiple of 5 at its last rating, and the firm suggested it would be difficult for the company to lower the multiple below 6 in the current ad market.

Source: thedeal.com, April 14, 2009.

Some firms attempt to persuade credit-rating agencies through metrics that they believe cast them in the most favorable light. For example, Sprint, in its fourth quarter 2009 press release, stated: "Net Debt is consolidated debt, including current maturities, less cash and cash equivalents, short-term investments and restricted cash. We believe that net debt provides useful information to investors, analysts and credit rating agencies about the capacity of the company to reduce the debt load and improve its capital structure."

A drop in the credit rating can affect both the cost of capital and the ability to receive supplies, as reported in Semco Energy's 2009 10K.

Example:

In March 2003, Moody's Investors Service, Inc. reduced the credit rating on the company's senior unsecured debt from Baa3 to Ba2. Since June 2003, Standard & Poor's Ratings Group has lowered the company's corporate credit rating from BBB– to BB–. These downgrades have required the company to pay higher interest rates for financing, increasing the company's cost of capital. Any additional downgrades could further increase the company's capital costs (including the rates for borrowing under the company's Bank Credit Agreement) and limit its pool of potential investors and funding sources, possibly increasing the costs of operations or requiring the company to use a higher percentage of its available borrowing capacity for ordinary course purposes.

In addition, on February 23, 2007, Moody's Investors Service, Inc., changed the company's ratings outlook to "Developing" from "Stable" upon the announcement of the company's entry into the Exchange Agreement.

Further credit downgrades or ratings outlook changes could also negatively affect the terms on which the company can purchase gas and pipeline capacity. As a result of the company's non-investment grade credit rating noted above, the interstate pipelines the company utilizes require prepayment for their services. In addition, certain of the company's gas suppliers may require the company to prepay or provide letters of credit for gas purchases over and above the levels of credit they may have extended to the company. The company can provide no assurance that suppliers will not impose additional requirements or restrictions on the conduct of the company's business.

Source: SEMCO Energy 2009 10K.

Example:

For insurance and other financial companies that are reliant on the debt market, there is a very direct measureable effect of a downgrade (upgrade), as illustrated for the Hartford Insurance Company.

Hartford Insurance Company: Presentation to Security Analysts

We are well-positioned to withstand both a decline in equity markets and significant investment-related impacts

	($ in millions)
Projected Sources of Capital	**2H 2009**
– Estimated 6/30/09 P&C and Life capitalization in excess of "AA-" ratings	$2,300
– Statutory earnings P&C and Life (excluding investment-related impacts)	700
– Q209 Holding Company resources (including CPP funds)	3,600
– Untapped contingent capital facility and bank lines	2.400
Total Sources of Capital	**$9,000**
Potential Uses of Capital	
– Global VA impact @ YE09 S&P 968 (including VA CARVM) [1]	1,300
– Investment-related impacts (2% of invested assets) [2]	1,600
– Holding company interest/dividends	300
– Expiration of Life DTA permitted practice	200
– Allianz payment	200
Total Potential Uses of Capital	**$3,600**
Equity Market Sensitivity	
– Global VA impact @ YE09 S&P 700 [1]	$2,100

[1] VA impacts include changes in surplus and required capital

[2] Based on approximately $90 billion of statutory invested assets at 6/30/09. Includes impairments, net realized gains (losses) from sales, mark-to-market, downgrades, partnership investment losses, and risk-based capital asset risk charges

The Hartford Financial Services Group, Inc. **12**

Source: Hartford Insurance Q2 2009 earnings conference call slides material.

The illustration, taken from a slide prepared by Hartford Insurance during a quarterly investor and analyst conference call, reveals the approximate amount of excess capital the company *believed* it had over an AA– rating, which was its credit rating prior to a cut to A. Nevertheless, Hartford compares itself to a company rated AA– because it is that level grade that it would like investors (and the agencies) to believe it deserves. Factors aside from capital position that rating agencies take into consideration when evaluating Hartford include earnings, cash flow, investments and potential losses in the investment portfolio, amount of hedging and reinsurance, market share, and trajectory of these factors.

Hartford, which sells annuities, although it is not a major player in the market, reinsures about 25 percent of that business, according to its second quarter 2009 10Q. As such, underperformance in the equity market versus what was promised its clients would be harmful to its business because its fee income hinges on the investment returns and hence its assets under management.

For the financial sector, and especially the insurers, ratings downgrades cause a capital drag, forcing such firms to raise additional capital needed for the capacity to write new business. Better capital efficiency allows for increased market share growth, as it did for one of Hartford's competitors, MetLife, when its competitors withdrew or cut back on their variable annuity business. MetLife has shown that business has a lot of earnings power but can eat up "risk-based capital"—if business deteriorates, it affects capital ratios.[27] State regulatory relief took place in 2009, helping insurers by allowing their insurance subsidiaries to operate with lower capital requirements resulting from mark-to-market accounting changes and reductions in their credit ratings.

FAIR-VALUE ACCOUNTING

Perhaps no accounting standard has received more publicity nor is better known to the lay investor than SFAS 157, *Fair Value Measurements*. While the FASB was understandably desirous of fairness in reporting practices and asset and balance-sheet values, the standard's application, when liquidity dried up during the worldwide financial and credit crises, resulted in distorted valuations.

In this section I provide a brief discussion of the fair-value rules and how two insurance firms, Hartford and MetLife, applied the accounting rules. The accounting promulgation would affect any entity with substantial investments.

Fair-value rules affected many companies holding low credit assets, and analysts are required to understand how a change in rated asset level tier would affect the financial structure. For these companies, it is often more a matter of understanding the value of their investment assets than of understanding their primary business. For example, during MetLife's fourth quarter of 2009, the company reported a significant improvement in the size of its unrealized losses. Unfortunately, the company also reported a smaller gain in the size of its unrealized gains, causing its stock to drop despite strength in its basic insurance operations (see following table).

[27] *Risk-based capital* is the required capital an insurance company must maintain based on the risks of its various operations.

Why is Use of Fair Value Controversial?

- Widely divergent and strongly held views
- Some (many users, academics, standard-setters) believe that current values (fair value) are more relevant than historical costs:
  - Greater comparability
  - Basic to economic theory/grounded in the reality of the market
  - Basis of investment decisions as reflect current data/expectations
  - More understandable — reduce complexity and improve transparency
- Many feel that the use of fair value measurements have been important and beneficial to investors during the credit crisis

Source: Marc Siegel, FASB, April 2008 presentation to security analysts.

The standards for fair-value accounting, contained in SFAS 157, as amended, were effective for both annual and quarterly financial statements issued under GAAP for fiscal periods beginning after November 15, 2007. SFAS 157 created a single definition of fair value, established a framework for measuring fair value, and required enhanced disclosures surrounding an entity's fair-value measurements.

Prior to SFAS 157, there were various definitions of fair value and limited guidance for applying those definitions within the realm of GAAP. The threshold for credit impairment was higher and was recognized only when such was probable. SFAS 157 eliminated the word *probable*. This former lack of guidance and the differences in what limited advice the guidance provided added to the ever-increasing complexity of applying GAAP. There was wide belief that this inconsistent application of GAAP, coupled with different views of how fair value should be measured, led to the standard that caused so much controversy with the outset of the 2007 financial crisis. Undoubtedly, both the FASB and investors in general believed that most investments were not listed at fair value, and hence SFAS 157 was adopted.

As spelled out by the FASB in its initial summary of SFAS 157:

> This Statement defines fair value, establishes a framework for measuring fair value in generally accepted accounting principles (GAAP), and expands disclosures about fair value measurements. This Statement applies under other accounting pronouncements that require or permit fair value measurements, the Board having previously concluded in those accounting pronouncements that fair value is the relevant measurement attribute. Accordingly, this Statement does not require any new fair value measurements. However, for some entities, the application of this Statement will change current practice.

Reason for Issuing This Statement

Prior to this Statement, there were different definitions of fair value and limited guidance for applying those definitions in GAAP. Moreover, that guidance was dispersed among the many accounting pronouncements that require fair value measurements. Differences in that guidance created inconsistencies that added to the complexity in applying GAAP. In developing this Statement, the Board considered the need for increased consistency and comparability in fair value measurements and for expanded disclosures about fair value measurements.

Source: FASB.

The theory behind the statement was to improve transparency because accounting rule makers felt that corporate officers were taking refuge in and taking advantage of the dark veil of GAAP to mislead investors and creditors through the placement of higher than realistic values on many of their less than liquid securities, with the cash flows from said assets not supporting the balance-sheet values. For instance, Enron took full advantage of mark-to-market accounting, using the rule to allow it to prop up values and, with it, record substantial profits.

During meetings with investors, many sound financial institutions made clear that it was neither their desire nor their need to sell assets that were forced under SFAS 157 to be written down owing to the then disorderly and illiquid marketplace where those assets traded yet whose underlying cash flows were, for the most part, coming in as scheduled. However, owing to application of the statement, as defined by the FASB (see application of Hartford), many firms and credit-rating agencies went scrambling. The capital of financial intermediaries, the largest owners of the affected financial instruments, was put into question, and banks were unable to furnish loans and other credits to worthy industrial and service firms, causing a severe economic shock wave to the rest of the economy.

The market for structured credit products[28] held in certificate form, which had grown so rapidly during the previous five years, was in chaos, often showing bids of 20 cents on the dollar for credits that had always been timely. Therefore, to comply with SFAS 157, the financial statements of the entities holding these securities had their net worth's taking deep hits, causing another round of cuts by

[28] A structured credit included portfolios of credit instruments that can include credit derivatives. For insurers, they were primarily collateralized debt obligations (CDOs), asset-backed securities made up from mortgage pools.

credit and equity analysts who questioned the ability of many of these financial companies to survive owing to a deterioration of their financial cushion (net worth). Liquidity spreads on even the highest credits increased to unprecedented levels. Asset prices were being set by weak institutions that had to dump their holdings to raise cash, but in so doing were setting a market not supported by long-term fundamentals.

Mark-to-market accounting required companies to set a value on most securities every quarter based on market prices. To credit analysts, if the asset is not up for sale, it is timely payment and probability for retirement of the obligations that matter. Cash-flow analysts would ask: *Are the statement of cash flows and the income statement telling the same story?* Impairments, to the extent that they are actual, should affect free cash flows; if they do not, they should not have been required to be written down.

If assets are impaired, *What do you expect the new cash flows to be, and what is the new capital structure?*

To others, including the chairman of Goldman Sachs, it was not fair-value accounting that failed but a disregard for risk. When assets are not impaired temporarily, the loss must be run through earnings, according to the statement. Financial institutions and the industrial entities with credit arms must show the loss related to both the changes in the credit and the noncredit portion in accordance with SFAS 115–2, which is explained in greater detail in the next section. Both the credit and noncredit pieces go through the income statement, but only the noncredit piece is shown in comprehensive income.

While very large errors in credit judgment were made by banks, there also was no question that SFAS 157 also was to blame by not allowing valuation based on the underlying assets cash flows and recognition of investors' desire to hold these assets long term. It was concluded, in March 2009, that the rule had been responsible for enough damage, and so it was modified.

In essence, the FASB pronounced, in a Staff Position in April 2009:

> **Previous Rule:** The holder of an investment must maintain the positive *intent and ability to hold* an impaired security to the recovery of invested principal in order to conclude that an impairment is temporary in nature and not reflected in earnings.
>
> **New Rule:** The entity must maintain that it *does not intend to sell,* or *will likely not be required to sell,* prior to invested principal recovery in order to conclude that an impairment is temporary.

The provision under SFAS 157 that lay at the center of the fair-value accounting controversy is tier 3 level assets. These are financial assets and liabilities whose values are based on prices or valuation techniques that require inputs that are both unobservable and significant to the overall fair-value measurement. Level 3 assets trade infrequently; as a result, reliable market prices may be unavailable. Valuations of these assets typically are based on management assumptions or expectations.

Of importance to the analyst and creditor when evaluating tier 3 assets (also see definition of levels 1 and 2 in Hartford footnotes below) is (1) how the assets were valued, (2) the size of the tier 3 capital, and quite importantly, (3) any migration of tier 1 and 2 assets into tier 3 assets. If assets are indeed migrating into tier 3, the entity indeed has had credit impairment, affecting prospective cash flows, the financial structure, and the cost of capital; such impairments are rare for industrial concerns unless they have financing arms or large investment accounts. One also must evaluate the discount rate used to value the tier 3 assets if those assets are priced using a cash-flow model.

Not included in SFAS 157 is the fair value of liabilities, which is being addressed in a new proposal for loans under existing standard SFAS 107, *Fair Value of Financial Instruments*.

Example:

The following footnote is from Harford Insurance company's 2008 10K, including an explanation of the three levels of pricing of their financial instruments as required under FAS 157.

THE HARTFORD FINANCIAL SERVICES GROUP, INC., NOTES TO CONDENSED CONSOLIDATED FINANCIAL STATEMENTS

Fair Value Measurements

The following financial instruments are carried at fair value in the company's condensed consolidated financial statements: fixed maturities and equity securities, available-for-sale ("AFS"), short-term investments, freestanding and embedded derivatives, and separate account assets. These fair value disclosures include the fair value measurement and disclosure requirements of SFAS 157 and related FSPs including FSP FAS 157–4 and FSP FAS 107–1.

The following section applies the SFAS 157 fair value hierarchy and disclosure requirements for the company's financial instruments that are carried at fair value. SFAS 157 establishes a fair value hierarchy that prioritizes the inputs in the valuation techniques used to measure fair value into three broad Levels (Level 1, 2, or 3).

Level 1 Observable inputs that reflect quoted prices for identical assets or liabilities in active markets that the company has the ability to access at the measurement date. Level 1 securities include highly liquid U.S. Treasury securities, money market funds, certain mortgage backed securities, and exchange traded equity and derivative securities.

Level 2 Observable inputs, other than quoted prices included in Level 1, for the asset or liability or prices for similar assets and liabilities. Most debt securities and preferred stocks are model priced by vendors using observable inputs and are classified within Level 2. Also included in the Level 2 category are derivative instruments that are priced using models with significant observable market inputs, including interest rate, foreign currency and certain credit swap contracts, and no or insignificant unobservable market inputs.

Level 3 Valuations that are derived from techniques in which one or more of the significant inputs are unobservable (including assumptions about risk). Level 3 securities include less liquid securities such as highly structured and/or lower quality asset-backed securities ("ABS"), commercial mortgage-backed securities ("CMBS"), residential mortgage-backed securities ("RMBS") primarily backed by sub-prime loans, and private placement debt and equity securities. Collateralized debt obligations ("CDOs") included in Level 3 primarily represent commercial real estate ("CRE") CDOs and collateralized loan obligations ("CLOs") which are primarily priced by independent brokers due to the illiquidity of this sector. Embedded derivatives and complex derivatives securities, including equity derivatives, longer dated interest rate swaps and certain complex credit derivatives are also included in Level 3. Because Level 3 fair values, by their nature, contain unobservable market inputs as there is little or no observable market for these assets and liabilities, considerable judgment is used to determine the SFAS 157 Level 3 fair values. Level 3 fair values represent the company's best estimate of an amount that could be realized in a current market exchange absent actual market exchanges.

In many situations, inputs used to measure the fair value of an asset or liability position may fall into different levels of the fair value hierarchy. In these situations, the company will determine the level in which the fair value falls based upon the lowest level input that is significant to the determination of the fair value. In most cases, both observable (e.g., changes in interest rates) and unobservable (e.g., changes in risk assumptions) inputs are used in the determination of fair values that the company has classified within Level 3. Consequently, these values and the related gains and losses are based upon both observable and unobservable inputs. The company's fixed maturities included in Level 3 are classified as such as they are primarily priced by independent brokers and/or within illiquid markets. Corporate securities included in Level 3 primarily relate to private placement securities which are thinly traded and priced using a pricing matrix which includes significant non-observable inputs. RMBS included in Level 3 primarily represent sub-prime and Alt-A securities which are classified as Level 3 due to the lack of liquidity in the market.

These disclosures provide information as to the extent to which the company uses fair value to measure financial instruments and information about the inputs used to value those financial instruments to allow users to assess the relative reliability of the measurements. The following tables present assets and (liabilities) carried at fair value by SFAS 157 Hierarchy Level.

	June 30, 2009			
	Total	Quoted Prices in Active Markets for Identical Assets (Level 1)	Significant Observable Inputs (Level 2)	Significant Unobservable Inputs (Level 3)
Assets accounted for at fair value on a recurring basis				
Fixed maturities, AFS				
ABS	$2,450	$—	$1,948	$502
CDOs	2,563	—	1	2,562
CMBS	8,290	—	8,092	198
Corporate	30,835	—	24,305	6,530
Government/government agencies				
Foreign	1,031	—	963	68
United States	4,240	271	3,969	—
RMBS	4,506	—	3,153	1,353
States, municipalities, and political subdivisions	10,953	—	10,739	214
Total fixed maturities, AFS	64,868	271	53,170	11,427
Equity securities, trading	30,813	2,285	28,528	—
Equity securities, AFS	1,308	241	839	228
Other investments				
Variable annuity hedging derivatives	604	—	3	601
Other derivatives	342	—	305	37
Total other investments	946	—	308	638
Short-term investments	12,701	10,478	2,223	—
Reinsurance recoverable for U.S. Guaranteed Minimum Withdrawal Benefit ("GMWB")	632	—	—	632
Separate account assets	131,069	98,229	32,167	673
Total assets accounted for at fair value on a recurring basis	**$242,337**	**$111,504**	**$117,235**	**$13,598**
Liabilities accounted for at fair value on a recurring basis				
Other policyholder funds and benefits payable				
Guaranteed living benefits	$(3,344)	$—	$—	$(3,344)
Institutional notes	2	—	—	2
Equity linked notes	(6)	—	—	(6)

	June 30, 2009			
	Total	Quoted Prices in Active Markets for Identical Assets (Level 1)	Significant Observable Inputs (Level 2)	Significant Unobservable Inputs (Level 3)
Total other policyholder funds and benefits payable	(3,348)	—	—	(3,348)
Other liabilities				
Variable annuity hedging derivatives	391	—	(143)	534
Other liabilities	(579)	—	(260)	(319)
Total other liabilities	(188)	—	(403)	215
Consumer notes	(4)	—	—	(4)
Total liabilities accounted for at fair value on a recurring basis	$(3,540)	$—	**$(403)**	**$(3,137)**
			$24,511	$31,159

Source: Harford June 30, 2009, 10Q, footnote 4.

Example: METLIFE

The following example illustrates how MetLife, the large life insurer, coped with and applied the FASB rules. Although I am illustrating another insurance company, the accounting rules apply to all companies covered under the standard. Industrial companies typically are less affected unless they have finance subsidiaries, like Caterpillar, which also footnotes its Level 1, 2, and 3 assets.

MetLife, which saw its stock trade as high as $70 per share in 2007, saw it fall to $11.37 in 2009, during the height of the credit crunch. The value of its fixed-income mortgage assets dropped owing to the adoption of fair-value rules and, resulting from weakened credits reflected in "ratings migration," the requirement that MetLife hold a greater amount of risk-based capital against those lower-rated assets.

For MetLife and other companies in its industry, SFAS 115 and the related follow-on standards had a pronounced effect owing to their investment portfolios being a large multiple of shareholders' capital. Even a small swing in MetLife's investment portfolio resulted in a substantial swing in book value and reported earnings because MetLife's balance sheet listed $211.5 billion in fixed-income assets relative to $27.6 billion shareholders' equity. Despite MetLife's $1.1 billion loss during their second quarter of 2009, the improved market pricing in its investment accounts (as seen through the comprehensive income section), resulting from shrinking yield spreads from the improved market for real estate mortgage instruments, allowed the company to record an 18 percent rise in book value that propelled a greater than 30 percent rise in its stock price.

MetLife's prior quarter's investment accounts were not, for the most part, the result of severely weakened underlying cash flows. It would, however, have affected potential and expected cash flows if the securities were forced to be sold prior to maturity.

Obviously, changing yield spreads have a pronounced effect on a financial enterprise but also can affect industrial enterprises if (1) they are levered, (2) they own a financial entity, (3) they have a large investment account, or (4) they or their clients rely on the credit markets. All these are true for MetLife.

MetLife's results for their second quarter of 2009 were influenced by adoption of SFAS 115 under its recognition of other than temporary impairments of debt securities. Under the FASB guidance, the credit loss or the portion of the decline in value that represents the reduction of expected cash flows is included as a change to net income, whereas the remainder of the decline in value or the noncredit portion is recognized within accumulated other comprehensive income (AOCI). As a result of the transition adjustment required by the guidance, equity as of April 1, 2009, was increased by $76 million after tax and DAC[29] with a corresponding reduction due AOCI.

This transition adjustment represented the noncredit portion of previously reported other than temporary impairments on debt securities. For the second quarter of 2009, the other than temporary impairments of debt securities in total were $566 million on a pretax basis, of which $332 million was included in realized investment losses, whereas the remaining $234 million was recorded in other comprehensive income. So again, the SFAS 115 adjustment would have been $234 million. This charge to shareholders' equity would be reversed as asset prices improved and had no effect on cash flow.

MetLife's consolidated statement of shareholders' equity reveals a $4.473 billion gain on the market value of its investments that did not flow through net income, in conformity with the SFAS pronouncement. The gain did boost net worth by 16.2 percent and represents investments that could be sold if MetLife decided it had a good use (or need) for that near cash, such as investments in higher-yielding instruments or to place additional cash on the balance sheet of its insurance subsidiaries, to fund additional growth. Some of these investments would in fact be sold later to help finance part of the firm's $15.5 billion acquisition of ALICO from AIG.

The financial statements on the following pages clearly show the impact of SFAS 115–2 and 124–2, *Recognition of Other than Temporary Investments*, on the various schedules. The standard is available at www.fasb.org and is discussed in the next subsection.

As MetLife wrote in its first quarter 2009 10Q:

> The above critical accounting estimates are described in *Management's Discussion and Analysis of Financial Condition and Results of Operations—Summary of Critical Accounting Estimates* and Note 1 of our 2008 Annual Report. We have updated the disclosures below due to the adoption of Financial Accounting Standards Board ("FASB") Staff Position ("FSP") No. FAS 115–2 and FAS 124–2, *Recognition and Presentation of Other-Than-Temporary Impairments* ("FSP 115–2"), which affects the recognition and measurement of impaired securities and significant changes in DAC estimates due to market volatility.
>
> ## Investment Impairments
>
> One of the significant estimates related to available-for-sale securities is the evaluation of investments for other-than-temporary impairments. The assessment of whether

[29]DAC refers to *deferred acquisition costs*, which in the case of large insurance companies include losses or gains above or below what was assumed they would be able to earn for investors on their annuities.

impairments have occurred is based on management's case-by-case evaluation of the underlying reasons for the decline in estimated fair value. The company's review of its fixed maturity and equity securities for impairments includes an analysis of the total gross unrealized losses by three categories of securities: (i) securities where the estimated fair value had declined and remained below cost or amortized cost by less than 20%; (ii) securities where the estimated fair value had declined and remained below cost or amortized cost by 20% or more for less than six months; and (iii) securities where the estimated fair value had declined and remained below cost or amortized cost by 20% or more for six months or greater. An extended and severe unrealized loss position on a fixed maturity security may not have any impact on the ability of the issuer to service all scheduled interest and principal payments and the company's evaluation of recoverability of all contractual cash flows or the ability to recover an amount at least equal to its amortized cost based on the present value of the expected future cash flows to be collected. In contrast, for certain equity securities, greater weight and consideration are given by the company to a decline in estimated fair value and the likelihood such estimated fair value decline will recover.

Additionally, management considers a wide range of factors about the security issuer and uses its best judgment in evaluating the cause of the decline in the estimated fair value of the security and in assessing the prospects for near-term recovery. Inherent in management's evaluation of the security are assumptions and estimates about the operations of the issuer and its future earnings potential. Considerations used by the company in the impairment evaluation process include, but are not limited to:

(i) the length of time and the extent to which the estimated fair value has been below cost or amortized cost;

(ii) the potential for impairments of securities when the issuer is experiencing significant financial difficulties;

(iii) the potential for impairments in an entire industry sector or sub-sector;

(iv) the potential for impairments in certain economically depressed geographic locations;

(v) the potential for impairments of securities where the issuer, series of issuers, or industry has suffered a catastrophic type of loss or has exhausted natural resources;

(vi) with respect to equity securities, whether the company's ability and intent to hold the security for a period of time sufficient to allow for the recovery of its value to an amount equal to or greater than cost or amortized cost;

(vii) with respect to fixed maturity securities, whether the company has the intent to sell or will more likely than not be required to sell a particular security before recovery of the decline in fair value below amortized cost;

(viii) unfavorable changes in forecasted cash flows on mortgage-backed and asset-backed securities; and

(ix) other subjective factors, including concentrations and information obtained from regulators and rating agencies.

The cost of fixed maturity and equity securities is adjusted for impairments in value deemed to be other-than-temporary and charged to earnings in the period in which the determination is made. For equity securities, the carrying value of the equity security is impaired to its fair value, with a corresponding charge to earnings. When an other-than-temporary impairment of a fixed maturity security has occurred, the amount of the other-than-temporary impairment recognized in earnings depends on whether the company intends to sell the security or more likely than not will be required to sell the security before recovery of its amortized cost basis. If the fixed maturity security meets either of these two criteria, the other-than-temporary impairment recognized in earnings is equal to the entire difference between the security's amortized cost basis and its fair value at the impairment measurement date. For other-than-temporary impairments of fixed maturity securities that do not meet either of these two criteria, the net amount recognized in earnings is equal to the difference between the amortized cost of the fixed maturity security and the present value of projected future cash flows to be collected from this security. Any difference between the fair value and the present value of the expected future cash flows of the security at the impairment measurement date is recorded in other comprehensive income (loss). The company does not change the revised cost basis for subsequent recoveries in value.

The determination of the amount of allowances and impairments on other invested asset classes is highly subjective and is based upon the company's periodic evaluation and assessment of known and inherent risks associated with the respective asset class. Such evaluations and assessments are revised as conditions change and new information becomes available. Management updates its evaluations regularly and reflects changes in allowances and impairments in operations as such evaluations are revised.

Source: MetLife August 3, 2009, 10Q.

METLIFE, INC.

INTERIM CONDENSED CONSOLIDATED BALANCE SHEETS

June 30, 2009 (Unaudited) and December 31, 2008

(In Millions, Except Share and Per-Share Data)

	June 30, 2009	December 31, 2008
Assets		
Investments:		
Fixed-maturity securities available for sale at estimated fair value (amortized cost: $225,494 and $209,508, respectively)	$211,563	$188,251
Equity securities available for sale at estimated fair value (cost: $3,679 and $4,131, respectively)	3,045	3,197
Trading securities, at estimated fair value (cost: $1,523 and $1,107, respectively)	1,471	946
Mortgage and consumer loans:		
Held for investment, at amortized cost (net of valuation allowances of $543 and $304, respectively)	48,229	49,352
Held for sale, principally at estimated fair value	4,271	2,012
Mortgage and consumer loans, net	52,500	51,364
Policy loans	9,907	9,802
Real estate and real estate joint ventures held for investment	7,295	7,585
Real estate held for sale	1	1
Other limited partnership interests	5,193	6,039
Short-term investments	8,117	13,878
Other invested assets	13,071	17,248
Total investments	312,163	298,311
Cash and cash equivalents	13,213	24,207
Accrued investment income	3,019	3,061

	June 30, 2009	December 31, 2008
Premiums and other receivables	16,730	16,973
Deferred policy acquisition costs and value of business acquired	20,323	20,144
Current income tax recoverable	253	—
Deferred income tax assets	3,856	4,927
Goodwill	5,036	5,008
Other assets	7,896	7,262
Assets of subsidiaries held for sale	—	946
Separate account assets	126,968	120,839
Total assets	$509,457	$501,678
Liabilities and Stockholders' Equity		
Liabilities:		
Future policy benefits	$132,823	$130,555
Policyholder account balances	147,883	149,805
Other policyholder funds	8,319	7,762
Policyholder dividends payable	881	1,023
Short-term debt	4,757	2,659
Long-term debt	12,940	9,667
Collateral financing arrangements	5,297	5,192
Junior subordinated debt securities	2,691	3,758
Current income tax payable	—	342
Payables for collateral under securities loaned and other transactions	24,607	31,059
Other liabilities	14,679	14,284
Liabilities of subsidiaries held for sale	—	748
Separate account liabilities	126,968	120,839
Total liabilities	481,845	477,693
Contingencies, Commitments, and Guarantees (Note 11)		
Stockholders' Equity:		
MetLife, Inc., stockholders' equity:		
Preferred stock, par value $0.01 per share, 200,000,000 shares authorized, 84,000,000 shares issued and outstanding, $2,100 aggregate liquidation preference	1	1
Common stock, par value $0.01 per share, 3,000,000,000 shares authorized, 822,359,818 shares and 798,016,664 shares issued at June 30, 2009 and December 31, 2008, respectively, 818,586,271 shares and 793,629,070 shares outstanding on June 30, 2009 and December 31, 2008, respectively	8	8
Additional paid-in capital	16,849	15,811
Retained earnings	20,472	22,403
Treasury stock, at cost, 3,773,547 shares and 4,387,594 shares on June 30, 2009 and December 31, 2008, respectively	(203)	(236)
Accumulated other comprehensive loss	(9,834)	(14,253)
Total MetLife, Inc., stockholders' equity	27,293	23,734
Noncontrolling interests	319	251
Total equity	27,612	23,985
Total liabilities and stockholders' equity	$509,457	$501,678

METLIFE, INC.

INTERIM CONDENSED CONSOLIDATED STATEMENT OF STOCKHOLDERS' EQUITY

FOR THE SIX MONTHS ENDED JUNE 30, 2009 (Unaudited)

(In Millions)

	Preferred Stock	Common Stock	Additional Paid-in Capital	Retained Earnings	Treasury Stock at Cost
Balance on December 31, 2008	$1	$8	$15,811	$22,403	$(236)
Cumulative effect of changes in accounting principle, net of income tax (Note 1)				76	
Common stock issuance—newly issued shares			1,035		
Treasury stock transactions, net			2		33
Deferral of stock-based compensation			1		
Dividends on preferred stock				(61)	
Change in equity of noncontrolling interests					
Comprehensive income (loss):					
Net loss				(1,946)	
Other comprehensive income (loss):					
Unrealized gains (losses) on derivative instruments, net of income tax					
Unrealized investment gains (losses), net of related offsets and income tax					
Foreign currency translation adjustments, net of income tax					
Defined benefit plans adjustment, net of income tax					
Other comprehensive income (loss)					
Comprehensive income (loss)					
Balance at June 30, 2009	$1	$8	$16,849	$20,472	$(203)

See accompanying notes to the interim condensed consolidated financial statements.

Accumulated Other Comprehensive Loss						
Net Unrealized Investment Gains (Losses)	**Other-Than-Temporary Impairments**	**Foreign Currency Translation Adjustments**	**Defined Benefit Plans Adjustment**	**Total MetLife, Inc.'s Stockholders' Equity**	**Noncontrolling Interests**	**Total Equity**
$(12,564)	$—	$(246)	$(1,443)	$23,734	$251	$23,985
	(76)					
				1,035		1,035
				35		35
				1		1
				(61)		(61)
					95	95
				(1,946)	(20)	(1,966)
(57)				(57)		(57)
4,624	(145)			4,479	(7)	4,472
		(6)		(6)		(6)
			79	79		79
				4,495	(7)	4,488
				2,549	(27)	2,522
$(7,997)	$(221)	$(252)	$(1,364)	$27,293	$319	$27,612

METLIFE, INC.
INTERIM CONDENSED CONSOLIDATED STATEMENT OF STOCKHOLDERS' EQUITY
FOR THE SIX MONTHS ENDED JUNE 30, 2008 (Unaudited)
(In Millions)

	Preferred Stock	Common Stock	Additional Paid-in Capital	Retained Earnings	Treasury Stock at Cost
Balance at December 31, 2007	$1	$8	$17,098	$19,884	$(2,890)
Cumulative effect of changes in accounting principles, net of income tax				27	
Balance at January 1, 2008	1	8	17,098	19,911	(2,890)
Treasury stock transactions, net			408		(1,157)
Deferral of stock-based compensation			141		
Dividends on preferred stock				(64)	
Dividends on subsidiary common stock					
Change in equity of noncontrolling interests					
Comprehensive loss:					
Net income				1,594	
Other comprehensive income (loss):					
Unrealized gains (losses) on derivative instruments, net of income tax					
Unrealized investment gains (losses), net of related offsets and income tax					
Foreign currency translation adjustments, net of income tax					
Other comprehensive loss					
Comprehensive loss					
Balance at June 30, 2008	$1	$8	$17,647	$21,441	$(4,047)

See accompanying notes to the interim condensed consolidated financial statements.

Accumulated Other Comprehensive Loss				Noncontrolling Interests		
Net Unrealized Investment Gains (Losses)	Foreign Currency Translation Adjustments	Defined Benefit Plans Adjustment	Total MetLife, Inc.'s Stockholders' Equity	Discontinued Operations	Continuing Operations	Total Equity
$971	$347	$(240)	$35,179	$1,534	$272	$36,985
(10)			17			17
961	347	(240)	35,196	1,534	272	37,002
			(749)			(749)
			141			141
			(64)			(64)
				(16)		(16)
				14	(65)	(51)
			1,594	71	(9)	1,656
(33)			(33)			(33)
(3,624)			(3,624)	(128)	(7)	(3,759)
	80		80	(3)		77
			(3,577)	(131)	(7)	(3,715)
			(1,983)	(60)	(16)	(2,059)
$(2,696)	$427	$(240)	$32,541	$1,472	$191	$34,204

As one can see, security analysis has evolved to a profession of requiring good credit analyst skills, especially for financial entities, given the size of their investment accounts in relation to their equity. Their holdings must be scrutinized as closely as one would go about an analysis of the operating company.

Without the credit foundation, it would be difficult to determine the risk to the cash flows and financial structure along with the potential for "unforeseen" surprises not discounted by investors in general. This is important in understanding industrial enterprises as well because they rely on the credit market to function properly. Even though an investor may have little interest in direct ownership of a financial security, understanding how to evaluate such securities will aid their analysis of other sectors. There have been many examples of this. For example, there have been construction cancellations and delays of large industrial projects owing to financial impairment of both the creditor and the builder. Many home builders were weakened or placed into bankruptcy owing to their financial subsidiaries' and joint ventures' leverage; large investor loss might have been avoided if such an analysis had taken place. The ability of a financial intermediary to produce sufficient and timely letters of credit also affects industrial concerns. The financial enterprise is expected to provide these funding requirements; if this support is not reliable or is weakened, the industrial entity is weakened as well.

Shifting market, financial, and economic conditions would be sure to cause a magnified affect to the equity of MetLife owing to changes in the market value of its large investment portfolio and the potential for ratings migration. Credit analysis, by forcing recognition of current risks with concurrent evaluation of the integrity of the financial structure, permits the analyst to place a more accurate discount rate onto the firm, yielding a fair value that can differ significantly from the current market value. In the case of MetLife, the company's financial strength was not being reflected in its cost of capital, forced on it by accounting regulation. The company had no need to sell assets at distressed levels given that both the cash flows from its high-quality investment portfolio and its operating businesses were holding up. The decline in its operating cash flows, as seen from its interim statement, resulted from a negative (hedge) bet the company made against itself by which it would gain if its yield spread rose. Such are the oddities of financial enterprises.

SFAS 115

SFAS 115–2 and SFAS 124–2, *Recognition and Presentation of Other-Than-Temporary Impairments on Debt Securities*, while chiefly affecting financial institutions, also affect entities having finance subsidiaries and other enterprises holding financial instruments. Where the predisposition to sell a financial instrument exists, the entire difference between the security's cost and fair value is recognized in earnings on the balance-sheet date. This practice is consistent with previous GAAP guidance, where the absence of intent to hold resulted in a write-down of the entire difference between amortized cost and fair value.

Where the ongoing intent of the organization is not to sell and the requirement to sell is unlikely, securities in an unrealized loss position that are identified for impairment on the balance-sheet date must have the difference between the security's cost and fair value bifurcated into two segments:

1. That attributable to credit loss, and
2. That attributable to all other factors

FSP SFAS 115–2 provides that an entity should use its best estimate of the present value of expected cash flows from the debt security to determine the presence of a credit loss. Contributing factors may include

- Length of time and extent to which the fair value has been less than the amortized cost
- Adverse conditions specifically related to the security, an industry, or a geographic area
- Historic and implied volatility of the security
- Payment structure of the debt security and the likelihood of the issuer's ability to make payments in the future
- Failure of the security issuer to make scheduled interest payments
- NRSRO rating agency changes to the security's rating
- Any subsequent events to the balance-sheet date that affect fair value

The credit-loss component then is recognized in earnings on the balance-sheet date, whereas all the other factor segments are carried in accumulated other comprehensive income.

One methodology to employ when estimating future cash-flow collections would be to follow the guidance prescribed in paragraphs 12 through 16 of SFAS 114, *Accounting by Creditors for Impairment of a Loan.* In this statement, the projected cash-flow collection is calculated using the present value of expected future cash flows discounted at the effective interest rate implicit in the security at the date of acquisition.

SFAS 166 AND SFAS 167

Adopted by the FASB in June 2009, for adoption beginning in 2010, SFAS 166, Accounting for Transfers of Financial Assets, and SFAS 167, Amendments to FASB Interpretation No. 46(R), change the method by which entities account for securitizations and special-purpose entities. SFAS 166 relates to the consolidation of variable-interest entities, and SFAS 167 amends existing guidance for when a company "derecognizes" transfers of financial assets. A variable-interest entity is a business structure that allows an investor to hold a controlling interest in the entity without that interest translating into possessing enough voting privileges to result in a majority. The new standard requires noncontrolling interests be reported as a separate component of equity and that net income or loss attributable to the parent and noncontrolling interests be separately identified in the statement of operations.

Example:

Marriot International, Inc., is a worldwide operator and franchisor of hotels and related lodging facilities. The company periodically sells notes receivable, on a nonrecourse basis, originated by its timeshare segment in connection with the sale of timeshare intervals and other timeshare-like products. The company continues to service the notes and transfers all proceeds collected to its special-purpose entities. If the notes have higher than projected default rates, there are provisions to which the cash flows of the pool will be maintained as extra collateral, affecting the cash flows to Marriott. The principal continues to be nonrecourse, however.

Even though nonrecourse notes legally remove Marriot from any default liability on the receivables, the company, based on the additional collateral it maintains, leaves doubt that it would allow the security holder to suffer a substantial loss. As such, a high default rate would negatively affect Marriott's cash flow.

For purpose of analysis, since the receivables are sold on a nonrecourse basis, the securitization pool would not be included as part of total liabilities, even though the debt from the SPE would be consolidated because Marriott exercises control over the subsidiary, in accordance with FSAS 166 and 167. Cash flow would remain the same, being the proceeds from the sale of the receivables and any interest not due to the note holders. If the owners of a timeshare default on their loan, Marriot could foreclose and resell the property. The following is from the company's 2008 10K:

> The company expects to adopt FAS 166 and 167 at the beginning of 2010, which will impact its accounting for securitized timeshare loans. Assuming the consolidation of the existing portfolio of securitized loans, the company expects assets to increase by $950 million to $1,025 million, liabilities to increase by $1,020 million to $1,120 million, and shareholders' equity to decline by $70 million to $95 million. Pretax earnings in 2010 would increase by $30 million to $50 million as a result of the accounting change, but no change in cash flow is anticipated.

LEASES

There are two major types of leases—capital leases and operating leases. Assets under capital leases are recorded as assets on the balance sheet with offsetting liabilities (usually denoted *capital lease obligations*) among the long-term liabilities of the firm. Assets under operating leases are not shown on the balance sheet as assets, nor are balance-sheet liabilities recorded owing to these leases.

From a credit viewpoint, operating leases should be capitalized to account for the acquired obligation while permitting comparability by taking into consideration all assets and liabilities, whether on or off the balance sheet. The capital base, by adjusting for the present value of lease commitments, more appropriately reflects actual returns on measures such as ROIC. To exclude operating leases would be to understate the capital base, especially relative to a firm that tended to sign capitalized leases, in both leverage and ROIC metrics.

To the cash-flow analyst, the signing of capital leases may artificially enhance operating cash flows. This is so because while the interest portion of capital leases is counted as an operating activity, the reduction in the lease, through those principal payments, is reported as a financing activity.

Weaker credit entities find it easier to enter operating leases because the credit hurdle is not as severe, especially since these obligations do not impair reportable shareholders' equity. Also, leasing assets, especially when technological innovation is rapid or if the entity is not completely sure the extent the asset is needed, may be preferable to an operating lease. Since lessees may not show imputed interest in fixed-charge coverage ratios, the analyst would need to include that charge in addition to typical interest expense in the calculation, although it is preferable to include the entire lease expense, that related to both capital and operating leases, because this is the cash payment actually due. Also, in the event the lessee has a low tax rate and thus the benefit of depreciation is enjoyed by the lessor, lower lease payments would result in additional cash savings to the lessee. In my credit model, I include the entire lease payment in fixed-charge coverage.

There is also greater flexibility to entering an operating lease because when the lease term is over, or if downsizing is required, the asset is handed back. If the same asset is purchased, it may be difficult to sell or can be sold only for a price that is less than its depreciated value. Such risk is borne by the lessor.

Information about operating leases is disclosed only through a footnote to the financial statements, hence the name *off-balance-sheet liability*. Accounting and disclosure requirements for leases are covered primarily by SFAS 13 and later pronouncements by the FASB that served to explain or slightly modify SFAS 13. It appears the FASB will, in the near future, modify existing standards because it is widely recognized by investors, credit-rating agencies, and the SEC (all of whom have voiced opposition to the current methodology) that operating leases represent a true liability. On March 12, 2009, the FASB and the IASB jointly issued a discussion paper, "Leases: Preliminary Views," that presents possible new approaches to lease accounting, including capitalizing operating leases. In August, 2010, the IASB and the FASB grew one step closer to the placement of operating leases on the balance sheet through the issuance of an exposure draft. The proposal requires a variety of assumptions in the estimation of the liability, and at this time a final standard has not been issued. Once issued, the analyst would need to monitor the lease expense versus any discrepancy in the reporting of cash flows.

Operating and capital leases are distinguished mainly though tests that are intended to examine whether the benefits and risks of ownership were in fact transferred from the lessor to the lessee. If they were, the lease is classified as a *capital lease*, and the asset with an offsetting liability is included on the balance sheet. Otherwise, the lease is classified as an *operating lease*, and the information is reported in the footnote. There are four major tests for the classification of leases as capital or operating leases. If any of these tests are satisfied, the lease is classified as a capital lease. The determination as to whether a lease should appear on the balance sheet is rather straightforward: Is it a right-of-use contract under which the user is legally bound to make periodic payments? Does the entity derive a perceived economic benefit? There is no question under current GAAP that similar transactions can be accounted for differently.

To the cash-flow analyst, the questions are rather straightforward: What are the entity's expected operating cash flows, and can they cover the liabilities assumed from undertaking the additional lease liability? What is the expected cash return, adjusted for taxes, for assuming the lease obligation and placing the asset in service under a variety of economic and business conditions? What is the effect of the additional liability on leverage ratios and ROIC? The question is not whether operating leases, even short-term leases, should be considered debt and placed onto the balance sheet—of course, they should! However, if the free-cash-flow yield from the asset under lease is above the firm's cost of capital, it is a value-enhancing proposition. If it is free-cash-flow-neutral, it is not rewarding to shareholders.

It is atypical to see an entity include equipment under operating leases in the property, plant, and equipment account through capitalization, although the number has been growing in recent years, especially because credit agencies have made it known that they take operating leases into account when constructing debt ratios.

Example: UPS

United Parcel Service (UPS), the world's largest package delivery company, while being a very large lessee, is also a lessor of aircraft. In its PPE account, the company includes equipment under operating leases for aircraft, which, in turn, the company may lease out, depending on its own needs. All the following tables for the UPS example to follow are taken from the UPS 2008 10K.

TABLE 6-20

United Parcel Service, Inc, and Subsidiaries

PROPERTY, PLANT, AND EQUIPMENT (In Millions)

	2008	2007
Vehicles	$5,508	$5,295
Aircraft (including aircraft under capitalized leases)	14,564	13,541
Land	1,068	1,056
Buildings	2,836	2,837
Building and leasehold improvements	2,702	2,604
Plant equipment	5,720	5,537
Technology equipment	1,620	1,699
Equipment under operating leases	136	153
Construction in progress	944	889
	35,098	33,611
Less: Accumulated depreciation and amortization	(16,833)	(15,948)
	$18,265	$17,663

Tests to Determine Whether a Lease Is Capital or Operating

1. If the lease life exceeds 75 percent of the life of the asset
2. If there is a transfer of ownership to the lessee at the end of the lease term
3. If there is an option to purchase the asset at a "bargain price" at the end of the lease term
4. If the present value of the lease payments, discounted at an appropriate discount rate, exceeds 90 percent of the fair market value of the asset

From a tax standpoint, the lessor can claim the tax benefits of the leased asset only if it is an operating lease, although the revenue code uses slightly different criteria for determining whether the lease is an operating lease.

If the lease is classified as an operating lease, at the end of the lease period, the lessee returns the property to the lessor. Since the lessee does not assume the risk of ownership, the lease expense is treated as an operating expense in the income statement with no effect on the recording company's balance sheet. In the lease is a capital lease, the lessee is deemed to assume some of the risks of ownership and enjoys some of the benefits. Consequently, the lease, when signed, is recognized both as an asset and as a liability (for the lease payments) on the balance sheet. The firm gets to claim depreciation each year on the asset and also deducts the interest expense component of the lease payment each year. In general, capital leases recognize expenses sooner than equivalent operating leases.

The analyst should thoroughly review the entity's footnotes to detect SPEs or other arrangements (*synthetic leases*) that were set up to avoid placing a lease liability directly on the balance sheet. Since analysts must look beyond the balance sheet when formulating liability ratios, a review of such financial circumventions must take place, and liability ratios must be adjusted accordingly. A synthetic lease allows the lessee to maintain ownership and receive the tax advantages of ownership while keeping the liability off the balance sheet. It can, for tax purposes, be set up to treat the lease payments as debt service, allowing the lessee to deduct interest expense and allow for depreciation of the asset. The synthetic lease belonging to an SPE must be considered as part of total debt, just as any operating lease. A strategy similar to synthetic leases is a sale-leaseback arrangement, whereby the owner sells the asset for cash and then leases it back for a specified time period.

Example:

Korean Air (KAL) is believed to have opted for a sale/ leaseback for the financing of one A330 delivery in November instead of bank debt or the possibility of another Japanese operating lease (JOL). KAL elected not to put the aircraft forward for export credit financing.

Source: Airfinance Journal, November 2000.

Example:

UPS typically enters into operating leases for its delivery equipment, such as trucks, vans, and warehouse equipment. Its capital leases are used primarily for aircraft, as shown in Table 6-21. In its property, plant, and equipment account on its balance sheet, the $2.080 billion from Table 6-21 will be included as part of the $18.265 billion in total PPE.

In a related financial strategy, UPS purchased high-investment-grade financial assets that allowed it to circumvent placing some capital leases on its balance sheet. The company has, in accounting parlance, *defeased* those liabilities, thus allowing it to receive interest on the related investments while improving leverage ratios. If UPS needed that cash for its operations, those investments could be sold, and the defeased capital leases would need to be placed back on its balance sheet as an asset and related liability.

TABLE 6-21

UPS Lease Obligations

Capital Lease Obligations

We have certain aircraft subject to capital leases. Some of the obligations associated with these capital leases have been legally defeased. The recorded value of aircraft subject to capital leases, which are included in Property, Plant, and Equipment, is as follows as of December 31 (in millions):

	2008	2007
Aircraft	$2,571	$2,573
Accumulated amortization	(491)	(416)
	$2,080	$2,157

These capital lease obligations have principal payments due at various dates from 2009 through 2021. Once the capital leases have been defeased, that is the company has placed a sufficient amount of cash into the highest grade investments to cover those payments, that debt associated with the lease no longer appears as a liability on the balance sheet.

We see in Table 6-22 that UPS deducted $115 million in imputed interest from its total minimum capital lease obligations. In the capital lease, part of the expense is presumed to be interest, which is an estimated portion of its total payment. For tax purposes, companies can deduct the imputed interest as well as current depreciation on the leased asset because the asset is deemed to be owned. UPS is using a 21.3 percent tax rate in its estimate of imputed interest, which is the $115 million divided by the $540 million. If the same asset had been purchased with cash, the firm would only be able to deduct the depreciation, which may be different from the imputed interest and depreciation expense. From time to time, to incentivize capital spending, Congress allows for quicker depreciation through the use of investment tax credits on the purchase of new long-lived equipment. The investment tax credit is calculated as a percentage of the equipment's cost and is a direct offset to taxes otherwise payable.

For analysts who look at EBITDA or operating income, imputed interest is added back, aiding those metrics, a practice I do not agree with because it does not reflect distributable cash.

UPS uses both operating and capital leases in its fleet of aircraft, although it leans more heavily towards capital lease obligations. We see its projected minimum lease payments for the coming five years, with a single line entry for the subsequent years, in Table 6-22. The company also reveals in its footnote: "We lease certain aircraft, facilities, equipment and vehicles under operating leases, which expire at various dates through 2055." The analyst should resolve how the company determines which assets it places under operating and which it places under capital leases to the extent its cash flows can be expected to change if the scheme for determining lease structure also changes.

TABLE 6-22

UPS Lease and Debt Maturity Schedule

The following table sets forth the aggregate minimum lease payments under capital and operating leases, the aggregate annual principal payments due under our long-term debt, and the aggregate amounts expected to be spent for purchase commitments (in millions):

Year	Capital Leases	Operating Leases	Debt Principal	Purchase Commitments
2009	$83	$344	$2,007	$708
2010	121	288	18	658
2011	29	217	5	667
2012	30	147	22	406
2013	31	109	1,768	—
After 2013	246	423	5,658	—
Total	540	$1,528	$9,478	$2,439
Less: Imputed interest	(115)			
Present value of minimum capitalized lease payments	425			
Less: Current portion	(65)			
Long-term capitalized lease obligations	$360			

As of December 31, 2008, we had outstanding letters of credit totaling approximately $2.132 billion issued in connection with our self-insurance reserves and other routine business requirements. We also issue surety bonds as an alternative to letters of credit in certain instances, and as of December 31, 2008, we had $262 million of surety bonds written.

From a credit point of view, the analyst should consider any legal and, in some instances, moral obligation necessitating a cash outflow—including operating leases—as debt (Table 6-23). These include commitments and contingency obligations, although the latter items might be more difficult to quantify because not all may result in a cash outflow. The obligation to transfer cash resulting from a lease payment in a future period should result in a liability on the balance sheet whether or not the leased asset is a de facto purchase. Similarly, the right to obtain benefits from use of the leased asset in the future should be construed as an existing asset on the balance sheet. On the other hand, the flexibility of an operating lease can prove of value should the asset no longer be needed or has declined in value.

Thus, in order to estimate the total debt of the firm, we need to estimate the future payments under operating leases because the present value under capitalized lease obligations is already included in the long-term debt of the firm. To do this, we use information that is available in the footnotes to the financial statements, as is shown for UPS in Table 6-23. To discount the operating lease obligations, we rely on present-value tables.

TABLE 6-23

Expected Cash Outlays

We have contractual obligations and commitments in the form of capital leases, operating leases, debt obligations, purchase commitments, pension fundings, and certain other liabilities. We intend to satisfy these obligations through the use of cash flow from operations. The following table summarizes the expected cash outflow to satisfy our contractual obligations and commitments as of December 31, 2008 (in millions):

Year	Capital Leases	Operating Leases	Debt Principal	Debt Interest	Purchase Commitments	Pension Fundings	Other Liabilities
2009	$83	$344	$2,007	$331	$708	$778	$74
2010	121	288	18	326	658	593	71
2011	29	217	5	326	667	828	69
2012	30	147	22	325	406	945	67
2013	31	109	1,768	285	—	964	65
After 2013	246	423	5,658	4,526	—	—	139
Total	$540	$1,528	$9,478	$6,119	$2,439	$4,108	$485

Source: UPS 2008 10K.

Unlike UPS, FedEx Corp. has been active signing operating leases as its preferred method of financing aircraft. As the company states in its footnote:

> The amounts reflected in the table . . . for operating leases represent future minimum lease payments under noncancelable operating leases (principally aircraft and facilities) with an initial or remaining term in excess of one year at May 31, 2009. In the past, we financed a significant portion of our aircraft needs (and certain other equipment needs) using operating leases (a type of "off-balance sheet financing"). At the time that the decision to lease was made, we determined that these operating leases would provide economic benefits favorable to ownership with respect to market values, liquidity, or after-tax cash flows.

The following table shows, in conformity with GAAP, the reduction in capital leases as a financing activity and represents only 2.2 percent ($328/$14,656) of expected payments of the company's operating leases.

UPS, in its last fiscal year had $51 billion in revenue, and FedEx had $35 billion in revenue. Yet, because of their differing financial strategies regarding non-balance-sheet-listed operating leases, FedEx showed just $2.5 billion in short- and long-term reported debt compared with $9.9 billion for UPS.

Contractual Cash Obligations

The following table sets forth a summary of our contractual cash obligations as of May 31, 2009. Certain of these contractual obligations are reflected in our balance sheet, while others are disclosed as future obligations under accounting principles generally accepted in the United States. Except for the current portion of long-term debt and capital lease obligations, this table does not include amounts already recorded in our balance sheet as current liabilities at May 31, 2009. Accordingly, this table is not meant to represent a forecast of our total cash expenditures for any of the periods presented.

Payments Due by Fiscal Year (Undiscounted)
(In Millions)

	2010	2011	2012	2013	2014	Thereafter	Total
Operating activities:							
Operating leases	$1,759	$1,612	$1,451	$1,316	$1,166	$7,352	$14,656
Noncapital purchase obligations and other	234	137	111	62	11	125	680
Interest on long-term debt	157	144	126	98	97	1,815	2,437

(Continued)

Payments Due by Fiscal Year (Undiscounted)
(In Millions)

	2010	2011	2012	2013	2014	Thereafter	Total
Required quarterly contributions to our U.S. retirement plans	350	—	—	—	—	—	350
Investing activities:							
Aircraft and aircraft-related capital commitments	964	791	527	425	466	1,924	5,097
Other capital purchase obligations	69	—	—	—	—	—	69
Financing activities:							
Debt	500	250	—	300	250	989	2,289
Capital lease obligations	164	20	8	119	2	15	328
Total	$4,197	$2,954	$2,223	$2,320	$1,992	$12,220	$25,906

Source: FedEx 2009 10K.

Back to UPS, the analyst would be required to make an adjustment to his or her cash-flow/total-debt model by increasing overall debt by the present value (Table 6-29) of the operating leases. In reality, UPS is a growing concern whose operating leases have been growing by 5.6 percent per year (Table 6-24), and to discount the operating leases as called for by GAAP (contractual cash obligations) would not reflect the historical underpinnings. For this exercise, we will assume that the minimum amounts reported in the company's 10K are correct, and we need to adjust its liabilities based on the reported amount of the current lease portfolio. If the analyst would like to account for growth in operating leases above the stated minimum, this would be both acceptable and, in many cases, necessary but I would caution that the growth rate should be no greater than shown historically, in this case 5.6 percent per year. Keep in mind that enterprises are required to report only the minimum expected lease liability, meaning the leases currently under contract.

As disclosed in the statements and footnotes that follow, UPS reports $7.8 billion in long-term debt, exclusive of operating leases, which is reflected on its balance sheet. Its footnote reveals that it has signed $425 million in capital leases, which seems low, inasmuch some of those leases are not due until 2055, which, when using present value, significantly lowers its adjusted value. Recall that UPS defeased some of its obligations under capital lease, which improved reported balance-sheet debt. Its operating leases, listed at $1.5 billion, or about

TABLE 6-24

Growth Rate in Operating Lease Obligations: UPS, 1998–2008

Fiscal Year	Five-Year Operating Leases	Percentage Change
1998	643	
1999	617	−4.0%
2000	975	58.0%
2001	1210	24.1%
2002	993	−17.9%
2003	992	−0.1%
2004	1,236	24.6%
2005	1,301	5.3%
2006	1,269	−2.5%
2007	1,222	−3.7%
2008	1,105	−9.6%
Annualized 10-year growth rate		5.6%

22 percent of its net worth, are not included on its balance sheet. It is important that we note that UPS's shareholders' equity dropped in good part related to a $3.6 billion addition to its comprehensive loss section of shareholders' equity, resulting mostly from its pension and postretirement plans (despite an increase in its discount rate). Table 6-25 reveals details of this comprehensive loss, which, we will soon see, may be added back, under certain conditions, to shareholders' equity, as if the loss were the result of a temporary impairment and not a reflection of higher expected normalized contributions. Comprehensive actuarial losses/gains are commonly associated with large annual swings, which, in most instances, would not impair long-term creditworthiness and would cause an imprecise and unstable estimate of ROIC, as I have defined it, if included.

TABLE 6-25

Accumulated Comprehensive Income: UPS, 2006–2008

Accumulated Other Comprehensive Income (Loss)

We incur activity in AOCI for unrealized holding gains and losses on available-for-sale securities, foreign currency translation adjustments, unrealized gains and losses from derivatives that qualify as hedges of cash flows, and unrecognized pension and postretirement benefit costs. The activity in AOCI is as follows (in millions):

(Continued)

	2008	2007	2006
Foreign currency translation gain (loss):			
Balance at beginning of year	$81	$(109)	$(163)
Aggregate adjustment for the year	(119)	190	54
Balance at end of year	(38)	81	(109)
Unrealized gain (loss) on marketable securities, net of tax:			
Balance at beginning of year	9	12	11
Current period changes in fair value [net of tax effect of $(33), $4, and $(3)]	(78)	6	(4)
Reclassification to earnings [net of tax effect of $5, $(5), and $3]	9	(9)	5
Balance at end of year	(60)	9	12
Unrealized gain (loss) on cash flow hedges, net of tax:			
Balance at beginning of year	(250)	68	83
Current period changes in fair value [net of tax effect of $(33), $(177), and $(4)]	(54)	(294)	(7)
Reclassification to earnings [net of tax effect of $118, $(14), and $(5)]	197	(24)	(8)
Balance at end of year	(107)	(250)	68
Unrecognized pension and postretirement benefit costs, net of tax:			
Balance at beginning of year	(1,853)	(2,176)	(95)
Reclassification to earnings (net of tax effect of $81, $73, and $0)	133	122	—
Net actuarial gain/loss and prior service cost resulting from remeasurements of plan assets and liabilities [net of tax effect of $(2,235), $111, and $11]	(3,717)	201	16
SFAS 158 transition adjustment [net of tax effect $(1,258) in 2006]	—	—	(2,097)
Balance at end of year	(5,437)	(1,853)	(2,176)
Accumulated other comprehensive income (loss) at end of year	$(5,642)	$(2,013)	$(2,205)

UNITED PARCEL SERVICE, INC., AND SUBSIDIARIES
CONSOLIDATED BALANCE SHEETS
(In Millions)

	December 31	
	2008	**2007**
Assets		
Current assets:		
Cash and cash equivalents	$507	$2,027
Marketable securities	542	577
Accounts receivable, net	5,547	6,084
Finance receivables, net	480	468
Deferred income tax assets	494	606
Income taxes receivable	167	1,256
Other current assets	1,108	742
Total current assets	8,845	11,760
Property, plant, and equipment, net	18,265	17,663
Pension and postretirement benefit assets	10	4,421
Goodwill	1,986	2,577
Intangible assets, net	511	628
Noncurrent finance receivables, net	476	431
Other noncurrent assets	1,786	1,562
Total assets	$31,879	$39,042
Liabilities and Shareowners' Equity		
Current liabilities:		
Current maturities of long-term debt and commercial paper	$2,074	$3,512
Accounts payable	1,855	1,819
Accrued wages and withholdings	1,436	1,414
Dividends payable	—	440
Self-insurance reserves	732	704
Other current liabilities	1,720	1,951
Total current liabilities	7,817	9,840
Long-term debt	7,797	7,506
Pension and postretirement benefit obligations	6,323	4,438
Deferred income tax liabilities	588	2,620
Self-insurance reserves	1,710	1,651
Other noncurrent liabilities	864	804

(Continued)

	December 31	
	2008	2007
Shareowners' equity:		
Class A common stock (314 and 349 shares issued in 2008 and 2007)	3	3
Class B common stock (684 and 694 shares issued in 2008 and 2007)	7	7
Additional paid-in capital	—	—
Retained earnings	12,412	14,186
Accumulated other comprehensive loss	(5,642)	(2,013)
Deferred compensation obligations	121	137
	6,901	12,320
Less: Treasury stock (2 shares in 2008 and 2007)	(121)	(137)
Total shareowners' equity	6,780	12,183
Total liabilities and shareowners' equity	$31,879	$39,042

TABLE 6-26

Debt Obligations and Commitments

Debt obligations, as of December 31, consist of the following (in millions):

	2008	2007
8.38% debentures	$741	$761
4.50% senior notes	1,739	—
5.50% senior notes	745	—
6.20% senior notes	1,479	—
Commercial paper	2,922	7,366
Floating-rate senior notes	438	441
Capital lease obligations	425	479
Facility notes and bonds	433	435
UPS notes	198	513
Pound sterling notes	730	989
Other debt	21	34
Total debt	9,871	11,018
Less current maturities	(2,074)	(3,512)
Long-term debt	$7,797	$7,506

The analyst might wonder why, when computing fixed-charge coverage's, we would compare today's cash flows against future debt requirements as it might be expected that cash flows in the future are also expected to grow, enabling UPS to more easily satisfy those obligations. It is so because operating cash-flow growth is not assured because UPS has seen its cash flows fall during recession and with spikes in fuel costs. Often creditors do build in growth in operating cash flows when making loan decisions, and many times those expected cash flows do not materialize, resulting in material loss.[30] Debt requirements, however, are legally obligated to be paid, and it is the operating cash flows that pay the interest but the free cash flow that pays the principal.

An analyst also might question the 8 percent discount rate in Table 6-27 used (as too high), which, if lower, would increase the debt added to the balance sheet. The discount rate for the capital lease obligations should be the cost of debt because we construe leases as a debt obligation. Also, it is normally wise to build some conservatism into the models, but note that UPS's bonds are not trading far from 8 percent (not tax adjusted for the 22 percent savings). The analyst would need to adjust the discounting of the payments for the period in the year the payments actually take place. In the example that follows, if one assumes that the $344 million of lease payments due in 2009 is to be paid in equal installments throughout the year, one would most likely discount those payments at a rate closer to 4 percent for that year because the first half-year payments will not be accruing interest for 12 full months. For the operating leases due after 2013, I used an 11-year average because UPS's footnote states that it has leases as far out as 2055, so an 11-year average is conservative. Another way of performing the calculation would be to divide the $109 million projected minimum lease obligations for the year 2013 by the $423 million remaining, or about four years, at the $109 million rate, and discount the $109 million at 8 percent for years 2013–2016.

It is best to use common sense in this analysis because it is most probable with UPS, unlike the table in the footnote, that operating leases will grow, not decline. Factoring in a 5 percent rate of growth in future operating leases would increase total debt by about $2.4 billion. Table 6-27 is based on a known stream of disclosed minimum future lease payments. If the company would share growth information, it would help in the model, although discounting many years out provides lower value added.

[30]For example, Tishman Speyer Properties, LP, and Blackrock Realty purchased Manhattan's Stuyvesant Town for a very rich price of $5.4 billion from MetLife. The bonds sold to help pay for the purchase were bought by investors who believed the cash flows from the rentals would increase over the coming years, but they were not realized.

TABLE 6-27

UPS Operating Leases Discounted at 8 Percent

Year	As Listed	8% Discount Rate
2009	344	319
2010	288	247
2011	217	172
2012	147	108
2013	109	75
After 2013	423	181
Total	**1,528**	**1,101**

Therefore, I would add $1.1 billion[31] to UPS's total debt to arrive at an adjusted debt of $10.971 billion (from the $9.871 billion of Table 6-26), which assumes that there were no further adjustments to be made. To properly capitalize operating leases, the analyst would need to know the terms of all the lease agreements, including their current value, useful life, guaranteed residual value, and how quickly they would depreciate. Technology equipment, for instance, would depreciate more quickly than delivery trucks and would have differing useful lives, even though the payments on the leases and the contracted lease period could be similar. One would think, but it is not always true, that the lease life and the asset life would be similar. These factors would need to be captured when capitalizing the lease, but they are not available to the analyst. It is therefore up to the accounting promulgators to adopt changes to lease accounting regulations, but in the meantime, analysts must use their best estimate based on reported information while placing the value of the operating leased asset on the balance sheet.

Another factor that needs to be considered is the residual value of UPS's capital leases. Residual value, aside from determining whether a lease is classified as an operating or capital lease, affects the realized amount when the asset is remarketed. If the value of the asset has declined to a greater extent than that estimated (considered other than temporary), it would affect net income and cash flow. When leases are large, as in the case of UPS and FedEx, the analyst should perform a sensitivity analysis, with estimates of the various impacts 10 percent changes in residual value to cash flow would have on the entity.

My cost-of-capital credit model is not biased toward shareholders' equity, but total debt and debt coming due in relation to the capacity, ease of, and time

[31] I am operating under the simple assumption that all the operating leases are added the same day and that UPS is receiving no added tax benefits.

period it would take the entity to repay its total debt, as well as the ability of the enterprise to satisfy its coming year's debt, from free cash flow and available resources. Adding the value of the assets under operating lease obligations to the PPE account does not reduce the cost-of-capital model as much as its associated debt adds. The debt is a guaranteed obligation, whereas future cash flows are not assured. Those operating lease assets are important to the extent that they produce free cash flow. Therefore, my credit model focuses on the debt component.

By including the present value of operating leases in total debt, I am recognizing it in my ROIC metrics. *To fail to do so would distort the financial returns, especially so in industry comparisons against peers such as FedEx, which would be given an unfair advantage if operating leases were excluded.*

Thus adjusted total debt for UPS (more so for FedEx) would have a significant effect on shareholders' equity and cash flow/total debt. No adjustment would need to be made to the cash-flow side of the equation because those assets are already in place and are contributing existing cash flows.

To calculate the revised leveraged ratios with the operating leases capitalized, one would add $1.1 billion to the long-term asset section as *assets under lease*. This assumes that the assets were not valued at depreciated value and were all placed into service at the balance-sheet date. In reality, this would not be the case, however—UPS does not do this for us.

UPS ADJUSTED DEBT/EQUITY INCLUDING OPERATING LEASE OBLIGATIONS	
Total debt (including operating leases)	10,971
Total equity (including operating lease assets)	6,780/12,422

We must evaluate the appropriateness of including pension and postretirement pension obligations, included as part of comprehensive loss section of shareholders' equity, to total debt. Shown to the right (above) as part of total equity, $12,422 includes the addback of the comprehensive loss, if the analyst believes that the loss represents temporary market conditions that did not impair the entity's cash flows but was the result of an accounting rule unlikely to affect cash or temporary market conditions having a negligible prospective economic impact. To this end, one could make that case for UPS, especially given that by the end of its 2009 first quarter it was apparent to many market observers that the worst-case economic scenario some had feared was not going to occur. For instance, UPS recorded a $78 million charge to equity based on fair-value accounting in addition to the large market impairment to its pension assets resulting from the fall in the financial markets during the year. Despite the large non-realized loss to the fund, UPS contributed less cash into its plans during 2008 than 2007, even considering the $5 billion decline in plan assets. During 2009, the plans rebounded strongly, coinciding with the general rise in equity prices, lending credence to not penalizing the strong cash-flow-producing entity's leverage ratios for noncash effects that may be viewed as temporary in nature, as all bear markets have proved to be. Not making the adjustment for other comprehensive loss only makes sense if the entity's cash flows are otherwise strong, allowing it the time for financial markets to normalize. This would not have been the case with General Motors, which had a high percentage of retirees/active workforce and whose operating business was not producing positive free cash flow.

Evidently the credit-rating agencies agreed because they rate UPS as AA– and Fedex, despite its lower balance-sheet debt/equity, as BBB. It is only when operating leases are included that Fedex and its $14.7 billion in operating leases shows much higher leverage. Capital lease obligations are roughly similar for the two firms, adjusted for their size.

The analyst also should note that capitalizing operating leases does not change net income or cash flows. The payments (cash outlays) on the leases do not change, and in the income statement, depreciation and interest expense on the lease are replaced with the lease expense. As stated, credit-rating agencies normally impute both an interest and depreciation component when calculating their adjusted financial ratios of fixed-charge coverages and EBITDA. Because I include the actual lease payment, no such adjustments are necessary. To calculate an imputed interest charge, credit agencies multiply the interest rate on existing debt by the current year's operating leases expense. In my model, I include the entire lease payment in addition to actual interest paid when evaluating fixed-charge converges.

Because operating leases run through the income statement as *lease expense* rather than interest, they can distort the credit metrics of analysts who consider interest-rate charge coverage an important indicator. For this reason, I include all lease payments in addition to interest expense to cover the omission. The reason I recommend including the entire operating lease expense and not just the imputed interest (also estimated as one-third the payment) is that the entire payment is required to be paid, just as interest is required to be paid on debt, even if principal payments in any particular year are not. Thus, in the case of UPS, we see

2008 interest expense	$359
2008 lease expenses (est.)	$344
2008 capital lease expenses (est.)	83
Total interest and operating lease expense	$786 million

In Table 6-23, management estimates the company's 2009 projected expense. The analyst should speak to the company's CFO for an estimate of more accurate lease expense payments for the coming five years, if the company is willing to do this. For example, for UPS, one would ask the number of new aircraft on order waiting delivery and those to be retired. The same logic would apply to other firms that use leases.

As seen in Table 6-28, UPS's normalized cash flows can easily service its interest and lease expenses, although, as seen in the table, the company's cash flows are cyclic and subject to the vagaries of the business environment. For its fiscal year 2007, UPS had negative free cash flow, and for the first quarter of 2009, its operating and free cash flow declined by a third despite a large cutback in capital expenditures. The operating and free cash flows reflected in the table are after lease expense. UPS, due to its financial strength, had access to the commercial paper market and other back-up credit facilities.

Companies that have high and growing amounts of operating leases as compared with their operating cash flows should be penalized with lower valuation multiples. As to be explained in Chapter 8, we indeed penalize such companies by

TABLE 6-28

UPS Cash Flow Items Including Discretionary Overspending

Year	Dec-04	Dec-05	Dec-06	Dec-07	Dec-08	Most Recent Quarter Mar-09	Previous Quarter Mar-08
Net Operating Cash Flow	5331.0	5793.0	5589.0	1123.0	8426.0	2196.0	3305.0
Capital Expenditures	2127.0	2187.0	3085.0	2820.0	2636.0	382.0	661.0
Sale of PPE	75.0	27.0	75.0	85.0	147.0	6.0	57.0
Free Cash Flow – Including Discretionary Items	3279.0	3633.0	2579.0	(1612.0)	5937.0	1820.0	2701.0
Free Cash Flow – Excluding Discretionary Items	3279.0	3633.0	2681.4	(1533.8)	6233.0	—	—
Discretionary Capital Expenditures	0.0	0.0	69.9	40.1	0.0	—	—
Discretionary R&D	0.0	0.0	0.0	0.0	0.0	—	—
Discretionary Cost of Goods Sold	0.0	0.0	32.4	38.1	296.0	—	—
Discretionary SG&A	0.0	296.0	0.0	0.0	0.0	—	—
Discretionary Advertising	0.0	0.0	0.0	0.0	0.0	—	—
Large Buildup (Reduction) in Accounts Receivable	0.0	894.2	(53.1)	(1040.3)	472.1	(1502.2)	(788.1)
Large Buildup (Reduction) in Inventory	(345.5)	0.0	0.0	0.0	0.0	0.0	0.0
Large Buildup (Reduction) in Accounts Payable	0.0	265.5	(135.9)	(1039.0)	(491.8)	(1169.7)	(414.0)

Source: UPS and CT Capital, LLC.

assigning them a higher cost of equity, in recognition of the increased financial burden. Of course, if the operating cash flows are growing as well, the credit would remain as is or perhaps strengthen.

Figure 6-7 depicts the fixed-charge coverage as defined by operating cash flows divided by interest and lease expense for both UPS and FedEx. The figure uses the actual interest expense from the statement of cash flows, not the amount reported on the income statement. FedEx covers its fixed obligations each year, but not with the great margin of UPS. To calculate the fixed-charge cover, I add back to the numerator (operating cash flow) the year's interest and lease expense, as I do in my worksheet for the cost-of-equity capital model in Chapter 8, to compute the number of times those charges were covered.

You will notice the sharp drop in coverage for UPS during 2007. The decrease in 2007 operating cash flows compared with 2006 and 2005 was due primarily to the $6.1 billion payment made to withdraw from the Central States Pension Fund in 2007. This was partially offset by reduced 2007 funding to its management pension and postretirement benefit plans. In 2007, the company funded $687 million to its pension and postretirement benefit plans as compared with $1.625 billion in 2006. This is another reason why I also consider power operating cash flows in

FIGURE 6-7

Percentage Coverage of Interest and Operating Leases

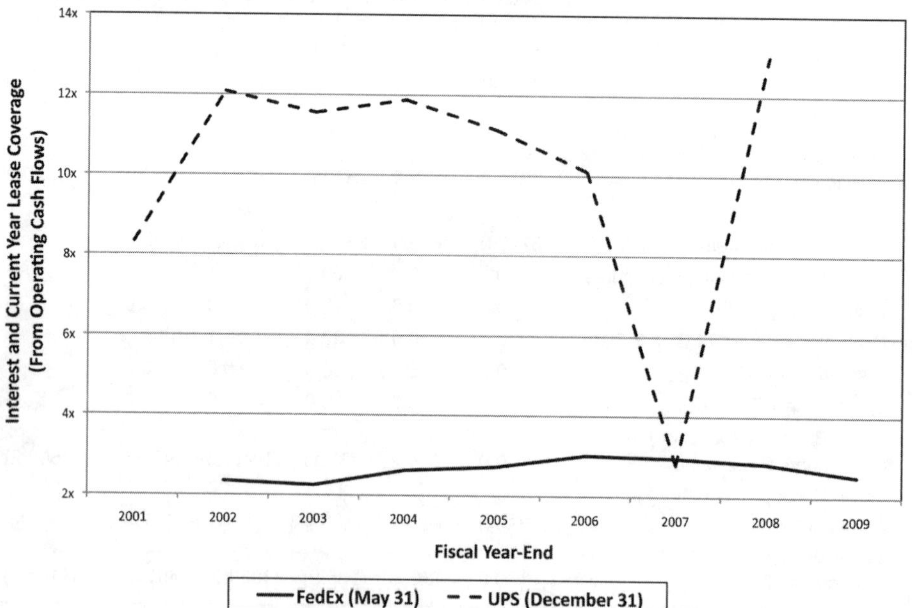

addition to the reported cash flow from operations. FedEx received a tax benefit related to the payment that resulted in a refund.

To calculate UPS's return on invested capital, we employ the definition espoused in Chapter 5 and the information contained in the appropriate charts (Table 6-29 also provides present value numbers):

ROIC = Free cash flow – Net Interest Income/Invested Capital (Equity + Total Interest Bearing Debt + PV of Operating Leases − Cash + Marketable Securities).

UPS had produced normalized $2.9 billion in free cash flow from which we exclude the $100MM in net interest income as we are seeking its return on capital employed.

= 2.9 − 0.1/6.78 + 9.87 + 1.1 − 1.05
= 2.8/16.7
= 16.8% excluding loss in comprehensive income
= 12.5% including loss on comprehensive income

Incorporating operating leases into the denominator lowers UPS's ROIC by about 6 percent. If the loss on comprehensive income (or part of it) were added back to shareholders' equity, the difference would have been meaningful, as shown. The company's ROIC is sufficiently above their weighted-average cost of capital (8.35 percent[32]) to state that UPS most likely has many value-adding investments it could make.

For FedEx, including its large operating leases into its ROIC metric quite substantially affected the ratio. Its three-year average free cash flow, when including excess expenditures, was $782 million; the company reported $26 million in interest income during its latest (2009) fiscal year and no comprehensive income or loss, so its

ROIC = 782 − 26/13,626 + 2,583 + 9,698 − 2,292
= 756/23,615
= 3.2%

The 3.2 percent was just for one recessionary year and is significantly below the company's three- and four-year average ROIC.

---

32 Calculated using the model in Chapter 8.

TABLE 6-29

Present-Value Table

Periods	PRESENT VALUE OF $1 — RATE PER PERIOD																
	0.25%	0.50%	0.75%	1.00%	1.50%	2.00%	2.50%	3.00%	4.00%	5.00%	6.00%	7.00%	8.00%	9.00%	10.00%	11.00%	12.00%
1	0.99751	0.99502	0.99256	0.99010	0.98522	0.98039	0.97561	0.97087	0.96154	0.95238	0.94340	0.93458	0.92593	0.91743	0.90909	0.90090	0.89286
2	0.99502	0.99007	0.98517	0.98030	0.97066	0.96117	0.95181	0.94260	0.92456	0.90703	0.89000	0.87344	0.85734	0.84168	0.82645	0.81162	0.79719
3	0.99254	0.98515	0.97783	0.97059	0.95632	0.94232	0.92860	0.91514	0.88900	0.86384	0.83962	0.81630	0.79383	0.77218	0.75131	0.73119	0.71178
4	0.99006	0.98025	0.97055	0.96098	0.94218	0.92385	0.90595	0.88849	0.85480	0.82270	0.79209	0.76290	0.73503	0.70843	0.68301	0.65873	0.63552
5	0.98759	0.97537	0.96333	0.95147	0.92826	0.90573	0.88385	0.86261	0.82193	0.78353	0.74726	0.71299	0.68058	0.64993	0.62092	0.59345	0.56743
6	0.98513	0.97052	0.95616	0.94205	0.91454	0.88797	0.86230	0.83748	0.79031	0.74622	0.70496	0.66634	0.63017	0.59627	0.56447	0.53464	0.50663
7	0.98267	0.96569	0.94904	0.93272	0.90103	0.87056	0.84127	0.81309	0.75992	0.71068	0.66506	0.62275	0.58349	0.54703	0.51316	0.48166	0.45235
8	0.98022	0.96089	0.94198	0.92348	0.88771	0.85349	0.82075	0.78941	0.73069	0.67684	0.62741	0.58201	0.54027	0.50187	0.46651	0.43393	0.40388
9	0.97778	0.95610	0.93496	0.91434	0.87459	0.83676	0.80073	0.76642	0.70259	0.64461	0.59190	0.54393	0.50025	0.46043	0.42410	0.39092	0.36061
10	0.97534	0.95135	0.92800	0.90529	0.86167	0.82035	0.78120	0.74409	0.67556	0.61391	0.55839	0.50835	0.46319	0.42241	0.38554	0.35218	0.32197
11	0.97291	0.94661	0.92109	0.89632	0.84893	0.80426	0.76214	0.72242	0.64958	0.58468	0.52679	0.47509	0.42888	0.38753	0.35049	0.31728	0.28748
12	0.97048	0.94191	0.91424	0.88745	0.83639	0.78849	0.74356	0.70138	0.62460	0.55684	0.49697	0.44401	0.39711	0.35553	0.31863	0.28584	0.25688
13	0.96806	0.93722	0.90743	0.87866	0.82403	0.77303	0.72542	0.68095	0.60057	0.53032	0.46884	0.41496	0.36770	0.32618	0.28966	0.25751	0.22917
14	0.96565	0.93256	0.90068	0.86996	0.81185	0.75788	0.70773	0.66112	0.57748	0.50507	0.44230	0.38782	0.34046	0.29925	0.26333	0.23199	0.20462
15	0.96324	0.92792	0.89397	0.86135	0.79985	0.74301	0.69047	0.64186	0.55526	0.48102	0.41727	0.36245	0.31524	0.27454	0.23939	0.20900	0.18270
16	0.96084	0.92330	0.88732	0.85282	0.78803	0.72845	0.67362	0.62317	0.53391	0.45811	0.39365	0.33873	0.29189	0.25187	0.21763	0.18829	0.16312
17	0.95844	0.91871	0.88071	0.84438	0.77639	0.71416	0.65720	0.60502	0.51337	0.43630	0.37136	0.31657	0.27027	0.23107	0.19784	0.16963	0.14564
18	0.95605	0.91414	0.87416	0.83602	0.76491	0.70016	0.64117	0.58739	0.49363	0.41552	0.35034	0.29586	0.25025	0.21199	0.17986	0.15282	0.13004
19	0.95367	0.90959	0.86765	0.82774	0.75361	0.68643	0.62553	0.57029	0.47464	0.39573	0.33051	0.27651	0.23171	0.19449	0.16351	0.13768	0.11611
20	0.95129	0.90506	0.86119	0.81954	0.74247	0.67297	0.61027	0.55368	0.45639	0.37689	0.31180	0.25842	0.21455	0.17843	0.14864	0.12403	0.10367
21	0.94892	0.90056	0.85478	0.81143	0.73150	0.65978	0.59539	0.53755	0.43883	0.35894	0.29416	0.24151	0.19866	0.16370	0.13513	0.11174	0.09256
22	0.94655	0.89608	0.84842	0.80340	0.72069	0.64684	0.58086	0.52189	0.42196	0.34185	0.27751	0.22571	0.18394	0.15018	0.12285	0.10067	0.08264
23	0.94419	0.89162	0.84210	0.79544	0.71004	0.63416	0.56670	0.50669	0.40573	0.32557	0.26180	0.21095	0.17032	0.13778	0.11168	0.09069	0.07379
24	0.94184	0.88719	0.83583	0.78757	0.69954	0.62172	0.55288	0.49193	0.39012	0.31007	0.24698	0.19715	0.15770	0.12640	0.10153	0.08170	0.06588
25	0.93949	0.88277	0.82961	0.77977	0.68921	0.60953	0.53939	0.47761	0.37512	0.29530	0.23300	0.18425	0.14602	0.11597	0.09230	0.07361	0.05882
30	0.92783	0.86103	0.79919	0.74192	0.63976	0.55207	0.47674	0.41199	0.30832	0.23138	0.17411	0.13137	0.09938	0.07537	0.05731	0.04368	0.03338
35	0.91632	0.83982	0.76988	0.70591	0.59387	0.50003	0.42137	0.35538	0.25342	0.18129	0.13011	0.09366	0.06763	0.04899	0.03558	0.02592	0.01894
40	0.90495	0.81914	0.74165	0.67165	0.55126	0.45289	0.37243	0.30656	0.20829	0.14205	0.09722	0.06678	0.04603	0.03184	0.02209	0.01538	0.01075
50	0.88263	0.77929	0.68825	0.60804	0.47500	0.37153	0.29094	0.22811	0.14071	0.08720	0.05429	0.03395	0.02132	0.01345	0.00852	0.00542	0.00346

The companies relative stock price performance quite accurately reflected its financing leverage and credit health surrounding the deep 2007–2009 recession. The equity security of UPS substantially outperformed FedEx going into and during the bottom of the recession, whereas the equity security of FedEx outperformed UPS as the stock market recovered. Investors believed that UPS's superior financial strength and total debt, including operating lease obligations, would enable the company to survive the economic downdraft, whereas investors in Fedex were, unsurprisingly, more concerned. The differences are clearly captured in the companies' stock prices (Figure 6-8).

Table 6-30 lists companies having high operating lease obligations relative to both their market value and total debt. If one excludes entities that were selling at very low prices (<$2 per share), such as Air Tran Holdings and Stein Mart, whose stocks jumped on the belief that the recession was over and were part of a wave of very leveraged companies trading near bankruptcy, the balance of companies underperformed the general market by a wide margin, indicating that even though rating agencies consider operating leases as part of their analysis, investors in general may not. It would appear, then, that analysts who capitalize operating leases may be able to avoid large, underperforming stocks, especially during periods of slow or negative economic growth. The table also might reflect weaker firms' preference for operating leases.

FIGURE 6-8

Cumulative Return: UPS versus FEDEX

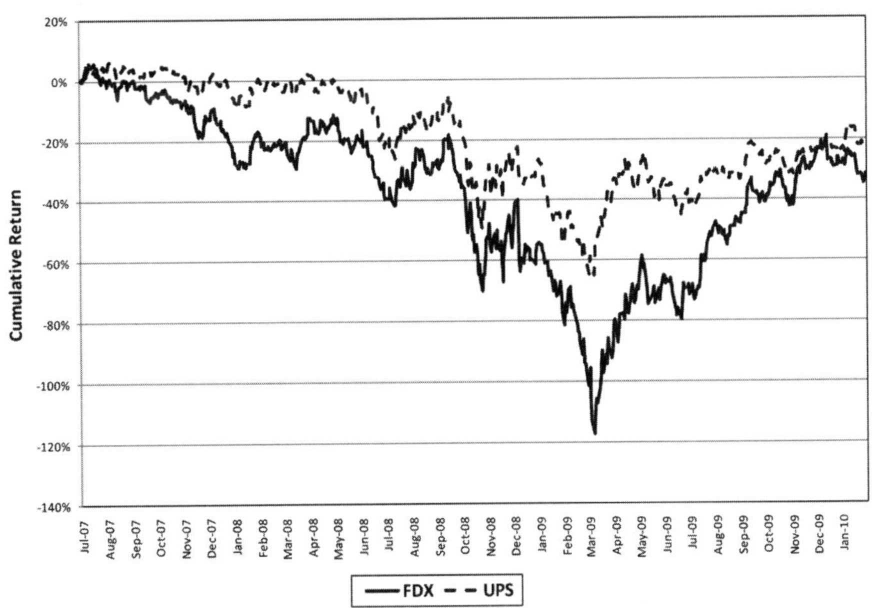

TABLE 6-30

Companies with Large Operating Leases Relative to Total Debt

Company Name	Ticker	Operating Leases/Total Debt	Operating Leases/Market Value	One-Year Total Return
Airtran Holdings, Inc.	AAI	2.8	6.0	147.9
American Apparel, Inc.	APP	3.5	2.8	−34.7
AMR Corp./DE	AMR	0.8	3.1	−40.8
Arden Group, Inc.–CL A	ARDNA	106.7	0.3	4.7
Big 5 Sporting Goods Corp.	BGFV	3.2	2.9	70.5
Brown Shoe Co., Inc.	BWS	3.2	4.2	−50.0
CBIZ, Inc.	CBZ	0.9	0.4	−20.1
Charming Shoppes, Inc.	CHRS	3.0	7.6	−11.4
Chicago Bridge & Iron Co.	CBI	1.8	0.3	−57.2
Conn's, Inc.	CONN	2.8	0.6	−19.7
Continental Airlines, Inc.–CL B	CAL	2.5	7.5	−18.6
Corinthian Colleges, Inc.	COCO	6.8	0.5	−2.0
CRA International, Inc.	CRAI	1.3	0.4	−28.4
Delta Airlines, Inc.	DAL	0.8	3.5	−8.1
Duff & Phelps Corp.	DUF	3.5	0.2	5.8
Ensign Group, Inc.	ENSG	2.0	0.4	35.0
Great Atlantic & Pacific Tea Co.	GAP	1.6	9.8	−63.7
Great Lakes Dredge & Dock CP	GLDD	0.6	0.6	−9.5
HHGregg, Inc.	HGG	4.6	0.9	83.3
Infineon Technologies AG–ADR	IFNNY	0.6	0.3	−34.8
Jetblue Airways Corp.	JBLU	0.6	1.1	−3.0
Jones Lang Lasalle, Inc.	JLL	0.9	0.5	−19.3
Ligand Pharmaceutical, Inc.	LGND	20.8	0.3	−15.0
Live Nation, Inc.	LYV	1.2	2.4	−53.7
Madden Steven, Ltd.	SHOO	4.4	0.3	42.6
Moduslink Global Solutions	MLNK	161.3	0.1	−41.7
Movado Group, Inc.	MOV	1.3	0.5	−32.8
Pep Boys–Manny, Moe & Jack	PBY	2.2	5.2	40.6
PHI, Inc.	PHIIK	1.0	1.0	−45.6
Pricesmart, Inc.	PSMT	3.4	0.2	−28.7
Rehabcare Group, Inc.	RHB	3.1	0.7	45.3
Res-Care, Inc.	RSCR	0.9	0.5	−14.9
Rigel Pharmaceuticals, Inc.	RIGL	40.5	0.5	−67.2
Saks, Inc.	SKS	0.7	1.3	−49.8
Skechers USA, Inc.	SKX	32.8	0.9	−26.8
Steak N Shake Co.	SNS	0.9	0.6	48.3
Stein Mart, Inc.	SMRT	3.8	7.7	146.8
Switch & Data Facilities Co.	SDXC	1.9	1.3	−17.5
Talbots, Inc.	TLB	2.0	8.6	−61.9
UAL Corp.	UAUA	1.3	7.4	−50.4
US Airways Group, Inc.	LCC	1.9	8.5	−42.1
Village Super Market–CL A	VLGEA	3.5	0.4	41.2

Source: CT Capital, LLC, August 10, 2009.

GUARANTEES

Guarantees can take many forms, and any guarantee potentially involves a cash settlement. For instance, in order to induce Hertz to buy cars from them for its fleet, General Motors made certain guarantees regarding the price it would repay Hertz on return of the cars. This represented a risk to both GM and Hertz—for GM regarding the price for which it could resell those used cars and for Hertz regarding whether GM was able to follow through on the guarantee. As indicated, the amount is substantial.

> Any default or reorganization of a manufacturer that has sold us program cars might also leave us with a substantial unpaid claim against the manufacturer with respect to program cars that were sold and returned to the car manufacturer but not paid for, or that were sold for less than their agreed repurchase price or guaranteed value. For the year ended December 31, 2008, the highest outstanding month-end receivable balance for cars sold to a single manufacturer was $249.1 million owed by General Motors. See "We face risks of increased costs of cars and of decreased profitability, including as a result of limited supplies of competitively priced cars."
>
> *Source:* Hertz 2009 10K.

The most common form of guarantee involves a financial guarantee. Specific accounting regulations may prevail depending on the transaction involved. Guarantees are covered by Interpretation No. 45, *Guarantor's Accounting and Disclosure Requirements for Guarantees, Including Indirect Guarantees of Indebtedness of Others*—an interpretation of SFAS. 5, 57, and 107 and rescission of FASB Interpretation No. 34. This statement does not apply to certain financial contracts, such as those issued by insurance companies. It also clarifies that a guarantor is required to recognize, at the inception of a guarantee, a liability for the fair value of the obligation undertaken in issuing the guarantee.

FASB summarized the reason for Interpretation No. 45:

> This Interpretation clarifies that a guarantor is required to disclose (a) the nature of the guarantee, including the approximate term of the guarantee, how the guarantee arose, and the events or circumstances that would require the guarantor to perform under the guarantee; (b) the maximum potential amount of future payments under the guarantee; (c) the carrying amount of the liability, if any, for the guarantor's obligations under the

> guarantee; and (d) the nature and extent of any recourse provisions or available collateral that would enable the guarantor to recover the amounts paid under the guarantee. For product warranties, instead of disclosing the maximum potential amount of future payments under the guarantee, a guarantor is required to disclose its accounting policy and methodology used in determining its liability for product warranties as well as a tabular reconciliation of the changes in the guarantor's product warranty liability for the reporting period. Disclosures under current practice, which generally include only the nature and amount of guarantees, do not provide the same level of useful information as required by this Interpretation.
>
> This Interpretation also clarifies that a guarantor is required to recognize, at the inception of a guarantee, a liability for the obligations it has undertaken in issuing the guarantee, including its ongoing obligation to stand ready to perform over the term of the guarantee in the event that the specified triggering events or conditions occur. The objective of the initial measurement of that liability is the fair value of the guarantee at its inception.
>
> *Source:* FASB.

It is common practice for a parent organization or holding company to guaranty the loans of its wholly owned subsidiaries. This could pose a problem for an analyst because guarantees of nonconsolidated affiliate debt may not be incorporated onto the guarantor's balance sheet. If the nonconsolidated subsidiary or affiliated company for whom the guaranty is made does not produce free cash flow, the analyst should add the amount of guaranteed debt to total debt of the company making the guaranty. The analysis also should take into account the legal distinction between the entities, especially if the subsidiary is subject to additional regulation that might require additional cash outlays or an increase in its capital. If regulations or the financial condition of the subsidiary changes, it could affect the parent or holding company, which might be required to provide additional funding, rework covenants to its debt agreements, or pay higher rates of interest on upcoming debt.

To the extent that a parent wishes to legally isolate itself from an operating division, the subsidiary may have nonrecourse debt on its books. This may occur, for example, if the parent wishes to protect the cash flows and financial integrity of another division. In the example that follows, all subsidiaries of the borrower, Red Mortgage Capital, are guaranteeing the debts of each other.

Example:

Notwithstanding anything contained in this Agreement or the other Loan Documents to the contrary (but subject to the provisions of Section 14.01, the last sentence of this Section 14.04 and the provisions of Section 14.11), each Borrower shall have joint and several liability for all Obligations. Notwithstanding the intent of all of the parties to this Agreement that all Obligations of each Borrower under this Agreement and the other Loan Documents shall be joint and several Obligations of each Borrower but subject to the provisions of Section 14.01, each Borrower, on a joint and several basis, hereby irrevocably guarantees on a non-recourse basis, subject to the exceptions to nonrecourse provisions of Section 14.01 to Lender and its successors and assigns, the full and prompt payment (whether at stated maturity, by acceleration or otherwise) and performance of, all Obligations owed or hereafter owing to Lender by each other Borrower. Each Borrower agrees that its non-recourse guaranty obligation hereunder is an unconditional guaranty of payment and performance and not merely a guaranty of collection.

Source: Master Credit Facility Agreement, Red Mortgage Capital 8K.

Often the risk regarding a financial guaranty may not be well known. The guarantee to support borrowing of an unconsolidated affiliate or third party is not recorded on the guarantor's balance sheet unless it meets certain tests regarding probability of payment or control. The guarantor also can choose to record the lowest amount in a wide range of outcomes, such that if it has a 70 percent chance of paying nothing and a 30 percent chance of having to pay $100 million, the company obligation in its footnotes could be just $30 million. It is thus up to the analyst to determine what a $100 million payment would mean to the entity's financial health and if it has the financial flexibility if funds need to be raised to pay that sum.

Example:

Pursuant to provisions included in the company's 2005 acquisition of Precision, the company guaranteed the value of 304,878 shares at $3.28 per share of the company's common stock used as consideration in that acquisition as of the second anniversary, which occurred on July 28, 2007. Based on the July 28, 2007 stock price, that guarantee requires the company to issue $963,000 of cash or an equivalent number of its shares (7,825,000) to the prior owners of Precision. The company has tried to issue the shares; however, the prior owners have initiated legal proceedings to compel issuance of cash instead. In addition, pursuant to provisions included in the company's 2005 acquisition of Long Term Rx, the company guaranteed the value of 182,183 shares at $3.28 per share of the company's common stock used as consideration in that acquisition as of the second anniversary, which occurred on July 28, 2007. Based on the July 28, 2007 stock price, that guarantee requires the company to issue $465,000 of cash or an equivalent number of its shares (3,880,000) to the prior owner of Long Term Rx.

Source: Standard Management 2009 10K.

Another guarantee is a performance guarantee. Normally, the cash outlays to satisfy such a guarantee are small, but not always. To the injured party, an inability to perform is normally covered by a surety bond. If this is not the case, economic damage would result. For the company issuing the guarantee, failure to perform could result in lost cash flows and lawsuits. Performance guarantees are common in the construction trade.

Example:

The Shaw Group is a provider of technology and engineering to utilities, oil companies, power producers, and governments. Many of its contracts provide for specific performance guarantees, for many of which the liabilities are difficult to quantify. The following is from the company's 2009 10K:

> Our approach to estimating liability provisions related to contractual performance guarantees on sales of our technology paid-up license agreements requires that we make estimates on the performance of technology on our projects. Our historical experience with performance guarantees on these types of agreements supports estimated liability provisions that vary based on our experience with the different types of technologies for which we license and provide engineering (for example, ethylbenzene, styrene, cumene, Bisphenol A). Our liability provisions range from nominal amounts up to 100% of the contractual performance guarantee. If our actual obligations under performance guarantees differ from our estimated liability provisions at the completion of these projects, we will record an increase or decrease in revenues (or an increase in costs where we are required to incur costs to remediate a performance deficiency) for the difference. Our total estimated performance liability remaining at August 31, 2009 and 2008 was $13.0 million and $16.1 million, respectively. The estimated liability provisions generally are more significant as a percentage of the total contract value for these contracts when compared to contracts where we have full EPC responsibility, and, as a result, these differences could be material.

If there is a dispute on performance and the amount sought by the injured party is substantial, the analyst may choose to add the guaranteed amount to debt. The new financial structure must be evaluated in light of the entity's ability to satisfy the guarantee and any additional costs, such as legal expenses and insurance.

CONVERTIBLE BONDS

Convertible bonds have the characteristic of a straight-debt bond plus an additional option to purchase a specified number of shares of the common stock at a fixed price. Thus the holder of a convertible bond enjoys a fixed interest payment until the bond reaches maturity (or is converted to equity) and, at the same time, enjoys the option of partaking in the capital appreciation of the stock if the stock were to rise above the conversion price. If the price of the stock increases in value to a point above the price implicit in the convertible bond, then the bondholder is likely to exercise its option and convert the bond to common stock. In such cases, the convertible bonds could be viewed as equity, and the analyst would adjust the entity's debt ratios accordingly, as well as any changes in free cash flow saved from the difference (tax-adjusted) of interest and dividend payments. This would be true for all convertible securities, including those which are required to be converted (mandatory convertibles). Where conversion is mandatory, the security always would be treated as equity, even prior to conversion. Also to be considered in the cash-flow projection are any common stock dividend payments resulting from the additional shares.

If, however, the price of the equity is well below the conversion price, the holder is unlikely to convert, and the bond should be considered as debt. *If the price of the common stock is somewhat above the conversion price, unless the conversion is forced, the analyst should not assume that conversion will take place.*

As with all bonds, holders must be aware of any provision or covenants that could affect the value of the bonds. For example, many issues are callable at par, even though, if interest rates fell, the bond would trade higher. On the other hand, holders may have the option to require the company to redeem the bonds as of a certain date. If the entity does not have the financial flexibility to retire these obligations, equity holders could see the value of their investment diluted, sometimes significantly.

Example:

The following is from Genesco Corporation's 2009 10K:

> On June 24, 2003 and June 26, 2003, the company issued a total of $86.3 million of $4^{1}/_{8}$% Convertible Subordinated Debentures (the "Debentures") due June 15, 2023. The Debentures are convertible at the option of the holders into shares of the company's common stock, par value $1.00 per share: (1) in any quarter in which the price of its common stock issuable upon conversion of a Debenture reached 120% or more of the conversion price ($24.07 or more) for 10 of the last 30 trading days of the immediately preceding fiscal quarter, (2) if specified corporate transactions occur or (3) if the trading price for the Debentures falls below certain thresholds. The company's common stock did not close at or above $24.07 for at least 10 of the last 30 trading days of the fourth quarter of Fiscal 2009. Therefore, the contingency was not satisfied. Upon conversion, the company will have the right to deliver, in lieu of its common stock, cash or a combination of cash and shares of its common stock. Subject to the above conditions, each $1,000 principal amount of Debentures is convertible into 49.8462 shares (equivalent to a conversion price of $20.06 per share of common stock) subject to adjustment. There were $30,000 of debentures converted to 1,356 shares of common stock during Fiscal 2008.

Since, as of this writing, the shares of Genesco were trading at $23 per share, the convertible securities were trading as equity, their price being above the $20.06 conversion price. In leverage ratios, the convertible could be considered equity because it can be reasonably expected, but not certain, that it will be converted. However, since the common stock is sufficiently close to the conversion price, both the current and pro forma financial structures should be included in the analysis. If the stock were to fall and the bonds were put to the company, Genesco would currently need to sell debt or stock to cover the liability, although the cost might be considerable to equity holders. Another option would be to pay bondholders with a payment in kind (PIK), where, instead of cash, they would receive additional bonds or shares of common stock.

Because convertible bonds offer less collateral protection than nonsubordinated bonds, they normally carry lower credit ratings. This would be true in the case of Genesco, which is a moderate credit and has not been a consistent generator of free cash flow. Thus it would appear that the company would be pleased to see the bonds converted to equity and, with it, enhance its credit status.

Sometimes convertible bonds are issued in conjunction with an upcoming equity offering. The issuer does this to gain needed cash while the offering is being prepared. Unlike a typical convertible bond or preferred, where the conversion price is above the current market price, under this offering, it is granted at a discount.

Example:

In anticipation of an upcoming IPO of its Macau subsidiary, Las Vegas Sands sold $600 million in convertible bonds that were to be converted, at the company's option, to equity in the subsidiary at a 10 percent discount to the offering price. If the company did not convert the debt to equity, because the company had the right to redeem the bonds, holders would be entitled to warrants to purchase stock for the number of shares to which they otherwise would have been entitled under the proposed offering.

FASB Staff Position APB 14–1

The advantages of convertible securities have become important to many firms needing to provide investors with an added incentive to purchase their debt securities. For convertible instruments that may be settled partially or wholly in cash, the FASB, in May 2008, approved, through a technical release, APB 114–1.[33]

Under the rules, an issuer must separately account for the liability and equity components of a convertible debt security. The issuer must value the liability component by measuring the fair value of a similar straight (nonconvertible) debt security. If the convertible debt security contains additional "substantive" embedded features,

[33] The staff position may be read at www.fasb.org/pdf/fsp_apb14–1.pdf.

such as put and call options, the issuer must take these into account in assessing fair value. The issuer may disregard a nonsubstantive feature or one the exercise of which is improbable.

An issuer must compute the carrying amount of the equity component of the convertible instrument by deducting the value of the liability component from the initial proceeds received at issuance. The equity component should be recorded as additional paid-in capital on the issuer's balance sheet. The issuer then must allocate transaction costs proportionately between the liability and equity components. This new bifurcated approach may result in the liability component having a temporary basis difference for income tax purposes. The FSP requires that this difference be recorded as an adjustment to additional paid-in capital.

Micron Technology, an early adopter, reported the following in its December 2009 earnings announcement: "The rule has no effect on cash flow, but could on leverage ratios, depending on the bifurcation ratio of debt to equity." To the credit and cash flow analyst, there should be no change in the analysis because the new rule has no credit impact over what previously existed. You will see from my credit model that available liquidly is compared with the amount of fixed obligations coming due.

Example:

In the first quarter of fiscal year 2010, the company adopted the FASB's new accounting standard for convertible debt instruments that may be settled in cash on conversion, including partial cash settlement. The new standard was applicable for the company's $1.3 billion 1.875 percent convertible senior notes issued in May 2007 and requires the liability and equity components of such instrument be accounted for separately in a manner such that interest cost will be recognized at a nonconvertible-debt borrowing rate in periods subsequent to issuance of the instrument. Amounts prior to fiscal year 2010 have been recast for this adoption in connection therewith. As of the issuance date of the $1.3 billion convertible debt, there was a decrease in the carrying value of the debt of $402 million, an increase in the carrying value of additional capital of $394 million, and a decrease in the carrying value of deferred debt issuance costs (included in other noncurrent assets) of $8 million. In addition, through fiscal year 2009, there was a decrease in retained earnings of $94 million and accretion of the carrying value of long-term debt of $107 million as a result of the new standard.

PREFERRED STOCK

Preferred stock has greater claim to the assets of an entity than common stock shareholders in the event of liquidation and so for years was referred to as *preference stock*. However, unlike common stock, because preferred dividends are fixed, like bonds, and not normally entitled to the free cash flow, the price of preferreds does not fluctuate as greatly. An exception would be a preferred that has a participating feature that entitles owners to receive the common dividend. A preferred stock carries no voting rights.

Holding preferred stock is riskier than owning fixed debt. Preferred dividends are paid at the discretion of the issuer, and the preferred represents a deeply subordinated claim in the event of bankruptcy.

From the issuer's point of view, preferred dividends, like common dividends, are paid from earnings and are not a deductible expense either for shareholder reporting or on the tax return. It is a charge against capital. Firms, however, may prefer to sell preferred stock because it avoids earnings dilution.

There are many types of preferred stock, and depending on their characteristics, they could be treated either as equity or debt or even perhaps as a hybrid. If the preferred stock has a maturity, it will be viewed as debt unless the security has a convertible feature and the common stock is trading above the conversion price.

When it is likely that the preferred will be recast as debt, it should be treated as such in the capital structure, as should a preferred that is exchangeable for debt at the company's option. When treated as debt, preferred dividend payments also should be considered in the fixed-charge coverage ratios. When it is likely that a preferred will be converted into common stock, it should be treated as equity and fixed-charge coverage calculated accordingly.

Because preferred dividends are not tax deductible, an entity might choose to redeem a preferred, whenever possible, to replace with debt. An issuer may chose to redeem a preferred security if there are any restrictive covenants associated with their issue that may be interfering with a capital spending program. Such was the case with SCANA Corp., a utility company that needed to redeem preferred stock to sell debt that had a lower cost of capital, aside from the resulting lower cash outlays. Entities often redeem their convertible preferred shares if the equity sells above the conversion price, saving the entity cash payments on the preferred dividends while adding to equity. If the common shares do not pay a common dividend, the savings can be significant, as was the case with NRG, a wholesale power company, when it forced a conversion.

An auction of preferred stock is one in which the dividend payments are reset each period based on the results of an auction, normally held every seven weeks. These instruments should be considered (short term) debt in the capital structure and also go by the name of *floating-rate preferreds*.

If an issuer has, by virtue of poor operating cash flows, preferred stock dividends "in arrears," that amount must be added to total debt in the computation of its capital structure. If the issuer redeems the preferred or it is apparent that it will do so, the new financial structure will depend on the means of financing. If replaced with another preferred issue, the interest-charge coverage may be affected. When a firm replaces bonds with preferred stock, shareholder reported profits will increase because the interest on the bonds is both tax deductible and appears on the income statement. Cash flow will change by the difference in after-tax cost of debt and the dividend payment. If preferreds replace bonds, net income and EBITDA will rise, pointing out yet another shortfall of using EBITDA and not free cash flow.

The analyst must determine the characteristics, issuer intent, and prospective redemption possibilities in determining how preferred securities fit into the capital structure and the determination of appropriate leverage ratios. A forced redemption on the part of the creditor must be considered as part of short-term debt with an analysis of funding outlets. Any special features, such as preference or auction preferred, will cause the capital structure to change more frequently and may affect the cost of capital if interest rates experience a dramatic shift.

When calculating free cash flow per share, all dilutive securities must be considered, including convertible preferred, convertible stock, stock options, and warrants.

CHAPTER 7

Cost of Equity Capital

As central as it is to every decision at the heart of corporate finance, there has never been a consensus on how to estimate the cost of equity and the equity risk premium. Conflicting approaches to calculating risk have led to varying estimates of the equity risk premium from 0 percent to 8 percent—although most practitioners use a narrower range of 3.5 percent to 6 percent. With expected returns from long-term government bonds currently about 5 percent in the US and UK capital markets, the narrower range implies a cost of equity for the typical company of between 8.5 and 11.0 percent. This can change the estimated value of a company by more than 40 percent and has profound implications for financial decision making.

McKinsey Quarterly, July 2005

I have discussed financial structure and free cash flow and have shown that obligations such as operating leases, commitments, contingencies, guarantees, and hedges must be considered. I also detailed, throughout this text, the limitations of earnings before interest, taxes, depreciation, and amortization (EBITDA) while explaining how free cash flow should be defined and why free cash flow, making adjustments to various discretionary areas, is superior to the commonly used practices that are popular today. Understanding the cost of equity capital and its significance in assigning fair value is now explored in detail because it is the by-product of those previous chapters.

Unfortunately, because they are not based on fundaments, the primary methods to determine the cost of equity used today often results in widely disparate outcomes. Illustrated both in this chapter and in Chapter 8 are areas of risk the analyst should be concerned with and needs to consider when evaluating the cost of equity in the establishment of fair value. In order to arrive at a fair-value estimate for an equity security, the analyst, for a going concern, must discount its free cash flow. I stress *going concern* because analysts use other measures to arrive at fair value, notably market value of the individual parts, liquidation value, price/sales, price/earnings, and price/book, most of which are tied into generally accepted accounting principles (GAAP) accounting but are limited in scope and *do not provide what equity investors are really seeking—the maximum amount of cash that could be returned to them without sacrificing the growth or value of the enterprise.* Book value has proven to be an unreliable metric if the book consists of assets where buyers at fair market prices are absent. What is the value of an asset for which there are either no buyers or buyers at unreasonably low prices? It is the free cash flows that then must be discounted. But at what rate?

Book value thus has little to do with cash that could be provided to shareholders unless those assets generate cash flows or can and should be sold and fair-price buyers exist. If assets are written down, stock repurchases occur at greater than current book value, dividends are greater than net income, and in any number of other circumstances, book value will decline, but this result in changes in capital, not necessarily free cash flow. Book value, unless assets are written down or fully depreciated, is more often a measure of management spending, not always their ability to earn a positive economic return on assets.

To this end, once I have determined what I believe is the entity's normalized free cash flow, the firm must be brought to present value using a fair approximation of its cost of equity capital. I discount by the cost of equity capital, not the weighted-average cost of capital, because the free cash flows represent cash that could be distributed to the equity holders. All others holding economic interests in the firm theoretically have been paid already. Inherent in the cost of equity is the magnitude and risk to the free cash flow, which include its consistency and growth rate. As you recall, I used the cost of debt to bring to present value the firm's operating lease obligations.

First, I will present some background on the cost of equity capital itself.

COST OF EQUITY NECESSARY FOR VALUATION

It is odd that a measure of such consequence as the cost of equity capital remains open for definition. While generally defined as the opportunity cost investors expect on their investment, a thoughtful introspection leads to a superior methodology for its calculation. The root of the proposed methodology lies in variables that might cause impairment or strengthening of the expected free cash flow.

McKinsey & Co.[1] believes that the cost of equity should be based on forward-looking projections implied by current stock prices relative to earnings, cash flows, and expected growth. Such is the return required by investors.

[1] *McKinsey on Finance*, Autumn 2002.

$$P_t = \frac{CF_{t+1}}{k_t - g}$$

where
P_t = price of a share at time t
CF_{t+1} = expected cash flow per share at time $t + 1$
k_t = cost of equity
g = expected growth rate of cash flows

The predicament from a practical viewpoint of the McKinsey approach is (1) if the growth rate is greater than the cost of equity, the results are empty, and (2) attempting to arrive at cash flows, McKinsey recommends a proxy of earnings multiplied by the payout ratio. This is a very crude and imprecise measure of cash flows that perhaps might have some validity when looking at a large sample but likely would be way off the mark for many individual entities. Many entities have positive earnings growth but no distributable cash flows.

It is also useful, *from the entity's standpoint*, to depict the cost of equity capital as the after-tax rate of return the company would need to earn on a new investment to prevent cash flow or earnings dilution as a result of additional equity issuance to finance said investment. This is further defined in the upcoming example on Sunoco, where the company is considering constructing a new refinery and needs to sell equity to finance the project. While this is not the cost-of-equity-capital method as defined by McKinsey and others, it is one that makes sense in the marketplace by those actually needing to issue equity capital. Since investors have no project under consideration when undergoing their analysis, I will look at other methods as well.

The cost of equity should be used as the denominator in conjunction with stock-valuation models, the most common of which is the dividend growth model or some variation typically employing earnings or cash flow.

THE CONSTANT-GROWTH-DIVIDEND MODEL

The dividend-growth model in use by many investors today implies that an entity is worth the present value of its dividends. For entities that do not pay a dividend, one may be estimated by substituting a percentage of earnings or operating cash flows. This valuation method often brings faulty results because (1) companies may borrow to pay their dividend (i.e., they do not generate positive free cash flow), (2) it ignores the capital requirements of the firm, (3) it ignores leverage and other credit metrics, (4) it ignores working capital requirements or balance-sheet management, which would allow the entity to pay a dividend, (5) it ignores overspending in discretionary areas, and (6) the required return (discount rate) is arbitrary.

The constant-growth-dividend model assumes that the price of a security is equal to the present value of dividends that are received on the security throughout its life. The main assumptions in this model relate to the discount rate used to value future dividends in current dollars and the pattern of cash dividends in the future. Most models assume that the discount rate is constant across periods, and as you have noticed, such models are merely a reformat of the equation in the preceding section.

$$\text{Value per share of stock} = \sum_{t=1}^{t=\infty} \frac{E(DPS_t)}{(1+k_e)^t}$$

where

DPS_t = expected dividends per share

k_e = cost of equity

In this equation, the value of a share of stock of the firm at the end of period t is equal to the present value of the dividends discounted at an appropriate rate. Note that the equation takes the sum of all future dividends (indicated by the summation sign Σ) from the following period ($t + 1$) through infinity (∞). In each period i, the dividend is discounted by dividing by one plus the discount rate to the power of $t + n$, which is equal to the number of periods the dividend is paid. For example, the dividend at period $t + 2$ will be discounted to the end of period t by dividing it into $(1 + k_e)$ to the power of 2.

In practice, it is less desirable to estimate valuation based on dividends because firms hesitate to reduce payments even though it is obvious the cash flows and business prospects do not support the current yield. Investors normally recognize this and will adjust the current share price accordingly, causing a further disparity with the artificial fair value estimated by the constant-growth-dividend model. Therefore, some investors prefer to discount earnings, but as the cash flow analyst knows, GAAP-reported earnings are also subject to financial engineering. As the growth rate under this model approaches the cost of equity, the value of the company reaches infinity.

I therefore focus on free cash flow. Even though management can "create short-term free cash flow" through various means, such as allowing accounts payable to age and reducing capital expenditures, such tactics can go on for only so long because such a firm would be in de facto liquidation. We also saw how UPS's free cash flow was negatively affected by the large payment of a pension contribution to terminate a plan. In addition, if management does attempt to squeeze the assets and expenses to create free cash flow, my credit model will pick this up because the power operating cash flows adjust for normalized working capital items.

THE COST OF EQUITY CAPITAL

Cost of equity capital represents the last frontier in security analysis, for without an appropriate discount rate, estimating free cash flow loses much of its significance. Cost of equity is at the very center of valuation. And valuation provides an assessment of a particular security's attractiveness as an investment; to the firm, it represents the cost to place additional equity. Only after it is established is the equity investor able to compare fair value with current value and determine whether the gap is sufficient to warrant investment. If the security's current market price and assessed value are in accord, the investor may decide to either hold or sell the security. If the assessed value is lower than the current market price, an investor may wish to sell or short the security.

The importance of cost of equity can be seen with a simple example. If an investor knew the exact free cash flow for the coming five years for a particular security, would the analyst know its precise fair value? The answer, of course, is no. It depends on the entity's cost of capital. Is inflation 2 or 12 percent? If inflation is at the high end, real after-tax ROIC will not be adequate to replace depreciated assets, which, when placed into service, are set in nominal terms. Are the free cash flows threatened by a series of lawsuits? Will the company's patents be running out? Is the company's free cash bolstered by underfunding of pension and other retirement benefits? Is the company possibly in violation of any debt covenants?

When Sunoco needs to raise equity capital to build a refinery, if it does so by selling 12 million shares instead of 16.8 million, owing to a lower cost of capital, the value of the firm to shareholders certainly is enhanced because dilution is reduced. A similar position should be taken by the portfolio manager in making portfolio decisions. The portfolio may be selected on the basis of criteria that point out undervalued securities based on potential return, as measured by the entity's free cash flow discounted by their cost of capital, return on invested capital (ROIC), and other factors relevant to the analyst. For instance, the portfolio manager may select rules that include other restrictions on firms on the portfolio. For example, the portfolio manager may place restrictions regarding minimum size, growth rates, market share, industry restrictions, dividend yield, or trading volume. Some clients specifically rule out investments in particular industries. Others may wish to invest in only certain industries. Regardless of the restrictions, cost of capital will determine if a firm is investing in value-enhancing assets.

Before I delve into the common cost-of-capital models, Table 7-1 vividly illustrates the importance of the cost of equity capital (discount rate) in equity analysis.

TABLE 7-1

Cost of Equity Capital

Fair Value	Current Free Cash Flow per Share	Growth Rate	Discount Rate (Cost of Equity Capital)
$42.00	$1.20	5%	8%
$31.50	$1.20	5%	9%
$18.00	$1.20	5%	12%

Causing fair value to change (Table 7-1) is the cost of equity capital—current free cash flow and its growth rate remain identical. As evidenced, a one-percentage-point change, from 8 to 9 percent in the cost of equity equates to a staggering 25 percent decline in fair value. If the entity's risk rises further, to a 12 percent cost of equity, the stock should be expected to fall by 57 percent. Such is the importance of the discount rate and the reason it must be established precisely to calculate fair value. If an entity's cost of capital rises, its share price must, by definition, fall until it reaches its new lower fair value, as shown in the table.

One might ask, If the current free cash flow and growth rate are known, why would fair value differ? It differs because the numerator is only a guess, even if an educated one supported by appropriate research and investigation. There are risks to any free cash flow or earnings estimate—patent or customer loss, volatility in input costs, foreign or exchange rate risk, asset risk, rollover of debt risk, and so on—and these are captured by the cost of equity. The fewer and less serious these risks, the more certain we can feel about the numerator—the free cash flows. For such an enterprise with above-average normalized free cash flow and moderate leverage, lower cost of equity normally will place the entity in a position to add value-adding projects with more facility than its competitors.

Popular Methods for Calculating the Cost of Equity Capital

Although I present the four most popular approaches to calculating the cost of equity, academia has devised other models as well, all of which are variations of these four. For example, one model adds a size premium and another a several-stage growth model. As you will see, except for the credit model, they all fall short in deriving an accurate equity cost of capital and in applying the commonsense logic of building up a risk profile from the risk-free rate. After all, the discount rate is meant to measure the risk to the numerator.

Later in this chapter I will explore another commonly used model, which I will refer to as the *project method*. It is simply the yield necessary to maintain the current level of earnings per share owing to new share issuance to finance a project.

Most Widely Practiced Cost-of-Equity-Capital Models

1. Capital Asset Pricing Asset Model (CAPM) using an estimate of beta[2]
2. Dividend-growth model
3. Implied cost of equity using a stock-valuation model, given known stock price and expected growth rate
4. Bond yield plus risk premium approach

COST OF EQUITY USING THE CAPITAL ASSET PRICING MODEL

By far the most commonly used model for estimating the discount rate, or required return, is the capital asset pricing model (CAPM), which, as pointed out in this book's introduction, was borne out of finance theory. Under the CAPM, the expected rate of return on any specific security *j* is provided by the following equation:

$$E(R_j) = R_f + \beta_j \times (R_m - R_f)$$

where $E(R_j)$ is the expected return on security *j*, R_f is the rate of return on a risk-free investment, β_j is the relative risk of the firm as measured by the beta coefficient, and R_m is the rate of return on the market portfolio.

Most data services that analysts rely on for use in their stock-valuation models estimate a beta with either five years of monthly returns or two to three years of weekly returns.[3] A five-year interval, it is believed, ensures against possible aberrant shocks to the beta owing to unusual short-term events. Others believe that a shorter risk interval may be more appropriate because it reflects the company's current risk profile; especially if the company's business or operating environment has changed, recognizing a shortened time period may unduly overweigh market

[2] The capital asset pricing model (CAPM) should not be confused with the Sharpe ratio, which is used to determine how volatility relates to return. The Sharpe ratio is used by many financial institutions to compare investment returns, adjusted for risk. I have found one instance, however, of a public entity, the Federal Home Loan Bank of Cincinnati, using the Sharpe ratio to evaluate return on equity. For more information, see its 2009 10K.

[3] Bloomberg, the most widely disseminated service, uses weekly data over two years.

misperceptions. Some services adjust the beta toward 1 on the theory that beta moves over time to a market risk.

In the stock-screening models employed at CT Capital, we use the 10-year Treasury note as the risk-free rate because it (10 years) is the approximate horizon period associated with many capital projects and long-term equity investor time horizons.

Since the risk-free rate is itself a leading credit metric, one may wonder why the CAPM went astray from the logic of its own application. My cost-of-equity credit model adds to the risk-free rate, the extent depending on the risk profile of the entity under consideration. The risk-free rate is used in the CAPM precisely because it represents a guaranteed rate of return. Why, then, does the model go on to measure volatility of stock price, which may not capture free cash flows and their associated risk? My model follows the logic.

To understand the relationship established by the CAPM, let me first explain the relative risk measure β_j. The CAPM posits that the expected return on each security varies systematically with the expected return on all securities in the marketplace, that is, the market portfolio. However, some stocks are defensive—their beta is lower than 1, and they fluctuate less on average than the market portfolio. Some stocks are more aggressive—their beta is greater than 1, and they fluctuate more than the market. With a beta of 1, the theory posits, the security is expected to fluctuate identically with the entire market.

The CAPM theory also posits a linear relationship between expected excess return on security *j* and the expected excess return on the market portfolio. In practice, as you will see in the Sunoco example that follows, this relationship is unlikely to hold up for anything but the shortest period. In fact, it is more common than uncommon for the beta to bounce around without regard to changes in the entity's risk profile. While empirical tests show support for the theory, it is much stronger at the portfolio level and generally has been unreliable at the individual-security level. Also, the literature documents several systematic deviations from the CAPM, such as the effect of the dividend yield, size, and book/market ratio on security returns.

A glaring weakness of the CAPM when calculating beta is that it does not, to the degree required and necessary, capture operating and financial risk, it being a measure of stock volatility. For instance, at the time that General Motors' debt was downgraded to "junk" by the three major rating agencies, its beta, according to the most widely used service, Bloomberg, was 1.4. At the same time, Bloomberg listed many companies having investment-grade debt with higher beta coefficients, such as IBM (1.6) and Intel (2.3). This variation is also seen in security analyst research reports. For instance, in a July, 13, 2005, research note from a large brokerage firm, the security analyst following IBM

TABLE 7-2

Beta and Leverage

Beta Lower Than	Average Market Value ($M)	Number of Companies	Total Debt/Net Worth Ratio
0	601	214	38.3[a]
0.5	499	585	64.9[b]
1.0	2,502	1,122	448[c]

[a]114 companies had both negative net worth and negative free cash flow, making the average 38.3 percent misleading.

[b]183 companies had both negative net worth and free cash flow and a beta < 0.5.

[c]322 companies had both negative net worth and free cash flow and a beta <1. 0.

used a beta of 1.1 in his calculation of fair value, a significant variation from the Bloomberg beta.

As business conditions change, so too should the firm's beta. However, as we saw with General Motors, this might not be the case. Many analysts prefer to use a historical beta as the firm's stock price is regressed against an index. However, because stock prices often fluctuate wildly, often for no fundamental reason, beta also moves wildly, unreflective of fundamental factors, issuing a false signal related to the cost of capital.

Many very weak credits have betas lower than 1. Table 7-2 shows that as of December 23, 2009, over 200 U.S. public companies had a beta of below 0, negative free cash flow, an average $600 million market value, and either a total debt/total equity of greater than 100 percent or negative equity, meaning that they had a cost of equity below that of the Treasury rate! A total of 183 companies had a beta of 0.5 or lower, were burning cash, and had a negative net worth.

Because the cost of equity capital, under this model, is calculated through the formula $K = R_f + \beta(R_m - R_f)$, it implies that companies that have a beta of close to 0 have a cost of equity capital that is close to the risk-free rate, hardly a plausible assumption. And for companies such as Interpharm Holdings that have a negative beta, the equity risk premium is negative $(R_m - R_f)$, implying a cost of equity that is *less* than the rate on Treasury bonds, even though that company has never turned a profit or generated positive cash flows.

An offshoot of the CAPM, called the build-up method, begins with the risk free rate, and then adds (builds on other risk factors), the long-term equity risk premium, small stock premium, industry risk premium, and any company specific risk premium. The long-term equity risk premium is normally equal for all entities, having averaged 6.35 percent according to data from Ibbotson Associates.

Risk Free Rate [a]	4.35 %
+ Long term Equity Risk Premium [b]	6.35 %
+ Smaller Stock Risk Premium [c]	1.67 %
+ Industry Risk Premium [d]	0.10 %
= Market Cost of Equity	12.47 %
+ Company-Specific Risk Premium [e]	5.0 %
= Concluded Cost of Equity	17.47 %

Source: Appraisal Report. Belk, Inc, February 2, 2008, filed as part of Tender Offer Statement.

I would therefore argue against the use of the CAPM when calculating the cost of equity capital, even though it is by far the most widely used and followed technique by security analysts, consultants, and publicly held companies.

IBM STUDY OF COST OF EQUITY USING POPULAR APPROACHES AND CREDIT METHOD

IBM, in conference call materials presented to security analysts, creditors, and investors, calculated its cost of equity, as shown Figs. 7-1 and 7-2. IBM executives had a mere 68 percent confidence level that the firm's beta was in a range of 0.4 through 1.2—a very wide span, especially for an A+ credit-rated company with strong, predictable cash flows and high recurring service revenues. The reader might appropriately ask, If IBM had a low confidence level that its cost of equity capital was between 7.89 and 11.7 percent, what does that suggest for the balance of all public companies?

For example, if IBM had free cash flow of $10 per share that would grow by 5 percent for five years and then 2 percent growth thereafter, its fair value would

FIGURE 7-1

An IBM Regression Analysis

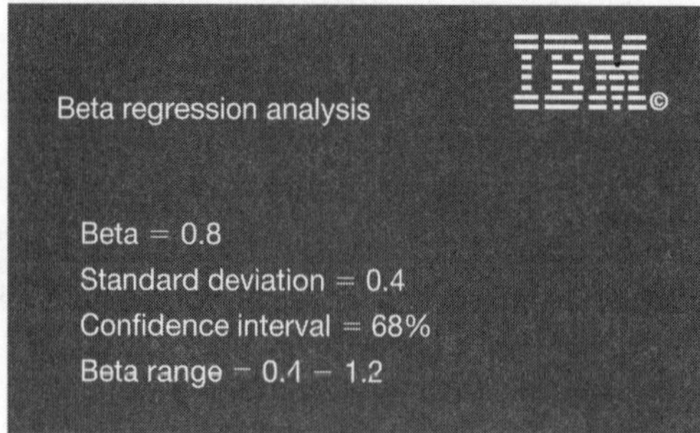

Source: IBM.

FIGURE 7-2

IBM Calculation of the CAPM Cost of Equity

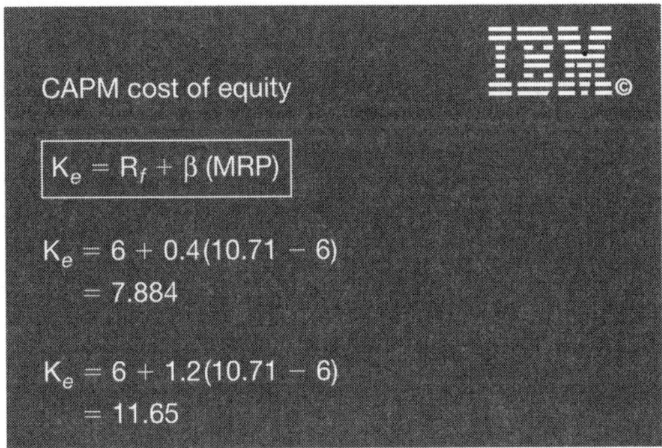

Source: IBM.

be in a range of $114 and $190 (excluding net debt), given the wide gap the company admits to in its equity cost of capital. Obviously, this is an unsatisfactory result, indicating a fundamental weakness of the CAPM the company used at its investor conference.

DIVIDEND-GROWTH MODEL TO CALCULATE COST OF EQUITY

Under the dividend-growth model, we solve for K_e by adding the dividend yield and growth rate in the dividend. Dividends serve as a measure of the free cash flows. This serves as a proxy for the required return to shareholders.

$$P_0 = \frac{D_1}{(K_e - g)}$$

Rearranging the terms, we get

$$K_e = \frac{D_1}{P_0} + g$$

where

K_e = cost of equity

$D_1 = D_0 - (1 + g)$

D_0 = four-year average of dividends paid

P_0 = year-end stock value

g = growth rate of dividend (or return on equity × retention rate)

Thus, for IBM, with its \$2.20 per share dividend and a stock price of \$115, we see

$$K_e = \left(\frac{2.2}{115}\right) + g$$

$$K_e = 1.9\% + 4.0\%$$
$$= 5.9\%$$

If one were to estimate dividend growth of 4 percent for the next five years and 2 percent thereafter, the cost of equity capital of 5.9 percent, significantly lower than that derived under the CAPM, would result in a net present fair value for IBM stock of \$286.28.

But *g* is sometimes calculated as the firm's return on equity multiplied by its retention rate, the theory being that payout could be distributed in the form of dividends. One would assume that the capital structure remains constant. IBM, however, has a small capital base compared with its earnings (and cash flow), which is not unusual for a service-oriented business that has repurchased a significant amount of stock for treasury.

Using that formula for *g*, we get

$$\text{Retention rate} = \frac{\text{retained earnings for the period}}{\text{after-tax earnings}}$$

We calculated IBM's retained earnings for 2008 by taking the difference in total retained earnings from its balance sheet between fiscal years ending 2007 and 2008 or

2008 Total retained earnings		\$70,352
2007 Total retained earnings	Less:	60,640
	2008 Retained earnings:	9,712

And IBM's after-tax earnings for 2008 were \$12,334 million. Therefore, its retention rate was

$$\text{Retention rate} = \frac{9{,}712}{12{,}334}$$
$$= 78.7\%$$

For the final step, IBM's return on equity was 72 percent based on its year-ending shareholders' equity of \$13,465:

$$\text{Return on equity} = \frac{9{,}712}{13{,}465}$$
$$= 72\%$$

We now see that IBM's cost of capital using the dividend-growth model was

$$K_e = \left(\frac{2.2}{115}\right) + 0.72 \bullet 0.787$$
$$= 1.9\% + 56.7\%$$
$$= 58.6\%$$

Obviously, this results in a very biased cost of equity, resulting from IBM buying back about $28 billion in stock over the past two years compared with $13 billion in shareholders' equity. This small equity base compared with its free cash flow provides an inconclusive result—IBM cannot be reasonably expected to raise its dividend by 57 percent per year. This model results in a fair value for IBM shares of about $19.39.

There are other faults with this model. First, dividends are a board decision and can be fixed despite the inability of the entity to cover them. And for companies that do not pay a dividend, the selection of one is arbitrary, even if one were to choose a low payout of operating cash flows. For instance, for expanding companies or those more leveraged, how does one estimate a fair payout ratio when all or most of their operating cash is being consumed at a time when they show good GAAP earnings?

IMPLIED COST OF EQUITY MODEL

The implied cost of equity is simply the present-value formula where the current stock price is known, the earnings or free cash flow are estimated, and we solve for the denominator, which is the cost of equity. The formula is identical to the dividend-growth model except that free cash flow is used instead of dividends.

$$Pt = \sum_{t=1}^{t=\infty} \frac{E(FCFt)}{(1+K_e)^t} \quad P_t = \text{price of share at time } tFCF_t$$
$$= \text{expected free cash flow per share } K_e$$
$$= \text{cost of equity}$$

The model calls for solving for K_e.

For IBM, discounting its projected free cash flows and using its current stock price, we get

$$115 = \frac{10.00}{K_e} + \frac{10.50}{(1+K_e)} + \frac{11.03}{(1+K_e)^2} + \frac{11.58}{(1+K_e)^3} + \frac{12.15}{(1+K_e)^4} + \frac{12.76}{(1+K_e)^5} + \cdots$$

TABLE 7-3

Cost of Equity Capital for IBM

Price, IBM	Implied Cost of Equity (%)
88	15
96	14
104	13
115	12
128	11
144	10
165	9

The current price of the stock is one of the three determinants in the model, the others being the cash flow forecast and the last, cost of equity, which we solve for. Table 7-3 is a matrix showing the cost of equity based on changes in the stock price using the same $10 in current free cash flow with 5 percent growth for the upcoming five years and 2 percent thereafter.

Using a growing annuity program that is programmed to solve this equation, we obtain a cost of equity of 12 percent.

While it might make intuitive sense that the higher the stock price, the lower is the cost of equity capital, perhaps the telling questions are

1. Should short-run stock price volatility have such a profound effect on a firm's economic decisions? On its ability to make long-term investment projects?
2. Why should the analyst not use a more discriminating measure of financial and operating risk in the cost-of-equity-capital calculation?
3. Should not cost of equity for a high-investment-grade-rated entity with predictable future cash flows exhibit greater stability than a model based on stock price? It would seem that this model is one of the tail wagging the dog.
4. What if the entity's stock price drops owing to factors unrelated to its cash flows and credit? Does the price fall really reflect the true cost of equity?

The skeptic might answer the last question as yes. In reality, however, if a board of directors knew the business and its prospects not to be realistically reflected in the stock price, it would finance asset acquisitions with as much debt as possible, staggering the maturities, and wait for its financial results to unfold. If reality still was not reflecting the firm's free-cash-flow generation after several years, it should have little problem with creditors and credit-rating agencies allowing the firm to roll over the debt coming due. Given consistent profitability, its tax shield will provide them with good long-term, low-cost financing, even though the CFO might view the company's capital structure as not where he or she would like. During this time, the CEO would need to convey the company's desired capital structure to shareholders and indicate why it would be unwise to sell equity at current levels.

Another limitation of this model is that security analysts and investors typically overestimate the long-term growth rate of earnings. This being the case, actual cost of equity will be higher than if using the analysts' exaggerated forecasts.

BOND YIELD PLUS RISK PREMIUM MODEL

The theory behind this simple model is that increases in a company's business risk are captured immediately by its bond yield. Of course, this model would not be appropriate if the entity, such as Apple Computer, has no long-term debt or if its debt securities were privately placed, closely held, or inactively traded. This model is just another approach and not one advocated as a primary method.

Using this approach, the analyst would add a "normal" spread over the firm's bond yield, typically 3 to 4 percent, because equity holders are last in line in the event of a Chapter 7 bankruptcy, the section of the code in which a business sells its assets and settles its liabilities.

If the bond yield was not readily available, the analyst could approximate it. For example, Fig. 7-3 shows the yield spread of AAA long-term bonds over similar Treasury securities. The analyst then would use a basket index of similar credits for the entity under review to calculate a cost of equity under this method.

IBM has many bonds on its books, including $1 billion principal amount, which at the time of this writing was yielding 5.4 percent to maturity. Adding 3.5 percentage points would yield a cost of equity capital under this method of 8.9 percent. Had no bonds been available, the analyst would have needed to add 3.5 percentage points to a basket of A+ credit ratings, IBM's credit.

FIGURE 7-3

Yield Spread of AAA Long-Term Bonds versus Similar Treasury Securities, March 2009–August 2009

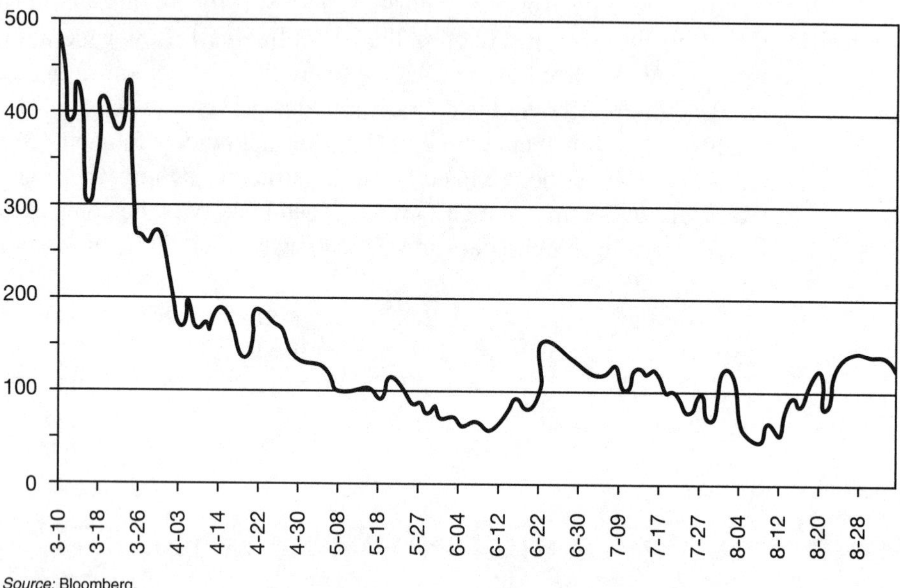

Source: Bloomberg.

COMPARISON

I now compare the cost of equity capital using the four most popular methods of benchmarking and an estimated 5 percent growth rate for the coming five years and 2 percent growth thereafter. Also included is the credit-model method, detailed in Chapter 8, which rendered an 8.4 percent cost of equity capital.

Method	Cost of Equity Capital (%)	Implied Fair Value of Stock ($)
CAPM	7.9–11.7	114.14–188.97
Dividend growth	5.9	286.26
Implied cost of equity	11.6	115.00
Bond yield plus risk premium	8.9	141.00
Credit model	8.4	168.00

There is such a wide gap is provided by the results of these models that it might be difficult to place, with confidence, a fair value for IBM equity shares within a reasonable range. Even the company itself found the limitations of the most popular model to be unacceptable. It is for this reason that I place greatest confidence in the company's fundamental characteristics, as reflected by its cash flows and credit. They are the real-world economic factors that should influence the cost of capital, cash flows, and investment decisions over the long term and are least influenced by short-term stock volatility and economic fear.

SPREAD VERSUS COST OF CAPITAL

The fact an enterprise does not show a positive spread (ROIC) in a particular year over its cost of capital should not necessarily signify its imprudence as an investment, especially if the current level of free cash flows are deemed to be temporary or underperforming assets could be shut down or sold, resulting in a boost to the ROIC yield. Since the marketplace normally overreacts to shortfalls, high returns could be forthcoming when normal conditions return or the underperforming division is disposed of. Divisional analysis could be a key consideration.

When ROIC is measured in conjunction with the entity's cost of capital, the analyst will be in possession of the most important factors in the evaluation of whether management is doing its part to create value for shareholders. If the company is not able to earn a return on its invested capital at least equal to its cost of capital, its stock will trade at a price reflecting the negative gap, especially if investors do not believe a turn is in the offing. If the entity is able to produce returns on its invested capital above its cost, it creates value, and its stock price should, over time, increase along with growth in the capital base. *Managers are placed in office to create value for their shareholders, and they accomplish this by maintaining the positive spread.* For the low-return company, if there is a need to raise new capital, it will be reflective of the underperformance gap, and add-on capital would be expensive compared with companies that are able to earn returns on invested capital in excess of its cost. *For this reason, restructurings are often part of a capital raise for underperforming firms. Investors and creditors examine the entity and force actions which they believe will bring about the positive spread.*

When an entity is considering a project whose ROIC is greater than its cost of capital, it then must weigh the additional benefits versus the increase in financial risk resulting from the project. If the project is sufficiently large, requiring a substantial debt financing that affects target capital and leverage ratios, it should consider speaking to credit-rating agencies prior to final approval. Credit agencies do not like surprises—unless they are unquestionably positive.

Example:

Figure 7-4 shows the ROIC and cost of capital for Altera Corporation, a manufacturer of specialized semiconductor equipment, one of the companies in Table 5-6 that showed a high recovery rate. The company's high ROIC and declining cost of capital were not lost on investors as its stock price has outperformed the general equity market by a significant margin. Trend lines are included owing to the cyclicality.

FIGURE 7-4

Altera Corporation: Cost of Capital versus Return on Invested Capital, with Trends

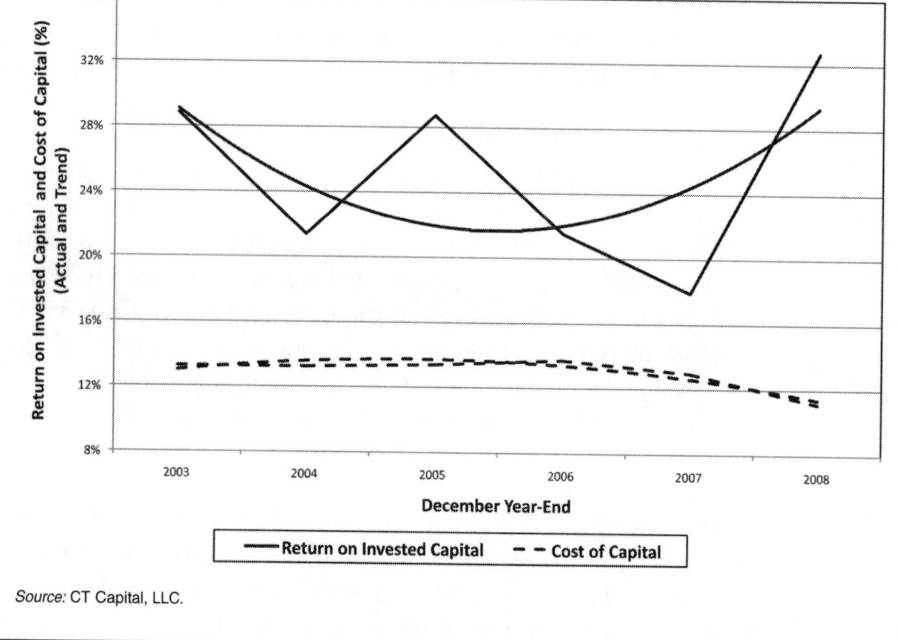

Source: CT Capital, LLC.

Advanced Micro Devices (AMD) is in a similar industry to Altera, but its stock lost 77 percent of its market value over the same period. Unlike Altera, however, AMD was not able to earn its cost of equity capital and therefore had to be categorized as a value-destroying entity, and as such, its stock price has declined. Notice in Fig. 7-5 how AMD, unlike Altera, has seen its cost of capital rise over the time period, reflecting its weakening credit posture.

You also can see how the real cost of capital was not picked up by analysts relying on the CAPM because, despite AMD's severely weakening credit posture during the period, its beta (Fig. 7-6), the central determinant of the CAPM, has been steadily decreasing, indicative of an entity with lessened risk.

FIGURE 7-5

Advanced Micro Devices: Cost of Capital versus Return on Invested Capital, with Trends

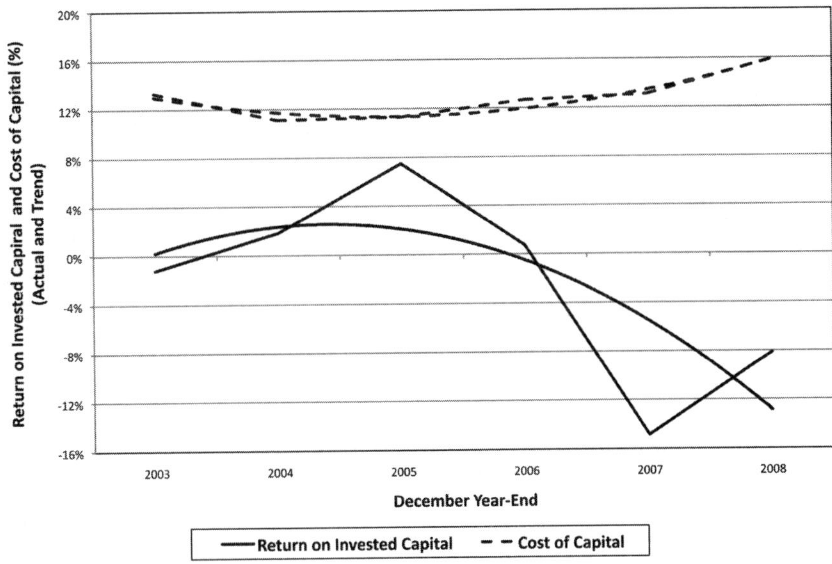

Source: CT Capital, LLC.

FIGURE 7-6

Beta Coefficient: Advanced Micro Devices

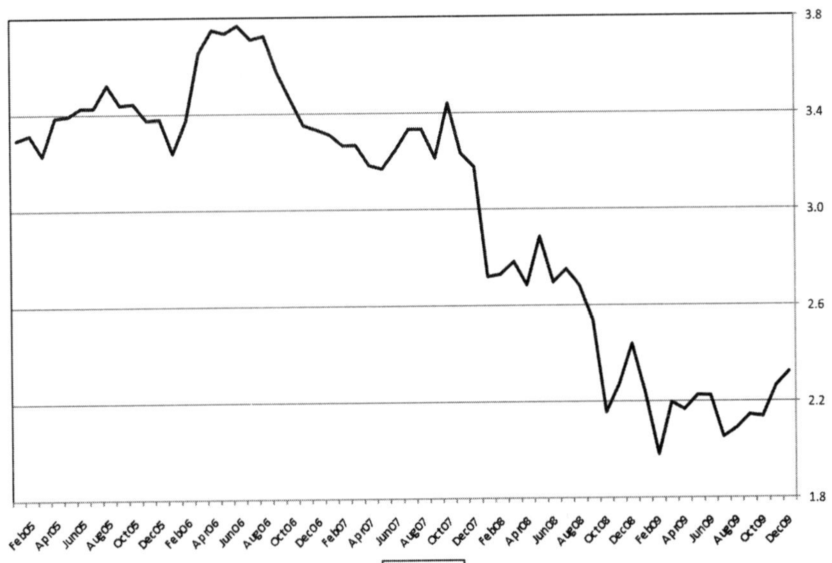

DIVISIONAL COST OF CAPITAL

Calculating a divisional cost of capital can prove vexing, especially if using the CAPM to estimate a beta. In order to calculate a division's cost of capital, it must be reviewed as a separate entity, not to assign a beta, but to estimate its cost of debt and equity through an evaluation of its cash flows and financial structure. The firm's beta is inappropriate because the cost of equity of the division under review should be set by its cash-flow and credit metrics.

The cost of debt can be reasonably estimated as that of the after-tax cost of the parent or, if the division is unconsolidated, the rate at which it borrows, adjusted for an estimated tax rate. If the division or special-purpose entity (SPE) files with the Securities and Exchange Commission (SEC), the appropriate rate would be that of its current after-tax yield unless it is being influenced by the parent, such as with guarantees. If the division is not reflecting a normalized balance sheet, that must be considered because often the parent will take excess cash from the division or in some other way alter its normal stand-alone financial structure. If the parent borrows on behalf of the division, it should be at the parent's cost of debt because this is the rate at which those funds are invested by the division. If the division is to be sold, the acquirer must estimate the division's new cost of debt when determining whether to proceed with the purchase.

The cost of equity must be estimated using the credit model in Chapter 8. Since most of the information to evaluate a division will not be available, a best estimate is required. Segment data often will provide just a partial picture and include many divisions.

For the parent or holding company, of course, such data are available. Typically, entities use the CAPM when computing a segment or divisional cost of equity by taking an average of other pure-play or similar public companies. This would be incorrect.

CASE STUDY: SUNOCO

During 2005, I prepared an analysis on Sunoco, Inc., using a fair estimate for cost of equity capital undertaken for the possibility of the company building a new refinery. At the time of the analysis, the general belief was that additional capacity would be needed within five years because demand was growing by 2 to 3 percent per year. It had been many years since a large refinery had been constructed in the United States. Looking back four years later, I evaluate how the model fared. The materials presented during the remainder of this chapter are excerpts based on that analysis. Several of the concepts of the study are repeated from earlier chapters, but their importance nonetheless bears reiteration in relation to the example.

From the point of view of the entity, the *cost of capital* may be defined as the return managers of the business must attain if they desire to prevent dilution resulting from additional equity issuance. Management's intent to actually follow through by selling additional equity is irrelevant when calculating the cost of equity capital but nevertheless should be quantified to have a better appreciation of investors' attitudes and risk perception of the company.

For this type of analysis, management would need to know the cost of all forms of capital to determine the appropriate financing mix of a project that cannot be financed from existing cash flow from operations.

While it is important to understand the weighted-average cost of capital (WACC) for the firm, which includes all means by which the entity is being financed, for equity investors, it is the cost of equity capital that is used in the discounting of free cash flow. Payment of principal on loans also derives from free cash flow if those obligations cannot be extended. Other outflows, such as interest payments, are paid from operating cash flows.

Having knowledge of all available costs of capital is vital in the evaluation and valuation process to (1) determine the least expensive cost of capital to the firm should current or future financing be necessary and (2) evaluate how raising funds through a particular source will affect the cost of capital of the remaining outlets. For instance, when financial companies raised substantial amounts of debt following the nadir of the worldwide credit crisis, their cost of equity capital declined substantially as their stock prices soared. This then allowed those firms to sell additional equity that was used to repay some of that high-cost debt, lowering the cost of equity even further.

The cost of total capital is the weighted-average cost of the entity's outstanding securities.

The computation for the cost of debt capital is often unambiguous and most often readily available, being the after-tax cost. If the entity is not profitable, it is the coupon rate of a bond divided by the net price to the entity. Thus, if a bond is issued at par with a 7 percent coupon rate, the cost of debt to that firm would be 7 percent.

In nonstressed economic periods, investment research reports on companies with leveraged capital structures typically use an unrealistically low weighted-average cost of capital owing to the entity's large debt allocation. Such companies realistically should see higher, not lower, weighted-average costs of capital despite the tax benefits of debt and indeed would if the analyst used the current market prices of the debt securities instead of prices and interest rates when the debt was originally issued. If the analyst uses a bond-spread estimate, which, at times, is unavoidable owing to illiquidity of the issue, it needs to be a conservative estimate comprised of securities having a fair comparable credit rating. Since rating agencies are not constantly evaluating and updating all securities in the fixed-income universe, the analyst might need to make changes to the current implied bond rating to reflect a more accurate and realistic assessment of its credit position.

Example:

The following was found in a research note for Centerpoint Energy, a very leveraged company:

> Using a bond spread of about 100 basis points and Citigroup Investment Research's equity risk premium of 3.5% yields a weighted average cost of capital (WACC) of 4.7%. The low WACC is a result of the company's high debt to total market capitalization, which results in a WACC more closely weighted to CNP's after-tax cost of debt.

Source: Citibank.

The projected cost of Sunoco's new refinery was $1.5 billion, which at the time this analysis was prepared was equal to about 20 percent of its current market capitalization. From the vantage point of Sunoco's finance department, it was imperative that the company know its current WACC to determine the least expensive method to fund the project.[4]

In order to calculate its cost of equity, the analyst in charge of the project decided to look at the project from several perspectives, including earnings dilution, the CAPM, and my credit model. The cost of capital must be determined with precision because it determines whether the project should proceed, having already estimated the project's ROIC. Some companies simply do not have access to capital, while for others, the cost is high in relation to a conservative estimate of its expected ROIC. Firms with a low cost of capital normally do not have a problem being overtaken by competitors because they can accept projects that their weaker peers cannot, as well as accept a smaller positive spread between the ROIC and the WACC.

As with any capital project, the uncertainly of the cash flows is the central determinant. The outlook for inflation is also crucial because it affects both cash flows and cost of capital. Assumed here is that inflation will remain about 3 percent. If the inflation rate were to increase beyond expectations, cost of capital would need to be adjusted up accordingly through the risk-free rate of the CAPM, whereas for the credit model, a further increase in the cost of capital would be added because it affects consumer demand not captured by the CAPM. An important point often overlooked by users of the CAPM is that lower interest rates do not always lead to a lower cost of capital. **In fact, contrary to popular thinking, a rise in inflation cannot often be overcome by a similar rise in revenues or net income—it must be overcome by a similar rise in free cash flows (which include the tax impacts), or else cost of capital will increase. During periods of higher inflation, the real ROIC often fails to keep up with cost of capital, hence a decline in stock value.**

[4] Sunoco has never been a client of mine or any entity affiliated with me. This was an independent analysis.

Often, the driver of cost of equity is the risk-free rate, which, if economic uncertainty abounds, generally would force cost of equity higher because the prospective free cash flows and credit are affected by the perception of the economic environment. For the CAPM, the drivers are the risk-free rate, stock volatility, and the expected return on stocks.

Calculating Beta under the CAPM

Since Sunoco's beta had been very volatile, resulting from the large swings in the price of oil, the company analyst decided to weight the beta, with the results shown in Table 7-4.

It is logical that Sunoco, given the large swings in the price of crude and refining margins, should have seen greater volatility over more recent periods, and an adjusted beta of 0.925 is probably closer to its true value. Of note is the wide range in the beta over the five-year period, not unusual for cyclic concerns. Intuitively, one would suspect that Sunoco's beta should be at least of the S&P's 1.0 beta.

Using a risk-free rate of 4.1 percent, the cost of equity capital for Sunoco using the CAPM is 8.6 percent, derived as follows:

$$\begin{aligned}\text{Cost of equity} &= 0.041 + 0.925 \times (0.09 - 0.041)\\ &= 8.6\%\end{aligned}$$

Making improvements to the beta has been the subject of much academic research. The primary limitation to the embracement of beta as a capital tool is that analysts are looking for a quantitative solution to a fundamental problem. The *equity risk premium*, defined as the expected return over the risk-free rate, is not designed to *forecast* future growth in cash flows or dividends—the numerator of

TABLE 7-4

Reweighting Sunoco Beta*

Year	Weight	Beta	Weight × Beta	Weighted Beta
2004	35%	1.30	0.35 × 1.30	0.455
2003	25%	0.85	0.25 × 0.85	0.210
2002	20%	0.50	0.20 × 0.50	0.100
2001	10%	0.54	0.10 × 0.54	0.050
2000	10%	1.10	0.10 × 1.10	0.110
			Weighted beta (total)	**0.925**

*Sunoco's weekly prices for 52-week periods were regressed against the Standard and Poor's (S&P) Industrials.

the discount model does that. The CAPM starts with the risk-free Treasury rate and implores the analyst to add on from there. This is perfectly logical. Where it fails is in its central assumption that security-level volatility represents a total and accurate manifestation of operating and financial risk, including free-cash-flow impairment. Clearly, this is not the case by virtue of the vast number of entities that are poor credits, including those in default or technical default, yet have low beta coefficients. These poor credits having a low cost of equity are not consistent with the theory underlying the CAPM. And the same is true for many higher-beta stocks. They have good fundamental outlooks with investment-level credit ratings, yet they are awarded an unfairly high cost of capital owing to the vagaries of their underlying stock trading patterns.

Table 7-5 illustrates the cost of capital using the CAPM and the comprehensive credit model for companies across the credit spectrum. Notice how, for these firms, the cost of equity is more closely aligned with the credit model than with the CAPM. For example, Eddie Bauer, a company in bankruptcy that is currently attempting to reorganize under the bankruptcy code, overwhelmed by massive debt, has an unjustifiably low cost of equity capital according to followers of the most popular cost-of-equity model; the company's cost of capital is lower than those of General Electric, 3M, and many other AAA-rated companies.

Cooper Industries (beta = 1.7), eBay (beta = 2.0), and Assurant (beta = 1.6), all well-known, actively traded credits with an accurate cost of capital under my credit model, show a high cost of capital (owing to stock volatility) if one were to follow the CAPM. Observe that eBay, despite its higher credit rating than Cooper Industries, has a lower cost of equity when using the credit model. Also of interest is that Caterpillar had a higher credit rating than eBay yet, according to its credit, deserves a considerably higher cost of capital.

TABLE 7-5

CAPM versus Rating Risk Equity Premium*

Company	Beta	Cost of Equity (CAPM)	Credit Rating	Cost of Equity (Credit Model)
Assurant	1.6	12.3	BBB+	8.8
eBay	2.0	14.5	A−	9.1
Caterpillar	1.9	13.95	A	11.1
Radio One	0.12	4.2	CCC+	19.1
Cooper Industries	1.7	12.9	A	8.2
Eddie Bauer	35.0	5.4	D	33.7

*Assumes 9 percent return on the market and a yield on 10-year Treasury bonds of 3.5 percent, which was the yield at the time this table was prepared, not the time the Sunoco analysis was undertaken. Credit ratings are those of Standard and Poor's.

Cost of Debt and Preferred

When computing the cost of debt, the analyst must establish the interest rate the entity would be required to pay to replace its existing debt under current conditions. Since interest is tax deductible, we need to multiply that coupon (or effective interest) rate by one minus the marginal rate. Thus, if the yield on the entity's bond, when issued at par, is 7 percent. and the company is in the 30 percent cash tax rate, the true after-tax cost to the firm is 4.9 percent. The shield on the outstanding securities does not change if interest rates, after issuance, change.

Using similar logic, the cost of equity capital is not directly affected by the tax rate because the company would not be afforded a tax benefit for shares it issued. A change in the tax rate will affect the free cash flow (if absorbed), which affects the cost of equity—hence there is an indirect impact.

The cost of preferred stock is the after-tax current yield on its existing instruments. Since preferred dividends are, like common stock dividends, paid after taxes, no tax deduction is available to the corporation.

For a profitable enterprise, the cost of debt capital almost always will be lower than equity because debt (1) is generally better secured with assets, (2) holds a higher security position in the event of default, (3) has tax-deductible interest payments, (4) has generally lower underwriting costs, and (4) new equity typically has substantial market impact. If warrants to purchase stock are issued as part of a financing (debt or equity), they may serve to lower the cost of those forms of capital or even permit outside financing to occur at all. Sunoco did not have warrants outstanding.

For debt trading at a large discount to the stated amount on the balance sheet, there could be a considerable variation between the cost of debt as currently priced in the market and that stated by the balance-sheet value. Such is the case in the following example involving MGM, with the data taken from its 2008 10K.

Example:

MGM stated that its weighted-average interest rate was just 6 percent, hardly befitting a company near bankruptcy at the time. For this Standard and Poor's (S&P) CCC-rated entity, the cost of equity capital based on my credit model was 17.3 percent. During the height of the financial crisis, MGM's 7.625 percent bonds due in 2017 yielded 33 percent. Six months later, after the financial crisis had passed, the bonds still yielded 13.71 percent to maturity. And during February 2010, MGM's lenders needed to defer principal payments on its debt for two years, referred to as *forebearance*. Without the forebearance, the foreclosure process would have begun.

From MGM's 2008 10K:

The following table summarizes information related to interest on our long-term debt:

	Year Ended December 31 (In Thousands)		
	2008	2007	2006
Total interest incurred	$773,662	$930,138	$900,661
Interest capitalized	(164,376)	(215,951)	(122,140)
Interest allocated to discontinued operations	—	(5,844)	(18,160)
	$609,286	$708,343	$760,361
Cash paid for interest, net of amounts capitalized	$622,297	$731,618	$778,590
Weighted-average total debt balance	$12.8 billion	$13.0 billion	$12.7 billion
End-of-year ratio of fixed-to-floating debt	58/42	71/29	66/34
Weighted-average interest rate	6.0%	7.1%	7.1%

TABLE 7-6

Sunoco, Inc.

SUNOCO, INC., AND SUBSIDIARIES
CONSOLIDATED BALANCE SHEETS
(Million of Dollars)

	At December 31	
	2004	2003
Assets		
Current assets		
Cash and cash equivalents	**$405**	$431
Accounts and notes receivable, net	**1,271**	1,056
Inventories (Note 6)	**765**	494
Deferred income taxes (Note 4)	**110**	91
Total current assets	**2,551**	2,072
Investments and long-term receivables (Note 7)	**115**	143
Properties, plants, and equipment, net (Note 8)	**4,966**	4,405
Prepaid retirement costs (Note 9)	**11**	11
Deferred charges and other assets (Note 2)	**436**	422
Total assets	**$8,079**	$7,053
Liabilities and Shareholders' Equity		
Current liabilities		
Accounts payable	**$2,109**	$1,365
Accrued liabilities	**461**	435
Short-term borrowings (Note 10)	**100**	—
Current portion of long-term debt (Note 11)	**3**	103
Taxes payable	**349**	242
Total current liabilities	**3,022**	2,145

	At December 31	
	2004	**2003**
Long-term debt (Note 11)	**1,379**	1,498
Retirement benefit liabilities (Note 9)	**539**	604
Deferred income taxes (Note 4)	**755**	602
Other deferred credits and liabilities (Note 12)	**247**	208
Commitments and contingent liabilities (Note 12)		
Minority interests (Note 13)	**530**	440
Shareholders' equity (Notes 14 and 15)		
Common stock, par value $1 per share		
Authorized—200,000,000 shares		
Issued, 2004—139,124,438 shares		
Issued, 2003—136,801,064 shares	**139**	137
Capital in excess of par value	**1,656**	1,552
Earnings employed in the business	**2,895**	2,376
Accumulated other comprehensive loss	**(164)**	(187)
Common stock held in treasury, at cost		
2004—69,796,598 shares		
2003—61,420,158 shares	**(2,919)**	(2,322)
Total shareholders' equity	**1,607**	1,556
Total liabilities and shareholders' equity	**$8,079**	$7,053

	December 31 (Millions of Dollars)	
	2004	**2003**
9.375% debentures, payable $16 in 2014 and $20 in 2015 and 2016	**$56**	$200
9% debentures due in 2024	**65**	100
7.75% notes due in 2009	**146**	200
7.60% environmental industrial revenue bonds paid in 2004	**—**	100
7.25% notes due in 2012 (Note 13)	**250**	250
7.125% notes paid in 2004	**—**	100
6.875% notes due in 2006	**54**	150
6.75% notes due in 2011	**177**	200
6.75% convertible subordinated debentures due in 2012 (Note 14)	**9**	10
4.875% notes due in 2014	**250**	—
Floating-rate notes (interest of 2.17% at December 31, 2004) due in 2034 (Note 10)	**103**	—
Revolving credit loan, floating interest rate (2.94% at December 31, 2004) due in 2009 (Note 10)	**65**	65
Floating-rate notes (interest of 2.72% at December 31, 2004) due in 2006 (Note 10)	**120**	120
Revolving credit loans, floating interest rate (3.42% at December 31, 2004) due in 2006 (Note 10)	**6**	28
Other	**85**	85
	1,386	1,608
Less: Unamortized discount	**4**	7
Current portion	**3**	103
	$1,379	$1,498

Since Sunoco's bonds listed in the 10K are *not* actively traded, I estimated, based on available yield spreads at the time relative to the company's BBB rating, that Sunoco's cost of debt of was approximately 6.6 percent, or an after-tax cost of 4.03 percent, based on an implied 39 percent cash tax rate. The use of the effective tax rate would not be appropriate given that we are using cash-based metrics. This cost of debt is derived as follows:

$$= 0.066 \times (1 - 0.39)$$
$$= 4.026$$

Sunoco has a simple capital structure consisting primarily of short- and long-term debt and equity capital. If preferred stock were part of this structure, the logic would be the same; that is, derive its current yield and plug it in based on its percentage of the capital structure.[5] Sunoco also is a lessor and lessee of operating leases. Netting the two and using the current after-tax 4.03 percent as a discount rate adds approximately $323 million to total debt, which I add to the balance-sheet debt ($1,479) included in Table 7-7. About a third of the leases were for marine vessels.

I do not include in this analysis short-term trade obligations as part of the capital structure. Such business expenses, such as payables and payroll, are met from the normal operating cash-flow cycle. On the other hand, operating leases

TABLE 7-7

Sunoco-Weighted Average Cost of Capital

		Credit-Rating Method ($ Millions)		
		Weight	Cost	Weighted Average
Debt	1,802	0.20	4.00%	0.80
Equity	7,410	0.80	8.96%	7.20
Total	$9,212		Weighted-average cost of capital:	8.00

[5] A quick note on its balance sheet. As we see, Sunoco conforms to SFAS 115, "*Accounting for Certain Investments in Debt and Equity Securities.*" Debt and equity securities not classified as either held-to-maturity securities or trading securities are classified as available-for-sale securities and are reported at fair value, with unrealized gains and losses excluded from earnings and reported in a separate component of shareholders' equity and found as *other comprehensive income (loss)*. Four years later, this statement, we now know, would be increasingly important for financial institutions and their investors and creditors.

should be included. If the entity has no bank debt, the analyst must impute an interest rate based on its credit rating. If the entity has no credit rating, one must be implied based on its credit metrics and S&P's adjusted financial ratios (see Table 6–6), which must be compared with like credits, or use the one-third of operating lease rule as the imputed interest rate and then determine the after-tax cost.

When I run through my credit model in the next chapter, I arrive at a cost of equity capital of 8.96 percent, and thus I determine Sunoco's WACC as shown in Table 7-7.

The $7.410 billion equity is the market value of Sunoco stock at the time. Preference is made to use market value as opposed to book value because it represented a closer relation to the assets values and capital strength than the depreciated balance-sheet value. Sunoco's gross PPE was $8 billion, with $3.7 billion in depreciation, resulting in the $4.966 billion balance-sheet figure. At the time, it was generally believed that industry capacity constraints were just a few years away, and this was being reflected in the strong performance of Sunoco stock relative to the S&P 500 (Fig. 7-7).

FIGURE 7-7

Cumulative Return: SUNOCO versus S&P 500 Index

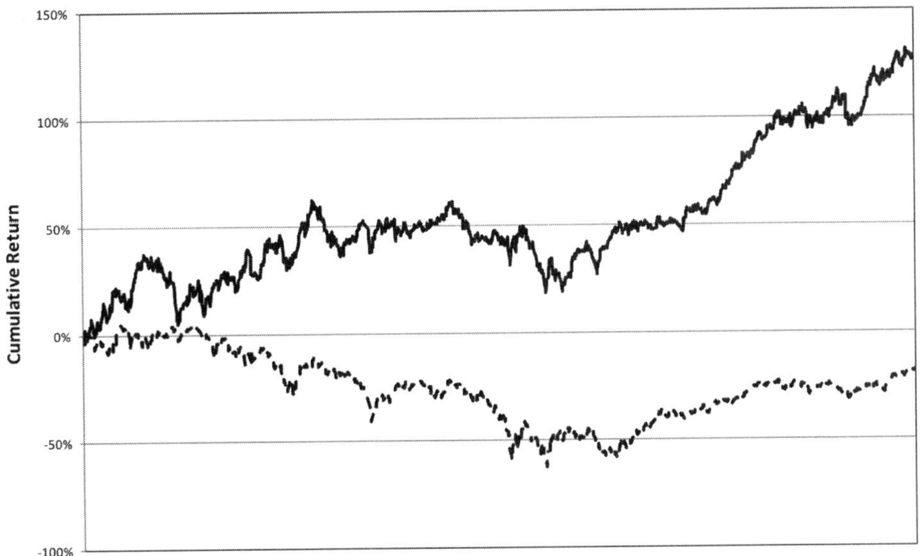

Cost-of-Equity Project Method

The cost of equity also can be calculated by determining the "hit" to earnings per share resulting from undertaking a new investment project. This method, although simple, is a common tool, although it does not address cash flow. Again, presume that Sunoco wishes to build that new oil refinery having a cost equal to 20 percent of its current market value, or $1.48 billion. Assume that to complete the new equity offering successfully, the company needs to sell its shares at a 12 percent discount to the current market value of $100 per share, which includes all underwriting, legal, accounting, and other costs. This amounts to 16.8 million additional shares (Table 7-8).

Some managers or board members like to see, as part of the analysis, the percentage reduction to earnings so, with a 10 percent increase in pretax income the following year, the cost of capital would be 10.4 percent (7.31/8.16), which represents the new estimated earnings divided by the new outstanding shares. It is a shareholder-reported GAAP number, assuming that the entity was able to grow its pretax income by 10 percent. This analysis would make more sense if

TABLE 7-8

Sunoco

NEW CAPITAL REFINERY ANALYSIS

		Increase in Pretax ($ Millions)			
	2004* (With New Refinery)	10%	15%	35%	50%
Pretax income	995	1,094	1,144	1,343	1,492
Provision for taxes (39.2%)	390	429	449	527	585
Net income	605	665	715	836	925
EPS	8.16	7.31	7.64	8.98	9.97
Common dividends	86	124.5	124.5	124.5	124.5
Shares outstanding	74.1	90.9	90.9	90.9	90.9
Addition to retained earnings	519	540	590	711	800
Addition to retained EPS	7.00	5.94	6.28	7.61	8.61

*Actual for 2004. Addition to retained earnings is from operations (not shareholders' equity) only and assumes that the refinery began operation in the next period or was purchased. It excludes, for instance, purchase of treasury stock, which likely would occur if the projection were met. Also, since Sunoco purchased $568 million in treasury stock during 2004, the shares outstanding do not match the 69.1 actual shares outstanding at the end of the fiscal year. The 74.1 million shares used is basic or average weighted shares outstanding during the year from which earnings per share reported to shareholders was calculated. Because of the fewer shares outstanding, earnings and cash flow per share would be boosted automatically, all else equal. Also, small movements in refining margins would have a large impact on profits, cash flow, and cost of capital. For the purpose of this example, we presume that margins are constant. Sunoco raised its dividend in March 2005, but for purposes of comparison, I left it unchanged.

the project would contribute immediately to earnings, a dubious assumption with a multiyear project.

Such analysis, however, omits the extra dividend paid on the new shares. It is for this reason that I choose to look, in this method, at the cash effect of the project based on the difference in additional retained earnings per share (Table 7-8), which would include the cost of the added dividend payments on the common. If the company paid preferred dividends, I also would need to include that cost in the table. Owing to the dilution and extra dividend requirement, pretax income would need to rise about 27 percent to return to the same addition to retained earnings as prior to the dilution.

An internal rate of return (IRR) was not used in the study owing to its severe limitation regarding interim-period cash flows. The IRR is useful only when there are no interim cash flows or if any interim cash flows can be reinvested at the IRR rate, hardly a plausible assumption for a company such as Sunoco. In fact, the assumed reinvestment rate is often the driving force behind the IRR analysis because over 10 years it accounts for a large majority of the return.

Clearly, the cost of this mammoth project might meet with some skepticism by Sunoco's board. However, the projected 10 percent increase in pretax profits shown in the first column of Table 7-8 is just for year one, and it could be argued by those in management and those of the board of directors favorably disposed that such a large expansion would lead to, over 5 to 10 years, much greater increases in income and cash flows depending on the growth in demand for refined products and the *crack spread*, which is the margin between the cost of crude and the price realized for product. We will see when looking at Sunoco's ROIC that refining margins are notoriously unstable.

Another way of looking at the project would be the yield needed to return the same earnings to shareholders (exclusive of the dividend) as prior to undertaking the project so that

$$\begin{aligned}\text{Required yield} &= \frac{\text{current earnings}}{\text{price of new shares to be sold}}\\ &= \frac{\$8.16}{\$88}\\ &= 9.3\%\end{aligned}$$

where \$88 is the price of the new shares to be sold, and \$8.16 is current earnings. The newly issued shares must each earn \$8.16 to result in the total firm earnings per share. Being earnings per share, it is an after-tax requirement. Pretax, it is a 15.3 percent requirement. This is greater than the prior method of 10.4 percent because it does not consider any increase in earnings resulting from the project.

However, as noted in Table 7-8, Sunoco also will need to pay dividends on the additional 16.8 million shares, or

$1.20 (current rate per share) × 16.8 (additional shares) = $20,16 million

Or a pretax requirement of $33.16 million because dividends are paid after-taxes, and we are measuring the cash needed to pay the additional dividend with balance-sheet cash remaining at its prior level.

$$\frac{\$20.16}{(1-0.392)} = \$33.16$$

Given Sunoco's 39.2 percent tax rate, it would need to earn $33.16 million added cash (in addition to the current $8.16 per share) to pay the new dividends and have retained earnings unchanged. The dividend requirement is ignored as this method typically is computed[6]; it is merely concerned with maintaining the earnings per share, not cash flow or change in shareholders' equity.

I now show the blended cost of capital using the three methods discussed. The 8.95 percent WACC (Table 7-10) averages the results of the three cost-of-equity methods shown. I did not include the implied cost-of-capital method or other methods reviewed earlier in this chapter because they are used infrequently compared with the CAPM, and I wanted to introduce the project method because investor conference calls normally focus on the earnings impact when accretion can be expected and the extent, if any, of dilution. If the analyst wished to include the implied cost of capital as another method when evaluating the firm's cost of equity, it would be averaged with the other estimates of Table 7-10.

TABLE 7-9

Sunoco

	$ Million	Weight	Cost	Weighted Average
Debt	1,802	0.20	4.0%	0.80
Equity	7,410	0.80	9.3%	7.44
Total	$9,212		Weighted average cost of capital:	8.24%

[6] This method was popularized by Erich Helfert in his landmark book, *Techniques of Financial Analysis* (Richard D. Irwin), originally published in 1963.

TABLE 7-10

Sunoco

WEIGHTED BLENDED COST OF CAPITAL

		Cost	Weight	Weighted Average
Equity:	CAPM	8.6%		
	Credit-rating method	8.96%		
	Project method	9.3%		
	Average cost of equity:	8.95%	0.80	7.16
Debt		4.0%	0.20	0.80
		Weighted-average cost of capital:		7.96%

The closeness in the results is surprising, but as the years unfolded, the credit-rating method remained relatively stable, whereas the CAPM cost of equity actually declined, resulting from a fall in Sunoco's beta.

We now have the cost of capital (7.96 percent) that Sunoco would compare with its ROIC, assuming that project financing is raised in the same allocation as its current capital structure. If the capital raise is dissimilar to the existing capital structure, it is that cost weighting that will be measured against the expected ROIC from the project. If the projected free cash flow based ROIC comfortably exceeded the WACC for the project, it would be brought to committee and the board.

Sunoco's 2004 ROIC

Sunoco and the refining group in general at the time the study was prepared were earning a high ROIC, and their stocks were reflecting this, as we saw from the stock chart. Using my formula to compute ROIC, we get

$$\text{ROIC} = \frac{\text{four-year average free cash flow} - \text{net interest income}}{\text{invested capital (equity + total interest-bearing debt + present value of operating leases} - \text{cash and marketable securities)}}$$

$$= \frac{591 - 10}{1{,}607 + 1{,}802 - 405}$$

$$= \frac{581}{3{,}004}$$

$$= 19.3\% \text{ (ROIC for 2004)}$$

Although 2000–2004 had been good to the refiners, during the period 1988–2004, there were eight years when Sunoco's ROIC was negative owing to low "crack "spreads and/or slack demand for its products.

Sunoco ROIC and Market Values 1988-2004

Year End (December)	ROIC (%)	Market Value ($M)
1988	(3.9)	3,420
1989	(2.5)	4,359
1990	0.1	2,969
1991	2.2	3,234
1992	(5.3)	2,976
1993	(5.4)	3,131
1994	(6.0)	3,073
1995	(7.2)	2,054
1996	(0.4)	1,779
1997	1.6	3,009
1998	(5.1)	3,373
1999	11.2	2,120
2000	14.3	2,864
2001	20.1	2,935
2002	11.8	2,533
2003	17.1	3,951
2004	19.3	5,975

A Final Decision

The team responsible for bringing the project forward now should have the beginning information necessary, including site design and financial projections, prepared in consultation with outside engineers and attorneys. An integral part of the approval process is overcoming the necessary legal obstacles from local and federal authorities. The internal team might consist, among others, of Sunoco's financial unit, project engineers, vice president of marketing, vice president of refining and supply, and chairman (who is also the CEO) because a project of this magnitude is a challenging, time-consuming, extremely costly, and risky process. The CFO will initiate discussions with the company's investment banker and credit-rating agencies, whereas the board of directors will continue to be made current on the project status. The board, by this time, will have seen reams of information related to the long-term supply and demand outlook for the industry, including percentage forecasted utilizations, legal requirements, tax effects, incentives, crude days of supply, inventory for all products, and so on.

The CFO must decide what avenue(s) of capital raises to pursue and then report back to the board for final approval. Given the information from the preceding, including current leverage ratios, the lower cost of debt capital, projected growth of earnings and cash flow, and Sunoco's good credit rating, one might expect the company to raise the majority of the new offering via the debt markets. However, as you recall, I used the current equity market value in the calculation of the capital structure, and some board members might prefer the capital structure be based on the book value, which would have resulted in a total debt/shareholders' equity of closer to 100 percent. Sunoco's investment bankers also will provide advice on current market conditions for all forms of capital. Most likely, however, given the extreme volatility of cash flows associated with the industry, the board would prefer equity financing whenever possible, avoiding a fix charge coverage issue if product prices collapse, as the company's ROIC history has shown.

Firms with more stable cash flows generally would prefer debt financing, perhaps in obligations maturing in 3, 10, 12, and 20 years, which allows for uncertainties in the fixed-income markets at the time the bonds mature. Otherwise, it would be expected that the raise would be similar to the existing capital structure.

It would be important that Sunoco have the credit-rating agencies on its side because a lower rating would affect (raise) the cost of debt capital and perhaps the equity capital as well. A drop to BB+ from BBB certainly would cause a market impact. S&P defines BB+ as an entity that faces "major ongoing uncertainties or exposure to adverse business, financial, or economic conditions which could lead to inadequate capacity to meet timely interest and principal payments." This contrasts with BBB, which S&P defines as an entity "having adequate capacity to pay interest and repay principal."

Often the ultimate decision is not based on the least expensive route but rather on which form of capital is more easily obtainable. For example, if refining-sector securities were experiencing strong institutional demand, as was the case at the time the study was prepared, Sunoco's investment bankers might suggest a greater percentage of the capital be raised via equity, even though it has a higher cost. If the equity route is not as available, then debt might be the only means open until the new debt can be replaced with equity. If the project is under way but not expected to produce free cash flow for the foreseeable future, the equity analyst must decide if such a company has investable long-term value, given that such a scenario would raise its cost of equity above the 8.96 percent reflected under the credit method.

Project Free Cash Flow and Stock Valuation

In a project this size, the manager spearheading ("owning") the project would estimate a wide range of free-cash-flow outcomes for a five- to ten-year period with the subsequent assumption that afterward the firm's free cash flow will grow at a rate equal to either the historical growth rate in gross national product (GNP) or the long-term expected growth rate for the industry. Undoubtedly, such estimates will prove a daunting task because it is normally difficult for refiners to forecast its free cash flows accurately. The analysis and financial projections will serve as a guideline because the decision will rest on comfort levels, investor's interest in the securities to be offered, and the belief that the capacity is needed.

Table 7-11 shows the net present value of Sunoco shares resulting from the Chapter 8 cost-of-equity-capital credit model. I show it for Sunoco both exclusive and inclusive of net debt. If Sunoco had net cash, I would add the value per share to the current present value, net of required working capital. For simplicity, I show fair value prior to consideration of working capital needs, which would be a function of the time of year the project began, because Sunoco generates greater cash flows during the summer as demand for gasoline is greater, margins are typically higher, and there may be less maintenance work on the refineries located in the Northeast as they prepare for winter distillates.

Assuming that Sunoco realizes 5 percent growth in its free cash flow, total firm free cash flow would increase to $754 million (from the $591 million four-year average in 2004) by 2009. Certainly, if one believed that 2004's 19.3 percent ROIC would continue, the decision would be an easy one given Sunoco's cost of capital. However, as pointed out, eight of the prior 17 years saw negative ROICs, a disturbing instability.

Given this scenario, it would seem that the project would meet with detractors because the $163 million in additional annual average free cash flow, given 5 percent growth over the 2004 four-year average, would be roughly equal to the company's cost of equity. The $95.01 net of debt value at the bottom of Table 7-11 represents the current fair value to equity holders given a projected 5 percent annual current growth (beginning 2005) and 90.9 million shares outstanding. As the table shows, fair value currently would be, given the dilution, roughly where the stock is currently trading, $100 per share.[7] If upcoming growth of the total firm's free cash flow were expected to be lower than 5 percent per year, the project would not cover its cost of capital, and Sunoco's current stock price would be expected to decline. Those in favor of the project would argue that a project of this size could be expected to result in excess of 5 percent annual growth over existing free cash flow given projected industry demand growth of about 2 to 3 percent per year and the absence of other major refineries being contemplated.

Given Sunoco's WACC of 7.96 percent, one would doubt the needed 5 percent or more growth from the current level of free cash flow to have the level of certainty

[7] The price when the study was conducted. For projects having more certain free cash flow, the payback period is often used. The payback period is defined as the time required after revenues are first received to achieve break-even cumulative cash flow. Because of normal regulatory delays and volatility in price realization, a payback period was not utilized in this example.

to go forward.[8] While the approximate $11 million in after-tax interest expense, given the $ 270 million in debt that would need to be raised, would not appear to be much of a hurdle for Sunoco, the larger question is the severe share dilution. Those expected free cash flows could, if realized, pay off the bonds rather quickly, which is fine for creditors, especially given the conservative financing. For stockholders, the risk is obvious—that of the free cash flow not materializing. Is the project worth the possibility of a dramatic fall in the stock price, as implied by the table?

A more stable cash flow entity would tend to be more favorably inclined to proceed with a large project having a small gap between cost of capital and ROIC. In general, it is doubtful a company in the refining industry would approve any project with a ROIC of less than 15 percent. This is a multiyear project where cost overruns are not uncommon, and cash inflows uncertain. And as Table 7-11 shows, if the price of refined product were to fall, resulting in a 10 percent decline in free cash flow, Sunoco's stock price could be expected to fall by almost two-thirds. For this reason, many companies, unless they can raise funds inexpensively, prefer to sit on their capital rather than invest in projects offering returns slightly above their cost. The margin for error should not be taken lightly.

TABLE 7-11

Sunoco: Fair Value of Equity Security Based on Various Growth Rates in Free Cash Flow

Assumptions: $591.3 million average four-year free cash flow (years 2000–2004)

Thereafter, 3 percent

Cost of capital of 8.96 percent

Net debt of $13.14 per share derived from $1,649 in fixed debt minus $405 in cash

Assumptions					
Average free cash flow	$591.30				
Growth rate in free cash flow	−10%	−5%	0%	3%	5%
Cost of capital	8.96%	8.96%	8.96%	8.96%	8.96%
Growth after five years	−5%	−3%	0%	2%	3%
Value per share	$36.48	$48.28	$65.90	$88.15	$108.15

Fair value with 5% growth = $108.15

Fair Value net of debt = $ 95.01

[8] During March 2009, after years in the planning stage, Kuwait decided to scrap a new $15 billion refinery project, calling it "not feasible." Their decision was due to the global fall in the prices of refined products.

Follow-Up to the Sunoco Study

Four years after this example was prepared, Sunoco's stock was selling at $55 per share, not adjusting for its poststudy two-to-one stock split. What went wrong with the credit model? Nothing, so far as the cost of equity is concerned—Sunoco's cost of capital under the credit model budged up just slightly to 9.4 percent. Its free cash flow suffered a precipitous drop owing to a large fall in demand and margins associated with the severe recession. The fall in the price of its stock was seen in the study as a real risk if free-cash-flow growth did not materialize. Sunoco had negative free cash flow during 2008 and 2009, not unusual given its historical instability. In the original analysis, the conclusion was that a project of this size was not recommended given that historic volatility in the company's free cash flow made the expected ROIC too uncertain owing to the potential risk to the stock.

Sunoco and other companies in its sector saw their stock prices drop by very sizable percentages during the ensuing five years. A look at the present-value table reveals that given the cost of capital picked up by the credit model, if one had fairly estimated Sunoco's free cash flow, the current $55 split-adjusted price is indeed approximated by the model, had those shares been issued. Of greater interest is how the credit model picked up the volatility in Sunoco's credit metrics, including cash flows, resulting in its stable discount rate over the ensuing years. If the poststudy volatility had been a surprise, the model's cost of capital would have increased more than it did. This contrasts with its four-year post analysis (2009) beta, as reported by Bloomberg, of just 0.58, indicating that risk had been reduced over the years. Clearly, this has not been the case, leading one to believe that the closeness of the initial CAPM cost of equity capital with that estimated by the credit model was coincidental. One could not conclude, given the weakness in and volatility of Sunoco's free cash flows, that its cost of equity capital declined during the ensuing four years; thus devotees of the CAPM would have been using a poor approximation of risk.

This leads us to the credit model itself.

CHAPTER 8

Cost-of-Equity-Capital Credit Model

During the course of my career, I have been fortunate to have had exposure to all facets of securities analysis, including the evaluation of business combinations and the writing of fairness opinion letters. I held various positions ranging from lending officer, security analyst, credit analyst, pension analyst, portfolio manager, and research director, followed by the founding of what became a successful investment advisory firm grounded in the analysis of free cash flow.

I believe that the most glaring weakness in investment and security analysis relates to the assessment of risk—the determination of a proper cost of equity capital. *The analysis of risk represents the single most important underexplored factor in security research and the primary reason for investor disappointment in their investment returns.*

The cost of equity capital, while known as a measure of investors' attitudes toward risk, more aptly should represent the uncertainty to the cash flows investors can expect to receive from their investment in the security being considered. Only through an accurate and reliable cost of equity capital can fair value be established, as well as the determination of whether management is creating value for shareholders, as measured by the return on invested capital (ROIC) in comparison with its cost.

Because security analysts are not confronted with the daily barrage of problems and hazards that managers and executives working directly for the entity face, and rarely are many such problems or hazards mentioned during investor presentations, a wide swath of "hidden" risks tends to be ignored or not calibrated properly. Investors need to think and behave like corporate insiders to truly appreciate this multitude of exposures so as to accurately place a cost of capital that takes into account these uncertainties, of which any one could damper cash flows or even threaten the entity's survival. On the other hand, if investors were to overweigh such risks, the entity's valuation multiple would depress, leading eventually to outsized investment performance for investors who weighed them properly.

The *analytical edge* will go to the continual student of the free cash flow and credit metrics listed in this chapter because they have greater depth of understanding and better establishment of the financial markets' placement of value in relation to the asset's real value. They understand the numerator and that it represents just half the present-value equation.

An *important investor edge* of the credit model is that it leads to lower portfolio turnover. This is so because credit risk normally shifts more slowly than does beta. Credit does not shift wildly, as do stock prices, in response to transient events, and thus the cost of equity often remains within a narrow band for long periods, especially for companies with established brands that offer predictable operating cash flows. It is no wonder that successful investors hold assets over very long periods of time. They inherently estimate a cost of equity and feel comfortable throughout normal stock market and economic conditions, including periods of great stock volatility.

Shown in Table 8-1, for Burlington Northern Railway, which agreed to be acquired by Berkshire Hathaway, is the company's beta and cost of equity capital, as established by its credit. As depicted, despite a 70 percent rise in its beta, its cost of equity capital has remained in a very narrow range, indicative of a credit quality whose financial metrics have indeed remained strong despite wide stock price movement. It is no wonder that Warren Buffett was attracted to the company because historically he has achieved success with such high credits, including Coca-Cola and McDonalds.

Since cost of capital represents the risk to the cash flows, U.S. government securities theoretically would have the lowest cost of capital. Entities that have greater risk to their cash flows than the U.S. government's 10-year note should have progressively greater cost of equity capital.[1] Bankrupt firms, because their

TABLE 8-1

Cost of Capital Based on Credit and Beta for Burlington Northern Santa Fe

	December Year End				
	2004	2005	2006	2007	2008
Cost of capital (historical)	9.59	9.64	9.79	9.70	9.47
Beta	0.60	0.65	0.83	1.19	1.00

[1] At the time of this writing, sovereign debt, including that of the United States, was being considered for a possible downgrade by the major credit-rating agencies. If the U.S. 10-year note offered a higher yield than an active AAA corporate credit, the analyst would decide which instrument offered the more assured cash flows.

cash flows are the most uncertain, should have the highest cost of capital, both equity and debt. This line of thinking contrasts with the popular methodology used by almost every firm reporting cost of capital in their security filings with the Securities and Exchange Commission (SEC). I have shown many examples of how companies under the microscope of the capital asset pricing model (CAPM) can be near bankruptcy yet have a cost of capital consistent with an investment-grade rating. I have shown how use of the implied-cost-of-equity model does not produce an accurate outcome because it too falls victim to stock price volatility.

Investors typically are consumed with the top (revenue) line, with insufficient time spent on the risk parameters—until they are forced to do so. A hurricane or lawsuit will force a refocusing on insurance or litigation risk or a poor quarter on a loan covenant. Although these and other type risks are constantly present, it normally takes a precipitating event for the investment community to place them in proper perspective. For example, while an analyst may not be able to predict a hurricane, recession, or commodity price spike in a given year, an examination of the stability of operating cash flows over an economic cycle or two (or more) often will show that these events are both real and that they do repeat. Just like Sunoco and the refining group were operating under ideal conditions during 2000–2007, by the end of the decade, history repeated. Firms that are prepared for a wider array of risk deserve, all else equal, a lower cost of capital.

In the cost-of-capital model, about half the weighting is on cash flows. If the operating cash flows are strong and consistent, reflecting superior products and management, an entity can normally work out of trouble caused by overleverage. And it can take appropriate actions to enhance its free cash flow, such as reducing costs, using assets better, or planning taxes more appropriately. Financial intermediaries will work with firms having prospective strong cash flow from operations. The same cannot be said for entities with weak operating cash flows or sales instability. If the entity cannot compete effectively or its profit margins are inherently unsatisfactory, this will show in the cash flow and sales metrics included in the model, and the entity will have difficulty if it enters a period of distress.

Throughout this book, there have been perhaps too many allusions to the limitations of the CAPM. However, as seen with IBM, the company itself, using the CAPM, could not reasonably appraise its cost of capital within an acceptable band. Defenders of the model believe that it encompasses all available information, including cash flow, credit, and other miscellaneous items. According to its devotees, the uncertainty of a firm's free cash flow is inherent in its stock's oscillations.

You will find that several of the variables of the credit model are residuals or closely related to other variables; however, after long research and application, including economic expansions and recessions, one will find that each is a necessary component for inclusion and analysis. Several of the cash-flow and debt metrics might appear overly restrictive, and they are. But the intent is to rate all entities, even firms possessing the highest credit or holding too much cash. Intuitively, one would think that since free cash flow and operating cash flow are included in several forms, why would the model include a cost-of-sales variable? Wouldn't the stability of free and operating cash flows be a function of cost-of-sales variability? The answer, I have found, unsurprisingly, is sometimes yes and sometimes no. There have been many instances when free cash flows were stable and growing, yet the cost of sales was showing signs of instability, which later manifested to unstable free cash flow.

The same logic applies to cash tax rates, balance-sheet management, and many other variables that I now will explore. Many metrics are indeed related to others, but at times, I have found, those strong correlations become weakened.

If one were to design software using the elements in the model, some variables, by their nature (e.g., debt that needed to be satisfied or loan covenants) would be accorded greater weight. Those with difficult hurdles would be weighted progressively lower. One would expect cash flows, stability of the tax rate, leverage, or the auditor's opinion to have greater weight in the model than insurance adequacy, productivity, country of origin, or the ability to repay all debt within a short time period from operating cash flow and cash and equivalents. This does not mean that the more difficult hurdles are unimportant and could not pose a threat to the firm's survival. It is just that they are less apt to do so.

Readers may wish to devise a scoring system or perhaps merely evaluate the metrics in light of how they believe investors in general are assessing the entity's risk. At CT Capital, we employ a scoring system to evaluate the metrics, which, as will be seen in Chapter 9, has been shown to outperform the general market with considerably less risk. About two-thirds of the cost-of-capital metrics could be programmed and modeled because they rely on historical numbers; about a third, depending on the number in the "other" category, are subjective or rely on a recent event that has not yet been captured by a filing with the SEC. Also, the leading data services, including Standard and Poor's Compustat service, do not collect all necessary data the model calls for. An example is the health care cost trend rate.

One simply may choose to evaluate the worksheet metrics by comparing an entity with its peers or its trend relative to its historic pattern. Since many of the variables are subjective, opinions might differ, but they are not subjective to the extent the conclusions would differ drastically.

Each entity under review will be its own island—have its own unique set of risk attributes that might require a particular metric to be weighted more heavily.

This is understandable and makes common sense. For this reason, I use the phrase *a penalty is assessed* throughout this chapter, not the range of the penalty. Most penalties, however, are in the range of 0.1 to 0.5 add-ons to the cost of equity.

Consistency in scoring must be applied and, if so, will yield a true representation of the equity security's underlying risk. *Important metrics, such as superior credit strength and consistency of free cash flow, could result in points deducted under my scoring system*, resulting in a low cost of equity. Although I am not revealing my scoring system (in full recognition that academicians would not approve) for competitive reasons, I do allude to it in the explanation of several variables. Analysts will find that by focusing on the cost-of-capital metrics, differences between current investor sentiment and their own opinions will become more frequent, both positive and negative. The model might force them to alter their current thinking.

I am gauging risk to the cash flows, just as a debt holder would evaluate the risk of payment of interest and repayment of principal. If the entity is overcapitalized yet has poor or inconsistent free cash flow, its cost of capital could, by my measure, be greater than the average entity. Such an enterprise would benefit from its short-term ability to weather economic events, but unless cash flows improved, it would risk losing that flexibility.

One might ask why management, given its influence over the firm's cash flow and credit, is not listed in the model as a separate line entry. The sway of managerial decisions is already weighted and manifested through the cash-flow and credit metrics. For many, management quality is subjective; to my model, management's weight is felt throughout. If, however, there is a (prospective) change in management, as we saw with Hewlett-Packard and NCR, it would be reflected in the miscellaneous section in the other category.

With this, let me proceed by describing the cash-flow, debt, tax, and miscellaneous metrics. You will see many of the definitions are repeated throughout the chapter in relation to other variables. This is done so that readers can refer to that metric without having to go elsewhere.

Also shown is an illustration of the model using Apple Computer as an example. I respectfully ask you to be sensitive to the fact that the example is based on a report dated June 2009 and that conditions almost certainly will have changed for Apple, a consumer-based technology company, by the time you read this.

I begin by showing the cover page and its basic information. The number of flags indicates the variables (indicated with X marks) for which the company under review had its cost of capital raised above the risk-free rate, the 10-year Treasury note. The report does not specify the variables contributing to the lowering of the cost of capital. Indeed, Apple, owing to its superior financial strength, had points deducted for several debt metrics.

COST-OF-CAPITAL WORKSHEET

Cover Page

A SPECIAL REPORT BY CT CAPITAL, LLC

Apple, Inc.			
This report is based on data as of	6/29/2009		
The company is in the primary industry of	Computer hardware	Electronic computer manufacturing	
Primary SIC code	3571	11	
			Rank in the Industry
Market value ($ millions)	$126,653		1
Total debt	$0		11
Operating cash flow	$9,596		1
Power operating cash flow	$6,409		1
Free cash flow (four-year average)	$4,418		1
			Industry Median
Debt/equity	0.0%		0.0%
Debt multiple (total debt/four-year average free cash flow)	0.0		0.0
Free-cash-flow multiple (market value/four-year average free cash flow)	28.7		(1.3)
Number of cash-flow flags	4		13
Number of debt flags	3		7
Number of other flags	6		7
Cash-flow ranking	A	Adjusted cost of capital	8.5%
Debt and miscellaneous ranking	A	Adjusted ROIC	36.6%
Combined ranking	A		

A SPECIAL REPORT BY CT CAPITAL, LLC

Apple, Inc.	**Flags**
Cash Flows:	
Operating cash flow-annual	
Operating cash flow-LTM	
Operating cash flows over 10 years	
Growing operating cash flows – recent 5 years	
Operating cash flow in the most recent quarter	
Power operating cash flow	

Power operating cash flows over 10 years	X
Growing power operating cash flows – recent 5 years	
Power operating cash flow in the most recent quarter	
Free cash flow	
Free cash flow-LTM	
4-year average free cash flow	
Free cash flow multiple (P/4-year average FCF)	
Free cash flows over 10 years	
Growing free cash flows – recent 5 years	
Free cash flow – most recent quarter	
Stability of revenues (sales)	X
Stability of free cash flow	X
Stability of OCF	X
Accounts receivable flag	X
Accounts receivable flag – based on the most recent quarter	
Inventory flag	
Inventory flag – based on the most recent quarter	
Accounts payable flag	X
Accounts payable flag – based on the most recent quarter	
Discretionary capital expenditures	X
Discretionary R&D	
Discretionary cost of goods sold	
Discretionary selling, general & administrative	
Discretionary advertising	
Cash burn rate – last fiscal year	
Cash burn rate – LTM & recent quarter	
Debt:	
Growth in total debt – recent 10 years	
Growth in total debt – recent 5 years	
Growth in total debt – most recent quarter	
Debt/(4-year average FCF) multiple	
Debt/(4-year average OCF) multiple	
Ability to repay total debt from 4-year average of (OCF-2/3 capital expenditures)	
Ability to cover current debt by free cash flow	
Ability to cover current and next year's debt from all sources, incl asset sales	
Ability to cover current debt from all sources, except asset sales	
Ability to cover current and next year's debt from normalized FCF	
Ability to cover current and next year's debt from FCF in the last 12 months	
Ability to cover current debt from net working capital	
Ability to cover current and next year's debt from net working capital	
Ability to cover current debt from 4-year average OCF	
Ability to cover current and next year's debt from twice 4-year average OCF	
Ability to cover current and next yr debt from twice 4 yr avg OCF+ net working cap.	
Ability to cover current debt from 4-year average OCF + net working capital	
Ability to cover current and next year's debt from 4-year average OCF+ net working capital	

Deterioration in net working capital to total debt	X
Deterioration in net working capital to total debt current quarter	X
Interest and lease coverage from working capital and FCF	
Interest and lease coverage from working capital and FCF current quarter	
Debt covenants	
Operating leases/total debt	X
Pension underfunding/total debt	
S&P commercial paper rating	
S&P senior debt rating	
Increase in benefit (health care) expense	
Health care cost trend rate	
Increase in postretirement benefit (healthcare) liability	
Credit spread	
Tax:	
Tax expense / pretax income	
Tax payment / pretax income	X
Stability of tax rate	X
Tax expense / pretax income. Most recent quarter	
Miscellaneous:	
Country code (non US>0), flagged if non-U.S.	
Qualified audit opinion	
Inflation	
Auditor change	
Growth in F.G Inventory > Growth in sales	X
Growth in total Inventory > Growth in sales	
Extraordinary items	
Pension gain	
Interest income	X
Significant acquisitions	
Decrease in order backlog	
Reinvestment indicator	
Reinvestment indicator – most recent quarter	
Ability to pay dividends from operating cash flow	
Pension fund-assumed return on assets increased from the prior year	
Pension fund-assumed rate of salary Increases decreased from the prior year	
Increase in the spread between the assumed return on pension assets and salary increases	
Reliance on major customer/supplier	
Litigation/legal	
Stability of COGS	
Insurance	
Other	
Productivity:	
Sales / employee growth – recent 5 years	X
Sales / net PPE growth – recent 5 years	X

Cover Page

This report is based on data as of:

This is the date on which the stock price is available. It is important for determining the current market value of equity. The company is in the primary industry as defined based on its primary SIC code. This information is taken from the description of the company by S&P's Compustat database. It is based on the segment with the largest proportion of revenues.

Primary SIC Code

The SIC code is a four-digit code assigned to an industry by the government. The code relates to the largest segment of the company in terms of revenues. The company may sell products that belong to more than one SIC industry.

Rank in the Industry

This is the company's rank among all companies in the same four-digit SIC industry. A rank of 1 indicates that the company has the largest amount (e.g., market value) of equity. Rank of 2 indicates the second largest, and so on.

Companies in the Industry

The number of companies in the same primary four-digit SIC industry.

Market Value ($ Million)

This is the market value of equity. It is based on the price per share times the number of outstanding shares as of the most recently available report. The data are reported in millions of U.S. dollars.

Total Debt

Total debt is the sum of current and long-term debt available from the most recently available annual 10K form of the company. It includes pension and postretirement liabilities, operating lease obligations, and all other obligations, outside of normal trade debts, for which probability is assured, as defined in the subsection to follow. It is stated in millions of U.S. dollars.[2]

---

[2] The dollar amounts in the report are all measured in millions of U.S. dollars unless stated otherwise. The actual data are not shown because the report on Apple is meant as a template and would be stale at the time of your reading.

Operating Cash Flow

The operating cash flow is taken from the most recently available annual and interim statement of cash flows and may include an adjustment. It is stated in millions of U.S. dollars.

Power Operating Cash Flow

Power operating cash flow (OCF) is my proprietary definition of "normalized" cash flow if the company would have maintained accounts receivable, inventories, and accounts payable at levels (in proportion to sales) that the company experienced in the previous five years. The power OCF also may normalize any other unusual working-capital items, such as taxes. It attempts to remove from reported operating cash flows unusual increases or decreases.

Free Cash Flow (Four-Year Average)

Free cash flow (FCF) is my proprietary definition of the cash flow that the company can distribute back to shareholders without affecting its current growth. It is based on normalized operating cash flow minus capital expenditures plus any proceeds from the sale of property, plant, and equipment (PPE). It also adds back discretionary capital expenditures and discretionary expenditures on research and development (R&D), cost of goods sold (COGS), selling, general, and administrative expenses (SG&A), and advertising. The free cash flow on the cover page is averaged over the most recent four years.

Industry Median

The industry median is the value for the company in the same four-digit SIC industry that represents the 50th percentile. The median typically is a better statistic (than the average) when ratios are reported because it is less affected by a few extreme observations.

Debt/Equity

The debt/equity ratio is the book value of total debt (short- and long-term debt, as defined in the subsequent debt metric section) divided by the shareholders' equity. It is a measure of financial leverage. The higher this ratio, the more financial risk a company assumes. It is advisable to examine the ratio in comparison with the industry median to determine if the company assumed a higher degree of financial risk than its industry peers. Also examined is the debt/equity ratio using market values when that is appropriate. For Clorox, market value would have been used owing to the aberrant effect of the large-stock buyback on shareholders' equity and the firm's ability to service its fixed obligations satisfactorily.

Debt Multiple (Total Debt/Four-Year Average FCF)

The debt multiple indicates how many years of free cash flow are needed to pay off the entire debt of the company. It is based on total debt divided by the four-year average free cash flow, unless the business composition has changed. If such is the case, I will use a more appropriate period. The higher this ratio, the longer it will take for the company to pay down debt, and the more financial risk the company assumes. For companies in certain stages of development, free cash flow typically is negative.

FCF Multiple (Market Value/Four-Year Average FCF)

The free-cash-flow multiple is the ratio of the market value of equity divided by the four-year average free cash flow, unless the business composition has changed. If such is the case, I will use a more appropriate period. Typically, companies in the S&P 500 Index trade at FCF multiples of 20 to 25. For companies in their growing stages or undergoing capital expansion programs, free cash flows are negative, and this ratio will show a negative number.

Number of Debt Flags

The number of flags raised (indicated by X) in the debt section of the report. The greater the number of flags, the greater is the credit risk of the firm and its commensurate cost of equity capital. See relevant sections for detailed explanations of the debt measures and how they affect cost of capital.

Number of Cash-Flow Flags

The number of flags raised (indicated by X) in the cash-flow section of our report. The larger the number of flags, the greater is the chance of operating problems associated with operating and free cash flow. See the next section for detailed explanations of the cash-flow measures and their effect on cost of capital.

Number of Other Flags

The number of flags raised (indicated by) in the report but not in the debt and cash-flow sections. The larger the number of flags, the greater is the general operating risk of the firm. See relevant sections for detailed explanations of these metrics and how they affect the cost of capital.

Cost of Capital

The cost of capital is derived using the proprietary system of CT Capital LLC., employing all the determinants listed in the body of the report. Apple's cost of capital of 8.47 percent compares with a 10.2 percent cost of capital when using the CAPM, based on its beta of 1.45. Even if the reader is unable to match the credit model's cost of capital in the Apple example or disagrees with my analysis, it should be apparent that Apple's cost of capital is lower than that derived using the most popular methodology employed today when using a credit-based model.

WORKSHEET: EXPLANATIONS AND DEFINITIONS

Cash-Flow Metrics

I begin the cost-of-capital analysis with the cash-flow metrics, followed by debt metrics, tax metrics, and finally, miscellaneous metrics. *Extraordinary events, even though they are not mentioned explicitly in each metric, are always considered to ensure that the result is a true representation of the credit health of the entity and its ability to return cash, through free cash flows, to shareholders.*

The cash-flow metrics are designed to capture the health of the firm's operating and free cash flows, including magnitude, growth, and stability. Power operating cash flows are included to account for unusual balance-sheet changes and whether it produces a conflicting story with operating and free cash flows. Revenues are investigated because they provide information regarding market share, innovation, marketing, and management. It provides the raw material for the starting point of the cash-collection process, which is cash collections on accounts receivables.

Discretionary expenditure areas are also considered in this section because they represent potential sources of cash.

Operating Cash Flow—Annual

The operating cash flow (OCF) of the company is from the most recent 10K. Cost of capital is penalized if operating cash flow is negative. For some items, such as postretirement benefits and other retirement obligations, I include the net cost for the period rather than actual cash outflows in order to separate what I view as financing of these obligations from the operating cost component.

Adjustments to the operating cash flows may be made to the extent that current reporting obscures the ability of the analyst to place a correct economic valuation on the enterprise. For example, the sale of accounts receivable would be picked up under operating cash flows if reported as a financing activity. Capitalizing interest would, be reclassified from investing to operating cash flow, as might interest, dividends and taxes that have been reported as investing or financing activities. The signing of capital leases may artificially enhance operating cash flows. This is because that while the interest portion of capital leases are counted as an operating activity, the reduction in the lease, through those principal payments, are reported as a financing activity. We typically make adjustments to reported operating cash flow to remove items we consider nonrecurring and include those we consider recurring, so the historical financial ratios will be more indicative of future performance. These adjustments cover items including discontinued operations; effects of natural disasters; gains or losses on asset sales and sale/leasebacks; and one-time charges for asset write-downs, restructurings, and plant shutdowns. Other adjustments could be made to allow for better comparability among peer companies and to derive actual cash from operating activities that may be included as financing or investment activities. The nature of any adjustment is to more accurately reflect the ability of the enterprise to satisfy its obligations and enhance forecasting. When making adjustments, they must be applied consistently, or comparability will be lost.

Typically, companies need to generate cash from their operations in order to survive. However, businesses may from time to time show negative operating cash flows in trough years, and these should be offset by larger positive operating cash flows in good years. Similarly, a company occasionally may have, owing to adverse business conditions or changes in balance-sheet items, a year in which cash from operations is negative. However, an enterprise cannot sustain negative operating cash flows for long periods without obtaining additional financing, liquidating assets, or falling into bankruptcy.

Operating Cash Flow—LTM

The operating cash flow of the company is retrieved from the four most recent 10Q forms, representing an annualized operating cash flow for the latest 12 months (LTM). For some items, such as postretirement benefits and other retirement obligations, I include the (net) cost for the period rather than actual cash outflows in order to separate what I view as financing of these obligations from the operating cost component. Other adjustments, as stated earlier, are incorporated.

The recent operating-cash-flow figure may indicate negative (or positive) trends in the business. The 12-month rolling OCF offsets any seasonal patterns in the company's operations. If OCF is negative, the entity is penalized. Typically, companies need to generate cash from their operations in order to survive. However, businesses may from time to time show negative operating cash flows in trough years, and these are offset by larger positive operating cash flows in good years. Similarly, a company occasionally may have, owing to adverse business conditions or changes in balance-sheet items, a year in which cash from operations is negative. However, an enterprise cannot sustain negative operating cash flows for long periods without obtaining additional financing, liquidating assets, or eventually falling into bankruptcy.

Operating Cash Flows—10 Years

I examine the annual operating cash flows, as defined earlier, beginning from the 10Ks over the most recent 10 years. If there are at least three years among the most recent 10 years in which operating cash flows are negative, I flag the company and penalize cost of capital.

The greater the number of years in which operating cash flows are negative, the greater is the penalty. Typically, companies need to generate cash from their operations in order to survive. However, businesses may from time to time show negative operating cash flows in trough years, and these are offset by larger positive operating cash flows in good years. Similarly, a company occasionally may have a year in which cash flow from operations is negative owing to balance-sheet items or unusual events. However, an enterprise cannot sustain negative operating cash flows for long periods without obtaining additional financing, liquidating assets, or eventually falling into bankruptcy. The entry represents the number of years in the most recent 10 years in which the operating cash flow is negative. This is a measure of frequency, which has shown to be quite useful in setting cost of capital. Investors demand higher returns for investments in firms that produce operating cash flows with less frequency.

Operating Cash Flows—Recent 5 Years

The operating cash flows of a low-cost-of-capital company should increase over time. If they decline or are negative consistently, the company may be liquidating slowly. If they stay constant, the company may be losing market share or undergoing pricing flexibility and will see its valuation multiple decline, resulting in higher financing cost. Since years one through five are also included in the prior metric (if operating cash flow is negative), this variable carries greater weight. This metric also will result in a penalty if there was an absolute decline, which is not true of the 10-year variable, which requires a negative period of cash flow from operations for a penalty to be assessed.

This item results in a penalty if annual operating cash flows declined (over the prior year) in two or more years over the most recent five years. The item also results in a penalty if operating cash flows have not grown by the general price rise for the industry or were negative. This entry represents the number of years in which those events occurred and is weighted more heavily than the prior metric because it may signal a change in product acceptance.

If the firm's business is contracting, managers will attempt to extract cash through "working" the balance sheet, in which case we will see weaker power operating cash flow and net income than GAAP reported cash flow from operating activities. In these instances, power operating cash flow metrics would be accorded greater weight than operating cash flow metrics.

Positive Operating Cash Flow in the Most Recent Quarter

The quarterly operating cash flow is retrieved from the most recently available 10Q. Adjustments, as stated, may be made, including those based on changes in working capital items when the firm reports operating cash flow as a single line entry.

This metric results in a penalty if negative to highlight potential problems and negative trends within the company. However, in seasonal businesses, a company actually may incur negative operating cash flows in quarters where collections are low. For entities that rely on a seasonal period for the majority of cash flows, weakness could signal a change in longer-term client demand, along with weakened cash flows. Thus an understanding of the individual entity is very much required with this metric.

Positive Power Operating Cash Flow—Annual

Power operating cash flow is my proprietary definition of "normalized" cash flow if the company would have maintained accounts receivable, inventories, and accounts payable at average levels (in proportion to sales) that the company experienced in the previous five years. It attempts to remove from reported operating cash flows unusual increases or decreases.

Any other unusual balance-sheet items biasing normalized operating cash flows also may be included in power operating cash flows, such as taxes. This item results in a penalty if power operating cash flow is negative in the most recent year.

Normalizing power operating cash flows allows for the ability to make varying assumptions and comparisons with peer companies. If the firm's business is contracting, the firm's managers will attempt to extract cash through "working" the balance sheet, in which case we will see weaker power operating cash flow and net income than GAAP reported cash flow from operating activities. In these instances, power operating cash flow metrics would be granted greater weight than operating cash flow metrics. However, businesses may from time to time show negative power operating cash flows in trough years, and these should be offset by larger positive operating cash flows in good years. Similarly, a company occasionally may have a year in which power operating cash flow is negative owing to other balance-sheet items or unusual events. Typically, companies need to generate cash from their operations in order to compete and survive. However, a company cannot sustain negative power operating cash flows for long periods without obtaining additional financing, liquidating assets, or eventually falling into bankruptcy.

Positive Power Operating Cash Flows Over 10 Years

I examine the annual power operating cash flows from the 10Ks over the most recent 10 years and make, if required, necessary adjustments. Next, I normalize the important working capital items, as stated. If there are at least three years among the most recent 10 years in which the power operating cash flows are negative, I flag the company and penalize its cost of capital. Additional negative years result in a greater penalty.

The entry represents the number of years in the most recent 10 years in which the power operating cash flow is negative. It is a frequency measure.

In the example, Apple was penalized because it had four of the past 10 years of negative power operating cash flow; however, the preponderance of the negative power operating cash flow took place over five years ago, prior to introduction of new and very successful product lines that grew revenues considerably. This illustrates the importance of considering the cyclicality of the industry, even when the company is meeting with the success of an Apple Computer.

Growing Power Operating Cash Flows—Recent 5 Years

This item penalizes cost of capital if annual power operating cash flows declined in two or more years over the most recent five years or power operating cash flows have not grown at the same or greater rate than the general price rise of the industry. The entry represents the number of years in which annual power operating cash flow either declined, grew less than its industry from the prior year, or was negative over the most recent five-year period. The five-year metric is more heavily weighted than the prior metric because years one through five are also included in the prior metric if power operating cash flows are negative. This metric also will result in a penalty if there was an absolute positive decline, which is not true of the 10-year variable.

Apple had one year of negative power operating cash flow during the past five years and was penalized.

Positive Power Operating Cash Flow in the Most Recent Quarter

I measure this item by using quarterly levels of accounts receivable, inventories, and accounts payable relative to the quarterly sales compared with the average quarterly ratio of the same quarter in the most recent five years. Other important working-capital items also may be included. This item is penalized if negative to highlight potential problems and negative recent trends within the company. However, in seasonal businesses, a company may incur negative power operating cash flows in quarters where collections are weak. Thus caution should be used when interpreting this metric. If the most recent quarter is normally seasonally strong, this metric will carry greater weight.

If the firm's business is contracting, the firm's managers will attempt to extract cash through "working" the balance sheet, in which case we will see weaker power operating cash flow and net income than GAAP reported cash flow from operating activities. In these instances, power operating cash flow metrics would be granted greater weight than operating cash flow metrics.

Free Cash Flow—Annual

Free cash flow (historic) is my proprietary definition of the cash flow that the company can distribute back to shareholders (Chapter 4) without affecting its current growth. It is based on adjusted operating cash flow (as stated earlier) minus capital expenditures plus any proceeds from sale of PPE. It also adds back discretionary capital expenditures and discretionary expenditures on R&D, COGS, SG&A, and advertising.

When projecting free cash flow, I typically make adjustments to a company's historic free cash flow to remove items that I consider nonrecurring and include those I consider recurring, so the historical financial ratios will be more indicative of future performance. These adjustments cover items including discontinued operations, effects of natural disasters, gains or losses on asset sales and sale/leasebacks, one-time cash effects of asset write-downs, restructurings, and plant shutdowns.

I review each potential nonrecurring item and determine whether an adjustment is appropriate and will aid forecasting prospective free cash flow.

This item is flagged if free cash flow was negative during its past fiscal year or is expected to be so in the current fiscal year. Typically, mature companies generate more cash from their operations than they need to invest in capital and other expenditures and hence have positive free cash flow that can be used to pay down debt, to further investments in the business, or to be distributed back to shareholders. However, companies in certain stages may need to invest in building capacity in excess of their generation from current operations, resulting in negative free cash flow. While not necessarily a negative indicator for growing companies or otherwise well-financed companies, it should be noted that these companies cannot sustain negative free cash flow for long periods without obtaining additional financing or restructuring their business. If current projects are considered value-enhancing—ROIC in excess of their cost of capital—the markup will be less significant. For mature companies, free cash flow may be negative during large capital expenditure programs or as a result of a catch-up payment used to fund a pension liability. Unusual outflows are considered; if the normalized operating and free cash flows are otherwise historically strong, the cost of capital is slightly penalized with a single year of negative free cash flow.

Free Cash Flow—LTM

The free cash flow of the company for the most recent 12 months is based on adjusted operating cash flows retrieved from the four most recent 10Qs minus capital expenditures from the same reports. It also adds back discretionary capital expenditures and discretionary expenditures on R&D, COGS, SG&A, and advertising.

This figure may indicate recent negative (or positive) trends in free cash flow; however, the rolling 12 months offsets any seasonal patterns in the company's operations. It is penalized if negative, with a stronger penalty when not accompanied by strength in cash flows from operations. Companies cannot sustain negative free cash flow for long periods without obtaining additional financing.

The trailing 12-month free cash flow is compared with the prior 12-month period to detect changes in trend, product acceptance, markdowns, and so on.

Free-Cash-Flow Multiple (Price/Four-Year Average FCF)

The free-cash-flow multiple is the ratio of the market value of equity divided by the four-year average free cash flow. If the business composition has changed, a more appropriate period will be used. Entities having consistent and growing free cash flows with higher free-cash-flow multiples typically will have lower cost of equity capital and greater access to the capital markets. An exception would be entities that have minimal free cash flow.

Entities that trade at lower (or negative) free-cash-flow multiples owing to weakness in their operations almost always have a higher cost of capital. This would be especially true if they also exhibited instability in sales, cost of sales, and taxes.

Strong producers of free cash flow that trade at higher than market multiples traditionally will have lower costs of equity capital and can finance their operations more easily, including new investment projects.

Apple, selling at a high free-cash-flow multiple, would be able to raise equity at a lower cost of capital than the average industrial entity. It would be highly unusual for a company such as Apple to be selling equity, given its extreme cash balance.

Positive Free Cash Flow Over 10 Years

I examine the annual free cash flow over the most recent 10 years. If there are at least three years among the most recent 10 years in which the free cash flow was negative, I flag and penalize the company. The entry reports the number of years in which annual free cash flow was negative over the most recent 10 years. The greater the number of years above three, the greater the cost of equity is raised. This metric is weighted slightly less than the 10-year operating and power operating cash-flow metrics owing to the greater stability of those metrics but is nonetheless a key variable. A firm's free cash flow becomes an investor's income, so the more consistency in this variable, the more assured is the payback on the investment.

Growing Free Cash Flow—Recent 5 Years

This item results in a penalty if annual free cash flow declined (over the prior year) in two or more years over the most recent five years. The entry represents the number of years in which annual free cash flow declined or was negative over the most recent five-year period. A higher penalty is accessed progressively for each year above two. Because years one through five are also included in the prior variable, this metric carries additional weighting. This metric also will result in a penalty if there was an absolute decline relative to the prior year, which is not true of the 10-year variable.

Positive Free Cash Flow—Most Recent Quarter

The free cash flow of the company for the most recent quarter is based on operating cash flows, as adjusted, and is retrieved from the most recent 10Q, minus capital expenditures from the same report. It also includes an amount for corporate overspending to the extent that such occurred in certain discretionary areas, such as R&D, advertising, capital spending, and COGS. This figure may indicate recent negative (or positive) trends in free cash flow. It is penalized if negative, with a stronger penalty if it is unusual for the entity to incur negative free cash flow during this quarter.

If the entity sells products or services that are seasonal, a given quarter could impair or improve the cost of capital but should not be given to overreaction. If, however, free cash flow in a given quarter reflects a shift in operating performance, this metric will result in larger markup/down to cost of capital relative to its prior quarter.

Stability

Stability of annual, rolling 12-month, and yearly quarter-over-quarter results is measured for sales, cost of sales/sales, free cash flow, operating cash flows, and tax rate. The greater the variability outside normal levels, the greater the entity is penalized. Corporate results are, by their nature, uneven, and thus a wide band is used in determining the penalty assessed to cost of equity capital. Sales stability is weighted more heavily, followed by stability of taxes, operating cash flow, cost of sales/sales, and then free cash flow. Although free cash flow and leverage are the two central rudiments of the credit model, sales stability should be less volatile than free cash flow because entities normally could lower product prices to enhance sales, even if those sales did not result in free cash flow.

Instability could be a function of the entity's industry, product demand, competitive position, market share, growth rates, and financial structure. It could be a result of government support, geography of receipt of income and cash flows, customer satisfaction, management and sales staff, or barriers to entry. Regardless of reason, stability is a prime determinant of cost of capital and financial structure. Changes in stability metrics must be investigated as to cause, whether it is possible to forecast their duration, and their impact on free cash flow and capital structure.

Seasonal companies and enterprises that have more irregular cash flows throughout the year are also slightly penalized relative to entities that receive their free cash flow more evenly throughout the year because external events are more likely to affect the entity's financial metrics whose cash flows are more heavily concentrated into fewer periods.

For stability of cost of sales, free cash flow, and operating cash flow, I assign a penalty based on their reliability and predictive value. For instance, quarterly instability of operating cash flows for consumer goods companies would be penalized more heavily than instability of that measure for steel manufacturers.

Stability of financial performance is the central element of risk analysis; predictability and reliability lead to a more accurate assessment of cost of capital and fair value for all enterprises.

Stability of Revenue

Revenue growth and stability reflect the demand for and depth of a firm's products, services, and marketing, as well as the reliance on and importance of a particular product or service to the firm's total operations. For example, Jackson Hewitt Tax Service was very negatively affected when its bank partner cut off most of the money it used for tax refunds, which covered about 75 percent of the company's financial products program. Firms that have many products and services, such as 3M, exhibit more stable revenues and are less likely to experience disappointments.

This measure also reflects the impact and contribution of R&D, competition, and the labor force; weakness of any of these items finds its way to the "top line." Once the analyst is comfortable that the method of revenue recognition is sound and applied consistently, an analysis of revenue stability is called for. As expounded in Chapter 4, growth in sales and cost of sales are fundamental determinants of an appropriate level of discretionary expenditures. Revenue is considered to be operating in nature, and thus interest income is not included in the measurement of this item and ROIC measures.

Revenue stability can be affected by events unrelated to the primary business, such as a business interruption resulting from a strike or natural disaster or a dictum associated with a government, especially for entities operating under heavy regulation or subject to an unpredictable foreign authority. The firm's relations with its unions, including strike history, average settlement (including pension, insurance, vacation), and procedures for dismissal, must be reviewed.

Illustrated in the tables are sales revenue stability tables for two retailers, Kroger, the supermarket retailer, and Macy's, the clothing retailer. As one would expect, Kroger exhibits consistent increases in yearly sales. If stores had been sold or closed, I would adjust for continuing operations, if significant, although, normally, growing retailing companies only prune underperforming stores or divisions. If stores were closed because of underperformance, then presumably one would see improved prospective free cash flow.

Unlike Kroger, Macy's shows higher than normal sales volatility because sales have declined in half the periods shown, and in two of the years, 2005 and 2006, revenues received a large boost resulting from acquisitions. Once the acquisitions were absorbed, revenues began to decline again. This could have been a result of underperforming locations or disposals (Macy's did sell one of its chain stores) in order to improve free cash flow and raise cash (to delever), but again, keep in mind that the benefits from cash flow and leverage metrics will be captured elsewhere. Here I am concerned only with sales stability. The closing or sale of units is normally, but not always, an admission of error. Sometimes units must be sold as a condition of regulatory approval.

In my zero- to five-point rating system for this metric (zero is most stable), I add 0.1 to cost of capital for each point to three; for a four ranking, I add 0.4 to the cost of equity capital; for a five, I add one full point. For Kroger, no penalty is assessed based on this measure because the company has shown consistent growth each year, whereas I assign a three to Macy's because of its inconsistent sales pattern.

A quick word on the interpretation of standard deviation: The higher the growth rate, the higher is the standard deviation, including when the growth rate accelerates. Obviously, an increase in standard deviation will have negative consequence if sales are declining, but high acceleration also can result in a penalty because high growth often requires cash and tends to attract competition.

A company whose growth rate accelerates, resulting in a high upside standard deviation, would be more prone to downside risk and probably would be awarded a penalty for success, the extent depending on the uniqueness of the situation. A drug manufacturer that was recently awarded a 20-year patent for a blockbuster drug would see little penalty. That Apple received a penalty, with its revenues growing from $13.9 billion to $42.9 billion in four years, is a tacit recognition that whatever goes up often reverts, and if this were to occur, investors would swiftly mark up their required return. In Apple's case, the penalties to the three stability measures were moderate. Another risk to upside volatility is that the firm's cost structure normally increases along with the higher levels of success. Apple has been diligent on the cost side and, as such, is awarded the moderate penalty.

Instability of sales, without growth, will reflect a high standard deviation, and the standard deviation/average becomes more significant. An analysis of stability statistics requires careful and sometimes considerable understanding of their limitations. Other times, stability measures only tend to reconfirm the obvious.

The stability measure cannot always be quantified properly through a statistical computer program. It must be reconfirmed fundamentally through careful assessment of any underlying contributory factors. When evaluating the standard deviation/average (coefficient of variation) for IBM, one sees a very stable sales indicator. Since the coefficient of variation is a normalized measure of dispersion, it provides a useful measure when comparing the volatility of one series with that of another. For IBM, sales growth is below norm, which has suppressed this metric. Because of its lack of growth, a penalty would be assessed to IBM (3 rating). I also should state that the standard deviation/average is not to be confused with the Sharpe ratio, which is the return over the risk-free rate divided by the annualized standard deviation. While both measures quantify volatility, the Sharpe ratio is used more appropriately as a measure of investment returns.

For the credit model stability metrics (i.e., cost of sales, tax, or cash flows), I also would recommend a table, where appropriate, of quarterly data (relative to prior years similar quarters) to determine if there is a change in stability during those interim periods. Changes in these variables during interim periods can signal a shift in the underlying fundamental business of the entity under analysis. If such variability has increased, management should be questioned as to the reason, if not apparent.

TABLE 8-2

Macy's, Inc.: Sales Stability

Ticker:	m		Cutoff:	0%		
Company Name:	**MACY'S INC**		**Industry Avg:**	**9,639.0053**	**DEPARTMENT STORES**	
	Sale	**% Change**	**Downside Volatility Only**	**% Change**	**Upside Volatility Only**	**% Change**
Y08	24,892.0000	−5.40%	24,892.0000	−5.40%		
Y07	26,313.0000	−2.44%	26,313.0000	−2.44%		
Y06	26,970.0000	20.46%			26,970.0000	20.46%
Y05	22,390.0000	39.21%			22,390.0000	39.21%
Y04	16,084.0000	2.56%			16,084.0000	2.56%
Y03	15,682.0000	−0.67%	15,682.0000	−0.67%		
Y02	15,788.0000	−1.40%	15,788.0000	−1.40%		
Y01	16,012.0000	−14.63%	16,012.0000	−14.63%		
Y00	18,756.0000	3.16%			18,756.0000	3.16%
Y99	18,181.0000	12.38%			18,181.0000	12.38%
Standard Deviation	**4600.0741**	**0.1525**	**5378.9184**	**0.0573**	**4282.2459**	**0.1513**
AVERAGE	20,106.8000	0.0532	19,737.4000	(0.0491)	20,476.2000	0.1555
ST. DEV/AVE	0.228782009	2.865173309	0.272524161	−1.16675004	0.209132843	0.9728411

TABLE 8-3

Kroger: Sales Stability

Ticker:	kr		Cutoff:	0%		
Company Name:	**KROGER CO**		**Industry Avg:**	**16,136.6207**	**GROCERY STORES**	
	Sale	**% Change**	**Downside Volatility Only**	**% Change**	**Upside Volatility Only**	**% Change**
Y08	76,000.0000	8.21%			76,000.0000	8.21%
Y07	70,235.0000	6.24%			70,235.0000	6.24%
Y06	66,111.0000	9.18%			66,111.0000	9.18%
Y05	60,553.0000	7.30%			60,553.0000	7.30%
Y04	56,434.0000	4.91%			56,434.0000	4.91%
Y03	53,791.0000	3.92%			53,791.0000	3.92%
Y02	51,760.0000	3.32%			51,760.0000	3.32%
Y01	50,098.0000	2.24%			50,098.0000	2.24%
Y00	49,000.0000	8.04%			49,000.0000	8.04%
Y99	45,352.0000	60.80%			45,352.0000	60.80%
Standard Deviation	**10046.9793**	**0.1750**			**10046.9793**	**0.1750**
AVERAGE	57,933.4000	0.1142			57,933.4000	0.1142
ST. DEV/AVE	0.173422919	1.533267222			0.173422919	1.5332672

TABLE 8-4

IBM: Sales Stability

Ticker: ibm   Cutoff: 0%

Company Name: INTL BUSINESS MACHINES CORP   Industry Avg: 1,270.6599   CMP PROGRAMMING, DATA PROCESS

	Sale	% Change	Downside Volatility Only	% Change	Upside Volatility Only	% Change
Y08	103,630.0000	4.90%			103,630.0000	4.90%
Y07	98,786.0000	8.05%			98,786.0000	8.05%
Y06	91,424.0000	0.32%			91,424.0000	0.32%
Y05	91,134.0000	−5.36%	91,134.0000	−5.36%		
Y04	96,293.0000	8.04%			96,293.0000	8.04%
Y03	89,131.0000	9.79%			89,131.0000	9.79%
Y02	81,186.0000	−5.45%	81,186.0000	−5.45%		
Y01	85,866.0000	−2.86%	85,866.0000	−2.86%		
Y00	88,396.0000	0.97%			88,396.0000	0.97%
Y99	87,548.0000	7.20%			87,548.0000	7.20%
Standard Deviation	**6600.1952**	**0.0580**	**4976.8954**	**0.0147**	**6098.6746**	**0.0369**
AVERAGE	91,339.4000	0.0256	86,062.0000	(0.0456)	93,601.1429	0.0561
ST. DEV/AVE	0.072260111	2.267699554	0.057829186	−0.32222393	0.065155985	0.6585063

TABLE 8-5

AMD: Sales Stability

Ticker:	amd		Cutoff:	0%		
Company Name: ADVANCED MICRO DEVICES			Industry Avg:	1,216.1533	SEMICONDUCTOR, RELATED DEVICE	
	Sale	**% Change**	**Downside Volatility Only**	**% Change**	**Upside Volatility Only**	**% Change**
Y08	5,808.0000	−3.41%	5,808.0000	−3.41%		
Y07	6,013.0000	6.44%			6,013.0000	6.44%
Y06	5,649.0000	−3.40%	5,649.0000	−3.40%		
Y05	5,847.5771	16.92%			5,847.5771	16.92%
Y04	5,001.4351	42.12%			5,001.4351	42.12%
Y03	3,519.1680	30.48%			3,519.1680	30.48%
Y02	2,697.0291	−30.70%	2,697.0291	−30.70%		
Y01	3,891.7539	−16.20%	3,891.7539	−16.20%		
Y00	4,644.1870	62.52%			4,644.1870	62.52%
Y99	2,857.6040	12.41%			2,857.6040	12.41%
Standard Deviation	**1273.7665**	**0.2779**	**1488.9827**	**0.1300**	**1257.5306**	**0.2110**
AVERAGE	4,592.8754	0.1172	4,511.4457	(0.1343)	4 ,647.1619	0.2848
ST. DEV/AVE	0.277335309	2.371053722	0.330045576	−0.96823511	0.270601859	0.7408589

TABLE 8-6

Texas Instruments, Inc.: Sales Stability

Ticker:	txn		Cutoff:	0%		
Company Name: TEXAS INSTRUMENTS INC			Industry Avg:	1,216.1533	SEMICONDUCTOR,RELATED DEVICE	
	Sale	**% Change**	**Downside Volatility Only**	**% Change**	**Upside Volatility Only**	**% Change**
Y08	12,501.0000	−9.64%	12,501.0000	−9.64%		
Y07	13,835.0000	−2.54%	13,835.0000	−2.54%		
Y06	14,195.0000	6.00%			14,195.0000	6.00%
Y05	13,392.0000	6.45%			13,392.0000	6.45%
Y04	12,580.0000	27.92%			12,580.0000	27.92%
Y03	9,834.0000	17.31%			9,834.0000	17.31%
Y02	8,383.0000	2.22%			8,383.0000	2.22%
Y01	8,201.0000	−30.85%	8,201.0000	−30.85%		
Y00	11,860.0000	25.26%			11,860.0000	25.26%
Y99	9,468.0000	11.91%			9,468.0000	11.91%
Standard Deviation	**2261.7639**	**0.1732**	**2944.2461**	**0.1473**	**2185.9495**	**0.0996**
AVERAGE	11,424.9000	0.0541	11,512.3333	(0.1434)	11,387.4286	0.1387
ST. DEV/AVE	0.197967942	3.20514151	0.255747124	−1.02706441	0.191961645	0.7184558

Above are stability tables for Advanced Micro Devices (AMD) and Texas Instruments (TXN), two leading manufacturers of semiconductors (Tables 8-5 and 8-6). I will present stability tables on these companies throughout the balance of this chapter. I also examine IBM as a model of consistency in an industry known for cyclicality.

AMD's standard deviation of sales is more than twice that of Texas Instruments; both have shown large year-to-year changes, although AMD's changes are considerably greater. Two of the past three years have seen negative sales growth for both. I assigned a three to AMD and a two to Texas Instruments, thereby adding 0.3 and 0.2 to cost of equity capital, respectively.

Stability of Free Cash Flow

Free-cash-flow stability is measured by appraising its deviation relative to itself, the average company, and its peer group. Measurement is most effective using statistical stability benchmarks, such as those shown, and the analyst's background studying the company and industry. Any special factors that might be contributing to instability will be considered, such as lumpy or unusual outflows as a payment related to a contingent liability, tax issues, pension prepayment, or settlement of a lawsuit. A mathematical model may, during shortened periods, be ineffective at capturing stability of free cash flow, or it may be revealing; true analytical judgment is required with the many moving parts, including the capital expenditure program, debt maturity, timing of expense payments and other obligations, and changes in working capital, that enter into the computation of free cash flow. Free cash flow also should be normalized over three or four years to allow for the effects of the operating cycle.

Even with their limitations, statistical measures provide a good guidepost from which the educated decision can be made regarding the stability component of the analysis. It is not crucial whether the company is assigned a 3 or a 4 but rather that the (in)stability be recognized and cost of capital adjusted appropriately.

An entity that has had an above-average history of instability may have taken recent measures to improve its circumstance, such as asset disposals or reduction in leverage. Larger instability of free cash flow deserves a higher penalty because investors cannot count on a return of their investment. If the entity has altered its business mix or credit profile, the analyst also would take that into account such that more recent data would carry a larger weighting in the analysis. Of all the factors in the credit model, the stability measure is both the most difficult to quantify and the easiest to spot. For one company, a change in the pension and postretirement risk might have an outsized weight affecting stability because contributions can be a large percentage of free cash flow. For most companies, this area is insignificant.

The analysis of company or industry groups undergoing life-cycle changes is an integral part of the stability measure. For instance, drug manufacturers, for so long considered a bastion of stability and predictability, can find that their free cash flows undergo pressure with competition. Pfizer, the largest drug company in the United States, saw its stock price fall precipitously as two of its strong and growing free-cash-flow-producing drugs came under scrutiny by the Food and Drug Administration (FDA) and when its largest cash-flow producer, Lipitor, drew competition from other manufacturers, which affected its cash flows, stability, and cost of capital.

Smaller health care companies are associated with more unpredictable free cash flow because their R&D budgets are large compared with revenues, and their prospects are often hinged to government drug approvals, the purchase of pipeline drugs, or marketing arrangements with their larger peers. Such companies often see their cost of capital rise or fall depending or such actions, which can lead to years of very predictable and stable cash flows.

Even world-class organizations whose products enjoy high inelasticity of demand, such as ExxonMobil, see periods of free-cash-flow instability; in three of its past 10 years through 2008, Exxon's free cash flows have declined. Even so, those years saw very strong nominal cash flows. During the same period, Exxon's operating cash flows have twice declined, once insignificantly and the other year by 7.1 percent, reflective of the cyclicality of a commodity business. I assigned a one rating to free-cash-flow stability and a one rating to operating-cash-flow stability for Exxon, thereby marking up those measures by 0.2 over the risk-free rate (Tables 8-7 and 8-8).

Compare ExxonMobil's percentage changes and standard deviation/average with those of Tesoro, a large energy-refining company. Tesoro shows very large and frequent drops in free cash flow, with similar but not quite as consistent drops in operating cash flows. Tesoro also shows positive operating cash flows in each year and just one year of negative free cash flow. Tesoro is typical for companies in the refining business, requiring constant and expensive upgrades along with high maintenance costs to its plant and equipment, and its cash inflows are affected by realized product price. As such, I assigned a 3 rating for operating cash flow stability and a 3 for free cash flow to Tesoro, indicating a 0.6 markup for these measures (Tables 8-9 and 8-10).

Tables 8-11 through 8-14 show cash flow stability for Advanced Micro Devices (AMD) and Texas Instruments. Cash flow from operations is represented in the tables as "oancf" and free cash flow as "fcf." For further comparison, Table 8-15 shows the data for IBM. AMD exhibits considerably greater instability of cash flows than Texas Instruments, especially so for free cash flow. As the tables reflect, IBM shows a fraction of the instability of Texas Instruments.

TABLE 8-7

Free-Cash-Flow Stability: ExxonMobil

Ticker:	XOM		Cutoff:	0%		
Company Name: EXXON MOBIL CORP			Industry Avg:	4,267.7096	PETROLEUM REFINING	
	FCF	% Change	Downside Volatility Only	% Change	Upside Volatility Only	% Change
Y08	41,629.9124	13.70%			41,629.9124	13.70%
Y07	36,615.0000	8.25%			36,615.0000	8.25%
Y06	33,824.0000	−1.38%	33,824.0000	−1.38%		
Y05	34,299.0000	20.07%			34,299.0000	20.07%
Y04	28,565.0000	63.91%			28,565.0000	63.91%
Y03	17,426.8279	66.41%			17,426.8279	66.41%
Y02	10,472.2405	−18.82%	10,472.2405	−18.82%		
Y01	12,900.0000	−10.98%	12,900.0000	−10.98%		
Y00	14,491.0000	162.49%			14,491.0000	162.49%
Y99	5,520.5168	51.49%			5,520.5168	51.49%
Standard Deviation	**12792.7458**	**0.5382**	**12838.8244**	**0.0873**	**13267.0491**	**0.5305**
AVERAGE	23,574.3498	0.3551	19,065.4135	(0.1039)	25,506.7510	0.5519
ST. DEV/AVE	0.542655299	1.51553705	0.673409174	−0.84006374	0.520138729	0.9612765

TABLE 8-8

Operating-Cash-Flow Stability: ExxonMobil

Ticker:	XOM		Cutoff:	0%		
Company Name: EXXON MOBIL CORP			**Industry Avg: 10,298.2622**		**PETROLEUM REFINING**	
	OANCF	**% Change**	**Downside Volatility Only**	**% Change**	**Upside Volatility Only**	**% Change**
Y08	5 9,725.0000	14.85%			59,725.0000	14.85%
Y07	5 2,002.0000	5.51%			52,002.0000	5.51%
Y06	4 9,286.0000	2.38%			49,286.0000	2.38%
Y05	4 8,138.0000	18.71%			48,138.0000	18.71%
Y04	4 0,551.0000	42.29%			40,551.0000	42.29%
Y03	2 8,498.0000	33.99%			28,498.0000	33.99%
Y02	2 1,268.0000	−7.08%	21,268.0000	−7.08%		
Y01	2 2,889.0000	−0.21%	22,889.0000	−0.21%		
Y00	2 2,937.0000	52.78%			22,937.0000	52.78%
Y99	1 5,013.0000	35.79%			15,013.0000	35.79%
Standard Deviation	**15704.9070**	**0.2029**	**1146.2201**	**0.0486**	**15729.0605**	**0.1811**
AVERAGE	3 6,030.7000	0.1990	22,078.5000	(0.0365)	39,518.7500	0.2579
ST. DEV/AVE	0.435875711	1.019716417	0.051915669	−1.33303409	0.398015131	0.7024128

TABLE 8-9

Free-Cash-Flow Stability: Tesoro

Ticker:	TSO		Cutoff:	0%		
Company Name: TESORO CORP			Industry Avg:	4 ,267.7096	PETROLEUM REFINING	
	FCF	**% Change**	**Downside Volatility Only**	**% Change**	**Upside Volatility Only**	**% Change**
Y08	424.5549	−55.03%	424.5549	−55.03%		
Y07	943.9943	11.06%			943.9943	11.06%
Y06	849.9890	70.00%			849.9890	70.00%
Y05	500.0000	−1.17%	500.0000	−1.17%		
Y04	505.9000	45.81%			505.9000	45.81%
Y03	346.9591	562.71%			346.9591	562.71%
Y02	(74.9846)	−709.77%	(74.9846)	−709.77%		
Y01	12.2973	−58.65%	12.2973	−58.65%		
Y00	29.7388	−35.76%	29.7388	−35.76%		
Y99	46.2903	1985.81%			46.2903	1985.81%
Standard Deviation	**356.5162**	**7.0311**	**263.5872**	**3.0144**	**367.9239**	**8.4197**
AVERAGE	358.4739	1.8150	178.3213	(1.7207)	538.6265	5.3508
ST. DEV/AVE	0.994538887	3.873842223	1.478158827	−1.75183318	0.683077937	1.5735524

TABLE 8-10

Operating-Cash-Flow Stability: Tesoro

Ticker:	TSO		Cutoff:	0%		
Company Name: TESORO CORP			Industry Avg: 10,298.2622		PETROLEUM REFINING	
	OANCF	% Change	Downside Volatility Only	% Change	Upside Volatility Only	% Change
Y08	716.0000	−45.84%	716.0000	−45.84%		
Y07	1,322.0000	16.07%			1,322.0000	16.07%
Y06	1,139.0000	50.26%			1,139.0000	50.26%
Y05	758.0000	10.61%			758.0000	10.61%
Y04	685.3000	53.21%			685.3000	53.21%
Y03	447.3000	673.88%			447.3000	673.88%
Y02	57.8000	−73.04%	57.8000	−73.04%		
Y01	214.4000	137.17%			214.4000	137.17%
Y00	90.4000	−19.79%	90.4000	−19.79%		
Y99	112.7000	−3.26%	112.7000	(0.0326)		
Standard Deviation	**447.1820**	**2.1669**	**315.3236**	**0.3056**	**414.8551**	**2.5730**
AVERAGE	554.2900	0.7993	244.2250	(0.3548)	761.0000	1.5687
ST. DEV/AVE	0.806765489	2.711183127	1.291119193	−0.86137922	0.545144677	1.6402501

TABLE 8-11

Texas Instruments, Inc.: Stability of Cash Flow from Operations

Ticker:	txn		Cutoff:	0%		
Company Name: TEXAS INSTRUMENTS INC			Industry Avg:	258.0503	SEMICONDUCTOR, RELATED DEVICE	
	OANCF	% Change	Downside Volatility Only	% Change	Upside Volatility Only	% Change
Y08	3,330.0000	−24.42%	3,330.0000	−24.42%		
Y07	4,406.0000	79.11%			4,406.0000	79.11%
Y06	2,460.0000	−34.78%	2,460.0000	−34.78%		
Y05	3,772.0000	19.90%			3,772.0000	19.90%
Y04	3,146.0000	46.26%			3,146.0000	46.26%
Y03	2,151.0000	7.98%			2,151.0000	7.98%
Y02	1,992.0000	9.51%			1,992.0000	9.51%
Y01	1,819.0000	−16.75%	1,819.0000	−16.75%		
Y00	2,185.0000	7.69%			2,185.0000	7.69%
Y99	2,029.0000	62.19%			2,029.0000	62.19%
Standard Deviation	**881.8489**	**0.3728**	**758.3867**	**0.0905**	**973.7838**	**0.2928**
AVERAGE	2,729.0000	0.1567	2,536.3333	(0.2532)	2,811.5714	0.3323
ST. DEV/AVE	0.323139957	2.379216232	0.299009067	−0.35742808	0.346348602	0.8809806

TABLE 8-12

AMD: Stability of Cash Flow from Operations

Ticker:	**amd**		**Cutoff:**	**0%**		
Company Name: ADVANCED MICRO DEVICES			**Industry Avg:**	**258.0503**	**SEMICONDUCTOR, RELATED DEVICE**	
	oancf	**% Change**	**Downside Volatility Only**	**% Change**	**Upside Volatility Only**	**% Change**
Y08	(692.0000)	−123.23%	(692.0000)	−123.23%		
Y07	(310.0000)	−124.09%	(310.0000)	−124.09%		
Y06	1,287.0000	−13.21%	1,287.0000	−13.21%		
Y05	1,482.8550	36.48%			1,482.8550	36.48%
Y04	1,086.5210	267.58%			1,086.5210	267.58%
Y03	295.5860	432.46%			295.5860	432.46%
Y02	(88.9100)	−153.03%	(88.9100)	−153.03%		
Y01	167.6450	−86.09%	167.6450	−86.09%		
Y00	1,205.5520	363.82%			1,205.5520	363.82%
Y99	259.9200	79.98%			259.9200	79.98%
Standard Deviation	**749.1842**	**2.1447**	**748.4788**	**0.5399**	**556.1340**	**1.7326**
AVERAGE	469.4169	0.6807	72.7470	(0.9993)	866.0868	2.3606
ST. DEV/AVE	1.595988951	3.150846952	10.28879299	−0.54025178	0.642122729	0.7339669

TABLE 8-13

AMD: Stability of Free Cash Flow

Ticker:	amd		Cutoff:	0%		
Company Name: ADVANCED MICRO DEVICES			Industry Avg:	127.2889	SEMICONDUCTOR, RELATED DEVICE	
	fcf	**% Change**	**Downside Volatility Only**	**% Change**	**Upside Volatility Only**	**% Change**
Y08	(689.7782)	53.15%			(689.7782)	53.15%
Y07	(1,472.1858)	−1487.65%	(1,472.1858)	−1487.65%		
Y06	106.0917	−60.05%	106.0917	−60.05%		
Y05	265.5896	440.45%			265.5896	440.45%
Y04	49.1419	139.90%			49.1419	139.90%
Y03	(123.1675)	80.27%			(123.1675)	80.27%
Y02	(624.2971)	−35.44%	(624.2971)	−35.44%		
Y01	(460.9269)	−210.20%	(460.9269)	−210.20%		
Y00	418.2506	240.29%			418.2506	240.29%
Y99	(298.1423)	47.28%			(298.1423)	47.28%
Standard Deviation	**558.5659**	**5.2517**	**652.8264**	**6.9717**	**400.9768**	**1.5212**
AVERAGE	(282.9424)	(0.7920)	(612.8295)	(4.4834)	(63.0177)	1.6689
ST. DEV/AVE	−1.974132679	−6.630806557	−1.065265892	−1.55500316	−6.362927376	0.9114894

TABLE 8-14

Texas Instruments, Inc.: Stability of Free Cash Flow

Ticker:	txn		Cutoff:	0%		
Company Name: TEXAS INSTRUMENTS INC			Industry Avg:	127.2889	SEMICONDUCTOR, RELATED DEVICE	
	fcf	**% Change**	**Downside Volatility Only**	**% Change**	**Upside Volatility Only**	**% Change**
Y08	2,608.5384	−30.46%	2,608.5384	−30.46%		
Y07	3,751.0414	193.52%			3,751.0414	193.52%
Y06	1,277.9311	−49.28%	1,277.9311	−49.28%		
Y05	2,519.3858	36.33%			2,519.3858	36.33%
Y04	1,848.0000	32.17%			1,848.0000	32.17%
Y03	1,398.2387	9.78%			1,398.2387	9.78%
Y02	1,273.7209	97.58%			1,273.7209	97.58%
Y01	644.6742	120.56%			644.6742	120.56%
Y00	292.2915	−61.40%	292.2915	−61.40%		
Y99	757.2099	30.68%			757.2099	30.68%
Standard Deviation	**1060.4545**	**0.8002**	**1162.3970**	**0.1559**	**1092.6424**	**0.6605**
AVERAGE	1,637.1032	0.3795	1,392.9203	(0.4704)	1,741.7530	0.7437
ST. DEV/AVE	0.647762806	2.108604515	0.834503598	−0.3314007	0.627323384	0.8881549

TABLE 8-15

IBM: Stability of Free Cash Flow

Ticker:	ibm		Cutoff:	0%		
Company Name: INTL BUSINESS MACHINES CORP		Industry Avg:	209.2528	CMP PROGRAMMING, DATA PROCESS		
	fcf	% Change	Downside Volatility Only	% Change	Upside Volatility Only	% Change
Y08	15,236.9845	20.14%			15,236.9845	20.14%
Y07	12,682.7624	8.10%			12,682.7624	8.10%
Y06	11,732.9248	−6.30%	11,732.9248	−6.30%		
Y05	12,522.1263	1.02%			12,522.1263	1.02%
Y04	12,395.6787	9.65%			12,395.6787	9.65%
Y03	11,305.0260	18.76%			11,305.0260	18.76%
Y02	9,519.2006	−5.90%	9,519.2006	−5.90%		
Y01	10,116.1294	79.17%			10,116.1294	79.17%
Y00	5,646.0007	0.52%			5,646.0007	0.52%
Y99	5,616.9308	27.16%			5,616.9308	27.16%
Standard Deviation	**3077.7808**	**0.2512**	**1565.3394**	**0.0028**	**3439.2221**	**0.2547**
AVERAGE	10,677.3764	0.1523	10,626.0627	(0.0610)	10,690.2048	0.2056
ST. DEV/AVE	0.28825253	1.649132666	0.147311325	−0.04655163	0.321717136	1.2384781

Accounts Receivable

The accounts receivable metric indicates whether accounts receivable show an unusual increase or decrease relative to sales. Subtracting from the most recent ratio of accounts receivable to sales, the average ratio over the prior four years, and multiplying by the most recent sales yields an estimate of the increase or decrease in accounts receivable. An unusual increase or decrease is noted when such an increase or decrease exceeds 10 percent of the absolute value of the prior four years. An unusual increase in accounts receivable may indicate collection problems owing to credit or a dispute. An unusual decrease in accounts receivable may indicate a temporary reduction that is likely to reverse in the future, such as through factoring, selling accounts receivable, or quicker collections. A firm that recently had entered a securitization program would see a large drop in the balance-sheet entry and a commensurate increase in operating cash flows.

A company is penalized if it had an unusual increase/decrease in accounts receivable in the most recent year or in at least two of the most recent three years. The weight of the penalty depends on the amount of the unusual increase or decrease in accounts receivable, and no penalty is levied if the increase/decrease is not unusual.

In the example, Apple was penalized because of large accounts receivable growth. In Apple's case, the unusual growth was traced to widespread acceptance of newly introduced products, and therefore, the company was assessed a minor cost-of-capital penalty.

Accounts Receivable—Based on the Most Recent Quarter

The accounts receivable metric indicates whether accounts receivable show an unusual increase or decrease relative to sales. Subtracting from the most recent ratio of quarterly accounts receivable to quarterly sales, the average ratio over the same quarter in the prior four years, and multiplying by the most recent quarterly sales yields an estimate of the increase or decrease in accounts receivable. An unusual increase or decrease is defined as where the absolute value of the difference between the ratio in the most recent quarter and the one derived from the average of the same quarter in the prior four years is at least 10 percent. An unusual increase in accounts receivable may indicate collection problems in the most recent quarter. An unusual decrease in accounts receivable may indicate a temporary reduction in the current quarter that is likely to reverse in the future, such as through factoring, selling accounts receivable, or quicker collections. A company is penalized if it had an unusual increase/decrease in accounts receivable in the most recent quarter.

In the example, Apple's accounts receivable for the quarter was within normal limits.

Inventory

The inventory metric indicates whether inventories show an unusual increase or decrease relative to sales. Subtracting from the most recent ratio of inventories to sales, the average ratio over the prior four years, and multiplying by the most recent sales yields an estimate of an increase or decrease in inventory. An unusual increase or decrease is where such an increase or decrease exceeds 10 percent of the prior four-year average. An unusual increase in inventories may indicate problems of falling demand or a poor estimate of demand, including problems with a large customer. An unusual decrease in inventories may indicate a temporary reduction that is likely to reverse in the future, such as production problems, inability to obtain raw materials, strikes, poor planning, or weakness in cash flows. The company would not be penalized if inventory levels were unimportant to the firm's activities or were reduced as part of a planned effort to aid cash flows and not induced by ongoing weaknesses in operations. If inventory levels increased greater than 10 percent owing to an inventory build related to anticipated sales, the entity could, unless such sales were relatively assured, be penalized slightly. Otherwise, a company is penalized if it had an unusual increase/decrease in inventories in the most recent year or in at least two of the most recent three years.

Inventory Metric—Based on the Most Recent Quarter

Similar to the preceding, the inventories metric indicates whether inventories show an unusual increase or decrease relative to sales. Subtracting from the most recent ratio of quarterly inventories to quarterly sales, the average ratio over the same quarter in the prior four years, and multiplying by the most recent quarterly sales yields an estimate of the increase or decrease in inventory. An unusual increase or decrease is defined as where the absolute value of the difference between the ratio in the most recent quarter and the one derived from the average of the same quarter in the prior four years is at least 10 percent. If a change in inventory occurred because of the company's accounting method and is not a reflection of the true market value of inventory, it would be considered. An unusual increase in inventory may indicate problems of falling or a poor estimate of demand, including problems with a large customer. An unusual decrease in inventory may indicate a temporary reduction that is likely to reverse in the future, such as production problems, strikes, cash flows, an inability to obtain raw materials, or poor planning. A company is penalized if it had an unusual increase/decrease in inventory in the most recent quarter and had predictive value—the inventory level was important in evaluating future performance. This metric reports the amount of the unusual increase or decrease in quarterly inventory, if one occurred. Apple had no unusual inventory change and as such is not assessed a penalty.

Accounts Payable

The accounts payable metric indicates whether accounts payable show an unusual increase or decrease relative to sales. Subtracting from the most recent ratio of accounts payable to sales, the average ratio over the prior four years, and multiplying by the most recent sales yields the estimate of an increase or decrease in accounts payable. An unusual increase or decrease is where such an increase or decrease exceeds 10 percent of the prior four-year average. An unusual increase in accounts payable may indicate liquidity problems. An unusual decrease in accounts payable may indicate problems in obtaining suppliers' credit or surplus cash. A company may be penalized if it had an unusual increase/decrease in accounts payable in the most recent year or in at least two of the most recent three years. This metric reports the amount of the unusual increase or decrease in accounts payable or nothing if the increase/decrease is not unusual.

Apple is flagged because of an unusual reduction in payables but is not penalized because it was due to its strong operating cash flows, not a credit problem.

Accounts Payable—Based on the Most Recent Quarter

Similar to the preceding, the accounts payable metric indicates whether accounts payable show an unusual increase or decrease relative to sales. Subtracting from the most recent ratio of quarterly accounts payable to quarterly sales, the average ratio over the same quarter in the prior four years, and multiplying by the most recent quarterly sales yields an estimate of an increase or decrease in accounts payable. An unusual increase or decrease is defined as where the absolute value of the difference between the ratio in the most recent quarter and the one derived from the average of the same quarter in the prior four years is at least 10 percent. An unusual increase in accounts payable may indicate liquidity problems. An unusual decrease in accounts payable may indicate problems in obtaining suppliers' credit or surplus cash. A company may be penalized if it had an unusual increase/decrease in accounts payable in the most recent quarter. This metric reports the amount of an unusual increase or decrease in quarterly accounts payable, and a penalty is assessed if the quarter had reliable information content.

Discretionary Capital Expenditures

The discretionary component of capital expenditures is derived according to the methodology outlined in Chapter 4. It is based on the difference between the growth rate of capital expenditures and COGS times the most recent level of capital expenditures. Discretionary capital expenditures indicate the amount of additional free cash flow the firm could free up if needed to meet outstanding obligations. This item results in a penalty it if the discretionary component represents at least 10 percent of current capital spending. If the overspending continued, the entity would see a rise in its cost of capital, indicating excessive and unwarranted growth in relation to its growth in units or cost of sales.

Apple was penalized because of high capital expenditures, adding 0.3 to its cost of capital. One might wonder why, with Apple's success as of this writing, I would penalize the company for success, especially given Apple's $23.4 billion in cash and no debt (outside trade). Success runs in cycles, even for a company as successful as Apple has been of late. If it were to continue to spend greater amounts on capital relative to its growth rate, free cash flow eventually could turn negative, and it is the return on productive assets that influences valuation, which, in turn, influences cost of capital.

Discretionary R&D

The discretionary component of R&D expenditures is derived according to my proprietary definition outlined in Chapter 4. It is based on the difference between the growth rate of R&D expenditures and COGS times the most recent level of R&D expenditures. This item is flagged if it represents at least 10 percent of the most recent R&D expenditures. Excessive spending in R&D could lead to an increase in the cost of capital for a firm that is not able to convert such expenditures into increased sales. For some firms, this ability is integral to the cost of capital. This has been particularly true in the pharmaceutical industry.

Other firms, however, have been successful buying R&D through acquisitions. For entities that have successfully levered purchased R&D to sell into its client base, such as Oracle and Cisco have done, the penalty would be less severe. Not all purchased R&D returns its cost of acquisition, though. I exclude the depreciation component of R&D, if given, because doing so may better reflect the discretionary component.

Discretionary Cost of Goods Sold

The discretionary component of COGS is derived according to my proprietary definition, as explained in Chapter 4. It is based on the difference between the most recent ratio of COGS to sales, the average ratio in the prior four years, times the most recent level of sales. Cost of capital may be penalized if the difference represents at least 10 percent of the most recent COGS. As outlined in an earlier chapter, many items make up cost of sales such that individual areas may reveal upcoming weakness or strength and should be taken into consideration in relation to changes in the level of risk. An increase in discretionary COGS could signal a change in the ability of the entity to generate cash flows or could be a temporary aberration associated with events such as a strike or an overheated economy. I typically exclude the depreciation component of COGS, if given, because doing so may better reflect the discretionary component.

Discretionary Selling, General, and Administrative Expenses

The discretionary component of SG&A is derived according to my proprietary definition. It is based on the difference between the most recent ratio of SG&A expenses to sales, the average ratio in the prior four years, times the most recent level of sales. This item results in a penalty if the excess represents at least 10 percent of the most recent SG&A expenses. If the entity exhibits consistent overspending in SG&A, management may not recognize a shift in market conditions or product acceptance. This would add risk because it may force higher debt levels to finance the overspending, though the markup to cost of capital should take place as soon as the overspending is recognized. I exclude the depreciation piece of SG&A, if given, because doing so may better reflect the discretionary component. An increase in leasing payments, if included in SG&A, could cause this measure to rise, reflecting additional risk.

Discretionary Advertising

The discretionary component of advertising expenses (ADV) is derived according to my proprietary definition. It is based on the difference between the most recent ratio of ADV expenses to sales and the average ratio in the prior four years times the most recent level of sales. This metric results in a penalty if the excess represents at least 10 percent of the most recent ADV expenses. The penalty to cost of capital typically is minor for this item, but not always.

Growth of the internet has reduced (the growth in) advertising spending in relation to sales for many entities. Even with the shift in advertising patterns, the total amount of advertising dollars is large and, for competitive and consumer goods industries, normally represents a significant percentage of their discretionary budget.

Cash Burn Rate—Last Fiscal Year

This item represents the number of days it will take until the company will use up all the cash and marketable securities it has on hand on its operations and new investments in capital expenditures. It is calculated as the magnitude of the negative free cash flow by the number of days, so if the entity had a negative free cash flow, as defined, of $80 million for the year and had $40 million in cash and investments, its cash burn would be 182 days. If the entity had bank credit facilities in place, depending on their reliability and dates the facilities run out, they also could be added to the balance-sheet cash. The cash burn is sometimes calculated as 365 (days) multiplied by cash and marketable securities divided by the difference between capital expenditures and operating cash flow. For example, if cash and marketable securities are $30 million, capital expenditures are $50 million, and net operating cash flow is $30 million, the cash burn rate is 547 days [365 × 30/(50 – 30)]. If the firm is burning cash, an evaluation would be made as to the upcoming quarter's expected burn rate and the firm's plan for remedy.

This item is not shown if the firm generates positive free cash flows because cash is not likely to be depleted. It is penalized if the cash burn rate is below two years, indicating that the firm may need to find new sources of financing for its operation in less than two years or be forced to sell assets or cease operations.

Even though negative free cash flow would be penalized under a separate metric, a positive (two-year) cash burn is more serious because it represents an inability to service all liabilities. If the cash from operations exceeds capital expenditures, cash still could be depleted if a substantial liability is due that requires a cash settlement that cannot be satisfied from available resources. This measure is closely related to debt and financial flexibility measures that I will examine under debt metrics.

Cash Burn Rate—LTM and Recent Quarter

This item represents the number of days it will take until the company will use up all the cash and marketable securities it has on hand on its operations and new investments in capital expenditures. It is calculated as the magnitude of the negative free cash flow by the number of days, so if the entity had a negative free cash flow, as defined, of $40 million for the quarter and had $160 million in cash, its cash burn would be one year. If the entity had bank credit facilities in place, depending on their reliability and the dates the facilities run out, they also could be added to the balance-sheet cash. It is also sometimes calculated as 365 (days) times quarterly balance of cash and marketable securities divided by the difference between the quarterly capital expenditures and quarterly operating cash flow. For example, if cash and marketable securities are $30 million, capital expenditures are $50 million, and net operating cash flow is $30 million, the cash burn rate is 547 days [365 × 30/(50 – 30)].

If the entity generates positive free cash flows, cash still could be depleted if a substantial liability is due that requires a cash settlement for which it does not have the resources to satisfy. If the firm is burning cash, an evaluation would be made as to the upcoming quarter's expected burn rate and the firm's plan for remedy.

Both the last 12 months and most recent quarter are analyzed to determine if there is a change warranting a (greater) charge to the cost of capital or, conversely, a lessening or removal of a charge. An LTM or quarterly positive cash burn may result in a markup in the cost of capital, especially if there are no extenuating circumstances. The quarterly cash burn should be compared with prior year quarters to see if it was due to seasonal or other factors, such as capital spending or an unusual outflow of cash. If the cash burn resulted from a shift in consumer preferences foretelling an upcoming liquidity issue, the markup to the cost of capital could be significant, even though the time period is limited.

Debt Metrics

This section enumerates the debt metrics included in the report, which are intended to evaluate the ease in which the entity can service its liabilities and satisfy covenants and the extent the entity's credit position has altered or is likely to be altered. Included are measures of financial risk designed to capture upcoming obligations and a concurrent shortfall to service those obligations. Incorporated is the ease of conversion of assets into cash and the ability to repay liabilities when due, fund growth of operations, and meet contractual and moral commitments, including those related to subsidiaries and special-purpose entities (SPEs).

You will find several metrics listed in this section that fewer than 10 percent of all S&P 500 companies can achieve. This is no reason they should not be included. A sustained economic recession may force even the most creditworthy entity to draw on available credits or issue debt and equity that were not contemplated in order to satisfy their funding needs. A tightening of the credit markets and periods of low liquidity in the financial markets will affect all entities regardless of current financial strength, and this model is designed to capture those possibilities. In this event, the cost of capital for almost all firms will rise.

Where one of the determinants of a metric is included elsewhere, care must be taken not to overweight. A reasonable penalty should be assessed when appropriate, even though it may appear that the correlation between the variables is strong.

Thus factors affecting the ability of an enterprise to raise capital are also explored. *Extraordinary factors and events, even though they are not mentioned explicitly under each metric, are always considered so as to ensure that the result is a true representation of the credit health of the entity and its ability to return cash, through the free cash flows, to shareholders.*

Growth in Total Debt—Recent 10 Years

Total debt consists of short- and long-term debt, including operating lease obligations, unfunded pension liabilities, unhedged derivatives agreements, and other legal liabilities such as payment due on settlement of a lawsuit, tax judgments, workers' compensation claims, and cash guarantee payments on behalf of another party, including affiliates or SPEs. It also includes possible forced redemptions (i.e., preferred stock) or other calls on cash if not already included as debt. Considered are any moral obligations that may need to be paid, including nonrecourse debt for which the entity is not legally bound but for which it may be in its best interest to pay.[3]

The metric results in a penalty if total debt grew from the prior year in at least four of the most recent 10 years; for additional years above four, the greater is the markup to the cost of capital, regardless of other financial metrics, including growth in cash flows. A company that continuously increases its borrowings is more likely to have a greater financial risk, even if its cash flows are currently strong or are expected to be so. Such an entity becomes increasingly dependent on the debt markets to grow and refinance its coming maturities. If business conditions unexpectedly decline, firms that make constant trips to the credit markets are more seriously imperiled, especially if they are weaker credits without strong backup bank facilities.

Cyclical companies are expected to reduce borrowings with the positive cash flows produced in good years and perhaps sell equity. Companies that are growing revenues and operating cash flows can raise external capital more easily. *This metric has been found to be particularly important in setting the cost of equity, even though it is not based on a leverage measure but on a frequency-of-use leverage measure.* The entry reflects the number of years (out of the most recent 10) in which total debt grew from the prior year.

All debt metrics in this section include commitments and contingencies under which there is a reasonable prospect of a cash outflow.

Growth in Total Debt—Recent 5 Years

Total debt consists of short- and long-term debt, including operating lease obligations, unfunded pension liabilities, unhedged derivatives contracts, and other liabilities outside normal trade payables, as specified earlier. A company is penalized if its total debt grew by more than 10 percent annually over the most recent five years. The growth rate in total debt is also compared with the growth rate in cash flows—operating and free—with the size of the penalty depending on the information content.

A company that continuously increases its borrowings is more likely to have a greater financial risk. Cyclical companies are expected to reduce leverage ratios by using the positive cash flows in good years. I take into consideration whether

[3] *Total debt*, as the term is used throughout this chapter, may include moral liabilities depending on the relationship between the issuer and the creditor, especially the need of future reliance.

the growth rate in total debt is the result of a business acquisition or capital program with a long period to complete, although a penalty will be assessed in every case. This variable will have a lower weighting than the growth over 10 years but is important owing to the overlap between the two.

Growth in Total Debt—Most Recent Quarter

A company could be penalized if its quarterly total debt grew by more than 10 percent from the same quarter in the prior year. Factors including the use of proceeds and changes in debt maturity schedule will be considered, as will the match between expected cash flows and debt repayment. A business combination or capital project may be value-adding and will allow for a smaller penalty. Debt assumed to satisfy a derivatives agreement may result in a higher penalty.

A company that increases its borrowings in a given quarter (aside for seasonal needs) is more likely to have a greater financial risk if the growth is due to a downward shift in demand for the entity's products or services. Where the possibility of a forced redemption (i.e., preferred stock) or other calls exist, for which debt is incurred, the penalty could be greater, unless the capital structure is consistent with the firm's ability to service its obligations. The quarterly total debt is compared with the same quarter in the prior year, especially important for seasonal concerns. Also reviewed is the growth rate of quarterly total debt from its prior quarter for entities of a nonseasonal nature or those in the growth stages of development.

Debt/(Four-Year Average FCF) Multiple

This is the ratio of total debt in relation to the four-year average free cash flow. Total debt consists of short- and long-term debt, lease obligations, postretirement debt, and all other obligations outside the normal trade and operating cycle, as has been defined at the beginning of this section. Free cash flow is my proprietary definition of the cash flow that the company can distribute back to shareholders without affecting its current growth.

The debt multiple indicates how many years of free cash flow are needed to pay off the entire debt of the company, recognizing that debts typically are rolled over. The higher this multiple, the longer it will take for the company to pay down principal debt, and the more financial risk the company assumes, resulting in a greater assessment to the cost of capital. For companies in their growing stages that have unusual payment obligations, large working-capital changes, or large multiyear capital expenditure programs, free cash flow could be negative, and this ratio will show a negative number. Power operating cash flow normalizes the working-capital items. I penalize a company that either has a negative free cash flow or has a multiple in excess of 10, with progressive penalties imposed, taking into consideration that negative OCF entities are also penalized elsewhere. By comparison, as of January 2010, the median entity in the S&P 500 had the capacity to repay its total debt from four-year average free cash flow in 7.3 years. Enterprises with negative free cash flow or high debt to average free cash flow will have a higher cost of capital.

Debt/(Four-Year Average OCF) Multiple

This is the ratio of total debt to the four-year average operating cash flow. Total debt consists of short- and long-term debt, as described previously, including any other expected outflows outside normal trade, such as settlement on a lawsuit, purchase commitments, guarantees, unhedged derivatives, unusual payments, or other financing commitments. Operating cash flow is based on the average annual net operating cash flow as reported in the 10Ks of the most recent four years plus any adjustments, as specified earlier in the section "Cash-Flow Metrics."

The debt multiple indicates how many years of operating cash flows are needed to pay off the entire debt of the company. Enterprises with negative operating cash flows and those with a higher multiple will need a longer period of time for the company to pay down debt, and the more financial risk the company assumes. I penalize a company that either has a negative operating cash flow or has a multiple in excess of 8, taking into consideration that negative OCF entities are also penalized elsewhere. By comparison, the median S&P 500 company, as of data available in January 2010, reported a debt/four-year average operating cash flow of 4.8; the higher the number in either direction, the greater is the penalty. Since interest on debt and operating leases is serviced from cash flow from operations, this variable is critical in the evaluation of the cost of capital and has a high weighting, especially for very high and negative ratios.

Ability to Repay Total Debt from Four-Year Average of (OCF – 2/3 Capital Expenditures)

This is a measure of minimal operating cash flow minus total debt. A firm is penalized if it is negative, indicating that the company cannot pay off its debt from available operating cash flow. Total debt consists of short- and long-term debt and other liabilities as described throughout this section. Operating cash flow is based on the average annual net operating cash flow as reported in the 10Ks of the most recent four years, including adjustments, if necessary. The minimal free cash flow is calculated by subtracting two-thirds of average capital expenditures in the most recent four years, essentially assuming that one-third of the capital expenditures is not necessary to continue the growth of the company. The reported number is the four-year average of (operating cash flow minus two-thirds of capital expenditures) minus total debt. Companies with strong operating cash flows and small capital requirements and/or lean manufacturing or subpar growth opportunities more easily pass this hurdle.

Companies that cannot pass this hurdle typically are operating with less financial flexibility and would be penalized.

Ability to Cover Current Debt from Free Cash Flow

This is a measure of four-year average free cash flow minus current debt. It is penalized if it is negative, indicating that the company cannot pay off its current principal debt from normalized free cash flow. Current debt consists of all debt that becomes due in the next 12 months. It also includes possible forced redemptions (i.e., preferred stock, settlements on derivatives agreements) or other calls on cash if not already counted as debt, as specified earlier. Free cash flow is my proprietary definition of the cash flow that the company can distribute back to shareholders without affecting its current growth. A negative number indicates that the company needs to find alternatives to service its current debt if its free cash flow is insufficient, such as extension, additional borrowing, raising new equity, or selling off assets. This is a variable typically passed by entities having strong free cash flows or modest amounts of current debt due. It does not take into account cash holdings or other calls on capital, such as bank facilities.

Ability to Cover Current Debt from All Sources of Liquidity, Excluding Asset Sales

All sources include cash on hand and available operating cash flows including tax refunds, settlements from lawsuits, and credit agreements. Asset sales are excluded unless the entity has a definitive sale agreement and a closing date set with a reputable and creditworthy buyer.

Inherent in this variable is whether the entity is relying on credit lines (rolling over debt) to satisfy the obligation and if such lines are subject to change or cancellation prior to the debt coming due. The conditions under which such lines can be pulled prior to the obligations are also reviewed. The analyst also must estimate the borrower's relationship with its bank(s) or financial intermediary, as well as the credit condition of the creditor(s). If the entity is relying on available cash and credit lines, it must be determined if its use limits the operations of the entity such that future cash flows will be compromised. If working-capital ratios fall below normal patterns, the cost of capital would be affected. The probability of extending the debt is assessed.

Asset sales are excluded because it may not be possible to realize cash within the coming year, or the amount received from a forced sale may be insufficient to satisfy the obligation. Standard accounts receivable securitization programs are included in this metric. If the entity is unable to pass this hurdle and extension of debt is in doubt, the penalty to the cost of capital could be severe.

Ability to Cover Current and Next Year's Debt from All Sources Including Asset Sales

Under this metric, probable asset sales are included because the entity has two years to prepare for the obligation(s), assuming that creditors allow for deferment until the asset sales take place. The probability of extending the debts is assessed.

Because even seemingly healthy companies face adversity, such as a strike, general financial market illiquidity, large litigation judgments, or crises, all sources of liquidity strength are appraised. If the entity is forced to take down its entire line of credit to satisfy obligations, a credit review is undertaken to determine if sufficient remaining financial flexibility exists, including an analysis of working-capital needs and the extent to which expected cash flows are compromised resulting from a sale. If an asset is sold and the remaining assets produce negative or more volatile cash flows, this would be covered under the appropriate cash-flow section, including *stability*. Likewise, if an important contributor of cash flows is sold, raising the remaining risk level, this would be covered under the appropriate cash-flow metric section or in the *Other* entry of the Miscellaneous section. If an entity is unable to pass this hurdle, and extension of debt is in doubt, there will be a severe penalty to the cost of capital, the amount depending on probability of default and bankruptcy. In all likelihood, other metrics would have indicated such a possibility many periods prior to a breach of this metric.

If the entity can pass this hurdle, even with a sale of assets, no penalty is assessed. If bankruptcy is threatened, the analyst must determine the likely value remaining to shareholders, taking a conservative estimate based on the firm's assets, liabilities, and dilution in favor of creditors. According to the U.S. Bankruptcy Code, creditor claims are paid prior to shareholders (first preferred, then common) in the following order:

1. Secured claims
2. Administrative expenses of the bankruptcy
3. Unsecured debts in an involuntary bankruptcy
4. Claims for payment of unpaid wages for employees and salespersons (These wages must have been earned within 180 days of the bankruptcy but only to the maximum of $10,950 for each individual. Claims in excess of $10,950 will be general unsecured claims unless they qualify for some other special treatment.)

5. Contributions to employee benefit plans, up to a maximum of $10,950 per employee
6. Recent taxes, including sales, income, employment, and gross tax receipts

If there are classes of common stock, each must be reviewed for priority, but if it is deemed to be unlikely that shareholder remains have value, a cost-of-capital designation is inappropriate. If the entity emerges from bankruptcy, the analyst then can estimate prospective free cash flow and cost of capital for the new concern.

Ability to Cover Current and Next Year's Debt from Normalized FCF

This is a measure of twice the four-year average free cash flow minus the debt that becomes due in the following two years. Although often a difficult hurdle to surpass for most firms using leverage, there is a penalty if it is negative, indicating that the company cannot pay off its debt obligations over the next two years from free cash flow in those two years. Current and next year's debt consists of all contractual and moral debt becoming due in the next 24 months. The reported number is twice the four-year average free cash flow minus the coming 24 months' debt obligations. A negative number indicates that the company may need to find alternatives to service its debt in the next 24 months if operating cash flows are insufficient, such as additional borrowing, raising new equity, rolling over debt due, or selling of assets. This is a stringent variable normally met by entities having small amounts of debt and other obligations coming due. Its importance lies when credit conditions tighten for all borrowers and if free cash flows are adequate to repay such obligations without requiring the entity to enter into costly credit agreements. Entities meeting this variable also can more easily prefund obligations, such as other postretirement benefits, and have adequate financial flexibility.

Ability to Cover Current and Next Year's Debt from FCF in the Last 12 Months

This is a measure of twice the last 12 months' free cash flow minus all debt that becomes due in the following two years. It is penalized if it is negative, indicating that the company cannot retire all its debt obligations over the next two years from the current level of free cash flow. Current and next year's debt consists of contractual debt that becomes due in the next 24 months. It also includes possible forced redemptions (i.e., a sinking fund) or other calls on cash. A negative number indicates that the company may need to find alternatives to service its debt in the next 24 months, such as additional borrowing, extend maturities, raise new equity, or selling off assets. This is a stringent variable for most companies having use of leverage and normally is passed by entities having small amounts of debt, and as such, the penalty assessment during periods of financial normalcy is low.

Ability to Cover Current Debt from Net Working Capital

This is a measure of the company's ability to pay its current debt from its net liquid assets (modified working capital). Current debt consists of all contractual and moral debt that becomes due in the next 12 months. Modified net working capital is computed as cash and equivalents plus accounts receivable plus inventories minus accounts payable and accrued expenses minus income taxes payable. It is penalized if it is negative, indicating that the company does not have sufficient liquid assets to pay its current debt. The company may either generate cash from operations in the next 12 months to pay the current debt or be forced to raise new equity, borrow additional amounts, extend maturities, or sell off assets. The reported number is the modified net working capital minus current debt, with restricted cash taken into account. Restricted cash is unavailable to the enterprise. Under unusual economic conditions, similar to the worldwide credit crisis of 2008, firms that meet this variable normally can survive. The weighting for this metric is low and results in a slight deduction to the cost of capital, if not passed. If the company shows investment-grade strength, this can result in points being deducted from the cost of capital.

Ability to Cover Current and Next Year's Debt from Net Working Capital

This is a measure of the company's ability to pay its current and next year's debt from its net liquid assets (modified working capital). Current and next year's debt consists of all contractual debt that becomes due in the next 24 months. Modified net working capital is computed as cash and equivalents plus accounts receivable plus inventories minus accounts payable and accrued expenses minus income taxes payable, adjusted for restricted cash because that is unavailable to the enterprise. The firm is assessed a slight penalty if it is negative, indicating that few leveraged companies have sufficient liquid assets to pay their debt that becomes due in the coming 24 months from existing working capital. The reported number is the modified net working capital minus current and next year's debt and any other nonoperating outlays. Under unusual economic conditions, similar to the worldwide credit crisis of 2008, firms that meet this variable normally can survive. Other entities must be able to roll over their debt, even if the cost is high. Companies that pass this hurdle and have free cash flow and/or minimal obligations due normally have a very low cost of capital. If the company shows investment-grade strength, this can result in points being deducted from the cost of capital.

Ability to Cover Current Debt from Four-Year Average OCF

This is a measure of four-year average operating cash flow minus current debt. It is penalized if it is negative, indicating that the company cannot pay off its current contractual and moral obligations from its average operating cash flow and must rely on the credit markets to extend maturities, raise equity, or draw down working capital to satisfy current claims. Current debt consists of all debt that may need to be satisfied in the coming 12 months. Operating cash flow is based on the average annual net operating cash flows, including any adjustments, including assets sales, other changes to operations, and other factors discussed under the section on operating cash flows.

The reported number is the four-year average operating cash flow minus current debt. Companies having healthy cash flows typically roll over debt; however, this may not be possible for weaker entities, which must raise equity capital or pay a higher cost (interest rate) to do so. Otherwise, the firm may need to use its balance sheet (cash or other assets) to retire the obligations.

Ability to Cover Current and Next Year's Debt from Twice Four-Year Average OCF

This is a measure of twice the four-year average operating cash flow minus the debt that becomes due in the following two years. It is penalized if it is negative, indicating that the company cannot pay off its anticipated debt obligations over the next two years from operating cash flows. If the four-year period does not reflect the current business composition's cash flows, a more appropriate time period will be used. Current and next year's debt consists of all contractual and moral obligations that become due in the next 24 months. Operating cash flow is based on the average annual net operating cash flow of the most recent 16 quarters. The reported number in the worksheet is twice the four-year average operating cash flow minus current and second-year's debt. A negative number indicates that the company may need to find alternatives to service its debt in the next 24 months, such as additional borrowing, extended maturities, raising new equity, or selling off assets. Companies having healthy cash flows typically roll over debt; however, this is not possible for other entities, which must sell equity capital or pay a higher cost (interest rate) to do so.

Ability to Cover Current Debt from Four-Year Average OCF plus Net Working Capital

This is a measure of four-year average operating cash flow plus modified net working capital minus current debt. The firm is penalized if it is negative, indicating that the company cannot pay off its current debt from its operating cash flow, even after allowing for its net liquid assets. For entities having large amounts of debt coming due and for which rollover risk is deemed slight, the penalty will be minor. Current debt consists of all contractual and moral debt that becomes due in the next 12 months after the balance-sheet date. Operating cash flow is based on the average annual net operating cash flow, as defined, of the most recent four years. Modified net working capital is computed as cash and equivalents plus accounts receivable plus inventories minus accounts payable and accrued expenses minus income taxes payable. The reported number is the four-year average operating cash flow (unless the business composition has changed) plus the modified net working capital minus current debt. A negative number indicates that the company is likely required to find alternatives for servicing its current debt, such as extending maturities, raising new equity, or selling off assets.

Ability to Cover Current and Next Year's Debt from Twice Four-Year Average OCF plus Net Working Capital

This is a measure of twice the four-year average operating cash flow plus modified net working capital minus current and next year's debt. The firm is penalized if it is negative, indicating that the company cannot pay off its current and next year's debt from its operating cash flows, even after allowing for its net liquid assets. For entities having debt coming due where extension is probable, the penalty will be slight. If credit agreements need to be called on, the penalty will be higher.

Current and next year's debt consists of all contractual and moral debt that becomes due in the next 24 months. Operating cash flow is based on the average annual net operating cash flow, as defined, of the most recent four years unless the business composition has changed. If this is the case, I will use a more appropriate period. Modified net working capital is computed as cash and equivalents plus accounts receivable plus inventories minus accounts payable and accrued expenses minus income taxes payable. The reported number is twice the four-year average operating cash flow plus the modified net working capital minus current and second-year's debt. A negative number indicates that the company is likely required to find alternatives for servicing its current and second-year's debt, such as extending maturities, raising new equity, or selling off assets.

Deterioration in Net Working Capital to Total Debt

This item is based on the ratio of modified net working capital to total debt. It results in a penalty if this ratio deteriorated from the prior year or interim reporting period. Modified net working capital is computed as cash and equivalents plus accounts receivable plus inventories minus accounts payable and accrued expenses minus income taxes payable. Total debt consists of all short- and long-term debt plus any off-balance-sheet liabilities. The ratio indicates what percentage of total debt can be paid off with the current levels of net liquid assets. Deterioration in the ratio can serve as a signal that the ability of the firm to service its total debt has deteriorated. The entry to be looked at is the ratio (in percentage) of modified net working capital to total debt.

Interest and Lease Coverage from Working Capital and FCF

This item represents the sum of modified net working capital and free cash flow divided by the most recent annual cash interest payment and total lease obligations. It is also computed for the current quarter based on the last 12 months. The total lease obligations are included, not the estimated interest portion (typically one-third of the payment), because the total lease expense for the period is due to be paid. The cash interest payment is as reported for the most recent year in the statement of cash flows or footnotes. Modified net working capital is computed as cash and equivalents plus accounts receivable plus inventories minus accounts payable and accrued expenses minus income taxes payable. Added back to free cash flow are the cash interest and lease payments to arrive at the multiple. I penalize cost of capital if the sum of modified net working capital plus free cash flow is not at least three times the annual payments. If a company does not have net liquid assets plus free cash flow in excess of three times the payments, its fixed-charge coverage becomes questionable for certain entities. Deterioration in the trend is a more important credit determinant in setting the appropriate markup in the cost of capital. This is an important metric in my credit analysis and has been found to be particularly effective at diagnosing upcoming credit distress.

Debt Covenants

Debt covenants pertaining to the entity's most restrictive requirements must be calculated in each reporting period, and all covenants that are disclosed must be reviewed for closeness to violation. Each quarter I determine which debt, income, working-capital, and other covenants might be exposed over the coming two years. If the entity might be required to raise capital to reduce leverage to avoid violating a condition, the likelihood of such a raise must be appraised, as should the need for and probability for success of (including cure resulting from) an asset sale. The violation of a covenant requires the assistance of investors and creditors, and thus the relationship with such parties also must be assessed. Although some covenant violations are relatively easier to cure than others, such as a violation caused by a change in an accounting standard, the entity must stand ready to address remedies to any current or future violation.

The effect and possibility of cross-defaults must be explored, including an examination of the entity's holders of debt securities should the possibility of breach exist. Any forebearance issued would result in a large penalty to the cost of capital. If the entity is unable to bring its debt payments current, foreclosure and bankruptcy are imminent. Even if the entity can satisfy its creditors, this often comes at a large cost to equity holders.

If the analyst believes that more likely than not a violation will occur and a remedy will be questionable, the entity's cost of capital would be marked up at least 2 percentage points, with the amount depending on the severity and likelihood of a cure. If a probable violation could result in bankruptcy, the markup to the cost of capital could be in excess of 20 percentage points. At this stage, analysis becomes one of asset and liquidation values and reorganization cost estimates rather than the metrics covered in this chapter.

Operating Leases/Total Debt

This item represents the percentage increase to total debt if the off-balance-sheet liability created by operating leases would have been treated as balance-sheet debt. To capitalize the operating leases, I discount to the present each annual lease payment for the next five years using an appropriate discount rate. If necessary, I adjust the minimum lease obligations to a more realistic requirement, allowing for probable growth. I then divide this amount by total debt, as defined. The entry is the percentage increase in total debt owing to the capitalization of operating leases. Ignoring this off-balance-sheet liability may severely understate the financial leverage of a company. When this item results in an increase in total debt of over 10 percent or operating leases continue to grow as a percentage of total debt, a markup in the cost of capital is warranted because normally weaker credits will grow their operating lease obligations. If total debt coverage is adequate (greater than three times modified working capital plus free cash flow as defined previously), no markup will result. All leases, including synthetic leases through an SPE, are used for this calculation, if not consolidated with the leased assets for use by the entity.

Apple is flagged in the report owing to its growth in operating leases; however, the company is seeing a moderate penalty (0.2) to the cost of capital because the total value of all operating leases ($1.9 billion), before discounting, represents a small percentage of available liquidity.

Pension Underfunding/Total Debt

Defined-benefit pension plans are sometimes underfunded; that is, the assets in the plans are insufficient to cover the pension obligations. However, because of accounting rules, this underfunding may not be captured on the balance sheet, and in some cases, the balance sheet may show an asset for prepayment of pension benefits, even though the plans are underfunded. SFAS 158, *Employers' Accounting for Defined Benefit Pension and Other Postretirement Benefits*, effective December 31, 2006, requires an employer to recognize the funded status of each of its defined-benefit pension and postretirement plans as a net asset or liability The discount rates or salary assumptions may be altered, allowing for an improvement when such is not warranted. See Chapter 6 for more detail.

This item compares the balance-sheet (or footnote) reporting of the pension asset/liability to the actuarial estimates of the accumulated and projected benefit obligations. To the extent that the actuarial estimates indicate that the net funded status of the company is worse than reported on the balance sheet, the difference is divided by total debt. The entry reports the percentage increase in total debt owing to the pension liability. Total debt consists of short- and long-term debt. Ignoring this off-balance-sheet liability may severely understate the financial leverage of a company. I flag this item and penalize the cost of capital if the increase in total debt is greater than 10 percent.

S&P Commercial Paper Rating

The entry reports the S&P rating of the company's commercial paper (if it is rated by S&P). If the rating is below A2 or has deteriorated from the prior reporting period, I penalize the cost of capital. SEC Regulation 2(a)7 severely restricts lower-rated commercial paper from being held by U.S. money-market funds. It is important for many firms to have open access to the commercial paper markets and rely on this low-cost capital to fund their ongoing operations. A downgrade or closing of this capital outlet could have serious implications for a firm's cost of equity, including the possible forced sale of equity or strategic assets. The commercial paper market normally is open only to large institutional investors and, as such, is not as reliable as the long-term debt markets.

S&P Senior Debt Rating

This entry reports the S&P rating of the company's senior debt (if it is rated by S&P). If the rating is below A– or has deteriorated from the prior reporting period, the cost of capital is marked up. *Credit-rating agencies may have confidential access to information shared by the enterprise that is not reflected in current risk assessment.* The lower the credit rating, the greater is the penalty assessment because the credit rating has a significant effect on the cost of doing business. For example, many companies selling outside the United States rely on their credit rating when basing their purchase decisions. Other companies have their cost of debt significantly raised or lowered owing to a change in their credit rating, whereas financial and regulated companies may be required to commit more capital to subsidiaries if their ratings are lowered. Also, ratings affect the entity's supplier and customer decisions regarding their willingness to supply or order if the ratings change.

If a customer's ratings are lowered, its business could be negatively affected. Adverse downgrades could require additional collateral to be placed with creditors and counterparties. The effect of a change in the credit rating on cost of capital will vary from insignificant to very significant.

Standard and Poor's Ratings: Long-Term-Issuer Credit Rating

Long-Term Issuer Credit Ratings

AAA

An obligor rated AAA has an extremely strong capacity to meet its financial commitments. AAA is the highest issuer credit rating assigned by S&Ps.

AA

An obligor rated AA has a very strong capacity to meet its financial commitments. It differs from the highest-rated obligors only to a small degree.

A

An obligor rated A has a strong capacity to meet its financial commitments but is somewhat more susceptible to the adverse effects of changes in circumstances and economic conditions than obligors in higher-rated categories.

BBB

An obligor rated BBB has an adequate capacity to meet its financial commitments. However, adverse economic conditions or changing circumstances are more likely to lead to a weakened capacity of the obligor to meet its financial commitments.

BB, B, CCC, and CC

Obligors rated BB, B, CCC, and CC are regarded as having significant speculative characteristics. BB indicates the least degree of speculation and CC the highest. While such obligors likely will have some quality and protective characteristics, these may be outweighed by large uncertainties or major exposures to adverse conditions.

BB

An obligor rated BB is less vulnerable in the near term than other lower-rated obligors. However, it faces major ongoing uncertainties and exposure to adverse business, financial, or economic conditions that could lead to the obligor's inadequate capacity to meet its financial commitments.

B

An obligor rated B is more vulnerable than the obligors rated BB, but the obligor currently has the capacity to meet its financial commitments. Adverse business, financial, or economic conditions likely will impair the obligor's capacity or willingness to meet its financial commitments.

CCC

An obligor rated CCC is currently vulnerable and is dependent on favorable business, financial, and economic conditions to meet its financial commitments.

CC

An obligor rated CC is currently highly vulnerable.

Plus (+) or minus (−)

The ratings from AA to CCC may be modified by the addition of a plus (+) or minus (–) sign to show relative standing within the major rating categories.

R

An obligor rated R is under regulatory supervision owing to its financial condition. During the pendency of the regulatory supervision, the regulators may have the power to favor one class of obligations over others or pay some obligations and not others. Please see S&P's issue credit ratings for a more detailed description of the effects of regulatory supervision on specific issues or classes of obligations.

SD and D

An obligor rated SD (selective default) or D has failed to pay one or more of its financial obligations (rated or unrated) when it came due. A D rating is assigned when S&P believes that the default will be a general default and that the obligor will fail to pay all or substantially all of its obligations as they come due. An SD rating is assigned when S&P believes that the obligor has selectively defaulted on a specific issue or class of obligations, excluding those that qualify as regulatory capital, but that it will continue to meet its payment obligations on other issues or classes of obligations in a timely manner. A selective default includes the completion of a distressed exchange offer, whereby one or more financial obligations is either repurchased for an amount of cash or replaced by other instruments having a total value that is less than par.

NR

An issuer designated NR is not rated.

In Chapter 6, Table 6–6 listed the key financial metrics under which S&P credit ratings fall. If a company under analysis has seen its credit ratios fall below several of the median credit ranges as set forth in the table, it could be subject to a downgrade along with a substantial rise in its cost of debt and equity capital. If it is apparent that capitalization is weak for the rating, a downgrade is often the result. The analyst therefore should monitor the firm in relation to the ratios in the table because a ratings change most likely would result in a significant revaluation of the equity multiple owing to a reassessment of risk, including causing stock sales by pension funds that may only own securities possessing a minimum credit grade.

Increase in Benefit (Health Care) Expense

As burdensome as the pension expense is for many entities, an inescapable and significant expense for almost all public companies is health care costs. The entity is flagged with the metric resulting in a penalty to the cost of capital if the expense for expected health care benefits has increased from the prior year or has increased in at least two of the most recent three years at rate greater than total compensation expense. Increasing expenses for health care benefits indicate increases in the liability for future payments. Because health care costs can increase quickly, this item is important in assessing the financial obligations of the firm. Of particular sensitivity are companies that assume a large percentage of the increase in such costs, firms with a quickly growing labor force or a high ratio of retired/active employees, and firms with a high percentage of their workforce under labor unions.

Companies can increase their free cash flow by putting into effect changes to their employee benefit plans, including the elimination of benefits. These entities can see reductions to their cost of capital on recognition of the savings, if material. For instance, elimination of drug reimbursement to retirees who would be covered by Medicare and Medicaid has added to cash flows for companies that otherwise would have seen impairments owing to a loss in the tax subsidy under the federal health care act.

Example:

Effective July 1, 2007, the company amended its nonpension postretirement plan to discontinue the subsidy for medical and dental insurance premiums. In connection with this amendment and curtailment of benefits, the company recorded a gain of $3.7 million in its fiscal 2007 consolidated statement of operations. This gain recognizes the $4.0 million reduction to benefit obligations listed in the preceding table net of fiscal 2007 actuarial losses totaling $0.3 million.

Source: JDS Uniphase 2009 10K.

Health Care Cost Trend Rate

Health care cost trends often result in significant expense, especially for entities which have promised its current and retired population benefits above those that may be required by law. When health care cost inflation exists, it can result in a significant liability to an enterprise, both in terms of cash flows and on the postretirement benefits obligation.

If the projected trend rate is understated so that a one percentage point increase either lowers its normalized (3 or 4 year) free cash flow by 5 percent or greater, or increases the projected benefit obligation by 5 percent, the item results in a penalty. To determine the probability of an understated trend forecast, analysis versus a peer group having a similar workforce as well as health care cost increases announced by insurance companies, would be taken into account.

Increase in Postretirement Benefit (Health Care) Liability

This item results in a penalty if the balance-sheet liability for expected health care benefits to retirees has increased in the most recent year from the prior year or has increased in at least two of the most recent three years, adjusted for an increase in the total compensation expense. Increasing liabilities for health care benefits indicate increases in expected future payments to retirees. Because health care costs can accelerate quickly, this item is important in the determination of financial leverage of the firm and in assessing cash flows. Of particular sensitivity are companies with an aging labor force, many retirees, and labor-intensive operations. For more information, see Chapter 6, where pensions and postretirement expenses are discussed. Under SFAS 158, healthcare obligations require recognition on the sponsor's balance sheet, and can cause a significant or unplanned drain to cash flows, including if the entity steps up funding. This could result in lower fixed-charge coverage, increased debt, and reductions in capital spending or available cash for other productive uses. The actuarial assumptions of the plan, listed in the 10K, must be reviewed because payments represent a call on cash flows. If the entity uses liberal assumptions, historical and current cash flows will be overstated. An analysis should include the magnitude of increase in non-U.S. health care costs because they may be less subject to control. The effects of inflation also must be considered on the projected obligation and benefit expense.

Credit Spread

This metric compares the company's long-term (minimum 10 years) debt yield relative to similarly dated maturity Treasury instruments and other similar-grade credits, the gap representing the risk (cost) to the firm associated with its credit in the marketplace. The greater the spread, the greater is the cost of debt, thus increasing the leverage (risk), weighted-average cost of capital, and cost of equity. Cost to the firm is lost financial flexibility if the spread increases or additional flexibility if the spread falls. The firm's cost to acquire its outstanding debt will be affected by the spread.

Where the entity has outstanding long-term bonds that are not actively traded, a surrogate spread index measure is used with an appropriate markup/down based on the entity's implied rating, based on Table 6-6**.** Where no long-term fixed-income instruments exist and the entity has three times modified working capital plus normalized free cash flow to interest and lease expenses, no penalty is assessed for this metric, although one may be assessed for the following metric. If it is unlikely that the firm will need to raise capital (equity or debt) within the coming two years, including the extension of existing debt maturities, no penalty is assessed. The next metric addresses these entities.

Even when investors are incorrect in their market judgment, resulting in a widening of the yield spread, the extra cost to the firm gives rise to an increase to the cost of equity capital. As discussed in Chapter 6, credit spreads present real-time market information that provides useful data that may not yet be reflected in an entity's financial filings. As seen during the worldwide financial crisis, credit spreads increased significantly and returned to normal levels notably prior to fundamentally reported changes. The spread narrowing brought credit relief to many hundreds of companies, whereas the increase in spreads cost them many billions of dollars in extra cost. The effect on the cost of capital resulting from increased credit spreads took hold several quarters prior to both credit-rating agency changes and observed credit deterioration from financial filings. As yield spreads closed, equity multiples expanded.

A penalty is accessed for each 25 basis point widening of the entity's long-term or comparable-maturity U.S. Treasuries. If the entity's long-term bonds yielded 400 basis points to maturity over U.S. government bonds, the markup could be up to 200 points. Normally my model uses up to half the difference because many of the factors accounting for the spread are captured in other metrics. Only if the quoted price of the issuer's fixed obligations is not being fairly reflected would the gap be adjusted or the following metric used. Common sense must be applied. If the yield spread falls to that level observed by higher credits, the cost of capital accordingly should be reduced.

Yield Spread Index

This measure captures the interest-rate yield spread for entities that either do not have long-term bonds outstanding and therefore the long-term-debt yield spread is unable to be calculated, where the entity's fixed-income securities are inactive or not publicly traded or when there are no observable yields of similar long-dated securities. Where no fixed-income instruments exist and it is not probable that the entity will be active in the capital markets within the coming 12 months, and the entity has three times modified working capital plus normalized free cash flow to interest and lease expenses, a penalty is assessed as the spread over its implied credit rating increases, with adjustments for each 25 basis points, based on the surrogate index of high-grade contracts or a more representative index that approximates the entity's credit.

A firm's cost of equity can rise or fall owing to changes in the perceived risk for the market as a whole. Even companies rated AA or AAA could see their cost of capital rise if the general health of the economy is deteriorating; that is, yield spreads, in general, are widening. One manner of evaluating this metric for investment-grade firms such as Apple is via the Chicago Board of Trade CDR Investment Grade Derivatives Index. As shown in the following chart, overall risk jumped almost threefold for the high-grade index during the height of the credit crisis as capital all but dried up for even those high credits, resulting in a rapid ascent in the cost of capital. These AAA credits, according to the chart, would have seen a 200 basis point increase to their cost of capital over an 8-month period. Other such baskets exist for other credits.

U.S. Investment-Grade Index

Source: Credit Derivatives Research.

Even though the entity may have no need to raise debt, a rise in yield spreads affects the cost of capital for all firms that may not be reflected in the risk-free rate because U.S. government securities are normally bid up during times of economic and financial stress. For example, as depicted in the chart, the 200 basis point increase between August 2008 and February 2009 would have raised Apple's cost of equity by 150 basis points, half the difference. By August, it would have resulted in a 50 basis point penalty. If Apple had been a lower credit, its markup, despite its having no outstanding debt issue, could have been marked up greater than 100 basis points, in line with the spread in those credits, per the prior metric. This is common for new firms that have raised large amounts of equity and have a cash burn of less than three years.

Bloomberg LP, other data providers, and security trading exchanges track yields and yield spreads from which this variable may be reasonably estimated based on the credit or the implied credit gleaned from Table 6-6.

This metric is used only if the actual credit does not have an observable issue; otherwise, the prior metric is used.

Tax Metrics

The significance of taxes in cash-flow and credit analysis is often underestimated while differing from entity to entity. This set of metrics attempts to capture tax implications, relying on various views of analysis. The signals tax payments (refunds) and rates reveal are wide reaching, from the cash outlay of a tax payment to managerial operating decisions, such as a firm's geographic location, to the value of tax deductions of stock options on exercise. Many large U.S. companies manufacture and hold profits in low-cost jurisdictions while running many of their tax-deductable expenses (i.e., interest) domestically as a tax-saving maneuver. Transfer pricing schemes are also used to shift profits out of high-tax countries by trading between affiliated companies. The ability of an entity to hold onto a low tax rate should be evaluated, especially when non-U.S. income is an important contributor to total income and cash flow.

Regardless of the tax-minimization programs employed, it will be picked up by the actual tax payments, and hence the tax footnote section underscores all underlying business decisions and the financial condition of the firm.

An increase in the instability measures resulting from the granting of new tax credits or legislation should not, by itself, result in a penalty to the cost of capital. If, however, the instability results from operations, it would result in a markup to the cost of capital.

Extraordinary factors, even though they are not mentioned explicitly under each metric, are always considered to ensure that the result is a true representation of the credit health of the entity and its ability to return cash, through free cash flows, to shareholders.

Tax Expense/Pretax Income

The reported tax expense on the income statement is divided by the reported pretax income to calculate the effective reported tax rate of the firm. The entry represents the average tax rate over the most recent three years. It is flagged if it is lower than 20 percent or greater than 50 percent, indicating that the firm may be or was temporarily benefitting from credits or low (high) tax jurisdictions. It might indicate potential changes in free cash flow not generally assumed by investors. Some companies manufacture in and receive the benefit of various tax breaks associated with low-tax geographies. They also might hold cash in these jurisdictions, subject to a low rate. To the extent that such cash is repatriated back to the United States or Congress changes tax laws, cash flow will be affected. Of the tax metrics included in the model, this variable (effective tax rate) has the lowest weighting.

Tax Payment/Pretax Income

In this measure, the actual tax cash payment during the year (as reported in the statement of cash flows or footnotes) is divided by the reported pretax income to calculate an approximate (cash) tax rate of the firm. The entry represents the average (cash) tax rate over the most recent three years. It is penalized if it is lower than 20 percent or greater than 40 percent, indicating that the current tax payments deviate widely from a "normal" statutory rate. This may be due to some unusual items and require further study, including tax-loss carryforwards, timing differences, settlement of an IRS dispute, foreign tax credits, or use of last in, first out (LIFO) during rising prices. Of greater importance is the stability of the tax rate because an entity can receive the benefits of tax havens for long periods of time. Thus the stability of the tax rate has higher information content and is accorded a higher weighting.

Stability of the Tax Rate

This item measures the stability of the cash payments for taxes. Instability of cash flows and factors of operations likely translate into erratic tax payments and a higher cost of capital, although, as noted earlier, they could be due to extraneous factors such as foreign tax credits or settlement of a tax dispute. There is a strong relationship between cost of capital and an unstable tax rate. To measure the stability of tax payments, I examine the cash tax rate—the actual tax cash payment during the year (as reported in the statement of cash flows or footnotes)—divided by the reported pretax income. Normally, an entity whose tax rate changes less than 10 percent from year to year will not see its cost of equity capital marked up unless it is part of a long pattern of volatility.

Example:

Tables 8-16 through 8-18 for AMD, Texas Instruments, and IBM disclose their respective cash tax payments/pretax income. The tax payments are from each company's supplemental cash-flow information, with pretax income abstracted from the income statement. When assigning a rating to the tax payment/pretax income metric, I evaluate the cash rate compared with the statutory rate and also look at other firms in its industry to determine if a trend is industry-wide and perhaps due to new tax law or other event.

My model also will add back permanent timing differences to the pretax income where appropriate, such as certain amortizations, to arrive at the cash tax rate, but even this will be an approximation and not normally add much information depending on the entity under consideration. The taxes reported on the income statement are considered a current tax provision, not a real tax rate. An analyst cannot add back amortization to pretax income carte blanche because not all amortization results in a permanent timing difference. Amortization of goodwill under the purchase method is deductable for tax purposes, not book purposes, an example of a permanent timing difference. Thus, in most cases, I will divide cash taxes paid by pretax income as the cash rate.

As we see in the tables, IBM has the lowest standard deviation and highest average tax rate, followed by Texas Instruments and then AMD.

TABLE 8-16

Cash Tax Payments/Pretax Income: IBM

Ticker: ibm			Cutoff: 0%			
Company Name: INTL BUSINESS MACHINES CORP		**Industry Avg:**	**0.1295**	**CMP PROGRAMMING, DATA PROCESS**		
	txpd/ni	**% Change**	**Downside Volatility Only**	**% Change**	**Upside Volatility Only**	**% Change**
Y08	0.1712	−31.63%	0.1712	−31.63%		
Y07	0.2503	14.90%			0.2503	14.90%
Y06	0.2179	−13.31%	0.2179	−13.31%		
Y05	0.2513	15.33%			0.2513	15.33%
Y04	0.2179	−3.20%	0.2179	−3.20%		
Y03	0.2251	−56.24%	0.2251	−56.24%		
Y02	0.5144	74.31%			0.5144	74.31%
Y01	0.2951	−11.45%	0.2951	−11.45%		
Y00	0.3333	34.98%			0.3333	34.98%
Y99	0.2469	−19.01%	0.2469	(0.1901)		
Standard Deviation	**0.0959**	**0.3658**	**0.0407**	**0.1904**	**0.1243**	**0.2791**
AVERAGE	0.2723	0.0047	0.2290	(0.2247)	0.3373	0.3488
ST. DEV/AVE	0.35218047	77.94333652	0.177877107	−0.84731494	0.36840921	0.8000084

TABLE 8-17

Cash Tax Payments/Pretax Income: Texas Instruments, Inc.

Ticker:	txn		Cutoff:	0%			
Company Name: TEXAS INSTRUMENTS INC			Industry Avg:	0.1181	SEMICONDUCTOR, RELATED DEVICE		
	txpd/ni	% Change	Downside Volatility Only	% Change	Upside Volatility Only	% Change	
Y08	0.4021	45.75%			0.4021	45.75%	
Y07	0.2759	−34.56%	0.2759	−34.56%			
Y06	0.4216	65.77%			0.4216	65.77%	
Y05	0.2543	81.32%			0.2543	81.32%	
Y04	0.1402	−30.86%	0.1402	−30.86%			
Y03	0.2028	66.13%			0.2028	66.13%	
Y02	0.1221	130.30%			0.1221	130.30%	
Y01	(0.4030)	−200.85%	(0.4030)	−200.85%			
Y00	0.3996	35.71%			0.3996	35.71%	
Y99	0.2945	−26.02%	0.2945	(0.2602)			
Standard Deviation	**0.2402**	**0.9253**	**0.3272**	**0.8525**	**0.1251**	**0.3334**	
AVERAGE	0.2110	0.1327	0.0769	(0.7307)	0.3004	0.7083	
ST. DEV/AVE	1.13852339	6.972903146	4.25530737	−1.16672843	0.416553557	0.4706405	

TABLE 8-18

Cash Tax Payments/Pretax Income: AMD

Ticker:	amd		Cutoff:	0%		
Company Name: ADVANCED MICRO DEVICES			Industry Avg:	0.1181	SEMICONDUCTOR, RELATED DEVICE	
	txpd/ni	**% Change**	**Downside Volatility Only**	**% Change**	**Upside Volatility Only**	**% Change**
Y08	(0.0036)	53.85%			(0.0036)	53.85%
Y07	(0.0077)	92.49%			(0.0077)	92.49%
Y06	(0.1024)	−142.50%	(0.1024)	−142.50%		
Y05	0.2410	−34.53%	0.2410	−34.53%		
Y04	0.3681	1282.22%			0.3681	1282.22%
Y03	0.0266	133.60%			0.0266	133.60%
Y02	0.0114	101.01%			0.0114	101.01%
Y01	(1.1261)	−2506.01%	(1.1261)	−2506.01%		
Y00	0.0468	126.91%			0.0468	126.91%
Y99	(0.1739)	−561.74%	(0.1739)	(5.6174)		
Standard Deviation	**0.4019**	**9.4899**	**0.5858**	**11.5253**	**0.1456**	**4.8283**
AVERAGE	(0.0720)	(1.4547)	(0.2904)	(8.1119)	0.0736	2.9835
ST. DEV/AVE	−5.583270679	−6.523603453	−2.017644478	−1.42078306	1.978651258	1.618354

Tax Expense/Pretax Income—Most Recent Quarter

The reported quarterly tax expense on the income statement is divided by the reported quarterly pretax income to calculate the tax rate of the firm during the quarter. The entry represents the average effective quarterly tax rate of the most recent quarter and the same quarter in the prior two years. It is penalized if it is lower than 20 percent or greater than 50 percent or if it is 10 percent greater or lower than the prior year's period, exclusive of extraordinary factors. The analyst also should assess whether the entity has a patterned history of higher (lower) estimated tax rates early in its fiscal year followed by a reversal as the quarters evolve. This pattern indicates that cash flows are understated earlier in the fiscal year.

Miscellaneous Metrics

Country Code

Companies that are subject to certain jurisdictions may be riskier (political, currency, taxes) for investors than U.S.-based companies. This was acutely reflected during the fiscal crises in Greece during 2010, with almost immediate repercussions throughout Europe, Asia, and the United States. The resultant weakness in the euro impacted U.S. entities with operations in Europe or sold into that market with the U.S. dollar based goods. On the other hand, the price of oil dropped since its price is quoted in dollars. During the period the crisis was at its peak, many entities which had planned to enter the debt markets to raise capital were not able to do so. The conditions under which a company operates and has major facilities or markets will influence cash flows, consistency measures, and leverage. As we have seen, energy exploration companies have had their operations nationalized, whereas many companies have been harmed by high inflation outside the United States. If an entity receives a significant portion of its cash flows from a non-U.S. geography, the risk to those cash flows must be assessed, with a markup to the cost of capital where appropriate. This is especially true for companies operating in emerging markets, where a markup to the cost of capital is always made, even if the cash flows from those areas are currently strong and without incident.

All possible threats and the entity's sensitivity to any related factors must be considered, including sanctions, tariffs, threat of retaliation for U.S. government actions, stability of currency, exchange control, inflation, threat of neighboring countries, restrictions, and so on.

Qualified Audit Opinion

This item is flagged with a very large penalty to the cost of capital if the auditor issued an opinion that questioned the viability of the company as a going concern (usually issued when there is doubt that the firm can meet all its financial obligations in the next 12 months) or when the auditor cannot form an opinion on the financial statements for various reasons (e.g., restriction on the scope of the audit, lack of independence, etc.). A qualified audit opinion signals extreme risk unless there are extenuating circumstances.

Inflation[4]

Lower interest rates on the 10-year Treasury (risk-free rate) do not always lead to a lower cost of capital. This was seen clearly during 2008 as interest rates fell, yet the cost of capital rose because credits and cash flows weakened owing to the effects of the recession and illiquid credit markets. Conversely, higher rates may not always lead to a higher cost of capital because particular industries benefit from (the fear of) inflation and price increases relative to costs. Where the yield spread and risk-free rate do not capture inflation on the security level, it is reflected here.

Contrary to popular thinking, a rise in inflation cannot be overcome by a similar rise in revenues—it must be overcome by a similar rise in free cash flows, or cost of capital will increase. Also to be taken into account is the effect of inflation on capital to be replaced. If the cost of such capital has increased at a rate greater than the increase in free cash flows, this metric would result in a greater penalty. For this reason, when inflation is running higher than expected, the real ROIC often (unless overcome with margin improvement) falls below the cost of capital.

The inflation rate affects economic and business risk, including the value of balance-sheet inventory, which may be severely understated for firms using LIFO accounting. And, as history has shown (see the following figure), the impact of inflation is not always divined accurately in the risk-free rate, which is used as the beginning building block for the cost-of-equity-capital model. Also, the inflation rate and the expected rate of inflation affect firms differently, and thus this metric may need to be adjusted for those groups. Enterprises with high leverage and sensitivity to commodity price swings, or enterprises that own significant investments whose values are tied (directly or indirectly) to interest-rate levels, will be more greatly affected by changes in the expected rate of inflation than entities that can pass along its consequences, such as some utilities.

---

[4] The Federal Reserve banks have studied various models' ability to forecast inflation and the risk-free rate, including investor forecasts of the implied inflation rate, as measured by nominal yields, compared with those offered by TIPS. The conclusions are mixed. For one such study, see the Federal Reserve Bank of Dallas, "Accounting for the Bond Yield Conundrum," *Economic Letter—Insights*, Vol. 3, No 2, February 2008.

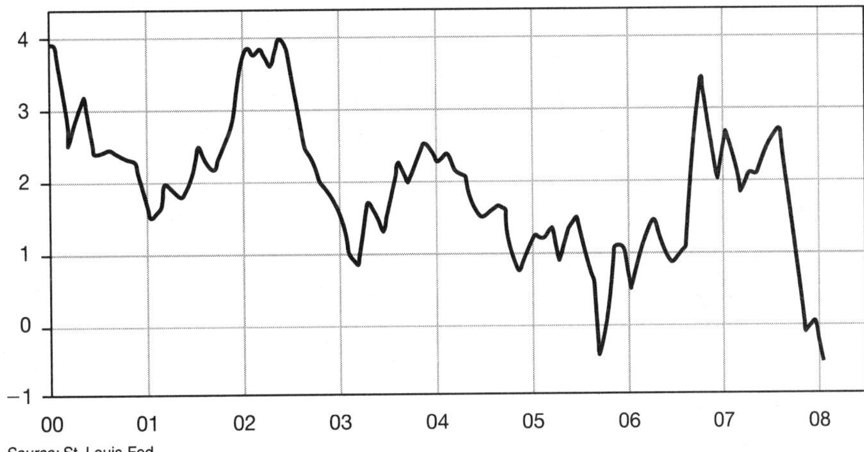

Source: St. Louis Fed.

Normally, I would raise the cost of capital by half the difference between the consumer price index (CPI) and the 10-year Treasury bond, recognizing the effect of real interest rates in the cost structure and effects on cash flow of such entities, whether directly for borrowers, their clients, or the ultimate consumer. For example, if the CPI-U were currently 3 percent and 10-year Treasury bonds yielded 5 percent, I would add 1 percentage point to the cost of capital. If the CPI were higher than the current 10-year note, this metric is ignored, unless very unusual circumstances exist, such as that which took place during the early 1980s. This measure is intended to adjust for the effects of inflation on an entity's cash flows not properly reflected in the risk-free rate, not its borrowing costs, which are covered under the yield spread.

Other effects of inflation are also picked up in the health care trend rate and cost of sales stability, and thus care should be exercised not to double count.

Auditor Change

This item is flagged and always results in an increase in the cost of capital unless the change is due to a merger of either the entity or the auditing firm. Special circumstances are considered, such as a negative event associated with the auditor. Because of the high costs incurred in a first-time audit engagement, auditors usually are replaced very infrequently. A change in auditor may be caused by disagreements with the prior auditor, material weakness, or because the prior auditor assessed the audit risk as being too great and dropped the client. However, it also can occur because the firm has decided to replace its auditor periodically to improve the independent verification process. The reason for an auditor change must be established if no reason is given in the Form 8K or other filing. If the change is due to a disagreement, the charge to the cost of capital will be large and almost always will result in a total cost of capital that is higher than for the median entity because the financial statements and footnotes could be compromised.

This item will be result in a penalty if there has been a change in the auditor within the past two years or one is anticipated for reasons related to the enterprise.

Growth in Finished Goods Inventory > Growth in Sales

This item represents the growth rate of finished goods inventories from the prior year (or total inventories, if finished goods inventories are unavailable) minus the growth of sales from the prior year. If it is positive, it may indicate that the firm has excess inventory that it cannot sell or problems in inventory management. This item is flagged and results in a penalty if the growth rate in inventory exceeds that of sales in the most recent year or in two of the most recent three years. No penalty will be assessed if inventory is not a useful predictor of future operating cash flows.

Inventories can be used to raise cash when demand is softening by not producing back to former levels. Care must be taken if goods are dumped into the market, having the effect of tarnishing a brand image or lessening consumers' desire to pay full price on future merchandise. If such is the case, it should be reflected here with a slight markup to the cost of capital. Adjustment will be made if the metric is biased owing to accounting method.

Growth in Total Inventory > Growth in Sales

This item represents the growth rate of quarterly total inventory from the prior quarter minus the growth of quarterly sales from the prior quarter. If it is positive, it may indicate that the firm has excess inventory that it cannot sell or problems in inventory management. This item is flagged if the growth rate in inventory exceeds that of sales in the most recent quarter and may result in a penalty depending on the importance of the quarter or on inventory as a predictor of cash flow and credit.

Inventory draw can be used to raise cash when demand is softening. Care must be taken if goods are dumped into the market, having the effect of tarnishing a brand image or lessening consumers' desire to pay full price on future merchandise. Adjustment will be made if the metric is biased owing to accounting method.

Extraordinary Items

This item represents the percentage of extraordinary items on the income statement (whether positive or negative) to operating cash flow unless it is reversed under that activity. It is flagged if the absolute value of extraordinary items exceeds 5 percent of the absolute value of operating cash flows. If extraordinary items represent such a significant proportion of operating cash flows, a further investigation into the quality of operating cash flows, durability of and implications for prospective operating cash flows, and stability measures are warranted. This normally would result in a minor penalty unless part of a trend.

When real estate prices are high, industrial and other enterprises whose primary business is not real estate may continually sell off parcels, and investors come to expect these sales to provide a flow of cash. These firms' cost of capital often does not reflect the potential instability of their operating results. When property prices fall, so too do the stock prices of these companies because the sellers of the stock did not recognize a risk that is manifested in every economic cycle.

Pension Gain

This item represents the percentage of pension plan net gains to pretax income. Typically, pension plans represent an expense to the company because employees have earned additional benefits for an additional year of service to the firm. However, in some cases, the pension plan investments yield a high rate of return that exceeds the additional benefits owed to employees for the additional year of service, and the pension expense becomes pension income (gain). Also, changes in actuarial assumptions may create a pension gain. If pretax income has increased from such pension gains in the most recent year or in two of the most recent three years, this item is flagged and may result in a slight markdown to the cost of capital because the risk of a large liability is reduced.

Interest Income

This item represents the ratio of interest income to pretax income, operating cash flow, and free cash flow. A firm may be penalized if this ratio exceeds 5 percent for either measure for the most recent year or for at least two of the most recent three years. A high contribution of interest income may indicate lower quality of cash flows by many investors who would lower their valuation measures, especially if the ROIC is below the cost of capital. There is the risk of the cash being poorly deployed. Since I do not include interest income in my ROIC, it does not affect that measure.

Apple is assessed a 0.2 penalty owing to it having 9 percent of pretax income as interest income.

Significant Acquisitions

This item is flagged if the company engaged in a significant acquisition(s) during the current year or in at least two of the most recent three years. A *significant acquisition* is defined as an acquisition that contributed at least 10 percent to total sales or if the consideration for the acquired companies exceeded 20 percent of current market value. Larger acquisitions result in a greater penalty.

Acquisitions typically are value-destroying undertakings for shareholders and are considered a negative signal for shareholders and creditors.[5] Many companies look on acquisitions as a growth strategy without a clear plan for synergies and the creation of additional free cash flow. Most acquirers overpay. While financially flexible firms often have the capacity for acquisitions during economic downturns, when prices would be lower, they most often wait for economic expansion. The most successful business combinations are those which build on established core competencies.

Underperforming entities that attempt to improve their performance by buying well-regarded competitors normally run into trouble because a "best practices" approach typically succeeds when both parties to an acquisition are already successful.

This metric is the average contribution of acquisitions to sales in the most recent three years or the three-year average consideration for acquisitions divided by current market value at the time of the acquisition or business combination.

There are many notable examples of large companies failing in a business combination: AT&T's purchase of NCR, Time Warner's purchase of AOL, Applied Material's acquisition of Etec, and Daimler's acquisition of Chrysler. In each of these cases, the entity being acquired had a cost of capital in excess of its ROIC.

When final demand in a particular industry shows signs of slowing or firms have excess cash on their balance sheets, it is not unusual to see merger activity pick up. At this stage, most failed mergers take place.

But not all mergers are value-destroying. Acquisitions grounded on cash flow, as opposed to "filling in gaps" or shortfalls in revenues or product, have a greater probability of success. And if the acquirer can easily reduce the cost structure, free cash flow can increase significantly, lowering the cost of capital. Exxon's purchase of Mobil resulted in points deducted from the cost of capital.

---

[5] Many mergers are initiated because of perceived synergies that were believed would result in enhanced cash flows. Mark Sirower, however, in his book, *The Synergy Trap: How Companies Lose the Acquisition Game*, has shown otherwise. In this book, Sirower found that two-thirds of deals destroyed shareholder value. Robert Eccles, Kersten Lanes, and Thomas Wilson, in "Are You Paying Too Much for That Acquisition?" (*Harvard Business Review* 1999), stated that "well over half of mergers and acquisitions failed to create their expected value" and "in 59% of the deals, the total market-adjusted return of the acquiring company went down on announcement. That means the market thought the deal would destroy rather than create value for the shareholders." A McKinsey study of more than 100 mergers in Britain and the United States in the 1990s found that about 60 percent earned returns on capital less than the cost of capital and that only a quarter of acquisitions ever recovered the costs of the merger. A 2003 KPMG study of about 100 companies found that 34 percent of deals added value and 32 percent destroyed it.

Some of the more easily cut costs are duplicative departments and cost savings in key expense areas, such as finance and treasury, advertising, technology, insurance, and employee benefits. Manufacturing, including the supply chain and transportation, also can result in significant savings. If the acquired entity has been mismanaged, new management can quickly turn the cash flows in a positive direction.

Successful business combinations are marked by experienced managers who have shown a history of success with such integration. When this is the case, the merged entities combine various departments and put additional pressure on vendors for cost savings. Difficulties are overcome more easily because experienced teams work together toward a common goal, pulling in employees who can solve unique problems. Vendors often feel obligated to cut their selling prices under the fear of losing the relationship. Landlords are also under pressure to hold back increases as leases come up for renewal because good, strong tenants are often difficult to replace and also act as a draw to the property. It is thus important that the analyst weigh the effect of a business combination on tertiary parties. If a supplier is weakened resulting from a business combination, the price for an important input could rise.

Decrease in Order Backlog

This item is flagged if the order backlog decreased from the prior year. Such a decrease may indicate that future sales and cash flows could decrease as well, and the company's financial conditions may deteriorate. The significance of the order backlog varies and must be assigned by the analyst. It can range from very important, such as with entities requiring long lead times to complete the production process (Boeing), to unimportant.

Reinvestment Indicator

This item indicates the extent of reinvestment of the company in its fixed assets. It is calculated as the three-year sum of capital expenditures minus the three-year sum of depreciation and amortization. It is flagged when it is negative, indicating that the company may not be replenishing the operating capacity it loses owing to depreciation and amortization. This variable must be evaluated in light of outsourcing, manufacturing efficiencies, and supply-chain improvements. It will result in a penalty if it imparts adverse information regarding the entity's cash flows.

Reinvestment Indicator–Most Recent Quarter

This item indicates the extent of reinvestment of the company in its fixed assets in the most recent quarter. It is calculated as the sum of quarterly capital expenditures in the most recent quarter and the same quarter in the prior two years minus the quarterly depreciation and amortization in the same quarters. It is flagged when it is negative, indicating that the company may not be replenishing the operating capacity it loses owing to depreciation and amortization. This variable must be evaluated in light of outsourcing, manufacturing efficiencies, and supply-chain improvements. Its weighting is normally low and will only result in a penalty if of significance to the entity.

Ability to Pay Dividends from Operating Cash Flow

Companies tend to maintain dividends at a constant level and increase cash dividends only when future operating cash flows warrant such an increase. A dividend decrease is interpreted as a negative signal for the firm's prospects because often, operating decisions are made with the dividend in mind. Companies sometimes borrow funds to sustain the cash dividend at its current level if operating cash flows deteriorate and there is a belief that current conditions are temporary. Operating cash flows that are insufficient to pay existing dividends imply additional borrowing and additional financial risk because shareholders' equity declines in relation to the uncovered dividend. This item is flagged if net operating cash flow was insufficient for dividend payments in any of the most recent five years, with the penalty graduating for each additional reporting period (including interim reporting periods).

Dividends that are omitted or reduced, providing needed cash that helps the entity to navigate a difficult operating environment, are viewed as a positive development. In most cases, the financial markets anticipate a dividend cut some time in advance.

Pension Fund–Assumed Return on Assets Increased from the Prior Year

This item represents the change in one of the most fundamental assumptions made by actuaries in calculating the pension liability and expense. The assumed rate of return on pension plan assets forecasts the growth of these assets, which will be used to satisfy future obligations to retirees. If the firm increases the assumed long-term rate of return on pension plan assets, it forecasts larger available future assets to satisfy the liability, as well as lower current expenses. This may be done in an effort to increase earnings and operating cash flows (via lower contributions) and lower liabilities and should be investigated in more depth. The item is flagged if the assumed rate increased from the prior year.

Pension Fund–Assumed Rate of Salary Increases/Decreases from the Prior Year

This item represents the change in one of the most fundamental assumptions made by actuaries in calculating the pension liability and expense. The assumed rate of salary increases determines the amount of future benefits that the company will have to pay its retirees because pension benefits are often calculated on the basis of the average salary prior to retirement. A decrease in the rate causes the pension expense and liability to decrease. A change may be assumed in an effort to increase earnings and operating cash flows and lower liabilities and should be investigated in more depth. To the extent that an inappropriate change occurs, cash flows are overstated. The item is penalized if the assumed rate decreased from the prior year or there was an increase in the spread between the investment and salary assumptions. The entry represents the most recent rate assumed by the company compared with the prior year. In the following template, Wyerhaeuser assumed no change in its salary assumption.

Example:

As Table 8-19 shows, Weyerhaeuser's (WY) pension plan's funding weakened as a result of the recession, losing almost $2 billion in plan asset market value, thus placing its plans into an underfunded status from being overfunded the year before. Although WY reduced its expected return on plan assets, the discount rate (Table 8-19) is still higher than it was during the bull market. Therefore, the company contributed over $100 million additional cash into the plans over the prior year. As a result of the new, higher funding requirements caused by fund underperformance, the cost of capital would be marked up. Given WY's weak free cash flow during the past three years, the cash required to be placed into its pension plans is significant. Plan underfunding is also confounded by the large weighting of the plan in alternative investments, as shown.

TABLE 8-19

Pension Plan Data: Weyerhaeuser

Annual data as of:	Y08	Y07	Y06
Benefit Obligation			
Vested Benefits	@NA	@NA	@NA
Accumulated Benefit Obligation	4,200.000	4,400.000	5,000.000
Pension Plan Assets			
Beginning Plan Assets	6,853.000	6,567.000	5,643.000
Acutal Return	(1,972.000)	777.000	888.000
Employer Contributions	28.000	36.000	67.000
Participant Contributions	0.000	0.000	3.000
Benefits Paid (–)	544.000	496.000	354.000
Other	(233.000)	(177.000)	2.000
Plan Assets	4,132.000	6,707.000	6,249.000
Pension- Funded Status	(294.000)	1,914.000	843.000

(Continued)

TABLE 8-19 *(Continued)*

Pension Plan Data: Weyerhaeuser

Annual data as of:	Y08	Y07	Y06
Balance Sheet Reconciliation			
Long-term Asset **	308.000	2,084.000	1,035.000
Current Liability (–) **	20.000	17.000	18.000
Long-term Liability (–)**	582.000	153.000	174.000
Pension- Funded Status	(294.000)	1,914.000	843.000
AOCI-Related			
Unrecognized Prior Service Cost	@NA	@NA	254.000
Other Adjustments	@NA	@NA	(277.000)
Net Pension Cost (Credit):			
Service Cost	98.000	129.000	147.000
Interest Cost	302.000	282.000	291.000
Return on Assets	(581.000)	(530.000)	(478.000)
Other Periodic Cost Components (Net)	75.000	96.000	58.000
Periodic Pension Cost	(106.000)	(23.000)	18.000
Pension Expense			
Pension Expense	(54.000)	30.000	90.000
Assumptions Used For Pension Plans			
Discount Rate			
Minimum	@NA	@NA	@NA
Maximum	@NA	@NA	@NA
Discount Rate	0.063	0.065	0.058
Conpensation Rate – Obligation			
Increase – Minimum	0.030	0.030	0.030
Increase – Maximum	0.035	0.035	0.035
Compensation Rate Increase	0.033	0.033	0.033
Asset Return Rate – Periodic Cost			
Minimum	0.048	@NA	@NA
Maximum	0.095	@NA	@NA
Asset Return Rate	0.071	0.095	0.095
Periodic Cost Discount Rate			
Discount Rate – Maximum	0.083	@NA	@NA
Discount Rate – Minimum	0.055	@NA	@NA
Discount Rate	0.069	0.058	0.059
Asset Allocation			
Asset Allocation – Debt	0.094	0.114	0.155
Asset Allocation – Equity	0.364	0.247	0.272
Asset Allocation – Real Estate	0.053	0.033	0.039
Asset Allocation – Other	0.489	0.606	0.534
Employer Contributions Expected Next Year	126.000	20.000	37.000

Source: Weyerhaeuser 10Ks.

Stability of COGS/Sales

This measure examines the firm's input costs and pricing power. During periods of price instability, it also will be a function of FIFO versus LIFO accounting, where the most recent costs are reflected in COGS. I attempt to exclude the depreciation component of COGS, if given, because doing so may better reflect the discretionary component.

Cost of sales includes direct costs of production but also may include some labor, rent, insurance, heat, and electric, among many other items. If the entity does not report a separate cost-of-sales line, other important input costs should be substituted in the numerator; such would be the case, for example, for fuel expenses for airlines, which do not report cost of sales. For other firms, it may be sales and marketing expense or R&D. Some firms may combine COGS, as Whole Foods does with occupancy costs. Since Apple does report COGS, I show it in the worksheet.

The greater the variability over periods of time, the less predictable will be the cash flows and the higher will be the cost of capital. When using the standard deviation of this measure, the analyst should include both 10 years of quarterly numbers and 10 years of annual numbers. Aside from a numerical solution, as is shown in Table 8-20, it is easy to "eyeball" the numbers because outliers are obvious. Changes in the cost of sales/sales must be evaluated to determine if input costs are rising, holding steady, or declining. As with all stability measurements, judgment is required, especially for recent events that may temporarily force up an important cost.

When this metric remains in a fairly narrow range for a long time period and then falls out in either direction, it normally reverts back to its mean. Entities that can permanently reduce this ratio relative to their peer group place themselves at a distinct competitive advantage and will have their cost of capital lowered.

Tables 8-20 through 8-23 display historical (COGS/sales) ratios for Advanced Micro Devices (AMD) and Texas Instruments (TXN). The ratios' year-over-year percentage change is also calculated and classified as either decreasing ("Downside Volatility") or increasing ("Upside Volatility"). One preferably would like to see this ratio stable and declining. If this were the case, all observations would be classified as downside volatility (because COGS is an increasingly smaller percentage of sales), and the entity would not be penalized for instability.

The standard deviation, average, and coefficient of variation (standard deviation divided by the average) are also displayed for each series. Since the coefficient of variation is a normalized measure of dispersion, it provides a useful measure when comparing the volatility of one series with that of another. In the case of AMD and Texas Instruments, they have similar average COGS/sales ratios. However, AMD has exhibited greater instability (reflected by its coefficient of variation being more than double that of Texas Instruments). Seen in the comparison are, for AMD, four years when COGS/sales rose versus three for Texas Instruments, including twice by more than 20 percent.

TABLE 8-20

IBM: COGS/Sales Stability

Ticker:	ibm			Cutoff:	0%	
Company Name: INTL BUSINESS MACHINES CORP			Industry Avg:	12.7406	CMP PROGRAMMING, DATA PROCESS	
	COGS/SALE	% Change	Downside Volatility Only	% Change	Upside Volatility Only	% Change
Y08	0.5098	−3.30%	0.5098	−3.30%		
Y07	0.5271	−0.04%	0.5271	−0.04%		
Y06	0.5274	−3.03%	0.5274	−3.03%		
Y05	0.5438	−5.65%	0.5438	−5.65%		
Y04	0.5764	−0.53%	0.5764	−0.53%		
Y03	0.5795	−0.35%	0.5795	−0.35%		
Y02	0.5815	0.09%			0.5815	0.09%
Y01	0.5810	−0.19%	0.5810	−0.19%		
Y00	0.5821	3.04%			0.5821	3.04%
Y99	0.5649	−0.39%	0.5649	(0.0039)		
Standard Deviation	**0.0277**	**0.0238**	**0.0279**	**0.0206**	**0.0004**	**0.0209**
AVERAGE	0.5574	(0.0104)	0.5512	(0.0169)	0.5818	0.0157
ST. DEV/AVE	0.049773156	−2.301114479	0.050523437	−1.22445128	0.000759826	1.3354447

TABLE 8-21

AMD: COGS/Sales Stability

Ticker:	AMD		Cutoff:	0%		
Company Name: ADVANCED MICRO DEVICES		Industry Avg:	19.2722	SEMICONDUCTOR, RELATED DEVICE		
	COGS/SALE	% Change	Downside Volatility Only	% Change	Upside Volatility Only	% Change
Y08	0.4134	−8.51%	0.4134	−8.51%		
Y07	0.4519	23.55%			0.4519	23.55%
Y06	0.3657	−4.37%	0.3657	−4.37%		
Y05	0.3825	5.78%			0.3825	5.78%
Y04	0.3616	−4.43%	0.3616	−4.43%		
Y03	0.3783	−24.39%	0.3783	−24.39%		
Y02	0.5004	−0.65%	0.5004	−0.65%		
Y01	0.5036	20.84%			0.5036	20.84%
Y00	0.4168	−17.80%	0.4168	−17.80%		
Y99	0.5070	3.02%			0.5070	3.02%
Standard Deviation	**0.0586**	**0.1509**	**0.0518**	**0.0917**	**0.0583**	**0.1039**
AVERAGE	0.4281	(0.0070)	0.4060	(0.1003)	0.4612	0.1330
ST. DEV/AVE	0.136963263	−21.65477912	0.127678123	−0.91440755	0.126344196	0.7817057

TABLE 8-22

Texas Instruments, Inc.: COGS/Sales Stability

Ticker:	TXN		Cutoff:	0%		
Company Name: TEXAS INSTRUMENTS INC			**Industry Avg:**	**19.2722**	**SEMICONDUCTOR,RELATED DEVICE**	
	COGS/SALE	**% Change**	**Downside Volatility Only**	**% Change**	**Upside Volatility Only**	**% Change**
Y08	0.4144	5.50%			0.4144	5.50%
Y07	0.3928	−5.76%	0.3928	−5.76%		
Y06	0.4168	−0.05%	0.4168	−0.05%		
Y05	0.4170	−2.66%	0.4170	−2.66%		
Y04	0.4284	−0.69%	0.4284	−0.69%		
Y03	0.4314	0.53%			0.4314	0.53%
Y02	0.4291	−11.54%	0.4291	−11.54%		
Y01	0.4851	18.64%			0.4851	18.64%
Y00	0.4089	−1.10%	0.4089	−1.10%		
Y99	0.4134	−9.68%	0.4134	(0.0968)		
Standard Deviation	**0.0244**	**0.0845**	**0.0124**	**0.0460**	**0.0369**	**0.0936**
AVERAGE	0.4237	(0.0068)	0.4152	(0.0450)	0.4436	0.0822
ST. DEV/AVE	0.057482744	−12.40703917	0.02980174	−1.02406494	0.083188604	1.1379069

TABLE 8-23

IBM: COGS/Sales Stability

Ticker: ibm			Cutoff: 0%			
Company Name: INTL BUSINESS MACHINES CORP		**Industry Avg:**	**12.7406**	**CMP PROGRAMMING,DATA PROCESS**		
	COGS/SALE	**% Change**	**Downside Volatility Only**	**% Change**	**Upside Volatility Only**	**% Change**
Y08	0.5098	−3.30%	0.5098	−3.30%		
Y07	0.5271	−0.04%	0.5271	−0.04%		
Y06	0.5274	−3.03%	0.5274	−3.03%		
Y05	0.5438	−5.65%	0.5438	−5.65%		
Y04	0.5764	−0.53%	0.5764	−0.53%		
Y03	0.5795	−0.35%	0.5795	−0.35%		
Y02	0.5815	0.09%			0.5815	0.09%
Y01	0.5810	−0.19%	0.5810	−0.19%		
Y00	0.5821	3.04%			0.5821	3.04%
Y99	0.5649	−0.39%	0.5649	(0.0039)		
Standard Deviation	**0.0277**	**0.0238**	**0.0279**	**0.0206**	**0.0004**	**0.0209**
AVERAGE	0.5574	(0.0104)	0.5512	(0.0169)	0.5818	0.0157
ST. DEV/AVE	0.049773156	−2.301114479	0.050523437	−1.22445128	0.000759826	1.3354447

In only two years has IBM's COGS/sales ratio risen, and no times during the past six years because IBM has been very successful at taking advantage of outsourcing in all phases of its business, events captured under the table. IBM also has been successful at transforming itself into a software from a hardware company, with the former having greater profit margins, cash flow, and stability metrics.

Looking at the stability metrics of cost of sales/sales and free and operating cash flows, my model has me assign higher than market instability to AMD, average to Texas Instruments, and below average to IBM. AMD has shown greater volatility in all measures, although Texas Instruments also has shown some instability, especially in cost of sales/sales. Texas Instruments has exhibited positive operating and free cash flow in every year shown.

Example:

The analyst would need to be aware of any special factors influencing COGS. As written in the 2009 10K of Ulta Salon and Cosmetics, Inc., a very large beauty salon having over 300 locations:

> Our cost of sales may be negatively impacted as we open an increasing number of stores. We also expect that cost of sales as a percentage of net sales will be negatively impacted in the next several years as a result of accelerated depreciation related to our store remodel program. The program was adopted in third quarter fiscal 2006. We have accelerated depreciation expense on assets to be disposed of during the remodel process such that those assets will be fully depreciated at the time of the planned remodel. Changes in our merchandise mix may also have an impact on cost of sales.

Example:

Many industries owe their instability to changing input costs, resulting in a large negative impact to cash flows. Perhaps no industry, though, see's greater volatility in its input prices than the airlines. While a few airlines have been effective hedging that risk, most have not, resulting in a high number of bankruptcies.

High and volatile oil prices have been the nemesis of the airlines, with the industry, owing to its high capital intensity, decidedly leveraged. Aside from their capital intensity, airlines are labor intensive as well. Typically, fuel and wage expenses account for about half of industry revenues.

Delta's September 20, 2004, 10Q showed that fuel expense rose 63 percent when revenues rose just 6 percent.

				Percentage of Total
Year	**Gallons Consumed (Millions)**	**Cost[1] (Millions)**	**Average Price per Gallon[1]**	**Operating Expenses**
2001	2,649	$1,817	68.60¢	12%
2002	2,514	1,683	66.94	12
2003	2,370	1,938	81.78	14

[1]Net of fuel hedge gains under our fuel hedging program.

> Delta went on to state in its 10Q:
>
> Aircraft fuel expense increased 15% in 2003 compared to 2002. Total gallons consumed decreased 6% mainly due to capacity reductions. The average fuel price per gallon rose 22% to 81.78¢ as compared to 2002. Our fuel cost is shown net of fuel hedge gains of $152 million for 2003, $136 million for 2002, and $299 million for 2001. Approximately 65 percent, 56 percent, and 58 percent of our aircraft fuel requirements were hedged during 2003, 2002, and 2001, respectively. In February 2004, we settled all of our fuel hedge contracts prior to their scheduled settlement dates. For more information concerning the settlement of our fuel hedge contracts, see Note 22 of the Notes to the Consolidated Financial Statements.
>
> Our aircraft fuel purchase contracts do not provide material protection against price increases or assure the availability of our fuel supplies. We purchase most of our aircraft fuel from petroleum refiners under contracts that establish the price based on various market indices. We also purchase aircraft fuel on the spot market, from offshore sources and under contracts that permit the refiners to set the price.
>
> To attempt to reduce our exposure to changes in fuel prices, we periodically enter into heating and crude oil derivative contracts. Information regarding our fuel hedging program is set forth under Item 7. "Management's Discussion and Analysis of Financial Condition and Results of Operations—Market Risks Associated with Financial Instruments—Aircraft Fuel Price Risk" and in Notes 3 and 4 of the Notes to the Consolidated Financial Statements.
>
> Although we are currently able to obtain adequate supplies of aircraft fuel, it is impossible to predict the future availability or price of aircraft fuel. Political disruptions or wars involving oil-producing countries, changes in government policy concerning aircraft fuel production, transportation or marketing, changes in aircraft fuel production capacity, environmental concerns and other unpredictable events may result in fuel supply shortages and fuel price increases in the future
>
> Our results of operations can be significantly impacted by changes in the price and availability of aircraft fuel. The above table shows our aircraft fuel consumption and costs for 2001–2003.

In the September 2004 quarter, Delta's fuel expense rose to 18.3 percent of operating expenses from the prior year's 14 percent. As a result, Delta reported very large negative cash flows. The airline already had a higher cost of equity capital than Southwest Airlines, which essentia lly hedged much of the input cost risk.

Not all hedges work out. For instance, many gold producers hedge against declines in the price of the metal. When gold prices rise above the hedged price, the company's forfeit free cash flow but are willing to sacrifice opportunity profits for stability. As long as the entity is consistent in its hedging strategy, its cost of capital will benefit. The stability metrics will outweigh a temporary increase in free cash flows because investors prefer returns having less variability.

Major Customer or Supplier

If the loss or gain of a customer or supplier would affect cash flows by 5 percent or greater, the cost of capital would be affected. Even if the new customer results in a minor positive impact on free cash flow, it can result in greater brand recognition, leading to follow-on customers at greater margins. It also can weaken its competition and allow for higher resource utilization. Accepting a large contract at a loss normally would raise the cost of capital. An exception is if positive free cash flows were assured later in the contract or some other benefit was to be realized, such as follow-on customers or a contract renewal at greater margins.

If goods have already been shipped, the loss of a major customer could be severe because the accounts receivable may be uncollectable. Risk of such loss must be considered carefully, as should the risk of a competitor buying out an important supplier, which could affect the entity's ability to conduct business. The effect of loss of a supplier is an important consideration in risk analysis, although it does not occur as often as loss of a customer. As Biotrove, Inc., explained in its S1 registration statement, "If we were to lose this supplier, we would be required to obtain a license to certain intellectual property held by the supplier or redesign the cartridge. If we ran out of inventory before we could arrange for a new supply source, our ability to provide RapidFire services and products would be compromised."

The gain of a new low-cost supplier also would have a positive impact on free cash flow and hence the cost of capital.

Example:

Also, as described in Note 10, the company lost a major customer contract effective July 1, 2009 (see Note 10). This Contract contributed 43 percent of the company's revenue during the first half of 2009. As a result of the loss of this contract, the company anticipates substantially reduced cash flow over the balance of 2009, and throughout the first half of 2010, with the likely result that it will face difficulty meeting its future debt service and covenant requirements.

Source: PNG Ventures, Inc., August 13, 2009, 10Q.

Example:

Boeing's largest customer, ILFC, buys their aircraft and then leases the equipment to airlines. When AIG, the troubled insurer and ILFC's parent, ran into financial difficulties, ILFC was closed out of the markets for public debt and bank loans, affecting Boeing.

Example:

During the fourth quarter of 2009, WW Grainger wrote off an investment in India owing to loss of a supplier.

Insurance and Litigation

The role of insurance is an often underappreciated and underanalyzed area of security analysis that could affect the cost of capital if it were insufficient or its cost grew greater than the rate of growth in operating cash flows. Regarding uninsured losses, current accounting rules require a company to disclose "specific quantitative and qualitative information" about loss contingencies but does not require it to provide for the fair-value impact losses would have on earnings or cash flows. Insurance adequacy is, unfortunately, rarely discussed during investor conferences.

Needing to be uncovered are:

- How is the company protected in the event of major damage to its computer system or warehouse?
- What coverage is there for product liability?
- How is the company protected for a worst-case scenario in the event of a cyber attack or business interruption owing to a strike, fire, or power outage?
- Is key man life insurance required to attract a replacement executive?
- Is the company attempting to save cash by underinsuring?
- Does the firm require backup facilities or other redundancies? Are such redundancies adequate to allow the company to continue providing goods and service?

Example:

Murphy Oil had large uninsured damage affecting free cash flow during 2006: Uninsured damage, higher insurance premiums, settlement of class-action oil spill litigation, and other hurricane-related pretax costs in the company's North American operations were \$3.0 million in 2007 and \$107.3 million in 2006. The hurricane expense in 2007 was caused by a downward adjustment of expected insurance recoveries based on an updated loss limit published by the company's primary insurer.

Security analysts are typically late in their evaluation of insurance adequacy, relegating their questioning to an event that has already occurred or is forecast and necessitating a review. Not true for the entity itself. For this reason, all large companies have dedicated employees, if not departments, whose sole purpose is to handle the insurance for the organization. If not for insurance, many companies would have filed for bankruptcy, the policies allowing them to collect cash resulting from large lawsuit awards or other catastrophic events. Many firms with facilities on the Gulf Coast of Louisiana certainly would have been out of business as a result of damage from Hurricane Katrina had it not been for property and business-interruption insurance. If an entity not having the resources to cover potential claims exposes its productive capital by being underinsured, its cost of capital should be increased.

Companies have lost large awards resulting from nonawareness of legal liabilities predating their acquisition of a business and for which they did not possess adequate insurance coverage. Other times, new scientific studies determined that a company was selling a product that was later found to be unsafe. Such was the case with asbestos, which drove scores of previously financially healthy companies into bankruptcy, including Armstrong World Industries, which did not recognize the problem at its asbestos division at the time it was purchased. In fact, the U.S. government, at the time Armstrong acquired the company, required that its buildings *contain* asbestos. Armstrong was a very strong and consistent producer of free cash flow, but eventually the asbestos liabilities became too great for its balance sheet and calls on capital. When the lawsuits began, Armstrong did not buy sufficient insurance, estimating that it could work its way out of the problem with its strong operating cash flows.

When the price of insurance rises, entities may choose to self-insure part of the risk; the analyst must determine the soundness of self-insurance given a catastrophic event.[6]

Example:

Self-Insurance: The company utilizes a combination of insurance and self-insurance for a number of risks including workers' compensation, general liability, automobile liability and employee related health care benefits (a portion of which is paid by its employees). Liabilities associated with the risks that the company retains are estimated by considering historical claims experience, demographic factors, severity factors and other actuarial assumptions. Although the company's claims experience has not displayed substantial volatility in the past, actual experience could materially vary from its historical experience in the future. Factors that affect these estimates include but are not limited to: inflation, the number and severity of claims and regulatory changes. In the future, if the company concludes an adjustment to self-insurance accruals is required, the liability will be adjusted accordingly.

Source: Bed Bath & Beyond 2009 10K.

[6] Because they were self-insured, BP PLC was virtually unprotected against the large oil rig explosion in the Gulf of Mexico in 2010.

Example:

The marketing and sale of our products may involve product liability risks. Although we currently have product liability insurance, we may not be able to maintain our current coverage at an acceptable cost, if at all, and there is no guarantee that our insurance coverage will be adequate to meet all types of product liability claims we may encounter. In addition, our insurance may not provide adequate coverage against potential losses. If claims or losses exceed our liability insurance coverage, we may go out of business.

Source: ecoSolutions 2009 10K.

Most companies have key man whole-life insurance on their top executives. Such policies are a tax-deductible expense while the cash surrender value most often grows significantly over time. These policies belong to the company, and as such, their cash surrender values are placed on the balance sheet, although the amount is often hidden with other assets. This cash can be called on by the entity at any time, if needed, but normally is used to fund key executives' retirement benefits.

Not only must the current adequacy of insurance be considered, so too must the risk of litigation that, if it took place, would result in a weakened financial condition. Some industries are, by their nature, more subject to lawsuits, whereas other industries may evolve to become of higher risk. An increase in such risk is not to be taken lightly, as was seen by the toy industry during 2006 when lead paint was found in many of their products, resulting in free cash flow that could not be reasonably estimated. As was discussed earlier under "Contingent Liabilities," a thorough review of such prospects (including adequacy of product liability insurance) needs to be explored.

If legal costs exceed or are expected to exceed 5 percent of normalized (three- or four-year) cash flow from operations, a penalty is assessed. If, in the opinion of the analyst, an existing lawsuit or the threat of one that the analyst believes has merit that will result in a payment of greater than 5 percent of normalized operating cash flows, a penalty is assessed. Potentially large payments that could emanate from manageable small lawsuits for which a payment has been made would result in a large penalty. Often, however, a firm is reluctant to discuss payments associated with lawsuits to discourage publicity.

Insurance inadequacy will penalize the cost of capital, the amount depending on the risks involved. Firms that underinsure workers' compensation are especially at risk.

Workers' Compensation

Workers' compensation insurance is required by law to protect workers who are injured or disabled in connection with their jobs. It also protects companies from being sued by employees for the workplace conditions that caused such an injury or illness. Most states give businesses the choice of buying workers' compensation policies either directly from the state or from a private insurer, with the individual states determining their own system's payment schedules, employee eligibility requirements, and rehabilitation procedures. Some states' workers' compensation regulations are more onerous than others and should be reviewed because the cost can be significant. For instance, California is well known to have more onerous workers' compensation provisions than most other states.

Workers' compensation expense normally is included in either cost of sales or SG&A. Incurred liabilities are reported on the balance sheet based on the present value of the estimated claims. Under GAAP, liabilities resulting from a workers' compensation claim are recorded on the company's balance sheet under other liabilities, based on an actuarially determined present value of known and estimated claims. These obligations represent a claim on prospective cash flows.

Big Lots, a large closeout retailer, wrote in its May 2, 2009, 10Q that its SG&A expense was higher than anticipated owing, in part, to its "insurance and insurance-related expense ... due to higher workers' compensation expense."

Example:

Insurance expense increased approximately $97,000 or 11.4% for the nine-month period and $30,000 or 10.2% for the three-month period compared to the same periods in 2003 due to increased premiums for workers compensation and general liability insurance.

Source: Canterbury Park Holding Corp. September 2005 10Q.

Other

Any event or factor not specifically listed or implied heretofore that would have resulted in a markup or markdown to the cost of capital should be considered here. For instance, loss of legal protection (patent), license, legal ruling, or other like event would be covered under this section, as would the loss of a key employee, whereas a positive event could lower the cost of capital, such as the announcement of sale of an asset that would result in marked lower leverage or greater financial flexibility not otherwise present. For an energy company, the announcement of substantial reserve additions could provide enhanced operating cash flows for many years, providing stability, greater fixed-charge coverage, and higher equity valuation.

A management succession plan, in the event of loss of a key employee or employees that would negatively affect the business, would be reviewed and addressed in this section. A change in tax status, nationalization, or new competitive entrant might negatively affect the cost of capital. A bill introduced in the House of Representatives can suppress or expand valuation multiples and yield spreads and thus affect the cost of debt and equity capital.

Delays in regulatory filings, executive management changes, and loss (reliance is covered separately) of an important contract or customer is also covered here. If there is a delay in a regulatory filing owing to weakness in the firm's internal controls, the cost of capital would be raised, the amount depending on the cause and strength of the remaining metrics, assuming credibility still existed. For an entity with rising demand for its products that also possesses financial strength and stability in cash flows and debt coverage, the markup would be small relative to a firm with weaker characteristics.

An announcement of an important acquisition would be considered here. The deferral of a preferred dividend or interest payment also would be covered under this section if not having been incorporated elsewhere.

Included in this section are assets and/or liabilities not reflected at fair value on the balance sheet. Prior to the outset of the worldwide credit crisis, many financial companies and those with financial subsidiaries were grossly overstating the value of their investments; to the extent that this is evident, the cost of capital must be marked up, depending on the entity under consideration and the importance of the assets to the firm's operations. Firms holding valuable assets that are not reflected at fair value could see a markdown to their cost of capital only if it is highly probable that the assets will be sold within 12 months. The intent to sell the assets is not sufficient because their anticipated market value may decline subsequently.

An entity that is using hedging or derivative instruments outside the scope of a fair-value or cash-flow purpose is considered here, as would be any other financial risk outside the normal business operations of the entity. The potential loss or actual loss of a bank credit facility is also covered under this section.

A negative change in the make-up of the board of directors would be covered here. For example, losing a director who is highly regarded and instrumental in the success of the firm, or a committee, could have a deleterious impact on the direction of the enterprise.

This section is one requiring judgment, with the ultimate assessment taking into account the short- and long-run implications for the entity and whether the metric is assessed elsewhere.

Productivity Metrics

Sales/Employee Growth—Recent 5 years

This is a measure of employee productivity. The entry indicates the ratio of total sales to number of employees and indicates the annual dollar sales per employee. This item is flagged if the ratio decreased from the prior year or in at least two of the most recent five years. A reduction in productivity, for a free-cash-flow producer, indicates that operating inefficiencies may result in lower cash flows and weaker debt metrics. As shown in Chapter 2, productivity enhancements have greater significance to already cash-flow-positive entities and entities that are likely to soon be cash-flow-positive.

Apple was flagged because of large employee growth associated with its retail operations and was penalized 0.1. The company still reported a strong and growing $925,000 in sales per employee. If Apple had not been producing free cash flow, this metric would have been ignored.

Sales/Net PPE Growth—Recent 5 Years

This is a measure of company productivity in using its fixed assets. The entry indicates the ratio of total sales to net PPE. The higher this ratio, the more sales that are generated from the same operating capacity, and the more efficient are the company's operations and utilization of fixed assets. This item is flagged if the ratio decreased from the prior year or in at least two of the most recent five years. A reduction in productivity indicates operating inefficiencies that are likely to result in lower cash flows as well as weaker debt metrics. Productivity variables have greater weight for free-cash-flow producers than for firms that are not.

Apple was flagged because of the large growth rate in PPE. However, it was coming off a low base, and thus Apple was penalized only 0.2. If Apple had not been producing free cash flow, this metric would have been ignored.

CONCLUSION

The cost-of-capital model assigned an 8.47 percent cost of equity to Apple, considerably lower than that estimated by the CAPM (10.2 percent), given its beta determined by Bloomberg and the risk-free rate of the 10-year Treasury yield. As the worksheet illustrated, Apple's violations were minor. Its cash-flow, debt, and miscellaneous metrics all were below the norm for the industry and equities in general because the credit model's median cost of capital for the S&P 500 is 8.8 percent compared to the CAPM's 9.4 percent. Apple has no bank debt and almost $23 billion in cash on its balance sheet. Including pensions and leases, the company has $780 million in debt when its leases are discounted at 8 percent. Their cash flows have been growing consistently and strongly. The company's step up in its capital expenditures has resulted in the company having $305 million in discretionary capital spending excess during its latest fiscal year, which may be unrecognized by investors using common definitions of free cash flow. Even though its products are subject to the vagaries of the consumer, Apple has been a very strong and consistent generator of operating and free cash flows for at least the past six years, resulting in below-normal stability metrics.

Almost regardless of the credit-based scoring system one might have employed in the evaluation of Apple's risk profile, with use of the model, it is quite apparent that the result would be superior to the CAPM's 10.2 percent, which is higher than that of the median S&P 500 entity; in reality, based on cash flow and credit, Apple has considerably less risk. Apple's beta of 1.45 does not reflect its true cost of equity capital and therefore would be an inferior tool for use as a discount-rate method. The credit and cash-flow model results in the analyst possessing a more accurate discounting mechanism from which to establish fair value from the estimated free cash flow.

CHAPTER 9

Portfolio Selection

On the last trading day in 2007, CT Capital selected an investment portfolio based on the processes and methods outlined in this text. The portfolio was rebalanced the last trading day of each subsequent quarter, with no portfolio turnover intra-quarter, and it was held for the duration of the following quarter. Because of the strictness of this requirement, I believe that the results presented are quite conservative.

Additions to and sales from the portfolio for the follow-up quarters were presumed to have taken place at the closing prices each quarter. The portfolio remained fully invested, and no trading commissions or management fees were charged.

To be included in the portfolio, a company was required to have

1. A current (rolling 12-month) and three-year average free-cash-flow yield of 20 percent greater than the then-existing 10-year Treasury yield. In the the actual management of accounts, one would slide the 20% spread depending on the interest rate on the 10 year note. As rates fell, the 20% would widen up to 40%, as was the case in the fall of 2010. As rates rose, it could fall to as low as 10%.
2. A return on invested capital (ROIC) greater than its cost of equity capital, as defined in Chapters 5 and 8.
3. The ability to retire total debt within 10 years from free cash flow (This requirement is also included in the cost-of-equity-capital model.)
4. Normalized positive annual rate of growth in free cash flow and operating cash flows, as measured by its three-year average.
5. Stability in its cost of capital, as defined in Chapter 8.
6. Banks and airlines are excluded owing to instability, leverage, and management discretion of important accounts not picked up by my credit model software.
7. Minimum shareholders' equity of $500 million to ensure liquidity and to enhance the reliability of the reported returns.

8. No more than three years of negative annual free cash flow during the prior 10 years but positive normalized free cash flow for every year based on its three-year average.

FIGURE 9-1

Investment Performance

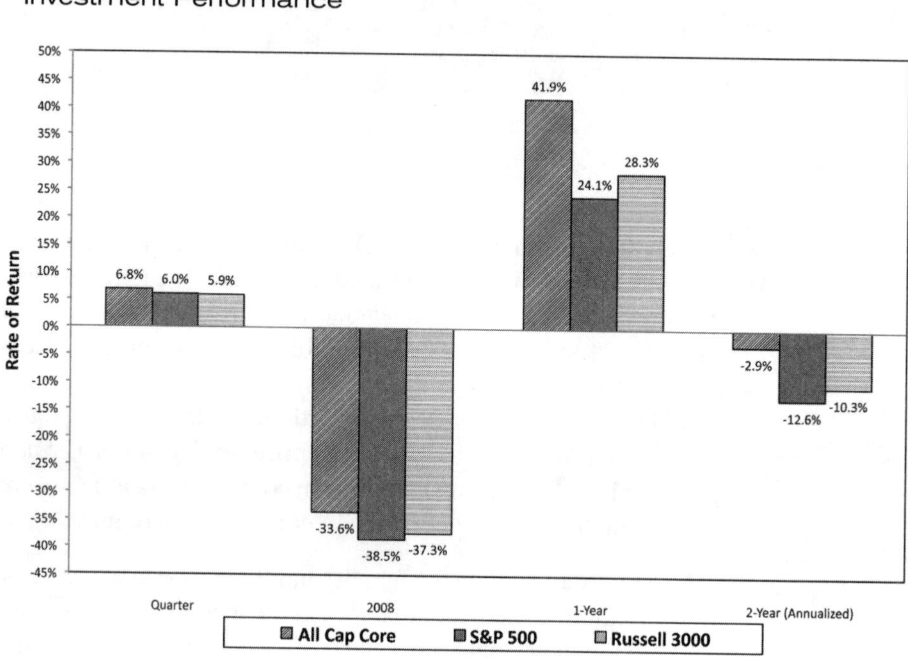

TABLE 9-1

Portfolio for Upcoming Quarter, January 1, 2010–March 31, 2010

Company Name	Total Debt/FCF	Mkvalc/ Threeyravgfcf	Market Value	Cost of Capital	Return on Invested Capital
ABB LTD -ADR	0.741	19.693	47,022.723	8.750	26.671
ACCENTURE PLC	0.000	10.363	27,270.123	8.550	83.402
ACE LTD	0.852	13.804	16,393.649	8.322	25.267
ANALOG DEVICES	0.954	15.811	8,747.104	9.101	13.235
ASTRAZENECA PLC -ADR	1.482	10.063	71,662.863	7.617	29.179
AUTOMATIC DATA PROCESSING	0.521	14.875	21,446.818	7.250	25.986
AVNET INC	0.904	6.024	4,362.771	9.750	30.674
BAE SYSTEMS PLC -ADR	2.002	9.652	21,287.099	9.150	12.554
BECTON DICKINSON & CO	1.664	17.275	18,252.856	7.858	17.027
BIOGEN IDEC INC	0.861	13.416	15,720.858	8.977	18.286
CARDINAL HEALTH INC	2.985	9.951	11,831.175	8.743	13.886

Company Name	Total Debt/FCF	Mkvalc/ Threeyravgfcf	Market Value	Cost of Capital	Return on Invested Capital
CHINA UNICOM (HONG KONG)-ADR	1.666	13.649	30,613.089	13.180	15.273
CHUNGHWA TELECOM CO -ADR	0.005	9.599	19,788.078	6.291	16.522
CISCO SYSTEMS INC	1.117	14.465	143,526.999	8.361	17.775
COACH INC	0.055	17.822	11,959.800	9.391	35.132
DANAHER CORP	1.457	15.277	24,792.916	8.125	15.048
DOVER CORP	2.482	11.160	8,644.198	7.924	16.775
EBAY INC	0.410	13.591	29,582.970	8.880	21.036
EMC CORP/MA	1.151	15.603	37,063.566	8.667	16.979
ENDURANCE SPECIALTY HOLDINGS	0.961	3.932	2,091.222	8.683	18.669
EXPEDIA INC	3.686	10.546	6,068.308	10.015	11.259
FLUOR CORP	0.216	16.836	8,985.248	8.854	24.011
FOREST LABORATORIES -CL A	0.000	8.263	9,460.364	9.400	24.127
FRANKLIN RESOURCES INC	0.189	21.277	25,458.213	8.133	8.411
GAP INC	0.051	11.426	13,620.461	9.900	22.073
HUMANA INC	2.785	7.376	8,155.333	9.303	13.291
INTEL CORP	0.336	17.775	118,612.557	8.476	13.019
INTL BUSINESS MACHINES CORP	2.226	13.149	173,802.813	8.039	45.234
JOHNSON & JOHNSON	0.971	14.619	179,617.412	7.148	24.424
KING PHARMACEUTICALS INC	2.449	7.829	3,219.699	9.978	17.317
LABORATORY CP OF AMER HLDGS	2.688	14.068	8,168.904	8.762	19.987
MATTEL INC	2.852	14.352	7,403.110	9.446	12.836
MCGRAW-HILL COMPANIES	1.174	7.917	10,498.766	14.084	46.421
MICROSOFT CORP	0.347	15.674	274,897.581	7.317	39.596
NATIONAL OILWELL VARCO INC	0.443	14.450	19,645.105	9.036	14.747
NIKE INC -CL B	0.574	16.480	25,831.055	8.550	15.457
NOBLE CORP	0.948	16.491	11,721.681	8.716	15.250
NOVARTIS AG -ADR	0.907	13.832	141,508.480	7.788	14.854
NOVO-NORDISK A/S -ADR	0.072	14.470	35,353.148	8.628	40.516
NTT DOCOMO INC -ADR	0.982	10.218	66,188.703	7.900	13.310
NUCOR CORP	1.713	8.545	15,082.690	7.953	17.753
NVIDIA CORP	0.183	16.785	9,782.887	12.389	14.240
OMNICOM GROUP	2.585	8.584	11,861.433	8.384	18.580
PARTNERRE LTD	0.746	6.175	5,900.396	8.317	25.838
PAYCHEX INC	0.000	18.142	11,330.110	6.400	46.786
POLO RALPH LAUREN CP -CL A	0.786	8.363	4,806.332	9.150	19.305
PRECISION CASTPARTS CORP	0.338	20.834	16,231.222	9.150	17.915
PRICE (T. ROWE) GROUP	0.000	22.972	14,108.536	8.400	26.192
QUALCOMM INC	0.029	19.963	81,049.401	12.393	32.208
SHIRE PLC -ADR	1.577	13.262	11,405.469	11.856	36.472
STRYKER CORP	0.019	25.579	22,289.349	8.547	17.946
TAIWAN SEMICONDUCTOR -ADR	0.090	13.593	56,297.925	11.410	33.130
TD AMERITRADE HOLDING CORP	2.481	15.077	10,730.541	8.848	12.864
TENARIS SA -ADR	2.772	20.174	27,984.629	8.647	11.964
TEXAS INSTRUMENTS INC	0.000	12.160	30,958.492	8.650	27.156
TRAVELERS COS INC	1.899	6.066	26,925.260	8.305	11.611
YPF SOCIEDAD ANONIMA -ADR	0.599	11.524	17,711.558	10.925	34.661
ZIMMER HOLDINGS INC	0.733	18.345	13,360.173	8.769	9.975

Although the two-year period for which I have made advance investment selections under the process is admittedly of short duration, the results are encouraging because the portfolio outperformed the Standard and Poor's (S&P) 500 Index by a wide margin.

The period under study began with the United States and world economy in deep financial and credit turmoil, with many companies experiencing severe stress. During this period of financial trauma, the portfolio outperformed the S&P 500 and the Russell 3000 indexes, which are its benchmarks.

During the period beginning in March 2009, when equity securities began to rally strongly, through the remainder of that year, the portfolio also outperformed its benchmarks.

It is understandable that a high-quality portfolio would show relative outperformance during periods of economic strain, but why it outperformed during the initial stages of a bull market are less clear. It is noted that several companies on the list appear would to have higher than expected cost of capital, such as McGraw-Hill and China Unicom. For these firms, their ROIC have enjoyed a consistent postiive spread over their cost of equity. Their total debt (column 1) is easily serviced from the operating and free cash flows. Normally, outperformance at the initial stage of a bull market is reserved for entities for which the risk of bankruptcy is reduced, as illustrated in Fig. 9–2, which is a portfolio consisting of all companies having

FIGURE 9-2

Weak Credits versus S&P 500 Index

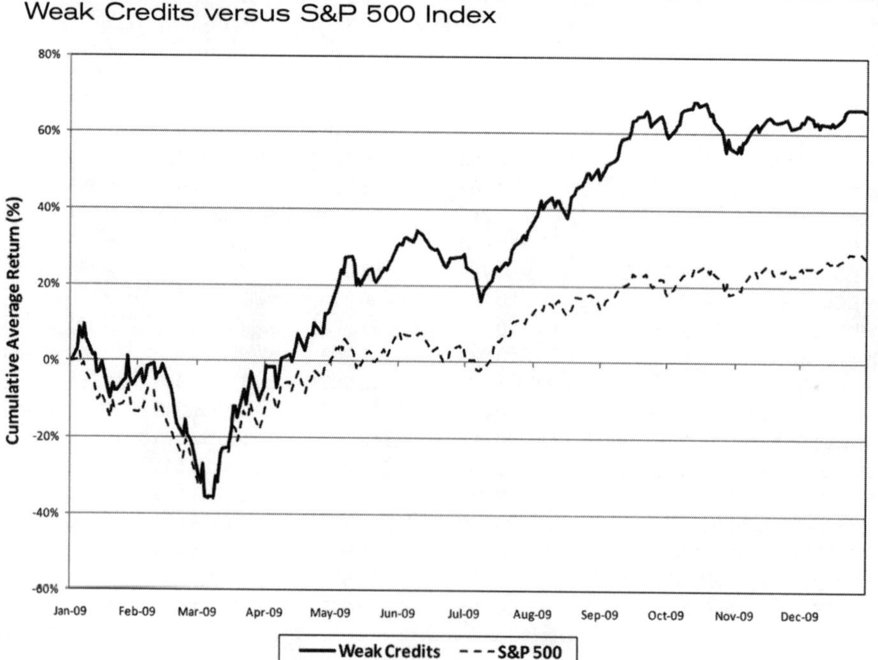

(1) greater than $100 million market value, (2) either a deficit shareholders' equity or total debt/shareholders' equity greater than 300 percent, and (3) negative three-year average free cash flow.

The most likely reason for the superior performance is that the high-quality portfolio of companies has been able to grow market share owing to financial flexibility, high ROIC, and low cost of capital. In looking through their individual financial results, one can see that these entities have sustained positive operating cash flow growth, positive and growing free cash flow, and some top-line growth despite the economic downdraft. Perhaps as a result of industry weakness, these companies will see long-term benefit, and such is being reflected in their stock prices. They are able to grow their market share owing to greater business leverage and pricing power and stronger free cash flow. Their competitors will take, in some cases, years to deliver. Their customers have come to appreciate their financial strength. Their employees are relatively happier than those of their peer group of companies because layoffs, to the extent that they have taken place within these firms, have not been as severe. Their managements likely have done a good job advising them of their financial superiority.

All this has not been lost on investors, as seen in the second-quarter 2009 investment performance, a period where the S&P rose 15.2 percent, but the investment portfolio rose by 21.9 percent. Significant outperformance also took place during the

FIGURE 9-3

CT Capital–Simulated Portfolio Performance

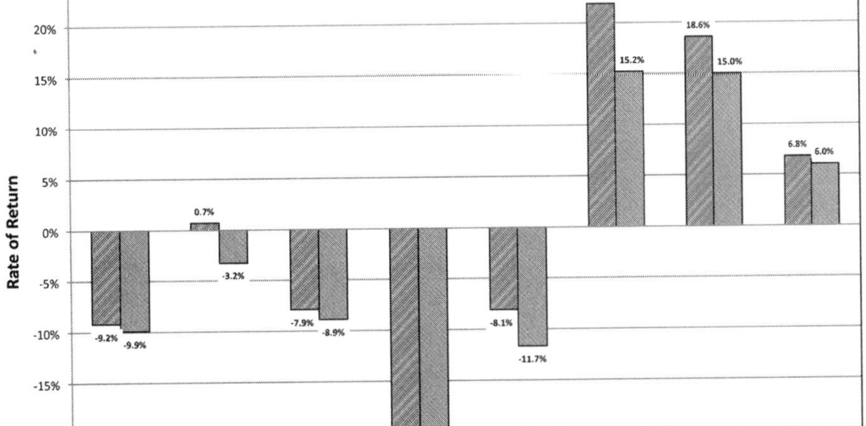

year's third and fourth quarters, a period where the preponderence of U.S. economists and investment strategists were raising their forecasts for the following year's gross national product (GNP) and target for the S&P 500. Growing market share should, for these entities, lead to rising free cash flow and, given their competitive cost of capital, allow them the facility to accept projects, including acquisitions, which many of their competitors cannot.

INDEX

Page numbers followed by *f*, *n*, or *t* indicate material contained in figures, footnotes, or tables respectively.

Nominal > Real Interest Rate

200K loan at 3% w/2% inflation

Nominal Interest Rate = Real Risk Free Rate + Expected Inflation Rate = 3%

Real Interest Rate = 3% - 2% = 1%

Required Int. Rate on Security = nominal risk free rate + default risk premium + liquidity premium + maturity risk premium (bonds longer will be more subject to this risk).